# The Shaping of American Higher Education
### Third Edition

# The Shaping of American Higher Education

Emergence and Growth of the Contemporary System

THIRD EDITION

Carrie B. Kisker
Arthur M. Cohen

**JB JOSSEY-BASS**
A Wiley Brand

Copyright © 2024 by John Wiley & Sons Inc., All rights reserved.

Published by John Wiley & Sons, Inc., Hoboken, New Jersey.
Published simultaneously in Canada.

No part of this publication may be reproduced, stored in a retrieval system, or transmitted in any form or by any means, electronic, mechanical, photocopying, recording, scanning, or otherwise, except as permitted under Section 107 or 108 of the 1976 United States Copyright Act, without either the prior written permission of the Publisher, or authorization through payment of the appropriate per-copy fee to the Copyright Clearance Center, Inc., 222 Rosewood Drive, Danvers, MA 01923, (978) 750-8400, fax (978) 750-4470, or on the web at www.copyright.com. Requests to the Publisher for permission should be addressed to the Permissions Department, John Wiley & Sons, Inc., 111 River Street, Hoboken, NJ 07030, (201) 748-6011, fax (201) 748-6008, or online at http://www.wiley.com/go/permission.

Trademarks: Wiley and the Wiley logo are trademarks or registered trademarks of John Wiley & Sons, Inc. and/or its affiliates in the United States and other countries and may not be used without written permission. All other trademarks are the property of their respective owners. John Wiley & Sons, Inc. is not associated with any product or vendor mentioned in this book.

Limit of Liability/Disclaimer of Warranty: While the publisher and author have used their best efforts in preparing this book, they make no representations or warranties with respect to the accuracy or completeness of the contents of this book and specifically disclaim any implied warranties of merchantability or fitness for a particular purpose. No warranty may be created or extended by sales representatives or written sales materials. The advice and strategies contained herein may not be suitable for your situation. You should consult with a professional where appropriate. Further, readers should be aware that websites listed in this work may have changed or disappeared between when this work was written and when it is read. Neither the publisher nor authors shall be liable for any loss of profit or any other commercial damages, including but not limited to special, incidental, consequential, or other damages.

For general information on our other products and services or for technical support, please contact our Customer Care Department within the United States at
(800) 762-2974, outside the United States at (317) 572-3993 or fax (317) 572-4002.

Wiley also publishes its books in a variety of electronic formats. Some content that appears in print may not be available in electronic formats. For more information about Wiley products, visit our web site at www.wiley.com.

*Library of Congress Cataloging-in-Publication Data:*

Names: Kisker, Carrie B., 1977- author. | Cohen, Arthur M., author.
Title: The shaping of American higher education : emergence and growth of the contemporary system / Carrie B. Kisker, Arthur M. Cohen.
Description: Third edition. | Hoboken, New Jersey : Jossey-Bass, 2024. | Includes bibliographical references and index.
Identifiers: LCCN 2024000470 (print) | LCCN 2024000471 (ebook) | ISBN 9781394180899 (cloth) | ISBN 9781394180905 (adobe pdf) | ISBN 9781394180936 (epub)
Subjects: LCSH: Education, Higher—United States—History. | Universities and colleges—United States—History.
Classification: LCC LA226 .C66 2024 (print) | LCC LA226 (ebook) | DDC 378.73—dc23/eng/20240110
LC record available at https://lccn.loc.gov/2024000470
LC ebook record available at https://lccn.loc.gov/2024000471

Cover Design: Wiley
Cover Image: © Kevin Dodge/Getty Images
Author photo: © Alexandra Turshen

For Harry Kisker, who first put a history of higher education into my hands, and who set an example—as an educator, spouse, and parent—to which I will always aspire.

# Contents

Preface ix
Acknowledgments xv
About the Authors xvii

Introduction: A Framework for Studying the
    History of Higher Education 1

1 Establishing the Collegiate Form in the
    Colonies: 1636–1789 13
      *Societal Context • Institutions • Students • Faculty
      • Curriculum • Governance • Finance • Outcomes*

2 Diffusion of Small Colleges in the Emergent
    Nation: 1790–1869 57
      *Societal Context • Institutions • Students • Faculty
      • Curriculum • Governance • Finance • Outcomes*

3 University Transformation as the Nation
    Industrializes: 1870–1944 105
      *Societal Context • Institutions • Students • Faculty
      • Curriculum • Governance • Finance • Outcomes*

4 Mass Higher Education in the Era of American
    Hegemony: 1945–1975 187
      *Societal Context • Institutions • Students • Faculty
      • Curriculum • Governance • Finance • Outcomes*

5 Maintaining the Diverse System in an Era of
    Consolidation: 1976–1993 305
      *Societal Context • Institutions • Students • Faculty
      • Curriculum • Governance • Finance • Outcomes*

6  Equity, Accountability, Distrust, and
   Disinvestment in the Contemporary
   Era: 1994–2023                                                425
      *Societal Context • Institutions • Students • Faculty*
      *• Curriculum • Governance • Finance • Outcomes*
      *• Summary and Trends*

References                                                      605
Name Index                                                      639
Subject Index                                                   645

# Preface

This book had its origins in a History of Higher Education course that my co-author, colleague, mentor, and friend, Arthur M. Cohen, taught for many years in UCLA's Graduate School of Education and Information Studies. As he related, and as I saw the year I was his teaching assistant, few of the students who enrolled each term had much prior knowledge of American history, and fewer still were aware of the roots of the collegiate tradition in our country. As the course evolved, it became apparent that a useful text would need to both encompass the entire scope of American higher education—from the Colonial Era to the present day—and set the developing colleges in the context of their times, all within the span of a 10-week quarter. Furthermore, the review of nearly 400 years of continuous expansion in enrollments, staff, curriculum, finance, and other aspects of the system had to be organized so that students and other readers could digest its component parts and come to understand how they influence one another. The matrix described in the Introduction to this volume has helped serve that purpose.

*The Shaping of American Higher Education: Emergence and Growth of the Contemporary System* was first published in 1998, and a second edition appeared in 2010. Both focused primarily on the Mass Higher Education Era (1945–1975) and the Consolidation Era (1976–1993), as most of the trends that had developed earlier either matured or transformed during these periods; the second edition also provided an early analysis of the Contemporary Era (then spanning the years between 1994 and 2009). While this third edition exhibits a few modifications in the system's history based on recent scholarship, its chief contribution is its synthesis of the Contemporary Era, which now encompasses the turbulent years between 1994 and 2023. In addition, unlike the other major texts on the history of American higher education, this book gives appropriate consideration to the development and contributions of the institution in which 40% of undergraduates first enroll: community colleges. These open-access institutions have been an essential thread in the fabric of American education since the early 1900s yet receive little mention in other major histories of colleges and universities in the United States.

## New in the Third Edition

A new edition of *The Shaping of American Higher Education* is warranted now, as several shifts in the system's functioning have occurred in the past three decades, along with numerous changes in public perception and support of America's colleges and universities. In particular:

- Like a snake biting its own tail, states and localities have continually disinvested in higher education and the institutions have responded by raising tuition and becoming increasingly entrepreneurial in their search for funds. Accordingly, the burden of paying for college has shifted ever more away from government and toward students, parents, corporations, and philanthropic donors. As a college degree has become viewed predominantly as a private good, the foundation on which the system was built and has been supported for nearly four centuries—the idea that higher education is essential for societal well-being—has begun to erode.

- Nearly all institutions have implemented equity-minded approaches to teaching, learning, and student support and some have sought to alter longstanding structures and policies that have precluded social and economic mobility for racially marginalized groups. As a result, access, persistence, and completion rates improved across the board. However, a vitriolic backlash to the concept of structural racism, as well as recent rulings against affirmative action and legislation in some states to ban diversity, equity, and inclusion programs and practices, have (at a minimum) complicated institutional efforts to provide welcoming and inclusive learning environments and may ultimately thwart higher education's ability to provide equitable support for marginalized or minoritized learners.

- Along with the growing tendency to hire part-time and non-tenure-track faculty, frontal attacks on tenure and academic freedom in some states accelerated the trend toward faculty de-professionalization and now threaten institutional autonomy.

- Over the past several decades, demands that institutions be held accountable for their stewardship of public funds and the outcomes of their students multiplied, contributing to rising administrative costs and entire units dedicated to compliance and reporting, not to mention a wealth of data from which to cherry-pick numbers to critique the system.

- New pedagogical and technological approaches to teaching and learning were introduced, forcing a reckoning about the costs and purposes of higher education, as well as the skills and competencies that students need to succeed in the workforce and in a democratic society.

- The COVID-19 pandemic exacerbated and laid bare what many in higher education have known for years: that unconsciously high numbers of students suffer from basic needs insecurities or mental health challenges. Institutional responses to providing new services or connecting students to resources in the community were publicly championed but often privately criticized as falling outside higher education's social role and responsibility.

- Reflecting (and sometimes feeding) high levels of political polarization and social fragmentation across the nation, student activism has reached a fervor not seen since the 1960s and early 1970s. America's colleges and universities are once again battlefields on which America's culture wars are fought, yet unlike in previous eras, now they are also the targets of ideologically inspired attacks by politicians or commentators. As a result, public distrust in institutions of higher education has reached an all-time high, threatening the perceived legitimacy of a system that has long been the envy of the world.

The era from 1994 through the present is thus one of the most fascinating and—for its supporters—disquieting periods in the history of American higher education. Yet the roots of each of these and other contemporary issues can be traced through previous eras, along with institutional responses and systemic adjustments. The system is pliant; it rarely moves quickly or abandons that which has come before, yet somehow shapeshifts to meet emerging societal pressures and needs. For this to continue, institutional leaders—faculty and administrators alike—must embody the *Sankofa* and look both to the future and to the past. They must identify innovative solutions to contemporary problems, yet stand together to protect the great strengths of American higher education, including institutional autonomy, academic freedom, equal access, and equitable support.

It is my hope that this book provides college and university faculty, administrators, trustees, and students—as well as scholars, policymakers, and commentators—with a nuanced understanding of the trends and events that have shaped American higher education over the past 400 years and a renewed appreciation for the complexity and vital importance of our diverse and multipurpose system.

# Acknowledgments

I have been blessed in life to have the support and love of several generations of family members and friends, including especially my husband, Sean, my exceptional children, Meredith and Grayson, my parents, Lucie and Rick Bourdon, and all my siblings and their spouses (Jackie and Clint Kisker, Hansell and Mac Woods, Allen and Lindsay Bourdon, Leland Bourdon and Megan Ash). But of all the intergenerational relationships I have been lucky enough to experience, the friendship, support, and love of my mentor, colleague, co-author, and friend Art Cohen has been perhaps the most surprising and—at least from a career perspective—monumental.

Art was four months shy of 50 years old when I was born, already well established as the grandfather of community college studies and a respected professor of higher education at UCLA. When I entered graduate school at age 25, he was three times my age and two years away from becoming emeritus. It was an unlikely friendship, but we recognized something in one another and for nearly 20 years Art advised me, encouraged me, debated with me, and eventually asked me to collaborate in the revision of his crown jewels: *The American Community College* and *The Shaping of American Higher Education*. Working with Art on the sixth and second editions, respectively, of these books taught me more than all my graduate courses put together; Art was a wealth of (sometimes esoteric) knowledge, and while I did not always agree with him, he taught me to listen, to hear, to reconsider, and then to formulate an iron-clad counterargument. Sometimes I even convinced him.

Art passed away in December 2020 at the age of 93, after months of COVID-induced separation in which I was able to visit him only once. Yet over the past 18 months, as I have written the seventh edition of *The American Community College* and the third edition of this book, I have heard his voice in my head almost daily, and his presence has been constant, shining through in sentences that only he could write as well as those that we composed together. For this, and for all that came before, I am ever so thankful. This book is much like our relationship was: a joining of scholarly thoughts and ideas, an amalgamation of our training and lived experiences. The only difference is that in this edition, when our perspectives differed, I always got the final word.

Writing a book such as this—especially when your co-author is deceased—can be a lonely venture, but several people provided support and camaraderie. Lauren Kater offered exceptional research assistance. Drs. Mark D'Amico and Reed Scull, who have both taught *The Shaping of American Higher Education* for years, provided encouragement and useful feedback on the new Contemporary Era chapter. (Indeed, the idea of urging readers to begin with the final chapter originated with Dr. D'Amico.) Many more—especially those mentioned in the first paragraph—gave me the love, time, and carpool assistance I needed to finish this treatise on the past, present, and possible futures of American higher education. Thank you all.

CARRIE B. KISKER<br>
LOS ANGELES<br>
SEPTEMBER 2023

# About the Authors

**Carrie B. Kisker** is president of Kisker Education Consulting in Los Angeles and managing director of the Center for the Study of Community Colleges (CSCC). She received her BA (1999) in psychology from Dartmouth College and her MA (2003) and PhD (2006) in higher education from the University of California, Los Angeles (UCLA). Drawing from her own and others' research, she regularly consults with college leaders on issues related to entrepreneurship and innovation, program and policy development, strategies for student equity, strategic planning and accountability, and civic learning and democratic engagement. Kisker is author of the sixth and seventh editions of *The American Community College* (2014, 2023), written with Arthur M. Cohen and Florence B. Brawer, *Creating Entrepreneurial Community Colleges, A Design Thinking Approach* (2021), and the second edition of *The Shaping of American Higher Education: Emergence and Growth of the Contemporary System* (2010) with Arthur M. Cohen.

**Arthur M. Cohen** (1927–2020) was professor of higher education at UCLA from 1964 until 2004. He received his BA (1949) and MA (1955) in history from the University of Miami and his PhD (1964) in higher education from The Florida State University. He was director of the ERIC Clearinghouse for Community Colleges from 1966 to 2003, president of CSCC from 1974 to 2007, and longtime editor-in-chief of *New Directions for Community Colleges*. Over the course of his career, Cohen served on the editorial boards of numerous journals and wrote extensively about community colleges, including 21 books; more than 80 book chapters, journal articles, and essays in edited volumes; and untold numbers of conference papers, journalistic pieces, and research reports.

# Introduction
## *A Framework for Studying the History of Higher Education*

Reading the history of higher education teaches appreciation for the power of tradition. Practically every aspect of the contemporary system can be traced to the formation of universities in the latter part of the nineteenth century, and many to the colleges in the Colonial Era. Some aspects were present in the universities of medieval Europe. This great weight of history and tradition is one of the system's strengths, but the stability of form over nearly 400 years also ensures a rather slow pace of change. New ideas—no matter how laudable—must always contend with the conflicting mandates, needs, and priorities of administrators, faculty, students, and other stakeholders. And all institutional decision-making occurs within the context of changing societal norms and public expectations about the purposes, costs, and outcomes of higher education.

Understanding the history of colleges and universities in America is thus essential for those who would reform the contemporary system or institutions within it. Publications calling for completely revising governance, teaching, funding, or student support appear frequently. An industry of innovation is apparent. But the practices, policies, and pedagogical approaches that are most likely to be adopted and institutionalized are those that build on what has come before, anchor themselves in the historic missions and purposes of the institution, incorporate incentives for each stakeholder group, and otherwise leave intact anything that does not directly conflict with the new approach. Even the most consequential event to have ever affected American higher education—the COVID-19 pandemic and its aftermath—did not result in fundamentally changed institutions: courses were moved online but remained part of the same programs, tied to the same institutional calendars and number of credit hours; student services personnel were asked to identify new ways to support learners at a distance, but the percentage of expenditures dedicated to student support did not increase commensurately.

Throughout its history the system has successfully resisted, co-opted, or absorbed—eventually changing but with the glacial majesty befitting a venerable structure. However, higher education has become more vulnerable to external forces over the last several decades. In particular, the slow but steady disinvestment in public institutions by states and localities, as well as fiscal repercussions stemming from the Great Recession of 2007–2009, have accelerated trends toward privatization and entrepreneurship. New governance players have exercised greater demands for accountability in both institutional actions and student outcomes. And intense media scrutiny of colleges and universities, driven in large part by the voracious demands of a 24/7 news cycle, clickbait headlines, rapidly rising tuition levels, and growing distrust of government and public institutions, has put higher education under a microscope. Public perception (whether it is rooted in fact or takes context into account) reigns supreme, and much institutional decision-making now takes place within a political arena.

In addition, colleges and universities have once again become flashpoints for conflict over changing American values. But unlike the student activism of the 1960s and 1970s, the social fragmentation and widespread distrust of *the other* that has thrust colleges and universities into the culture wars of the Contemporary Era threatens the perceived legitimacy of the system. And the emergence of new entry points to the workforce and different ways of "doing college" (Gaston and Van Noy, 2022, p. 28) threaten the necessity of a system designed around linear, sequential pathways.

For nearly 400 years, American colleges and universities have held a near-total monopoly on providing access to a better life; for the first time in history, prospective students may be turning the other way or at least delaying entry.

Thus, 25 years into the twenty-first century, higher education is faced with a decision; either it gathers its cloak of history and tradition around itself in an attempt to insulate against an onslaught of public accusations and demands, in the process feeding the perception that college is for some people and not for others, or it spreads its arms, ensuring transparency, inviting innovation, and enveloping new approaches and ideas alongside time-honored values and institutional mores. One choice leads to a society in which U.S. institutions of higher education were once the envy of the world; the other to a future where they still are. The challenge, however, lies in recommitting to that decision every day, in every corner of every college, even in the face of reduced funding and politically motivated attacks.

Fortunately, many of the most fraught issues in higher education today have been debated since the colleges began. What shall be taught? Who shall learn it? Who shall pay? And who gets to decide? Such questions are grounded in the stories of each institution and historical responses differ according to the societal context in which they were considered. Today's challenges are related to yesterday's practices, and tomorrow's decisions must be informed by an understanding of what has come before.

## A Framework for Studying the History of Higher Education

The history of higher education is taught in most graduate programs that prepare faculty or administrators for positions in colleges or universities, and it is increasingly appealing to those seeking to understand how and why such institutions frequently become symbols of societal discord or settings for social activism. Most courses and texts on the subject utilize a chronological approach; students and readers learn about colleges in the Colonial Era and then are led through the development of universities on into the present. Many also take a topical approach, pointing out changes in the number and types of institutions, students attending, working conditions for faculty, curriculum, patterns of governance, and public and private financing. These topics are often supplemented by subtopics of interest: the rise of women's colleges, Historically Black Colleges and Universities (HBCUs), intercollegiate sports, training for the professions.

Within these topics, various key events are noted. The founding of certain types of institutions—state colleges, graduate and professional schools, and community colleges, for example—may be accorded separate sections. Legislation, including the Morrill Acts and the Servicemen's Readjustment Act (popularly known as the GI Bill), is given space along with important court decisions such as the Dartmouth College case, which protected institutional independence. The courses and texts also show how certain trends have been pervasive: greater access for students, a trend toward occupationally relevant curricula, secular governance, and state-level coordination of higher education.

This book's approach is to define trends and events chronologically under topical headings and within six major eras, and to detail interrelationships among them. Exhibit I.1 displays the framework for this book. While many readers will choose to start at the Colonial Era (Chapter 1) and trace the history of American higher education as it is presented chronologically, others may elect to begin at the Contemporary Era (Chapter 6)—the time period with which they are most familiar—and then go back in time to learn about various antecedents to the modern system. This edition has been revised to better facilitate such an approach. Still other readers may elect to take a deep dive into particular topics, skipping from era to era to understand how curriculum, governance, or finance, for example, has evolved over nearly four centuries. All approaches are welcomed, and all six chapters conclude with several questions relating to trends and events associated with that era; these issues may serve as discussion topics in class or as starting points for student essays or dialogues.

As Exhibit I.1 shows, each of the topics illustrated has at least one major trend associated with it. Many of the tendencies have lengthy histories. The institutions have grown steadily larger and adopted more varied purposes and specialties. The trend for students has been in the direction of greater access; ever-increasing numbers of 18-year-olds and adults have matriculated. In recent years, attention to student equity has also come to the fore. In general, the faculty moved steadily toward professionalization, although this trend slowed and began showing distinct signs of reversal late in the twentieth century. Curriculum has become more directly related to workforce entry, as one occupational group after another began demanding additional years of schooling for its initiates. Throughout the first 350 years of American higher education, governance tended toward broader systems and a diminution of church-related control, but in the past three decades it has become increasingly decentralized and bureaucratized, with an ever-expanding number of governance actors demanding some level of accountability for student and institutional outcomes. Similarly, institutions became more and more dependent on public funds until the late twentieth century, when disinvestment in public institutions accelerated, the forces of privatization took hold, and colleges and universities were forced to broaden their search for support. Higher education's outcomes have been directed increasingly toward producing a skilled workforce, enabling people to move out of the social class into which they were born, and conducting scientific research that yields useful products and processes.

Not all topics show such distinct trends. The context varies as public perceptions reflect contemporary societal concerns. In general, the expectation that higher education will contribute to economic growth has found its way into the mainstream of public thought.

Exhibit 1.1. Trends and events in American higher education.

| Eras | I<br>Colonial<br>1636-1789 | II<br>Emergent Nation<br>1790-1869 | III<br>University Transformation<br>1870-1944 | IV<br>Mass Higher Education<br>1945-1975 | V<br>Consolidation<br>1976-1993 | VI<br>Contemporary<br>1994-2023 | Overall Trends | Recent Adjustments |
|---|---|---|---|---|---|---|---|---|
| Topics | | | | | | | | |
| Societal Context | | | | | | | Expanding nation and economy; increased demands and expectations | Social fragmentation; distrust of government and public institutions |
| Institutions | | | | | | | Diverse; multipurpose | |
| Students | | | | | | | Access | Attention to equity |
| Faculty | | | | | | | Professionalization | Part-time, fungible labor |
| Curriculum and Instruction | | | | | | | Vocational and varied | |
| Governance and Administration | | | | | | | Secular; larger units | Decentralization; accountability |
| Finance | | | | | | | Public funding | Disinvestment; privatization; entrepreneurship |
| Outcomes | | | | | | | Individual mobility; societal and economic development; advancement of knowledge | |

But the belief that it can or should ameliorate social problems or that access and equitable support for everyone should be pursued is affected by the short-term mood of the nation, its media, and its national administration.

The six eras reflect the evolution of the trends. In the Colonial Era, 1636–1789, the college form was established on Old World models. The Emergent Nation Era, 1790–1869, saw hundreds of small colleges established and the beginnings of access for different types of students. In the University Transformation Era, 1870–1944, the research university made its appearance, faculty professionalization took a leap forward, and the role of the state expanded. The Mass Higher Education Era, 1945–1975, was marked by greater size and number of institutions, augmented student access, and an increased reliance on federal funding. The Consolidation Era, 1976–1993, saw a flattening of growth in faculty professionalization, fewer institutional openings, and lower public per capita funding, matched by a greater reliance on state-level governance and increases in tuition and fees.

The era since 1994 is especially significant from a historical perspective, as it can be characterized by course changes in several of the trends evident throughout the first five eras. Namely, institutions became increasingly entrepreneurial in their search for funds as the historical reliance on public coffers shifted to corporations, individual donors, and students themselves. Faculty professionalization essentially came to a halt as colleges and universities employed ever greater numbers of part-time and non-tenure-track instructors and as legislators in some states mounted a frontal attack on tenure. Large, centralized public systems gave way to autonomous units and all institutions faced demands for greater accountability. A commitment to equity and to understanding the historic structures and policies that have precluded social and economic mobility for various racial and ethnic groups led to a widely publicized and at-times ugly backlash against the system, along with accusations that colleges and universities were anti-White. And the for-profit sector grew astronomically (and then shrank considerably) as federal regulations either supported the expansion of or cracked down on the sector's abuses.

For several of the topics, major events cluster around the cleavage lines separating the eras. The year 1790 marked the beginning of a rapid expansion in number and type of institutions. The first state colleges and the first technical institutes were formed shortly thereafter, and the curriculum was opened well beyond the liberal arts to include a broader array of emphases. Within a few years on either side of 1869, the Morrill Land Grant Act was passed, graduate study was introduced along with the first HBCUs, and the first sizable philanthropic donations were given to establish universities. The year 1945 marked the opening of the Mass Higher Education Era because the GI Bill, the President's Commission on Higher Education report, and the formation of the National Science Foundation all occurred around then. In the years surrounding 1976, America finally disentangled itself from the conflict in Vietnam, the gap between rich and poor began widening for the first time since the 1950s, and the rate of college-going turned up once more. However, the Consolidation Era was notable less for major events than for planting the seeds of change that would alter or even reverse historical trends in the years that followed. The beginning of the Contemporary Era in 1994 coincided with intensified public preferences—both at home and abroad—for smaller government and greater reliance on individual responsibility and free markets. Even though these preferences have weakened as people sought government aid to stimulate the economy or provide pandemic relief, together with increased access, escalating costs, and greater emphasis on efficiency, they have led to adjustments in several of the trends that had undergirded the previous 350 years of higher education in America.

This book accords approximately equal emphasis to each of the eight topics. But the eras are treated differentially. Because other works have covered the years prior to World War II rather completely, this book devotes only 30% of its total to those eras: 15% to the Colonial and Emergent Nation Eras together and 15% to the University Transformation Era. Roughly 20% each is devoted to the Mass Higher Education and Consolidation Eras, and about 30% of the book discusses the trends and events of the past 30 years.

The book is less a history than a synthesis. Several general history books from McMaster (1909) to Jordan and Litwack (1994) were consulted relative to the societal context for the period prior to 1945, but no attempt was made to uncover new information regarding debatable issues. A rich literature traces social reform; the background and effect of immigration policies; sources of the expansionist mentality in the nineteenth century; the oppression of Indigenous peoples; economic, social, and political issues related to slavery; and so on. As Nash, Crabtree, and Dunn (1997) documented, all have been reinterpreted repeatedly and are not repeated here. Controversies also persist over most major events within higher education: whether the Dartmouth College case of 1819 truly altered relations between states and private institutions; who was most influential in Congress's passing the Morrill Act of 1862; the extent to which the Civil War constrained the expansion of higher education in the South; the importance of various collegiate forms that were tried early in the twentieth century; which institutions deserve the lion's share of credit for preserving general education—to name only a few. Thorough treatments of each of these issues are available elsewhere.

This work traces higher education's first few centuries by synthesizing prevailing views without iterating the debates over motives, causes, or prime movers. It recounts the story of the early eras only to establish a background to the past 80 years for readers unfamiliar with the ways higher education developed. It centers on what was and what is, with a minimum of what ought to be. However, biases do appear throughout; absolute objectivity is an impossible conceit. In particular, we are unapologetic advocates for preserving and protecting at all costs the major pillars upon which higher education has rested for nearly 400 years, including institutional autonomy, academic freedom and free expression, and a commitment to acting for the public good. To these mainstays we add the (relatively) newer concepts of equal access and equitable support as essential aspects of the system. Over four centuries, American higher education has experienced numerous trends in curriculum, pedagogy, financing, and other characteristics, but these principles provide a through line from 1636 to the present and protect the ideals upon which this country was founded; abandoning them would be nothing short of abdicating higher education's role in the preservation of our democracy.

Not all of postsecondary education is treated here. People always have learned outside the formal system; apprenticeships, ateliers, and academies have been prevalent throughout history. Today, industry-granted nondegree credentials, noncredit courses, proprietary schools, and virtual universities (both non- and for-profit) surround the core enterprise and involve millions of learners. But this work considers primarily the sector that the National Center for Education Statistics calls higher education and that most people mean when they say they went to college: public and private, nonprofit community colleges, four-year institutions, and universities.

This book is useful as an overview for faculty, staff, and students in all institutions of higher education who may benefit from knowledge of the broad currents affecting their work. It draws on numerous historical and contemporary sources; unless otherwise cited, most statistics on the institutions and their students, faculty, governance, finances, and outcomes are from the U.S. Department of Education's *Digest of Education Statistics* or similar, broadly available publications. Since the first edition of this book was published in 1998, it has been adopted widely in undergraduate and graduate education and social science courses, providing students with an understanding of the institution in which they are engaged and where they might spend their careers. This book also may appeal to readers outside the postsecondary realm who are concerned with higher education's contributions to democracy, its role in reflecting and propelling major social movements, and what its trends, events, and priorities portend for the future of America and its place in the world.

## Supplementary Reading on the History of Higher Education in America

A few books are indispensable for a rounded view of the history of higher education. Rudolph (1962, 1991) reviewed numerous single-college histories, anecdotal accounts of college life, and reports of collegiate functioning to produce *The American College and University*—a detailed account of colleges in the eighteenth and nineteenth centuries. The transformation of the university has been documented in several basic texts. Bledstein's (1976) *The Culture of Professionalism* traces one of the pillars on which the university system was built. Veysey's (1965) *The Emergence of the American University* carries through the conversion of colleges and the development of new universities. Geiger's two-volume account of the research function, *To Advance Knowledge* (1986) and *Research and Relevant Knowledge* (1993), analyzes how the growth of research stimulated and was itself furthered by universities from the nineteenth century through the Consolidation Era. Thelin's (2021) *Essential Documents in the History of Higher Education* presents a collection of many primary sources critical to understanding the development of higher education in the United States.

Some texts examine the history and contemporary issues associated with particular institutional types. These include Lovett's (2015) *America's Historically Black Colleges and Universities: A Narrative History* and Harris's (2021) *The State Must Provide: Why America's Colleges Have Always Been Unequal—And How to Set Them Right*; Harwarth, Maline, and DeBra's (1997) *Women's Colleges in the United States: History, Issues, and Challenges*; Kisker,

Cohen, and Brawer's (2023) *The American Community College*; and Geiger and Sorber's (2013) *The Land-Grant Colleges and the Reshaping of American Higher Education*.

Several books focus on particular topics within higher education. College students and their lives have been examined repeatedly, including in Levine and Dean's (2012) *Generation on a Tightrope: A Portrait of Today's College Student*. College costs and outcomes have been considered from many perspectives. Goldrick-Rab's (2016) *Paying the Price* examines how college costs and financial policies perpetuate an inequitable system. Bowen's (1980) *The Costs of Higher Education* displays various ways of analyzing costs, and his 1977 book *Investment in Learning* traces individual and societal benefits as revealed in numerous studies of college outcomes. The effects of college on individual students are reviewed by Feldman and Newcomb (1969), Astin (1977, 1993), Pascarella and Terenzini (1991/2005), and Mayhew et al. (2016). Kaplin's reviews of court decisions and legislation affecting higher education have appeared in six editions of *The Law of Higher Education*; the most recent of these succinct summaries (Kaplin et al., 2020) reveals how every aspect of the college is embedded in a legal structure. Excerpts from all these books, along with relevant journal articles or contemporary journalistic pieces, can be assigned alongside this text to provide students with both a broad understanding of the shaping of American higher education and opportunities to dig deeper into issues of interest in their lives and their studies.

# 1

# Establishing the Collegiate Form in the Colonies: 1636–1789

Three characteristics of the English colonies in America most affected their development. First was the settlers' determination to form a way of life different from the governmental and familial rigidities they had left in Europe. Second was the land—the limitless horizons for which dissidents and new immigrants could reach whenever they tired of their previous stations. Third was the religious spirit of the time—Protestantism and Anglicanism newly separated from Catholicism and continually reforming, yielding variations in patterns of observance from deism (later Unitarianism) to fervent religious sects established in reaction to the eighteenth-century Enlightenment.

## Societal Context

The distance between Europe and the New World allowed the colonists to build their own societies with varying degrees of oversight from the parent country. Although explorers and immigrants had been arriving in the Western hemisphere for more than 100 years, no lasting English settlement occurred until the beginning of the seventeenth century. Under British sovereignty, Virginia, the first colony, was settled in 1607, and all but one of the colonies was formed by the end of the century. Georgia, the last of the original 13, was settled in 1732.

Each colony differed from the others as a consequence of its climate and the religion, mores, and social patterns characteristic of its early settlers. Among these groups were Puritans, who brought a high interest in literacy and a strong theological bent to Massachusetts. Next were distressed Royalists who saw Virginia as an extended export farm to be worked by indentured servants and enslaved Africans. The Society of Friends (Quakers) who emigrated from the English Midlands to the Delaware Valley were the most willing to interact peaceably with Indigenous peoples and to base their communities on religious toleration. The last groups were from Scotland and the north of England and Ireland, who emigrated to escape poverty in the mid-seventeenth century and settled the Appalachian back country. Each group stamped its lifestyle so definitively on its environment that its speech patterns and accents, attitudes toward learning and aging, child-rearing practices, and many other folkways (Fischer, 1989, names over two dozen) persist to this day.

Whereas the seventeenth century was characterized by an influx of English families, adventurers, and indentured servants, along with Africans who were brought unwillingly, in the eighteenth century, sizeable numbers of Germans, Scots, and Irish arrived. From around 250,000 in 1700, the colonial population quadrupled by midcentury and increased by as much as 30 to 40% each decade thereafter. The settlements were widespread; Boston, the largest city, had 7,000 people in 1700, and by the end of the Colonial Era it, Philadelphia, and New York each had as many as 10,000. The more Europeans who arrived, the greater the need for land, hence the forced displacement of native peoples as the immigrants conquered the wilderness. This expansionism was a continuation of the brutal colonialism that had characterized the Spanish in the Caribbean and Central and South America, and that the English and other European powers subsequently pursued in Australia and parts of Africa. The colonists began enslaving and importing people from Africa because they could not entice or coerce the Indigenous to work in farms or industries. The policy of removing Indigenous peoples persisted until the end of the nineteenth century, when the remnants of native populations had all been assimilated through intermarriage or sequestered on reservations.

For most of the settlers, the New World represented a chance for a new start. Some came as indentured servants who had escaped prison or penury and bought their passage by promising to work for the plantation owners for several years after arrival. Others were disinherited children who saw greater promise on a continent where land was cheap and a farm and family could be built anew. The desire for religious freedom brought groups from England and the European continent during an era of religious turmoil and conflict.

In their social and cultural context, the colonies were decidedly English. For a half-dozen generations after the founding of Jamestown and the landing at Plymouth Rock, they retained the characteristics of the motherland. The Germans brought their own language and customs, but the colonial laws, dress, culture, religion, professions, government, and child-rearing and educational practices were modeled on English forms. However, the years in America effected modifications in all areas of life. Some were necessitated by the challenge of living in a land where the wilderness and geographic remoteness posted a substantial threat. Others were shifts in thinking, as a unique American consciousness took shape. Distance from the mother country, reckoned in terms of the several weeks that it took for messages to pass between England and the American seaboard, allowed for new ideas in religious observance and acculturation of the young to take shape.

Religion and the churches are worthy of a special note because they were so close to the daily life and thought of the colonists. Anglicanism and various Protestant sects dominated seventeenth-century England, hence the English colonies as well. The Bible was the major text, often the only book in the home. God and the devil were real to believers. As the witchcraft trials in Massachusetts and Connecticut supposedly demonstrated, people could be possessed and have occult powers (although a good dose of misogyny was clearly also at work). The New England Puritans had fled the dictates of the high church of the home country and its links with the crown. They abhorred the idea of a theocracy, but the secular states they established had strong ties to their churches and in some areas of social control were more rigid than those they had left.

The Puritans especially felt they had a mission to create "a city upon a hill," as John Winthrop exhorted even before his congregants reached shore. If they failed to establish God's Kingdom, he later preached, they would be turned out of the land. In other words, fail and you're damned. This thesis, modified toward secular pursuits, became so engrained that 200 years later Alexis de Tocqueville commented on how ambition was the universal feeling in America.

By the middle of the eighteenth century, European concepts of the Enlightenment and deism modified thought. Many of the leaders born in the first half of the century—Washington, Jefferson, Franklin—adhered to rationalist ideas, read political philosophy that espoused the rights of man, and had less attachment to organized religious observance. To them, the Bible was not revelation but a text. Reaction to the eighteenth-century Enlightenment came with a religious backlash known initially as the Great Awakening, dating from around 1750 and reappearing subsequently under different identifiers. This religious fervor led to the continual splintering of established churches into various sects.

The major peculiarity of the North American continent—its limitless land—influenced the way the colonies and eventually the nation developed. The country was large enough to allow for continual reformation in all aspects of colonial life. New forms of religious observance and fresh ideas in everything from the building of settlements to child rearing could emerge in the vast spaces available. The boundless horizons affected family life. The general outlook, especially in the New England colonies, was that everyone should live in family units. But the restless son, chafing under the domination of parents who might have little patience with a rebellious child, could always strike off on his own. The frontier, new opportunities, a different environment always beckoned. In a land where cash was scarce, a child had little reason to hope for an inheritance, but although nearby farmland was not free, the frontier was ever expanding and a young man could work his way into a homestead of his own. Accordingly, a sense of optimism grew. The sons could expect to have more wealth than their fathers; a young man could become a professional even if his father was not. There were few barriers to men on the move. Roles for women were more limited; most opportunities other than domestic service as wife, maid, or private nurse were still in the future.

The geographic openness of the land was reflected also in the way people could reinvent themselves. There were few restrictions on entering the professions. Lawyers, physicians, and theologians occasionally attempted to control entry into their professions, but in few communities was anyone eager to examine the credentials of a newly arrived practitioner; public licensing was seldom seen. Apprenticeships were the major form of access to the professions. A lawyer could take a young person to read with him, and that person could hang up a shingle and enter practice at any time. In medicine, a few physicians tried to form groups to judge who was entitled to call himself a doctor, but apprenticeships and the subsequent opening of practice were not regulated. According to Handlin and Handlin (1971), "Only one colony, New Jersey, in 1772, actually limited by law the right of anyone to assume the title of Doctor" (p. 39). Clergymen were both preachers and teachers, and congregations tended to value those who were schooled. Numerous preachers ascended to the pulpit without formal schooling, but "university graduates who could hurl about quotations in the original Hebrew and Greek and loftily demonstrate their superior familiarity with Scripture enjoyed a strategic advantage" (Handlin and Handlin, 1971, p. 43). Teaching required no specific preparation; anyone who could read and write could show others how to do it.

The development of literacy did not depend on schooling. Today's children are exposed to language on television, billboards, emails, texts, even the promotional material on cereal and toy boxes; regardless of the emphasis in their homes, they are surrounded by words. But although the colonists in the coastal cities saw books and newspapers, many who lived on the margins of civilization had little association with print other than in the family Bible. Their familiarity with ideas came through words delivered by a preacher or itinerant peddler. For the vast majority of young people, the family was the source of education in social mores, morality, and ways of behaving. Under the circumstances, the extent of literacy is remarkable. Their orthography was crude, but the colonists were more familiar with language than were their European social-class counterparts.

The American Revolution was born as the colonists gained a sense of uniqueness. Strung along the Eastern Seaboard from Massachusetts to Georgia, oriented to the sea across which the immigrants had come, most colonists saw England as the mother country. All the main towns were on bodies of navigable water, and most of the commerce was waterborne trade among the colonies themselves, the English colonies in the West Indies, and Britain. The reasons for the American Revolution have been discussed countless times. Was it commercial interests? Blundering by the English rulers? A by-blow of the French–British rivalry? The revolution has gained particular status as a mythic quest for freedom from oppression by the crown. Taking a cynical view of the latter reason, Samuel Johnson contemporaneously asked, "How is it that we hear the loudest yelps for liberty among the drivers of negroes?" (Bate, 1975, p. 193). Most colonists had no trouble holding compartmentalized notions of freedom—one for themselves, another for the enslaved and servants. Views of parity were further stratified to account for what were perceived as natural differences among wealthy and poor and men and women. The "all men are created equal" phrase in the Declaration of Independence proved rather a qualified statement—one that was to be debated and reinterpreted countless times throughout the new nation's history.

## Institutions

Table 1.1 shows a statistical picture of the conditions surrounding American higher education in the Colonial Era. Between 1700 and 1789, the number of institutions grew from two to nine, and the number of students and faculty increased 600% or more. Still, the roughly 1,000 students enrolled at the end of the Colonial Era comprised a miniscule portion of the free population.

The nine colleges that were organized in the colonies were modeled on educational forms that had been developed in Europe over the prior 500 years. This development has been traced well by Rashdall (1936), Herbst (1982), and more recently, Lucas (2006). One incipient university form was organized by groups of students who established their own organizations and assemblies, employed the faculty, decided on how they would spend their funds, and set rules governing the courses of study, examinations, and awarding of degrees. Such institutions were organized as early as the twelfth century in Italy and subsequently in Spain, Portugal, and central Europe. The curriculum included the classical writers along

Table 1.1. Statistical Portrait of the Colonial Era, 1700–1789 (estimates).

|  | 1700 | 1789 |
|---|---|---|
| Colonial population | 250,000 | 3,800,000 |
| Free population |  | 3,123,600 |
| Enslaved population |  | 676,400 |
| Number of students | 150 | 1,000 |
| Number of faculty (professors and tutors) | 5 | 133 |
| Number of institutions | 2 | 9 |
| Number of degrees earned | 15 | 200 |

Sources: Rudolph, 1962; Snyder, 1993; U.S. Bureau of the Census, 1791.

with studies in the liberal arts and natural science. They awarded bachelor's degrees and, if a graduate chose to stay on for another year or two, the master's. A teaching license would be awarded somewhere between receipt of the bachelor's and the master's. The student-led institutions also established rituals surrounding graduation, including academic robes and commencement exercises.

A second type of European institution developed within the church. Allied closely with the priesthood, these institutions were dedicated to training clergymen. Their curriculum was based in church doctrine with students learning the words of doctrinal authorities and principles of theology. They were professional schools operated by and for the purposes of the centralized church. The University of Paris exemplified the form.

In retrospect, the threads of the colonial colleges and of higher education subsequently were apparent in both groups. The institutions incorporated the conceptual precision that would later lead to empirical investigation, the use of ancient texts as enhancing intellectual curiosity, and humanistic thought that led toward secularized study. Elements of all the institutional types can be found in higher education today. However, at the time of the founding of the colonial colleges, the pattern of curriculum and faculty-student relations stemming from church-related institutions was most prominent. The European universities were lagging in the development of science, and the colonial institutions had little to do with science until the end of the era. The students and the faculty had no say in governance matters; authority ran from the institution's board of governors to the college president. Curriculum centered on classical texts and the foundations of Christian doctrine. The humanities, as studied in classical writings as literature and the fine and performing arts, had to await a later day. Similarly, experimental science as an area of inductive inquiry could not emerge until scientists freed themselves from reliance on doctrine and prior authority and from the search for universal truths as revealed in classical writings.

The eighteenth-century Enlightenment did not have an immediate effect. The anticlerical ideas that were filtering into the thinking of Europeans from French and English philosophers to literate laypeople were slow to penetrate the universities. Gradually, however, the idea of the university as the seat of all learning came to fruition in Oxford and Cambridge. And slowly across the continent, the university as an agent of the state was born. Still, science as a path to understanding through experimentation and verification was developing outside the universities and remained there well into the nineteenth century. Except for theologians, few scientists, philosophers, or leading thinkers were working within the formal higher education structure in Europe or in the colonies.

The colleges in the American colonies were modeled on an amalgamation of ideas and forms coming from Europe, but they emerged in their own way. Boorstin (1991) commented that the colonists settled the continent before they had a system for dealing with it. Hence they had to reinvent governmental and educational forms as they went along. The idea of lay governing boards was transplanted from Scottish universities and the curriculum and residential pattern from Cambridge. None of the colleges followed the continental pattern of students in charge of the institution, and none was strictly controlled by a dominant church. They all developed around notions of acculturating the young, passing on the wisdom of the classics, and preparing people for service as clergymen or public servants.

Around 130 university-trained men were in the first generation of immigrants to Massachusetts Bay Colony. Thirty-five were graduates of Emmanuel College, Cambridge, and when they established Harvard, they followed the Emmanuel pattern. Control was to be in the hands of church elders; curriculum was similar to the Cambridge curriculum, and the residential pattern was suited for shaping immature youths. The college centered on teaching, not on the advancement of learning, and saw no contradiction in preparing young people to take their place as public officials and as ministers in a community where church and state were closely aligned. Because any institution could constitute itself as a college and grant the degrees that it chose, Harvard began awarding degrees even before it was legally incorporated.

The colleges formed in the other colonies followed the Harvard pattern but with some major distinctions. Soon after Virginia was settled, the colony received a grant of land for college purposes from the crown, but the College of William and Mary did not open until after it received a royal charter in 1693. The college was to prepare civil servants and clergymen for the Anglican church. Scottish influences were seen in the development of William and Mary, as its control was established in a board of trustees representative more of laymen than of church officials. William and Mary also had a mission of Christianizing and civilizing the Indigenous, as did Harvard and Dartmouth. But their efforts were largely unsuccessful. Few Native Americans enrolled; in Dartmouth, for example, which had begun with a specific intention of bringing the Indigenous into the fold, perhaps 50 enrolled between 1769 and the end of the nineteenth century.

The combination of church influence blended with lay control became the pattern. There was a link between the established churches and the teaching of morality or the good life, and as new churches were formed, the colleges came along with them so that the young could be instructed in proper conduct. Each of the colonies was founded by "a considerable infusion of men who had received in the European universities a liberal culture, which they desired to reproduce on these shores" (Ten Brook, 1875, p. 17). Dartmouth and Yale were formed by Congregationalists—spin-offs from the Massachusetts Puritans. The dominant religious groups in the other colonies formed their own institutions: the College of New Jersey, later Princeton, by the Presbyterians; the College of Rhode Island, later Brown, by the Baptists; Queen's College, later Rutgers, by the Dutch Reformed church; and King's College, later Columbia, by the Anglicans (but with a strong minority of other religions represented on its first governing board). The College of Philadelphia, later the University of Pennsylvania, was the most decidedly nonsectarian of the colonial institutions (see Table 1.2).

Much has been written about these institutions; each has its own history, which Rudolph (1991) summarized well. In general they consolidated trends coming from England and Scotland. College governance, finance, faculty-student relations, curriculum, and instructional practices were all codified in this era, so that when hundreds of new colleges were founded after the formation of

Table 1.2. The Nine Colonial Colleges.

| Original Name | Current Name | Year Established | Primary Religious Affiliation |
|---|---|---|---|
| Harvard College | Harvard University | 1636 | Puritan |
| College of William and Mary | College of William and Mary | 1693 | Anglican |
| Yale College | Yale University | 1701 | Congregationalist |
| College of Philadelphia | University of Pennsylvania | 1740 | Nonsectarian |
| College of New Jersey | Princeton University | 1746 | Presbyterian |
| King's College | Columbia University | 1754 | Anglican |
| College of Rhode Island | Brown University | 1765 | Baptist |
| Queen's College | Rutgers, the State University of New Jersey | 1766 | Dutch Reformed |
| Dartmouth College | Dartmouth College | 1769 | Congregationalist |

the United States, they followed the model even as their emphases shifted. Although they were connected with the churches, the colleges were not as much religious as educative, founded to produce a learned people. They would train clergymen, and because most clergymen were community leaders, they would prepare statesmen.

Trow (1989) traced other reasons for establishing colleges: the idea of perpetuating a civilized society in frontier communities; the growing need for better-trained people not only in law, medicine, and theology but also in commerce and navigation; community pride; and idealism and philanthropy on the part of community leaders. The absence of any restraining political force helped. There was no centralized government to establish standards. Each colony was free to set its own rules, and although each college resembled the others because of the power of imitation, the institutions were free to develop in idiosyncratic patterns. The colonists could have sent their young to England for university schooling, and many did, but the trip was long and perilous and the expense was great. Coupled with the desire to build communities with a strong religious orientation and to fit youth for public employment in the civil state, the colleges developed indigenously. They followed Harvard, the first, but Harvard never set rules for the others.

The ease with which religious sects formed as splinters from existing churches also influenced the development of higher education in the colonies. Rivalry between religious sects certainly played a part, as a half-dozen different church groupings were represented among the nine colonial institutions. Except for the College of Philadelphia, each had a church connection, although as at King's College, it might be so tenuous that the institution was effectually interdenominational. Church influence was never absolute, and a tradition of lay governance was established early on.

If the colleges were not needed to prepare people for professions, the impetus for their founding must be sought elsewhere. In general the colonists wanted to build communities that integrated religion with society, and religion depended on an educated laity.

They needed institutions to assist in acculturating the young, and the notion of civilizing the Indigenous population was not far from the surface. Furthermore, the colleges brought prestige to communities that needed to show that they were centers of civility, not merely rude outposts. The desire to build unified communities with strong religious orientation was powerful, and the belief that civil government needed educated leaders was prominent as well. For all these reasons the colonists built colleges—only three prior to the middle of the eighteenth century but six more between then and the founding of the nation. As few as they were, they effected lasting public perceptions of what a true college should be.

Toward the latter part of the Colonial Era the religious orientation waned, and the idea of a civil community centered on principles of morality and public service, apart from an established church, grew. The colleges emphasized public service, acculturation of the young, and the civil community. Benjamin Franklin ([1749] 1931) detailed these purposes in his *Proposals Relating to the Education of Youth in Pensilvania*, in which he outlined the institution that would become the University of Pennsylvania. The college would center on the education of youth for the purpose of supplying qualified men who would serve the public with honor. These youth would be prepared in writing, drawing, arithmetic, geography, and history, including natural history and the history of commerce. The rector would be a learned man, a correct and pure speaker and writer in English, and would have tutors serving under him. The scholars and students would live together and keep their bodies sound through frequent exercise. The English language would supersede Latin as the tongue of instruction. All would center on the good life for the students and the betterment of the community without reference to church doctrine. Here was the foundation of the institution that could sustain all the best purposes of the other colleges without reliance on doctrinal connection. William Smith, who published a similar plan for a college based on a broad curriculum, became the College of

Philadelphia's first leader. More than any other colonial institution, it seems to have presaged the institution that epitomized the American college.

## Students

Few young people in the American colonies went to college. Either they had no need to go or college was not accessible to them. Few families had the cash to pay tuition, low as it was, and support their children through a course of study. More likely, they depended on their sons for assistance on the farm or in the family business. Except in New England, education was not compulsory even in the lowest grades, hence there was no groundswell of demand for further study; few students attended school past the primary years.

College as an avenue of career preparation had limited appeal because few careers depended on further study. All the crafts and trades, as well as farming and business, could be learned through imitation or apprenticeships. The incipient professions—law and medicine—were learned in similar fashion. Only theology demanded some further schooling, and even there, most of the preachers were not college-trained. Of the few careers available to women, none required classroom learning.

Enrollments were small. By the end of the Colonial Era, scarcely 1 in 1,000 colonists had been to college. The total number of resident students at any of the colonial colleges was usually less than 100, and the graduating classes could be numbered in single digits. Harvard, the largest college, graduated 64 students in 1771, but it was well out in front of the others. Rudolph (1977) noted, "Not until 1759 did the handful of colonial colleges graduate, among them, more than a hundred young men in any one year" (p. 25). Some of the wealthier families, especially in New England, sent their children to the mother country for higher education, but even adding those into the college-trained population, the numbers remained consistently small.

The careers followed by those who had been to college give an indication of the purposes for which students attended. Most became either ministers, physicians, teachers, lawyers, public servants, or a combination of these. However, their numbers were so sparse that they did not form alumni groups or otherwise interact with each other in terms of the institution they had attended. They were likely to associate in the literary societies formed in Boston and Philadelphia that enlisted members from any college in America or England, or from none.

The paucity of public schools meant that most of the young people who had any formal training studied with tutors—educated people who would take on a few students as a means of supplementing their own livelihood. In Virginia, the planters' sons sometimes boarded with preachers who would provide instruction in English grammar, Latin, mathematics, and natural science. Meriwether Lewis commented that finding a place with tutors was not easy because the rudimentary schools that they operated could house only a few pupils at a time. He had to stay away from home for long periods of time so that he would not lose his place as a student in the home of a person who was teaching him English grammar and arithmetic (Ambrose, 1996). Lewis's experiences as a member of a plantation-owning family were typical; most students were sons of landowners or professionals. A few were from the families of artisans or tradesman; very few were from among the owners of small farms.

College life was designed as a system for controlling the often exuberant youth and for inculcating within them discipline, morals, and character. Each student was to attend the lectures and tutorials, obey the rules, and avoid the company of base people. Yale issued a set of rules describing the rigor with which the college expected its students to attend to a way of life: "No Student of this College Shall attend upon any Religious Meetings either Public or Private on the Sabbath or any other Day but Such as are appointed by Public Authority or Approved by the President. . . . If Any

Student shall Prophane the Sabbath by unnecessary Business . . . or makeing any Indecent Noise or Disorder . . . He Shall be punished. . . . No Student Shall walk abroad, or be absent from his Chamber, Except Half an hour after Breakfast, and an hour and an half after Dinner" (Dexter, 1896, pp. 4–5). Further regulations described penalties, fines, or at the ultimate, expulsion, for swearing, cursing, blaspheming, playing cards, singing loudly, associating with disorderly people, and the like. First-year students were also obliged to go on errands if so instructed by students in superior classes. There were no provisions for grievance proceedings.

The family that sent its youngster to college expected that the institution would take charge of the boy's life. Frequently the 14- or 15-year-old already had been identified by his parents as being in need of some greater discipline than a father or mother could provide. The colleges were truly to act as surrogate parents and to enforce behavior that the boy's parents might not have been able to instill. Youngsters who could not accept the form of discipline that the college imposed might be sent home.

The admissions requirements imposed by the colonial colleges further limited the number of students who could attend. Harvard required that the applicant be able to speak Latin verse and prose and to decline Greek grammar. At William and Mary an applicant was to be at least 15 years old and to have studied Latin and Greek in the college's preparatory section if he had not attained a working knowledge of the classical languages previously. Admissions requirements at Yale were the same as at Harvard; students were to be "skilful in construing and grammattically resolving both latine and greek authors and in making a good and true latine" (Broome, 1903, p. 28). The only real change in admissions requirements by the end of the era was when Yale added an understanding of arithmetic in 1745 along with "Sufficient Testimony of his Blameless and inoffensive Life" (p. 30). Princeton added arithmetic to its requirements in 1760; King's College began in 1754 with requirements in Latin, Greek, and arithmetic.

There were no written admissions tests. Students were examined orally by the college president or the tutors. Students were sometimes exempt from one or another requirement, especially because all the colleges needed students and could not afford to adhere too strictly to their written admissions statements. Most of the books in use were written in Latin, hence knowledge of that language was certainly to be expected. But the colleges that required their students to converse exclusively in Latin were considerably less successful in enforcing the rule. Broome (1903) cited a record of a visitor to Harvard in 1680 who found the students hardly able to speak a word of Latin. However, Latin was used on formal occasions.

Patterns of student life, some of which persisted well into the University Transformation Era, were set in the colonial colleges. The right of upperclassmen to haze first-year students; college responsibility for student conduct; the residential nature of the institution, with students expected to obey rules set down by the college authorities; pranks played on faculty by students; punishment for mischief making—all the elements of adolescence displayed by boys living in isolated communities were present. The rules of conduct typically were those found in a monastery or a reform school run by a religious order.

Rudolph (1991) summarized the formation of what became a particular way of combining living and learning: "The collegiate way is the notion that a curriculum, a library, a faculty, and students are not enough to make a college. It is an adherence to the residential scheme of things. It is respectful of quiet rural settings, dependent on dormitories, committed to dining halls, permeated by paternalism. It is what every American college has had or consciously rejected or lost or sought to recapture" (p. 87). He rationalized this form of community by pointing out that in the Colonial Era the population was so scattered that for colleges to develop they had to form their own communities. But he also pointed out: "By the time that the colleges in Philadelphia and New York were under way, the collegiate pattern was not a necessity, for there were cities. But by then what had been a necessity had become a tradition" (p. 88). Although young people living together led to excesses such as rowdiness, it continued to be justified as the best arrangement for maintaining control over the developing adolescents, merging the extra curriculum with the formal program, enhancing relationships among all the people involved, and in the more recent vernacular, merging cognitive and affective growth. Belief in the virtue of the isolated community persisted. "Supporting this belief was the attachment of the American people to an agrarian myth, to a view of the world that saw the land as the source of virtue and as the great moving force in history" (Rudolph, 1977, p. 95). Nice to have a myth that fits the landscape.

## Faculty

Throughout the era, the teaching profession was struggling to be born, but there were too few faculty to form a critical mass of like-minded colleagues. Most faculty were tutors, typically recent graduates who were awaiting positions as ministers. They received little pay and might have been thankful for subsistence. Early on, the college president and the two or three tutors who served at his pleasure taught all the subjects to all the students. Subsequently, professors began to specialize in various subjects and nascent academic disciplines.

A review of the leading colleges reveals the situation. The president of King's College hired a tutor in 1755 and a professor two years later; the three taught the entire curriculum. Queen's College opened with one tutor in 1771 and employed another even before appointing a president; one tutor left, but the other taught all the classes and, in 1773, organized a student literary society. William and Mary had a total of 10 professors over a 40-year span. Five principal masters teaching natural philosophy, moral philosophy, oratory, languages, and mathematics served the College of Philadelphia.

Yale and Harvard, which were older and larger, employed a combination of tutors and professors. Between 1702 and 1789, approximately four tutors a year worked at Yale; their tenure was typically three years. A professorship of divinity was endowed in 1746. Harvard had six professorships endowed between 1721 and 1783: divinity, mathematics and natural philosophy, Hebrew and other Oriental languages, rhetoric and oratory, anatomy and surgery, and theory and practice of physics. In addition, a total of 63 tutors were employed from 1643 on; all were Harvard graduates. The president and professors lived in their own houses, but the tutors, who were not allowed to marry, lived at the college and monitored the students 24 hours a day.

The idea of college teaching as a profession developed gradually and at different times in the early colleges. But none of them entertained the European idea that faculty constituted a corporate body possessing authority, privilege, and functional independence. Finkelstein (1983) conceptualized academic careers as having three strands: disciplinary, institutional, and external. Until the middle of the eighteenth century, the academic disciplinary strand had virtually no effect, and there was not much to the faculty member's involvement with the institution from the standpoint of autonomy, permanent appointments, and other elements of making a career. Toward the end of the eighteenth century, the institutional aspect of the academic career took form as a permanent faculty made up of professors appeared. However, the external career—the consultations with government and industry—was more than a century in the future.

Both professors and tutors tended to come from professional families; their fathers were in law, medicine, or the ministry. Faculty acted both as instructors and as custodians responsible for student behavior. The tutors usually taught all subjects to a single class, whereas the professors taught in a particular subject, often one in which they had some post-baccalaureate training. The relative permanence of the professors was another distinguishing characteristic; a professor might plan a career at a single institution, but few tutors remained at a college long enough to see their class through to graduation. In a few cases, a tutor was promoted to professor; in most, the professor was appointed from the outside.

The low wages paid to tutors and professors set a pattern that persisted until the second half of the twentieth century. The faculty were similar to clerics in that they were expected to teach for the privilege of affiliating with the college. Unlike lawyers or physicians who expected to be paid for their ministrations, faculty were more like volunteers engaged in public service. Few social institutions, except churches, could command that type of loyalty. At any rate, for some, tutoring and attempting to shape young people had more appeal than the drudgery of farming.

## Curriculum

In his foreword to Rudolph's 1977 book, *Curriculum: A History of the American Undergraduate Course of Study Since 1636*, Clark Kerr offered a definition of curriculum as "nothing less than the statement a college makes about what, out of the totality of man's constantly growing knowledge and experience, is considered useful, appropriate, or relevant to the lives of educated men and women at a certain point of time" (p. xxi). Whether curriculum is defined as a set of courses or the totality of experiences that the college designs for its students, it is always rationalized as being practical. The curriculum responds to society and in turn shapes society, sometimes lagging, sometimes leading.

Curriculum is directed toward acculturating young people—their character formation, preparation for careers, access to society, language, and manners. Over time and among institutions, the emphasis on one or a combination of these purposes shifts. Except for the rarest of programs, learning for the sake of learning has not been used as a curriculum rationalization. Practicality and usefulness, whether for building critical skills among students or equipping them to obtain certain jobs or make more money, have been the goals; curriculum always has purpose.

The definition of what is practical shifts from era to era. A knowledge of rhetoric, classical scholarship, and the Bible was occupational preparation for lawyers, ministers, and statesmen in the Colonial Era. Science and mathematics entered the practical curriculum toward the end of the era, as many of the students prepared for commercial careers. Colleges do not change curriculum readily. The drawback of having a stable curriculum with only minor changes is seen when students begin using the college for purposes other than those for which it was designed, and the curriculum does not shift rapidly enough. If the college curriculum is designed to turn out clergymen or public servants, for example, and businessmen come out of the college, has something gone wrong with the curriculum? Or has society changed its mind? By the end of the Colonial Era the defenders of classical studies were hard put to justify their favored curriculum, as proportionately fewer graduates entered the clergy. But those studies persisted through several additional generations.

The colonial curriculum did not rest on vast numbers of courses. A few courses, required for all students, sufficed. The curriculum has since expanded dramatically, not necessarily because of the expansion of knowledge (a justification often placed on the overblown college catalogue of our times; there was much to be learned in the Colonial Era as well). But several forces acted to keep the colonial curriculum restricted: there were few students, as most young people entered society through learning outside the colleges; study was not for the purpose of advancing knowledge but for preserving what was already known; few occupations demanded specific preparation; and the colleges were dominated by religious organizations with a limited view of the scope of knowledge.

Principles of scientific inquiry were slow in penetrating the curriculum. Meriwether began his 1907 text by saying, "To-day science dominates our schools. Our colonial ancestors studied and taught in an atmosphere of religion which they had inherited from the middle ages. For centuries the pedagogic aim had been to point the road to Heaven" (p. 13). Education was a matter of authority; truth was derived from omniscience; individuality or creativity was not part of the plan. The classics and biblical texts dominated the curriculum throughout the Colonial Era because they proceeded from a well-organized base.

The classics could be justified as practical training for all careers. Because apprenticeship was the mode of training that led people toward every occupation, those who went to college would expect to advance in the higher reaches of the professions that they had entered through academic apprenticeship. A knowledge of rhetoric and Greek and Latin could certainly be justified as useful for practitioners in law and medicine as well as theology. No one was required to go to college to enter professional practice, and occasional efforts to restrict access to the professions had little effect. The label of practicality, then, was as easy to justify as it was difficult to prove. None of the professions demanded content examinations; modern foreign languages were no more or less useful than Greek, Latin, and Hebrew; chemistry had no more or less practical relevance than rhetoric.

The curriculum in the colonial colleges was a direct import from Europe with little modification until the latter half of the eighteenth century. Rudolph (1977) traced it to both the Renaissance and the Reformation, whereas Lucas (2006) took it back to the Roman Empire and the library and scholarly enclave at Alexandria. From the Renaissance, the colleges taught Greek and intended to bring their charges toward adopting the role of gentlemen and scholars. Medicine and theology were the vocational studies of the time. From the Reformation, the colleges took the study of Latin in preparation for the clergy. Both movements had been incorporated in Cambridge, where young men were prepared not only for the clergy and scholarship but also for public service. "Emmanuel at Cambridge, a Puritan foundation, was the model for Harvard; Queen's at Oxford was the model for William and Mary" (Rudolph, 1962, p. 24). Additional imports were the four-year baccalaureate and the names for the freshman, sophomore, junior, and senior classes, along with the organization of curriculum into courses with finite time blocks and the notion of a master or teacher who would dictate to his charges.

The curriculum derived from the seven liberal arts: in Latin, the trivium (grammar, rhetoric, and logic) and the quadrivium (astronomy, arithmetic, geometry, and music), which were said to lead students to a unified understanding of reality. These seven subjects did not encompass everything that was known in Greece and Rome or even the curriculum as it was taught in the schools of the time, but they did appeal to the medieval church, not least because they were especially suited to the intellect and to spiritual concerns, as differentiated from the mundane or secular. Butts (1939) traced the codification of the seven liberal arts to the Roman scholar Varro in the second century BCE. Along with Lucas (2006), Rashdall (1936), and others, Butts tracked the development and modification of this essential curriculum form from its earliest days through the medieval church, the Reformation, and on across the Atlantic.

What is noteworthy is the way liberal arts studies were adapted to religious purposes, modified to add various forms of philosophy and ethics, and prescribed for all who would count themselves among the learned. At Oxford, the four-year baccalaureate program included grammar, arithmetic, rhetoric, logic, and music. Students who would go on to the master's degree would read prescribed books in geometry, astronomy, and philosophy—the latter including physical science, ethics, and metaphysics. Thus, the tradition of a prescribed curriculum was set before the American colonies had been founded.

Tracing curriculum in any precise form is difficult because the meaning of course names changes. Arithmetic, logic, physics, and philosophy were all present in the colonial curriculum, but content in those areas was different from the areas of learning into which those studies evolved. Latin in the seventeenth century was studied as a medium of communication, whereas by the eighteenth century it had been transformed into drill in composition and grammar. Science was certainly not as it is currently construed: an inductive process that involves discovering knowledge through theory building, hypothesis testing, and experimenting. Notes left by teachers of science in the Colonial Era show how painfully they attempted to straddle the worlds of observation and reliance on doctrine. They explained weather, the senses, and elements such as air and water deductively, with a combination of observation and a heavy reliance on prior teachings. By the middle of the eighteenth century, Harvard had various types of apparatus for teaching science, including scales, pulleys, rulers, mirrors, and cylinders—the equipment found in a middle-school classroom 2 centuries later. Science teachers could demonstrate the force of gravity, a vacuum, and the rotation of the planets; thus, the capacity for showing how experimentation and observation could yield understanding was present and undoubtedly used. Appliances to measure sound and electricity were meager, but space, time, and optics were well covered. Nonetheless, Meriwether (1907) noted, "Of the scientific attitude as it is cultivated to-day, of cold, dispassionate study of nature without the lingering flavor of authority or of religion, our colonial ancestors knew nothing" (p. 224).

Barriers to a common curriculum across institutions stem from the earliest days of the colleges. Each college staff thinks it has a unique approach because of the special predilections of the teachers, students, and community from which they come. However, there is much imitation in curriculum formation. The two forces—uniqueness and imitation—are constantly at odds. But regardless of whether the colleges imitated or went their own way, the curriculum in the colonial colleges was serious. No frivolous courses decorated the catalogues with promises of divertissements for the young people. They went to college and they were expected to study. What happened on their own time may have been frivolous, but the college demanded rigorous involvement with what the masters felt was appropriate. Rudolph (1977) reported that "the official catalogue of the Yale library in 1734 listed the works of Shakespeare, Pope, and Spenser under the heading, 'Books of Diversion'" (p. 25).

A view of the colonial curriculum is available in the earliest schedule printed by Harvard, around the year 1638. It shows classes laid out from Monday to Saturday for students in the first, second, and third year of their studies. The first year included logic, physics, rhetoric, divinity, and the history and nature of plants, along with Greek etymology and Hebrew grammar. In the second year, the students were presented with ethics, politics, and Greek prose and dialectics, along with a continuation of rhetoric, divinity, and plant taxonomies. The third year introduced them to arithmetic, astronomy, and geometry while they perfected their composition in Greek (Meriwether, 1907, p. 52). Although Harvard started with a three-year program, by 1654 it had adopted a four-year plan.

Yale modeled its curriculum on that of Harvard, and William and Mary picked up elements of that curriculum but added more science and mathematics. However, the College of Philadelphia (later the University of Pennsylvania) laid out a three-year curriculum in 1756 that deviated somewhat. There, students studied more arithmetic, including algebra; more science, including architecture, mechanics, optics, and astronomy; more natural science, including both plant and animal history; and more chemistry. Such innovations as studies in navigation, surveying, civil history, law and government, and trade and commerce were brought in as well. Even so, students were expected to follow classical and rhetorical studies with Greek and Latin literature at the core. And disputation (oral debate) was still important; the plan showed afternoons of the third term for seniors held aside "for composition and declamation on moral and physical subjects" (Snow, 1907, p. 71).

The other colonial colleges, all founded in the 30 years prior to the revolution, kept the study of the classics and the Bible but added modifications of their own. Most of the changes were in the direction of natural philosophy and greater emphasis on mathematics. William and Mary was the first to establish a professorship in science, and by the end of the era, all the colleges had professors of mathematics and natural philosophy or physics. Ethics became an important area of study. It had been present from the start in courses in moral philosophy, which were central to the study of divinity, but as ideas from the eighteenth-century Enlightenment penetrated, the importance of reason and human nature began to supplant biblical studies. Ethics courses, often taught to seniors by the president of the college, included elements of science and religion; all were concerned with questions about the proper conduct for people to follow. Ethics had to be defended continually against those who contended that faith and religious texts pointed the way. Still, the writings of modern philosophers such as John Locke were incorporated into the courses, and by the end of the era a professorship in moral philosophy had been endowed at Harvard.

Evolution of the curriculum continued as King's College in New York (later Columbia) opened with a distinctive bent toward commerce. Soon after the revolution, Jefferson, an alumnus and member of the board of visitors, tried to reorganize the College of William and Mary by abolishing professorships in divinity and adding medicine, natural history, and modern languages to the curriculum. His plan even included the introduction of electives, but it had only limited success. Throughout the era the champions of science fought continually against the religious orientation to which college founders and their successors had adhered. Plans for complete curriculum reorganization were usually defeated, and those who would introduce new studies would have to wait until separate professorships could be established. Then, as later, the disputes centered on what courses of study should be required of all students.

A view of curriculum in the Colonial Era shows, above all, how the colleges were struggling to break away from the influence of the church and adherence to the classics. Literature and history were introduced even at Harvard. Logic was studied as a key to understanding the scriptures but evolved so that it became more readily applied to human affairs. The early studies of science were dominated by recourse to authority; the works of Aristotle were scanned for reference to physical phenomena. As the era progressed, however, the teachers of science became more ready to base their curriculum on observation and experimentation. Languages that were studied as a way of learning literature and philosophy evolved so that they became objects of study in their own right. By the middle of the eighteenth century, the classics were still at the core of the collegiate experience, but the study of political philosophy and science in the form of astronomy, mathematics, physics, chemistry, and geology was present in all the institutions. The establishment of professorships in the various disciplines revealed how the curriculum was splitting. Yale had both apparatus for teaching science and a professor of divinity, suggesting that the college leaders recognized the necessity for separating these areas of thought.

Throughout the era, issues of freedom of thought and the value of experience over authority were at the heart of curricular battles. The Scottish universities were reforming themselves throughout the eighteenth century and had begun to influence the colonial colleges. In particular, they assigned specific subjects to professors, thus laying the foundation for academic specialization. They also broke away from the idea of a prescribed curriculum, with each student studying the same subjects, and they added scientific studies. William and Mary had been founded as an Anglican institution, but because its first president had come from the University of Edinburgh, its curriculum was never as strict as that in the New England institutions. The first provost at the College of Philadelphia was also influenced by the Scots; he had attended the University of Aberdeen. The very idea that curriculum had to be justified as being for practical use effected other changes. At King's College and the College of Philadelphia, navigation, geology, the study of government, and mathematics were central and pushed divinity and the classics to the side. A broader curriculum that tended away from a primary reliance on deductive reasoning was emerging.

**Instruction**

Methods of instruction are central to studies of curriculum. Both what is taught and *how* it is taught are at the core of the collegiate experience. Complete descriptions of teaching methods are not available, but the pedagogy of the time can be pieced together from reports of students describing their experiences in the classes, the rules governing instruction, and the reminiscences of the tutors.

Grammar was learned through memorization and analogical reasoning. Classifications of words, paradigms for declension and conjugation, and syntactic structures had to be learned by heart. Long passages or even the complete speeches of celebrated orators were assigned for students to recite. More advanced students were required to compose their own orations. The study of rhetoric included training in the finding of suitable subject matter, arranging a debate or declamation, memorizing material, and developing the style and form of delivery. Students might have constructed their own speeches by taking extracts from the texts they were using. Education in rhetoric balanced reading and memorization with composition and performance.

Until the latter part of the era, few textbooks had been written especially for college teaching. The tutors lectured, the students gave recitations, and readings were assigned in whatever books the college was able to acquire for its small library. Some of the professors gave laboratory demonstrations, and a few may have employed the Socratic method. The paucity of books made tutors, and eventually the professors, the primary source of information. The president lectured as well. When textbooks did appear, they reflected ideas of the Enlightenment; written in English, they were thus subversive of Latin as the language of instruction.

Each of the colleges had a library, often with the core collection donated by a local book collector. Except for Harvard's 12,000 volumes, the holdings averaged around 2,000. Most of the books were reprints of classical texts. Shores (1966) calculated the average annual rate of acquisitions to be less than 100 volumes, some funded by student fees. The risk of fire or water damage was high.

Although much instruction, especially in the early years, was in Latin, few students spoke it outside of class. Most could no more speak Latin than can contemporary students who have studied a year or two of a modern foreign language speak readily in that language. Writing in Latin was similarly difficult for the students. They may have been expected to read classics in the original, but translation guides in English were usually available. Students were supposed to be able to translate from Greek to Latin to Hebrew to English and so on, but few could do more than parrot the passages in the various languages. A professorship in Hebrew was established at Harvard in 1764, but "by 1775 the subject was almost extinct at Yale" (Meriwether, 1907, p. 108).

Scholasticism, a medieval philosophy centered on traditional teachings and doctrines, undergirded instruction that valued arguments based on authority. An archaic form of pedagogy, disputation clashed with the notion of experimentation and free inquiry as ways of discerning knowledge, but it held on throughout the era, possibly because it was popular, fitting the enthusiasms of young boys who may have seen it as verbal fighting in the classroom. Argument from authority, vehement rhetoric, and debates all blended with the boyish desire to harangue in ringing terms. (Today we would call it an in-your-face method.) The intention was to see who could argue most convincingly.

Harvard demanded two disputes a week from students in their first three years and one a week from the seniors. Disputation was even part of the entrance examination, and student debates were featured in graduation ceremonies where a thesis might be given to two students who would apply their powers of deduction to establish its validity. The rules were carefully spelled out in great detail, specifying exactly how the adversaries should conduct themselves.

The reliance on a pedagogy centered on scholasticism grew steadily weaker throughout the era as students began studying empirical methods. Astronomy changed as students were introduced to the Copernican system, wherein the Earth spins on its axis and the planets revolve around the sun, instead of the Ptolemaic system in which the Earth was thought to be the center of the universe. But the old methods of learning from authority died hard and could be observed for more than a century after experimental science entered. Furthermore, the scholastic method was based on the rigor of logic and a reliance on rhetoric—two ways of organizing and displaying learning that served well for their time.

Gradually the new pedagogy of experiments and experimental evidence became prominent. Descartes, Bacon, Newton, Locke, and Hume were studied. The colleges now had telescopes and other scientific apparatus. Mathematics evolved to become a foundation for surveying and navigation. Early experiments with electricity were conducted. By the end of the era, the philosophy of experience and experiment had pushed scholasticism quite to the side; if not for the religious tradition, it would have disappeared even earlier. Instruction was being carried on in English, and even at Harvard and Yale—the colleges that clung to Latin the longest—the ancient language had weakened its hold on students and faculty alike. Latin would have disappeared completely except that many of the available books were written in Latin. Instruction in Hebrew was no longer required, and consequently the language was used only at ceremonial occasions.

The classics survived, and even though science was clearly in the ascendancy at the end of the era, Greek and Latin texts were still being studied. The rationale for reading those texts had shifted. Studying the classics in the original Greek and Latin had replaced the texts emanating from the church. The humanists were the progressives of the time, arguing against strictly religious studies. They held sway through much of the era, even as engineering, navigation, and modern foreign languages were being introduced. The evolution of curriculum in the Colonial Era is shown in the change from a curriculum based on church doctrine, to one based on secular humanism revealed through Greek and Latin texts, to one in which science replaced divine revelation as the ultimate standard. Each in its time had been justified as practical: the teachings of authority represented orthodoxy and were necessary to bring young people into understanding Church doctrine and to leading a blameless life. Humanistic studies, classical Greek, and Latin were necessary to demonstrate how the Protestant churches had broken from medieval orthodoxy and were certainly important for people who would display the garb of erudition. Science was the foundation of engineering, hence necessary for people who would go into the emergent professions. Study of language and literature would well fit the incipient statesmen and lawyers. Faith in the power of science, the reformation of social institutions, and belief in the intrinsic goodness of man were making their mark.

## Governance

The governance of colonial institutions foreshadowed issues of governance in higher education throughout its history. The colleges were founded with a combination of public and private control, with a tilt toward the latter; the extent of influence by the lay board and the members appointed by the colonial court or legislature was always an issue. Similarly, the extent of control to be exerted by the board of trustees, as contrasted with the members of the college community itself, was always in question, although the board was certainly in control of all the important issues. A dominant president appointed by the board and responsible to it alone also dates to the Colonial Era.

These governance features came about because of the time when the colonial colleges were established and the peculiarities of the English colonies in America. In Europe, the universities had evolved from self-governing groups of teachers and students or from within a court or church hierarchy itself. In the self-governing institutions, the masters and students received charters similar to those granted to the medieval guilds. The university properties and management were quite modest. But in the colonies, there was no class of faculty, masters, teachers, or professors to organize its own institutions. The colleges founded in the Colonial Era were governed by outsiders—boards of overseers that were made up of clergymen or magistrates. The only teacher represented in the governing body was the president, and even he served at the pleasure of the board. Subsequently, when the colleges were incorporated, the notion of adding faculty as members of a governing body was raised. However, the faculty were never in a position of power and certainly far from having self-governing status. The combination of lay boards of trustees, strong presidents, a weak professoriate, and the absence of a central ministry of higher education throughout American history served to perpetuate these early-established governance patterns.

A short review of the governing principles in some of the colonial institutions serves to illustrate the nature of governance. The General Court (that is, the legislature) in the Massachusetts Bay Colony agreed to establish Harvard and in 1639 arranged for a committee of overseers to be the initial governing body. Members of this committee included the governor, deputy governor, and treasurer of the colony as well as three magistrates and six ministers. The overseers were not actually a governing board but were subject to the General Court, which itself hired the first president of the institution. This president taught the entire curriculum on his own and presided over the first graduation with no explicit authority until the General Court granted a college charter in 1650.

Under the charter, a corporation consisting of the president, fellows, and treasurer was formed. As a corporate body, it had the right to self-succession and to hold property, appoint other officers within the institution, and be exempt from taxes. However, the corporation exercised its rights only in the presence of the counsel and consent of the overseers who, after 1642, included the colonial governor and deputy governor along with the college president, nine assistants of the court, and nine pastors and teachers from adjoining towns. Thus, although Harvard had two governing boards—one a lay group, the other comprising the college's administrators and faculty members—the lay board was clearly in charge.

The College of William and Mary, organized in Virginia toward the end of the seventeenth century, took a slightly different form. Virginia was a royal colony dependent on officials in London, and the colony itself was dominated by plantation owners, many of whom did not rank public education as a high priority. In 1691, the head of the Anglican church in Virginia traveled to London and, on behalf of the Virginia assembly, petitioned the bishops for a grammar school and a college. James Blair returned to Virginia with a charter authorizing 18 Virginia gentlemen to act as college trustees. This board, whose members were called visitors, would be augmented by additional members nominated by the general assembly. The visitors were authorized to draw statutes for the college and to arrange for their own successors. They also were to form a corporation made up of the college masters. But the board of visitors could elect members of the corporation and in effect had far greater authority over the faculty than had been the tradition in European universities. Like the lay board at Harvard, William and Mary's lay board had ultimate power with the corporation subordinate to it.

The third colonial college, Yale, was formed by Congregational ministers in Connecticut. The Connecticut General Court appointed 10 clergymen as trustees to organize the institution. They were given the power to manage the funds and property, to appoint the college rector and officers, and to grant degrees or licenses. The 1701 charter thus established a college operating without the direct participation of secular officials, even though the General Court promised to grant an annual sum to sustain the institution.

Toward the middle of the eighteenth century, the trustees were incorporated as "The President And Fellows Of Yale College" under a charter that gave the General Court the right to inspect the college laws and to disallow those they considered improper. The charter upheld the ultimate authority of the General Court but also guaranteed the college's autonomy within certain limits. Because the 10 trustees were still church ministers, the charter reaffirmed the original intention of the college planners to protect the established religion by keeping the secular authorities away from direct governance.

The charter of Rhode Island College, later Brown, similarly gave authority to a governing board that was made up of clergymen but had an ecumenical tone. The Baptists were a majority of the board, and the president was to be a Baptist, but positions were reserved also for Quakers, Congregationalists, and Episcopalians. The Baptists dominated, not because they were the official religion of Rhode Island but because they outnumbered the other sects and were the original sponsors and chief supporters of the institution. The Rhode Island charter also stated that there should never be a religious test administered to anyone wanting to teach in or attend the college. Accordingly, the college developed as a blend of religious ecumenicalism with a strong tilt toward single-sect dominance in the governing board and in the person of the president.

The College of New Jersey, later Princeton, was organized under a charter granted by the king and approved by the colonial legislature. It advocated religious freedom, specifying that the masters and students be from any religious denomination. The trustees were required to take an oath of loyalty to the king and were entitled to receive land and funds from which they could draw their salaries and pay the president, tutors, and college officers. The trustees were responsible for employing the staff and were authorized to award degrees. Staff included not only the president but also tutors, professors, a treasurer, a clerk, an usher, and a steward.

King's College, renamed Columbia after the revolution, received a royal charter in 1754. As evidence of the public interest in supporting and monitoring higher education, the legislature established the University of the State of New York (USNY) 30 years later to provide oversight to Columbia and other colleges incorporated thereafter. USNY's regents were empowered to visit and inspect New York's colleges, to award degrees, and to distribute state funds.

Benjamin Franklin's plan for organizing the College of Philadelphia was not followed exactly, but it is notable for what it says about governance powers and the detail with which it specified institutional functions. The college was not to be church-based but was to be formed by collecting money from a group of subscribers who would then choose trustees; the trustees in turn adopted a constitution. The plan thus provided for the formation of an institution without seeking permission from any outside governmental authority. It specified everything from tuition to the appointment of faculty and the president, from plans for a library to rules for the deportment of students, from the management of funds to salaries to be paid to the staff. The trustees were to have power over all those functions and also would engage people who would teach modern foreign languages, writing, mathematics, and natural and "mechanical" philosophy (Franklin, [1749] 1931, p. 29). Franklin's plan also provided for a variant curriculum with one program based on Latin and Greek, another on English; an early acknowledgment of the importance of having both traditional and modern programs in the same institution.

The colonial institutions reflected the social organization within the colonies: a major religion or combinations of sects; reliance on a legislative body for at least initial if not continuing control through appointing trustees; and funding to be derived from a combination of donations or subscriptions and legislative appropriations, supplemented by whatever tuition they could collect from the students. Some colleges received royal charters, and others began with charters issued by the colonial authorities. In three of the institutions—Harvard, William and Mary, and Rhode Island College (later Brown)—a dual governing structure was established in which the lay board of trustees shared power with an internal group of college fellows consisting of the president and members of the faculty. In the other six colleges, the lay board had authority over all functions. The influence of organized religion was evident in the composition of the lay boards. Several of the charters provided for trustees to be drawn from certain religious denominations, but none required that control remain in the hands of the founding denominations. Only three specified that the college president be a member of a particular religious group.

Perhaps most in contrast to European institutions, the American college president was the unquestioned authority. He was the liaison between members of the college and the governing board and was responsible for all college operations. Most of the presidents were ministers who taught classes, raised money, recruited and disciplined students, and presided over all college functions. Much of their energy was devoted to ensuring that the college had enough students and funds to sustain itself. Many were homegrown; Harvard had six presidents in its first 50 years, four of whom were alumni of the institution. Many of the presidents of other colleges had been trained in Scotland, including the founding leaders of William and Mary, the College of Philadelphia, and the College of New Jersey.

Whether or not one religious denomination was dominant in a colony, the colleges tended to emphasize interdenominational freedom. Harvard, William and Mary, and Yale had been founded with an emphasis on preparing ministers, but in their original charters several of them mentioned the importance of interdenominationalism: "those of every Religious Denomination may have free and Equal Liberty and Advantage of Education in the Said College" (Princeton), and "all the members hereof shall forever enjoy full, free, absolute, and uninterrupted liberty of conscience" (Brown) (Hofstadter and Smith, 1961, pp. 83, 135). As Herbst (1981) noted, "It was a case where the religion of the people rather than of the sovereign determined the religion of the college" (p. 46).

Regardless of whether the colleges were established by the colonies or via royal charter, the concept of a lay board of governors was central. As time passed, the social composition of boards shifted and clergymen were eventually replaced by businessmen and politicians. Even though the faculty subsequently gained a measure of self-governance, taking charge of curriculum and admissions requirements, they never were granted more than token representation on boards of trustees. And when the first state universities were organized soon after the formation of the United States, their governance followed the pattern established previously: lay boards were responsible for fiscal matters and for appointing a president who would manage the day-to-day affairs of the institution. The main difference in the state institutions was that church influence on the governing board and curriculum was abolished. Otherwise, these institutions functioned similarly to their private predecessors.

## Finance

How did the colleges sustain themselves? In general, they depended on voluntary contributions and on combinations of funds from various other sources. Support was received from sponsoring church groups, from subscribers or private donors, and from governmental bodies. This combination of public and private financing led Rudolph (1991) to coin the term *state-church colleges* to describe Harvard, William and Mary, and Yale.

Harvard received money from the Massachusetts General Court, including a tax levy and a donation of land. The court also assigned revenues from the Charlestown Ferry; years later, when the ferry was replaced by a toll bridge, Harvard continued to receive revenue from it. The college itself was named for the Reverend John Harvard, who contributed money and what was then a sizable library of 400 books. In the latter years of the seventeenth century, more than half of Harvard's annual income was provided by the government; less than 10% came from tuition.

When William and Mary was chartered in 1693, the Virginia legislature awarded funds to it from a tax on tobacco and from export duties on furs. Subsequently, monies from a tax on peddlers were granted to it. As additional evidence of legislative support, the students were granted immunity from taxes and military service.

Exemption from taxes and military service was granted also to students at Yale as a way of making the college more attractive to the young people it was attempting to enroll. The Connecticut General Court also donated special funds from time to time. The institution was named in honor of Elihu Yale, who donated goods that yielded an endowment of around 500 pounds, a goodly sum at a time when 50 or 60 pounds might support the entire staff for a year.

The College of New Jersey (Princeton) and Queen's College (Rutgers) did not receive regular financial support from the legislature, although they and other colleges that were formed in the middle of the eighteenth century might appeal for ad hoc donations from time to time. Legislative support was capricious anyway because when a colonial assembly became dissatisfied with a college, it might reduce or omit an annual appropriation. Still, the colonies had a hand in assisting most of the institutions—some by donations of land, which they had in surplus. And the colonies helped in other ways, such as by granting permission for the colleges to operate lotteries.

The College of Philadelphia was founded with donations from individual subscribers. Around 400 pounds total was pledged per annum for the first five years by 25 donors, Benjamin Franklin among them. Even so, in most of the colonies, substantial donations were hard to attract, and the colleges had to depend on student fees for their survival. A family that could afford to send its sons away to school could usually also spare some money for tuition. Fees, room, and board ranged from 10 to 50 pounds at a time when a journeyman mechanic earned 50 pounds per year and a prosperous attorney from 200 to 300 pounds. Obviously, college was not for the sons of the poor. However, few students were expelled if they could not pay the tuition; the notion of work-study was in place early on.

Thus, the pattern of funding from multiple sources was established. Philanthropy, regular or occasional support from legislative bodies, and tuition all played a part. None of the colonial colleges were well endowed; the pattern of trying to raise money continually, of spending all that could be raised, and of living in genteel poverty continued well into the future for practically all colleges in the nation.

## Outcomes

The few extant colleges with their small numbers of students were certainly less influential than the churches of the era, but some effects were apparent. These included career preparation, individual mobility, assistance in child rearing, the idea of the institution as an archive, and such intangibles as community pride.

Some of the long-term trends noted in the Introduction to this book were already apparent. The nation was certainly expanding. The twin forces of continued immigration from Europe and large families led to phenomenal population growth; the estimated 1.1 million people in 1750 had become nearly 4 million by the time of the first U.S. Census 40 years later. But larger numbers of diverse institutions and access for greater numbers of students were not yet on the scene and several generations had to pass before more than a scant handful of women were allowed to enroll. And although the colonial colleges employed a few professors, the group remained far from any semblance of professionalization. Yet a curriculum leading to various occupations had begun, especially in the colleges with a more secular bent, and public funding was also apparent.

Career preparation was especially notable in two areas: preparation for the ministry and for public service. Although many graduates became neither ministers nor public servants, a high proportion entered those callings. In the early years of Harvard and Yale, more than half their graduates became ministers, a percentage that dropped to about one-third by the end of the Colonial Era. Although this group did not account for the majority of the people who took up pulpits, it was a force because many of the alumni returned to the institution as tutors while they were awaiting reassignment, and because ministers who had been college trained often were selected for the most prestigious church positions. The collegiate function of preparing students for the ministry dropped as a percentage of the whole as new colleges were opened and new programs were added, but it remained significant; as late as the Civil War, 20% of Yale graduates were ministry-bound.

Graduates of the other colonial institutions were less likely to enter the ministry. A record exists of the progress of students at King's College, which admitted between 6 and 11 young men in each of its early years. Few of those students completed the course of study; they went into business or into the army; they left because of illness or transferred to other institutions. One student "after three years went to nothing" (Schneider and Schneider, 1929, p. 244). These different career outcomes reflected the different orientation of King's, as well as some of the other institutions that had less stringent church affiliations than Harvard and Yale.

A sizable proportion of graduates became influential in public service. Fewer than 5,000 people graduated from the nine colonial colleges between 1636 and 1789, but 25 of the 56 signers of the Declaration of Independence and 31 of the 55 members of the Constitutional Convention were lawyers, along with 10 of the first 29 U.S. senators and 17 of the first 65 congressmen. Not all the lawyers had graduated college, and some had been trained in England, but in an era when the colleges awarded approximately one bachelor's degree per year per 25,000 people, their influence was well out of proportion to their size. Five of the first six presidents of the United States were college trained—the two Adamses at Harvard, Jefferson and Monroe at William and Mary, and Madison at Princeton. Several justices of the Connecticut Supreme Court were Yale graduates. William and Mary produced the first president of the Continental Congress, the principal author of the Declaration of Independence, a delegate to the Constitutional Convention, several senior officers in the Continental Army, a chief justice, a governor of Maryland, the first governor of Virginia, and several early congressmen. This suggests not only the importance of the early colleges but also that the nation was founded by an educated minority whose writings evidenced their dedication to classical and then-contemporary political philosophy.

The graduates who entered civil service, the ministry, or other activities were similar in many respects. The distinction between one profession and another or between people in the professions and those who were managing estates or businesses was not nearly as clear as it would become later. The curriculum was not distinguished by barriers between academic disciplines. Young men studied the liberal arts along with science, classics, and classical languages. On a continent where social and professional roles were not rigidly differentiated, the manner of preparing people for particular callings was not differentiated either.

People had to be versatile. Men prepared for the ministry often entered public service or managed estates. Most changed vocations as opportunity or circumstances beckoned. The colleges prepared learned men, using a liberal arts curriculum that was considered the best preparation for anyone who would take their place in society. A curriculum centering on rhetoric, the classics, and grammar was useful for ministers, lawyers, or statesmen, all of whom frequently embellished their arguments with quotations from the ancients. The importance of rhetoric alone cannot be discounted as an essential for politics and the pulpit. Specialized curriculum for any endeavor was slow to develop.

Individual mobility was enhanced through college attendance. The colonial institutions brought the young person into society in a fashion similar to the function that later institutions sustained. At issue was the proper way of rearing children. Could a family raise sons with all of the necessary skills and connections that an aspiring member of the elite should have? Many could not, and they depended on a college to properly prepare them.

The early colleges created several arrangements to acculturate their charges. The living quarters included tutors as male role models and, because the students lived together, peer pressure was strong. Students met others who could help them with social connections; a sample of students from the College of New Jersey, College of Philadelphia, and King's College suggests that around one-fourth of them married sisters of classmates or daughters of trustees or college presidents. These personal connections also led to beneficial apprenticeships as the students met professional people who helped them connect with the proper physicians or attorneys with whom they might study (Vine, 1997). Elaborate graduation ceremonies were another way that students connected with the community. Commencement exercises were a rite of passage, and the colleges that were formed in the latter part of the Colonial Era all had rules about conducting the ceremonies written into their charters.

Although their libraries served as archives and their curriculum tended to perpetuate knowledge, the early colleges were far from being centers of scholarship and research. Nor was there much interaction among professors at different institutions; more likely, any discussions about scientific research or philosophy took place in learned societies such as the Boston Philosophical Society and the Philadelphia-based American Philosophical Society. Various other specialized societies were formed outside the colleges in the Colonial Era; prominent among these were marine societies in Boston and Salem.

The colleges continually strived to demonstrate their value to the broader community. They petitioned repeatedly for public funds and wrote into their charters or regulations promises that they would fit young people for public employment. Certainly the colleges were valuable because of the status that was gained by someone who became conversant with the classics. Communities took pride in the number of erudite people among them. Even though the degree was not required for any particular vocation, a community with a number of college graduates serving as teachers, ministers, lawyers, and members of the town council was considered to be of high social status. Liberal education had a connection with community mores.

Thus the colleges provided an avenue of mobility for young men, prepared ministers, and assisted in the formation and maintenance of an elite group of public servants at a time when there was no specialized training for government, teaching, librarianship, or medical practice. Overall, they served as symbols of community pride; an institution of higher learning distinguished a civilized community from an unlettered settlement in the wilderness.

Among the many questions regarding the colonial colleges, a few stand out.

- Would the rules governing student behavior in the colonial colleges have been less strict if the students were older?

- Given that few families sent their sons to college in the Colonial Era, how might one account for the predominance of college-trained men in the colonial legislatures and the Constitutional Convention?

- Why were the colonial colleges so little concerned with science and only marginally connected with the advancement of knowledge?

- Even today, the nine colonial colleges are among the most prestigious institutions of American higher education. What factors might account for their longevity, their ability to remain at the top of nearly all college and university rankings, or their continued popularity among aspiring students and their families?

Vestiges of the colonial colleges are most readily apparent today on the campuses of small liberal arts colleges, yet their influence extends deep into even the largest, most diverse, and occupationally oriented universities. This consistency of form both stymies radical organizational change and demonstrates the power of tradition.

# 2

# Diffusion of Small Colleges in the Emergent Nation: 1790–1869

Several events occurred around the time the nation was formed that separated the Colonial Era from the Emergent Nation Era. Most notable were the opening of the West—punctuated by the treaty ending the revolution in 1783 and the Louisiana Purchase 20 years later—the rapid organization of dozens of new colleges in the newly acquired territories, and the establishment of the first state colleges soon after the U.S. Constitution was ratified.

## Societal Context

The opening of the West marked the new nation. In the latter years of British hegemony, the colonists were forbidden to settle the lands over the mountains. But as soon as the British were expelled and even before the Treaty of Paris in 1783 had specified that the Northwest Territories be ceded to the new nation, population moves toward the West were under way. By the time of the second national census in 1800, 1 million of the 5.3 million Americans were living west of the Appalachians.

Soon after the turn of the century, the Louisiana Purchase in 1803 nearly doubled the size of the nation. By 1820, 2.5 million people lived in the West, and by 1830, 3.5 million, accounting for 37% of the entire population of the United States. Gaining Florida, Texas, and Oregon, along with territory ceded by Mexico in 1848, added so much land that nothing stopped a single person or a family from going West and making a new start. The acquisition of new territory and a sense of optimism fed on each other. Both built on the millennial outlook of the early colonists, especially the New England settlers, who felt their expansion into the New World was justified by scripture. "It is our manifest destiny to possess the whole of the continent which Providence has given us for the development of the great experiment of liberty," proclaimed a New York journalist in 1845. And that was followed by expressions such as, "Go West, young man, and grow up with the country," the title of an 1851 editorial in an Indiana newspaper (subsequently popularized by Horace Greely, editor of the *New York Herald*).

The nation became conscious of itself as an American people, integrating waves of European immigrants. Many newcomers, especially the Irish Catholics, suffered from discrimination, but only African Americans were excluded completely from the bounty and optimism of the expanding nation. Their enslavement marked the entire era, from their being noted in the Constitution as three-fifths of a person for purposes of apportionment, to the pattern by which new states were brought into the union, to fundamental disagreements about the ethics and economics of enslaving human beings that culminated in the Civil War.

The nation was one politically but its sections developed separately. The emphasis on manufacturing in the North and agriculture in the South began in the Colonial Era, as Virginia's economy centered on tobacco and the economies of the New England and mid-Atlantic states were based on fishing, shipping, and manufacturing. By 1810, the United States was producing more than $125 million in manufactured goods per year, most of them in the Northern states. In the 1820s, in Massachusetts alone, the output of the textile mills rose more than tenfold. During the same decade, cotton production in the South more than doubled, as farmers and plantation owners moved into the fertile lands of Alabama and the Mississippi Delta. Exports of agricultural products were high, with cotton supplanting in value the colonial crops of tobacco, rice, and indigo. (Forced labor by enslaved people, of course, contributed to the profitability of the cotton industry.)

The ties binding West to Northeast grew stronger each year as the main railway lines were built between those sections. People and institutions followed the tracks. By the middle of the century, the telegraph and the railroad had become so widespread that for the first time in the history of civilization, people and ideas could move faster than an animal could carry them. Other elements in the nation's infrastructure were growing. The Bank of the United States was founded, along with a national currency, a post office, copyright law, and patent and bankruptcy laws. Tensions with Europe and the vast amount of land to be developed turned the nation inward. At the same time, rivalry between North and South was accelerating. One region was building cities, being populated by waves of European immigrants, expanding its industry. The other was building its agricultural capacity, exporting its products, and coalescing its thinking around slavery—its most peculiar and shameful institution.

Growth in power of the federal government was limited by the determination of the Southern states to maintain their independence. Even so, the federal government helped develop canals and railroads by giving land to private agencies. Canal construction was further enhanced by the Army Corps of Engineers, formed in 1824. Although contemporary capitalists like to claim that free enterprise built the nation, around 70% of the cost of the canals and 30% of the cost of the railroads was advanced by federal and state governments. The government was land rich; the value of its public lands was probably greater than everything that was owned in the private sector; certainly that was true after the Louisiana Purchase. The movement of people to the West was enhanced by the government's selling off its lands in small pieces or, more often, in large tracts to speculators who would in turn sell small freeholds. Eventually, with the passage of the Homestead Act in 1862, millions of acres were simply given away to anyone who would settle on them.

The early nineteenth century was notable for expansion not only in population, territory, and manufacturing, but also for the continued evolution of forms of religious observance. Any alliance between church and state had been written out of the federal Constitution; Article VI says that no religious test shall ever be required as a qualification for any office. And the First Amendment to the Constitution says that Congress shall make no law respecting an establishment of religion. The states wrote similar provisions into their constitutions, although in a few states where a single church was predominant, separation took a little longer. Despite the dominance of Puritanism in New England in the Colonial Era, by the time the nation was founded, the largest denominations were the Anglicans, Presbyterians, and Congregationalists.

Church membership grew, from around 1 in 15 people at the beginning of the Emergent Nation Era to 1 in 7 at the end of it. And church affiliations shifted around so that among the Protestants, the Methodists and Baptists were the most prominent after the middle of the century, followed by the Presbyterians, Congregationalists, and Lutherans. The Episcopal church, successor to the once-prominent Anglicans, fell to eighth place. Catholicism, fueled by new congregants each time a ship arrived bearing immigrants from Ireland or Central Europe, became the largest single denomination by the end of the era.

Not only did church membership increase but the splintering of denominations into various sects spawned numerous new churches, especially in the West. As the people moved over the mountains, the bonds they had with their prior cultural institutions, organizations, and churches broke down. Religious multiplicity became the norm, and church membership became fluid, with people joining different sects depending on where they moved and their feelings of comfort with a group. The fractionated churches had an additional effect; because many of them were based on emotional appeals and literal readings of the Bible, they suppressed general understanding of scientific discoveries, especially the theory of evolution. Most of the colleges formed during the era, and all of those formed by religious sects, were slow to build modern science into their curricula.

Social reform movements grew all through the nineteenth century. Groups calling for the abolition of slavery became ever more vocal. A temperance movement spread, along with activities to ameliorate child labor and conditions in prisons and mental institutions. Support for expanding the years of compulsory schooling grew, varying in strength from locality to locality and state to state. The U.S. government remained essentially aloof from the support of schooling at any level, although it founded military and naval academies and supported the Smithsonian Institution, another type of educational structure.

Overall, the conflict between North and South, resting on different views of the morality and economics of slavery and political control of that system, dominated the era. Any act of Congress was judged on whether it seemed to enhance or preclude the spread of slavery. The idea of Manifest Destiny—that the United States was ordained to spring from the Eastern Seaboard to the Pacific Ocean—could not be held back, and eventually questions of whether and how far slavery should spread into the new territories triggered armed conflict between North and South. The Civil War (1861–1865) intensified when President Lincoln issued the Emancipation Proclamation on January 1, 1863, freeing all enslaved people in rebelling states, but it was not until June 19, 1865, that slavery, "an institution so influential and corrosive that it both helped create the nation and nearly led to its demise" (Hannah-Jones, 2021, p. xix), would come to an end. On that day, 2.5 years after the Emancipation Proclamation, a Texas general issued an order proclaiming freedom for the last enslaved people in that state. And in December of that year the states officially abolished slavery by ratifying the Thirteenth Amendment to the U.S. Constitution, although African Americans would be systematically excluded from full participation in democracy and in American society for at least another 100 years.

One of the myths that was furthered during the Emergent Nation Era was the idea of individual betterment and its concomitant, free enterprise. People could be more prosperous than their parents; an expanding economy almost mandated that they gain more wealth. People could move out of the class or social status into which they were born. They could join any occupational group that they chose. The less governmental interference with a person's drive for self-improvement, the better. This myth held that the West was settled by people acting on their own. It neglected the realities of government donations of land and sizable subsidies for the railroad and canal builders, as well as the limited opportunities available to Black, Indigenous, and immigrant populations, especially those from Asia. The dark side of the myth was that if all people had the opportunity to better themselves, anyone who did not was considered a failure. Those who did not advance beyond the station into which they were born must have done something wrong. And because that was too much for most individuals to accept, the tendency to blame outside forces grew, fueling disaffection at times with "the rich," at other times with "the government."

In sum, the period from 1790 to 1869 was characterized by territorial expansion that, except for a few islands, brought the nation to its current size; by continued cultural and economic divergence between North and South culminating in armed conflict; by social reform movements; and by optimism that encouraged speculation, entrepreneurship, and the growth of businesses, churches, and educational institutions of every stripe.

## Institutions

Table 2.1 shows a statistical picture of the conditions surrounding American higher education in the Emergent Nation Era. Note how the free population increased more than tenfold and the enslaved population by seven times in 80 years (figures for the latter are taken from the 1860 Census).

Hundreds of colleges were formed in the three-quarters of a century following the founding of the nation. In the first 20 years

Table 2.1. Statistical Portrait of the Emergent Nation Era, 1790–1869 (estimates).

|  | 1790 | 1869 |
|---|---|---|
| U.S. Population | 3,929,326 | 38,558,000 |
| Free population | 3,231,629 | 27,489,561 (in 1860) |
| Enslaved population | 697,697 | 3,953,760 (in 1860) |
| Number of students | 1,050 | 61,000 |
| Number of faculty (professors and tutors) | 141 | 5,450 |
| Number of institutions | 11 | 240 |
| Number of degrees earned | 240 | 9,200 |

Sources: Herbst, 1981; Snyder, 1993; U.S. Bureau of the Census, 1791, 1864.

alone, twice as many colleges were opened as had been organized in the entire Colonial Era. By the 1860s, well over 500 colleges had been established, and between 210 and 250 were still functioning. Questions about the number of institutions are difficult to answer because of the nature of the data. When speaking of the founding of an institution, do we use the charter date, the year classes were first offered, or the year the first degree was awarded? What about colleges that were chartered and never opened or those that provided classes but never awarded degrees? Herbst (1981), who studied the founding of colleges in this era extensively, listed 52 degree-granting institutions chartered between 1636 and 1820. He also traced the various name changes and reorganizations that most of the colleges endured and pointed out how some of them were chartered and never opened, others closed before awarding any degrees, and still others had no data indicating whether or not the college was still in existence in 1820.

Imprecise definition adds to the question of numbers. The name *college* might be applied to an academy, technical institute, professional school, specialized training center, atelier, seminary, or group of apprentices studying with a practitioner. This plethora of institutional forms foreshadowed the contemporary pattern of postsecondary education, which includes technical schools, adult learning centers, community colleges, university extensions, and research institutes, in addition to liberal arts colleges and comprehensive and research universities.

The great flurry of institution building occurred for several reasons. The distances between settlements were great. The splintering of religious denominations continued, and each sect had to have its own college. In each newly formed community, town boosters felt they needed a college to legitimize their settlement. The field was open for philanthropic groups, churches, and community developers. But the overriding reason had to be the general feeling of expansiveness that swept across the United States in the first few generations after independence. When the West opened, the population expansion was so great and the attitude of conquering the continent so strong that the nation reached for the frontiers. High immigration fueled the growth. And the attitude was that everything was open, anything could be built, conquered, accomplished. Crossing the mountains and reaching the Pacific included taking your institutions with you, if not in the first generation, surely in the second. The desire to imitate older communities was strong.

The colleges were formed without any superordinate agencies attempting to impose order. Accreditation was far in the future. Some colleges attended primarily to disciplining young people whose families could not control them. Others provided supplements to apprenticeship programs. Some had special vocational programs; others centered on the professions of engineering, law, and the ministry. As Jencks and Riesman (1968) noted, "Hundreds of colleges owed their existence to the energy and dedication of a single man who felt a call to found a college and was able to rally a few supporters for his cause" (p. 3).

The religious groups were most vigorous in establishing institutions. Proselytizing by the established Eastern institutions was a powerful force. Princeton and Yale especially sent alumni, religious zealots, and evangelists westward to establish Christian colleges. This desire to spread the faith carried with it the patterns of curriculum, instruction, and governance that had been established during the Colonial Era. As the various denominations grew and splintered, more colleges were formed and each competed for students. Whereas in 1810 more than 85% of the enrollment was in colleges formed by three denominations—Congregational, Presbyterian, and Episcopal—by 1860 the share of the enrollment enjoyed by colleges under those auspices had declined to one-half, with the Baptists, Methodists, Catholics, and other denominations (along with state institutions) making up the difference (Burke, 1982).

The spread of colleges included specific types. Some colleges were formed for women, as in Georgia in 1839, but most institutions open to females were finishing schools whose curriculum, designed for homemakers, was far from the contemporary notion of collegiate. The first teacher-training schools appeared; one was founded in Vermont in 1823. Municipal colleges supported partially by local taxation, administered by local governing boards (usually appointed by the mayor), and designed for commuter students were formed in Cincinnati in 1819, New York in 1847, and subsequently elsewhere. Only a few were still extant in the late twentieth century, most notably City College of New York, which had spawned several sister institutions (Brooklyn, Hunter, Queens, Baruch). Most of the others had reverted to private status or state funding and control.

In the absence of regulations, it was easy to form colleges. Any group could solicit funds, write a declaration of principle, obtain a business license, employ a few reasonably learned people, and open for instruction. As long as they could attract a steady trickle of tuition-paying students and collect enough donations to pay the staff and buy food and firewood, they could sustain the enterprise.

Much depended on the entrepreneurial skills and persuasiveness of the organizers. Most of the schools were continually on the edge of bankruptcy.

The federal government enhanced the free and open market in two major ways: first, through the conspicuously absent mention of education in the Constitution and the failure to form a national ministry of education or a national university, and second, through the Supreme Court's decision in the Dartmouth College case of 1819, in which corporations were held to be inviolable. Even though the first six U.S. presidents supported the idea of a national university, and four of them sent requests to Congress for that purpose, it was never established. The arguments in favor of a national university suggest what it might have been. In 1788 Benjamin Rush published a proposal for a federal university that would prepare young people for public life, going so far as to say that after the university had been in existence for 30 years, only its graduates should be appointed to federal office. George Washington mentioned a national university in his first and last messages to Congress, saying that it would promote national unity and, by concentrating resources, be able to employ the best professors. He too saw the institution as having as its primary objective the study of the science of government. President Madison asked Congress to develop an institution that would expand patriotism and strengthen the national government. In President Monroe's administration, a congressional committee endorsed a national university, saying that because there was a surplus in the treasury and plenty of land that could be allocated to it, such an entity should be built. The committee concluded that the undertaking was within the power of Congress to legislate, but many members of Congress, along with President Monroe, believed that a constitutional amendment would be necessary; the House voted against such an amendment.

Had a national university been established it would have had a marked effect on higher education. It would have served as a beacon, setting standards for curriculum, degrees, professorial qualifications, and possibly even for college admissions. Without it, colleges developed capriciously, free to choose the patterns manifest in the older and more prestigious institutions. Absent a national ministry of education, the principle of *anything goes* guided their development.

The Dartmouth College case also affected the development of institutions. The point at issue was whether the state of New Hampshire would be allowed to reform Dartmouth College according to a bill passed by the legislature. The rationale for proposing such changes was that the college had been established as a private corporation designed to benefit the public, hence the public should be able to guide its operations. The counterargument was that once a charter had been granted, the state could not abridge or revoke it. In his remarks to the Supreme Court, Daniel Webster famously is said to have stated, "It is, Sir, as I have said, a small college, and yet there are those who love it" (Hurd, 1966, p. 21). And in 1819, the Court held that the original colonial charter served as an inviolable contract. Even though education was a public matter, the teachers were not public officers, and donations given to the college were not public property subject to the caprice of the legislature. The basic proviso was that once a corporation had been established, it had a right to manage its own affairs, hold property, and exist indefinitely. The decision in effect gave a license to any church or philanthropic group to apply for a corporate charter and organize itself under a self-perpetuating board of trustees without fearing that the state would intervene by appointing trustees, rescinding the charter, or otherwise jeopardizing the autonomy of the institution, regardless of the extent to which the college might offend the sensibilities of state officials. Not only the colleges but any church or private corporation was protected from capricious legislative interference operating apart from rules of due process.

The federal government's refusal to shape higher education by creating a national university and the Supreme Court's limiting of state power over private colleges "constituted a kind of license for unrestrained individual and group initiative in the creation of colleges of all sizes, shapes, and creeds" (Trow, 1989, p. 12). And so the race was on, and colleges were founded in every state. Before the Civil War, 43 were established in Ohio, 46 in Tennessee, 51 in Georgia, 85 in Missouri. Most suffered from financial failure, unfavorable location, fire, or dissensions among faculty, the president, and trustees and failed to survive. But enough did so that the type and character of institutions remained as varied as the communities in which they were located, the purposes for which they were founded, and the groups that established them.

The states became prominent in establishing institutions, and the principle of state support to higher learning gradually emerged. Vermont chartered a state college in 1791—the same year that it entered the union. In Tennessee an act was passed for the promotion of learning, even while the upper east section of what is now Tennessee was known as the state of Franklin in 1785. While Kentucky was still part of Virginia in 1780, the legislature offered 8,000 acres of land for a publicly supported institution. Georgia and North Carolina also chartered state colleges before the turn of the nineteenth century. Further west, public universities were chartered in most of the territories before statehood had been granted: 20 years prior in Michigan; roughly 25 years prior in Arizona, Colorado, and Washington; and 50 years prior in Hawaii and Utah. In all, state universities were formed in 17 states during the era.

Finding money was the biggest problem for both public and private colleges. Most states awarded land. Dartmouth was endowed with 44,000 acres; Maine gave 115,000 to Bowdoin. However, the sale of lands yielded little. Typically, university supporters had to return to the legislature time and again to petition for more funds. It took a couple of generations before most states had sufficient income and legislative desire to support public colleges of any stature.

The federal government also awarded land to help state colleges get started. The contract for the sale of 750,000 acres negotiated in 1787 between a congressional committee and the Ohio Company included a proviso that "two complete townships . . . be given perpetually for the purposes of an University . . . so that the same shall be of good land, to be applied to the intended object by the legislature of the state" (Peters, 1910, p. 40). Manasseh Cutler, a principal in the Ohio Company, modeled the institution that became Ohio University on his alma mater, Yale. Although it did not open until 1809, it was, in effect, the first educational institution endowed by Congress.

The colleges tended to be exceedingly weak—underfunded, too small to support a broad curriculum, too poor to pay their staff more than a subsistence wage, and, in many cases, too marginal even to survive. Hofstadter (1952) commented, "The census of 1840 showed that there were 173 colleges which shared 16,233 students or an average of 93 students per college; the figure reached 120 by 1860. It can be left to the imagination what kind of a faculty could be supported by 93 students or fewer" (p. 119). The colleges were hardly agencies of social integration. They drew their board members and their funds from those whose interests they promised to serve. They were not as influential in defining American life as their supporters might have hoped, probably playing a smaller role than the churches did.

Because of the great number of struggling colleges, each had to promise something to attract students. Numerous brochures and catalogues were distributed to show the special features of an institution, usually depicted as sitting on the brow of a hill with an expanse of landscape around it, sending the message that one's child would be safe from the evil influence of the city. Each college claimed that its alumni went on to superior positions in society. Each pointed to the erudition of its president and tutors. Each touted the virtues of student life, the associations that students would make, the benefits they would carry with them.

All such assertions were based on anecdotal data; a group running a separate professional school or specialized institute might have some follow-up information, but a liberal arts college was hardly in position to make reliable claims. Boasting that graduates obtained moral virtue could go only so far. The schools that trained for particular skills were on sounder footing in a nation that valued commerce and money-making vocations. Nonetheless, the allure of social prestige and particular sets of manners remained strong. Although many colleges foundered for lack of support, others were able to sustain their liberal arts–based curriculum, claiming all the while that young men and women were the better for having experienced it.

The growth and spread of institutions was typically American: no restrictions, try anything, graft new ideas on old. European influence was sporadic. Instruction in French was offered as early as 1779 at Columbia, and French-style arts and sciences academies were founded. French influence was seen also in the formation of the University of the State of New York in 1784, an institution that would supervise all branches of higher education in the state, even while doing no teaching or degree granting of its own. Jefferson's model for the University of Virginia with no attachment to the church reflected the teachings of the French philosophers. However, the flirtation with French ideas died out because of opposition to French liberalism and because of the rise of the German universities. Both French and English higher education essentially had neglected science, while the Germans placed maximum emphasis on it.

As the era moved toward its close, the German universities more and more became models for the college system. The ideas they exported included scholarship as a profession in its own right, education reform as a state prerogative, and professors as civil servants. Professorships in numerous branches of science and the arts were established, and the professors were expected to conduct research and to bring the fruits of their investigations into their teaching. Although only a few hundred American students had traveled to German universities by 1850, a sizable proportion of them returned to become professors at American colleges. The more the colleges pursued science, the more they looked to Germany. The German universities tended also to attract major thinkers, while in France and England few of the intellectual leaders were associated with the colleges. The German universities were also early in expecting the PhD as evidence of preparation for teaching at a time when the English institutions did not even offer advanced studies. Across the United States, science and research, along with advanced training—the German model—was appended to preexisting institutions that more closely resembled English boarding schools for adolescent boys.

Several attempts were made to establish universities apart from the colleges, but they were not successful. The colleges that developed as specialized institutions—the engineering schools and military academies—were professional schools, not graduate- or research-based schools. Although professors of medicine were seen at the University of Pennsylvania and at King's College during the Colonial Era, in the early nineteenth century many colleges of medicine were established on their own. Applied sciences were taught in numerous institutes, some freestanding—such as Stevens Institute of Technology and Michigan State Agricultural College—others affiliated with or organized by established institutions: University of Virginia Department of Applied Chemistry, Lafayette School of Mines, University of North Carolina School of Applied Science, and many others. A number of religiously controlled Midwestern schools attempted to start agricultural programs in the 1840s and 1850s but without much success. A professor at a college in Illinois proposed the idea of an industrial university that would serve agricultural, mechanical, and industrial workers of the state, but conservative traditions kept that from getting off the ground. Still, experimentation was everywhere, and with hundreds of colleges opening and closing and trying different ideas to attract support, the variety in institutional type that was to become the hallmark of American higher education was present.

## Students

The trend toward access was marked by a broadening of the student base. The Emergent Nation Era opened with around 1,000 students, all white males. It ended 80 years later with 61,000 students, including some women and a few African Americans. The median age of students at entry changed. In the early 1800s, between one-third and one-half of the entrants were younger than age 17, but by the 1850s the ratio of younger matriculants had declined to around 15%. People from more varied backgrounds began attending. Even in the old-line institutions in the East, students from the lower and middle classes far outnumbered those from wealthy families. Tuition charges were sufficiently modest so that students from all but the most destitute families could attend. The $90 per year charged by Columbia was quite the exception. Annual tuition was $55 at Harvard, $40 at Princeton, $33 at Yale, and between $25 and $40 at most other institutions. Although the colleges had supplemental charges for room and board, they all had provisions whereby students could work to cover a portion of their expenses.

Growth in the number of students looks impressive until it is judged against growth of the American population. The nation began with about 3.9 million people; by 1860 the population had expanded eightfold to 31.4 million. Furthermore, the students were spread across many more colleges; hence, the institutions remained small, with most of them proud if they could boast as many as 100 students. The number of bachelor's degrees awarded remained at around 50 per 1 million of the total population until 1820 when it began a gradual climb. Overall, the ratio of students to the number of 18-year-olds in the population hovered at or below 2% in the first two-thirds of the nineteenth century and did not increase substantively until after the universities came on the scene.

Public secondary schools were slow in developing, hence the students applying to college came from private academies, Latin grammar schools, proprietary schools, and private tutors. A few well-qualified students skipped the first year, often comprising a remedial sequence, and entered as sophomores. During the latter part of the era, preparatory schools expanded, growing fourfold between 1860 and 1870. Although the high schools were not organized especially for preparing students who wanted to go to college, their net effect was to elevate the desire for more schooling and to hold younger students away from college so that the median age of entrants increased.

At the start of the era the admissions requirements typically included arithmetic in addition to Latin and Greek. Algebra was specified in many of the prestigious Eastern institutions toward the middle of the century, and English grammar was added as a requirement as well. By the time the University of Michigan opened in 1841, geography had been added, and history was included at Harvard in 1847. By the end of the era, many colleges required "geography, English grammar, algebra, geometry, ancient history, physical geography, English composition, and United States history" (Broome, 1903, p. 46). The list of subjects generally required for admission masked the specialized requirements that grew as the colleges added programs. But most of the colleges did not strictly enforce the requirements; they needed the students and could not be too particular about whom they admitted.

The early nineteenth century was marked not only by changes in residential patterns but also by notions of child rearing. There was a steady migration to the cities as people left farms to find opportunity in the expanding factories. This was accompanied by a dramatic rise in choice of occupations and in differentiation of economic opportunities available. In preindustrial society, children provided parents with a form of social security, but the early nineteenth century saw increasing numbers of young men becoming more independent and moving away from their parents.

Within the colleges, this youthful independence often translated into raucous behavior. The hazing of younger students by upperclassmen, harassment of instructors, and various forms of youthful hedonism were accentuated by the sequestered, residential pattern that led to student subcultures in every institution. Battles between students and faculty and attendant efforts at disciplining the rowdy young were reported frequently. In the Colonial Era, the only way students with grievances could gain recourse was to leave the college, but subsequently both formal and informal groups bound the young people together into a self-aware student body.

College discipline revealed an obsession with order. The concept of *in loco parentis* (that college staff would act in the place of parents) did not fully describe the disciplinary measures the colleges attempted to install because most of them were considerably more stringent than what parents would have prescribed. The students were rebellious at every turn, refusing to inform on their peers, using the ideas of human rights to establish the notion that being a student was a limited status, and that faculty rules had to be eased. The colleges issued lists of rules, but the students reacted, declaring independence even while accepting the hierarchical nature of college organization. The colleges could go only so far in demanding order. They needed the students, and even when the administration threatened suspension or expulsion, the students were willing to take the risk because losing students was a costly proposition. Future U.S. president James Buchanan entered the junior class at Dickinson College in 1807 but was so disobedient that at the end of his first year, the principal of the college wrote to his father that the boy would not be welcomed back. A member of the board intervened, and he was received for his senior year, graduating in 1809. In 1851, he was an intermediary between the Dickinson College students and faculty after the entire junior class was dismissed for mischievousness and insubordination. Even well-established colleges like Harvard, which occasionally resorted to expulsions, had to reinstate most of their rebels.

Whether students resisted overly strict disciplinary efforts by the president and faculty or whether the restlessness of youth who were expected to lead monkish lives directed them toward unruly behavior can be argued either way. But not all students were miscreant, and not all colleges were places of rebellion. The students in state colleges and smaller Midwestern institutions, especially those closely affiliated with churches, were more conforming. Coming from families of more modest income, these students tended to be industrious and goal directed. They had little excess money to spend and were more likely to work to help defray the costs of attending college than they were to be engaged in mischievous behavior. Nonetheless, many students at the older institutions continued their prankish behavior, careless attitude toward studies, and disrespect for professors. The colleges were central to the development of a culture of rebellious adolescence.

Although the colleges at one time might have been places where families sent their unruly boys to be disciplined, the purposes of college-going and the social strata from which the students came had broadened so that the repressive rules seem to have outlived their necessity. In general, the colleges presented students with a form of daily living quite in contrast to their home life. Their residence halls were spartan—little different from military barracks. Their meals were served in dining halls, with students required to be deferent to upperclassmen and tutors. In most institutions morning prayers and Sunday chapel attendance were mandatory. Typically, there were no infirmaries, and when a contagious disease hit, many were affected. A young person who maintained enrollment for a full four years had to have a strong constitution.

The Eastern colleges had many dedicated students as well as mischievous ones. As evidence of students' pursuit of higher learning, they formed literary clubs, debating societies, and other groups suggesting a seriousness of purpose. These student societies, most with Greek names, date from the middle of the eighteenth century. By the end of the Colonial Era, chapters of Phi Beta Kappa had been organized at William and Mary, Harvard, and Dartmouth. By the early years of the nineteenth century, such organizations had been formed in well over a dozen institutions: Philologian (Williams), Dialectic (North Carolina), Adelphic (Union), Athenaean (Bowdoin), and Phoenix (Hamilton), to name a few. They provided a home for students who wished to study beyond the curriculum provided by the college and a fraternal organization for those who wished to associate with one another for serious purpose.

The importance of peer-group relationships was revealed also in fraternities that were formed less for intellectual relationships than for bringing fellows together. For most students, college was their first sojourn away from home, and as they bonded with peers, they formed groups devoted to sports and activities through which they could share experiences. College presidents tended to look kindly on fraternal associations that imposed a form of order on their members because it allowed the college to devote its energies to areas other than discipline. But the progress of fraternities was not always smooth. Some college leaders feared the secret societies because of the control such groups had over their members at a time when the colleges themselves were responsible for students' character and moral development. From time to time, governing boards passed resolutions forbidding membership in secret societies. For example, in 1849 the faculty at the University of Michigan "announced to the members of two societies that their connection with the University would cease at the opening of the ensuing term unless they renounced their connection with their respective fraternities" (Ten Brook, 1875, p. 196). Misbehavior might be tolerated in the young, but only to a point. Organized misbehavior was too much for many college administrations to accept. But colleges often depended on fraternities and sororities to provide living quarters for their students at a time when institutions could not afford to build their own residence halls.

Women entered the colleges—not in great numbers, but enough so that their presence made a difference. Oberlin College was the first to enroll women to study alongside men. Fewer than a half dozen other colleges became coed before the end of the era. More popular was the separate institution, the first of which was the Georgia Female College (now New Wesleyan), which opened in 1839 (although it was predated by several female "seminaries"). By the 1850s, over 40 degree-granting colleges for women had been established, most in the South. The first sorority dates from 1851. Subsequently, as state colleges grew, they began admitting women; the University of Iowa did so in 1855, the University of Wisconsin in 1863, and nearly all the newly formed universities in the West followed suit.

Female students were not welcomed widely, however, and misogynistic prejudice was frequently the norm. Dating from the Colonial Era, women who ventured outside the home were mistrusted. Illustrating this sentiment, Park (1978) wrote, "Women seemed to have a weakness for heresy and were therefore not thought reliable in doctrinal matters . . . education was not considered to be a remedy for these deviationist tendencies" (p. 14). Well into the latter part of the nineteenth century, commentators on higher education argued against enrolling women. Ten Brook (1875), who wrote a history of the University of Michigan shortly after women were admitted in 1870, reacted in a manner typical to the era, saying, "Intelligent and strong-minded women have expended their strength unduly upon formal efforts to prove their equality with men. . . . But the question will arise whether the public ought to bear the expense of the professional education of a class whose services will not be required. . . . Lifelong public occupations will be nearly all in the hands of men, for the marriage of women will always be deemed to disqualify her for such. . . . It may be doubted whether the relative occupations of the sexes will ever be essentially changed" (pp. 359–362).

In sum, while a great many colleges opened during the era, young people were not clamoring to get in. Student numbers failed to maintain stride with the expanding population. Compulsory schooling beyond the elementary grades and a widespread system of secondary schools were still in the future. The residential pattern established in the Colonial Era persisted, but too many colleges competed for too few students. And too many segments of the population were systematically excluded.

## Faculty

The trend toward faculty professionalization was apparent as the nineteenth century began. Although tutors were still in the majority, a core of full-time professorships had been established at the leading institutions, usually through philanthropic bequests. By 1800, permanent faculty were in place at most colleges. The professors had teaching responsibilities, but they were older and more highly educated than the tutors. They taught in an academic specialty and saw the professoriate as a career rather than as a way station to a better opportunity. By around 1825, professors outnumbered tutors by a 3-to-1 ratio.

The rise of the professor can be attributed to many influences, especially the introduction of advanced courses in mathematics, natural science, and the arts. Teaching those subjects required a faculty better trained than those who could be drawn from the ranks of recent graduates or from the pool of clergymen who typically taught on an interim or part-time basis. The colleges had expanded their role beyond that of maintaining custody of the young and attempting to instill spiritual and moral values. There were secular tasks to be done: training for careers other than the pulpit; providing general education for an enlightened citizenry; and passing on a shared cultural heritage that centered on American values. Lovett (1993) pointed out that these goals were "achieved less through changes in the curriculum, which remained largely focused on the Western classics, than through a redefinition of faculty roles and responsibilities" (p. 28).

Other characteristics of the time contributed to faculty professionalization. One was size; as the institutions grew, so did the number and role of faculty. A second was a general acceptance of the idea that a professorship was a worthy occupational goal in its own right, something a person might aspire to as a lifelong career. Emerson (1838) expressed that view eloquently. A third was that many ministers who in the Colonial Era might have served a parish for a lifetime found that they were being displaced within a few years. Accordingly, some clergymen sought the better opportunity afforded by a professorship in the local college, a reversal from the time when the tutors stayed on only until they could find a pulpit. The majority of faculty came to the profession from nonacademic jobs, primarily the ministry but also law and medicine, and without specialized post-baccalaureate training.

Beginning in the first quarter of the century a number of American college graduates went to Germany for further study and returned with Germanic notions of the professor as an independent researcher responsible for guiding students in a particular subject and for conducting inquiry in that field according to his own determination of the value of topics to study. An institution might appoint a tutor as a professor and then send him to Europe (at his own expense) to do postgraduate study in a specialized subject. By the 1830s nearly half the Harvard faculty had received such training. In the 1850s several of the faculty at Brown took leaves of absence so that they could study abroad. By the end of the era, half or more of the faculty at Williams and Dartmouth had received graduate training in a specialized area.

Early in the era, few faculty members had sufficient disciplinary commitment to be involved with learned societies or scholarly publications. The professors published, but their works were not in the form of research and scholarship known in a later time; they were more likely to be collections of sermons or orations delivered at public occasions. A sizable number of professors were still involved in occasional preaching, while others were active in community affairs. However, by the mid–nineteenth century, half or more of faculty at the leading institutions published in their field and participated in the activities of professional organizations. Furthermore, the first evidence of faculty allegiance to an academic discipline being greater than to a single institution appeared at this time, as a senior faculty member might leave one college for a position at a rival institution. One more indicator of specialized knowledge as an element in the faculty role appeared as the number of faculty involved in itinerant preaching dropped and those who applied their subject-area expertise to local community and state issues grew. In the main, these extramural activities centered on public lectures in which the faculty brought their opinions to public view and informed their listeners and readers of their latest discoveries.

Finkelstein (1983) argued that the academic career began early in the era with traditional professions splitting, so that some practitioners or clinicians maintained their service while others reduced or eliminated clinical functions to become full-time academicians. A class of permanent senior faculty members grew, and the specialized subject-centered professor became prominent toward the end of the era, preceding the emergence of the university in the next. The professorship grew as a career toward which college-trained individuals would aspire, holding greater loyalty to disciplines than to institutions, increasing involvement with disciplinary societies and specialized publications, and entering directly into the profession from graduate training. The lines of the profession were rather clearly drawn before the institutions were ready to provide a permanent home, pay, facilities, and status for the members of the group. In this regard, the professionalization of the faculty was a major input to the formation of the university. Even so, most professors still held outside jobs, many as clergymen, chiefly because salaries were quite low and the honor of serving might be considered recompense enough. Besides, a college could always find a recent graduate to teach classes for little more than room and board. College salaries in this era were "never adequate to support a middle-class lifestyle" (Lovett, 1993, p. 28).

Toward the end of the era, a career-ladder pattern emerged, as a few colleges employed instructors as junior faculty members with the expectation that they might move into the senior professor ranks. Thus, the professorship took on one of the characteristics of a profession—the notion of career advancement. It took on another characteristic as well: loyalty to the academic discipline began to erode loyalty to the institution. Still, most of the professors remained leading members of the community, taking part in civic affairs, local literary societies, and clubs.

## Curriculum

The trend toward a varied, vocationalized curriculum continued, but the struggle between advocates of classical studies and those who would introduce practical studies for a variety of people and purposes did not abate. Throughout the era, the curriculum was splitting, fragmenting, separating, becoming specialized. Remnants of the integrated studies common in the Colonial Era were present along with new studies in the sciences, social sciences, and fine arts. Curricula designed especially for those who would enter engineering, agriculture, mechanics, and manufacturing occupations entered along with all kinds of practical studies. The foundation was being laid for specialized programs and colleges, the elective system, training for every profession and occupation, and numerous avocations. A curriculum that offered anything that anyone wanted was being formed.

The organizing principles for this curricular variety can be traced to the separation of philosophy from religion, the rise of the scientific method, and a breakdown in the notion of privilege, hence of a curriculum designed only for a few people who would be civic leaders. One mode of thought was not superseded by another; all was additive. The philosophers who postulated different ways of accounting for human affairs did not replace the religionists with their appeals to authority. All they did was pave the way for social science, which itself organized into subfields of economics, sociology, psychology. Science kept the observations of astronomy and geology but added experimental physics and chemistry. Statistics was introduced as a way of verifying, on one hand, and predicting on the other. Applying scientific methods to human affairs led to studies in morality—no longer a struggle between good and evil but a consequence of competing interests. A belief in science emerged to rival the belief in religion. Research and experimentation provided ways of gaining knowledge quite different from the knowledge gained from spiritual revelation. Social science promised understanding of human behavior. Humanism, which began as anticlericalism, was transformed into study in the humanities. Freedom of thought was put forth as an antidote to dogma or orthodoxy. Inside the colleges and in the community in general, people learned to allow religion and different patterns of thought to coexist.

These shifting thought patterns—changes in the way people viewed themselves and their environment—worked themselves out in numerous social organizations. Because the colleges were expanding rapidly, there was room within them for all the patterns of scientific thought, philosophy, and humanities to be refined. The colleges were becoming centers of intellectual ferment as well as schools for the molding of young minds. Although the full development of science and curricular election had to await the dawning of the university, the foundations were apparent in the Emergent Nation colleges.

No college was large enough to support scholars to teach specialized courses exclusively. Chemistry, mathematics, natural history, and geology were prominent in most of the institutions, but typically anyone skilled in any branch of science would also teach the others. As the social sciences developed, the same instructor would teach all of them. The idea of electives, with professors teaching in their specialties and with students studying what they wanted, was suggested but gained little ground. Similarly, the idea of scholarship or in-depth study in specialized fields was put forward, but it too made little headway. The faculty began preparing themselves to specialize, but there was not a sufficient student body to accommodate a full range of curricular specialization. Science made its most notable inroads in the newly formed technical colleges, especially the U.S. Military Academy (West Point) and Rensselaer Polytechnic Institute (RPI). The curriculum at West Point centered on mathematics, chemistry, and engineering. RPI taught science through laboratories and fieldwork. Graduates of these institutions went on to build the railroads and to open the mining and manufacturing industries that developed rapidly in the second and third quarters of the century.

Curricular expansion was revealed also in the teaching of modern foreign languages, prevalent not so much because of their practicality (although they were useful for foreign travel and for study in Europe) but because they provided a respectable replacement for the Latin and Greek that were falling out of favor. Most colleges appointed professors of modern languages, but few students studied with them unless they were required to do so. The classical languages held on, and Greek and Latin were still taught in most institutions throughout the era.

Not surprisingly, the expanding curriculum had its adherents and detractors. Students at Yale, for example, typically studied Greek and Latin along with a modified version of the liberal arts, including mathematics, astronomy, grammar, and rhetoric, along with French and German. Experimental sciences (chemistry, physics) shared the curriculum with observational sciences (geology, botany). Theories of evolution were slow to penetrate, not least because of most colleges' continued affiliation with organized religion. This blend of the old and the new led to a schism among faculty and administrators, with defenders of the traditional clashing with those who would bring the curriculum into a scientific mode. One result was the well-known Yale Report of 1828 (reprinted in Wechsler, Goodchild, and Eisenmann, 2008), in which the president of the college and a committee of professors confronted the issue of studying ancient languages and the liberal arts. The report took the position that young people should be required to study a variety of topics so that all the areas of their mind would be exercised. Each subject assisted the development of a different part of the mind, one leading to the ability to reason, another toward taste, a third to accuracy in expression, and so on. The report provided an example of a statement of educational philosophy that eschewed recourse to religion as the centerpiece of the college. Here was an argument around which defenders of the historic curriculum could gather—one that rationalized it by reference to psychology and views of human thought and behavioral processes.

Across the nation, educators frequently referred to the Yale Report to justify their own programs. It was quoted and paraphrased repeatedly, and the principles on which it was based became the foundation for curriculum in numerous institutions. The report proved especially useful to small denominational colleges, providing them with a way of justifying a curriculum that straddled the liberal arts and experimental science while holding to Latin and Greek as proper studies for the educated man. When the College of the Western Reserve opened in Ohio, it was to be "the Yale of the west," with a curriculum modeled on that of its predecessor institution (Snow, 1907, p. 145). In 1854, the faculty of the University of Alabama quoted the report in their justification of mandating certain studies as "furnishing the best discipline for the mind, and such as are indispensable to a man of liberal education" (Snow, 1907, p. 142). The curriculum built strong minds through mental discipline. All subjects had to be studied lest the entire system be upset. A uniform curriculum required for all students held its appeal throughout the era, even as new arrangements were being introduced.

Jefferson's plan for the University of Virginia included curricular differentiation. That institution opened in 1824, just before Jefferson's death, with a faculty subdivided into specialties of languages, mathematics, history, and others, but with no professorship of divinity. The plan was to have each of the various schools organize separately with its own professors, students, and space. Soon after it opened, however, the university abandoned some of the more far-reaching innovations such as separate diplomas awarded by the individual schools and settled back to become a college that awarded bachelor's degrees for study in a variety of subjects.

Elsewhere, reforms in curriculum proceeded with greater or lesser success. Electives were added along with new types of bachelor's degrees, separate curricular tracks, and courses of study for students who did not intend to complete four-year programs. Yet most of the innovations had to be modified if not abandoned outright as traditionalists resisted the changes. The colleges could not reform fully yet could not hold rigorously to the classical curriculum. They tried to straddle but, as Rudolph (1977) put it, "It sometimes seemed in the 1820s and 1830s that failure was a certain prospect for any curriculum that held to the past and for any curriculum that dared to move off dead center" (p. 80).

Throughout the era, the colleges fought for their own survival and struggled to sustain support. Those blessed with enlightened leadership were sometimes able to install curricular reforms and make them stick. Union College, for example, had a strong president, one who served for 62 years, from 1804 to 1866. Eliphalet Nott's tenure thus straddled almost the entire era, and he was able to introduce and sustain many of the changes necessary to bring his institution to the fore. Union College allowed students to take classes even if they were not headed for degrees and introduced parallel programs for those who did not want to study classical languages. The college had a strong emphasis on science, and one of its programs encouraged students to study mathematics and modern languages in a form that looked much like the distribution requirements that would appear a century later in most American institutions under the guise of general education. The college broke with tradition by awarding bachelor's of arts degrees to students who completed either its classical program or its scientific program. President Nott taught the senior-level capstone course in moral philosophy, integrating the various lines of study. The college was successful; its enrollments and graduating classes were among the top five in the nation throughout Nott's tenure.

Despite Union College's success, Harvard, Yale, and Princeton were more influential on the course of higher education. Each supplied leaders for the colleges that were developing across the nation and where the curriculum resembled the programs in the colleges from whence the new presidents came. Uniformity in curriculum was apparent, even though variations in emphasis and sequence were tried. Toward the middle of the century, the president of Brown was able to state that the curricula "in all the Northern Colleges are so nearly similar that students, in good standing in one institution, find little difficulty in being admitted to any other" (Snow, 1907, p. 141). The classics, mathematics, science, history, and philosophy—all were represented. Few college leaders dared suggest that any of the traditional subjects be eliminated. The power of tradition was manifest. Each field of study had its supporters, and little justification could be found for eliminating anything. At most, the time devoted to studying one or another subject might be reduced.

Those who would model education after changes in thinking and in student expectations were continually at odds with those who felt that an anchor with the past was important. Presaging curricular debates in later eras, college leaders contended that if enrollments were to remain high, programs more suited to what young people wanted were necessary. A new curriculum was proposed to serve "that large class of young men, who are not destined to either of the learned professions, and carry them through a course, which they think better adapted to their future plans and prospects" (Snow, 1907, p. 155). The faculty of Amherst College even suggested a department of education in which teachers might be trained—this in 1827 when teaching had by no means developed as a profession and when the idea of a separate baccalaureate program to prepare teachers had few adherents.

The spread of different programs illustrates how curriculum changes: not by revolution, but by accretion. The inauguration of Josiah Quincy as president of Harvard in 1829 was the occasion for an address suggesting that a curriculum modeled on the past was not sufficient for a modern institution. Using terms such as the *spirit of the age,* he suggested that more students be admitted into special or parallel courses of study so that the "long-established standards of collegiate education" not be upset. He also proposed a set of courses centering on science that would be useful for a variety of students and purposes (Snow, 1907, p. 168). But Harvard did not abandon the classics; after much debate it added a separate program in science.

For at least a half-century the parallel curriculum solved the problem presented by the desire to introduce new courses and attract more students while maintaining the classical program so that traditional standards would not be compromised. Separate programs open to students who were not prepared in the classical languages were organized at several institutions. One such program at Columbia dates from 1830. Termed the "Scientific and Literary Course," it involved three years of study but led to no degree. Students could be admitted if they knew French grammar, mathematics, and geography. In 1833, Union College established a scientific program, but its admissions requirements were similar to those for the classical course. Eventually the college opened the scientific program to students who needed no prior preparation greater than English grammar and arithmetic.

Parallel courses leading to separate degrees were formed at many other institutions: Brown and Harvard in 1851; Yale, Dartmouth, and Rochester in 1852; Michigan in 1853; Columbia in 1864; and at Cornell when it opened in 1869. New degree titles were invented to indicate the difference between these programs and the classical curriculum. The bachelor's of science or bachelor's in philosophy was often the culminating degree. These parallel courses were not unitary; Cornell, for example, offered nine different programs leading to degrees.

Thus, the curriculum remained in flux. A few of the more than 500 colleges established during the era experimented with modernized curriculum, including sciences and broader applications of mathematics, but most maintained Latin and Greek, moral philosophy, English grammar, and requirements modeled on those that had been established in the Colonial Era. The colleges were not large enough to sustain a varied curriculum, with some students studying science, others humanities, and still others the basics of literacy. Too few students could function as independent scholars—choosing electives and following lines of modern thought. Too many were young and ill-prepared. And student complaints about curricular dryness were prevalent. McLachlan (1974) noted, "No single reason why the former curriculum could not have been made interesting to students is immediately apparent" (p. 467).

Where students were present in sufficient numbers to form literary societies, they were able to build what was essentially their own curriculum. These societies engaged student interests through providing reading materials, debate activities, and helping to build an intellectual climate. In some institutions they were elaborately organized and self-governing—colleges within colleges. They enrolled most of the students, awarded diplomas, and operated their own libraries. The most current materials might not be found in the classrooms and the college libraries, but the literary societies typically collected the latest periodicals along with books of history, literature, science, poetry, and public affairs. These societies flourished from the middle of the eighteenth century to the middle of the nineteenth century when they were replaced gradually by fraternities. Toward the end of the era, formal curricular and instructional practices had been modified to accommodate many of the principles on which the literary societies had been founded.

The fraternities had a different agenda, which was considerably more reliant on social activities.

The classical curriculum survived not only because of tradition but because it had purpose. It fit with the religious revivalism that swept through sections of the nation periodically and found adherents and a ready audience in the colleges. Some colleges had been founded by revival-oriented ministers, and many presidents found that revival fervor could work to the advantage of the institution by directing youthful emotions and enthusiasms into constructive avenues. The courses in moral philosophy assisted in this channeling. Furthermore, the classical curriculum opened to allow courses in science, fine arts, and social studies. Latin and Greek might form its core in the first two years, but the upper division was much broader. The classical curriculum also retained its utility as training for the professions of law, medicine, and the ministry.

And thus, the curriculum in the Emergent Nation Era was a collectivity of old forms centering on the classics, science splitting and growing, vocational subjects, and remedial efforts; in brief, it was a microcosm of the curriculum in the eras to follow. The colleges gradually absorbed many functions that had been performed previously by other institutions: literary societies, academies of science, seminaries, libraries, and formal apprenticeships. They opened programs for a greater variety of students, not least those whose prior education had ill prepared them higher learning. The conflict between science and religion was not yet a great problem because scientists and moral philosophers alike held the conviction that "by studying the laws of nature scientists confirmed the existence of God, the author of nature, and glorified him in his works" (Sloan, 1971, p. 236). Science was itself in great ferment as new branches continued emerging. Social change was occurring more quickly than the colleges could adjust to it, possibly because they "were not organically knit into the fabric of economic life . . . . Although college training was an advantage, it was not necessary in the early nineteenth century to go to college to become a doctor, lawyer, or even a teacher, much less a successful politician or businessman" (Hofstadter, 1952, p. 21). Higher education was still a luxury.

Francis Wayland (1850), Brown's forward-thinking president in the second quarter of the century, attacked the curriculum, low admissions standards, the superficiality of teaching, and institutional irrelevance, claiming that although there was a great demand for civil engineers to help build railroads, industry, and the mines, the colleges were doing little to prepare such practitioners. More courses should be organized, including professional curricula and certificate programs for those who did not want or need to study for a full four years. Abandoning the fixed four-year program of study, introducing a purely elective curriculum, and awarding degrees based on successful completion of examinations could be justified by broadening the base of students served by the institutions. If Latin and Greek could not attract sufficient enrollments, they did not deserve to be offered. President Wayland proposed 15 courses of instruction: Latin and Greek for those who wanted them, and separate programs in English language and rhetoric, teaching, agriculture, chemistry, and modern languages. He mentioned with favor how New York and Massachusetts had considered establishing agricultural institutions. College leaders did not rush out to introduce the programs that he sketched, but he did summarize the way that curriculum was evolving into separate programs designed for every interest.

Instruction evolved as well. The reliance on recitation and disputation—hallmarks of the colonial colleges—first gave way to the lecture method, then to the laboratory. As instructors moved from a tutorial group to a career as professors and specialists, they relegated recitation and disputation to the lower schools, where the latter quickly died out. Their lectures were used to supplement texts by conveying information, generating understanding, and stimulating interest; they also transmitted attitudes and values, intentionally or otherwise. Lectures became popular most quickly in the sciences; they were often accompanied by demonstrations of experiments. The combination lecture and demonstration usually started with the enunciation of some specific principle and then moved to a concrete illustration. Professors stimulated the students with enthusiasm for their specialties and, gradually, as they conducted research of their own, by conveying their latest findings.

The laboratory also emerged during this period as a way of teaching the sciences. Students listened to lectures and watched demonstrations and then performed the experiments on their own. Another innovation was the written examination, replacing public recitations or debates with private demonstrations of acquired knowledge. This also led toward uniformity in instruction, as all students responded to the same set of questions. The beginnings of the university as we know it—and of managing sizable numbers of students—were clear.

## Governance

The pattern of college governance with control vested in a nonacademic board of trustees had begun in the Colonial Era. There were not enough scholars to form a self-governing body, but a group of laypeople could organize an institution and employ a president to manage it. The president held office at the pleasure of the board, and as long as the board supported him, he could do what he wanted within the institution; he could employ the tutors and design the curriculum. These characteristics continued as new colleges were founded in the Emergent Nation Era and marked what would become a lasting pattern of college governance.

The colleges were formed typically under one of three patterns. The first was the civil corporation. Here a group received a charter—essentially a license to do business—from a state legislature. When the states began founding public institutions, the legislature typically described the parameters of the college, defining how trustees would be appointed and often providing a seat on the board for the governor, attorney general, or other state official.

Another form was the private college founded by a religious group. Typically, a church would organize a college, appoint a number of trustees from within or outside the denomination, and apply to the state for a charter or a license to do business. Such charters were readily awarded. It remained then for the board to find funds, employ a president, and begin offering classes. This form of organization was most responsible for the great number of colleges organized in the Emergent Nation Era because as churches expanded into the western territory, they formed colleges in every population center.

A third group of colleges "depended on organized community effort which might, or might not, involve one or several Christian denominations in addition to civic or professional groups" (Herbst, 1980, p. 15). This set included colleges formed under municipal auspices, as well as private, nondenominational institutions.

Regardless of sponsor, the private colleges all shared similar characteristics. If they were closely affiliated with a denomination, church members were urged to contribute funds. If nondenominational, they might be supported by people who responded to appeals on the basis of civic pride. In either event, private institutions did not have to beg for funds from legislatures that might from one year to the next have different views of what the colleges ought to be doing. Herbst (1980) pointed out that partisan rivalries often "prevented legislatures from responding to the demands for additional public colleges," thus allowing private initiative to fill the space. Boosterism was important because "in the United States anyone with enough capital or enthusiasm could become a college founder. As capitalism built towns, canals, and bridges and private business empires, so it also financed and directed higher education" (p. 18).

The president increasingly came to be seen as a representative of the trustees and less as a member of the faculty. Many presidents continued teaching, but more devoted most of their time to fundraising and community relations. The faculty gradually gained a sense of independence and self-worth, especially as professors replaced tutors. Professors in specialized institutions, such as medical schools, were first to gain some measure of control over the curriculum and internal workings of the colleges. But the faculty role in academic governance was not yet established and, of course, the students had no say in institutional conduct.

This pattern of governance was well established before the faculty became a self-conscious professional group. By the time the higher education professoriate developed its own internal hierarchy, tendency toward research and scholarship, and, most important, autonomy, it was too late to change the mode of institutional organization and to acquire the prestige accorded to scholars in Europe. Faculty gained responsibility for appointing professors and deciding on curriculum but never the power to appropriate funds, manage the institution, or even to have the final word on students to be admitted. They did not become self-governing in the fashion of the medieval guilds or even as some of the other learned professions in the United States.

Because nearly all the managerial power rested with the president, when additional administrators were needed, they became attached to the president's office. In the long run, this helped institutions maintain their autonomy, as college officials responsible to state authorities have never been welcome on campus. Trow (1989) concluded, "Strong presidents and their administrative staffs could act in pursuit of self-interests of individual institutions and lay boards could ensure that those institutions would continue to be responsive to the larger society, and to its markets for students and graduates, rather than to the state or professional guilds" (p. 15). However, faculty and administrative interests continued moving in different directions. From the professors' point of view the president was the spokesman and representative of the board of governors, not the leader of the faculty.

Mercantile and professional people made inroads on the boards of trustees as the percentage of clergymen diminished. Alumni and donors also began to influence board membership. Governance became secularized even as most of the colleges retained their nominal status as church-related institutions. One of the major inputs to secularization was the fact that few colleges were controlled strictly by a single church group; most were interdenominational or nondenominational, bringing onto the institution's board, faculty, and student body anyone who could assist in keeping the institution afloat.

One of the more prominent characteristics distinguishing public institutions from private was that the former often specifically excluded clergymen from the governing board except to the extent that such individuals were prominent members of the community who might be appointed regardless of their clerical affiliation. In private colleges it was almost axiomatic that the president be a cleric; many institutions had that proviso in their charter. In state universities, it was considered important to have a prominent figure who could negotiate for institutional support.

It was not uncommon for a small institution to pay a substantial amount to a prestigious individual, hoping that, as president, he might garner institutional prestige and support. Henry Tappan, a graduate of a theological seminary, had been a professor at New York University before taking office as president at the University of Michigan. He had visited Europe, written several works in philosophy, and published a treatise on university education. In 1852, his first year in office, the total budget of the university was less than $13,000, but he received a salary of $1,500 plus traveling expenses. By his second year, his salary was raised to $2,000 a year, a figure that still approximated 12% of the university budget. Paying a large sum to an influential leader was an investment in institutional growth.

Thus, the governance forms established in the colonial colleges solidified as self-perpetuating or legislatively appointed governing boards that maintained control and responsibility. Some of the presidents emerged as prominent leaders taking their colleges into new areas of service. The faculty developed their own codes without gaining voice in institutional management. The stage was set for boards to be dominated by business leaders, the presidents to become innovators, and the faculty to pursue their own interests.

## Finance

The financing of colleges followed patterns established in the Colonial Era, with funds coming from private donors as well as the state. Students paid little tuition; the low-paid faculty cost little and colleges were subsidized by whatever funds the presidents and boards of trustees could garner. Money was scarce, and nearly all institutions—private colleges and the newly formed state colleges alike—survived from year to year, if they survived at all.

The colleges depended on private donors for a major portion of their revenue, with most coming in the form of small pledges. Many colleges were started when a founding body was able to find enough subscribers to put together a fund sufficient to open the institution's doors. The College of Philadelphia had been formed that way, and most of the later colleges were similarly endowed. Williams College was founded by $14,000 in small contributions and Amherst with $50,000. The existing institutions similarly collected small amounts from as many donors as they could attract. Princeton launched a major fundraising campaign in the 1830s; the top donation received was $5,000. Columbia raised $20,000 from a benefactor.

Fundraising campaigns took various forms. For the most part they rested on individual solicitations conducted by the college president or faculty. Any donation was welcome. Cash was preferred, but the colleges were pleased to receive farm produce to keep the staff and students fed or books to augment the library. Frequent sales of homemade artifacts were conducted, along with fairs and lotteries. Some colleges sold perpetual scholarships entitling the owner to free tuition for one person in perpetuity, but these never became popular because the colleges usually priced them too low and were then forced to charge additional fees when the students materialized. Few colleges were fortunate enough to have a president as wealthy as Eliphalet Nott, whose investments yielded more than half a million dollars and made Union College the most highly endowed institution of the era. Yale organized a Society of Alumni in 1828, which contributed $100,000 over the next few years. Harvard collected $2.2 million in 1869. But overall, little cash was available; as late as 1870, the colleges of the nation were collectively receiving approximately $8 to $9 million per year through private donations.

In cases where the college was closely affiliated with a church, fundraising might be undertaken in tandem. Rudolph (1991) described the American Education Society, founded in 1815 "to raise funds in the Congregational churches and to help send promising ministerial candidates to the appropriate colleges" (p. 183). Similar organizations were founded by other churches that might sponsor students of their faith or, in some cases, collect cash. Some of the Catholic colleges received funds from European missionary groups. But regardless of denominational affiliation or the lack thereof, nearly all the colleges were impoverished.

The states provided some support to private institutions. Tax exemptions represented a continuing subsidy, and some states gave cash. Harvard received a total of $100,000 from the Commonwealth of Massachusetts in the decade following 1814, and Williams and Bowdoin received around $40,000 each. New York gave over $100,000 to Columbia. The University of Pennsylvania received nearly $300,000 from its home state, and Dickinson College even more. In these cases and in others where states were slow in organizing public institutions, private colleges were able to tap into the public treasury, a pattern traced in detail by Herbst (1982).

The states had land that they were willing to donate, but generally it was not worth much. Whether the proceeds of land sales went to private institutions or to the newly formed public colleges, it was difficult to turn land into cash. In every state, mismanagement and fraud stained the conversion. Surveys were often found to be inaccurate, and deeds frequently were litigated because of conflicting claims. Land that was supposed to sell for $20 an acre might go for as little as $2. Millions of acres of land that had been donated by Congress to the states carved out of the Northwest Territories often sold at $1 per acre or less. By 1821, the awarding of great blocks of land to the Western states spurred arguments that the older, Eastern states should receive lands of similar value so that they too could build publicly supported institutions. But it was to be 40 years before such a plan was enacted. Congress could afford to be more profligate with land in the West; it held title to more of it. In the East, the public lands were considerably more likely to be owned by the states themselves.

Occasionally, public institutions were able to obtain larger sums. The first sale of land that had been deeded to the newly formed University of Michigan yielded only a few thousand dollars, but by the time Michigan became a state in 1837, land values had increased so that the state was able to sell off property at $20 or $25 per acre. Overall, though, public and private institutions alike had to rely on supportive legislators to find ways of keeping the colleges alive. The narrowly sectarian institutions were least successful in obtaining state monies, as the legislatures were careful not to give the appearance of supporting one denomination over another.

One indication of the weakness of college budgets and physical plants can be seen in a report on college library holdings in the middle of the nineteenth century (see Table 2.2). Only eight colleges, all in the East, had close to 10,000 volumes, although when the literary society libraries were added in, another 10 Eastern institutions crossed that mark. During the decade of the 1840s, only three of the institutions for which data are available had an

Table 2.2. American College Libraries with the Largest Collections, 1849.

| Institution | Estimated Number of Volumes | | | Estimated Average Annual Expenditure for Books 1840–1849 |
|---|---|---|---|---|
| | College Library | Society Libraries | Total | |
| Harvard | 56,000 | 12,000 | 68,000 | – |
| Yale College | 20,500 | 27,200 | 47,700 | $1,620 |
| Brown University | 23,000 | 7,200 | 30,200 | $2,500 |
| Georgetown College | 25,000 | 1,100 | 26,100 | $350 |
| Bowdoin College | 11,600 | 9,900 | 21,500 | $200 |
| South Carolina College | 17,000 | 1,400 | 18,400 | $2,000 |
| University of Virginia | 18,400 | – | 18,400 | $550 |
| College of New Jersey | 9,000 | 7,000 | 16,000 | $400 |
| Dickinson College | 5,100 | 9,500 | 14,600 | $100 |
| Union College | 7,800 | 6,800 | 14,600 | $400 |
| Amherst College | 5,700 | 8,000 | 13,700 | $300 |
| Columbia College | 12,700 | – | 12,700 | $200 |
| University of Vermont | 7,000 | 5,300 | 12,300 | $60 |
| University of North Carolina | 3,500 | 8,800 | 12,300 | – |
| Wesleyan University | 5,600 | 5,500 | 11,100 | $100 |
| Williams College | 6,000 | 4,600 | 10,600 | $190 |
| Hamilton College (NY) | 3,500 | 6,800 | 10,300 | $60 |
| Franklin College (GA) | 7,300 | 3,000 | 10,300 | $600 |

*Source:* Hamlin, 1981.

annual expenditure for books estimated at greater than $1,500. With few exceptions, the libraries were open but a couple of hours per week (Hamlin, 1981).

Low salaries for staff helped keep the marginally funded colleges afloat. By the end of the era, a few senior professors at the larger institutions earned as much as $1,500 or $2,000 a year, but most less than $1,000 per year—a salary comparable to that of a journeyman mechanic. And even then, the professors were not always paid. Occasionally, a college would close for a year to allow faculty to go out and raise money, or it would defer payment until such time as it had the funds, which often as not never came. Sometimes a professor was appointed with the understanding that half his salary would be provided by his friends in the form of donations. Or the faculty would agree to have their pay contingent on the receipt of tuition. If a professor had an outside source of income, he would be expected to serve with no pay at all, just for the honor of being affiliated with the college.

Exploitation of the faculty was rationalized on the grounds that the colleges provided a public service, brought the young to maturity, and acted as a point of pride and honor to the community—all justifications similar to those the churches had used for centuries. The colleges could not ask students for much money lest they lose all their enrollment. That, too, was rationalized on the grounds that the community owed its young an education for as many years as it took for the person to profit from it. Few colleges wanted to be seen as rich men's institutions; they did not want to be accused of turning away poor but worthy students. And the supply of faculty was never in jeopardy. There were always recent graduates who could be found to teach classes for little more than room and board.

Thus, beginning in the Colonial Era and continuing through the Emergent Nation Era, professors were severely underpaid in terms of the years of education it took before they became qualified. However, they were not the only such group; clergymen also were expected to live in genteel poverty. One of the aspects of the professoriate that slowed its professionalization was this exploitation in the name of a higher calling, with schoolteachers and professors alike underpaid well into the middle of the next century. As long as the supply was greater than the demand, and so long as there were no contracts to enforce payment of a living wage, the colleges lived on the backs of their staff members.

## Outcomes

Higher education's outcomes in the Emergent Nation Era were similar to those yielded by the colleges of the Colonial Era: individual mobility, preparation for careers, assistance in child rearing, and community pride. However, the expanding nation and the growing economy placed additional demands on higher education, and so further outcomes can be traced, especially preparation for newly emergent professions and the development of a collegiate style that marked the young people who had been to college with particular ways of acting and viewing the world.

Higher education as an essential component of professional preparation grew during the era. The percentage of lawyers and physicians taking up practice without having been to college dropped steadily, as apprenticeships alone were no longer sufficient for people who wanted to move ahead rapidly in their chosen field. However, as the splintering of religious denominations and formation of new sects accelerated, the percentage of college-trained ministers actually declined. New church groups sought charismatic leaders who could appeal to a congregation's emotions and effect religious fervor—qualities not typically enhanced in college classrooms. These country preachers were found more in the South and the West than in the New England states, where traditional churches continued to dominate.

Most of the colleges formed under church auspices attempted to build a faith with teachings directed toward knowledge of the

Bible. Connections were formed between populist democracy and religious fundamentalism, merging the notion that the intuitions of the common man were to be trusted more than the rationalizations of the intellectuals. Religious revivalism reappeared in different parts of the country at various times, splintering established churches and precluding advances in scientific thinking. Church-founded colleges were certainly not going to advance inductive reasoning; therefore, an argument might be made that higher education actually delayed the general adoption of science as a way of organizing knowledge.

The number of young people going to college to advance their personal wealth and movement in society grew, and the notion that college was a good personal investment overtook the idea of college as a social investment. Education's contribution to forming an elite group remained prominent, but fewer graduates entered public service. Although 5 of the first 6 presidents of this nation were college graduates, only 4 of the next 11 attended college. The men who formed the nation had been scientists and classicists, using their knowledge of history and politics to solve problems. But by the time Jackson was elected in 1828, popular democracy had become so ascendant that no politician ever after was able to claim status as an intellectual as a condition for winning public office. One had to be a man of the people, self-taught, self-made, rooted in the soil, born poor but risen through adversity. The notion that intuitive folk wisdom was superior to an educated intellect grew strong. Common sense as exhibited by ordinary men shouldered its way in as an ideal qualification for public office, just as charisma and emotion became the basic characteristics of successful church leaders. Even so, because the secondary schools had yet to take hold, especially in the South, many civic leaders emerged from the newly formed colleges. South Carolina College included among its graduates future governors and congressmen from several southern states.

The emphasis on individual mobility and the rise of self-educated leaders did not supersede the social value of higher education completely. The colleges still taught moral philosophy—a course that probably did much in shaping the thinking of civic reformers and social activists. The courses covered logic, rhetoric, natural law, politics, and aspects of philosophy. Their aim was to produce a supply of virtuous men who could counter the professional politicians and vulgar businessmen who were becoming increasingly influential in public affairs. College-affiliated learned societies engaged students in considering social issues such as gender equality, universal suffrage, abolition, temperance, child labor, and reform of social institutions. Many of the most influential writers of the time, including Emerson, Hawthorne, and Thoreau, were college graduates. The old gentry were diminished with the rise of businessmen and self-trained politicians, but many among them did not relinquish their concern for social reform. In fact, according to Giele (1995), "Among the major temperance and suffrage leaders, more than half had the equivalent of some college education" (p. 80), including Elizabeth Cady Stanton and Lillian Wald, as well as college graduates Lucy Stone (Oberlin), Carrie Chapman Catt (Iowa State), and Jane Addams (Rockford).

Engineers prominent in building the canals, railroads, and public works of the era came from the new colleges established especially to train them. The U.S. Military Academy and RPI prepared a sizable majority of the engineers; RPI allowed young people from every background to study engineering using laboratory experimentation and field study. The academy at West Point did not offer bachelor's degrees, but it had a rich collection of technical books, and its extensive publications on military subjects made it a national center of scientific study. Trained scientists came from many colleges, and toward the end of the era, additional schools—including the Polytechnic Institute of Brooklyn, the Massachusetts Institute of Technology, and Worcester Polytechnic Institute—added to the supply.

A research presence grew in the elite institutions. Joseph Henry, a physicist, developed important work in electromagnetism while he was a professor at Princeton prior to becoming the first director of the Smithsonian Institution. Asa Gray, professor of natural history at Harvard, effectually made that institution the center of botanical study in the United States. The colleges attracted scientists even as they delayed in developing graduate schools. Wolfle (1972) reported that 1,600 scientists published 9,000 papers in American journals between 1800 and 1860, with the most productive authors affiliated with the science divisions of Yale, Harvard, and the University of Pennsylvania. Overall, though, the colleges were slow to adopt laboratories, departments, and institutes for specialized research, and the German universities remained virtually the only places where a student could be trained in scientific or scholarly research. The contributions of science as fostered within the universities took a back seat to practical inventors in developing commercially useful products and processes.

The colleges changed notions of human development. In earlier eras, the transition from childhood to adulthood was direct, as young people left school at age 10 or 12 to go to work. As the period of schooling expanded, however, young people's development was suspended. Teenagers living together in colleges developed their own codes of conduct. Indolence, rowdiness, and disrespect for elders became social norms. Delaying entry to adulthood with its attendant responsibilities was now acceptable. Those colleges that acted as surrogate parents fostered the development of a culture of adolescence that was a major outcome of higher education in the Emergent Nation Era.

The era is fascinating when viewed from a contemporary perspective, and several questions remain unsettled.

- How were the churches able to retain such a prominent influence on college curriculum and management for so many years even after state colleges were formed and secular funding rose?

- Applied science strained to be born; what might explain its delayed emergence?

- Was faculty professionalization dampened because the colleges were small and lacked funds, or were there other reasons?

- How has the concept of *in loco parentis*, evident in both the Colonial Era and Emergent Nation Era, continued to influence college student behavior (as well as institutional attempts to control such behavior) in modern times? Why did college administrators look favorably on literary clubs and debating societies, while being suspicious of fraternities?

- What factors contributed to the slow enrollment of women?

- What might the nation look like today if African Americans (both free and enslaved) had been granted the same access to higher education during the Emergent Nation Era as Whites?

# 3

# University Transformation as the Nation Industrializes: 1870–1944

The Civil War—the cataclysmic result of persistent disputes over the economics and political control of a system based on the enslavement of human beings—was the most notable event marking the onset of the University Transformation Era. The College Land Grant (Morrill) Act, passed during the war, and the Servicemen's Readjustment Act, passed during World War II, bookended the University Transformation Era and were the two most important pieces of legislation ever enacted by the U.S. Congress in terms of their influence on the course of higher education. The first gave rise to the land-grant colleges, which turned higher education toward broader areas of service. The second—the GI Bill—inaugurated the Mass Higher Education Era by making college possible for millions of veterans.

## Societal Context

The conflict between North and South was the most immediately calamitous event in a rivalry that had been evident from the time the U.S. Constitution was drafted, with its deliberately ambiguous language regarding the relationship between the states and the federal government, its near omission of slavery, and its failure to draw a distinction between person and property. The era leading up to the Civil War—and well beyond—was marked by several political compromises regarding regulation of the slave trade or admission of new states to the union, and these inflamed either the North or the South, and sometimes both. Territorial expansion continued through the acquisition of Alaska in 1867. The 80 years following the founding of the nation saw its land area spread from the Appalachians to the Bering Sea and its population multiply tenfold. Moreover, the mentality of expansiveness continued through the end of the nineteenth century, extending now into the Pacific and Caribbean. The population continued increasing, with an incredible growth of 72% between 1850 and 1879 alone.

Industrialization was triumphant by the beginning of the University Transformation Era. It affected farming, where newly invented agricultural machinery enhanced yields, and hence exports. Oil had been found in Pennsylvania and, together with metals in the West, led to great individual fortunes. Railway building alone consolidated wealth. The connivance of the federal government was apparent, as the railroads received a total of 130 million acres of land in return for putting tracks through to the Pacific Ocean. And this was in addition to the 200 million acres that the railway builders had been awarded prior to 1860.

The growth in industry, capital, and population was substantially greater in the North and West than it was in the South. The South had clung to an agrarian tradition, while the North was shifting rapidly toward heavy industry and the growth of cities. The South was so devastated by the Civil War, which stripped it of at least half its wealth, that it could do little to catch up in industry, capital formation, or education. The Civil War had effected a $1.5 billion decrease in the value of its land, and every bank and insurance company in the region was essentially worthless. The loss in bank capital during the war approximated $1 billion, and the emancipation of enslaved people represented another $2 billion in lost capital (Adams, 1931). Few Southerners took advantage of the land made available under the Homestead Act, 2.5 million acres of which were claimed mostly by migrants from the North and East in the first two years after the act was passed; 12 million acres were so taken by 1870.

Expansion of wealth and industry in the years following the Civil War was marked by rampant speculation and fortune building that included numerous unsavory characteristics: fraudulent sales and surveys in the West; the forced or duplicitous removal of Indigenous populations; scandals and graft reaching into the highest levels of state and federal government; and price gouging, monopolistic practices, and disregard for public safety across the industrial sector. Meat packers, railroad owners, oil producers, iron and steel makers, clothing manufacturers, bankers, and business builders of every kind grew rich and gained political as well as economic power. The domestic market was fueled by population growth of 20 to 30% per decade, as well as increased foreign exports.

The speculative excesses and profiteering of the Civil War and its aftermath were not the only examples of avarice. Financial panics in 1837 and 1857 were followed by similar panics in 1873 and 1907. All were due to speculation, overextension of credit, failures in the banking system, and causes endemic to unregulated capitalism. Even prior to the Civil War, several factors had led to feverish expansion: the need for housing and land by large numbers of immigrants, the building of railroads, and the export of agricultural products to Europe. The expansion led to subsequent, although temporary, financial collapse.

The excesses of the industrialists were so egregious that a counterreaction set in and governmental attempts at regulation began to bear fruit toward the end of the century. For example, in 1887 the Interstate Commerce Act was passed to protect farmers and manufacturers from the ruinous multiple-pricing practices of the railroads. The Sherman Anti-Trust Act (1890), the Pure Food Act (1906), and the establishment of the Federal Reserve and the Federal Trade Commission (1913) also attempted to curb the actions of the industrialists and bankers. The constitutional amendment establishing an income tax, ratified in 1913, enabled the government to restrain some of the immense individual fortune building. Not incidentally, it led to the expansion of philanthropic foundations, which were established to provide a haven for wealth.

They later became useful in supporting research, scholarships, and several other areas within higher education.

The moral outrage of the Abolitionists did not stop with emancipation and contributed greatly to the Reconstruction Era. Curiously, the moral crusade hardly extended to Indigenous Americans. As Adams (1931) wrote, "The plight of the red man, for example, left Abolitionists cold, though they were willing to pull down the whole fabric of America, if need be, to free the black man" (p. 243). Similarly, for all their pleas on behalf of their enslaved brethren, Northerners and not a few Southerners launched periodic campaigns against Catholics and foreigners. The course of prejudice and moral indignation is never straight nor consistent.

The emancipation of enslaved people took place as a result of the Civil War, but it did not fully liberate the Black population. Jim Crow laws in the South kept the formerly enslaved and their descendants legally segregated for another 100 years, ensuring few pathways for social or economic advancement. Opportunities for African Americans were similarly constrained in the Northern states; although they had outlawed slavery much earlier than in the South, property-holding and voting restrictions could be found well into the Civil War. Thus, few Black people had the chance to rise higher than the working class at the lowest rungs of the economic ladder; in fact, those who developed large businesses were more likely to do so in Atlanta, Birmingham, or New Orleans than in New York, Boston, or Philadelphia. Discrimination based on race was by no means terminated with the emancipation of enslaved people any more than it was to subside when the Civil Rights Act was passed 100 years later. Ever-present xenophobia and racism against African Americans, Jews, and Asian immigrants festered for generations, and after World War I extended to newer arrivals, giving rise to laws that severely limited immigration from Southern and Eastern Europe.

The United States emerged from World War I as a wealthy, powerful player on the world stage. Because the nation was not a direct participant until the war had been under way for nearly three years, it was able to profit enormously by exporting agricultural products, manufactured goods, and explosives to the belligerents. By the end of the war, more than 20,000 new millionaires had been created. Sizable portions of the debt that was owed to European countries as they helped finance the growth of railroads and industry in the latter part of the nineteenth century were repurchased. And even after the United States became actively involved in the war, it escaped relatively easily. The Civil War had cost America more than 600,000 deaths in a population approximating 35 million. The United States lost fewer than 120,000 men in World War I, out of a population of 100 million.

The tension between private capitalism and public welfare was accentuated during the era. Is an economic good tantamount to a moral good? Should the people who earn the money be the sole determinants of how the money should be spent? Do all people, including intellectual workers, owe allegiance to business? How can spiritual values be reconciled with the values of the marketplace? All these questions affected the development of higher education and the role it played as universities transformed the enterprise. One thing was certain: the city on the hill, the light unto the world, the moral beacon that was the dream of a few influential colony builders had been thrust totally to the shadow.

## Institutions

Prior to the Civil War, continued disaffection with a narrow conception of higher education had slowed the expansion of colleges. Those who moved to the frontier spent their first generation building communities. Even though they often started colleges as emblems of community pride, higher education was not essential for solving problems of subsistence, nor was it a major contributor to growth. At the beginning of the University Transformation Era there were fewer college students in proportion to the population than there had been when the century began. There were no graduate schools, and the agricultural and mechanical colleges authorized in the Morrill Act had barely begun. Colleges were small; few taught religious doctrine, but fewer still appeared to be centers of inquiry.

However, all that changed after 1870. The 75 years of the University Transformation Era saw greater shifts in higher education than in the preceding 235 years combined. Most of the change in institutional form occurred in the first 40 years, and the largest growth in enrollment in the last 35. As Table 3.1 illustrates, between 1870 and 1944 the number of colleges quintupled, the number of students grew from 63,000 to 1.6 million, the faculty from 5,500 to nearly 150,000. At the beginning of the era, just over 9,000 bachelor's degrees were awarded each year; by its end, more than 135,000 were awarded. Doctoral degrees awarded went from none to 3,300. Higher education's endowment grew from less than $50 million to $1.75 billion; its revenue and expenditures grew to $1 billion per year.

Table 3.1. Statistical Portrait of the University Transformation Era, 1870–1945 (Estimates).

|  | 1870 | 1945 |
| --- | --- | --- |
| U.S. population | 39,818,449 | 139,924,000 |
| Number of students | 63,000 | 1,677,000 |
| Number of faculty | 5,553 | 150,000 |
| Number of institutions | 250 | 1,768 |
| Number of degrees earned (bachelor's, master's, and doctoral) | 9,372 | 157,349 |
| Current-fund revenue (in thousands of current dollars) | 14,000 | 1,169,394 |

Source: Snyder, 1993.

Much of this expansion would have happened anyway because of population growth and wealth generation, but the main impetus was that both secondary and postsecondary schools expanded their offerings, presented new types of programs, and attracted students who in earlier times would not have considered education beyond the lower grades. New types of colleges were formed, including specialized colleges, junior colleges, and colleges serving particular interests or racial groups. But the most prominent element in the transformation was the emergence of the university—an institution complete with an undergraduate college, professional schools, graduate departments, an orientation toward research and knowledge creation, and a wide range of service components.

## Universities

Pressure to introduce elements of the university into American higher education had been building for a generation before the institutions came to the fore. The faculty had been transforming themselves into a professional group and scientific research was spreading. But before colleges could become universities and before new institutions could be founded with all the characteristics marking a university, several concepts to which the colleges had adhered since early in the Colonial Era had to be modified. In general, the colleges had to reduce their involvement with religion, especially sectarianism; effect liaisons with incipient professional groups; adopt a service-to-the-community role; encourage or at least allow a professionalized faculty to take form; value research and the advancement of knowledge as ends in themselves; elevate farming, mechanics, and industry to areas worthy of study; exalt science over humanities; move from the perpetuation of tradition and teaching from authority to the position that knowledge was ever-evolving; stretch the educational experience from four years to a greater length of time by organizing graduate schools and awarding advanced degrees; and gain access to sizable funds, both from the public treasury and from wealthy donors. All these characteristics fell into place between the 1860s and the end of the century.

The idea of converting colleges to universities can be traced to the men who had been influenced by direct contact with higher education in Germany. George Ticknor was the earliest, reporting back to Harvard in 1825 after having visited and studied at German institutions. Subsequently, Daniel Gilman, Andrew White, Charles Eliot, Theodore Woolsey, and G. Stanley Hall—influential in the forming or transformation of Johns Hopkins, Cornell, Harvard, Yale, and Clark, respectively—stand out. All had been influenced by the universities in Germany. Others were influential as well. Henry Tappan, president of the University of Michigan in the 1850s, attempted to establish graduate study by bringing in scholars to work on their own research and by accepting advanced students to work with them. Francis Wayland, president of Brown, had tried repeatedly a decade earlier to convert his college to an institution committed to a broader curriculum serving students with a greater variety of interests. But the notion of the university can actually be traced to Thomas Jefferson, whose plans for the University of Virginia included advanced study and a faculty organized according to academic specialty.

The American university dates from the founding of Cornell in 1869—an institution complete with the characteristics of the comprehensive structures that were to follow. Johns Hopkins, founded in 1876, was dedicated from the outset to research and graduate training, and hence also must be accorded status as a first of its type. Others followed soon thereafter, and many of the older colleges transformed themselves into universities by adding graduate and professional schools centering on research, scholarship, and public service.

As the universities were formed, graduate enrollment expanded notably. At the outset of the University Transformation Era, there were perhaps 200 graduate students in the nation. Twenty years later there were around 2,400. Twenty years after that, nearly 10,000, and by 1930, nearly 50,000 graduate students were enrolled. As Hofstadter (1952) concluded, "The entire system of graduate teaching and research had developed within the lifetime of one man" (p. 64). As for degrees, in 1876, around 25 institutions awarded 44 PhDs; in 1930, more than 2,000 doctorates were granted. The 16 leading institutions were averaging 100 PhDs each per year by 1939.

Higher education's association with occupational groups striving to professionalize themselves expanded notably in the latter years of the nineteenth century. Law, medicine, and theology—the venerable professions—continued to be taught, but taking their place alongside were schools of business, journalism, engineering, architecture, pharmacology, dentistry, agriculture, mining, forestry, librarianship, education, psychology, and sociology. The notion that one had to be specifically trained to enter practice grew rapidly, feeding on three factors: each group's desire to be seen as a profession requiring a lengthy period of training; the expanding knowledge base that was itself transforming practice; and the availability of schools in which the acolytes could be prepared. David S. Jordan (1903), founding president of Stanford, summed up the institutions' role with these words: "The value of the college training of today cannot be too strongly emphasized. You cannot save time nor money by omitting it, whatever the profession on which you enter" (p. 36).

An emphasis on research most characteristically marked the beginnings of the universities. The research universities were dedicated to discovering and codifying knowledge as well as to advanced studies, knowledge for practical use, and career preparation. Natural science obtained a foothold in the science schools founded at Harvard and Yale in the 1840s and 1850s. The Massachusetts Institute of Technology (MIT) was organized in 1865 as a separate institution dedicated to scientific study. Natural science, training for practical careers, and research-based graduate education were mutually reinforcing. Rationality was the mark of a modern university. An emphasis on religion, reliance on authority, and study of the classics were all in full retreat. The university was more than a college with a group of professional schools clustered around it; its crowning function was original research. The university was the home of scholars and scholarship.

By the time the Association of American Universities (AAU) was formed in 1900, the research universities had themselves become a special group among American institutions. Geiger (1986) noted that the founders of the association included five state institutions, five formerly colonial colleges, and five that were founded as universities committed to graduate study from the outset. These were the institutions that set the standards for graduate study and research. The universities of California, Illinois, Michigan, Minnesota, and Wisconsin were growing rapidly; they added to the value of their endowments, to their libraries, to the number of doctoral degrees awarded, and to their increasingly prestigious faculties. Yale, Princeton, Harvard, Pennsylvania, and Columbia were the transformed colonial colleges in the group. The institutions founded with a commitment to graduate study included Chicago, Cornell, Johns Hopkins, MIT, and Stanford; California Institute of Technology (Cal Tech) was added to the group roughly a decade after the AAU was formed.

The leading research institutions grew rapidly. In 1876, their libraries averaged under 50,000 volumes. At the turn of the century, they had grown to 171,000 volumes each, led by Harvard's 549,000. Twenty years later they averaged close to three-quarters of a million volumes, and Harvard had over two million. The University of Chicago opened in 1892; seven years later it awarded 43 PhDs, more than any other university in the nation. Stanford opened in 1891; eight years later its endowment of $18 million was the highest for any institution. By 1930, several of the research universities were among the largest institutions in terms of enrollment; leaders were Columbia with 15,000 regular full-time students, California with 17,000, and Minnesota and Illinois with around 12,500 each.

The universities were able to get off to such a fast start because of the funding they attracted. The coincidence of public funds available through the Morrill Act and private funds coming from the fortunes made during and after the Civil War gave a double boost. The Morrill Act of 1862 permitted every state to select 30,000 acres of federal land times its number of congressmen to set aside for universities; nearly 17.5 million acres were thus distributed (Nevins, 1962). Morrill money was used in founding the University of Illinois in 1867, the University of California in 1868, and colleges in a total of 30 states before 1900. Funds from private fortunes went to Johns Hopkins in 1876. Cornell received money from both: $500,000 from Ezra Cornell and New York's share of the Morrill money. The institutions' emphasis on science and research was a natural consequence of the Morrill Act's specifying that the funds be used to endow "at least one college where the leading object shall be, without excluding other scientific and classical studies, and including military tactics, to teach such branches of learning as are related to agriculture and the mechanic arts" (Hofstadter and Smith, 1961, p. 568). And although no such restriction was placed on private contributions, the railroad, steel, oil, and textile barons did not expect that their millions would be used to support the few young people interested in studying philosophy or religion.

Imitation was prominent. What the leading universities did was frequently adopted by other institutions across the nation. Harvard's elective system became all but universal, as did the academic department as the basic unit of college organization. Graduate and professional schools that were created within the institution but which operated separately from the undergraduate program became the norm. Requirements for the PhD took standard form, especially after the members of the AAU articulated expectations. In fact, within a few years of AAU's establishment, it was effectually accrediting other institutions by listing those whose bachelor's degree holders could be deemed ready for graduate study.

However, not all the leading institutions' practices were adopted; Harvard's experiment with a three-year undergraduate degree found few takers, and Johns Hopkins's initial concentration on graduate education never spread to other institutions to the extent that Hopkins pursued it.

Competition with other institutions became a driving force. The universities sought to grow large as a way of effecting prestige. And in private institutions, large size meant more money from tuition, which accounted for over half of all revenue. As the universities raced for status, they began adding specialized facilities: laboratories, football stadiums, residence halls, auditoriums, and carillon towers that served as focal points for the campuses. Nine of the most prominent (50,000-plus seat) football stadiums in use at the turn of the twenty-first century were built prior to 1930 primarily to entertain alumni and townspeople, as well as students who in many venues—Harvard and Yale, for example—would occupy no more than 10% of the seats if they all showed up for the games (Lombardi et al., 2003). Except for Cal Tech, MIT, and a few specialized research institutes, every major research university in the nation at one time had a renowned football team.

Each university claimed to be unique, but imitation and competition led them to adhere to the same rules about course attendance, time-to-degree, the nature of the degrees awarded, and the way students and faculty conducted themselves. Public relations offices, organized within some of the universities early in the twentieth century, pointed out the institutions' virtues, but in general the students and faculty were relatively homogeneous. They were drawn from among the same social strata; the students were transitory and had no political power; faculty freedom and the ability to move from one institution to another kept them relatively satisfied. The basic characteristics of the university had been established: boards of trustees, now made up of more businessmen than clergymen; a bureaucratically organized administration; a system of faculty ranking; relatively uniform standards for admissions and student progress; and academic departments.

The ostensible mission of the universities—the quest for knowledge and academic excellence—was always subordinate to the institutions' adherence to popular values. They could not stray too far from community mores lest they lose their support. For example, compulsory daily chapel for students was a feature in the early years of many state universities such as California, Illinois, and Michigan, a reflection of the hybrid, homogenized Protestantism that was a virtual cultural establishment of the time. Thus, instead of preparing social revolutionaries, they trained young people to take their place within the established community. Their admissions policies—which discriminated against women and students from various ethnic, racial, and religious groups—reflected the attitudes of the times and contributed to the solidifying of a caste system still apparent today.

The university's major contribution was the production of scientific research of a quality and variety that by the 1940s was preeminent in the world. American physical and natural science overtook the once-leading European institutions, especially after the 1920s. The universities had become involved in research for World War I in 1917, readily compromising their dedication to intellectual freedom and truth. The Reserve Officers' Training Corps (ROTC) was formed in 1916 and the Students' Army Training Corps (SATC) in 1918, both of which allowed male students to enlist, stay on campus, and receive military training. Research in explosives and industrial processes that would further the war effort was supported by governmental funds, and eagerly accepted by the institutions. Both research and military training foreshadowed a lengthy list of war-related relations that marked higher education during World War II and well beyond.

By the early years of the twentieth century, an enduring pattern of higher education had been established. All took place within the 40-year tenure of Charles Eliot, the president of Harvard, who in 1869 had articulated many of the principles on which the system was based. With greater or lesser emphasis on the various functions, universities both public and private exhibited several characteristics that they had inherited from earlier models. Their treatment of undergraduates followed the British form of residential colleges. Graduate study and research was adopted from the German universities. Service to the community and preparation of students for a wide number of occupations had developed indigenously. As Kerr (1963) described it, "The resulting combination does not seem plausible but it has given America a remarkably effective educational institution" (p. 18).

**Other Institutions**

Not all the colleges shared the growth in size, prestige, and programs and services exhibited by the universities. Many remained too small to offer much breadth in curriculum, let alone to construct modern laboratories or libraries. The colleges had to make vertical moves, extending themselves to graduate study if they were to attract the funding and faculty that would in turn lead to enrollment growth. Clark (1995) pointed out that a college might well add science to the undergraduate curriculum but "advanced research could hardly be put alongside tutoring in Greek and Latin" (p. 120). Some commentators at the turn of the century recommended that the smaller colleges close if they could not transform themselves into institutions with greater breadth. Thwing (1910) commented that "the presence of the poor college is a weakness to the whole college system" (p. 146). Chicago's president Harper suggested that the weaker institutions drop the upper division and become junior colleges that prepared students for entry into the universities; by 1940, 15% of the institutions that had enrolled 150 or fewer students in 1900 had become junior colleges, and an additional 40% had closed their doors or merged with other colleges. However, enough small liberal arts colleges survived so that the institution would remain part of the American educational scene for at least another century.

Other institutions showed high growth as they expanded their offerings, not necessarily in research and graduate education but in professional studies, a broader undergraduate curriculum, and involvement with public service. Many, especially those in urban areas, emphasized part-time and summer-session enrollment, so much so that by 1930, when Columbia, New York University, and City College of New York had the largest total enrollment in the nation, considerably fewer than half their students were full-timers (Geiger, 1986, p. 112). Several other urban institutions, including Hunter (New York), Northwestern (Chicago), the University of Southern California (Los Angeles), Northeastern (Boston), and Western Reserve (Cleveland), also had total enrollments in which regular, full-time students were in the minority.

Because the universities could not or would not matriculate everyone who sought upward mobility through higher education, several other institutional forms developed. Historically Black Colleges and Universities (HBCUs) were a notable example. Prior to the Civil War, scarcely two dozen African Americans had graduated from colleges in the United States, despite the fact that freedmen numbered close to 250,000 in 1825 and nearly 500,000 by the time the Civil War started. Few colleges in the North or South would consider enrolling them. Lincoln University in Pennsylvania and Wilberforce in Ohio formed in the 1850s, and Howard, a creation of the U.S. Congress in 1867, were organized especially to admit African American students. Soon after the Civil War several churches and philanthropic foundations funded the creation of private colleges especially for children of the formerly enslaved. Over 50 historically Black private, four-year colleges were founded. A few, such as Tuskegee and Fisk, became prominent, but most others remained unaccredited well into the middle of the twentieth century.

Publicly supported colleges for African Americans received a major boost in 1890 when the second Morrill Act stipulated that states must either demonstrate that admission to land grant institutions (established by the first Morrill Act in 1862) was not restricted by race or establish new institutions for Black students. As Gonzales and Robinson (2023) wrote, many southern states opted for the latter to "access new resources while maintaining a racially segregated system of higher education" (p. 457). Unsurprisingly, students enrolled in these first HBCUs "were not afforded learning opportunities commensurate to those of their white counterparts, as the curriculum was generally restricted to applied forms of education" (p. 457). This, in combination with Jim Crow laws in the South and policies of discrimination and exclusion of African Americans across the United States, slowed the development and evolution of HBCUs. Yet in the early twentieth century, several northern philanthropic organizations, in collaboration with the U.S. Freedmen's Bureau, provided matching grants to help selected HBCUs build a professorate and facilities "fit for the four-year collegiate level" (Lovett, 2015, p. xiii).

Women's colleges blossomed during the same period, some growing out of all-female seminaries, others started through benefactions. However, not until Vassar, Smith, and Wellesley opened in the 1860s and 1870s did this group of colleges take its eventual form. Women began entering higher education in greater numbers as liberal arts colleges and state universities, especially in the Midwest and West, opened to them. By 1900, more than two-thirds of the nation's colleges and universities admitted both men and women. But apparently many educators, as well as families, felt that young women would be better served in institutions of their own. The women's colleges adopted the collegiate traditions of professional faculty, a four-year curriculum, and dormitory living, but generally placed a greater emphasis on the arts, languages, and humanities. By the end of the century, Harvard, Brown, Columbia, and a few other old-line institutions that refused to admit women on equal status had organized Radcliffe, Pembroke, and Barnard as annexes for women to take supposedly equivalent classes and exams.

Junior colleges also emerged during this era, beginning with Joliet Junior College (Illinois) in 1901. Defined as institutions offering two years of collegiate instruction, they began originally with the support of a few university leaders who insisted that the universities would not become true centers of research and professional development as long as they retained their lower divisions. However, the foremost impetus for the growth of junior colleges was the pressure for further education occasioned by the rising number of high school graduates. By 1922, 207 junior colleges, 137 of which were privately supported, operated in 37 states. Most were quite small; total enrollment for all institutions was around 20,000. By 1930, 450 junior colleges could be found in all but five states; total enrollment was around 70,000. By the end of the University Transformation Era, more than 600 junior colleges were functioning, most still small, averaging around 400 students. California was an early leader in forming the colleges—in 1930, it boasted one-third of all the public junior college students in the nation. A large number were founded also in Illinois, Texas, and Missouri. Many private junior colleges in the East and Midwest served as finishing schools for young women who would not go on to university studies. Many others were designed to allow students to take the first two years of college in their hometown and eventually to transfer to a baccalaureate-granting institution. In the 1930s and 1940s, junior colleges began providing courses in numerous occupational areas and hence took on a hybrid form as institutions preparing people either for further collegiate studies or for immediate employment (Kisker, Cohen, and Brawer, 2023).

State colleges—sometimes characterized as comprehensive universities, and later as broadly accessible institutions—grew notably as various professional and quasi-professional groups began encouraging aspirants to obtain specialized preparation that required less than a doctoral degree. Approximately 100 public normal schools were opened in the last third of the nineteenth century. Most were transformed into state colleges offering bachelor's degrees, and eventually master's degrees, to young people who would become schoolteachers. These comprehensive institutions expanded into other professional areas, including nursing, accounting, business, and various trades and technologies. They also developed programs in home economics and several specialties within agriculture such as farm management, animal husbandry, and crop production.

Overall, the college population expanded so that any area of esoteric studies could find students to enroll in it, just as experimental colleges could survive by matriculating students who valued the institution's eccentricity or specialized focus. But not many such institutions were built as freestanding entities; more common was the university with an experimental college, a cluster of colleges, or a separate college within it. Here, a few students and professors could indulge in a wide range of studies, a modified curriculum, and different instructional forms without disturbing the broader institutional setting. The University of Wisconsin's Experimental College, centering on the few students and instructors who wanted to interact without concerning themselves with a fixed curriculum or instructional forms, opened in 1927 and lasted for five years, thus foreshadowing both in duration and intent many experimental colleges of the 1960s. The more successful General College of the University of Minnesota opened in 1932 and acted as a junior college. It tested and sorted students, provided orientation to postsecondary study, and passed students through to the upper division or provided them with what was called at the time a terminal general education. St. John's College also reorganized in the 1930s around a particular theme: the Great Books. Its hallmarks were seminars, a faculty made up of tutors without specialization, and a fully prescribed curriculum. Entire colleges were built around the idea that young people should be creative. Bennington, Sarah Lawrence, Bard, Rollins, and Black Mountain, among others, all shared enthusiasm for artistic expression.

Various other specialized colleges survived despite the dominance of the universities. Postsecondary vocational schools maintained themselves by matriculating nearly anyone who chose to enroll and by teaching the trades (cosmetology, appliance repair, office skills, fashion design) that the other institutions ignored. Independent theological schools hung on as well: in 1897, they accounted for 13% of all colleges and enrolled over 4% of all students. But by 1934 they made up only 10% of institutions and enrolled less than 2% of students.

## Students

At the beginning of the University Transformation Era, fewer than 2% of the nation's 18-year-olds entered college. Of the 63,000 students enrolled, 1 in 5 was female. The numbers increased steadily along with the nation's population; by 1900, 250,000 students were enrolled. The ratio of women had gone up to 2 in 5 and was to reach nearly half the undergraduates by 1920; it fell back to one-third by the end of the era. Overall, the percentage of 18-year-olds matriculating increased steadily, reaching 3% in 1890, 4% in 1900, 5% in 1910, 8% in 1920, and 16% in 1940.

Enrollment growth was greatest during the 1920s. Most of the expansion took place in existing institutions, but the newly formed junior colleges and the transformation of teacher education into baccalaureate study contributed heavily. The number of high school graduates, which increased by 150% between 1920 and 1930 alone, contributed as well. Institutions and programs expanded at different rates. Engineering, law, and medicine declined as a percentage of the whole, while nonprofessional graduate education increased. Also contributing to the overall enrollment figures was an increased demand for professional training as more occupational groups began to expect some college education for their new initiates, and the increase in length of time required to complete a program; law increased to three years, medicine and teacher education to four years.

The belief that education could serve as a means of ascending from lower to middle class and from middle to upper class grew steadily. Bledstein (1976) commented, "In a nation without an effective apprenticeship system and without a significant gentry, the school diploma more and more served as the license with which an individual sought entry into the respectability and rewards of a profession. By 1870, there were more institutions in America awarding bachelor's degrees, more medical schools, and more law schools than in all of Europe" (p. 33).

**Admissions**

College admissions requirements broadened during the early years of the era. Academic merit was always at the top of the list, although a parent who was an alumnus of the institution or who had a deep pocket might well cause admission officers to look kindly upon an otherwise less-than-qualified applicant. An acquaintance with at least a dozen subjects was expected, although students were not expected to be similarly proficient in all of them. In the first years of the University Transformation Era, physical geography, English composition, physical science, English literature, and modern languages were added to the subjects that had been introduced earlier. Most of the innovations were led by Harvard, with Princeton and Michigan taking the lead in a few subjects.

Admission to bachelor's of arts programs at the leading colleges centered on a similar combination of subjects, although the amount or depth of preparation required differed. Harvard demanded the most mathematics, Michigan the least Greek. English had not been a requirement before the beginning of the era, probably because an interest in English literature was secondary to classical literature read in the original. Furthermore, because English was the vernacular language, the college leaders anticipated that students would come adequately prepared, especially as public school systems expanded. English composition found its way into admissions requirements at Princeton in 1870, Harvard in 1874, Michigan in 1878, and Columbia and Cornell in 1882. This requirement usually took the form of applicants' being required to write a short English composition—a requirement that survives in the essay that applicants have been expected to write ever since. The physical and natural sciences entered into admissions requirements; physical geography, which was introduced at Harvard and Michigan in 1870, was first. Cornell began requiring a knowledge of physiology in 1877, and botany and natural philosophy were part of Michigan's requirements in 1890. By the end of the century, physics was becoming a general requirement for admission to a bachelor's program.

The expansion in types of programs led to different requirements. The Lawrence Scientific School, founded at Harvard in 1847, required physics and chemistry for admission, but curiously the schools of science at Yale and Princeton were slow to expect their applicants to have prior knowledge of science. As late as 1888, Princeton's John C. Green School of Science required five books of Caesar and four orations of Cicero, and not until 1895 was botany introduced as an admissions requirement to the Sheffield Scientific School at Yale. The latter institutions clung to the notion that drill in the classics and mathematics was a well-disciplined preparation for studying science. Furthermore, not much science instruction was available in the secondary schools of the time.

As the University Transformation Era evolved, more changes in the amount or quality of study expected of entering students took place than were changes in the subjects themselves. The leading institutions, pushing toward advanced study and research, increased their expectations for first-year applicants. They also effected a downward pressure on the secondary schools to prepare students in various subjects. As for foreign languages, the actual use of the language and the ability to read literature in the original supplanted drill in grammar.

Toward the end of the nineteenth century, the U.S. Bureau of Education collected data on admissions requirements from 475 institutions and found that of the 432 that offered bachelor's of arts degrees, 93% required Latin and 73% Greek (see Table 3.2). This scaled down in the other programs; few institutions offering bachelor's of letters or bachelor's of science degrees required Greek, but 39% of them expected a modern language (Broome, 1903).

As pressure for college entrance increased in the 1920s, issues of access plagued the universities. Facilities and resources simply could not accommodate all who sought entry. The preservation of wealth and family position were contrary to the myth of egalitarianism and the idea that higher education enables individuals to move between social classes on the basis of their intelligence and demonstrated academic qualifications. The institutions looked for defensible criteria on which to discriminate. College presidents,

Table 3.2. Admissions Requirements for Various Bachelor's Degree Programs, 1897.

| Degree Program | Number of Institutions | Percent of Institutions Requiring | | |
| --- | --- | --- | --- | --- |
| | | Latin | Greek | A Modern Language |
| Bachelor's of arts | 432 | 93% | 74% | 14% |
| Bachelor's of philosophy | 123 | 81% | 6% | 42% |
| Bachelor's of letters | 98 | 68% | 2% | 39% |
| Bachelor's of science | 318 | 55% | 2% | 39% |

Source: Broome, 1903.

especially in the private Eastern institutions, posted finite numbers to which they would limit the size of their first-year class. In some colleges, these restrictions were undertaken in an attempt to limit the number of entering Jewish students—despite the fact that many exhibited the qualities of intellect and drive for achievement that the presidents otherwise lauded. Here the multiplicity of university roles came to the fore. Were the colleges places for individuals to study, learn, and move up in social class? Were they places for people to make contacts or gain access to an old boy's network? Were they to prepare students to feed the graduate schools? All came into play along with anti-Semitism and discrimination against African Americans and the children of southern Europeans. Colleges in the other parts of the country, especially the state universities in the Midwest, continued admitting sizeable numbers of students with minimal restrictions; for many, high school graduation was sufficient.

Karabel (2005) described admissions practices at America's leading colleges as "exceedingly strange" (p. 1) because over time they have included athletic ability; family wealth; where one's parents went to college; and the applicant's race, ethnicity, gender, extracurricular activities, test scores, prior academic achievement, religion, and, vaguely, qualities of character or merit. What we laud as "equal opportunity" actually applies only in context of the entirety of the nation's postsecondary system. Within single institutions, "an admissions policy is a kind of negotiated settlement among contending groups [administrators, alumni, trustees, faculty, state and federal officials], each wishing to shape admissions criteria and the actual selection process to produce the outcome they prefer" (p. 6).

Examining changes in requirements for entering students reveals an evolution of expectations, but it begs the question of why colleges select students on the basis of academic merit. All colleges have limited resources and hence must restrict enrollment. However, academic capabilities, defined as prior school achievement or scores on entrance tests, have been by far the most widely employed criteria for the following reasons:

- Institutional reputation. The more highly prepared are likely to complete a degree and go on to more successful careers, hence make the college appear to have taught well.

- Ease of instruction. Better prepared students better fit the faculty ideal and keep faculty morale high.

- Higher return on investment. Greater learning occurs even with less effort in teaching.

- Individual motivation. Young people are rewarded for their academic efforts in the lower schools.

- Societal value. Aspiring young people are stimulated by researchers and encouraged to make their own contributions to advancing knowledge.

During the 1920s and 1930s, selective Eastern institutions adopted several forms of admissions criteria in addition to academic merit, as they feared that when Black, Jewish, Italian, Catholic, or other types of students made high scores on the exams and were admitted, the traditional students—those whose characteristics were favored by the board, administration, and alumni—would withdraw (Wechsler, 1997). When Columbia required its applicants to provide letters of reference, personal data, and aspirations with the understanding that the admissions office could accept or reject on the basis of subjective criteria, its percentage of Jewish students dropped in half. Harvard's president Lowell tried to establish a Jewish quota and, after the Harvard faculty rejected the idea, built subjective criteria into the admissions process. Geiger (1986) concluded, "Harvard's experience made it clear to other schools that overt quotas could not be publicly admitted; and Harvard seems to have learned from others that discrimination required a cloak of ambiguity" (p. 135). Princeton blatantly gave priority to social over intellectual qualifications, and only secondarily used examination scores for selection. The private institutions also gave preference to graduates of exclusive secondary schools and to children of alumni. The notion of *holistic evaluation*—later implemented in an attempt to maintain diverse student bodies in states where affirmative action had been banned—was used in the University Transformation Era as a way of keeping certain groups out. Same process, different goals.

Selective admissions based on a variety of criteria—never the same from one decade to the next or one institution to another—have been less of a problem in American higher education than in other countries because of the number of colleges in the nation. There are always institutions that accept nearly every applicant. Furthermore, the United States has never had a national examination, with all of its accompanying problems. However, the shifting basis for admissions frequently reflects the biases of institutions, especially those where alumni play a significant role or where an intra-collegiate belief system is relatively homogeneous. It also means that the order of prestige among institutions is to an extent dependent on the selection criteria they employ. The basis on which students are selected reflects the relative status of American social groups and the changes in social mores over time.

As selective admissions became more prominent in the 1920s, various standardized tests such as the Scholastic Aptitude Test (SAT) were developed. In the 1930s the College Education Examination Board developed examinations for use by prestigious institutions, and during that decade the Graduate Record Examination (GRE) was also installed. All these tests were used most frequently in the Eastern institutions, especially as those colleges tried to broaden their student base. The SAT rapidly gained favor because its standardized scores were comparable nationally, consistent each year, readily understandable to the public, and modestly predictive of graduation rates. During the 1930s, the number of students coming to Eastern colleges from private secondary schools shrank, and the colleges tried to become more national than regional. In 1934, Harvard began a program of scholarships awarded to high-achieving prospective students from the Midwest, and Yale and Princeton similarly sought students from across the nation. Academic merit was supposed to be the main criterion, and standardized tests were considered the best measure. Along with formalized courses of study, these types of admissions screens helped college educators convince the public that objective principles determined competence.

Race, religion, gender, ethnicity, family wealth, and social standing—all have been used as admissions screens despite the fact that these characteristics are inherent to the individual, not the result of effort or accomplishment, and thus are discriminatory on their face. Over time, universities began to reject these criteria as unfair or antiegalitarian; prior school attainment or scores on an achievement test appeared more acceptable as the University Transformation Era came to an end. Even so, as late as 1952, less than 13% of legacy applicants to Harvard were rejected (Karabel, 2005, p. 189).

**The Collegiate Way**

The idea of going to college as a way of life came into full bloom during the University Transformation Era. The residential experience and association with peers took center stage as aids to cultivating the maturing young person and helping individuals generate associations that would last a lifetime. Although part-time commuter students grew as a percentage of the whole by virtue of their attendance at junior colleges and universities that made special provision for them, students at the older, residential institutions increased their claim to exclusivity by developing a model for collegiate life that the commuters and part-timers could never duplicate.

The value of the four-year residential college experience became ingrained in the American psyche. This echo of the English undergraduate residential college, imported to the United States along with other English social institutions, refused to be quieted in the face of expanding graduate and research enterprises. A college had to provide tutorials, housing, and extracurricular activities if it was to remain true to its principles; the undergraduate experience had to be sustained, even within the broader university. The cost of constructing dormitories in rapidly expanding universities was a constraint; the first female students at the University of Washington roomed at the president's house. At the turn of the twentieth century, over half the students at the University of California were commuters, a ratio equaled or exceeded in other institutions located in cities where off-campus housing was available. Cal's first sizeable residence facilities opened when it was already one of the largest universities in the nation, a third of a century after its founding. When students lived in the surrounding community, institutions attempted to enforce rules on their behavior and conduct. In general, the notion that the college was responsible for the lives of its undergraduates remained strong, even as the institutions grew larger.

The idea of the four-year residential experience—complete with extracurricular activities—was so pervasive that it became synonymous with what college was supposed to be. Nearly all research on higher education or the effects of college on students focused on those in four-year, residential environments; the effects of college on part-timers or commuters was hardly studied at all. By the 1930s, a student personnel point of view had been codified; that is, the belief that a college was responsible for all aspects of a young person's life, including emotional and psychological characteristics as well as learning and cognitive development.

The four-year residential college had been present from the beginnings of higher education in America, and as the colleges expanded they constructed new residential facilities to sustain this special experience. The insularity exhibited in the curriculum, divorced as it was from most of secular life, extended to the extra-curriculum as well. Campus activities including sports, dramatics clubs, debating societies, fraternities, and religious observances expanded. The extra-curriculum became a form of surrogate involvement—a substitute for attendance at comparable activities in the outside world. College activities that reached beyond the walls associated the students with their counterparts elsewhere. This was the era in which organized sports and debating clubs grew into intercollegiate activities. Even religion followed suit, with the creation of the intercollegiate YMCA in the late nineteenth century.

The University Transformation Era saw intercollegiate athletics blossom into major endeavors. Athletics departments gained their own budgets; massive stadiums were erected; sporting events filled the pages of the newspapers and were broadcast nationally as radio became widespread. Athletics were part of the collegiate experience in English and German universities as well, but they were different in the United States because of commercialization. Once intercollegiate sports began in the latter part of the nineteenth century, they grew rapidly, as though they were "rushing in to fill an emotional vacuum" (Hofstadter, 1952, p. 113). Even in the Ivy League, where intercollegiate athletics were de-emphasized after the 1930s, a varsity-level athlete with a subpar academic record stood a good chance of being admitted. Athletics certainly displaced much of the rowdiness common among students in colleges of an earlier era and helped connect alumni to the institution, sustaining their loyalty and, not incidentally, their donations.

As the collegiate way became codified, student rebellions against the colleges' surrogate-parent status were seen, but were less acrimonious, relatively free of the violence and mayhem characteristic of student riots during the mid–nineteenth century. Part of the difference might be attributed to the fact that students in the latter part of the century faced greater economic opportunity—more professions from which to choose. "Students in the 1890s, especially those at prestigious colleges and universities, could confidently view college education as a pleasant interlude on a well-marked path" (Kett, 1977, p. 175). Gradually, as older students populated the campuses, the modes of control that had been installed to manage young adolescents were modified.

Not all of student life was athletics and socializing. Student involvement in social issues grew. Female students and faculty were involved with the suffrage movement; 15 colleges formed the National College Women's Equal Suffrage League in 1908. During the 1930s, antiwar activities included student protests against required participation in ROTC. Students also took part in strikes at coal mines and clothing manufacturers. Some joined clubs aligned with communist movements. The end of Prohibition took away the thrill of illegal drinking, and the Great Depression sobered students in other ways as they came to realize that fulltime, well-paying jobs were not going to be readily available. A popular song of the era featured a young man lamenting having to work his way through college in order to acquire knowledge he would most likely never use after graduation. The U.S. entry into World War II effected an even greater change in student life, as most of the young men were called into the armed services and as the campuses became centers of training for the vast numbers of military officers who were needed to pursue the war effort. But the collegiate way had already been established as the essence of the American college experience.

## Social Mobility

Throughout the history of higher education, students have expected college to contribute to their social mobility. The students in the University Transformation Era were no different.

As the curriculum broadened and the social milieu shifted, students found a mix of peers through which they could develop associations lasting a lifetime. Each of the colleges was a community apart, imprinting its own values on the developing youth and anticipating lifelong loyalty. Within these isolated enclaves, students developed their own codes of behavior, which were so powerful that by the 1920s the term *college man* had a ready reference: someone with an intense loyalty to his institution; a special mode of dress; the expectation that he drank socially, if not to excess; a devil-may-care attitude regarding young women; and a marginal association with the life of the mind—the latter being exemplified by the "gentleman's C."

Despite enacting discriminatory admissions criteria, the colleges continually put forth ideals of equality and egalitarianism, emphasizing that anyone with academic qualifications could attend. In Eliot's inaugural address as president of Harvard in 1869, he mentioned that the institution would never turn away any student who had the capacity and character for college work. However, he also pointed out that women were not yet welcome—not, he stated, because of any limiting notions about their innate capacities but because of the difficulty of establishing segregated housing facilities. (He was more discrete than one of his successors who, more than a century later, was forced to resign after he opined that women lacked the capacity for science.) Despite the leaders' progressive rhetoric, the colleges of the University Transformation Era reflected, more than led, their contemporary society.

## Faculty

At the beginning of the University Transformation Era, few of the 250 or so colleges in the nation employed more than two dozen instructors. Probably half the faculty had professorial status but differentiation into academic ranks, the formation of disciplinary departments and associations, academic freedom, and faculty autonomy were as yet but dimly seen. Along with other characteristics of the modern faculty, these were put in place less than a half century after the blossoming of the university. In fact, the universities and the faculty as a professional group grew in tandem in the late nineteenth and early twentieth centuries.

Efforts to define the concept of professionalism have had a long history. The problem of definition remains because occupational roles vary depending on the setting in which they are performed. Professions continually evolve, and different segments of society may view them as having more or less status. By most definitions, the professional works full time and has a lifetime commitment to a career. A professional gains a specialized body of knowledge during a long period of formal education. Ministry to a client population, autonomy of judgment, adherence to ethical standards, licensure or formal entry requirements, and associations that monitor all the above characterize the group.

As the University Transformation Era began, faculty had evolved from the status of tutors, expecting that they would spend only a short time teaching a variety of subjects, to that of professors, knowledgeable in a particular academic discipline with a commitment to long-term, full-time employment. The profession had been slow to form because of the tutors' low pay, low status, and lack of secure employment. State governments were indifferent to the instructors; nowhere did they enjoy status as civil servants, and their pay and working conditions were rarely the concerns of a governing body outside the institution. College presidents could hire and fire, paying only as much as necessary to attract a staff they considered qualified.

All that changed after 1870. One indication of the rise of faculty status is provided by William Rainey Harper's behavior as soon as he was appointed president of the fledgling University of Chicago. The university had been organized with sizable donations from John D. Rockefeller and several Chicago business leaders. Therefore, Harper had money to work with, and one of his first actions was to travel around the country seeking the best professors. He recruited faculty from Yale and employed several former college presidents, including the president of the University of Wisconsin. His raid on Clark University was notable. Shamelessly, without the president's knowledge, he met with the majority of the Clark faculty, offering to double their salaries. When the Clark president objected, Harper invited him also to join the Chicago faculty. When all settled, he had engaged 15 of Clark's professors, thus stripping the institution of most of its staff, as Clark had been open only three years at the time (Hofstadter and Smith, 1961).

Although universities differed in size and emphasis, most included an undergraduate college, a graduate division, and several professional schools. The rise of the faculty depended on the latter two characteristics; the faculty would not have become professionalized nearly as rapidly if they had been involved solely with undergraduate teaching. Yet despite the shifting emphasis, research could be conducted only after teaching responsibilities were fulfilled. Nonetheless, the number of hours that a faculty member was expected to spend in the classroom differed between research universities and liberal arts colleges. In the first decade of the twentieth century, professors at research universities averaged 8 to 10 hours of teaching per week, which was considerably less than the 15 to 18 hours spent in the classroom by their colleagues at most colleges. By 1920, the hours spent on teaching and research became further differentiated, with the prestigious, wealthy, and graduate-oriented institutions requiring progressively fewer teaching hours of their faculty. However, because the higher education system was differentiated, with junior colleges and teachers colleges growing rapidly, the overall student-teacher ratio of 10 to 1 did not change throughout the era. This average figure obviously masked a continual decline in the number of students per teacher at research institutions and the increasing enrollments and class size in undergraduate colleges.

Still, professors at all institutions continually sought reduced teaching hours. Faculty at broadly accessible institutions pointed to their counterparts at more selective universities; those at the leading institutions pointed to the teaching hours expected of the professors in Europe. However, even though the number of hours devoted to teaching and research varied between types of institutions, among departments in the same institution, and among faculty ranks, in few cases were individuals expected to devote all their time to one or the other endeavor. The notion that professors were supposed to be engaged at least some of the time in teaching and some in research became part of the ethos of the American university. All were supposed to be, at the same time, teachers and scholars.

Other characteristics of the profession appeared at various times. Sabbatical leaves began at Harvard around 1880. The practice spread so that by the turn of the century several other research universities were doing the same thing: offering professors every seventh year off, with some proportion of their pay sustained. Set in place originally so that professors would have time to engage in further study and remain current in their field, the sabbatical became a fringe benefit and bargaining chip as professors were recruited. In the first two decades of the twentieth century, the practice of offering intra-institutional funds for research expanded. The University of California included a budget provision for faculty expenses related to research in 1915. However, salaries did not increase commensurately. At the time of World War I, the assembly line workers at the Ford Motor Company earned as much as associate professors at the University of Michigan (Kreger, 1998).

The professionalization of the faculty meant that increasing numbers of learned people, especially scientists, took academic positions. In an earlier era, the most prominent scholars might have been freelancers, but the rise of the university drew them into the faculty ranks. One study conducted in 1906 showed that of the 1,000 "Leading American Men of Science," more than 400 were employed at 15 leading research universities and nearly 200 more at other colleges (Geiger, 1986, p. 39). All this had happened in but one generation after Eliot's inaugural address at Harvard when he said, "The university does not hold a single fund primarily intended to secure to men of learning the leisure and means to prosecute original researches" (Hofstadter and Smith, 1961, p. 617).

Research was clearly the endeavor that marked the rise of the professoriate, and by pursuing their studies into narrower channels, the professors became more and more specialized. By the 1890s, the special interests of the faculty led them to form departments organized along academic disciplinary lines. These specialized units resulted from the German influence, prevailing assumptions about the nature of knowledge, and the ambitions of young scholars looking for new fields in which to make a name for themselves. Furthermore, as the universities grew larger, the unitary supervision of curriculum, teaching responsibilities, and student progress toward degrees became inadequate. The rise of institutional administration also contributed to the formation of academic departments, as professors sought organizational units that would provide them with a power base from which they might counter untoward demands on their time and activities.

The rise of the academic department coincided with expectations of academic freedom. The German tradition of freedom for students to choose their own studies and freedom for professors to study and teach what they would was welcomed by the incipient faculty professionals. Administrators and governing boards were considerably less enamored of academic freedom, especially when the faculty conceived of it as the right to advance unpopular ideas. The struggle derived not from educational theory but from institutional relationships. Faculty proponents of academic freedom modified the original concept of freedom to study and to teach to include protection for professors who would comment on the affairs of government, business, and other trends and events away from the campus. Many presidents took a different view, contending that freedom to take positions was limited to the classroom. These disagreements presaged future court battles that would draw the boundaries of academic freedom and institutional autonomy in later eras.

A few celebrated cases of professors being dismissed for espousing unpopular views led to the forming of the American Association of University Professors (AAUP) in 1915. Much of the energy of this nationwide, cross-institutional association in its early years was devoted to addressing grievances of members who had been dismissed or who felt they were being treated unfairly by their institution's administration. In 1920, the AAUP's Committee on College and University Governance recommended that the faculty have a role in institutional governance, particularly in the selection of administrators, preparation of the budget, and in the formation of educational policy. Toward the end of the era, in 1940, the AAUP published a Statement of Principle, holding that faculty tenure was a right that could not be abrogated by an institution's governors merely because a professor expressed unpopular views. Competition among universities, each wishing to attract the most notable scholars in a field, and the relationships among scholars who interacted with disciplinary counterparts at other institutions also helped mitigate restrictions on what they could publish or proclaim, thereby reinforcing the concept of academic freedom.

Part of the faculty's difficulty in advancing ideas of tenure and job rights was that power would shift as people formerly regarded as employees took command of essential aspects of the workplace. A more subtle barrier was that standards for judging competence changed as reliance on religion and authority were replaced with ideals of rationality. The Enlightenment dream was that debates on justice and equity would take place in a public arena, that an ever-evolving quest for truth would replace tradition. Research, experimentation, and rational inquiry in the universities fit the dream. The faculty code of pursuing truth became a cornerstone of the profession, and within that code faculty claimed the right to maintain their own views and speak out on matters of public policy.

The faculty as a professional group differed from most other professions in that they did not appeal to the states to impose restrictions governing admission to practice. University instructors did not have the equivalent of a board of medical examiners, a bar examination, or state licensure requirements. They imposed their own standards within the context of their own institutions, hence the standards varied depending on institutional emphasis. Other professions depended on public recognition; the faculty practiced within an academy and as such were more dependent on its accepting them as professionals. Even so, the faculty soon adopted a practice of migrating between schools if they felt they could better their positions.

Faculty professionalization was furthered by the academic disciplines as inquiry became more and more specialized. Separate associations were formed to bring together members of different disciplines who could discuss scholarship in their own sectors, review each other's work, and advance knowledge along accepted lines of inquiry. Nearly all the inter-institutional disciplinary associations date from the early years of the University Transformation Era, from the American Philological Association, founded in 1869; through the Modern Language Association, American Historical Association, and American Economic Association, formed in the 1880s; the American Chemical Society and American Psychological Association, organized in the 1890s; and the American Philosophical Association, American Anthropological Association, American Political Science Association, and American Sociological Society, all dating from the first five years of the twentieth century. Eventually, associations concerned more with issues of teaching than with research were formed, with the National Council of Teachers of English as an example. The faculty now had colleagues in institutions other than their own—reference groups who judged their work according to national standards.

For much of the University Transformation Era, the faculty at the leading research institutions were appointed from among those who had earned their doctoral degrees at the same institution. Geiger (1986) reported that in 1930, between one-half and three-quarters of the faculty at Chicago, Illinois, Minnesota, Cornell, and Wisconsin universities and at MIT had received all or part of their graduate training at the university where they were employed. Several factors came into play. Graduate students were employed as teaching assistants and, because most appointments of junior faculty members were made on the recommendation of the academic department, the person known to the staff had the inside track when a faculty position opened. The expansion in employment opportunities that was occasioned by increased enrollments early in the century led to numerous faculty positions, and the academic departments often were reluctant to take a chance on an outsider. Concerns about this type of inbreeding developed only later, after the pool of candidates had broadened considerably.

The practice of ranking faculty from instructor through assistant professor, associate professor, and professor dates from the latter years of the nineteenth century. The University of Chicago began with an elaborate system of academic ranking, and other universities quickly fell into line. Instructors might be employed and kept at the lower ranks indefinitely. Only gradually did the idea take hold that professors had to be promoted or dismissed within a certain number of years. Not until the AAUP's 1940 Statement of Principle did the tendency of allowing junior professors only a finite time at one institution become widespread. The AAUP policy was that after a probationary period lasting not more than seven years, a junior faculty member had to be advanced to tenure or dismissed. Most institutions adopted some version of that policy, writing it into their codes, regulations, and faculty manuals.

As the faculty became more professionalized, they added public service to their responsibilities. The academic social scientists, especially, tended to seek a voice in affairs in the broader society, and public service was on the agenda when the leading social science disciplinary associations were formed. Independent social science departments were present in universities beginning with Cornell's founding and had gained stature at Johns Hopkins and with the establishment of a School of Political Science at Columbia. The early social scientists taught classic principles of social and political organization in a historical perspective, attempting to extend those principles to contemporary times and, depending on their students, to carry their message to the public. With the growth of professional associations, efforts to educate the public became more prominent. This was a time when great strides in explaining natural and physical science were perceived as leading to humanity's control of the world. If the scientists could do that for the natural and physical world, social scientists should be able to do that for the world of human affairs. Thus, social scientists began working with all types of governmental agencies and eventually became quite visible as members of President Franklin Roosevelt's Brain Trust. The progression of faculty members to federal service in the 1930s followed the appointments that many had held in state governments in the 1920s.

The professionalization of the faculty proceeded rapidly at the universities, less so at the liberal arts colleges and specialized institutions. But even at the leading institutions the faculty did not police their ranks as vigorously as they might have. A fully professionalized faculty would take measures to weed out the incompetents—the professors who should not have been appointed or who, with the passage of years, lost the ability to contribute either in teaching or in research. However, although the faculty exercised the right of initial appointment and promotion, they never developed a tendency to dismiss any but the most blatant miscreants, and even then relied on the administration and board to take action. As a group, the faculty acted more like a protective or welfare association for their members, relying on early socialization and amorphous codes of ethics to control individual functioning throughout a lifetime.

Early in the era, faculty in many institutions took over the responsibility for admitting undergraduates. In 1884, the academic senate of the University of California developed entrance exams for undergraduates and criteria for accrediting high schools, similar to measures at other state universities, especially in the Midwest. However, the faculty ultimately lost those prerogatives. They first lost control of accreditation standards, which were taken over by inter-institutional accrediting agencies on which university faculty might be represented but were far from a majority; then they lost the power to control admissions. As the institutions grew large and administrative positions proliferated, deans of students, registrars, and other administrative functionaries began enforcing criteria for admissions, which soon became intertwined with public relations and finances—areas outside the faculty's main purview.

By the end of the era, enrollments had grown so that, on average, more than 85 instructors were employed in each institution. An occupational group well on its way toward a high level of professionalization had arisen. It had specialized, formed disciplinary associations, gained power through academic departments, differentiated itself into academic ranks, employed and promoted its own members, and enjoyed much freedom of functioning. Except in the higher ranks of the professoriate and in a minority of institutions, the faculty were still underpaid relative to their length of training, but that too was changing along with the public's view of the profession.

## Curriculum

What is a curriculum? It is any set of courses—a summation of the syllabi and activities of students and faculty functioning in isolated units. It is a set of intended learnings. It is the totality of experiences designed for students and under college control, everything from libraries to residence halls. It is the courses required for a particular degree or certificate, whether granted by a two- or four-year college, technical, professional, graduate, or any other type of school. The term is as variable as any in higher education.

As the number of students increased, the curriculum trend toward vocations and variety accelerated. To state it most basically, the curriculum simply exploded. Most attempts to bring students to a general or integrated understanding of the world disappeared as one specialization after another was introduced. Allowing the faculty to teach what they wanted and the students to study what they wanted became exalted as a measure of freedom. Actually, it was a tacit admission that the colleges' unifying theme was based not on teaching common knowledge or values but on adding enrollments, preparing young people for various careers, providing a home for organized research in all areas, and gaining prestige. A unified curriculum was feasible when all the nation's colleges enrolled a total of a few thousand students. It takes a great stretch of imagination to visualize a million young people studying philosophy and the classics out of their own volition.

**Breadth**

The broadening of the curriculum was stimulated by several forces. One of the pressures came from the organizers of new institutions. Cornell prided itself on converting knowledge from abstract subject matter into education that students could use for practical interests. Not only did the universities propel students toward professional careers, it expanded the definition of professions to include such occupational groups as farming, social service, and teaching. But it sustained the study of history and philosophy with the argument that learning in those areas would be valuable for students entering political or social service. In college after college the retention of favored subjects was similarly justified on practical grounds. Johns Hopkins opened with a commitment to research, scholarship, and advanced learning. The curriculum in its graduate school was as specialized as its scholars wanted it to be. In its undergraduate school, it pioneered the academic major and minor, channeling students toward graduate specializations. Hopkins also broadened professional studies by furthering the idea that a doctoral degree was a necessary credential for university teaching.

The older institutions also transformed their curriculum. Liberal education at Yale included science, literature, and other modern studies as well as the classics. Its Sheffield Scientific School added preprofessional studies, especially a new premedical option. Harvard created a full-blown elective system, rationalizing it as that which allowed young people to follow their own interests and learn whatever they felt would be useful. It also enabled professors to teach in their own areas of interest. The elective system made such rapid headway in other institutions that by the turn of the century more than half of all course enrollments across the nation were in optional classes.

Vocationalism represented another force, as bachelor's programs in every conceivable occupation were organized. Departments of education were formed as teacher training became part of the university curriculum. Journalism and business joined the list early in the twentieth century, taking their place along with various subsets of engineering, forestry, and agriculture. Social work and public administration became popular as career opportunities in those areas emerged. Some occupational groupings such as radio repair, automotive mechanics, commercial art, and practical nursing were so ill-formed or so lacking in prestige that few universities were willing to mount baccalaureate programs around them, but they found a home in the junior colleges.

The faculty also exerted a force on curriculum transformation. Professors now came from ever more specialized graduate programs in which they learned principles within academic disciplines that had not been available to earlier schoolmasters and tutors. The political power they gained by organizing themselves into academic departments provided a base from which they could take the curriculum into narrower channels. By the 1890s, academic departments at the leading institutions controlled professorial appointments. The system thus fed on itself; graduate schools produced narrowly trained scholars, who were selected for employment by members of specialized academic departments, where they taught courses in their area of narrow expertise. The schools exalted the academic disciplines—intellectual domains with their own concepts, theories, and methods for gathering data and validating knowledge.

All areas of study were transformed. Experimentation was the hallmark of academic science. Professors in the social sciences engaged in the practice of inductive inquiry in imitation of the physical sciences and in reaction to earlier appeals to a moral authority. Once the notion dissipated that the study of fine arts was suitable only for women, departments of art, music, dance, and, subsequently, creative writing, film, drama, and art history and appreciation flourished. With church doctrine segregated to a specialized area of inquiry, philosophy and literature could emerge, along with numerous sub-specializations within each. The extent to which the curriculum formerly had been balanced and unified is debatable, but it is certain that during the University Transformation Era it spread in every conceivable direction.

This splintering made it impossible to sustain the moral philosophy course—the longstanding senior-year experience that attempted to tie together all threads of knowledge. Too many forces acted against it. All but a few presidents stopped teaching, and the faculty became so specialized that few had the ability to organize a unifying course. Which academic department could lay claim to moral philosophy? The sciences had taken completely different directions; chemistry, physics, and biology were held together only by their adherence to inductive inquiry; none alone could explain the world. The social sciences became so fractionated that no department could create a course that brought economics, political science, sociology, geography, and history together to explain how society functioned. Humanistic studies tended toward criticism, particularity, and subspecialties organized by author, artist, or era.

Recognition came early that the specialties and electives made a shambles of bachelor's degree requirements. But only in the smallest colleges could the staff specify degree requirements centering on the unification of knowledge. Most accommodated the broadening curriculum not by changing degree requirements but by adding new programs, degree titles, and paths to the old degrees. Even before the Civil War, bachelor's degrees in philosophy, science, and literature had been introduced in the older, Eastern institutions. In the West, bachelor's degrees in music, home economics, and agriculture were introduced, along with special bachelor's degrees for teachers and engineers. The University Transformation Era saw these variant degrees proliferate until a bachelor's degree in practically any specialized area of study was available.

**Preparatory Programs**

As degree titles and requirements expanded, requirements for admission to college shifted as well. In 1900, prior study in Latin was still required for admission to degree programs in philosophy, letters, and science in a majority of institutions, but French and German were gradually replacing it. Charges were raised early on that students who entered programs leading to the variant degrees were less well prepared than those who sought a classical curriculum. The leading institutions were giving more nonclassical degrees than they were awarding bachelor's of arts degrees anyway, but contentions of inadequate student preparation were widespread. As the different degrees with their different sets of learning requirements took over, admissions requirements shifted as well. When Stanford opened in 1891, it required only English for admission, along with any 10 subjects from a list of 25. As early as 1870, Harvard's president Eliot had commented that students with superior training in mathematics might use that as a substitute for deficiencies in the study of the classics. And few institutions required admissions tests; most accepted prior years of study in a subject as tantamount to ability in that area. However, as Harvard and Yale sustained their requirements for Latin until 1898 and 1931, respectively, they effectually excluded applicants from public schools, most of which did not offer Latin.

Attention turned to the public high schools, which year by year were graduating more students and sending many on to the universities. According to Rudolph (1977), by 1895, 41% of students admitted to college came from public high schools, 40% from the preparatory departments of the colleges themselves, and 17% from private preparatory schools. As public high schools took over the preparatory work, universities began abandoning it, but a dilemma was observed quickly: the public high schools were teaching increasing numbers of students who would not go to college, hence their curriculum had to be designed for broader purposes. They taught modern languages, applied science, agriculture, homemaking, manual training—not the areas the colleges preferred. If the founding of colleges and universities had followed—instead of preceded—the secondary schools, the colleges might have developed their curriculum as the natural outgrowth of that which was taught in high schools. But by the turn of the century, the lack of articulation between the late-blooming secondary school system and the college course of study, which had expanded into innumerable areas, was so evident that college leaders determined to rectify the situation. What they could not control in their own house, they would impose on the institutions sending people to it (a tactic still attempted today).

Under the auspices of the National Education Association, the Committee of Ten was formed in 1892. Made up of college presidents along with the U.S. Commissioner of Education, a college professor, two private school headmasters, and a public high school principal, the committee issued a report proposing a model high school curriculum, including recommended courses for each of the four secondary school years. Students were to take four years each of Latin, history, English literature and composition, and German or French; three years of Greek and algebra and geometry; and a year each of physics, chemistry, botany, geography, astronomy and meteorology, and anatomy and physiology.

The committee's recommendations came at an inconvenient time. Compulsory school attendance through age 16 spread in tandem with laws restricting child labor. Whereas in 1890 only 27 states had compulsory attendance laws that reached into the secondary school years, by 1918, all states had such mandates. But a minority of high school students graduated, with fewer still going to college. Only a rare high school principal could demand a strict college preparatory curriculum for all students. The colleges may have preferred that high schools serve as preparatory institutions, but high school diplomas were awarded for a variety of activities at far reach from the undergraduate curriculum. The schools were considerably larger and more widespread than the colleges. Public high schools alone graduated more than 61,000 students in 1900, of whom perhaps 30% followed a college preparatory curriculum.

The colleges' attempts to dictate curriculum in the high schools were criticized repeatedly. A major contention was that schools with requirements pointing toward subsequent levels of schooling did a disservice to the majority of students who would progress no further in the graded-education system. Flexner (1908) was particularly negative, saying that the high schools should remain free to innovate, that forcing students to study subjects (Latin, for example) that they would not pursue in college was wasteful, that prescribed entrance exams encouraged cramming and memorization, and that the list of required courses was not an educational program but a politically inspired compromise among contending groups within the universities. Furthermore, the rigid requirements did not prepare students for the colleges' own elective systems.

Still, the colleges continued attempting to impose their expectations on the secondary schools. Many universities set themselves up as secondary school accreditation bodies; the state universities in Michigan, Indiana, Wisconsin, and California were leaders in this activity. The Board of Regents of the University of California noted in 1884 that upon the request of the principal of any public school in the state, a committee of the faculty would visit the school and report on the quality of instruction there. By the end of the century, nearly 200 colleges were certifying high schools—a pattern that broke down only after the accreditation associations were formed.

As high school enrollments continued growing, the schools developed parallel tracks—one leading to college, the other leading to employment or to a person's place in the community as homemaker or good citizen. Thus a pattern of sorting young people at an early age was established. Prior sorting had been made on the basis of who went to school and who did not; now, with a majority of young people in school until age 16, the sorting took place within institutions. As for the colleges, dissatisfaction with the adequacy of preparation displayed even by students coming from the college preparatory programs led to other devices, especially admissions tests. The first entrance examinations administered by the colleges were idiosyncratic, reflecting the preferences or specialties of the few professors who devised them. Quickly though, the colleges moved toward developing examining boards that set standards across institutions. Formed early in the century, the College Entrance Examination Board held great promise because of its practice of applying tests uniformly across institutions and in various cities across the country. However, it was several decades before more than a small percentage of college applicants sat for those exams. Most colleges still administered their own.

The colleges' relations with secondary schools were confounded further by the types of teachers the schools employed. Teacher training had come into higher education as a separate area of study early in the nineteenth century, but at the outset of the University Transformation Era there were only a dozen or so normal schools. Even though the number grew rapidly, by the end of the century, only around 20% of schoolteachers were college trained. The early normal schools had a curriculum of two or three years that was presented to students entering after perhaps two years of high school. Accordingly, students graduated from normal schools with considerably less than a full college education. Even in 1940, only 18% of the nation's teachers college or normal school graduates had completed four-year programs. The universities, then, were attempting to dictate curriculum to a set of institutions in which the majority of teachers had not studied the subjects themselves.

As the percentage of young people in secondary schools expanded, and as the number of college students grew, the paths to college diverged. The curriculum endorsed by the Committee of Ten, picked up by only a minority of secondary schools, actually declined after the early years of the twentieth century. By the 1940s, only around 20% of high school enrollment was in college preparatory courses. For example, just under half of the public high school students took Latin in 1910, and fewer than 10% did so by the end of World War II. Less precipitous declines were seen in enrollments in modern foreign languages, mathematics, and science.

Because the colleges could not rely on public secondary schools to supply sufficient numbers of what they considered to be adequately prepared students, they shifted their sights. Most had reduced their reliance on their own preparatory departments as the high schools expanded, but they reinstated these activities under the guise of remedial or developmental education. Many, especially the Eastern institutions, reconciled the problem by selecting more students from private preparatory schools that adhered to a collegiate-type curriculum. Many others took the expedient of lowering admissions standards so they could enroll first-year students who were not as well prepared as they might have liked, especially when the number of tuition-paying students declined (as in the 1930s) and they needed the revenue. That way they could at least maintain enrollments. And many, especially public colleges in the Midwest, began admitting as many students as possible regardless of prior academic preparation, with the intention of dismissing half of first-year students within the first 12 months. But to a greater or lesser degree, all were involved with what is now called developmental studies, especially in their early years. The nineteenth-century curriculum in the state universities in Washington and Nevada was almost exclusively college preparatory. Even in California, the first state to develop a widespread set of junior colleges, UCLA had programs with a strong developmental emphasis leading to the associate of arts degree well into the 1940s.

### The Centrifugal Curriculum

It is rather indicative of the insularity of many college leaders that they thought they could impose a curriculum on the high schools even as they themselves embraced the elective system. Electives and subsequent major and minor requirements may have been necessary to effect the conversion of colleges into universities and to elevate research and the graduate schools to the prominent positions that they quickly attained, but they drove the undergraduate curriculum toward chaos. The main argument against the elective system was that the bachelor's degree referred to no patterned-learning experience. Two people could go through the same college at the same time without ever having taken a course in common. The degree signified nothing except that a person had accumulated 120 or so college credits, not necessarily from the same institution. Why this should be a problem has never been quite clear, except that expectations for the learning attained by a bachelor's degree holder became totally vague. The elective idea further gave the faculty a license to dissociate themselves from the growth of the undergraduates, to prepare courses in narrow areas of interests. The concepts of freedom to study and freedom to learn established the rationale for an environment in which everyone could do much as they pleased. The uniform college experience disappeared, along with the idea that the faculty in particular—or the curriculum in general—was in any way responsible for what became of the students.

The notion of curriculum as a set of disparate courses became the dominant definition. A major institution might offer 500 different courses, suggesting that knowledge could be splintered into minuscule pieces. Occupational courses took their place alongside the remnants of classical languages; preprofessional students sat next to those without a clear career orientation. And as the curriculum expanded, little was abandoned. There was no need to deny any course that a professor wished to teach and for which a few students could be found. All that had to be done was to make the degree requirements flexible. Then, an individual professor's popularity or a course that students perceived as being useful could become the dominant influence. The organization of curriculum into structural units, each signifying a number of hours of study and all to be aggregated into the requisite number for graduation, completely overcame any intention of equipping students with common understandings.

The idea that students should be allowed to pursue any course of study that fit their interests and aspirations was accepted widely. It was easy to justify. What could be more democratic than providing courses and activities of enough variety that any student might follow a desirable path? But the elective system was also a philosophical statement saying, in the main, that the college had no authority to prescribe a curriculum, that any course of study was as useful as any other, that no area of knowledge was of greater worth, that knowledge was ever-evolving. The system accommodated several powerful forces: ever-increasing numbers of students attending for occupational training; departments centered on academic disciplines with professors desirous of protecting enrollments—hence budgets—in their areas; and a paucity of institutional leaders willing or able to take the position that some areas of knowledge were more valuable than others, that students should leave college with certain areas of learning in common, and that their institutions contributed to the maintenance of a society unified around certain values and understandings—in other words, that colleges should be responsible for protecting and promoting cultural literacy.

### General Education

Reaction against the fractured curriculum coalesced in the idea of general education, which became especially prominent in the 1920s and 1930s. General education has been defined variously, but one of the more lasting definitions is that all students should gain a common body of knowledge so that they can take their place as members of a community with a shared understanding of the world. The problem that general education tried to solve was how to sustain a set of common values in an era of fragmented and specialized knowledge. In 1919, Columbia declared that there was a certain minimum intellectual and spiritual tradition that people must understand if they were to be called educated; the school built an integrated course in Western civilization. Courses that combined threads of knowledge that had been split into specialized areas became prevalent at other institutions. Integrated courses in the social sciences, with titles such as "The Individual in Society," were most prominent, with interdisciplinary humanities courses such as "Modern Culture and the Arts" in second place. The physical and life sciences had the most difficulty unifying strands of knowledge.

General education in the form of interdisciplinary courses actually reflected the moral philosophy courses that had all but disappeared as the professors tended toward disciplinary study. It made headway in institutions where academic or administrative leaders were willing to pursue it against the specialized interests that acted as centrifugal forces on the curriculum. Entire institutions such as Sarah Lawrence and Bennington were organized around integrated general education, and schools within schools were formed at several leading universities, notably Wayne State University and the University of Minnesota, for the same purpose.

However, in most institutions the ever-more-specialized faculty and professions continually subverted the notion of a unity of knowledge. Curriculum planners could not impose curriculum standards any more than the faculty could divorce themselves from the discipline-bound areas of learning they had come to enjoy.

As the era drew to a close, general education in most applications had been redefined as a set of distribution requirements. This provided the curriculum with a rationale: students should take classes in the humanities, science, social science, mathematics, and fine arts so they would have a breadth of knowledge. It satisfied the academic departments as well; they could list several specialized classes and allow students to choose from the menu. This form of curriculum distribution, that is, one or two classes from each of a set loosely organized under broad titles, went into effect in most institutions and remained the dominant model. Actually, the old classical curriculum provided more of a general education than the distribution requirements did. At least it had purpose and order. Majors and minors, fields of concentration, and various permutations among them gave the appearance of rationality but were in effect a compromise with the bureaucratic organization of the institutions. A fully integrated general education could not penetrate the power structure that faculty had built within their departments.

A related curriculum controversy emerged as a struggle between the humanists—successors to the classicists—and the vocationalists, for whom the highest calling of college was to prepare people for specific occupations. The former coalesced around the idea of liberal education—one leading to reflection and self-knowledge—and the latter around the purpose of education as preparing people for work. Curriculum centering on study of the classics, rationalized from the Yale Report of 1828, to the Great Books of the 1930s, sustained a small place in the overall fabric of higher education, mostly in such private institutions as St. John's College and some of the smaller Catholic colleges. Liberal or humanistic studies remained the centerpiece of the curriculum in institutions large enough to maintain them as separate programs, such as the University of Chicago, and in those that had neither the resources nor the desire to build graduate schools or to see themselves as occupational training centers. Vocational education became the hallmark of the junior colleges and of professional schools that prepared people for specific callings. Yet in most institutions, liberal and occupational education coexisted, with one or the other gaining in emphasis depending on the whims of institutional leaders and the demands of particular communities.

**The Collegiate Experience**

The colleges continually claimed that they offered more than courses; they determined lives. The liberal arts colleges especially rationalized that they provided culture, that they were places where small groups of young people would gain lifelong associations with peers of similar social standing. They put themselves forward as protectors of a tradition and molders of character. Concepts of loyalty to the alma mater, class reunions, successive generations matriculating in the same institution—all testified to a college experience that went far beyond the classroom. Social affairs, school colors, fight songs, and intramural activities all contributed.

Whether freestanding or under the umbrella of the university, the professional schools also built sets of experiences that reached beyond teaching the skills of the trade. They added ways of thinking and behaving and loyalty to the fraternity of professional practitioners. Less concerned with building school ties, they forged connections with groups of like-minded colleagues across the landscape of professional practice. They developed ceremonies and rituals and examinations that tested not only knowledge but also the candidate's ability to perform under stress. The internships they arranged, the professional association meetings they sponsored, the journals they edited, the placement services they provided for their graduates—all served ceremonial functions. The acolyte was indoctrinated into a select society. The importance of where one went to school had more than symbolic meaning.

Specialized institutions such as HBCUs and women's colleges built curricula deemed appropriate for their students. HBCUs—of which nearly 800 had been established in the 45 years after slavery—frequently imitated the liberal arts colleges, offering comparable courses along with a complete roster of fraternities, sports, and rituals designed to ensure the collegiate experience. However, because education for African Americans at all levels—especially in the South—had been slowed by Jim Crow laws, and because "Negro education was left out of . . . the standards, controls, and order for schools, colleges, and universities serving whites" (Lovett, 2015, p. xiii), most HBCUs were forced to develop intense programs in basic skills. Furthermore, because the careers open to African American graduates were so limited, HBCUs were obliged to sustain programs in manual training and industrial technology well after most four-year colleges abandoned them.

Similarly, although women's colleges followed the pattern of providing instruction in humanities, science, and social science, they elevated to the status of collegiate studies areas that were considered appropriate for women. Home economics and social work became prominent, along with music and art, childcare, and elementary school teaching. The programs offered a fit with the careers and activities that the nation expected of its women: librarians, social workers, nurses, and schoolteachers—areas in which women constituted 90% or more of the practitioners. And just as the professional schools populated largely by men taught ways of behaving, professional mannerisms developed through the curriculum at women's colleges were considered nearly as important as the skills acquired.

## Instruction

The University Transformation Era saw a broadening in instructional forms as well as in curriculum. Libraries remained open for longer hours as collections grew and as instruction centering on students' finding and reporting on sources became prevalent. Discussion groups became a favored form; they imitated the German university seminars, and they suggested that students were thinkers, not inmates of a reformatory. Laboratory work became required in the scientific fields. Correspondence courses opened up and field trips, especially in occupationally oriented institutions, began. Written examinations became prevalent, with the same tests given to all members of a class, as differentiated from the previous individual recitations. Honors programs were introduced as the larger institutions tried to accommodate an increasingly diverse student body. Beginning in the 1920s, courses by radio were tried, justified by innovators who claimed they were the wave of the future and eventually would replace the classroom.

The growth in student enrollment led to the necessity of managing and budgeting for large numbers of students. Class sizes grew. "As early as 1901 thirty-nine Harvard courses enrolled over 100 students, fourteen over 200" (Rudolph, 1977, p. 233). Princeton, along with a few other institutions, clung to a tutorial system, with preceptors or young instructors responsible for small groups of students. Elsewhere large classes, often with attendant small discussion sections, were brought forward to display the best lecturers.

Other ways of managing growing numbers of students were introduced. One that had been put forth in earlier eras and that had never died out was the idea that time-to-bachelor's-degree should be reduced to three years or even two. An idea that had somewhat greater success was the year-round calendar. Orientation programs became prevalent by the 1920s as a way of introducing masses of students to college, providing an introduction to the methodology of learning, helping the students sort themselves into programs consonant with their abilities and aspirations, and assisting them in making psychological adjustments to college.

Counselors and guidance personnel took over these responsibilities from the tutors of an earlier time.

The spread of variant instructional forms and of different ways of managing the numbers of students led to other educational formats. Several institutions, especially those in urban areas, developed extension courses and classes offered in the evening so that older, working students could attend. The University of Chicago pursued the idea of separating portions of its lower division into a junior college and, on the other end, establishing strong graduate schools not only in traditional scientific and professional areas but also in the fine arts and education. It pioneered the associate degree, which was awarded to students who completed a general education program in their first and second years. However, in institutions across the nation, growth rate, funding, and size remained the major determinants of curriculum and instructional forms, far outstripping governing-board philosophy.

The era saw also efforts to standardize examinations. The principle that exams be conducted by outsiders rather than by professors was mentioned repeatedly but was just as often resisted with the argument, "Who but the instructor knows what the students should know?" The professors may have been certain of the uniqueness of their courses, but the curriculum and instructional forms provided by various institutions made courses of comparable size and emphasis seem almost interchangeable. Students could and did transfer from one institution to the other, carrying course credits as readily as their clothing. Faculty trained in one university carried academic styles to the others. Textbooks marketed nationally lent uniformity to courses. No governmental control was needed to effect similarity in institutional functioning; imitation did the job.

Grades that purported to indicate the depth of student learning in particular areas were introduced. Whereas written statements of a student's progress were commonly provided in earlier eras, growing numbers of students precluded this form of assessment. Furthermore, written statements were subjective, whereas single letters or numbers suggested objectivity. A written commentary on a student's progress might encompass deportment and attitude along with cognitive learning; the grade mark collapsed all into a code usable by professors who might not recognize their students on campus but who could mark written examinations and reduce the results to letters or numbers. The computing of class ranks and grade point averages (GPAs) across courses spread. Letters from A to F were used along with numbers on 4-, 10-, or 100-point scales. No grading system was universally satisfying because too many purposes were subsumed within it: stimulating students, satisfying professors, encouraging scholarship, and, above all, providing a reference point or credential for institutions and programs to which the student might subsequently apply. Students' GPAs appeared on their transcripts along with the concentration of courses (the major) they had followed.

The other part of the credential was the standardized course unit or credit earned. Academic credits were tied to hours spent in class and, along with the grades earned, became academic tender. Students involved with such a system could transfer between institutions, satisfy the requirements of more than one program so that they could switch academic majors, or stop out and return to college while maintaining credits they had banked toward a degree. Higher education was on its way toward regimentation in handling students, taking on an industrial character even as curriculum and instruction became more varied.

The move toward uniform systems of accounting for the college experience was accelerated by national associations, regional accrediting bodies, and philanthropic foundations that became increasingly influential after the turn of the century. The Carnegie Foundation for the Advancement of Teaching, the Carnegie Corporation, and the Rockefeller Foundation restricted their grant-making activities to institutions that met minimum standards in faculty salaries or library holdings. The Carnegie

Foundation also listed a minimum number of units of high school credit that applicants must present for admission, a certain number of full-time professors, department heads with doctorates, a four-year program leading to the bachelor's degree, and a minimum-funded endowment as its criteria for a college that was worthy of receiving funds. The Association of American Universities published minimum requirements for libraries and laboratories. By 1919, the American Council on Education spelled out the expectations for a college: an institution that required for admission the completion of an accredited four-year secondary program, required at least 120 semester hours for graduation with a baccalaureate, had at least 100 students and 8 department heads, had professors who taught no more than 16 hours per week in classes averaging no more than 30 students, had an annual operating income of at least $50,000 and a library of at least 8,000 volumes. Nowhere in these criteria was there any comment about what or how much the students were supposed to learn. Order was coming to the system of higher education: not so much the curriculum, but to the display of quantifiable data regarding students, faculty, physical plants, and funding. In addition, the failure of institutions to tie degrees to passage of an academic examination furthered the widespread belief that the experience of attending college was evidence enough that the graduate's knowledge and attitudes had been shaped.

## Governance

The governance of higher education became increasingly secular during the University Transformation Era. Enrollments in state colleges grew at a far greater rate than those in the private sector. Within private institutions, church influence declined, especially in colleges that converted themselves into universities. The presidency and the ranks of the faculty, which had been dominated by clergymen in prior years, were filled by laymen. The idea that college was a business grew rapidly, along with institutional size and budgets.

Governance structures shifted notably in the direction of administrative hierarchies and bureaucratic management systems. Accrediting and professional associations acted as quasi-governmental entities to the extent that they could influence faculty-student ratios, laboratory size, and staff qualifications in specific programs. The faculty gained power in terms of hiring, curricular oversight, and degree requirements; trustees became corporate directors responsible for institutional maintenance; and the administrators became business managers. The larger the institution the more it developed conglomerations of component parts, each with a supervisor and a certain amount of responsibility for its own budgets and staffing.

The composition of governing boards shifted as businessmen were appointed in greater numbers. People were selected for any of several reasons, including having built successful businesses on their own, having social or political connections or access to wealthy donors, or being popular community figures. A few were scholars or clergymen, and some appreciated the opportunity to engage in public service. Trustees in public institutions were often appointed by the state governor, sometimes with confirmation by the senate. In private institutions, most were elected by a church body or, as growing numbers of private colleges reduced their dependence on the churches, by self-perpetuating lay boards. When term limits were specified, the norm was three to six years. In both public and private colleges, alumni might be represented; the University of California designated an alumni seat on its board beginning in 1915.

Governing boards maintained oversight in matters relating to the institution and represented the school to the public. In public institutions, the trustees often helped preserve institutional independence by acting as a buffer between university and legislature, serving as advocates even when the legislature, swayed by the politics of the moment, might have preferred different policies.

They solicited donations, pointed directions for construction, and approved institutional budgets. Most important, they employed the president.

**Presidents**

The exercise of presidential power varied among institutions. Some presidents behaved nearly autocratically, demanding that they have a part in all decisions. Others developed hierarchical management systems. Few maintained more than the semblance of a democracy. Their role was to guide the institutions in new directions while managing increasingly complex organizations. All could not sustain this dual effort with equal facility, but many built both strong academic programs and powerful administrative empires. Most were appointed more for their managerial skills than for their allegiance to any particular academic program. As in later eras, they tended to be pragmatists, empire builders, fundraisers, and experts at public relations. Although on ceremonial occasions they espoused individualism, academic freedom, and noble virtues, they were more likely to value those policies that brought prestige and, above all, income to the institution.

The leading presidents were key figures, standing astride the institutions, gaining power as budgets and enrollments grew. They were builders, converting the college form into that of the university complete with graduate and professional schools, a professionalized faculty, and a position of eminence it had not previously enjoyed. The era saw a number of influential presidents: in any list of the 10 most prominent presidents in the history of higher education, 8 would be from the University Transformation Era. They were not universally loved but they were effective.

Although clergymen had long been the majority of college presidents, by the end of the era not more than 10% had backgrounds in theology. Charles Eliot was the first nonclerical president in Harvard's 233-year history. Yale's first non-clergyman was appointed in 1899, Princeton's in 1902. The new presidents were cosmopolitan; they were students of the history of higher education, and, above all, observers of European practices. To a man, they were determined to build great universities that would serve the business, professional, and industrial interests of the nation. The classical curriculum might be tolerated for a time, but it certainly would not be allowed to stand in the way of the more practical emphases in which presidents and trustees were interested.

Each of the presidents put his stamp on his institution. Daniel Coit Gilman opened Johns Hopkins as a graduate school, enrolling undergraduates but with the majority of students and funds directed toward the graduate program. James Angell built Michigan's research and graduate emphasis in a way that his predecessor, Henry Tappan, had dreamed of but was unable to effect. Andrew White at Cornell and Frederick Barnard at Columbia led their institutions toward graduate education and also emphasized public service with programs for working professionals. William Folwell did the same for the University of Minnesota. David Starr Jordan and William Rainey Harper, founding presidents at Stanford and Chicago, respectively, manipulated the sizable funding at their disposal to create institutions that from their inception were leaders in research and graduate education, typifying what the major institutions were becoming. And the era of the strong president continued into the twentieth century, as Nicholas Murray Butler at Columbia, A. Lawrence Lowell at Harvard, Lotus Coffman at Minnesota, Benjamin Wheeler at California, and Robert Hutchins at Chicago followed their illustrious predecessors by taking their institutions into even broader areas of service.

Several characteristics linked these outstanding presidents. They were at once compromisers and autocrats, accommodating the trustees' desires while negotiating with the faculty, although their tendencies toward strong leadership often brought them into conflict with a faculty becoming aware of its own power. Butler's role in censuring the faculty at Columbia and Jordan's stance in a similar conflict at Stanford were major inputs to the formation of the AAUP. Above all, the strong presidents were innovators who converted small colleges into great universities by building new types of programs. Many of them had a vision of what they wanted their institutions to be and were able to remain in office long enough to see their ideas become reality. Eliot served 40 years at Harvard. Even when their vision differed from that of their predecessor, as when Eliot's successor, Lowell, wanted to emphasize undergraduate education at Harvard, they were able to merge their ideas without jeopardizing institutional status. But part of that is a result of what the universities had become—institutions with "a unique capacity for riding off in all directions and still staying in the same place," absorbing new ideas into what had become massive corporate bodies (Kerr, 1963, p. 17).

**Administration**

The University Transformation Era saw the rise of administrative bureaucracies. Just as large business enterprises emphasized functional organization and efficiency, the universities incorporated such practices. Authority was centered in the office of the president; deans were appointed to preside over schools; the academic departments had chairmen responsible for interpreting institutional policies; practices of faculty rank came to the fore; and an administrative bureaucracy filled with registrars, administrative officers, physical plant managers, alumni relations directors, and the like was spawned. In all but the smallest colleges, the vision of faculty and students meeting with the president to discuss academic affairs fell into the realm of nostalgia.

Student affairs developed as a separate category. The position of dean of women dates from the founding of the University of Chicago in 1892; by 1903 an association of deans of women had formed. Most institutions began adding deans of men in the first quarter of the twentieth century; in 1919, that group met to form an association. In 1934, the Council of Guidance and Personnel Associations entered the scene, and later in the decade *The*

*Student Personnel Point of View* was published (American Council on Education, 1937). Harvard's dean of students, appointed in 1890, and the subsequent deans of women and men now saw their work codified so that battalions of counselors, guidance personnel, admissions officers, alumni relations officials, and student affairs personnel became part of the bureaucracy.

The faculty resisted becoming quite so bureaucratized; even so, the academic department was established as the locus of power. Early in the history of the research university, the autocratic department head, modeled on the German system, was seen in some institutions, but that type of governance was short-lived. Academic departments became more democratic, with rotating chairs, equal voting rights, and equal voices for the members. Early in the twentieth century, the departments gained control of faculty appointments so that except in the smallest institutions, new instructors were employed on the recommendation of the department (although the trustees retained the final say). The departments developed their own curriculum and examinations and controlled the academic requirements for students who would gain a degree in their specialty. But organized faculty control did not become influential in the general pattern of university development. The faculty tended to stay within their own departments, and the departments were so competitive with each other for a share of institutional resources that general institutional direction continued to be set by the president and the trustees.

Several of the state universities provided for the formation of an academic senate and with the establishment of senates, the faculty eventually gained some measure of influence over university management. But these senates never took power to the same extent as administrators. Most important decisions continued to be made by governing boards, which, in the early years, may have micromanaged to the extent of revising curriculum. Formal agreements between faculty organizations and trustees typically limited senate powers to determining conditions for awarding certificates and degrees, adding or deleting courses, and appointing professors. In all other areas, the faculty senate had at most an advisory role, which effectually circumscribed its influence on educational policy and budget issues.

**Influences**

It is difficult to divorce governance from influences. Governance usually refers to the formal structure through which policies are developed and decisions made. But influence may come from many less-formal sources. Private grants made to an institution for specific projects or programs have an effect on institutional emphases. For example, a donor who provides funds to construct a laboratory for scientific research has a different effect on an institution from one who endows a theater or symphony hall. States can provide funds in greater or lesser amounts for different programs or different categories of students. State funds based on enrollment can lead to colleges recruiting as many students as they can handle without increasing costs.

A major influence on institutional conduct came as accrediting associations established standards for library holdings, classroom and laboratory size, programs, degrees, and numerous facets of institutional functioning. Regional associations made up of representatives from all colleges in an area formed; the Northeast Association of Colleges and Secondary Schools dates from 1885. By 1909, the North Central Association adopted explicit standards for the institutions in its region, and by 1924 associations functioned in the other regions. Institutional accreditation spread largely because the plethora of academic degrees was confusing to the institutions where students might transfer to do graduate work. What was a bachelor's of philosophy? Did a bachelor's of arts from one college suggest preparation similar to a bachelor's of arts from a different institution? Institutional accreditation developed especially so other institutions or outside agencies could estimate the value of a degree. The North Central Association published a list of accredited institutions in 1913, the Southern Association in 1921. The Association of American Universities maintained a list. The U.S. Bureau of Education attempted to produce its own list of accredited institutions but withdrew from the process in 1911 because of reaction against what the institutions perceived as government interference.

Other types of accreditation were conducted by the specialized cadres that grew out of academic disciplinary associations and professional groups. They worked continually to establish standards for curriculum and for entrance and graduation requirements, as well as to persuade states that graduation from an accredited program should be a prerequisite for licensure in an occupation. This form of external review grew to ensure that institutions met licensing requirements, maintained their eligibility to offer degrees and receive public funding, provided prospective students with information about programs and emphases, and assisted the institutions in assessing their own quality. A parallel form of internal review grew as well: tenure and promotion reviews, student evaluations, and peer reviews of research. The entire process is an example of how higher education attempted to regulate itself at a time of immense growth before an outside governmental force could be introduced—the type of regulation that most institutional leaders feared.

The students in American colleges and universities never developed the type of political power enjoyed by their counterparts in Europe and Latin America. Most institutions developed some form of student government, but only rarely did it grow past the stage of responsibility for extracurricular activities. Students exercised another form of power through the elective system, as they could choose which programs to enter and which faculty members' courses to enroll in, and thus had an effect on curricular directions and staff appointments.

The nature of institutions allowed for entrepreneurship. Program heads, whether faculty members or administrators, might see opportunity for new types of service. If they were resourceful, willing to work hard on their own time, able to enlist allies within or outside their college, and successful in finding funding, they could influence institutional functioning. External mandates were few; changes in areas of service typically came from staff members' desire to modify practices.

A less direct influence on institutional functioning was exercised by faculty associations, notably the AAUP, and by the various types of administrators who developed inter-institutional groups, from associations of university presidents to affiliations of registrars, trustees, business officers, and so on. By sharing ideas across institutions, the administrators brought home ways of organizing their affairs. Standards for curriculum and graduation were promulgated by the members of academic associations. All affected institutional development as though sets of national norms had been legislated.

Overall, however, the states—not the federal government—fostered institutional development, some vigorously, others laggingly. They were influential in the development of publicly supported junior colleges, as legislatures controlled public school districts' spending on post-high school programs. State boards of education that set requirements for teacher certification effectually managed the teachers colleges. State funds built the campuses and supported the programs. The major influence of the federal government was yet to come.

Out of all these direct and indirect forces grew a system of higher education held together considerably more by voluntary agreements, imitation, internal competition, and generalized rules of conduct than by legislation. A superficial view of the system may have shown waste, inefficiency, duplication, misdirection, a lack of economy. But the system's power lay in its variety of institutions and the way they competed with one another to serve the public. Its fluidity of form allowed for experimentation with different types of curricula, academic calendars, and management in all areas of institutional functioning.

## Finance

Who financed the new institutions? During the Emergent Nation Era, Brown's President Wayland commented that since the colleges were not self-supporting, they had two choices: either they could give people a product that they needed and were willing to pay for, or they could throw themselves on the mercy of the broader society and beg for funds like any charitable organization. His either-or argument was hyperbole, so stated because of his desire to see the colleges build curriculum suited to a broader population. As the colleges developed, the curriculum expanded, but institutions never had to choose between tuition and charitable fundraising; they drew from both sources and from public funds as well.

### Philanthropy

Philanthropy was essential in the formation or conversion of private universities. Each president solicited donations continually. Here, higher education's roots in the church paid off, as institutional fundraisers contended that the colleges elevated society, contributed to the development of high culture, and were noble enterprises. They said also that worthy students from less-wealthy families should not be barred and that students from wealthy families should attend because the country benefited when poor and rich people alike became enlightened. They argued both for unrestricted funds and for funds for special purposes such as buildings, scholarships, and book collections.

Private donations, always an important source of revenue, accelerated rapidly during the era, so that by the 1890s some institutions received $1 million or more. After the turn of the twentieth century, even before the tax laws changed, many large private donors organized philanthropic foundations as conduits for their funds. As income and inheritance taxes grew, foundations became even more prominent.

The donors' interests and the needs of the institution had to be balanced carefully. A few institutions that had access to sizable funds were in the fortunate position of being able to support all types of activities. Ezra Cornell's $500,000 donation was huge in 1869, but it was soon eclipsed by Vanderbilt's $1 million, Johns Hopkins's $3.5 million, the Stanford estate's $20 million, and Rockefeller's $30 million to the University of Chicago. Duke, Clark, Carnegie, Stetson, Vassar, Spelman, and Mellon, either personally or through testaments or foundations, also contributed substantially to the institutions that bear their names. But at most of the colleges, funds came in smaller increments, and donations might be made for distinct purposes such as scholarships for students, certain extracurricular activities, and books or funds for the library. Money for a gymnasium or classroom building with the donor's name prominently displayed at the entrance was usually welcomed; few colleges in the nation did not have such a building on campus.

At first, the support was solicited solely through personal contacts made by the president or a member of the board of trustees, but after the turn of the century fundraising became organized. The more prominent universities set up sophisticated solicitation systems, seeking funds from businessmen and industrialists and developing networks of alumni to whom they directed regular appeals. As the numbers of alumni grew larger, the funds they contributed grew as well. These organized campaigns rapidly replaced the occasional, individual appeal, but a potential wealthy benefactor could still be assured of a personal visit from the president.

Systematic fundraising efforts proved salutary as institutions became less dependent on single fortunes and as philanthropic foundations became prominent. The universities were diversifying their sources of funds; they were particularly vigorous in soliciting money from agencies that had been formed for the purpose of distributing tax-sheltered fortunes. The foundations often concentrated their giving for special purposes such as the education of Black students or research in the health fields. But whether the money came from a private donor or a foundation, the college's development personnel continually had to convince donors to support the university's general fund. Costs increased as professional schools sought their own buildings, faculty petitioned for salary increases, students needed scholarships, and library and laboratory construction became necessary. Donations earmarked for particular purposes have always been a problem for institutions because they force adherence to special requests, thus exerting a measure of control outside regular governance channels. Institutional expansion was so rapid that some institutions went into debt to expand their facilities and thus had to seek additional donations merely to maintain the debt service.

A few philanthropic foundations sought to raise institutional functioning across the board. Instead of—or usually in addition to—earmarking contributions for particular purposes, they promised to give money to institutions that met certain standards. Operating with Rockefeller money, the General Education Board was especially generous to colleges for African Americans and offered funds for permanent endowment on a matching basis to institutions deemed fiscally and educationally sound. By way of strengthening an entire sector, The Carnegie Foundation funded a nationwide review of medical education that culminated in the famous Flexner Report (1910), a document that revolutionized the training of physicians. The foundation also formed a pension fund (TIAA-CREFF) open only to faculty at colleges not affiliated with a religious denomination. However, for the smaller colleges, fundraising remained local, with institutions more likely to raise money from alumni and charitable people in their communities.

The prosperous decade of the 1920s enhanced the gifts from foundations and private donors. The $65 million donated to higher education in 1920 more than doubled to $148 million by 1930. Three-fourths of the 1920 funds were given for institutional endowment, but this ratio dropped to less than half by the end of the decade as more money went into buildings. The General Education Board had stimulated giving for endowment as it publicized a desirable standard of around $250 per student. However, even though the board offered matching money to all of higher education, few institutions could meet the $250 standard. The rich got richer as Chicago, Columbia, Harvard, and Yale gained the lion's share of the funds.

**Endowments and Appropriations**

The spread in income between the prominent institutions and the rank-and-file colleges grew wider around the turn of the century. Not only did Stanford, Chicago, and Johns Hopkins start with more money than most of the colleges had ever dreamed of, the older institutions that had successfully converted themselves into universities grew wealthy as well. Harvard, Columbia, Yale, and Princeton had access to well-developed networks of alumni and were skilled at obtaining funds from them. They also built research entities that attracted funds from the foundations. The national wealth was growing at a rapid rate, hence the research universities could ride an expanding economy and grow just as other industries grew, receiving a disproportionate share of the funds. Their physical plants and the size of their libraries expanded, far exceeding growth in the student body. As for the rest of the nation's colleges, most remained "still fairly small, even marginal operations, with annual incomes of less than $50,000" (Geiger, 1986, p. 40).

The leading public universities developed in parallel fashion. State legislatures began committing funds on a regular basis and, because the country was prosperous and the tax base was expanding, were able to support rapidly growing enrollments. A building boom, especially of laboratories and libraries, took place at most state universities early in the twentieth century. The states also helped support academic research, even if indirectly, as they funded buildings that could be used for research, as well as the salaries of faculty members who included research among their responsibilities. Overall, in most states, the notion that universities were permanent responsibilities was prevalent, and funds were appropriated in a fashion similar to the way other state agencies were supported. West of the Mississippi, where public institutions dominated, the states provided nearly half of all higher education funds from the 1920s to 1940s.

Income per student varied widely across types of institutions. The private research universities received more than the liberal arts colleges; the state universities, some of which had become major flagship institutions, received more than the lesser-known public colleges. Funding varied among states, which was often a reflection of their relative wealth. Accordingly, it is difficult to draw inter-institutional comparisons except among similar types. For the major private research universities, income at the turn of the century was around $150 to $300 per student; for the major state universities, $70 to $200 per student. The ratio changed somewhat toward the end of the era when the gap between the lower end of the public and private universities was reduced and that at the higher end widened. In 1937, the major state research universities received $350 to $450 per student and the private institutions $500 to $1,400 (Geiger, 1986, pp. 273–275).

The major private institutions were able to build sizable endowments as their professionally directed fundraising campaigns brought income greater than their annual expenditures. Harvard's endowment reached $20 million by the end of Eliot's presidency in 1909. A few fortunate institutions, such as Johns Hopkins and Stanford, that had been endowed with sizable funds from the outset received more than 70% of their funding from endowments. Several of the others had expenditures funded half from endowment income and half from tuition. The discrepancy between per-student charges at public and private universities was not as great early in the century as it would become later. Private institutions "charged from $100 to $160 per year, while state universities typically charged $30 to $40" (Geiger, 1986, p. 41). State funds bolstered tuition in the public institutions and endowment income added to tuition in the privates.

The proportion of receipts for endowment declined primarily because funds earmarked for physical capital and current expenditures increased. The 1920s saw a building boom across the landscape of higher education, both public and private. Fundraising and the extra-curriculum went hand in hand, as laypeople and alumni alike took pride in their institutions. Success on the athletic field brought sizable sums. Whether built through donations or funded through deficit financing, the giant football stadiums still in use at California, Illinois, Michigan, Minnesota, Wisconsin, and Yale were built in the 1920s. Some of the donations spilled over into buildings with other uses, including auditoriums, art museums, student union buildings, and residence halls. Overall, though, and in spite of the largesse of the foundations, institutions depended most on their alumni. Wealthy graduates gave sizable sums and other alums smaller gifts, but all were courted, especially those who would donate funds with no strings attached that could be used for general institutional purposes.

Higher education financing suffered during the Great Depression. State appropriations were considerably lower in the early 1930s than they had been in the 1920s. Foundation grants declined from $52 million in 1930 to $40 million in 1940. Capital spending almost disappeared entirely and across-the-board cuts became the norm. Faculty salaries declined by around 15% between 1931 and 1933 alone. Between 1930 and 1940, instructional costs per full-time equivalent faculty member declined by more than 10% at public institutions. Alumni giving declined and endowment income fell at the private universities, as dividend cuts and lower interest rates affected the amount they could garner from their endowments. However, higher education suffered less in the 1930s than did many other social institutions because the facilities built when funds were readily available in the 1920s were still in place, and its labor-intensive character meant that teaching assistants and postdoctoral fellows could be employed for very little money to replace higher-cost professors. Some colleges tried to force the retirement of older professors to lower costs, and others declined to promote instructors and lecturers to professorial positions and were thus able to accommodate increased enrollments with only slight increases in instructional costs.

The federal government, by now an important contributor of funds, took up some of the slack in institutional income. The Smith-Lever Act of 1914, which authorized funding for agriculture and home economics programs, and the Smith-Hughes Act of 1917, designed to provide money to higher education to train vocational education teachers, continued to be sources of income. In the 1930s, the Public Works Administration helped to construct residence halls, and the National Youth Administration funded part-time jobs for students. Funds authorized under the Morrill Act of 1890 were used to support land-grant institutions. Various federal agencies supported scientific research. Overall, the growth rate of federal funding between 1930 and 1940 was 6.6%—lower than it had been in prior decades but still greater than that of any other source of institutional income. When World War II began in the 1940s, federal funding of university-based scientific research accelerated dramatically. Questions of federal interference with institutional autonomy and of the extent to which geographic considerations should play a part in federal appropriations were set aside as research and personnel training for the war effort dominated the scene.

By the end of the era the pattern of finding funds from multiple sources was ingrained. Philanthropy remained an important source of funds for all institutions, but those that had benefited from industrialists' largesse early in the era maintained the healthiest endowments. State support varied depending on the economy. Federal funding expanded beyond the Morrill Act donations to include support for particular purposes. Higher education's leaders learned to be ever more nimble and creative in their pursuit of funding.

## Outcomes

Some outcomes of the University Transformation Era were continuations of effects that could be discerned in earlier times; others were new, as the institutions expanded more deeply into different areas. Community pride represented a continuing effect. Towns vied with each other to become the site of a new institution. Land developers donated property in the center of their tracts to colleges, assuming that the construction of classrooms, dormitories, and associated buildings would increase the value of the surrounding property. Colleges served as secure enclaves. Their campuses were well maintained, their buildings attractive beacons. They offered lectures, concerts, recitals, and sporting events to which the public was invited. Few people living in a community that included a college felt they were in a backwater.

Contributions to the war efforts were a new outcome. Many institutions served as military training centers in both world wars. They maintained officer training programs both for recruits and for servicemen upgrading from enlisted to officer ranks. Under government contract, they developed weaponry and processes enhancing the nation's military capabilities. The role of the universities in the two world wars can be contrasted with that of higher education during the Civil War, when a college would have been the last place a military procurement official would have looked to train soldiers or develop weapons.

Research in the natural sciences grew rapidly, in part because much more support could be found for it than for research in the humanities and social sciences. Donations for the latter typically came in the form of individual support for libraries and perhaps an endowed professorship or campus-based museum, whereas the natural sciences had more ready access to government and foundation funds. Much university-based research in the sciences was led by the medical schools, which converted to scientific research institutes in their own right as the old form of medical education through apprenticeship fell into disrepute. Scientific research led also to patentable industrial processes.

Research in agriculture took longer to develop. The early agricultural and mechanical colleges were slow to organize research efforts. Many of them assigned the teaching of agriculture or science to professors of divinity or classical languages, whose own fields were dying out but for whom work had to be found. That generation had to pass through before research in agriculture could gain a firm footing. The institutions were not overflowing with students of agriculture either, as farmers were slow to understand that colleges had anything useful to teach their children. Engineering students outnumbered students of agriculture in the agricultural and mechanical (A&M) institutions until the second decade of the twentieth century. Congress noted the slow development of agricultural research and passed the Hatch Act in 1887, funding federal experiment stations to assist the agricultural colleges in establishing research. Further federal intervention through the Smith-Lever Act in 1914 established an agricultural extension system—something the colleges should have been doing earlier. Those two additions to the land-grant colleges came 25 and 50 years after the institutions were authorized. Gradually, their assistance in increasing crop yields and in understanding animal husbandry proved notable in enhancing agricultural productivity.

Preparing individuals for service in the professions and adding to the professionalization of numerous occupational groups accelerated. The older professions of law, medicine, and theology, and the profession of engineering that came into the institutions in the first quarter of the nineteenth century, all continued to develop with the help of higher education. Many other learned professions were newly professionalized, in part by requiring more years of schooling for people aspiring to their ranks and by gaining prestige in the eyes of the public by having graduate schools especially designed to prepare their practitioners. National professional associations all had connections with the schools that were training their people. The professional schools were attentive to state licensure boards, and the licensing process itself often tied the award to graduation from the school. By the end of the nineteenth century, one-third of states required degrees from accredited medical schools before a physician would be allowed to practice. And the colleges regulated entrance to various medical subspecialties, including pharmacists, nurses, laboratory technicians and, eventually, medical secretaries.

Bledstein (1976) traced the culture of professionalism, showing how various groups began insisting that their practitioners receive theoretical training that included a degree from a recognized institution. Economists, librarians, dentists, psychologists, and at least 100 other groups all began insisting that before entering practice or apprenticeships, people aspiring to the field gain scholarly knowledge of it. Even public administration became professionalized, as college graduates began entering the service sector. Higher education became a social necessity for upwardly striving individuals, and the bridge between college and the professions grew at the same time that the new occupational groupings were taking on professional garb.

Thus, the training of professionals and the concomitant professionalization of numerous groups was undoubtedly a major outcome. The universities seized eagerly on this function, claiming service to society because the nation needed people trained to staff its clinics, pulpits, classrooms, and laboratories. The training of professionals also assisted the drive toward scientific specialization because the preparation of practitioners rested on their learning the scientific principles undergirding their specialties. It helped higher education break away from the churches, thus contributing to the system's secularization. It assisted in sustaining the ties of loyal alumni because practitioners could be enlisted as clinical professors. Earlier assumptions that liberally educated people could acquire professional skill on the job weakened as separate curricula were developed for various professional subdivisions, technologists, and support staff. Higher education became essential for professional practice, and the professions depended on it to prepare practitioners worthy of their ranks.

The longstanding purpose of assisting students to enter society accelerated during the University Transformation Era. As greater percentages of young people attended college the institutions channeled them into specific occupations, allocating them to positions that they otherwise would not have gained. At the same time, it held numbers of young people off the labor market, thus supporting the child labor laws that became increasingly stringent. College degrees came to carry special meaning: the bachelor's in engineering included channels for civil, mechanical, electrical, chemical, metallurgical, and so on through the range of specialties within the profession. Toward the end of the era, the junior colleges prepared young people for specialized trades and for positions as support staff for the professions. The system served the nation by preparing a trained workforce. It also contributed indirectly to a cultural mindset that held individual (though not group) mobility in the highest esteem.

The old liberal arts emphasis was not abandoned; professional and occupational curricula simply grew alongside it. Just as the professional and graduate programs certified competence in the practice of a profession, the liberal arts colleges—and the liberal arts programs within larger institutions—conferred the status of the educated on their graduates. As they always had, the colleges taught manners, cultural awareness, critical thinking, humanitarian impulses. Students gained literacy, awareness of societal concerns, the stamp of having attended college. Mental and moral discipline remained high on the list of outcomes. Artistic and literary standards were fostered along with the shaping of character. The well-rounded person able to function in various social settings—that is, the individual who could tolerate ambiguity and remain flexible—was identified in studies conducted by educators, psychologists, and sociologists from the 1920s onward. The liberal arts and general education programs did not abandon their mission.

College as an economic generator in its own right came to the fore. As enrollments and budgets increased and philanthropy and state appropriations grew, each institution became a fiscal engine. Funds coming into the colleges from state capitals and from distant donors were spent in local communities. The staff paid rent or bought homes; the college bought materials and services. Although such effects can be traced to the presence of any institution that attracts funds from outside the community, the colleges were distinctive because they brought not only money but also people who might command higher wages and thus spend more on goods and on taxes.

## Critiques and Commentaries

Higher education attracted some pointed criticism during the era. The earlier colleges had been narrowly based, touching the lives of only a minuscule portion of the population, but as institutions became more prominent they came in for their share of disapprobation. The criticisms ran the gamut, from the way colleges were organized and functioned to their educative goals and connections with industry. Institutions were accused of losing their soul because they provided too many curricular options. Businessmen on boards of trustees had little understanding of the institutions' missions but exercised considerably more control than the faculty. There was too much emphasis on occupations, too little on the liberal arts. Masses of young people enrolled, but only a few were fit for higher learning. The colleges shifted from pure research to applied research, and in developing weaponry they were party to mass destruction. Instead of assisting in building an equitable society, they enhanced the reproduction of preexisting social structures. Colleges were unwilling to take risks; accreditation standards made them all alike. The faculty were so concerned with their own professional growth that they lost touch with the young, turning them over instead to student personnel workers. The list of accusations was long and some of the diatribes were vicious, but the sheer fact that so many commentators felt compelled to critique the institutions only reinforced their growing importance to the economy and in American society.

Thorstein Veblen ([1918] 1957), an especially vituperative critic, contended that scholarship should be primary, that the teaching function belonged in the university only to the extent it facilitated inquiry by professors and equipped students for the process of inquiry. Veblen felt that technical and professional schools should not be associated with universities because the interests of university professors and those in the trade schools did not sufficiently overlap. In his mind, a university shouldn't even have an undergraduate school. Boards of trustees were unneeded as well; the faculty should be in charge, for so long as business principles guided the management of higher learning, the future of science and scholarship would be threatened. To Veblen, occupational training defeated the primary purpose of a university: the independent pursuit of knowledge.

Veblen's concerns were followed a few years later by Upton Sinclair's (1923) scathing assertion that the universities did not further the welfare of mankind but merely kept the capitalistic system with all its evils at the forefront of national thinking. University boards of trustees were comprised of lawyers, bankers, real estate owners, merchants, and directors of large corporations. University presidents cultivated the rich and the powerful, running back and forth between business and learning, moderating the clash between greed and service. Presidents and trustees alike were thus inimical to a free faculty and a student body engaged in scholarship. Sinclair also criticized the rampant prejudice against Jews and African Americans, arguing that it was symptomatic of the snobbery of college life. Alumni were more concerned with the success of the athletic teams than with the academic programs, and philanthropic foundations were part of the conspiracy, demanding institutional conformity before they would release funds. To Sinclair, freedom for both faculty and students was tied to the rise of the working class; faculty would have to unionize to hold on to power and students had to petition for change within the institutions.

Robert Hutchins, president of the University of Chicago, published an argument in 1936 in favor of a return to the first principles on which higher education was founded: a liberal education. Job preparation and vocationalism, as well as professional schools and business interests, should be sloughed off. Hutchins felt that rather than contributing to the academic life of the institution, the professional schools reduced the status of the enterprise. He believed that young people should be kept out of the university until they concluded their sophomore year at another type of college. That education should be based in the classics of Western civilization and the liberal arts, including grammar, rhetoric, logic, and arithmetic; students might be admitted to the university for research and specialized study in metaphysics, the social sciences, and the natural sciences only after they completed this milestone. Applied research should be conducted in institutes that might be attached to the universities but were not part of them. Similarly, the professions should be centered in technical institutes, leaving the universities to focus solely on pure research.

Flexner, whose 1910 report on the status of medical education in the United States exposed conditions that stimulated reforms revolutionizing the preparation of physicians, commented 20 years later, contrasting American universities with those in Europe. He believed that regardless of locale, higher education should be concerned with the conservation and interpretation of knowledge and ideas and with the search for truth and the training of students to think as scholars and scientists. The universities were only one of many educational structures; accordingly, they should not try to do everything but should allow other agencies to do that which fell outside the university's purview (Flexner, 1930).

These critiques are instructive because they reflect the magnitude of change in higher education during the University Transformation Era and the speed with which it occurred. But the critics had little effect. At most they caused a stir among a few students, faculty, and administrators; board members were probably less cognizant of these ideas. Overall, the commentators seemed unable to accept what higher education was becoming. They could not conceive that there was a place in America for research universities, liberal arts colleges, agricultural schools, junior colleges, professional schools, and numerous other permutations—sometimes all under the umbrella of a single institution. The explosion in enrollments, purposes, professional training, and involvement with the broader society was more than they could reconcile. It was much easier to postulate an institution with singular motive, concentrating only on pure research, the transmission of Western culture, professional training, or the application of knowledge to social problems—any of these, but certainly not all of them together.

Further questions amplify the commentaries.

- Did the establishment of HBCUs following the second Morrill Act serve to promote or preclude higher education opportunities for African Americans?

- In 2005, Karabel critiqued admissions policies in the University Transformation Era, noting similarities between educational credentials and "the direct inheritance of property as a major vehicle for the transmission of privilege from parent to child" (p. 3). In other words, he argued that families passed on educational advantage in the same way as economic advantage. Is this as prominent now as it was then?

- Bledstein (1976) showed how professions developed along with universities. Which gained more from the association? Would each have been able to develop without the other?

- Why did few if any public universities maintain specified, mandatory, integrated curricula? Would enrollments not have grown as rapidly as they did if universities had emphasized basic general education instead of exploding the curriculum into myriad elective pieces? What, if anything, was lost in the subjugation of liberal education to a broader, more applied curriculum?

- Written statements of student progress were supplanted by grades, ostensibly because of the need to assess larger numbers of students. What was gained thereby? What was lost?

# 4

# Mass Higher Education in the Era of American Hegemony: 1945-1975

The 30 years of the Mass Higher Education Era were the golden age for America's colleges and universities. Enrollments, finances, institutions—all aspects of the system expanded. Earlier eras had set the stage for this growth, which occurred as new campuses were opened, new types of students began attending, and new curricula were introduced. Trends established as early as the Colonial Era—including public funding, faculty professionalization, student access, and research for societal and economic advancement—all accelerated, in some cases peaking near the end of the era.

## Societal Context

The United States emerged from World War II as the most powerful nation on earth. Its population continued expanding and the economy, released from the depressing grip of the 1930s, enjoyed a prolonged rate of growth that had been seen previously only during occasional periods of prosperity. Although 400,000 American servicemen were killed during the war and more than $300 billion was spent prosecuting it, the United States' suffering was light compared with that of a devastated Europe.

### Communism and the Cold War

One of the major trends that characterized the Mass Higher Education Era was the search for security in a world made unstable by collapsing colonial regimes; the rise of the Soviet Union as a military power; the increase in nationalist expectations among ethnic and linguistic groups in Europe, Africa, and the Pacific; and fearsome new military capabilities, headed by atomic weaponry. A Cold War resulted, with the United States attempting to contain communism wherever in the world it seemed likely to appear.

In the first few years after the war, the United States was so influential that the United Nations functioned essentially as its arm. At the insistence of the United States, the UN General Assembly approved an international force to defend South Korea when it was invaded by its neighbor to the north. By keeping the idea of admitting the People's Republic of China (PRC) to the UN off the agenda, the United States was able to delay the PRC's admission until 1971, by which time the original 51 member nations had tripled in number. In 1947, President Truman convinced Congress that the United States should assist Greece and Turkey in opposing communism, and by 1950 the United States had sent more than $600 million to those two countries. The Marshall Plan, also developed in 1947, distributed $12 billion in aid to Western European nations to prevent the spread of communism and promote democracy and free-market economies. The North Atlantic Treaty Organization, the Organization of American States, and the Southeast Asia Treaty Organization all evidenced the American attempt to resist Soviet expansion.

The armaments race that accompanied this policy of containment not only yielded a massive buildup in war material but also spawned research on new weaponry, with a sizable proportion of the funds going to universities. Old questions about whether higher education should engage in basic, disinterested research or whether it should apply its research capabilities to specific problems receded. The universities had started working on combat-related research during World War I and were engaged deeply by World War II. Scientists in the academy might have thought it would be wonderful if the federal government granted money to universities for unrestricted research, but that was not the way most of the funds were dispersed; Department of Defense priorities did not extend to general science. The National Defense Research Committee spent $1.5 billion on radar, much of it at MIT, and the Army Corps of Engineers spent $2 billion on the atomic bomb, with university-based scientists involved. The Office of Strategic Research and Development coordinated other contracts. The idea that universities could take federal funds to work on national security and other applied projects had proven successful.

**Economic Prosperity and Changes in the Labor Force**

A postwar population surge contributed to major social changes. In the 30 years after World War II, the American population increased 60%, with the highest increases in the earlier years. Restrictive immigration laws reduced the size of the foreign-born population, but American families were larger through the 1950s. This was an era of optimism. Economic conditions were considerably better than they had been in the 1930s. The federal government subsidized interest rates for housing through loans guaranteed by the Veterans Administration and the Federal Housing Administration. Housing expanded into the suburbs as more Americans began owning homes than renting them. In 1950, 3.5 million babies were born—an increase of 1 million over the number born just 10 years earlier. This baby boom created a rising demand for dishwashers, freezers, clothes dryers, and garbage disposals—appliances that were luxuries in an earlier era but now available on easy credit. Business boomed as taxes were cut and wartime price controls removed. Inflation grew but was partially contained by productivity that expanded at an average rate of 2.8% per year throughout the era. Economic expansion led to disposable income and to a delay in the time when young people had to enter the workforce, both contributing to the massive increases in college enrollments.

The nature of work and the relationship of workers to the broader American society shifted. Heavy industry declined as a percentage of the whole. For example, in 1947, 85% of the nation's products contained some form of steel made in the United States, and 40% of the labor force depended either directly or indirectly on the steel industry. Steel production grew by around 40% during the era, but this was nothing in comparison to overall worldwide production, which expanded by 400%. Other heavy industries such as automobile production also declined as foreign nations built more efficient industries relying upon—at least initially—a lower-paid labor force. American corporations began moving plants overseas in search of cheap labor. By the mid-1970s only about 33% of the American labor force produced goods—down from more than 40% in the prewar era. The service sector increased from less than 60% to more than 67%. The fastest-growing occupations were professional and technical workers, increasing from about 30% of the labor force in 1940 to half of it by the end of the era.

The shift in industrial production and in labor force competition took place gradually. For the first generation after the war, the pent-up demand for goods was so high that American industry was able to coast on its previous strengths. Much of the manufacturing capability had been built prior to World War I, based on technologies that were already established. The inventions and industrial processes of the late nineteenth century spawned steel, automobile, and agricultural production capabilities. In agriculture alone, mechanization was so effective that whereas at the turn of the century half the labor force worked on the land, the number dropped to less than one-third by 1945, and by the 1960s to less than one-tenth. These shifts seem rapid in retrospect, and indeed they were disruptive at the time the nation was undergoing them. The heavy industries enjoyed a sizable domestic market, hence were slow to adopt new technologies, means of production, or relationships with their labor force. Workers who were pushed out of agriculture were able to make the transition to assembly-line jobs, but as these shrank in favor of professional and technical positions, many tended to be left behind for lack of skills.

The pattern of labor relations in the postwar era reflects some of these changes. The labor unions, whose power centered in the heavy industries, tried to hold on to the gains they had made during the prior half-century. By nature conservative, they were slow to adapt to the changing conditions of work. A backlash against the unions took form in 1947 with the passage of the Taft-Hartley Act. The act legalized so-called right-to-work laws passed by states in which requiring union membership as a condition of employment was prohibited. Labor's response was to merge the American Federation of Labor with the Congress of Industrial Organizations as a way of consolidating the former craft-based and industrial-based groups. By the late 1950s, nearly 40% of the private sector workforce was covered by union contracts, but that was the high-water mark—the proportion grew steadily smaller throughout the remainder of the twentieth century.

The unions changed direction in other ways as well. They became more politically sensitive, attempting to influence elections at every level. They also began organizing white-collar workers and government employees. The American Federation of Teachers and the American Federation of State, County, and Municipal Employees made great gains in membership and political power, as one state after another passed legislation allowing public employees to form bargaining units. Sanitation workers, firefighters, prison guards, public school teachers, and eventually postsecondary faculty all took advantage of the opportunity.

**Environmental and Social Concerns**

Concern about the environment grew steadily. In the decade from 1965 to 1975, "Congress enacted some twenty new major regulatory laws, governing clean air, clean water, toxic waste, occupational safety and health, highway safety, consumer-product safety . . . and creating an elaborate new regime for assessing environmental impacts" (Kuttner, 1997, p. 232). The Occupational Safety and Health Administration was formed in 1970. The Motor Vehicle

Safety Act in 1966 and the 1975 Energy Policy Conservation Act affected automobile safety and fuel efficiency. The Clean Air Act of 1970 required the Environmental Protection Agency to reduce pollution. Taking a broad view, all of these were an extension of the federal government's concern with the quality of life—concern that extended back to the Pure Food Act of 1906 but now reached into many more areas of life, from mandating warning labels on cigarette packages to providing massive sums for medical research.

Periodically, the United States goes through eras of witch hunting, super-patriotism, and repression of free speech. Such times are similar to religious revivalism; they occur when the nation is undergoing rapid change or when people perceive threats to mainstream ideas—most typically when they do not understand what is happening, when their formerly secure foundations seem shaken. The early 1950s were such a time. The United States emerged from World War II as the dominant power, but it was challenged almost immediately by the Soviet Union. The Soviets exploded their atomic bomb in 1949, thus demonstrating that the United States did not have an exclusive right to that fearsome weapon. In 1950, North Korea's invasion of South Korea was perceived to be a communist move toward world domination. Coupled with communist-led rebellions in Eastern and southern Europe and threats of governmental destabilization in Latin America and Southeast Asia, it seemed as though the United States was under attack. Fears that communist governments would be established across the globe under the leadership of the Soviets were voiced repeatedly.

This unease both arose from and fed the xenophobia that had materialized from time to time since the late eighteenth century, when the freedom-of-speech-limiting Alien and Sedition Acts were passed. Examples were the nativism of the mid–nineteenth century, which attempted to keep immigrants out of public office; the periodic, localized racism and violence of the Ku Klux Klan from the 1860s onward; and the subversive-chasing activities of

President Harding's justice department. These tendencies coalesced with full force in the early 1950s, as Wisconsin Senator Joseph McCarthy led a campaign to rid the nation of communists. The Communist Party in the United States was never very influential, but it served as a symbol of disloyalty at a time when the super patriots wanted everyone to swear allegiance to the flag. People were measured by the extent to which they proclaimed their patriotism. Candidates for minor public offices tried to show how they were more loyal than their opponents.

Even before McCarthy became the figurehead for the anticommunist crusade, Congress and the U.S. State Department had laid the groundwork for loyalty investigations. In 1947, President Truman ordered an investigation of all federal employees to determine if they had been associated with any of the 90 organizations considered disloyal. Within four years, more than three million records had been examined and around 3,000 civil servants had resigned. The House Un-American Activities Committee held hearings considering the political associations of people in any area that they considered influential in affecting the course of American thought, including academics, left-wing politicians, labor union activists, and those in the entertainment industry. Investigations in Hollywood led the studio heads to form a blacklist of people who refused to testify and were thereby deprived of their right to work in the film industry. Congress passed the McCarran Internal Security Act over President Truman's veto in 1950 and two years later passed the McCarran-Walter Immigration Act, again over the president's veto. Under the first act, individuals could be arrested if there was any suspicion that they might be considering an act of espionage or sabotage; under the second, subversives were to be screened out from among potential immigrants and deported, even after becoming naturalized citizens. President Truman characterized the measures as dangerous to the Bill of Rights, but Congress was reflecting the mood of the nation; most people favored making it a crime to join the Communist Party. Capitalizing on this national mood, Senator McCarthy continued making accusations, even implicating two American heroes, Generals Marshall and Eisenhower, in a plot to destroy the nation by furthering the cause of world communism. By 1954, the Senate had had enough and censured McCarthy for conduct unbecoming a member.

A different type of federal intervention gave rise to a major change in the way Americans viewed college, hence an eventual shift in the proportion of people attending. The Servicemen's Readjustment Act of 1944 ushered in the Mass Higher Education Era. The GI Bill, as it was called, was passed by a Congress fearful of mass unemployment when millions of servicemen were demobilized. The bill provided several veterans' benefits: a year of unemployment insurance; medical care; counseling services; and tuition, books, and living expenses while attending any educational program. Each veteran was entitled to one year of schooling as a full-time student plus an additional month for each month served in the armed forces. A veteran with two years of active duty could complete a four-year college program at governmental expense because the three years of credit translated into four 9-month academic years. Nearly half of the 15 million veterans participated; 29% went to college, the others to pre-collegiate, for-profit, or on-the-job programs (Committee on Veterans Affairs, 1973). Higher education enrollment doubled its prewar level, as over 2 million veterans attended in the six years following the war. Because the Veterans Administration paid the out-of-state tuition rate, state universities received a sizable windfall. Most important, the belief that everyone could go to college became firmly established in the minds of the American people; college was no longer reserved for an elite few.

## Civil Rights and Equal Opportunity

A social change of similarly long-lasting effect accelerated in the early 1950s. In the 1890s, various U.S. Supreme Court rulings had held either that the federal government had no jurisdiction over state laws regarding racial segregation or that equal rights were obtained if separate facilities were equal. During the 1930s and 1940s, the National Association for the Advancement of Colored People (NAACP) pressed legislators and brought suits in an attempt to gain equal employment and educational opportunities for Black people. As a result, some progress toward desegregation occurred. For example, in 1948 President Truman issued an executive order calling for racial equality in the armed services, and under his leadership various committees called for equality in other areas. Some gains were made also in postsecondary education with two Supreme Court rulings in 1950. *Sweatt v. Painter* held that separate law schools in Texas were not truly equal because the associations that students make during their school years affect their success in the workforce. And in *McLaurin v. Oklahoma State Regents for Higher Education*, the University of Oklahoma was directed to accord a Black doctoral student the same privileges and treatment as its White students. But segregation was still entrenched across the American landscape—de jure in the South, de facto in many institutions in the North.

The breakthrough challenge to the concept of separate but equal came in *Brown v. Board of Education* in 1954, when the Supreme Court ruled that separating children solely because of their race generates a feeling of inferiority, therefore separate educational facilities are inherently unequal; the Court extended the ruling to higher education in *Florida ex rel. Hawkins v. Board of Control* (1956). Based on the equal protection clause of the Fourteenth Amendment, the rulings overturned the legalities on which segregation had rested, but the Supreme Court did not specify when the schools should be desegregated; it left that issue to the local courts. Desegregation thus took place rapidly in the border states (former slave states that did not secede from the Union during the Civil War, including Delaware, Maryland, Kentucky, Missouri, and West Virginia), but most of the old Confederacy remained defiant. For example, in 1957, the governor of Arkansas blocked Black children from entering an all-White high school in Little Rock by calling out the National Guard. Similarly, the governor of Virginia ordered the closing of racially integrated schools. When local courts ordered the University of Mississippi and the University of Alabama to admit Black students, the governors of those states similarly defied orders.

Despite resistance from the Southern segregationists, efforts to expand equal opportunity continued in the 1950s. Civil Rights acts were passed, with the intent to guarantee that no one would be barred from voting or from employment because of race. But segregation and overt racism continued as states, municipalities, and private businesses used various stratagems to sustain the practices they had followed for the century that had passed since the emancipation of enslaved people. Civil rights leaders and groups favoring integration and equal opportunity kept up the pressure by staging sit-ins at segregated facilities, boycotting transportation facilities that segregated the races, and returning to the courts frequently. The segregationists countered with open defiance; they realigned school and voting districts and petitioned repeatedly for more time before they had to modify their conduct. The Civil Rights Act of 1964, passed during the first year of President Johnson's administration, brought together various strands of civil rights efforts by authorizing federal power to be brought to bear on the right of all people to vote, use public facilities, and obtain jobs according to their ability. It also supported colleges and schools in providing in-service training designed to assist staff in dealing with challenges caused by school desegregation. Some progress toward equal opportunity was made, but racial equality proved chimerical, with opportunities for African Americans and other people of color varying from community to community and region to region.

One of the notable effects of Civil Rights legislation was the federal bureaucracy set in place to enforce it. Hundreds of thousands of jobs were created to administer antipoverty programs, the

1965 Voting Rights Act, and numerous antidiscrimination efforts. President Johnson's Executive Order 11375 specified that beginning in 1968, every federal contract had to state that potential employees would not be discriminated against because of their race and that if contractors seemed to lag in employing people of color, they were to develop plans to rectify the situation. This led to an expansion in the Office of Civil Rights, which issued directives and investigated complaints. This, in turn, affected the colleges, most of which had not yet made substantial efforts to hire faculty and staff of color and whose employment ranks were predominantly White.

Title IX of the Education Amendments of 1972, which prohibited sex bias in any educational program or activity, similarly stimulated efforts to diversify faculty and staff along gender lines. The federal government seemed to champion social justice while the universities appeared to lag in their civic responsibilities. As would happen time and time again, one set of observers saw institutional resistance and inadequate progress toward parity, and another viewed the legislation as untoward pressure toward goals that were impossible to attain. Although it would be many decades before women achieved parity in higher education employment—most racial and ethnic groups still haven't—gender, racial, and ethnic categories became firmly entrenched and remained prominent throughout the era and beyond.

Successes won by the NAACP in the courts and legislatures led other groups to press for similar rights. People with disabilities gained a national voice and pushed legislation demanding equal access to public buildings, along with special facilities in schools. Women's groups founded the National Organization for Women in 1966, seeking in particular equal pay for equal work and equality in employment and education. Congress passed an Equal Rights Amendment to the Constitution that simply specified "equality of rights under the law shall not be denied or abridged by any state on account of sex." However, the amendment fell short of ratification by 3 of the 38 states needed; hence, it never became part of the

U.S. Constitution. Title VII of the Civil Rights Act, which banned discrimination in employment, and Title IX of the Education Amendments of 1972, which prohibited sex bias in college admissions and athletics, remained the key provisions by which women gained equal protection.

In 1970 a Texas district court ruled that Mexican Americans should be treated as an identifiable group, a first step in attaining equality under the law. Groups representing prisoners, mental patients, and LGBTQ+ populations sought such status but were less successful in attaining it. Even so, there was a shift in social relations as these groups, along with those representing specific ethnic, racial, and gender categories, continued petitioning for equal treatment in employment, educational opportunity, and enforcement of the laws.

A shift in the direction of equal opportunity cases came toward the end of the Mass Higher Education Era. In 1972, the Supreme Court ruled in the case of *Griggs v. Duke Power* that requiring a person to complete a certain level of schooling before being considered for employment was unconstitutional if the credential or required level was not relevant to the performance of the job and if the imposition of that requirement effectually discriminated against members of a protected group. Even when discrimination on the basis of race could not be proven, if it could be shown that an employment requirement had a *disparate impact* on people from a given demographic group, that requirement could be struck down. This ruling, and others that flowed from it, carried longstanding implications for college admissions and employment opportunities.

## Institutions

Table 4.1 shows a statistical picture of American colleges and universities in the Mass Higher Education Era.

The drive toward larger public institutions accelerated in the Mass Higher Education Era, and states that had not developed an

Table 4.1. Statistical Portrait of the Mass Higher Education Era, 1945–1975.

|  | 1945 | 1975 |
| --- | --- | --- |
| U.S. population | 139,924,000 | 215,465,000 |
| Number of students | 1,677,000 | 11,185,000 |
| Number of faculty | 150,000 | 628,000 |
| Number of institutions (including branch campuses) | 1,768 | 3,004 |
| Number of degrees earned (bachelor's, master's, and doctoral) | 157,349 | 1,665,553 |
| Current-fund revenue (in thousands of current dollars) | 1,169,394 | 39,703,166 |

*Sources:* NCES *Digest*, 1996; Snyder, 1993.

extensive public sector—those in New England for example—hastened to catch up. In the West and Midwest, where public institutions were already strong, the sector expanded by building branch campuses, converting specialized colleges to all-purpose institutions, and by opening community colleges. More than 600 public institutions were added, 500 of them awarding the associate as the highest degree. In the private sector, 650 new institutions opened, but half as many closed, for a net gain of 325.

This expansion was due to many factors not present in most other countries: institutional variety, decentralized authority, multiple funding sources, and a belief in open access. The move toward comprehensiveness continued: normal schools were converted to state colleges offering a full range of programs and, usually, the master's degree; few freestanding teacher education institutions remained by the end of the era. A major shift took place as well in single-sex institutions. At the start of the era, more than one-quarter of all colleges enrolled only men or only women. By 1970 this had dropped to 14% as many closed, merged with nearby institutions, or became coeducational.

The turning point in the ratio of enrollments in public and private higher education came soon after World War II. At the beginning of the 1930s, enrollments had been about equal in both sectors and remained at that level for more than a decade. The early years of the Depression were difficult for the state universities, but by the end of the 1930s, the drop in interest rates and in voluntary donations affected the private institutions more. During the war, inflation continued squeezing private institutions, but as the war ended, state colleges had sizable funds at their disposal. By the first decade after the war, expenditures for campus expansion in the public sector ran at least 50% higher than at the private institutions. Tuition paid by veterans attending under the GI Bill helped, but as their numbers declined in the early 1950s, the private institutions had to increase tuition notably, thereby diverting most of the increased enrollment to the public sector.

The trend toward secularization was steady throughout the era. Public institutions rose from 35 to 44% of all colleges and universities, and public enrollments went from 49 to 79%. This growth in the public sector was reflected also in degrees awarded. By 1975, public institutions awarded 88% of associate degrees, 69% of bachelor's, 66% of master's, 65% of doctorates, and 42% of first professional degrees. They conferred the majority of bachelor's degrees in every field except philosophy and religion. The private sector held on to its lead in the number of master's awarded in business, law, and psychology.

**Research Universities**

As measured by graduate program enrollments, most of the push for higher status, research funds, and more selective undergraduate admissions was made in the public sector, where aspiring universities could raise admissions requirements because they were able to divert less-qualified students to community colleges.

The availability of state funds made it possible for them to expand graduate programming, and federal money helped construct laboratories and research facilities. The University of Texas built on substantial revenues from oil lands. The University of Washington expanded its research and graduate efforts. The University of California, especially the Berkeley campus, was shaken by a loyalty-oath controversy in the late 1940s, but it was so strong in academic research that it maintained a preeminent position. State appropriations to the University of California increased by 24% per year for the first five years after the war, and the university also enrolled the largest number of veterans; hence, it was the foremost beneficiary of tuition payments coming from the GI Bill. New campuses made it a statewide university with nine branches by the 1960s. UCLA increased its stature as Los Angeles grew to become the second-largest metropolitan area in the nation. But for it to become a world-class research university, it had to relinquish many of the vocational and associate degree programs established in its early years.

Some of the stronger private universities also grew, and the gap between the haves and the have-nots expanded. Stanford was noted as a research university early on when it opened with a large endowment. But its funding was on a narrow base; it had few active benefactors and suffered more from the Depression than most other institutions of its stature. But when the Office of Naval Research and the Department of Defense began funding research on electronics in the late 1940s, Stanford rose quickly. Its distinguished faculty members in electronics studies and its close ties with private industry put it in a position to grow alongside the electronics industry.

Expansion in the number of institutions aspiring to be major research enterprises leveled off by the end of the era. Many institutions that had tried to develop strong graduate programs and major support for research efforts found that the fiscal climate was too difficult. Federal support for basic research had flattened out, the research effort itself had become too expensive, and the tone of higher education in general was in the direction of egalitarianism, access, civic engagement, and community relations. The leading state institutions in Florida and Arizona continued to advance because the expanding economies in those states made funds available to build extensive community college systems and to elevate the major universities. However, many of the private, Northeastern institutions that had once aspired to become major research enterprises withdrew from the race.

**Comprehensive Institutions**

The tier of state institutions known as comprehensive colleges, regional universities, or, more recently, broadly accessible institutions grew notably. They began as post–high school academies, normal schools, state-supported liberal arts colleges, schools of agriculture, institutions providing instruction in industrial arts and home economics, and as schools that emphasized engineering and business administration. Around 8% of them began as junior colleges, 25% as normal schools, and a few as four-year universities sponsored by municipalities. Nearly one-third of these institutions were founded in the Mass Higher Education Era; 300 were in place by 1970. Whether they developed into multi-college systems or continued as freestanding universities, in most states they educated a majority of teachers and technicians. By 1975, they enrolled one-quarter of all students in higher education and granted one-third of all bachelor's degrees, 30% of master's, 30% of first professional, and 5% of all doctoral degrees.

The California experience provides an example of the evolution of comprehensive universities. The state's six normal schools became teachers colleges in 1921; in 1935, they dropped the word *teachers* from their titles and became state colleges. In the 1960s, they were authorized to add the word *university* to their titles as an indication of the comprehensive programs they offered. By 1975, 18 campuses had organized themselves into a statewide group known as the California State College and University System, and many of them changed their name to reflect the new status. For example, Long Beach State College became California State University at Long Beach. San Diego State was on its way to becoming a regional university; the 1960 master plan that allocated functions among the state's public institutions precluded it from offering the doctorate until 1967, but it still secured sizeable funding for research. Sonoma State operated like a rural liberal arts college; Stanislaus State continued emphasizing agriculture. The university system prepared most of the state's schoolteachers.

Several specialized institutions remained within the comprehensive-school designation: military colleges such as The Citadel, technical and trade schools such as New Jersey Institute of Technology, municipal colleges such as the University of Akron, and many of the Historically Black Colleges and Universities (HBCUs). The designation thus covered a great spread in type, emphasis, and size; more than half the state colleges had fewer than 6,000 students, some of the others more than 30,000. And a variety of programs spanned the field. Although comprehensive institutions were most prominent in teacher education and agriculture, they were responsible for a sizable proportion of the degrees awarded in business, engineering, nursing, and all the trades and technologies. The institutions spanned a broad middle ground; 40% of them provided less-than-baccalaureate-level technical and occupational programs, whereas 15% offered the doctorate.

State colleges and universities were distinguished also by their patterns of funding and governance. Tuition, which covered around one-third of instructional expenditures, was lower than fees at publicly supported research universities but higher than in the community colleges. They derived half their current-fund revenues from state and local sources. The American Association of State Colleges and Universities, their major national organization, was formed in 1961 to give a voice to this rapidly expanding sector. In size, variety, and comprehensiveness, they resembled the community colleges except that they were even more aggressive in establishing programs because they covered a wider range of degrees and service areas.

**Liberal Arts Colleges**

The liberal arts colleges took a different direction. Most of them had been founded before the Civil War. To survive in the twentieth century, many began offering graduate or professional programs, thereby diluting their traditional undergraduate emphasis. But twice as many closed or became comprehensive in the five years from 1971 to 1975 as had opened in the prior 25 years. They could not compete with the lower-cost, publicly supported state universities and community colleges.

In many instances the lines between comprehensive institutions and liberal arts colleges became increasingly blurred. The Carnegie Commission (1973a) broadly defined a liberal arts college as an institution with a strong liberal arts tradition that also offered modest occupational programs, including engineering and teacher training. Additionally, any public institutions with enrollments under 1,000—and private institutions with enrollments under 1,500—were automatically considered liberal arts colleges, regardless of their course offerings. Using these criteria, the commission classified 719 public and private institutions as liberal arts colleges. In contrast, some researchers, such as Breneman (1994), considered liberal arts colleges to be only those private, small (enrollments under 2,500), primarily residential colleges that limited majors to fields in the humanities, languages, social sciences, physical sciences, and the arts. Less than one-half of the Carnegie Commission's liberal arts colleges conformed to this more restrictive definition.

Regardless of the definition employed, a decrease in the number of liberal arts colleges was apparent by the end of the era; the 719 liberal arts colleges operating in 1970 were reduced to 583 by 1976 (Carnegie Foundation for the Advancement of Teaching,

1994). Many students sought an education that would point them toward immediate employment and had little patience for the arts and humanities. No matter how much the liberal arts colleges attempted to convince prospective students that the degree they earned would fit them for employment in a number of fields, most were skeptical. Furthermore, public colleges costing several thousand dollars less per year were widely accessible, and it was difficult to assure students and their families that attending a liberal arts college was worth the higher tuition.

Drops in the proportion of students attending liberal arts colleges matched their decline in numbers. At the turn of the century, these colleges enrolled around two-thirds of all students in higher education. In the 1950s, this ratio dropped to roughly 25% and by the end of the Mass Higher Education Era to under 8%. The colleges tried to bolster enrollments by pointing to the benefits of small classes, single-purpose curricula, and residential life. Each sought to be considered unique and excellent so it could attract full-paying students, but most had to engage in price cutting, discounts, and other sorts of financial incentives. Few had sizable endowments to fall back on, and although half of them still had some affiliation with an organized religious group, they could not expect much help from that quarter.

Many that were unable to support more than a few students from college funds began restricting admissions to students who could pay full tuition through a combination of their own funds and grants and loans derived from state and federal sources. By the end of the era, the colleges accepted around 40% of all applicants, but this figure masked many differences within the group; some colleges enrolled 1 in 6; others, 1 in 2. Each college tried to maintain a certain size and usually did so by being more or less selective in its acceptance of applicants. The greatest competition for students was within the private sector, because once a family had decided that their young one should attend a liberal arts college, the decision of which one to attend might have been made on the basis of the most attractive aid package. A student bound for Kalamazoo College might be diverted to Albion, but Western Michigan University would not usually be a contender.

**Junior and Community Colleges**

Private junior colleges did not fare well in the Mass Higher Education Era. In 1922, 137 of the 207 junior colleges were private (66%). In 1947, half the 650 community or junior colleges were private, including 180 church-related, 108 independent non-profit, and 34 proprietary colleges. By 1975, the total number of community and junior colleges had reached 1,200, but the private institutions among them had dropped to 222 (19%); one-third of those closed in the next 20 years. The median enrollment at private colleges was fewer than 500 students, whereas the median public college enrolled nearly 3,000 students. Like the liberal arts colleges, they depended almost entirely on tuition revenue and had difficulty competing with lower-cost public institutions.

The community college sector, dominated by public institutions, was astoundingly diverse. Transfer rates were quite variable, depending in large measure on the proximity of a community college to a four-year college or university and on the restrictions universities placed on freshman enrollment. The colleges' relative vocational emphases varied between states and among colleges in the same state. Where the colleges had grown out of technical institutes and vocational training centers, as in Indiana and North Carolina, occupational programs and enrollments were high. Where the colleges were responsible for adult basic education, as in San Francisco and San Diego, literacy programs swelled enrollments. In some states, the colleges operated under the aegis of the university system, as in Kentucky and Hawaii, and provided both transfer and occupational studies. Pennsylvania State University and the Universities of South Carolina and Wisconsin built two-year branch campuses that emphasized pre-baccalaureate studies, but those states also organized separate comprehensive or technical college systems.

## Other Institutions

The spread of institutional types brought significant investments in colleges without walls. New York formed Empire State College in 1971 to accommodate students whose lives precluded residential experiences or who lived in areas too remote for commuting to a campus. Further expansion of adult education took place in programs sponsored by museums, libraries, corporations, extension divisions of the universities, and noncredit programs provided by community colleges. Figures are imprecise, but a reasonable estimate is that these types of educational arrangements outnumbered formal institutions by at least 5 to 1 and involved three or four times as many students.

The proprietary sector is the most difficult to describe. For-profit postsecondary structures gained enormously in the late 1940s as the GI Bill funded veterans who attended vocational colleges and technical institutes—schools teaching all types of trades. More than 5,000 proprietary schools were organized in the first five years after the war, but their enrollments were usually omitted from data on higher education. Only when Guaranteed Student Loans were made available following the 1965 Higher Education Act did the proprietary sector become an area of concern in studies of postsecondary education, as students in those institutions attracted more than one-quarter of the loan money and defaulted at considerably higher rates than students in other sectors.

Other types of institutions at the periphery of the traditional degree-granting, higher education sector included worker colleges and cooperative or community universities. Together with the proprietary trade schools, perhaps 10,000 such institutions operated during the Mass Higher Education Era, again with little public attention until they began tapping funds that might otherwise have run to students in the traditional sector.

Overall, several institutional shifts occurred during the 30 years of the Mass Higher Education Era. The public sector eclipsed the private in terms of enrollment. Propelled by funds for research, a number of public and private universities grew large and prestigious. Comprehensive state universities grew by expanding their business and technical programs, while the liberal arts colleges shrank due to a dearth of students willing to pay for the special experience they provided. Public community colleges showed the most phenomenal growth, reaching five million students in 1975—as many as had been enrolled in all of higher education a dozen years earlier. Private junior colleges all but disappeared, along with the normal schools whose function had been assumed by the comprehensive institutions. And single-sex colleges shrank as student and societal preferences changed and as formerly all-male institutions welcomed coeds to campus. Overall, the institutions grew large: the average college enrolled 4,000 students at the end of the era, compared with 1,200 at its start.

As higher education expanded its enrollments, it grew in power. Through admissions policies the institutions decided who would benefit, and through their programs and associations with professional groups, the colleges allocated matriculants to various positions within society. The sector steadily increased its ability to control access to opportunity and, through occupational, in-service, and adult education programs, to career advancement. Even matriculating more of the adolescent population was a form of power; institutions kept the young among their peers and steered the course of their development as adults. Led by the flagship universities, the system had become much more than a collectivity of students and professors. It was now a unique social force. The public willingly granted these powers to institutions of higher education because everyone now had a stake in their accomplishments.

## Students

The Mass Higher Education Era was marked by student access and activism. Enrollments increased phenomenally—in the 30 years between 1945 and 1975, they rose by more than 500%, from around 2 million to 11 million students. The public sector gained most; enrollment in public institutions was approximately equal to private at the start of the era but more than four times greater by its end. Public community colleges gained an increasing share, reaching nearly half of all first-time enrollments. High schoolers enrolling in college the year following graduation reached 49% in 1962 and hovered around the 50% mark for the next 20 years. The percentage of male and female students shifted. In 1940, 60% of the student body was male; in 1950, temporarily inflated by returning veterans, it was 70%. But female undergraduates nearly reached parity by the end of the era. Students aged 25 or older accounted for one-third of the total. The University Transformation Era set the framework for a modern era in which mass higher education was a reality; now colleges and universities—and, by extension, the entire nation—reaped the benefits.

By any measure, the growth was incredible. People who in an earlier era would not have thought of attending matriculated as colleges were opened in their hometowns. Those who could not afford the tuition took advantage of financial aid that was made available, first through the GI Bill, then through various state and federal grant and loan programs. Public community colleges charged little tuition, and in most cases their students were able to live at home and commute to campus. The doors to higher education swung wide and the population surged, so much so that college leaders—especially at public institutions—began to prioritize growth above all else and develop programs to ensure ever-greater access for recent high school graduates and adult learners alike.

## Access

One of the longest-standing questions in education has been, if a potential student chooses not to attend college, whose fault is it? In 1959, one-third of high school graduates aged 16 to 24 who were not enrolled in college reported that they had "no desire to go" (Harris, 1972, p. 49). Was this because their secondary schools had not adequately prepared or encouraged them to attend? Because their families had little experience with or did not value higher education? Because they did not know college was an option for them or believe they could succeed? Because the barriers to enrollment were too high? Or were there sufficient employment prospects that a college credential did not seem necessary or worth the cost?

Regardless of the answer, colleges continuously tried to attract students, to break down all academic, attitudinal, cultural, and economic barriers. For underprepared students, they expanded developmental programs. Most colleges had always had some provision for students who were not sufficiently prepared, but with the decline in ability displayed by high school graduates beginning in the mid-1960s, developmental programs grew so that by the mid-1970s all but the most selective colleges offered them. The best-prepared students tended to enroll in leading research universities and the most prestigious liberal arts colleges. Institutions that prided themselves on the qualifications of their entering classes competed for students with the highest scores. Most other colleges organized honors programs and scholarships for high-performing students so that they too might obtain their share of well-qualified individuals.

Family income was highly correlated with attendance patterns. The lower their family's income, the less likely a student was to matriculate. In 1967, 11% of American families with dependents had incomes under $3,000; their children accounted for fewer than 5% of first-year students. At the other extreme, 22% of entering students were from families in the top 12% of the income distribution. Faced with the stark inequality illustrated by these numbers, states and the federal government established grant and loan programs and expanded them throughout the era. In constant 1994 dollars, federal aid increased from just over $1 billion in 1963–1964 to nearly $16.5 billion in 1973–1974; state grants increased from $262 million to $1.1 billion; and institutional and other aid rose from $1.3 to $3.1 billion (Gladieux and Hauptman, 1995).

Throughout the era, major steps were taken to encourage the enrollment of Black students and, later, Hispanic and Indigenous students. These moves were made initially through the courts, as state legislatures and the U.S. Congress were slow in developing antidiscrimination measures. Low-income students also benefited from these decisions because many racial and ethnic groups were concentrated in the lower income tiers. In fact, most of the financial aid appropriated by Congress and state legislatures was rationalized on the grounds that it assisted underserved racial and ethnic groups.

Access for women also accelerated during the era, due in large part to changes in social relations; by the time specific legislation and court decisions on behalf of gender equity appeared, the enrollment of women had almost reached parity. The issue of equality for women then shifted to access to certain programs. Under Title IX of the 1972 Education Amendments, women could not be barred from matriculating in historically male fields such as engineering, construction trades, auto mechanics, and the sciences. Most of the law schools and medical schools did not have to be prodded by threats of legal action; they had opened to women already. However, the number of degrees conferred in those fields jumped in the years following the passage of Title IX. In 1972, women received 830 degrees in medicine: 9% of the total. Three years later that number had doubled to 1,629, representing 13% of the awards. The parallel figures for law showed women receiving 1,498 degrees (7% of the total) in 1972 and 4,415 (15%) in 1975. Women entered the field of dentistry at a slower pace. In 1972, 43 dentistry doctorates were awarded to women (1% of the total), and in 1975, 146 were awarded (3%).

Following federal legislation, people with disabilities also attended colleges at a higher rate. Section 504 of the Rehabilitation Act of 1973 prohibited disability-based discrimination in federally funded programs, including admission to institutions of higher education. A student with disabilities who otherwise met the academic and technical standards required for admission could not be refused. The law also required institutions to make reasonable accommodation to allow students with disabilities to participate in college programs. The Act's language "otherwise qualified" and "reasonable accommodation" led to subsequent cases circumscribing what must be done to make collegiate facilities and programs accessible for students with disabilities, including those with visual, auditory, psychological, or ambulatory challenges.

Numerous scholars traced the relationship between access and socioeconomic status, showing a high correlation between family income and college entrance and completion. A 1961 study showed that two-thirds of high school graduates whose fathers were professional or semiprofessional entered college, compared with one-quarter of those whose fathers were farmers, craftsmen, or unskilled workers (Harris, 1972). Another study showed a relationship between socioeconomic status and the type of college attended, with high-income students going to private universities or four-year colleges and lower-income groups attending public two- or four-year colleges (Harris, 1972). Higher education's response to this evidence of socioeconomic inequality was to increase the scholarships and fellowships awarded. The $172 million granted by all institutions in 1960 increased to $1.45 billion by 1975, and that did not include Pell Grants. But few low-income students enrolled in high-tuition colleges even after the institutions became sufficiently affluent to offer need-based scholarships and the states and federal government began offering a variety of aid programs. The percentage of students from the lowest income tiers never came come close to equaling its proportion of the nation's population.

The drive to broaden access also extended to high-performing students, as policymakers and educators expressed concerns that the nation was losing brainpower because some of its most talented young people did not go to college. Several studies conducted in the 1950s found that as many as one-half of students graduating in the top 20% of their high school class did not continue their schooling (Wolfle, 1954). Others reports showing that high-performing students were more likely to graduate led to a nationwide push to recruit more top students to college, especially those from low-income families. The National Merit Scholarship Program took a lead in enabling such students to matriculate. In 1957, more than 96% of the nearly 15,000 Merit Scholars, finalists, and semifinalists went on to college (Harris, 1972).

Most colleges that had selective admissions used some combination of high school rank and test scores to determine a student's qualifications. The highest correlation with achievement in college came when that performance was compared with performance in high school; the best way of predicting what people will do tomorrow is to view what they did yesterday. But the use of supposedly predictive tests of achievement grew; by 1964 more than one million prospective students took the SAT each year. Standardized tests were applauded as objective measures of a person's ability to succeed in college, and the highest predictions of success could be obtained by combining their high school grade point averages with their scores on the SAT. But what were the tests really measuring? Soon after IQ tests were introduced in the late teens and early 1920s, they were criticized for reflecting the taker's social and economic backgrounds. Similarly, by the 1940s, while defenders of achievement tests insisted that they measured "the one essential human ability," critics proclaimed that they only reflected the "existing class structure, in which the better-off economic and ethnic groups are found to be more intelligent and the worse-off are found to be less so" (Lemann, 1995, p. 84).

This controversy was only of academic interest until 1951, when a new military draft was instituted to provide troops for the Korean War. Because college students could obtain deferments from service on the ground that the nation needed scientific personnel and people with special skills, achievement tests indirectly helped to determine who would go to war. Questions of test fairness were raised continually and differences in average scores across various racial and ethnic groups were used to illustrate cultural bias. Despite this evidence, testing became entrenched as a way of selecting and sorting students for college, and its use continued to grow. The American College Testing Program, founded in 1959, developed a test similar to the Educational Testing Service's SAT. Both ETS and ACT expanded their repertoire and developed specialized tests that professional and graduate schools might use in screening applicants.

**Activism**

The campus scene shifted markedly during the Mass Higher Education Era. Whereas in the 1920s the prevalent view of undergraduates had been carousing, delayed adolescents, by the late 1940s—especially after enrollments of World War II veterans swelled the ranks—this view shifted to a vision of mature, serious students eager to graduate and get on with their lives. Some one-half to three-quarters of male students at the larger universities were veterans. Many were married, and a sizable proportion had children; they had little patience for fraternity hazing and other pranks associated with college life in an earlier time. In the 1950s, after most of the veterans had passed through the system, students came to be known as the Silent Generation because they seemed rather disinterested in social and political affairs. They were similarly criticized as conformists, lacking in independent thought, but these attributes all but disappeared among college students a mere decade later.

By the 1960s, the Baby Boomers who were then attending college were more determined to question social values and to take part in attempts to rectify injustices. Many were involved with the Civil Rights Movement and participated in numerous demonstrations for desegregation and voting rights. Students at HBCUs in the South were especially involved, but many White students from both Northern and Southern colleges participated as well.

Student activism extended to institutional policies, which took the universities by surprise. In Fall 1964, administrators at the University of California at Berkeley prohibited the solicitation of funds for off-campus political groups, and this decision sparked a student demonstration that resulted in numerous arrests. The movement spread to other colleges and included protests against parietal rules, college grading systems that seemed better suited to managing children, faculty who expected students to remain as passive learners, curricular irrelevance, civil rights, and, eventually, the draft and the Vietnam War. The targets shifted but the patterns were similar: raucous parades, sit-ins at campus buildings, demands for change. Failure to moderate the so-called Free Speech Movement at its outset may be attributable to missteps by the Berkeley administration and also to the nature of the community where there was a large, sympathetic nonstudent population adjacent to campus. However, other types of activism appeared on hundreds of campuses in the United States and in universities as far away as Paris, Mexico City, and Tokyo. Around the world, students in the late 1960s rebelled for a variety of reasons: an unpopular war, civil rights, access to college, curricular and instructional reforms, environmental issues, and the perceived evils of a corporate world.

The most virulent upheavals in the United States occurred where there was a resident student population and a strong subculture centered on students' feeling alienated from the rules and traditions governing the institution. Graduate students were less involved than undergraduates, commuter students less than resident, older students less than younger, part-timers less than full-timers, students in the sciences less than those in the humanities and social sciences. The self-styled revolutionaries such as those who signed the Port Huron Statement drafted by the Students for a Democratic Society probably never amounted to more than 1 or 2% of all students. Yet as many as 10 times that number took part in demonstrations on some campuses.

Not all of the activism was pointed at social injustices in the broader society or outmoded campus rules; membership in conservative groups such as Young Americans for Freedom grew as well. Indeed, in *Resistance from the Right: Conservatives and the Campus Wars in Modern America*, Shepherd (2023) illustrated how America's college campuses of the 1960s gave rise to a long tradition of conservative political activism, much of it focused on the same issues "that preoccupy conservative culture warriors today" (Ward, 2023). Thus, in the Mass Higher Education Era, campuses became politically polarized, even as the majority of students recognized that college was but a way station toward a better life and career.

Overall, the universities proved vulnerable to student demands. Dedicated as they were to freedom of speech and expression, they had little defense against students petitioning for social change. University administrators who previously might have referred student demands to committees were rarely able to effect any meaningful change with sufficient rapidity to satisfy demonstrators. In the manner of youth, students demanded immediate action, refusing to be set aside with promises that committees would investigate their concerns. Furthermore, student demands ranged from the trivial through the reasonable to the unattainable, from permission to set up a table and distribute literature, to demands that they be allowed to vote on faculty tenure, to insistence that the Vietnam War be ended. Faculty were often sympathetic. As one dean said to a group of students camped in his office, "OK, I agree that the United States should pull out of Vietnam. Where do I sign?" But the students who saw the university as complicitous with government and corporate interests were not to be mollified.

In response to demonstrations and sit-ins, some university administrators overreacted and called in local police forces, and the protests took a new form. One of the most prominent and tragic examples occurred on May 4, 1970, when the Ohio National Guard shot into a crowd of Kent State University students protesting the U.S. military's expansion into Cambodia. Four students were killed and 9 others injured, triggering outrage on campuses across the country. A mere 11 days later police shot and killed 2 Black students, injuring 12 others, outside a dormitory at Jackson State University in Mississippi, in a massacre with substantial racial overtones. These brutal responses to student demonstrations led President Nixon to establish a Commission on Campus Unrest and brought widespread attention and sympathy for the protestors, further dividing public opinion about the role of the United States in the Vietnam War. The faculty were also divided, with some supporting the protesters, others deploring their activities but not knowing what to do, a few meeting with students in attempts to defuse the situations, and others putting their heads in the sand.

What led to the unprecedented levels of student activism in the Mass Higher Education Era? No satisfactory answer is apparent. If the demonstrations had been confined to the United States, they might have been perceived accurately as a reaction to an unpopular war. But French, Mexican, and Japanese student activists were not threatened with a draft; their countries' troops were not in Vietnam. They too wanted less-rigid institutional forms, and in those countries subgroups often reacted vehemently against the protesters.

In the United States, student activism shifted back and forth from national to local concerns, from protests against the war and activism on behalf of civil rights to demands for institutional change. Students at many colleges demonstrated against ROTC and campus recruiting stations for the military. At Columbia, they protested campus expansion into the surrounding neighborhood. However, regardless of the numerous causes for which the students demonstrated, revulsion against the war proved the longest-lasting. A sizable percentage of draft-eligible young men were in college, and rumors about whether they would continue to enjoy deferments kept them on edge. The assassination of Martin Luther King Jr. in 1968 and the American military incursion into Cambodia in

1970 dropped oil on the flames. Demonstrations were fueled also by the popular media eager to publish lurid displays of every confrontation, and—foreshadowing events in the Contemporary Era—by commentators intent on tarnishing the idealism of young people and branding them as irresponsible or immoral, with little regard for traditional American values.

By one line of reasoning, the protests took place on college campuses because that's where the young people were and because institutional controls on their behavior had weakened. By this reasoning, universities relinquished their scholarly standing to one of immediate utility and thus lost their claim to a higher moral position. Riots took place in prisons and mutinies in armies, but short of a major revolution such as that in Russia in 1917, not with such widespread fervor and, most notably, with so little punishment for the rebels. Hardly any students were expelled from college as a result of their activism; hardly any faculty censured by colleagues for condoning students' behavior. Only a few chief administrators were dismissed by governing boards unwilling to tolerate campus unrest.

Student protests largely subsided with the end of the military draft in 1973. Whether or not they succeeded in shortening the war itself is uncertain. The progression toward enhanced civil liberties and an open society continued, but any link between student demonstrations and congressional actions or Supreme Court decisions in the mid-1970s is questionable at best. As for relaxation of parental-type regulations on student life, these had been eroding for decades; the student rebellion merely hastened them along. After the early 1970s, it became difficult to find a campus where strict rules limited the tendency of students to socialize in any way they chose. Many colleges opened residence halls where unmarried men and women lived together—arrangements that would have sent the deans of students of an earlier generation into catatonic shock. The broader rules of the general community came into play on campus and, except for sexual harassment, overt drunkenness, and disobedience of the prevailing civil code, few regulations remained to be enforced.

One marked but temporary effect of student activism during this era might have been the relationship between universities and the Department of Defense; Pentagon support for academic research declined "from a high of $279 million in 1969 to a low of $184 million just five years later" (Geiger, 1993, p. 241). Whether or not there was a direct connection between student activism and these reductions, they did evidence one point of the protests—the universities' complicity with the military, which might have been supported in peacetime but which was abhorred by many in the midst of an unpopular war in which more than 58,000 young American men lost their lives.

## Faculty

As enrollments surged, the professionalization of the faculty accelerated. Salaries increased steadily, so that by the end of the era they reached what might be called a living wage for the first time. The faculty took greater control by establishing collective bargaining units and by gaining a say in institutional governance. Their job rights were codified through legislation and court decisions. Academic freedom was no longer merely a concept that appeared in statements of principle; it became a privilege upheld by the courts.

Even so, toward the end of the era, several developments made it seem as though further gains toward professionalization would be more difficult to attain. The percentage of part-time instructors was growing, but they were not serving as assistants to full-time faculty in the manner that a profession might demand; instead, they were independent instructors with fewer responsibilities and lower pay. The move to unionize, which rose rapidly in the 1970s, may have weakened the public's view of the faculty as a professional group. The tenure system, long sought by the faculty as a way of protecting their members from capricious dismissal, began to be seen as a way of retaining members who were no longer productive. Faculty complicity in student activism raised further questions about professionalism. And the sheer growth in numbers removed the distinction of rarity and weakened the special status and aura of mystery that surrounds the most prestigious professions.

**Demography and Salary**

Growth in the faculty ranks was impressive. From fewer than 150,000 professors in 1940, overall head count rose to 565,000 by 1975. The percentage growth in student enrollment had been greater, however, and the ratio of students to faculty grew from its historic pattern of 10 to 1 to 17 to 1. The average number of faculty per institution, which had been less than 40 in 1910, reached 86 by 1940 and 200 by 1975. Much of the change in faculty relations with their peers, students, and institutions stemmed from this shift in institutional size. Relationships among people are one thing when there is face-to-face contact among most members of the community, quite another when a bureaucracy develops to manage massive structures.

The demographics of the faculty shifted. Women, especially, grew as a percentage of the total, from 20% early in the century to around 33% by 1975. Toward the latter part of the era, the number of faculty of color grew as well, reaching 8% in 1975. These percentages differed by institutional type and discipline. Women were most highly represented in community colleges and in university humanities and social science departments. Faculty of color were severely underrepresented in the sciences also and often clustered in the social sciences at public institutions. When colleges staffed up to meet surging enrollments, the percentage of young instructors increased, and the median age declined notably. After the 1960s, when relatively fewer new appointments were made, the median age gradually increased.

In the 1970s, two-thirds of all faculty were Protestant, 18% Catholic, and 9% Jewish; 4% reported "other" and 3% "none" (Ladd and Lipset, 1975). But the distribution across institutions was uneven. Nearly 20% of the faculty in the most prestigious universities were Jewish, with the proportions highest in law (36%), sociology (34%), economics (28%), and physics (26%). The Jewish instructors had benefited from a decline in publicly espoused anti-Semitism after World War II, just when academic jobs opened up in great numbers. The argument for diversifying faculty ranks turned not on the issue that the curriculum needed a Jewish perspective or that the students needed particular role models, but simply on the point that when prevailing professional standards were applied and an expanding academy needed talent, it became more difficult to justify excluding anyone. Women also benefited from a decline in prejudice and from their greatly increased attendance at all levels of higher education. For faculty of color, the road was bumpier and slower; increases in their ranks had to await legislation, court rulings, and targeted expansion in their educational preparation.

Sources of faculty remained the same, with one major exception. Faculty beginning employment at the community colleges tended to come from secondary school teaching positions, many with extensive teaching experience. Most of the recruits held master's degrees. In the mid-1970s, around 1 in 8 junior or community college instructors held a doctorate, and many of those had obtained it while they were teaching at the colleges. For them, the doctorate was not the beginning of a research career but served primarily to elevate them on the salary schedule at the institution where they worked already. For university faculty, graduate schools continued to prepare most new hires, with the number of master's and doctoral degrees awarded increasing tenfold during the era. Not until the early 1970s did the number of PhDs awarded exceed the number of new, junior-level faculty appointments at the universities. By the late 1970s, the employment of doctorates in government and industry outpaced the growth of employment within higher education, as increasing numbers of degree holders found jobs outside academe.

Affirmative action with regard to faculty employment and promotion revealed just how gradually but steadily the turn toward racial and ethnic diversity occurred. In 1972, Title VII of the Civil Rights Act of 1964 was expanded to forbid discrimination in employment on the basis of race, color, religion, sex, or national origin in public and private educational institutions unless it could be proven that the operation of the institution depended on people with particular characteristics. Claims of discrimination based on Title VII came in two forms: *disparate treatment* and *disparate impact*. In a claim of disparate treatment, individuals had to show that they were discriminated against in hiring, firing, promotion, or condition of employment based on their identity. In the case of disparate impact, plaintiffs had to show that they belonged to a protected group, that they were qualified for the job for which they applied, that despite qualifications they were rejected, and that after rejection the position remained open and the employer continued to seek applicants from people who had comparable qualifications.

The federal Office of Civil Rights began requiring that every institution draw up an affirmative action plan, set goals, and establish specific procedures by which faculty would be recruited and hired. Initially, the pool of women and candidates of color was too small to satisfy the affirmative action goals. Furthermore, there were questions about whether the goals should be institution-wide or enforced at the departmental level, and whether they should be applied to women and members of various racial and ethnic groups separately or in total. University responses to affirmative action mandates took several forms. Where the faculty in a particular academic area proclaimed that there were no qualified candidates from among the groups sought, the university might make additional slots available contingent on the department's finding women or faculty of color to fill them. New positions also were created to which people could be appointed without holding doctoral degrees or other specified qualifications. Nationwide searches were organized, letters written to the heads of academic departments from which students in particular fields were obtaining degrees, and advertisements placed in journals and newspapers. The number of position listings in the Chronicle of Higher Education made it appear as though that periodical was founded in the 1960s especially to provide a vehicle for these searches. But despite these efforts, results were slow in coming.

A more significant change in the composition of the faculty was the increase in numbers of part-timers. In 1960, the part-time faculty made up about one-third of the total—many of them employed even if they did not possess graduate degrees. Ten years later, when the number of people receiving master's degrees annually jumped from fewer than 75,000 to more than 200,000 and the number receiving the doctorate from fewer than 10,000 to nearly 30,000, the number of part-timers on staff declined to 2%. The prior decade had seen qualified people coming onstream, and the institutions were willing to grant them full-time status. But by 1975, the ratio of part-timers climbed back up to 30%, occasioned now not by a shortage of qualified candidates but by the desire of administrators to save money at a time of rapidly increasing expenditures. The growth of community colleges, where the use of part-time instructors has always been higher than the ratio for all of higher education, also contributed to this increase. The percentage of part-time instructors at community colleges was around 40% in 1970, but by 1975 it climbed to more than half of all faculty in that sector.

Salaries for full-time faculty continued increasing but at a slower rate. The median doubled from $6,015 in 1957–1958 to $12,710 in 1970–1971. It then increased to $15,622 in 1974–1975, a rise of 23% in 4 years. But when viewed in constant dollars, the gains in the early 1970s actually represented a decline of 6%. Salary increments were harder to attain, especially as the faculty were accused of complicity in the student activism of the time and as other public employees, who were better organized to present demands to the legislature, took more of the states' budgets. The faculty found they could not receive pay increments sufficient to keep up with inflation.

The faculty meanwhile had advanced their professionalization by solidifying control over many aspects of their work. In the universities, they spent time on teaching, research, and public service, often shifting from one to the other as they chose. This flexibility helped attract people to the profession. Few faculty took university positions because they wanted to tutor youth exclusively; more likely, they sought an environment where they might follow a variety of pursuits. Research and scholarship did not come into direct conflict with teaching because the rapidly expanding institutions could accommodate scholars while they also developed additional cadres of counselors, ombudsmen, advisers, registration officials, and the like to take care of students' general concerns. The downside for faculty was that these student personnel specialists took money that might otherwise have been used to increase professorial salaries. As for the faculty in community colleges and four-year institutions where expectation for hours spent in the classroom remained high, those who obtained positions immediately after graduate school did not expect to spend time on research, and for those who entered from secondary school positions, research had never been part of their professional life.

Working conditions shifted somewhat toward the end of the era. Bowen and Schuster (1986) listed four changes. First, in anticipation of declining student enrollments, many institutions cut back on support staff and reduced funds available for professional travel. Second, the greater number of inadequately prepared students forced the faculty to teach developmental classes, which few enjoyed. A third change was in student preference for fields that were strongly professional or practical: agriculture, business, health, trades, and technologies. This produced a poor distribution of professors, as those who had expected to teach in their areas of specialization, especially in the humanities or social sciences, found themselves teaching in areas only marginally related to the fields in which they had obtained their degrees. The fourth concern was that faculty participation in academic decision-making was becoming less direct as the larger institutions and newly formed statewide coordinating boards contributed to a decline in collegiality.

One more factor might be noted. The faculty were aware that their purchasing power had eroded and were inclined to blame legislators and trustees for their inability to obtain sufficient salary, especially as they saw other public employees gaining. The faculty also might have been demoralized by the variations in pay received by instructors in the different disciplines. Competition from the nonacademic sector drove faculty salaries up in such fields as business, engineering, and computer science, and soon those in the liberal arts fell behind.

**Academic Freedom**

The concept of academic freedom that had been gaining acceptance in the prior half-century was wracked by a loyalty oath controversy in the late 1940s, when several universities and state legislatures ruled that every employee had to sign a disclaimer stating that they were not communists nor members or supporters of any group that advocated overthrowing the U.S. government. The mass hysteria known as McCarthyism spread to what were supposed to be bastions of intellectual freedom. In 1953, a statement by the Association of American Universities, written by a committee chaired by the president of Yale, endorsed by 37 leading institutions, and titled "The Rights and Responsibilities of Universities and Their Faculties," described the university as comprised of scholars loyal to the nation and to its form of government. The document declared further that anyone belonging to the Communist Party had no right to remain on staff. Although the statement might have been issued as a sop for posturing politicians, it did suggest that the presidents did not think of themselves as sufficiently independent to say, "We understand that the nation is involved in a Cold War. Be assured that we have no intention of aiding the enemy. At the same time we will continue to respect the freedom of thought exhibited by the people around whom our institutions are built." Since the time their institutions' budgets passed the million-dollar mark, few presidents had the courage to make such statements, although Chicago's Hutchins, Harvard's Conant, and Boston University's Marsh did go on record as deploring witch hunts. By the end of the 1950s, the furor over party membership had subsided, but 15 states still had statutes requiring that employees refrain from membership in subversive groups.

The AAUP's contention that nothing in the nature of the teaching profession required the automatic exclusion of communists, and that college teachers should not be subjected to civic limitations not imposed on other citizens, was reflected in the major private universities' typically not imposing such requirements. But state legislators were not dissuaded. In 1946, the regents of the University of Washington succumbed to legislative pressure and dismissed eight professors alleged to be current or former members of the Communist Party. Thirty-one University of California professors were dismissed for refusing to sign a loyalty oath, but the board of regents rescinded the requirement in 1951. In 1952, the California Supreme Court ruled that the non-signers be reinstated, and in 1967, it invalidated loyalty oaths. In retrospect, it seemed that the controversy had been less about finding communists than about whether the center of power regarding the faculty should be in the governing board, administration, or academic senate.

When the student uprisings began in the mid-1960s, a number of instructors were sympathetic to the antiwar, anti-corporate, anti-capitalist, and eventually antiracist demands raised by students. Some even mimicked the young people in their charge, accepting their mode of dress, their opinions, and their tendency toward institutional disruption. But the profession as a whole did not attempt to sanction them. The venerable concept of academic freedom protected the professors, even those who joined their students in rebelling against the academy.

Even though many universities had effectively become extensions of the surrounding communities, faculty tended to behave as though the campuses were still sequestered enclaves. They abhorred the idea of police coming on campus to the student demonstrations. Such revulsion stemmed from the ancient pretext that the campus was a sacred environment, different from the surrounding community, deserving to be self-governing and to mete out its own sanctions. The notion that an institution with 40,000 students and staff members and billions of dollars in buildings and equipment was quite different from the small band of students and scholars from which the university sprang seemed to have eluded the faculty as well as those administrators who promised anything to students so long as they went away without breaking the windows of the administration building. As would happen time and time again, some parts of the institution evolved while others remained frozen; the professional schools, research laboratories, and mass enrollment of undergraduates put the university squarely in the middle of American society, but when it suited their purpose, liberal arts faculty acted as though they were the true scholars of antiquity, sitting in dingy rooms, reading classics with small groups of young people, with Do Not Disturb signs on the doors.

Academic freedom is a subtle concept, and it is not easy to draw the line between liberty and license. For years, the faculty sought rules forbidding that they be sanctioned for speaking out on controversial issues. Beginning in the 1950s, the Supreme Court developed a constitutional framework for this right, granted mainly under the freedom of speech and association guarantee of the First Amendment but also in the due process clause of the Fourteenth Amendment and the protection against self-incrimination of the Fifth Amendment. In 1957, the Supreme Court, in *Sweezy v. New*

*Hampshire*, overturned a contempt conviction earned when a professor refused to answer questions about a lecture he had delivered. In the 1960 *Shelton v. Tucker* case, the Supreme Court rejected as unconstitutional a state law requiring faculty at public institutions to provide information on their membership in or financial support of any organizations. Seven years later, in *Keyishian v. Board of Regents*, the Court ruled that state laws requiring faculty members to sign a certificate stating they were not and never had been communists were unconstitutionally vague and overly broad; therefore, faculty who had lost their jobs for refusing to sign had been terminated improperly. This case overturned a 1951 case that had upheld a New York State law excluding from employment teachers who were members of specified subversive groups.

In the late 1960s, the Court began extending its application of the constitutional principles of academic freedom from protection against state interference to issues of protecting the faculty from their home institution. In 1968, in *Pickering v. Board of Education*, the Court ruled on a case in which a teacher was terminated for writing a letter criticizing the school board's financial operating strategy. As Kaplin and colleagues (2020) summarized, the Court invalidated the teacher's termination because there was no working relationship between him and those he criticized; the letter was of public concern and had no detrimental impact; the teacher's performance was not affected; he wrote as a citizen; and the school board's interest in efficient operation of its schools was outweighed by the plaintiff's free speech interest.

### Tenure and Due Process

Tenure and the right to continuing contracts also came under Court review. In cases adjudicated in 1972, the Supreme Court decided that faculty at public institutions were entitled to a fair hearing under the due process clause of the Fourteenth Amendment when their contracts were not renewed and if they were deprived of property or liberty interests. In *Board of Regents v. Roth*, brought when a professor was given no hearing before his initial one-year contract at the University of Wisconsin was not renewed, the Court found no violation of due process, holding that the professor had not been deprived of a liberty interest because the university had made no charge against him nor was there any potential damage to his reputation. His one-year contract, made in accordance with state law, did not give him a reasonable expectation of continued employment; therefore he had no property interest in his position, and the institution did not have to grant him a notice of dismissal or a hearing.

However, in *Perry v. Sindermann*, a professor who had been employed by the Texas college and university system for 10 years on a series of one-year contracts was determined to have a reasonable expectation of continued employment. The institution had no formal tenure system, but its faculty guide did suggest certain assurances of continued employment. Thus, the Court ruled that Perry had been deprived of a property interest and was entitled to a hearing about why he was not retained. The property interest also was applied in the 1978 case of *McLendon v. Morton*: a faculty member at Petersburg Community College had fulfilled the institution's published criteria for tenure (six years as a full-time instructor and achievement of the rank of assistant professor) but was denied on the grounds of incompetence, without a hearing. The Court ruled that by satisfying the objective criteria, the teacher had gained a property interest in continued employment and was entitled to due process consisting of notice of grounds for discontinuation, a hearing before a neutral fact finder, and an opportunity to refute the charges brought against her.

Thus, by the 1970s, the Supreme Court had clearly established that faculty had a right to continuing contracts and the award of tenure if the institution had given reasonable expectation of continued employment or if the professor had followed the guidelines as stated in the institution's list of regulations. These decisions were rendered on the basis of both property and liberty interests;

the latter created when an institution, in the process of failing to renew a contract or denying tenure, charged a faculty member with conduct that "could seriously damage his or her reputation, standing, or associations in the community" or when nonrenewal was so damaging that the faculty member was precluded from obtaining employment elsewhere (Kaplin et al., 2020, p. 283).

**Collective Bargaining**

Tenure, working conditions, and salaries were all connected with the rise of faculty unions in the latter years of the Mass Higher Education Era. Laws governing the right of faculty to organize and be recognized as collective bargaining units depended on whether an institution was public or private. In general, public institutions were subject to state law, whereas private institutions came under the jurisdiction of federal law, specifically the National Labor Relations Act. This act, passed in 1935, "was amended in 1947 to exclude supervisors from the category of employees entitled to a protected right to organize and bargain" (Garbarino, 1977, p. 106). At the same time, it was amended to point out that professional employees could organize; professionals were defined as those employees engaged in predominantly intellectual work involving the consistent exercise of discretion and judgment—work of such a character that its results cannot be standardized and which requires advanced knowledge resting on prolonged, specialized study in an institution of higher learning (Garbarino, 1977). Thus, the 1947 amendment actually spelled out several characteristics of a profession and noted that professional workers were covered. However, not until 1971 did the National Labor Relations Board grant full-time college faculty at private institutions the right to organize into unions by classifying them as employees.

During this same period federal and state employees also gained the right to organize. An executive order issued in 1962 stipulated that federal employees could form bargaining units, and by 1970 more than half of the 2.7 million working for the federal government belonged to a union or employee association. Wisconsin was the first state to pass legislation enabling public employees to bargain collectively. By 1970, half the states had mandated collective bargaining for some sectors of public employees, whereas another 15 permitted negotiations; only two states specifically prohibited recognition of public employee organizations. Overall, in 1970, around one-third of all public employees in the United States were represented by bargaining organizations—a ratio slightly higher than the percentage of private, nonagricultural workers who were organized into unions.

Faculty unions followed closely on the laws governing public employee organizations. Milwaukee Technical Institute, a two-year college, was the first postsecondary institution to be organized in 1963. Three years later the first four-year institution to recognize collective bargaining was the United States Merchant Marine Academy, a federal institution. Faculty unions were recognized in the university sector beginning in 1968, led by state institutions in Michigan and Massachusetts and the City University of New York system.

From these beginnings, the unionization movement spread rapidly. In 1966, a total of 23 institutions—only one of which was a four-year college—had bargaining units, covering a total of 5,200 faculty. By 1974, 331 institutions (132 of them four-year colleges or universities) had organized units representing 92,300 faculty. These numbers included around one-eighth of all higher education institutions, with community colleges overrepresented: 25% of that group had faculty unions, whereas only 6% of four-year institutions were so represented. All the growth had taken place in less than a decade (Garbarino, 1975).

The rapid moves toward unionization drew much commentary and figurative hand-wringing. The faculty were professionals; what did they want from a union? They had gained in public esteem, prospered financially, attracted capable and ambitious individuals to their ranks. They made recruiting and hiring decisions and shaped academic content—functions that in earlier eras had been under the aegis of the president. The 1966 "Statement on Government of Colleges and Universities," issued by the American Association of University Professors (AAUP), American Council on Education, and Association of Governing Boards of Universities and Colleges (the leading faculty, administrative, and trustee organizations), said that the faculty had primary responsibility for curriculum, instruction, and research and that while the governing board or president had the power of review or final decision, it was to be "exercised adversely only in exceptional circumstances" (Carnegie Foundation, 1982, p. 18). No objections to it were raised. The statement further suggested that the faculty should participate in college governance whenever issues related to their primary responsibility might be discussed. Thus, the rush to unionize in the early 1970s struck many observers as untoward. What had happened to collegiality?

Numerous reasons for unionization were put forward. The faculty were young; in 1969 one-third were less than 35 years old, a reflection of the intense hiring of the late 1950s and early 1960s. Two-thirds of the faculty were in public institutions, most in large ones; in 1970, 209 colleges had more than 10,000 students each and 40 had more than 30,000. The number of multi-institutional systems had grown, as branch campuses were set up to accommodate the increased enrollments. A shift in level of control had occurred: in 1959, 17 states had no coordinating agency for higher education; 10 years later only two states had no coordinating body. Unionization had spread first in the public schools, and in the postsecondary sector was most prominent in the community colleges. Flush with victory and with treasuries bulging with contributions from new community college members, the unions campaigned to organize faculty in the senior institutions.

Presumably, the younger faculty were more militant, unused to deliberations and the slow pace of decision-making that was traditional in higher education. The faculty in large public institutions, especially those with multiple campuses, became isolated and felt apart from institutional governance; they wanted a voice. State-level coordinating agencies shifted the locus of control from individual campuses to larger units with greater responsibility; the faculty sought countervailing power. Bowen and Schuster (1986) commented that collective bargaining would not be needed in institutions where faculty members were treated with respect, played an important role in decision-making, received reasonable compensation, and were part of a genuine academic community. They ascribed much of the unionization push to deteriorating working conditions and the loss of real earnings, but still expressed a belief that collective bargaining was not appropriate in an environment in which collegiality and community were essential.

Surveys were conducted to gauge faculty attitudes. A report by Ladd and Lipset (1975) analyzed data from the national faculty survey conducted by the Carnegie Commission in 1969. In that year, 59% of all faculty supported unionization. And when asked to agree or disagree that "Collective bargaining by faculty members has no place in a college or university," the percentage disagreeing rose to 66% in 1972 (Garbarino, 1975, p. 52). Attitudes had obviously shifted as membership in faculty organizations grew. By 1974, the American Federation of Teachers (AFT) boasted 30,000 members in more than 200 higher education units. Although it had been active since 1916, the AFT formed a Colleges and Universities Department only in 1967 and became aggressive in recruiting members and establishing chapters in colleges across the country. The AAUP, begun in 1915 as a professional organization devoted to review and discussion of matters pertaining to faculty, now had 75,000 members. The National Education Association (NEA) also joined the ranks of agencies seeking recognition as bargaining units. Most of its members were in the public schools, but by 1970 it had 28,000 members on 234 college campuses, and by 1974 had reached parity with the higher education membership of the AFT. NEA had started as a professional organization in 1870, but like its higher education counterpart, the AAUP, it developed strong subunits seeking recognition at the colleges.

The AFT, AAUP, and NEA competed for the allegiance of professors, with each promising to negotiate benefits, especially pay raises, if the faculty members would vote them in as a unit to be recognized by the governing boards of the institutions. Their success was measured by the number of bargaining units they established, first in the strong labor states of Michigan and Wisconsin, then in the multi-institutional systems in New York, Florida, and Hawaii and in states where nonacademic state employees had organized, including Pennsylvania, New Jersey, Nebraska, and Minnesota. Traditional observers of the faculty might be horrified to see them marching down the same path as office clerks and prison guards, but so they did. Collective bargaining and traditional forms of academic governance coexisted. The faculty associations and academic senates, dependent on the institution for funding and support, continued discussing economic and academic issues and engaging in shared governance as appropriate. The newer organizations were supported by membership dues and were recognized by law as official organizations empowered to conduct formal negotiations and enter into written contracts covering everything from salaries to grievance procedures. The two processes, resting on difference approaches to academic governance and faculty rights, shared an uneasy alliance, but already potential conflict between the two was apparent. In 1975, Garbarino concluded that "any attempt to limit the scope of bargaining in order to provide separate compartments for academic government . . . is essentially unworkable" (p. 80).

Ultimately, the faculty moved toward professionalization by gaining control over many areas of practice that had been formerly held by administrators and trustees. In all but the community colleges, they were solidly in control of decisions pertaining to curriculum and instruction and participated in institutional governance to the point of being represented on boards of trustees in a few institutions. Cornell, for example, appointed four faculty members as voting trustees in 1956. Threats to tenure were countered both in the courts, which tended to protect it on grounds of due process and freedom of speech, and in practice when a contract achieved through collective bargaining spelled out rules for tenure in great detail. But by the end of the era, the faculty reached a plateau in their trend toward professionalization. Faculty lobbying in state capitals and negotiating collectively on the campuses made them appear as just another labor organization. Furthermore, mass higher education had removed the mystique from college-going, and the increase in part-time instructors weakened any image of a higher calling. But at least the faculty were no longer poverty-stricken scholars, as Harvard's President Eliot had characterized them a mere 100 years earlier.

## Curriculum

Patterns of curriculum that had developed in earlier eras persisted. The curriculum was divided into courses, with each course carrying a specified number of credits that usually were tied to a measure of hours spent with an instructor in a classroom. A specified number of credits led to a degree. Typically, the requirements included 60 units, or around 20 courses, for an associate degree and 120 units (40 courses) for a bachelor's. In addition to the specialized classes required for students in certain programs, most students took a few courses in the liberal arts, divided among science, social science, humanities, mathematics, and English. Whether a student attended a community college, liberal arts college, university, technical institute, or vocational school, the pattern was similar. The faculty controlled the curriculum. Student voices were muted; they took what the faculty prescribed to complete their programs and often were glad for the opportunity to add a few elective courses when their prescribed major left openings. The units usually were transferable between institutions, and they kept their value even as more students attended sporadically, stopping out and returning later to complete a degree program at the same or a different institution.

Within that framework, certain curricular emphases rose while others fell. During the University Transformation Era the curriculum swung in the direction of human capital formation—courses that had content directly applicable to the performance of jobs and the practice of professions. By the opening of the Mass Higher Education Era, the enrollment of more types of students and the splintering of academic disciplines into numerous subfields resulted in a greater variety of courses: more classes in the arts and sciences, subdisciplinary courses for nonmajors in a field, highly specialized classes centering on esoteric snippets of knowledge.

Knowledge—one of the university's main products—became a basis for economic and social growth. But knowledge takes many forms. The scientific idealism so prized in universities has never been accepted across the span of American higher education. Science as the application of intellect based on rationality has battled religion, intuition, and emotion. The long-standing dispute between science and humanism was overshadowed by other events of the 1960s but remained prominent within the academy, especially as funding for occupational training and scientific research increasingly put pressure on the liberal arts tradition. Many of the humanists were content to bask in the prestige that science and the professional schools brought to the universities and willingly accepted the pay increments that followed. But others grumbled, even as the 1958 National Defense Education Act provided funds for foreign language training and the National Foundation of the Arts and Humanities, created in 1965, effected a channel for federal grants. Their pleasant little campuses and meditative studies were compromised beyond hope of redress.

Should higher education serve society or should it center on some ideal vision of truth? Should it prepare people for the marketplace or create citizens who can make objective judgments based on evidence? How much should people's individualism and competitiveness be engendered in contrast to their commitment to assisting one another? Except in the few institutions dedicated almost exclusively to science on the one hand or to the liberal arts tradition on the other, these questions were not resolved. The vast majority of colleges attempted to do everything: to be social servants and knowledge seekers, to assist individuals and groups, to espouse freedom of inquiry along with development of the creative impulse. Still, the questions remained, affecting student and staff positions on every issue from admissions to program funding, public relations to staff appointments, presidential searches to plans for campus expansion.

One of the fascinating aspects of the Mass Higher Education Era is the reversal in the political dimensions of science and humanism. Early in the twentieth century, science was considered elitist because it attracted the brightest students and sent people on to high-paying careers. Later, humanism was called elitist because its programs centered on critique, self-examination, and traditions of literacy. The older America had seemed secure in its village society and industrial capitalism. Now it had to confront modernism in religion, literature, and art, along with relativity in morals. Might democracy be better served by assaulting a meritocratic tradition? Every curriculum change was justified as being practical, timely, and necessary for the different groups of students attending and for the purposes toward which higher education was directed. Personality and character formation took their place along with career and occupational skills as essential curricular elements. The humanities were practical because all citizens needed frames of reference on which to make judgments in the polity. Reading and writing were practical, else how could one function in society? Computational skills were practical because business demanded them. Women's studies and ethnic studies were practical because students could gain understanding of different cultures or perspectives and thus function better in an inclusive society. All changes were practical; all were relevant.

But claims of practicality were not sufficient to defend certain curricular emphases. The cultural heritage of Western civilization, formerly prominent, declined steadily, although its shadow could still be seen in required courses in the humanities. Home economics dropped out as women entered the workforce and as automated appliances and packaged foods liberated them from their kitchens. Farm management declined as family farms gave way to giant agricultural businesses. Journalism was folded into communications. Degrees earned at any level in philosophy, religion, or theology shrank to such a small proportion of overall awards that the National Center for Education Statistics began listing them along with home economics, ethnic studies, parks and recreation, and a few additional categories in a column called "Other."

By 1960, more than 2,400 differently named degrees had been awarded since Harvard introduced the bachelor's of science in 1851, and 1,600 of them were still being awarded, from the associate through the doctoral level; 43% were various kinds of bachelor's degrees. The student as consumer and the faculty as specialist were on full display. Few colleges were able to maintain general requirements beyond lists of courses in various broad areas from which students might choose. Whatever the students wanted to study became, for them, the collegiate experience. Whatever the faculty wanted to teach gained a place in the curriculum. The number of different courses offered reached into the thousands (see Table 4.2). By the 1970s, the 50 leading universities (as measured by federal support of academic science) averaged more than 4,500 different courses each—nearly 2,400 at the undergraduate level and more than 2,100 graduate courses. Other universities averaged between 1,000 and 4,000 courses, and many liberal arts colleges and community colleges listed 500 in their catalogues (Clark, 1995).

This mass of courses spread steadily so that specialization and electives ruled the day. Between 1967 and 1974, the number of institutions requiring at least one course in English for students receiving bachelor's degrees declined from 90 to 72%; those

Table 4.2. Undergraduate and Graduate Courses in American Institutions, by Type of University or College, 1977.

| Type of Institution | Average Number of Courses per Institution | | | Percent Undergraduate |
|---|---|---|---|---|
| | Undergraduate | Graduate | Total | |
| Research universities | 2,335 | 1,943 | 4,278 | 55% |
| Doctoral-degree-granting universities | 1,801 | 980 | 2,781 | 65% |
| Comprehensive universities and colleges | 1,050 | 203 | 1,253 | 84% |
| Liberal arts colleges | 540 | 8 | 548 | 99% |
| Community colleges | 463 | – | 463 | 100% |

*Source:* Clark, 1995.

requiring a foreign language declined from 72 to 53%; and those requiring a course in mathematics declined from 33 to 20% (Carnegie Foundation, 1977). Nearly 60% of students majored in professional or preprofessional areas, with the others divided into social sciences (11%), biological sciences (7%), arts (6%), humanities (5%), and physical sciences (4%). All other fields totaled around 8%. In general, the students divided their time almost equally between their major, electives, and the breadth or distribution requirements that the institutions imposed. The holistic, humanistic tradition, underwater since the University Transformation Era, was submerged completely.

## Forces on Curriculum

Student preparedness joined faculty interests as a force affecting curriculum. As the proportion of students entering college expanded, average literacy levels of matriculants declined. Among students taking the SAT in 1952, the average math score was 494. It increased to 502 in 1963, then declined to 480 in 1975. Verbal scores showed a similar pattern: 476 in 1952, 478 in 1963, 440 in 1975. The decline that began in the mid-1960s was attributed to many causes: the coming of age of the first generation of students reared on a diet of television; the youth counterculture, which glorified drugs and disrespect for authority; and a rise in the number of single-parent households. All were named as contributors. The public schools, too, were blamed as they reduced the length of the school year, began teaching driver education and other nonacademic subjects, expanded their pattern of passing through students who were not prepared for college, reduced the number of academic requirements for high school graduation, and deemphasized reading and writing. The percentage of high school students enrolled in English courses dropped from 95 to 71% between 1960 and 1972 and proportionately in social studies, science, and mathematics. The high school graduates of 1960 had averaged four years of English, their 1972 counterparts only three years. As these students entered college, the proportion diverted to developmental reading, writing, and arithmetic courses increased in all types of institutions, with the largest increase coming in the open-access community colleges. By the 1970s, around 3 in 8 English classes and nearly 1 in 3 mathematics classes at the community colleges were presented at below college level, and developmental classes accounted for 13% of the enrollments in chemistry (Kisker, Cohen, and Brawer, 2023).

Developmental studies were forced on the colleges by the matriculation of underprepared students, but career and occupational studies expanded for different reasons. Students have always gone to college as a way of gaining skills and certification enabling them to enter the workplace at a higher level, but the number of occupations requiring more years of schooling expanded so that more of the curriculum was taken up by specialized vocational classes. In the early colleges, prospective doctors, lawyers, and clergymen studied the liberal arts. Specialized programs and schools for engineers and professional schools for physicians, attorneys, architects, and others followed soon thereafter.

However, not until the Mass Higher Education Era did the expectations of employers and the modifications in college curriculum follow each other with such rapidity. More people stayed in school longer; therefore, the different occupational groups could demand more years of schooling. As apprenticeships and on-the-job training declined, the schools expanded the number of skills they taught. Specialized groups sought the prestige of college degrees. For example, nursing education moved from the hospitals, and police education moved from academies into bachelor's degree–granting institutions. The community colleges took on much of this vocational effort. In 1963, roughly one-quarter of their enrollments were in occupational programs from which students expected to enter the job market, not proceed toward the baccalaureate; that figure reached 35% by 1975. The curriculum became ever more occupational as students were seen as consumers, education was considered a commodity, institutions competed for enrollment, the public accepted the idea of human capital formation through education, and colleges attempted to enhance local economies by providing skilled workers.

The curriculum moved simultaneously toward precollege work, occupational studies, and academic subspecialties in a centrifugal pattern. No sector was immune; community colleges took on the majority of developmental and occupational studies; liberal arts colleges added business and preprofessional emphases; research universities expanded academic majors and graduate school specialties; and comprehensive colleges and universities attempted everything. In all institutions the curriculum reflected political influence, opportunism, the power and ambition of small groups of faculty, the abilities and desires of students, and the pressure exerted by legislators, benefactors, and chambers of commerce. Faculty remained the dominant force, slicing everything into disciplines and distribution requirements, fiercely maintaining their prerogatives, defending their favorite courses. The influence exerted by students paled in comparison; after all, a student attended for a few years at most, while the staff were there for a lifetime.

Even so, the idea of college as a place where values, judgment, and the examined life were exalted would not die. A vocal minority within higher education continued calling for an integrated curriculum, one that would assist students in developing a framework on which to place knowledge stemming from various sources and teach them to think critically, develop values, understand traditions, respect diverse opinions. The term general education, coined early in the century, was continually brought forward as the descriptor for this form of holistic education. It was difficult to argue for a set of coherent learnings; there were too many areas of knowledge, each with an equivalent claim on the curriculum, and most educators had given up on the concept. However, some faculty in the humanities and social sciences and a few administrators who believed in a tradition of rationalism spoke out repeatedly. The Mass Higher Education Era began and ended with the publication of two vigorous statements on behalf of integrated studies: General Education in a Free Society (Committee on the Objectives of a General Education in a Free Society, 1945) and Missions of the College Curriculum (Carnegie Foundation, 1977). But most institutions did little to guarantee their students an integrated learning experience; essentially, all they did was trot out the old distribution lists periodically and make new sets of courses from which students might choose to fulfill their general education requirements. The Carnegie Foundation report described what had happened to the curriculum, deplored the excessive specialization, and argued in favor of a common experience for the students, but acknowledged that general education was moribund.

Repeated calls for interdisciplinary studies that would unify patterns of learning echoed the Yale report of 1828, in which classical studies were justified for the discipline they imposed on developing minds. A latter-day liberal education would show students how to recognize commonalities among recurrent problems and to apply creative solutions. It would also help them tolerate ambiguity and teach them to organize their thoughts logically and to write and speak coherently. This would be done through independent study, honors programs, integrative seminars, work-study and study abroad, collaborative learning, and community or civic engagement opportunities. The colleges would regain their central purpose—one that had been lost in the rush to provide something tailored for each matriculant. Yet pleas for greater curricular focus on interdisciplinary study were to little avail; the curriculum had taken a Humpty Dumpty fall and could never be put together again.

At least a portion of the activism of the late 1960s was directed against a curriculum that students saw as unresponsive. They wanted courses relevant to their desires and aspirations, nestled in an institution that cared for them as sentient human beings, not as units to be processed. A few institutions reacted to what the students called a dehumanized undergraduate experience by developing smaller units, experimental colleges, colleges within colleges, and other configurations designed to bring students and faculty closer together. Some students and instructors were given an opportunity to recreate the personal relationships, the shared quest for common understanding that they believed had characterized institutions before higher education became bureaucratic, impersonal, and highly specialized. However, most of the settings in which students and instructors came together to design their own curriculum lasted but a short time. Desks replaced with pillows, faculty on call 24 hours a day, unstructured curricula, students operating with a minimum of guidance and a maximum of permissiveness—all reflected the fervor of righteousness, but few models could be sustained. Most students wanted to get on with their degrees and most faculty with their research and quest for promotion within the academic ranks. Several of the colleges named in Grant and Riesman's *The Perpetual Dream* (1978) and in MacDonald's *Five Experimental Colleges* (1973) sank without a trace or were so transformed that they hardly resembled the intentions of their founders.

The experimental colleges had a negligible effect on the curriculum. Reactions against the elective system pursued with such vigor earlier in the century led to the creation of interdisciplinary courses. Modifications brought forward in the name of satisfying student demands for a relevant curriculum did the same, for a while. But these changes were overpowered by ever-longer lists of courses from which students could fulfill degree requirements. The curriculum had no more direction, rigor, or overall coherence than it did before the students' cries for guidance and values on which they could construct their lives. When an institution has no basis for judging the relative worth among forms of learning, how can it deny any area of study?

In addition, a sizable number of faculty and increasing numbers of students became more vocal in espousing their views on the shortcomings of the broader community, especially those having to do with the rights and progress of women and people of color. By the 1970s, it was common for institutions to take positions on societal issues and especially to make proclamations against racism, sexism, and other social ills. After student activism brought these issues to the fore, the institutions could no longer afford accusations that they were unresponsive to social change or that they retained intellectual positions that opposed dominant themes in the broader community. The multiversity, so named by Clark Kerr in the early 1960s, was characterized as objective, neutral, and dedicated to the advancement of knowledge and service to the community. By the end of that decade and on into the 1970s, increasing numbers of students and faculty identified areas where they said higher education was not objective, where its practices of exclusion in admitting students and hiring faculty from particular groups—along with its Western-centered curriculum—revealed its values in ways the academy's claims to neutrality could not counter.

Controversies over the curricular canon accelerated. Faculty attempted to remain apart from and morally superior to the surrounding communities. In large measure that was why they had entered the university in the first place; the notion of the ivory tower was not born in the 1970s. Now they were being called on to use their exalted position to remedy social ills. Each time a change in the canon was made, a handful of faculty and commentators argued that it meant the end of the search for truth. For example, when the classics were abandoned early in the University Transformation Era, many critics claimed that the heritage of Western civilization had been debased. Toward the end of the Mass Higher Education Era when African American studies, women's studies, and studies of other cultures were proposed, the same accusations were leveled. But the institutions' leaders had learned to compromise, and it was not difficult for them to encourage the development of new, specialized courses in ethnic and women's studies. After all, what was the addition of another few classes to a catalogue that listed a thousand or more already?

Still, the controversies remained heated. When the classics were diminished, only a few scholars objected. When vocationalism squeezed the humanities, most objections came from instructors in those disciplines. Now the students, empowered by moral righteousness and using tactics learned in the activist period, kept the pressure on. And sympathizers among the faculty smoothed the path. Courses in area and ethnic studies, foreign languages, and women's studies did not engage a large proportion of students or staff, but they represented symbolic victories. Their introduction demonstrated how egalitarianism began to occupy a center position in the ethos of academe. The courses showed young people that every gender, cultural, or demographic group was as worthy as any other, but as the era ended, the campuses—and of course the broader society—were as fractured as they had been when it began.

**Instruction**

The Mass Higher Education Era encompassed a full slate of innovations in instruction. Some were new; more were variations on earlier practices. The lecture and the laboratory remained dominant, but they were surrounded by an array of pedagogical innovations. Some instruction was designed for students to proceed at their own pace, but most was conducted with groups in classes. The power of the faculty was absolute; each instructor was free to design a method of teaching following the procedures judged suitable for the subject area under the assent of their disciplinary colleagues. As had been true since the beginnings of schools, some instructors were creative, skilled at tailoring instruction to the situation, inspiring. Others were dull, lethargic, inflexible. One characteristic of the institution covered them all: peer evaluation was pro forma, and administrative evaluation was practically nonexistent. Only the students, voting with their feet, maintained an informal network of commentary about which instructor's classes were useful. Beginning in the 1960s, they published critiques based on classroom evaluations in an attempt to influence the pedagogy. But even that right was hard-won, as professors in many institutions abhorred the idea of being evaluated by their charges. Nonetheless, student evaluations eventually were accepted, and in many institutions the completed forms became part of each professor's dossier.

Innovations in instruction became pervasive. The College Level Examination Program, established by the College Board in 1967, spread so that students might earn credits without participating in courses. Awarding Pass/Fail grades and allowing students to withdraw from courses without penalty up until the last weeks of the term were introduced as ways of reducing grade inflation, avoiding penalties for not keeping up in the class, encouraging students to take courses in subjects outside their main interests, and leveling outcomes in required courses.

The Keller Plan was introduced in 1966 as a form of self-paced instruction. Learning laboratories in which students might proceed through self-instructional materials were popular. Computerized tutorials, auto-instructional workbooks, and a host of other technological aids to instruction were tried on the grounds that different students had different learning styles. In addition, the chimera of reduced instructional costs lured college administrators to fund new technology. Publishers brought to market programmed workbooks, audio-tutorial instructional systems, and various mechanized ways of presenting material. A few instructors adopted the innovative programs, changing their own teaching methods to accommodate the self-paced characteristic of the materials. Many other instructors acknowledged that the materials might be useful and urged libraries or learning laboratories to purchase them so students could use them as supplements. Most went on teaching as they had before the words *automated instruction* had been coined.

Supplemental Instruction (SI), an academic support program targeting courses with high dropout or failure rates, was introduced in the 1970s. Study sessions for students in those courses were led by students who had completed them successfully. SI has persevered as an effective strategy for enhancing student learning and improving grades in a variety of general education classes. Not least, the student tutors gained much from the experience, a finding demonstrating once again that the best way to learn something is to teach it.

The various forms of instruction attempted provided a splendid view of an institution attempting to accommodate numerous forces: a variety of students differing in levels of preparation, aspirations, and interests; academic disciplines splitting and re-forming continually; the need to keep costs under control; and professors who effectively modified the curriculum every time they organized a course. Curriculum committees tried to control course proliferation but could do nothing about instructional innovation; in fact, in most institutions new forms of instruction were encouraged and money set aside so that professors could develop or purchase different types of instructional materials. Colleges that did not introduce new programs or pedagogical practices were deemed stodgy; the professor teaching from yellowed lecture notes was a caricature; the catalogue that each year did not list numerous cutting-edge courses was archaic. The modifications continued in a never-ending kaleidoscope.

The effect of all this innovation was to give the appearance that higher education was responsive to changing social conditions, new types of students, and advances in knowledge. But did students learn more? No method was shown to be consistently superior to any other. The conditions of instruction were so fluid and the students and professors so varied that claims of greater learning outcomes proved impossible to verify. McKeachie (1963) summed much of the research on teaching by pointing out how it could say little more than in college A, on day B, instructor C used method D to teach subject E to students F. Modify any of the variables and the results would differ. Instructors continued trying different techniques and insisted that they improved student learning, even as they resisted deliberate attempts to measure it reliably.

Neither instructional innovation nor course proliferation could be brought under control. In most institutions, if a course was not presented over a period of a few years, it was removed from the catalogue. But for each one removed, more were added, with the presumption that if professors wanted to teach them, if students would take them, and if they did not substantially duplicate others, the courses must be worthy. Any form of instruction that did not increase per-student costs showed that the college was not afraid to experiment.

This atomistic approach to curriculum and instructional reformation was not without its critics: students needed more nurturing as they made their way into adulthood, hence the college should function more as a therapeutic center, said Rogers (1969); societal scales were unevenly weighted, and thus marginalized students should be taught how to combat the evils of their economic and social oppressors, said Freire (1970). All were given hearings and then thoroughly compromised by the magnitude of the system. Too much structure or too little, too many choices or too few, too much or too little adherence to the heritage of Western civilization, an excessive concern with liberal arts or with careers or with scientific research—all critiques were as marshmallows tossed at a juggernaut. The curriculum encompassed every bit of esoterica, every view of truth, every skill that anyone might need to have. The instructional forms sustained the debates, recitals, lectures, examinations, and independent study variations prominent throughout history. Added to them were all of the technologies that could be purchased and introduced. Yet overall, the system remained the same. Students came to college and attended classes; professors attempted to influence their learning; books were available in the library. Campuses persisted as places to be associated with the life of the mind.

## Governance

As public institutions increased in size and greater state-level coordination expanded, higher education came to be viewed as a public good. No state wanted to be left behind in the race to provide postsecondary education for as many of its citizens as possible. Plans were developed and efforts made to put a college within commuting distance of every resident, as evidenced by the reports emanating from commissions organized to review higher education at the state level and for the nation as a whole. Revealing the attitude of the era, these reports both reflected and influenced legislation.

For example, the 1947–1948 President's Commission on Higher Education recommended that at least half of all high school graduates could benefit from a minimum of two years of college to extend their general education and to gain occupational skills, thus encouraging support for community colleges. Not incidentally, the group also specifically denounced any restrictions on the enrollment of Jews and African Americans, a first for a high-level governmental commission. Two years later, the Commission on Financing Higher Education reiterated the view that half of all college-age students could benefit from enrollment and foresaw separate collegiate and occupational tracks. During the Johnson administration, the White House Conference on Education acknowledged that education was a primary instrument for solving societal problems. The Task Force for Reform in Higher Education released a report in 1970 suggesting that mass education should be the goal, and research and direct public service should be deemphasized so that higher education could accommodate more people. In the same year, the Assembly on University Goals and Governance recommended expanding general education while reducing attempts to serve the public directly. The Educational Policies Commission of the National Education Association similarly called for expansion and egalitarianism. And so it went through the era, as various conferences and commissions urged each state to broaden its higher education effort so that none would be left behind.

The most prolific group was the Carnegie Commission on Higher Education, which published more than 50 books in the late 1960s and early 1970s. Its general tone was that higher education should be expanded to include more of the population and that the system should sustain a proper balance between public and private and undergraduate and graduate education. The commission's books considered institutional growth, admissions policies, budgets, mission, and accounting practices, all of which they said should be under state-level coordination. The states should be judged on the extent to which they offered access and equality in educational opportunity. They should encourage educational diversity, preserving college autonomy even while insisting on public accountability. The states should prepare people for the workforce and provide incentives for institutional innovation. Statewide coordinating agencies should take precedence over boards of control. The commission's other recommendations covered the field:

- More people should be prepared for the health professions because that area was expanding, and fewer people should be prepared as teachers because public school enrollments would decline in the 1970s.

- The proportion of higher education income derived from federal sources should increase so that parity among the states might be approached.

- Enrollments should increase and tuition should be kept low so that universal access becomes the norm across the nation.

- Faculty salaries should increase to bring the wages of professors closer to those of comparably trained professionals in other fields.

- More curricular options should be explored, including developmental education for students underprepared by the lower schools.

- Intellectual competence should be nurtured and seen as the proper way of differentiating among people; all other types of discrimination were to be shunned.

The Carnegie Commission acknowledged that most state master plans made few provisions for the private sector and foresaw major difficulty in sustaining institutional diversity and a variety of possible educational experiences. Its reports came toward the end of an era in which public funding already had accelerated substantially. The states had built extensive college systems, and federal appropriations were going into research, facilities, professional study, financial aid for students at all levels, libraries, and instructional improvement. By accepting these funds, higher education had to follow state and federal mandates—characteristics of governance that would become more pronounced as the years went by.

The Carnegie Commission reports also followed developments in several states where plans for expanding and coordinating higher education were under way. Notable among these was the 1960 Master Plan for Higher Education in California, a voluntary compact (Clark Kerr, its principal author, called it a *treaty*) that divided responsibilities among the state's community colleges, comprehensive colleges, and universities. The University of California was to admit students from the top one-eighth of high school graduating classes and be the sole public provider of doctoral education. The state colleges would take students from the upper one-third of high school graduates and provide programs through the master's level. Anyone aged 18 or older would be eligible to attend the community colleges, which would provide general education through grade 14, along with occupational certificate programs. In short, the various public institutions would divide the territory. Each had developed separately—the university as a land-grant institution named in the state constitution, the comprehensive colleges as normal schools or occupational training centers, the community colleges as extensions of local school districts. Instead of competing, they would cooperate in providing education for every purpose. By 1970, California's colleges and universities enrolled as many students as did the public institutions of New York, Illinois, and Texas combined.

The federal government stepped up its involvement with and influence on higher education. Year after year, beginning with the GI Bill in 1944, more laws, more funds, and more regulations illustrated the government's attention to higher education. For example, in 1950, the Housing Act authorized loans to construct college residence halls. The 1958 National Defense Education Act authorized loans and fellowships for college students and funds to provide for foreign language study. In 1963, several acts expanded federal involvement, including the Health Professions Educational Assistance Act, the Vocational Education Act, and the Higher Education Facilities Act. The Higher Education Act of 1965 provided grants for several types of college services, including libraries and undergraduate programs; it also authorized guaranteed student loans. During the same year, a Medical Library Assistance Act added funds for libraries, and a National Vocational Student Loan Insurance Act expanded loan insurance programs. The Adult Education Act of 1966 and the Education Professions Development Act in 1967 expanded teacher training. The Vocational Education Act and the Higher Education Act were both amended in 1968 to expand their original scope and funding. In 1971, the Comprehensive Health Manpower Training Act and the Nurse Training Act expanded provisions in those areas. The Education Amendments of 1972 established the education division in the Department of Health, Education, and Welfare and authorized a Bureau of Occupational and Adult Education. The Education Amendments of 1974 established the National Center for Education Statistics.

This review of legislative action displays much of what the federal government was doing to increase access and to turn higher education ever more in the direction of professional and occupational training. And the list does not include the numerous programs that—although not directly pointed toward higher education—enhanced the funding available for applied research. Higher education had always been regarded as an agent of social change, first through its providing for individual mobility, then through its research on social issues and its role in economic development. But in the Mass Higher Education Era, its social role expanded as it conformed with rulings regarding discrimination, student aid, affirmative action, applied research, and institutions and programs for especially designated groups. The association between campus and state, which grew steadily after the beginning of the University Transformation Era, accelerated.

**State Coordination**

The Higher Education Act of 1965 was an omnibus bill, with sections covering financial aid to students, construction of facilities, aid to institutions that wanted to work on societal issues, and not least, the directive that each state establish a coordinating agency for higher education. This latter provision had a powerful and long-lasting influence. It forced coordination of all sectors, and state-level coordinating boards or boards of governors were erected or strengthened so that more decisions reaching deeper into institutional affairs were negotiated in state capitals, thus accelerating a trend toward consolidation that had been in place since the era began.

The states were quick to create boards or commissions to comply with Section 1202 of the Higher Education Act; within 10 years all but four had established a new commission or converted an existing agency into a commission in the form recommended. These groups were composed of members from all the sectors identified as part of higher education in each state: the public four-year institutions, public community colleges, public vocational or technical institutes, and private colleges, augmented by representatives of the general public. Each 1202 commission had between 8 and 29 delegates, with the median at around 15.

The 1202 commissions accelerated trends toward state-level coordination that had been developing in most of the states and stimulated action in others. They had several effects initially. They coordinated data collection, wrote position papers, and provided a forum for debate among representatives of various sectors. Gradually they began defining categories of higher education and recommending that one or another sector expand certain types of programs. The differences between universities, community colleges, and vocational-technical institutes were brought forward and attempts made at integration for planning purposes. In some states they were able to effect better coordination of higher education resources, but in most they found it difficult to gain cooperation among the various agencies responsible for one or another area of education. In particular, they often were not able to present a unified voice to the state legislature, as each sector and many of the interest groups within it maintained their own offices in the capital, sending representatives to the commissions but making their own demands and appeals to the legislature.

One of the effects of the move toward coordinating commissions was that most states developed comprehensive plans or studies of the financial need for higher education. The California master plan was developed under the Coordinating Council for Higher Education, and when that group was converted to the California Postsecondary Education Commission, new studies and ways of ironing out wrinkles in the master plan were pursued. The 1202 commissions were not legislative bodies. They could study and recommend, but any change in funding or control still had to work its way through traditional channels in the legislatures or in the institutions' governing boards. Coordination implied continuing autonomy for each institution, that is, the prerogative of the campuses to develop their own programs and areas of service. The trend toward state coordination was intact, but it had not yet reached a point where major decisions affecting programs on individual campuses were being made. Actually, increased state-level activity often improved the quality of campus decision-making by setting it in a broader framework. The tradition of individual campus autonomy, stemming from the earliest colleges, still dominated.

While the 1202 commissions studied cooperative relations, planning mechanisms, financial needs, and relationships among the sectors, a parallel trend toward state-level governance was developing. In several states, the universities were linked with a governing board managing all of them. The idea was that centralized governing boards would streamline the system, present a unified voice to the legislature, and reduce program duplication. Centralized management and budgeting would reduce waste. Operational guidelines would ensure that funds were allocated properly. Public relations statements promised greater efficiency as governing boards took command.

The results turned out somewhat differently. Merely because a multi-campus system evolved from a set of individual institutions did not guarantee change in the essential characteristics of the system. One area of contention came over the question of whether a particular campus should offer a graduate degree in a certain field. The tradition of individual campus autonomy was so strong that issues of curriculum and program modification usually were debated in the abstract, with campus representatives participating in discussions but with intramural groups—often allied with local supporters—making the final determination. For example, the University of California opened four new medical schools in addition to the one it already had, three of them in the 1960s alone. The system-wide governing board questioned program duplication, but local politics and campus ambitions won the day.

The governing boards found rhetoric easier than reality in other areas as well. Central administrations were supposed to be accountable to the state for expenditures across campuses, but individual units demanded and usually retained the flexibility to shift funds among programs. Campuses also clung to requirements for student admissions and graduation and to most issues related to curriculum. For example, getting a statewide, uniform course-numbering system in place proved to be a lengthy process and in many states did not reach fruition by the end of the era. However, the multi-institution governing boards did achieve program coordination in some areas, especially in occupational programs, probably because those were the ones most closely associated with employer demand and employment rates that could be calculated for the state as a whole. And in many multi-institution systems, staff salary schedules were set uniformly so that everyone at a certain level would earn the same regardless of the institution in which they were employed.

A general effect of the statewide boards was that institutions within a system were considered equal. The major research universities—Illinois at Urbana, Texas at Austin, Michigan at Ann Arbor—saw resources spread more widely across their states' higher education system. Part of this was inevitable as rising student populations in the comprehensive institutions demanded more resources. But where state budgets were limited, this diffusion seemed to penalize the flagship institutions that previously were at the front of the line in obtaining state funds. The leading universities' share of state appropriations declined, and support for sister institutions and state colleges rose significantly. Another effect was that the universities' budgetary requests became negotiable alongside the demands of other public agencies; in some states, higher education budgets grew much more slowly than did those for welfare and health services. The extent to which this would have happened in the absence of state governing boards is debatable; perhaps higher education would have suffered more if each college still had to make a separate budgetary plea.

The era also saw the public gaining influence over the conduct of institutions, which was not surprising. As higher education increased its expenditures as a proportion of gross domestic product, the public became more concerned. Governing boards were opened to people whose major concerns were more as watchdogs than as institutional spokespeople or fundraisers. More state-level boards meant that more officials were appointed by governors; in some cases the superintendent of public instruction, lieutenant governor, or governor became a member of the board automatically. The traditional idea of the governing board as an independent agency serving as a buffer between the campus and the public or legislature was compromised.

State-level governance did little to reduce competition among institutions or among groups within them. As the systems and each unit in the systems grew larger, the likelihood that the college reflected a community of people with shared interests and values grew more remote. Most institutions seemed more like business corporations, governmental bureaus, or agencies in which contending parties vied for a greater share of power. This view of the university as a center of conflict or political contentiousness received much attention in the early 1970s when student activism, faculty unionization, and program expansion were prominent. Competition among institutions was matched by competition within, as each department and each stakeholder—faculty, students, teaching assistants, deans, business officers, and other officials—sought more resources. Many groups formed statewide associations and presented their own requests to the governing board or directly to the legislature. Perhaps the idea of the college as a collegial community had been unrealistic; certainly the student rebellions of the nineteenth century suggested that a generational split was the norm. But until the Mass Higher Education Era, the various subgroups within each campus were not sufficiently large or well-organized enough to take their case to the next level.

**Institutional Management**

Greater size led to complexity in management, as each institution added administrators in greater proportions than it did faculty. Complying with state and federal regulations, managing financial aid and affirmative action, and providing assurances that the institution was accountable in everything from student admissions to pollution control demanded that additional offices be opened. The National Association of Financial Aid Officers was founded in 1966 and by 1969 was the largest higher education association in the country. Tasks that once were performed by the president and the faculty, along with many that were previously unknown, were assigned to middle management. Allocating economic resources and reforming educational programs necessarily brought administrators into conflict with faculty, students, and alumni groups. These tensions occupied much of the time that the parties might otherwise have spent on education—the essence of the enterprise—and additional offices were created to resolve issues among them.

Most institutions divided their administrative structure into three general functions: academic affairs, student affairs, and business affairs. Under academic affairs were the deans of the various schools, a director of the library, a registrar, and financial aid officers. Student affairs typically oversaw housing and food services, counseling, placement, student organizations, and student health. The business affairs office was concerned with financial operations, personnel, buildings and grounds, security, purchasing, mail, and administrative computing. These divisions varied across colleges. In one institution, the director of admissions might be under academic affairs, in another under student affairs, but one axiom held: the larger the institution, the more the administration was subdivided into smaller units.

In systems managed at the state level, campus administrative units were usually duplicated in statewide offices that provided a coordinating function among them. To a board of regents and president were added vice presidents for academic affairs, administration, health, and finance. Each supervised officials responsible for affirmative action, personnel policy, academic planning, liaising with faculty, admissions, library, and 5 or 10 other functions. The vice president for finance managed offices for alumni relations, budget analysis, long-range development plans, capital improvement, construction, gifts and endowments, governmental relations, and everything from space utilization to resource administration. The vice president for administration oversaw business operations, collective bargaining services, contracts and grants, accounting, faculty housing, patents, and several other services. Attempts to enhance efficiency in institutional management usually were negated by the demands for interoffice review, data, and assurance of compliance with system-wide regulations. The larger independent institutions were spared much of that type of reporting and oversight but had as many administrative offices within them. The smaller private colleges added administrators to ensure compliance with federal and state regulations regarding affirmative action, health services, and financial aid packages. No level or sector of higher education was exempt from administrative expansion.

Accordingly, the role of the president shifted notably from leader of the educational program to manager of the bureaucracy. The president who could stamp the institution with a specific academic style could no longer prevail against all the countervailing forces. The strong presidents of the University Transformation Era, those who followed the precept "Never retract. Never explain. Get the thing done and let them howl!" (Birnbaum and Eckel, 2005, p. 341), soon found it necessary to update their résumés and seek employment elsewhere. The academic senates became increasingly well organized and powerful. They had almost total responsibility for what happened within the departments and gained various university-wide responsibilities as well. A growing number of public institutions had faculty representation on the governing board. And within public and private universities alike, the faculty typically were responsible for determining what research and public service projects should be undertaken. They also determined admissions and graduation requirements in various schools; the appointment, promotion, and dismissal of professors; the purchase of books and journals by the library; and the allocation of departmental clerical and research support. In the larger institutions, the senates had their own committees, councils, and task forces to facilitate communication among departments and between faculty and administrators. Together with various administrator groups, the faculty senates ensured that the president's role was limited to macromanaging, fundraising, and representing the institution to the governing board and the public.

Student government changed as well. In the early American colleges, the students had no voice in institutional management, curricular affairs, or any other aspect of student life. Subsequently, colleges developed honor codes, making students responsible for their conduct. By the turn of the twentieth century, student governments had formed to include honor systems, advisory councils to the faculty, committees with power of discipline, oversight of residence halls, and management of extracurricular activities. It was easy to justify student involvement in governance; it was supposed to train for citizenship, give experience in policy making, provide for student expression, develop leaders, and in general enhance the morale of the college community. By the end of the University Transformation Era most institutions had a student government made up of an executive council, a lawmaking body with elected representatives, and a student court to adjudicate violations of regulations.

Subsequently, the scope of student participation in institutional governance expanded. One of the goals of the student activism of the 1960s was to gain a greater voice in academic management. Accordingly, students gained seats on institutional governing boards and on college committees where they could discuss admissions policies and faculty and administrative appointments. They might have been invited to sit on faculty and administrative committees, but there they found not centers of power where sweeping decisions were made but tedious, lengthy discussions of the most mundane details, seemingly without conclusions ever being reached—the real world of academic decision-making. Students who developed statewide associations and public interest research groups found that influence could be exerted more effectively. The goal of campus-level governance with students, faculty, and administrators meeting, conferring, and deciding together remained elusive, and student associations acted as one more pressure group among many.

## Accreditation

The GI Bill specified that veterans' educational benefits would only apply at institutions approved by state educational agencies, which solidified accreditation as an essential feature in higher education. Its successor bill, the Veterans Readjustment Act of 1952, directed the U.S. commissioner of education to publish a list of approved accrediting associations; from then on, access to federal funds was limited to institutions that were accredited by one of the agencies recognized by the U.S. Office of Education. As such, the influence of accreditation grew. Six regional associations took responsibility for certifying that a college met certain predetermined standards.

The process of institutional accreditation took many forms, but in general the accrediting group established standards, and each institution performed a self-study comparing itself to those standards. A team selected by the accrediting agency visited the institution or program to determine if the standards had been met; if the agency was satisfied, the institution was officially accredited. Accreditation might be for a period of a year or two or as much as 10 years. Programs that did not meet standards typically were put on probation and, after a time, visited again to see if they had come into compliance. All was designed to stimulate institutional self-improvement.

The accrediting of professional programs and special types of colleges proceeded along with the accreditation of colleges and universities. The American Medical Association, the first of the specialized accrediting groups, was organized in 1847. It challenged schools to improve their curriculum and to enforce stricter entrance and graduation requirements. The American Association of Teachers Colleges began accrediting teacher education nationwide in 1923. By 1948, it had become the American Association of Colleges for Teacher Education and accredited fewer than 250 of the 1,200 institutions then involved in preparing instructors. The National Council for Accreditation of Teacher Education took over in 1954 and was recognized as the sole accrediting agency for that field by the National Commission on Accrediting in 1956. Other fields became involved with accreditation, including the National League for Nursing, the American Dental Association, and at least 50 other groups. Some of them persuaded the states that graduation from an accredited program was necessary for licensure in that occupation, thus demonstrating considerable power in the management of higher education.

From the standpoint of institutional governance, the accreditation process segmented responsibility. It was criticized for emphasizing the interests of certain programs; for reinforcing the status quo by limiting deviation from conventional practice; for effectively requiring governing boards to spend funds for buildings, equipment, and staff when it specified faculty-student ratios and minimum square footage for program operation; and for having standards that tended to be quantitative rather than qualitative. However, the accreditation process has been higher education's way of managing itself in the absence of a national ministry of education found in most other nations. And in peculiarly American fashion, the U.S. Department of Education accredited the accreditors, ensuring that the federal government had only indirect control over college and university operations.

Toward the end of the Mass Higher Education Era, several themes became prominent in the higher education lexicon—accountability, efficiency, effectiveness, assessment, equity—as pressures from federal and state agencies and accreditors exerted greater influence on institutional processes. The institutions were asked to justify expenditures, to rationalize societal benefits and, as the Consolidation Era opened, to provide data in ever-finer detail. In the public sector, statewide coordinating or governing boards spread along with linkages among what previously had been independent colleges and universities. Expansion in campus-level administration occurred in both public and private institutions, as offices were created to manage the complexities of larger units and to satisfy demands for compliance with state and federal regulations. Accrediting associations gained quasi-official status when the federal government stipulated that colleges and universities must be accredited to be eligible for federal funds. The connections among higher education's thousands of institutions took the form of a gigantic spider web or a skein of yarn tossed by a kitten. All were interconnected yet at the same time functioned independently.

## Finance

Recounting finances over time is ultimately an exercise in storytelling. The gross numbers tell one story, those adjusted for inflation quite another. Data can be displayed for all of higher education, subdivided by sector or level, or compared with funding for some other public institution. Revenue can be considered by source and expenditures by category, and both can be broken out again on a per-student basis, for any number of years. Accordingly, it is possible to show that during the Mass Higher Education Era, finances for higher education increased, decreased, or remained the same. As the truism has it, torture the data enough and they will confess to anything. However, a realistic conclusion is that American colleges and universities did quite well in the 30 years following 1945.

### Sources of Support

The raw numbers are certainly impressive. In 1945, higher education received around $1.2 billion from all sources; by 1975, this figure increased to nearly $40 billion. Adjusting for inflation and using 1967 dollars as a base, the 1945 total would be $1.7 billion, and the 1975 figure would be $14.4 billion—a substantial increase. Using those same constant-dollar figures and dividing by the number of students enrolled yields an expenditure of around $850 per student in 1945 and $1,270 per student in 1975—a much more modest but still sizable gain.

The value of higher education property increased from $5 billion in 1945 to $75 billion in 1975. The total physical plant, land, buildings, and equipment equaled $3 billion in the earlier year, $62 billion in the latter, or $7,800 per full-time equivalent (FTE) student. The balance was made up by the value of endowments: $2 billion in 1945, $13 billion in 1975. Higher education added around $4.7 billion per year to its total capital base by the end of the era.

Patterns of financing most directly differentiate the public and private sectors (see Table. 4.3). Tuition is one example. Near the beginning of the era, private universities derived 57% of their current-fund income from tuition and fees, whereas the figure for public institutions was one-quarter. By 1975, the proportion of income derived from tuition had dropped to 48% in the private institutions and to 16% in the public sector (actually an increase from the decade prior, when tuition comprised 14% of current-fund revenue in the public sector; McPherson and Shapiro, 1991). Across all institutions, tuition accounted for roughly 20% of all revenues at the end of the era.

Similarly, as Table 4.3 illustrates, federal, state, and local governments accounted for about 16% of all revenue to private institutions near the start of the era and 69% in the publics. By 1975, private institutions received 29% of revenues from government, whereas the public percentage had increased to 79%, mostly from states and localities. Gifts and endowment earnings had made up 23% of income in the private sector, dropping to 19% by the end of the era. Not yet a major source of funding for the public sector, gifts and endowment earnings began and ended the era at 3%.

Within each sector, different types of institutions were more or less dependent upon various sources of revenue and showed different rates of change in each of them. Annual growth in gross tuition charged, which was 13% between 1940 and 1950, dropped to 5% between 1950 and 1960 and increased again to 14% between 1960 and 1968 when governmental grants and loans enabled the private institutions to increase tuition substantially. State appropriations went from $150 million in 1940, to $500 million in 1950, to $1.4 billion in 1960, to $5.8 billion in 1970, and to $12.2 billion in 1975. In the latter years, the share going to universities declined,

Table 4.3. Percentage of Current-Fund Revenue of Private and Public Universities, by Source, Selected Academic Years.

| | Percentage of Current-Fund Revenue | | | | | |
|---|---|---|---|---|---|---|
| | 1949–1950 | | 1965–1966 | | 1975–1976 | |
| Source | Private Institutions | Public Institutions | Private Institutions | Public Institutions | Private Institutions | Public Institutions |
| Governments, total | 16 | 69 | 32 | 77 | 29 | 79 |
| Federal | 12 | 13 | 30 | 23 | 25 | 18 |
| State and local | 4 | 56 | 2 | 54 | 4 | 61 |
| Tuition and fees | 57 | 25 | 43 | 14 | 48 | 16 |
| Gifts and endowment earnings | 23 | 3 | 18 | 3 | 19 | 3 |
| Other | 5 | 3 | 6 | 5 | 4 | 2 |

*Note:* Figures do not include revenue from auxiliary enterprises, sales, or services. Student aid is included under tuition.
*Source:* McPherson and Shapiro, 1991.

and that for community colleges rose as the states increased funding for the sector that was responsible for more of the rise in enrollment. In addition, half the states, led by New York and Pennsylvania, provided some institutional support to the private colleges. Federal expenditures for higher education (excluding student aid) rose from less than $40 million in 1940, to $500 million in 1950, $1 billion in 1960, $3.1 billion in 1970, and $5.5 billion in 1975. The percentage of current-fund revenue provided by the states to all institutions of higher education was 21% in 1950 and 31% in 1975. In contrast, the federal government provided 22% in 1950 and 16% in 1975, as its contributions swung from support for research and facilities construction toward aid to students (Snyder, 1993).

**Efficiency**

Efficiency is an index of how well an institution uses its funds in relation to its desired outcomes. However, there is no limit to the amount of money a college might spend to achieve educational excellence or gain greater prestige. Accordingly, each raises all the money it can and spends all it raises. This distorts concepts of efficiency because specific outcomes are rarely attributable to additional funds.

Efficiency is typically associated with gains in productivity, yet it has always been more difficult for higher education to enhance productivity than it has been for most other industries. Some service industries became more productive by adopting technology; banks, insurance companies, and brokerage firms that automated processes all led in this area. But the creative and performing arts, churches, and higher education have not been able to benefit from technology to nearly as great a degree. This may have been due to the nature of these professions, or to the fact that they touched sensitive aspects of people's lives, and best practice usually required personal contact. Just as health services requires the presence of physicians and nurses, instruction depends (for the most part) on teachers. Thus, few technological adoptions affected productivity in the Mass Higher Education Era. The colleges continually sought more funds to pay their staff, and when these were not forthcoming, saw wages fall behind those in industries that were less labor-intensive or where technology spawned productivity gains.

Comparatively large increases in revenue per student came to an end in the early 1970s, and the colleges and universities began reducing the rate of salary increases, deferring maintenance, and looking for other places to save money. They increased class sizes, employed more part-time instructors, added distance learning possibilities through television and radio, built audio-tutorial laboratories and computer-assisted instructional programs, awarded credit for independent study and for prior experience, and tried to enhance the use of buildings by offering courses for longer periods of the day and on weekends. Funds for libraries that had run at about 4% of total institutional expenditures began a steady decline. There were no data to show how much maintenance was deferred, but it seems likely that most institutions retrenched there; the paint may have been flaking off a building's walls but at least it was not pounding the table and demanding an increase in salary. Arguments were raised continually to the effect that further cost cutting would sacrifice program quality, but the budget makers had little choice. And overriding all the contentions about where to make cuts was the great unknown: the relationship between expenditures and outcomes. The cost of education per student was lower in some colleges than in others, but it was certainly not clear that cost-per-student or expenditures in any area had a direct effect on institutional outcomes.

Comprehensive reviews of costs and benefits were made by Bowen (1980), who subdivided colleges by type, level, control, size, and so forth and found wide variation in the allocation of funds. No matter how calculated—whether or not doctoral students, upper-division students, and lower-division students were weighted differently—the range among institutions of the same type was greater than the median differences among types of institutions. This variance was mirrored in the way institutions spent funds on different functions. Bowen's data showed that private liberal arts colleges allocated 38% of expenditures to teaching and research universities put 59% in that category. However, in the latter case, departmental research was calculated as part of instructional cost. Consistent with their claims of close relationships and enhanced student life, private liberal arts colleges spent more than other institutions on scholarships, fellowships, and student services.

Bowen found few differences in percentage allocations to various institutional functions among the wealthiest and most cash-strapped institutions in the same category. Apparently, as the colleges gained access to more funds, they spread them around so that almost all functions got a share. Every department, every section could always use additional money; whenever new funds came in, they all reached for them. The effect was that each institution's historical pattern of allocating funds tended to be perpetuated. The resource-rich institutions spent more on everything; the less well-endowed institutions made do with less across the board. The one exception was that the more affluent institutions seemed to "apply their incremental expenditures to successively less important purposes" (Bowen, 1980, pp. 150–151). They were more likely to have a larger number of administrators and clerks, more office equipment and supplies, and larger budgets for travel. In a preview of institutional critiques to come in later eras, Bowen felt that one useful way of analyzing institutions might be to focus on the ratio of nonacademic staff to students, instead of on the ratio of faculty to students. But he concluded, "The dispersion of costs is astonishingly great—so great that one may reasonably question the rationality or equity in the allocation of resources among higher educational institutions" (pp. 120–121).

Identifying the optimal size or number of students per institution proved elusive. Every college had to have some faculty and administrators, some buildings and books. The cost per student in each of these areas decreased as the number of students increased, hence, to a point growth seemed to suggest efficiency. However, as institutions grew, they often found that certain costs rose; in particular, it cost more to coordinate programs, ensure adequate administration of various functions within and across departments, and provide support for a greater number of students. Accordingly, costs per student seemed to decline sharply as an institution grew until a certain point of enrollment was reached and then they leveled off. The larger institutions spent more on administration and student services, less for plant operation and maintenance. Scholarships and academic support showed little relationship to size. The increase in funds dedicated to program coordination resulted from the growth in interdepartmental committees, personnel officers, formal newsletters, and other means of communication. Large institutions were still able to save money, however, because they could use their buildings more efficiently. In short, institutional size had a considerable impact on certain unit costs, but overall costs per student differed little. There seemed no way to calculate the most efficient size for an institution.

Nevertheless, legislators, coordinating boards, and other governing units continually tried to influence college allocations in the quest for efficiency. The extramural agencies often tried to micromanage expenditures, arguing that because colleges were not run as businesses and because educators continually sought more money, governing agencies must show them how to spend their funds. They often set up detailed financial controls and prepared impressive-looking reports, but these had little effect because the categories were elastic, and it was relatively easy for an institution to shift costs around within them. Bowen (1980) contended that public agencies wanting to control costs might focus on two things: "First, to establish in broad general terms the basic scope and mission of the institutions for which they are responsible, and second, to set the total amount of money to be available to each institution each year" (p. 24). When this was done the individual colleges could allocate resources according to their best determination. But in most states systemwide management had advanced too far to sustain that type of budgeting autonomy.

## Staff Salaries

In 1975, American colleges and universities employed almost 1.6 million people, including faculty, support staff, maintenance workers, and administrators. The payroll totaled over 57% of current-fund expenditures; fringe benefits alone accounted for nearly 19%. Salaries charged to instruction came to 34%—practically the same as at the beginning of the era. Even though the faculty had improved their compensation during the 1950s and 1960s, the costs of everything else that the colleges purchased had increased at a greater rate and accounted for more of the increase in per-student expenditures.

The higher education labor market is different from many others. Faculty may migrate from one college to another readily, but they rarely move out of higher education at large. They have invested much in their training, and the decision to become a professor is often tantamount to a lifetime commitment, not affected by temporary increases or decreases in compensation. Once in, the individual usually stays. This gives colleges some latitude when deciding whether or not to raise salaries. Within reasonable limits, a qualified staff can always be employed. Concerns that not enough professors could be found to staff the colleges when enrollments increased rapidly in the 1960s proved unfounded. The feared shortage never materialized.

For several decades, trends in faculty pay shifted only slightly in constant-dollar terms. The slow advance after the turn of the century turned into a decline during World War I. A rapid advance in the early 1920s slowed in the latter part of the decade but increased again in the early 1930s. A moderate decline during the latter 1930s turned into a sharp decline during World War II as inflation eroded faculty pay. The decline slowed in the late 1940s, and then in the 1950s and 1960s a marked, steady advance occurred. Early in the 1970s the trend turned down again. Because faculty salaries had started at such a low baseline—around $5,000 in constant 1967 dollars at the turn of the century—not until 1950 did they begin a rise toward what might be called a living wage.

Faculty pay rates have little to do with the supply of or demand for qualified instructors, and they are not closely associated with rates of inflation or deflation in the general economy. They relate more to public attitudes and the political power of professors. Because the faculty did not exhibit any significant bargaining ability prior to the late 1960s, the wage gains of the preceding decade cannot be attributed to such efforts. Similarly, if market forces operated properly, faculty compensation would decline along with student enrollments and with a growing supply of potential instructors. But the rise and fall in faculty salaries relative to wages paid to other professional groups showed little relationship to any of these forces.

Faculty compensation includes more than salaries and fringe benefits. In many private institutions, a faculty member's family may receive tuition remission. In most institutions, access to campus events and sports facilities, long vacations, sabbatical leaves, tenure, flexibility in responsibilities and schedules, and in some cases subsidized housing add to the pay package. Furthermore, most instructors have the opportunity to earn outside income. Some estimates in the 1970s were that three-fourths of the faculty on academic-year appointments earned outside income, which added about 20% on average to their base salary. Accordingly, when all the supplemental compensation was totaled, faculty earnings were comparable to their counterparts in government service.

Of course, the amount that faculty earn from second jobs is never calculated as a cost of higher education because it does not show up in expenditures. However, except for CEOs and coaches, administrators and other salaried employees do not receive outside income to a degree nearly comparable; thus, when total faculty income is compared with administrators' income, the difference between the two was not as great as it appeared. The recognition that faculty can and should earn money from other pursuits arose when professors were considerably underpaid; pay for administrators was set when they broke from the faculty ranks and were given additional stipends for administrative service. Although top administrators are sometimes paid to consult and to serve on corporate boards, compared with the compensation that middle managers in other industries receive, higher education administrators as a group are probably more underpaid than the faculty.

**Federal Support**

By the end of the Mass Higher Education Era, support for higher education shifted from research support to student aid, which expanded manifold after the Higher Education Act of 1965. But for two decades, expenditures for research grew even while enrollments soared. At the conclusion of World War II, federal contributions were evidenced by the pool of qualified researchers on staff at universities and the number of scientific and technical laboratories that were built. Not wanting to waste this accumulated wealth of talent and capability by retreating to prewar levels, the universities sought continuing support from the federal government. The conviction that the university was a proper setting for research was reiterated continually: in a report to President Roosevelt by Vannevar Bush, director of the Office of Scientific Research and Development during the war; in the formation of the National Science Foundation (NSF) during the Truman administration that omitted support for constructing governmental laboratories; in a Bureau of the Budget report to President Eisenhower maintaining that research and development that could be procured from the private sector ought not to be undertaken by federal agencies; and in a task force report to President Kennedy concluding that the government should continue relying on the private sector for its scientific and technical work. Accordingly, the government continually shifted its research and development from its own laboratories to external contracts, and the bulk of those contracts went to the universities.

The push for an enhanced research presence was most notable between 1950 and 1970. The NSF was established in the former year, with the universities well represented on its board of directors. Its appropriation in 1952 was only $3.5 million, but it grew steadily and by 1958 had distributed more than $75 million in research grants and graduate and postgraduate fellowships. The National Aeronautics and Space Administration (NASA), authorized in 1958, channeled additional funds for academic science. Overall, federal funds for academic research reached over $1.25 billion by 1964. Most of the early money supported basic research; nearly 60% of federal dollars came from the NSF and the National Institutes of Health (NIH)—agencies that typically did not direct programs but that funded institutions and allowed them to develop their own programs. However, by the late 1960s, applied research was added to the mission of the NSF, and the fervor of federal spending for undifferentiated purposes in higher education subsided as research solutions to specific problems were sought.

Other agencies that would bring federal assistance into various areas of inquiry were formed in 1946: the National Institute of Mental Health, the Office of Naval Research, and the Atomic Energy Commission (AEC). By 1950, the AEC spent nearly $100 million for research. The universities also sent in proposals to other agencies concerned with the Cold War; the Air Force had contracts with 50 institutions. Altogether, in 1950 federal support for research totaled around $140 billion, most of it for projects related to the nation's war-making capacity, a sizable proportion going to the universities, and much to faculty members soliciting support for their own studies.

As the Cold War continued, support for university research from federal agencies grew every year except for a downturn toward the end of the 1960s. The United States was committed to developing new types of weaponry, and entrepreneurial professors became the conduits through which vast sums of federal money flowed into the universities. The Cold War effort never turned on maintaining a large standing army or on stockpiling traditional weapons; it was fought with inventions and new technologies, better ways of targeting missiles, more powerful atomic bombs, new types of submarines and airplanes, and weapons that could find their own targets. Technological innovation was dependent on scientific expertise and large capital investment in laboratories; the universities were in a seller's market.

The NIH, a primary channel for federal funding of scientific research, led the shift toward applied inquiry. Whereas the NSF represented natural science in general, the NIH was concerned primarily with biomedical studies. Funds continued pouring into the NIH on the hope that the research it sponsored would eventually cure various health problems. In 1954, NIH appropriations were over $70 million. They increased to $98 million in 1956, and according to Geiger (1993), "for the next five years the average annual increase in the NIH budget was $96 million, and for the next six years the average rise was $156 million" (p. 181). By 1960, the NIH had surpassed the Department of Defense (DOD) in its support for academic research, and by 1965, it was three times larger than the NSF. NIH funds were used for numerous purposes in medical and biological science: as matching funds for capital costs of health-research facilities; to support graduate and postdoctoral students in the health fields; and for research grants—the latter accounting for half of all NIH appropriations in 1967. Medical education in general benefited; practically every medical school in the nation received at least $1 million dollars a year from the NIH.

Geiger's (1986, 1993) books—landmarks in examining the field of academic research—showed how federal funds transformed the landscape in health and other areas of inquiry. The National Institute of Mental Health, which separated from the NIH in

1967, provided more than 40% of federal support for studies in psychology and sociology. The National Defense Education Act supported research in languages and area studies. The AEC, DOD, and NASA supported academic research in the sciences; the latter agency funded more than $100 million in academic science in 1964. Many DOD subagencies funded academic research, but when the Vietnam War protesters and some members of Congress demanded that DOD-supported activities be abolished from campuses, that agency's support for research declined precipitously. The DOD had accounted for one-third of all federal support for academic research in 1960, but by 1975 it was down to just 8%. Overall, federal support for science was highest between 1958 and 1968 and support for students highest from 1963 to 1972. Geiger (1993) concluded, "The five years in the middle of the 1960s when both these revolutions overlapped appear in retrospect to have been the golden age for research universities" (p. 195).

Federal funding for research in science and social science had several effects. In 1968, 36 large, separately organized university research centers employed more than 12,000 professionals and graduate students and spent over half a billion dollars. Even education was represented with a set of research centers, laboratories, and ERIC, the Educational Resources Information Center. By 1970 the universities and their associated research centers collectively were responsible for 60% of the basic research and 10 to 15% of applied research conducted in the United States (Wolfle, 1972).

Wealth concentrated in the universities that received the largest research grants and charged the most for indirect costs. The top 20 institutions, beginning with Cal Tech, MIT, and the Universities of California and Chicago, received 61% of federal dollars in 1958, up from 32% 10 years earlier (Orlans, 1962). But as other universities, especially in the public sector, gained research capacity, the funds were spread more widely. By 1968, 40 universities received at least $10 million each—half the annual total of federal research funds. This reduced the disparity but by no means eliminated it; Cal Tech, Johns Hopkins, MIT, Chicago, and Stanford still received over one-fourth of the money. Centers of excellence in research were developed and the PhDs they trained sought positions in research-oriented institutions, thus reducing the talent available to small colleges. Although the proportion of students and faculty in the sciences did not increase, support for their work set them apart. "The most unfortunate consequence of federal science programs has been the cleavage they have engendered between the status and rewards of faculty in the sciences and humanities" (Orlans, 1962, p. 134).

Put into perspective with other higher education expenditures, activities related to research commanded a constant 8% of total current-fund expenditures between 1945 and 1975. Other current-fund expenditures are shown in Table 4.4. Even though the federal government provided the lion's share of funds for research, the universities gathered money from other sources, including their own endowments, state and local governments, industry, and philanthropic foundations.

Other federal programs were proposed but not enacted. A national foundation for higher education was debated in the early 1970s, but the prestigious research institutions were opposed to it because it would have spread funds for research and graduate education across the spectrum of universities. This was only one example of how higher education found it difficult to speak with a unified voice. Its different interests kept colliding with one another. The most prestigious universities wanted federal funds for research; community colleges wanted aid for low-income students; comprehensive institutions wanted funds deployed across a wider array of colleges and universities. Even the National Institute of Education, formed to sponsor and fund research in teaching, learning, student access, and student aid, died within a few years because of inept leadership and lack of support from the higher education community, although it was succeeded by the Office of Educational Research and Improvement. Defenses of institutional

Table 4.4. Expenditures of Institutions of Higher Education as a Percentage of the Total, 1945–1946 and 1975–1976.

| Purpose of Expenditures | Percentage of Total Expenditures | |
|---|---|---|
| | 1945–1946 | 1975–1976 |
| Administration and general expense | 10 | 13 |
| Instruction and departmental research | 34 | 34 |
| Organized research | 8 | 8 |
| Libraries | 2 | 3 |
| Plant operation and maintenance | 10 | 8 |
| Organized activities related to instruction | 6 | 3 |
| Extension and public service | 5 | 3 |
| Scholarships and fellowships | – | 4 |
| Other general expenditures | – | 1 |
| Independent operations | 22 | 12 |
| Auxiliary operations | – | 3 |
| Hospitals | – | 7 |
| Other | 2 | – |

Source: NCES Digest, 1996.

autonomy were raised continually, as mistrust of the federal government, coupled with the desire of elite private institutions to maintain their eminence, perpetuated the disunity. Senator Daniel Moynihan (1975) concluded that "initiatives concerning higher education arose primarily from the political interests and objectives of successive Presidents and their Administrations. Rarely did higher education act; it was acted upon" (p. 139).

Relations between colleges and universities collectively and the federal government resembled a couple of behemoths circling each other warily. Each kept doing things to verify the suspicions of the other. The federal government placed a requirement for a loyalty oath in the National Defense Education Act legislation, something many of the campuses opposed. Student demands that ROTC and military recruiters be banned from the campuses antagonized legislators. Even so, the federal government and higher education maintained mutual dependencies. Student aid became a lasting feature in federal appropriations, and funds for research continued to run to the universities through numerous channels. Most of the federal measures broadened access to higher education by providing funds to low-income and other marginalized students and allowed the institutions to increase tuition. It is amazing that all this happened without a concentrated political effort by institutions of higher education. In one respect, the sector rode the coattails of the well-organized elementary and secondary school associations. In another, Congress and the presidential administrations of the era responded to a broad public will that the benefits of higher education be made available to everyone.

By the end of the era, the Carnegie Commission on Higher Education recommended that federal support be increased across the board, saying that because of the rapidly increasing costs in higher education, additional federal funding was essential. The commission argued for many types of support, including direct payments to institutions, construction funds to accommodate increased enrollments, more money for research, and a national student loan bank that would make it possible for all students to go to college and repay their loans at low rates of interest over extended periods of time. The commission recommended increasing Basic Education Opportunity Grants that were authorized in 1972, making a plea for fully funding that program along with the college work-study program. Occupational training, libraries, graduate student fellowships: all should receive augmented federal funding. The commission acknowledged that federal funds in all those areas had increased but argued that the rate of inflation was accelerating even more rapidly, thus diminishing the actual support received from the federal government. However, the commission did not maintain a presence in Washington, and the influence of its scores of books and press releases was indirect at best. Nonetheless, federal support for graduate student fellowships dropped by 60% in the decade following 1967, and aid to undergraduates rose rapidly. The shift toward enhancing access was on.

**Philanthropy**

Voluntary support increased tenfold during the era. Alumni and other individuals, corporations, foundations, and religious organizations all stepped up their donations. Giving by high-income individuals was stimulated by income tax rates, which for a time were such that a $100 gift might cost the giver as little as $30. Led by the larger private institutions, the universities made notable appeals for this money. Harvard organized an $82 million drive in 1957, and shortly thereafter Stanford opened a $100 million campaign.

Corporate giving was particularly sought. A change in the federal tax code in 1935 allowing corporations to deduct up to 5% of their pretax net income for charitable gifts stimulated increased donations. However, only in 1945 did corporate contributions exceed 1% of pretax income. One of the problems was a lingering question over whether corporate gifts were subject to shareholder approval. That question reached the New Jersey Supreme Court in a case brought by the shareholders of the A.P. Smith Company, which had contributed $1,500 to Princeton University in 1951. The court approved the donation, allowing the company to make it without prior approval of the shareholders. Other corporations began various forms of support; Ford Motor Company announced a scholarship program for children of employees, and in 1955, General Electric began a matching gift program whereby employees might have their donations matched by the company. In 1975, around 1 out of every 6 donated dollars came from corporations.

Charitable foundations continued supporting higher education. The federal excess profits tax imposed during World War II and put into effect again during the Korean War stimulated corporations to form foundations as a way of sheltering income. Five times as many such foundations were formed during those years as had been established in all previous years, and some of the larger foundations were quite generous to higher education. After 1950, Ford Foundation donations eclipsed those made by the Rockefeller and Carnegie foundations, both of which had been prominent in the earlier part of the century. In 1953, Ford's contributions equaled more than one-third of total foundation giving, and three years later it made grants totaling over $200 million to the entire population of private colleges and universities. These funds were to be used for faculty salary increases, and they proved quite welcome, especially at the smaller private institutions where faculty salaries lagged. Ford also made funds available through challenge grants, whereby the private institutions put up matching funds to strengthen areas they wished to pursue.

The philanthropic foundations were generous to university research in general, and medical research in particular. They also supported research in the social and behavioral sciences, which was largely ignored by the federal government. Carnegie assisted the Russian Research Center at Harvard and other types of work on international studies elsewhere. Rockefeller helped establish a Russian Institute at Columbia, designed to train specialists for governmental work. Ford contributions addressed social concerns; its assistance to the Center for Advanced Study in the Behavioral Sciences at Stanford effected a major achievement in that area. The University of Chicago also received funds to support study in the social sciences.

Overall, as shown in Table 4.5, the proportion of voluntary support received from each source between 1949–1950 and 1975–1976 remained steady, with the exception that corporate giving increased from 12 to 16% of the total. However, because the public sector had grown large, the proportion of total support for higher education accounted for by private gifts declined from around 9%

**Table 4.5. Voluntary support for institutions of higher education, by source and purpose of support (in millions of current dollars).**

|  | 1949–1950 | 1975–1976 |
|---|---|---|
| Total voluntary support | $240 | $2,410 |
| Source (percent of total) | | |
| Alumni | 25% | 24% |
| Nonalumni individuals | 25% | 24% |
| Foundations | 24% | 23% |
| Corporations | 12% | 16% |
| Religions organizations | 7% | 5% |
| Other | 7% | 8% |
| Purpose (percent of total) | | |
| Current operations | 42% | 61% |
| Capital purposes | 58% | 39% |
| Voluntary support as percentage of total expenditures | 9% | 6% |

*Source:* NCES Digest, 1996.

of institutional revenue at the start of the era to 6% at the end. The percentage of revenue accounted for by endowment income and by sales and services, auxiliary enterprises, and hospitals declined as well; state and local government support became the primary source of revenue to institutions of higher education.

### Expenditures

Expenditures rose along with enrollments and revenue. The increases were not uniform; different time periods and expenditures for different purposes showed varying rates of acceleration. For example, during the 1960s, faculty salaries increased at more than double the rate of inflation as universities sought to play catch-up for a professional group whose wages lagged behind those of other groups with comparable training. Administrative costs increased as additional staff were added to manage the growing number of programs and responsibilities that did not exist in earlier times. The cost of utilities and supplies increased, and there were few ways to find new income to purchase them. The price of a new building might be obtained from a generous benefactor or governmental agency, but the building had to be heated, lighted, cleaned, and repaired forever thereafter. The colleges had to find more scholarship money to help them recruit a more diverse student body. Tuition discounts became widespread in the private sector, as gross tuition charges began pricing all but the wealthiest students out of the institutions. Campus infrastructure demanded investment as computers and communication equipment became vital. The shortfall between revenues and expenditures could not be rationalized away as a temporary phenomenon; costs in all areas rose more rapidly than income and, for at least part of the era, more rapidly than the rate of inflation. Between 1954 and 1967, educational costs per student credit hour increased an average of 3.5% per year, whereas the consumer price index rose by only half that much.

All these cost increases take on a different cast when placed in a longer time perspective. Between 1930 and 1976, total expenditures for all purposes, including capital improvements, increased from $632 million to $43.6 billion, an average annual rate of increase of 9.6%. But much of that was due to increased enrollments and to a decline in the value of the dollar. During the 46-year span, FTE enrollment increased from 890,000 to nearly 8.5 million while the purchasing power of the dollar declined by 70%. Putting those two figures together, the per-student cost grew on average by only around 1.4% per year.

As a percentage of gross national product, total higher education expenditures increased from 0.7% to 2.7% over those same years, primarily because of the nearly tenfold growth in enrollment. Bowen (1980) concluded, "The data hardly support the notion that higher educational costs rise steadily and inevitably over time . . . . When expressed in constant dollars, they have held steady or declined over long periods, for example, during the period 1929–1930 to 1949–1950, and also during the 1970s. Only in the golden years of the 1950s and 1960s did unit costs increase" (pp. 36–37). Indeed, from 1930 to 1950 expenditures per student declined slowly as measured in constant dollars, whereas from 1950 to 1970 they increased tremendously, and after 1970 again began a slow decline. The surge of expenditures in the 1950s and 1960s "was a unique event that lifted costs per student in constant dollars to a new and unprecedented plateau from which the higher educational system is now slowly receding" (Bowen, 1980, pp. 43–45). However, in comparison to expenditures per elementary and secondary school pupils, which increased 656% between 1950 and 1976 (not accounting for inflation or increased average daily attendance), the 429% increase in expenditures per FTE student was relatively small (Bowen, 1980).

Furthermore, several socially imposed costs rendered the institutions powerless to control certain expenditures. Security costs went up along with insurance and unemployment compensation for workers. Due process rulings, environmental protections, nondiscrimination clauses, sunshine laws, and associated demands that information be made public brought additional costs. These reflected basic changes occurring in society, new pressures effected by interest groups that led to governmental action, and shifts in social mores that prompted institutional change without governmental intervention.

External demands came with increasing frequency. During the 1930s, the Social Security Act and the Wagner Labor Relations Act caused some increase in the costs of staff. But these were modest in comparison with the legislation of the 1960s and 1970s, including Title VII of the Civil Rights Act of 1964, as amended by the Equal Employment Opportunity Act of 1972; the Affirmative Action Executive Order of 1965; the Occupational Safety and Health Act of 1970; Title IX of the Educational Amendments of 1972; and the Employment Retirement Income Security Act of 1974. These various acts prohibited discrimination either in admissions or employment on the basis of sex, age, or race; they controlled pension plans and workplace safety. In addition, local or state actions affected building codes and workers' compensation, both of which imposed additional costs. Some of the expenses appeared significant but were one-time outlays, such as making buildings accessible to people with disabilities, and were not very great when amortized over the life of a building. Other changes cost little initially but over the years turned out to be expensive—women's athletic programs developed to comply with Title IX, for example. The costs of compliance in supplying certain data seemed high initially, as the institutions adopted new procedures to compile it, but became lower as the provision of data became routine. Bowen (1980) estimated all these mandates effected additional expenditures of around $2 billion to $2.5 billion annually during the era.

A few observers deplored the socially imposed costs as an assault on academic freedom, but most contended that higher education was just being brought more in line with societal changes. At any rate, the institutions had little choice in the matter and could not pass the increased cost along to their consumers as profit-making corporations often do. In the case of public institutions, tuition might be regulated by a state legislature, hence, not easy to change merely because costs have gone up. And except for the most prestigious among them, private institutions could raise tuition only so much lest they price themselves out of the market. In both sectors, financial aid, student support, and other costs associated with a larger and more diverse student body added to expenditures.

An overview of expenditures in higher education for 1975 shows that around one-third of the total supported instruction and departmental research; one-quarter to student services, scholarships, and fellowships; and around 40% to organized research, public service, and auxiliary enterprises, including hospitals. Those figures conceal much variation among sectors. They are also subject to various interpretations because the categories are not distinct. In general, however, higher education was funded well, spreading its sources of revenue and controlling its expenditures despite inflation, paying its staff a living wage, and increased costs associated with federal, state, and local mandates. Contentions that the government impinged upon institutional autonomy continued, but they received little attention in an era in which higher education was embedded in American society and thoroughly dependent on diversified funds.

## Outcomes

Higher education's outcomes can be tabulated in many ways. The most common metrics are based on attainment and efficiency: the number of degrees awarded relative to the number of students matriculating, as well as the employment and salaries of graduates. A second set of measures associates student learning with changes in attitudes or perspectives during the college years. A third relates to the benefits that educated people bring to society. During the Mass Higher Education Era, university research became a fourth quantifiable outcome, as it contributed to the nation's knowledge base and to industrial and economic development.

### Degrees and Wages

The 500% enrollment increase between 1945 and 1975 naturally affected the number of degrees awarded. Associate degrees increased in number from 50,000 to 350,000 annually; bachelor's and first professional degrees from 135,000 to nearly 1 million; master's degrees from 20,000 to nearly 300,000; and doctoral degrees from 2,000 to 34,000. The fields in which degrees were awarded shifted, especially toward the end of the era. Between 1970 and 1975, bachelor's degrees in business increased by 30%, those in life sciences by 50%, and those in the health professions and communications more than doubled. At the same time, bachelor's degrees in mathematics declined by one-third, those in social sciences and history by 18%, and those in education by 12%. At the master's level, degrees in education and business increased by 40 and 65%, respectively, as requirements for entry into those fields ratcheted up. Library science showed a similar effect, as bachelor's awards declined by 17% but master's degrees rose by 15%. Some progress toward gender equity was evident in the number of degrees awarded: in 1945 men earned two bachelor's degrees for every one earned by a woman, but by 1975 women were earning 45% of all baccalaureates.

Increased production of doctoral degrees illustrated the push for additional years of schooling, as well as higher education's contributions to the professional workforce. A major impetus to the tenfold growth in doctorates was the impending increase in the 18-year-old population and the greater percentage attending college. In the late 1940s, it was clear that more professors were needed, but where would all these doctoral recipients come from? In 1953, around 30% of new faculty held the doctorate, a ratio that could not continue as enrollments swelled rapidly in the late 1950s and 1960s. Many universities—especially those seeking the greater prestige that accompanied doctoral programs—used the anticipated shortfall as a rationale to employ more highly qualified faculty, expand research, and appeal for more state funding. As a result, the number of doctoral-granting institutions increased, from around 100 in 1949 to twice that number by 1970.

Other measures for ameliorating the presumed crisis in doctoral degree production were brought forward. The doctor of arts in teaching was introduced, although it gained little ground beyond a few institutions. Several philanthropic foundations put additional funds into graduate study, and the federal government supported predoctoral students through the National Defense Education Act, the NSF, and NASA. By the 1960s, a sizable majority of full-time doctoral students received fellowship assistance. Some analysts advocated shortening the time-to-degree, arguing that if students completed doctoral programs more rapidly, the number of doctorates would increase, and more space would be available for future students. Students in the sciences typically earned the doctorate more rapidly than those in the humanities and social sciences, but those entering academic careers in the sciences often engaged in extensive postdoctoral work, so that the actual time from the beginning of doctoral study until the end of training was similar to that in other fields.

The question of program length provided another rationale for more funds: surely students' time-to-degree could be lessened if more had fellowships and did not have to take time away from their studies to earn money. But this proved not to be the case; students who took assistantships and similar jobs on campus often worked diligently and received their degrees at a similar pace as those supported by scholarships. Furthermore, faculty in the humanities and social sciences were not concerned about the length of time it took students to complete their programs; in Geiger's (1993) felicitous phrase, "In more ruminative subjects, like literature or philosophy, faculty thought it desirable that there be ample time for, well, rumination" (p. 228). Eventually the crisis subsided, not because substantially greater numbers of doctoral holders were produced, but because fewer 18-year-olds graduated high school in the 1980s and more and more students attended community colleges, where possession of a master's degree was considered sufficient training for a professor.

Numerous studies dating from the Mass Higher Education Era and the ensuing decades examined income in relation to schooling. In their compendium of research on students, Pascarella and Terenzini (1991/2005) showed that when intelligence, socioeconomic status, and work experience were held constant, attainment of a bachelor's degree provided a 25 to 30% advantage in earnings over students who left the educational system after high school. Indeed, Pascarella and Terenzini (1991/2005) concluded that "attainment of the bachelor's degree may be the single most important educational step in the occupational and economic attainment process" (p. 501). Although a number of studies have since confirmed the connection between higher education and greater earnings, the effects are not universally linear, and much of the difference in earnings depends on the time in a person's life when earnings are calculated: for example, within a year or two after leaving school or 5, 10, or 20 years later. And it has always been difficult to correlate earnings with capability in the many well-paying occupations for which possession of a degree is required before a person may be considered for employment—a phenomenon known as the sheepskin effect. There is no way of knowing how much people without degrees might have earned if they had been allowed to enter those fields.

**Personal and Social Benefits**

The personal and social effects of college attendance—also referred to as its public and private benefits—have been studied extensively. In the early 1970s, the Carnegie Commission (1973b) translated the traditional purposes of higher education—teaching, research, and service—into five sets of objectives spanning both public and private outcomes: (1) providing opportunities for the intellectual, aesthetic, ethical, and skill development of individual students; (2) advancing human capability in society at large; (3) expanding educational justice; (4) transmitting and advancing learning; and (5) critically evaluating society for the sake of society's self-renewal. However, it has always been easier to theorize the outcomes of higher education than it has been feasible to find data showing the extent to which college attendance produces the desired outcomes. In 1969, Feldman and Newcomb examined the impact of college on students by synthesizing studies conducted from the mid-1920s to 1967, finding that several characteristics change with considerable uniformity during the college years. In particular:

- Regardless of the characteristics that propelled an individual student toward a particular type of college, those same characteristics were likely to be reinforced and extended by the experience of attending that institution; in short, selection and impact were interdependent.

- Within the same college, experiences associated with different majors typically had effects above and beyond those that could be accounted for by initial selection into those fields.

- Although individual instructors were often influential, the faculty as a whole did not exert a campus-wide impact on students, except in settings where the influence exerted by peers complemented and reinforced the influence of faculty.

- Attitudes held by students when they left college tended to persist, possibly as a result of living in post-college environments that supported those same attitudes.

Similarly, Pace (1979) reviewed 10 major studies conducted between the 1930s and the 1970s and found positive links between college attendance and job satisfaction, participation in political activities (voting, campaigning), pursuit of cultural interests (attending concerts, reading, visiting museums), interpersonal relations, and development of personal values, goals, and philosophies. Pace also reported that the median family income of college graduates was twice that of the U.S. median and that between 70 and 90% of bachelor's degree holders were in professional or managerial positions (the difference depending on the number of years they had been out of college). He concluded that college graduates tended to have good jobs and higher incomes, that they liked their jobs and thought their studies were relevant to them, that they were more likely to participate in civic and community affairs, and that they typically agreed that their college experience had been beneficial.

Bowen (1977) also reviewed a number of studies, finding that college attendance led to greater openness to change, a realization that the prevailing conditions of society can be improved, greater involvement in public affairs, increased expectations for government and social institutions, and enhanced concern for the environment and tolerance for differences among people. Higher education also contributed to economic efficiency, improved international relations, better dissemination of technology and information, and a generally healthier lifestyle, including less violent behavior, more volunteerism, and a greater appreciation of the arts. Bowen's (1977) research also identified four societal benefits of higher education's research efforts, including public service; scholarship that preserves cultural heritage; scientific research that yields vaccines, medical techniques, electronics, computers, and agricultural products; social science research that results in a better understanding of the effects of public policy as well as societal criticism necessary to assist the nation in maintaining its values.

Another societal outcome of higher education—the development of human capital—was enhanced in more complex ways than merely training and shifting people into various avenues of employment. Developing individuals' skills and maintaining a properly educated workforce were seen as dual, overlapping purposes of higher education. The system developed talent, allocated people toward areas of greatest economic and social need, enhanced individual (geographic, occupational, and socioeconomic) mobility, and enabled people to continue developing throughout their lifetimes; all benefited both individuals and society. Furthermore, the Carnegie Commission

(1973b) argued that higher education contributed to a more just society by reducing barriers to individual advancement and helping individuals move between social strata. Access to college in the Mass Higher Education Era was far from equitable, but the system was more open by far than that of any other nation. In particular, the development of low-cost community colleges within driving distance of nearly every citizen did more to equalize opportunity than any other social institution.

**Differing Effects**

Attempts to demonstrate the differing effects of certain colleges, programs, instructors, or instructional methods were usually unconvincing, as variations in achievement among individual students completing the same program or attending the same institution were great. Even after controlling for all possible quantifiable variables, including students' gender, race, ethnicity, entering test scores, prior achievement, and socioeconomic status—and even for less reliable measures such as incoming attitudes and aspirations—researchers were left with little conclusive data about why certain students selected certain institutions, the effect of their on-campus experiences, and the impact of events and experiences that occurred off campus. Holding nearly every conceivable input variable constant, Astin (1977) found that the experience of attending full-time and residing on campus had the most marked effects on a student's likelihood of completing a degree.

Undoubtedly, students graduating from various institutions differed widely in terms of academic achievement, religious interests, and aesthetic sensibility. However, the differences among graduates from one institution or another, substantial as they were, could be explained largely by the differences among the same students at time of entry. The overlap among colleges in what they did and how they did it was so great that finding large differences in outcomes was highly unlikely. Even though the more affluent institutions appeared to generate higher graduation rates, they might have performed similarly with less money, and many more institutions might have achieved greater results with no additional funds. Some of the expenditures in high-cost institutions were "almost surely designed more largely for the students' satisfaction than for their educational growth" (Bowen, 1980, p. 167). Nonetheless, students attending more affluent institutions reported that they derived greater benefit—a finding that may have resulted from the extra money spent on student affairs and extracurriculars.

Such data beg the question: Does the public get its money's worth? Any consideration of the proportion of a state's resources that should be devoted to higher education brings an implicit comparison of the social benefits that might be derived if those funds were allocated to other agencies; an impossible task. And even within higher education it has been impossible to demonstrate that a dollar spent at a research university is more or less socially beneficial than one spent at a community college; the two types of institutions serve different students and provide different services.

Some analysts have contended that the greater support for research universities and graduate programs during the Mass Higher Education Era led to unequal benefits, and there is some data to support this assertion. For example, expenditures per FTE student in 1975–1976 totaled less than $1,800 at community colleges, compared to roughly $4,000 at highly selective public universities. At the same time, the median parental income of first-year community college students was $13,579, compared to nearly $22,000 for the parents of first-year students at highly selective public universities (see Table 4.6).

In 1969, Hansen and Weisbrod argued that because family income was related to the type of institution attended, and because the state allocated more to universities than to community colleges, wealthier families whose children were more likely to attend universities and highly selective four-year colleges received greater subsidies than lower-income families whose children more often

**Table 4.6. Institutional Expenditures and Median Parental Income of First-Year Students, by Type of Institution, 1975–1976.**

| Type of Institution | Expenditures per FTE Student | Median Parental Income of First-Year Students |
|---|---|---|
| Public institutions | | |
| Two-year colleges | $1,778 | $13,579 |
| Four-year colleges | | |
| Low selectivity | $1,741 | $13,895 |
| Medium selectivity | $2,071 | $16,593 |
| High selectivity | $3,888 | $17,802 |
| Universities | | |
| Low selectivity | $2,678 | $17,813 |
| Medium selectivity | $3,086 | $18,618 |
| High selectivity | $4,153 | $21,946 |
| Private institutions | | |
| Four-year colleges | | |
| Low selectivity | $2,627 | $13,978 |
| Medium selectivity | $2,485 | $17,977 |
| High selectivity | $2,835 | $20,150 |
| Very high selectivity | $4,275 | $26,117 |
| Universities | | |
| Low selectivity | $2,142 | $20,977 |
| Medium selectivity | $3,514 | $27,986 |
| High selectivity | $5,954 | $23,573 |

*Source:* Bowen, 1980.

enrolled in community colleges. Furthermore, they came to the "rather startling conclusion" that because university students tended to remain enrolled for longer, and because each year of attendance meant that students received an additional benefit,

9% of high school graduates received subsidies exceeding $5,000, while "more than half of California's young people receive[d] under $750 . . . and a substantial fraction—41 percent—receive[d] no subsidy at all" (p. 181).

Another issue was that higher education's outcomes could not reasonably be validated in the long term. What students learned while they were in college and the jobs they entered immediately upon graduation were amenable to measurement. But the colleges could not be held responsible for the jobs available to their graduates or for the particular jobs they took; students in one field might well enter a different one upon graduation. As the supply of college graduates grew, different types of businesses and newly emergent professions employed more of them. The more corporations required college degrees as prerequisite for employment, the more higher education became "the personnel office for white-collar America" (Lemann, 1995, p. 97). The framers of the National Defense Education Act rationalized that if more qualified students were recruited by top colleges, they would become scientists working on projects to enhance the nation's security. Instead, most of them went into law, medicine, finance, and teaching in areas other than science. Thus, the dream that by investing in higher education the government could develop the workforce and equalize access to economic opportunity was, as Lemann (1995) stated, "substantially realized in the intake, but not in the outflow" (p. 97).

## Research

From the beginning of the University Transformation Era, higher education leaders contended that research was good for industry, and the institutions gained support from industrialists. In the Mass Higher Education Era, they contended that research was essential for national defense, and they gained funding from governmental agencies. Funds from the states were acquired by pointing out that the universities would assist in economic development. In large measure, such rationalizations were based on true outcomes. Many industrial processes were pioneered in university research laboratories, and entire industries, such as electronics, were based on such efforts. The universities operated atomic research laboratories and conducted basic research that supported the development of weapons systems. Most state universities could point both to research in agriculture that led to better crop yields and land use, and to local industries that grew because of the state's trained workforce.

The research emphasis changed higher education. By combining undergraduate instruction, research, and professional training in the same institution, the universities gained strength and independence even while the contradictions among the three purposes resulted in internal tensions. Additional friction points emerged as separately organized research centers within universities began acting as independent organizations, sometimes competing with academic departments by providing research support to faculty members and, in effect, enabling them to buy their way out of teaching responsibilities. During the Mass Higher Education Era, the research effort was so stimulated and so successful that it became tantamount to the academic ethos; faculty in research universities became the normative group to which faculty in other institutions aspired. Because scientific research had become the *sine qua non* of a major university and because it was so expensive, the institutions leading in the research effort and those aspiring to move into the top ranks of research universities had to find increasing amounts of money to pay for faculty who taught fewer students and for the laboratories and equipment that research demanded.

One result of this effort was a symbiotic relationship between the research universities and the industries that both supported them and benefited from their work. The electronics industry was one of the first to grow along with university-based work in electrical engineering. Varian Associates and Hewlett-Packard both had close ties with Stanford. "What clearly had emerged by 1950 was a triangular nexus between electrical engineering at

Stanford, the Department of Defense, and the electronics industry" (Geiger, 1993, p. 121). Different types of university organizations and different relationships with governmental agencies and industries developed. Separate research centers, institutes, and laboratories that were organized within universities coordinated research, individual budgets, and the work of faculty members.

Some of these centers, institutes, and laboratories became dominant in their field. The Michigan Institute for Social Research and the Columbia Bureau of Applied Social Research, both dating from the 1940s, developed the methodologies and set the standards for sociological studies. The National Opinion Research Center at the University of Chicago similarly gained respect for the validity of its work. The Jet Propulsion Laboratory at the California Institute of Technology and the Lawrence Livermore Laboratory at the University of California took the lead in space exploration and nuclear physics development, respectively. MIT had several organized research units with military connections: its Research Laboratory of Electronics, Center for International Studies, and Instrumentation Laboratory were funded by and worked closely with military units, including the Air Force, CIA, and Office of Naval Research. In some of the research universities early in the era, budgets for funded research were larger than academic budgets.

Faculty who were interested in research thrived on the system. They maintained intellectual sovereignty in their fields and sought grants for projects that fit their expertise. The universities earned overhead on awards to faculty and often were able to support lesser-funded areas with the money provided. Faculty gained autonomy because they controlled allocation of the money they brought in. In addition, the universities gained prestige, which was useful in attracting donations, as well as the ability to sustain less-popular programs. Students gained support for their graduate studies, and the federal government and many large corporations gained the products of research without having to build their own research enterprises. The outcomes were manifold, complex, and interrelated.

**Critiques and Commentaries**

In 1974, the editors of *Daedalus*, the journal of the American Academy of Arts and Sciences, invited more than 100 people to write essays reflecting on the previous 10 years of higher education and to consider where the enterprise might be headed. Around 80 university professors and presidents, psychologists, theologians, and other authors responded. They were sobered by the upheavals that higher education had experienced in the prior decade. Little boosterism appeared; more prominent were comments on the problems colleges and universities faced and the need for (and likelihood of) reform. Most of the authors perceived the dawning of an era of consolidation, little or no further growth, and demands for institutional accountability, often perceived as a turn away from the freedoms that higher education had long enjoyed.

These articles both reflected the myriad concerns about higher education expressed in the preceding century and foreshadowed some that would be articulated in the ensuing decades. How much education should be general in nature and how much specialized? How can education for an elite be reconciled with equality in access and opportunity? Why do the institutions insist on the doctorate as preparation for their faculty when so few professors pursue a research agenda? Why does higher education devote most of its resources to educating young people when lifelong learning might be a more useful goal?

In a sign of the times, however, few of the authors called for racial equity or the development of a multicultural curriculum—those demands became more prominent in the years that followed. Although some noted that the rising tide of expectations would engulf the colleges eventually, forcing them to revise their positions on egalitarianism, they used the term diversity not in terms of the racial, ethnic, or gender makeup of a student body but to indicate a variety of types of programs and institutions. Further, despite a new focus on access to higher education, the idea of equity was still distant and many of the authors commented on it disparagingly, mentioning how attempts to rectify unequal treatment would exhaust the moral and intellectual energies of the enterprise. For example, in 1974, Bloom wrote, "What we are witnessing is the routinization or bureaucratization of the radical egalitarianism which was the essence of the student demands of the sixties" (p. 66). Some authors acknowledged that student activism had been influential in enhancing civil rights both within higher education and in the broader community, but few predicted that social justice activism would continue. Indeed, several noted that the ethnic studies courses that were introduced as a result of student demands were already subsiding. According to Notre Dame's President Hesburgh (1974), "Most of the Black studies programs introduced during the student revolution are either dead or moribund" (p. 69).

The authors acknowledged that the years of activism resulted in students' gaining representation on university councils but believed it had made little difference to institutional governance. Relaxing the rules governing student behavior was viewed as a mixed blessing. On the one hand it sent the message that students were adults and responsible for their own actions; on the other, it suggested that the institution did not care what the young people in its charge did. Hesburgh (1974) summed the activist era by saying, "The worst results of the happenings of the sixties were the crisis of confidence and loss of nerve they produced in the universities, coupled with a growing disdain and even contempt for the universities on the part of those who had loved them most: parents, alumni, benefactors, legislators, students, too" (p. 70). But neither he nor other authors translated this disdain into reduced support. They sensed that the university had lost some of its opacity and mystique but argued that its framework had survived. Its governance structures, faculty roles, and curriculum had been attacked and shaken, but with minor adjustments would continue as before.

In particular, few of the authors predicted that the loss of confidence in colleges and universities would lead to a time when the institutions had to struggle to maintain support. They did not anticipate the rapid rise of tuition such that its proportion of overall revenues would double. Even Clark Kerr, who saw the failure of several public bond measures as evidence of a loss of confidence in the sector, did not foresee the difficult fiscal times ahead. Some of the authors pointed out that institutional costs would continue to rise more rapidly than revenues because of pressure for salary increases and other inflationary factors that would not be accompanied by increased productivity. But overall, the shock of the student activism of the 1960s and early 1970s had the most marked effect on the commentary and predictions of *Daedalus* essayists.

The Carnegie Commission on Higher Education's publications of 1968 to 1973 were followed by another set of books published by its successor, the Carnegie Council on Policy Studies in Higher Education (1980). Together, the reports totaled 118 volumes offering essays on what colleges ought to be; providing examinations of every type of institution; speculating on the proper role of students, faculty, and administrators; and publishing statistical compendia verifying everything that had happened in higher education in the prior few decades. The resultant recommendations were rather straightforward: higher education deserved support as a valuable resource for the nation; its students should pay a higher percentage of the cost because they were the ones who benefited most directly; a wide array of institutions from community colleges to liberal arts colleges and universities, both public and private, should be sustained.

The Carnegie Commission straddled the fence about higher education's role and responsibilities in criticizing society. It supported academic freedom and social critique by individual students or faculty, but believed the system as a whole should temper its criticism, as too much would lead to ideological positioning and backlash from the institutions' main supporters. The commission thus advised against colleges and universities taking any direct action on an issue, favoring instead the development of rules to guide evaluation and analysis. Rather than specify changes, institutions should enhance society's capacity for self-renewal and recommend possible ways of addressing social inequities.

The Carnegie series, along with the essays in *Daedalus*, all written by authors frequently characterized as the intellectual elite, presented few alternatives to the existing structure of higher education. Many of them deplored certain aspects of how the system operated, but their commentaries usually concluded with pleas to support the status quo, or at least their favorite program, institution, or practice within it. Few changes that would address how the system reinforced or contributed to economic or racial inequities were mentioned. Affirmative action was but dimly seen. Community service was defined as opening access to all who wished to attend, thus enabling people to take their place as higher-paid members of the workforce and as responsible citizens. Other forms of direct social action were considered much beyond the scope or the purposes of higher education.

Many authors noted the impending decline in the number of 18-year-olds in the American population and, together with a leveling in the rate of college-going exhibited by recent high school graduates, predicted enrollment declines for the 1980s. Many deplored the tendency of higher education institutions to be managed like business corporations, with administrators making decisions based on economic principles and on satisfying a broad internal and external constituency. The differences between faculty who wanted the freedom to pursue their interests and governing boards or state officials who wanted to rationalize institutional costs and outcomes seemed irreconcilable. Several analysts insisted that a college should not be measured in terms of outcomes, impacts, or benefits, arguing that the nature of learning and the human experience could not be so readily captured.

The move toward secularization, community service, and activities on behalf of industry or government came in for its share of opprobrium. One commentator's view of the trend led him to conclude that it "means that the college or university as an institution is becoming less distinguishable from other institutions in this society such as business, government, deliberative bodies, or the Pentagon" (Tollett, 1975, p. 293). To Tollett, unionization and cost-benefit analyses made higher education like a business; programs designed for community uplift or social welfare made it like government; a preoccupation with shared governance and constituency formation made it like a deliberative body; and "proliferating bureaucracies and mindlessly escalating budgets are reminiscent of the Pentagon" (p. 293).

Despite these critiques, by the close of the Mass Higher Education Era, the system was so complex and so successful that it ignored criticism the way that a supertanker traveling at high speed shrugs off an errant wave. It was a huge economic engine devouring billions of dollars every year. It had (theoretically) mitigated the problem of access for everyone who wanted to attend by erecting 1,000 community colleges while preserving every type of institution that had ever been founded: residential and commuter, liberal arts and occupational, single-sex and coed, religious and secular. Its faculty gained raises that brought them into the category of adequately paid professionals. Its programs were so diverse that the logo "Any person, Any study," coined at Cornell 100 years earlier, was surpassed; the 3,000 institutions and branch campuses available meant that "Any person, Any study, Any place" was now a reasonably accurate description of the system. Colleges and universities engaged in basic and applied research, general education, developmental education, professional development, skills training, career upgrading, and personal interest studies. The system sustained its definition of productivity as passing more students through to graduation and its definition of prestige as high selectivity in student admissions, faculty publications and awards, and a sizeable amount of extramural grant funding. It had weathered attacks from within and outside. It was a marvel, if not the envy of the world.

As a result, the Mass Higher Education Era often has been characterized as the golden age for American colleges and universities. Indeed, several of the trends outlined in the Introduction to this book leveled or peaked around the end of the era. This prompts several questions:

- The ratio of part-time faculty climbed to 30% of the total by the end of the era. Did this, coupled with faculty unionization, presage the end of the century-long trend toward faculty professionalization? What other factors may have contributed to this reversal?

- Other nations saw population expansion and pressure for higher education enrollment but did not erect community colleges to accommodate the new students. What alternatives did they employ? Could the United States have accomplished its egalitarian goals without expanding a network of low-cost, open-access institutions that provided both transfer preparation and occupational training?

- Why were hardly any public liberal arts colleges formed during this period of massive institutional expansion?

- Student activism during the era was focused primarily on civil rights, the Vietnam War, and specific institutional policy and programmatic changes. Did the fervor of one cause feed the others? What factors contributed most to the sharp decline of activism around the end of the era?

- The years in which high levels of federal support for university research and large increases in federal student aid overlapped evidenced a high-water mark for governmental support of higher education. Did the enhanced aid to students contribute to a reduction in federal support for research or were other factors more responsible for this decline? Will America ever again make such a large public investment across the system or was this level of governmental support unique to the Mass Higher Education Era?

- In what ways were American colleges and universities affected by the communist witch hunts, super-patriotism, and repression of free speech during the 1940s and 1950s? Are there contemporary parallels to these events and have they had similar effects on higher education?

# 5

# Maintaining the Diverse System in an Era of Consolidation: 1976–1993

The period from the mid-1970s to the mid-1990s was marked by a continuation of several trends in American society and some events that could be considered turning points. The trends included an aging population, increased participation in education at all levels, and a higher ratio of women in the workforce. The events were the end of the Cold War, the demise of the Soviet Union, and on the domestic scene, revisions in the tax codes that led to an increased gap between the highest and lowest income quartiles. Some of the trends from the prior 30 years reversed: organized labor's influence diminished, the ratio of part-time to full-time jobs increased, the percentage of citizens participating in civic affairs decreased, and immigration accelerated, but with Central and South America and Eastern Asia, rather than Europe, accounting for most of the new arrivals.

## Societal Context

The 1980s marked a shift in America's relations with the rest of the world. U.S. troops had left Vietnam at the start of the era, but the communist threat was perceived as continuing. In 1983, President Reagan declared the Soviet Union to be an evil empire bent on world conquest—one that must be stopped by the United States as leader of the forces of freedom, light, and progress. Interventions were made in El Salvador, Nicaragua, and Grenada on the grounds that communist influence there had to be rooted out. Within

Eastern Europe, the Poles, Hungarians, and several other national groups held free elections and sent Soviet troops away. The Berlin Wall came down in 1989 after 29 years of dividing the city, and by the end of the following year, East and West Germany were united.

At home, the federal debt continued climbing, fueled in part by tax reductions enacted during the 1980s. The Reagan and George H.W. Bush administrations attempted to reduce domestic spending for welfare, health, and various other social programs, but because of continued increases in military spending and interest payments on the debt, as well as the growing costs of Social Security and Medicare occasioned by an aging population, the federal budget expanded. Annual growth in productivity slowed to 1%, but GDP growth averaged 3.9% per year, as it had since 1950 ("Making America Rich," 1998).

**Changes in the Labor Force and Income Inequality**

Deregulation became an article of faith in the 1980s. Spurred by President Reagan's promise to reduce governmental involvement, legislators restricted antipollution laws and those governing health and safety in the workplace. Organized labor was set back when the air traffic controllers went on strike in 1981 and were replaced by nonunion workers. Labor would not begin to recover until 1997 when the United Parcel Service strike was settled on terms favorable to the Teamsters Union. But by then only 10% of private sector employees worked under union contracts.

The weakened unions proved unable to protect full-time positions. A high proportion of new jobs created in the 1980s paid less than poverty wages; between 1981 and 1987 the number of people working for minimum wage grew from just over 5 million to nearly 8 million. The number of women working outside the home climbed, passing the 70% mark in 1990—a year when well over half of all mothers with children under the age of six were in the labor force. Many people were laid off because of so-called restructuring, which typically meant the dismissal of full-time employees in favor of part-timers who could be paid a lower wage, denied benefits and retirement packages, and dismissed whenever conditions warranted.

This change in the configuration of the workforce led to an increased disparity between the incomes of the wealthy and the poor. By 1989, there were around 1.5 million millionaires and at least 50 billionaires in the United States. "The share of national income going to the wealthiest 1 percent rose from 8.1 percent in 1981 to 14.7 percent in 1986 . . . . The bottom fifth of income distribution suffered a 1 percent decline . . . from 1973 to 1979, but a 10 percent decline from 1979 to 1987" (Jordan and Litwack, 1994, pp. 481–482). The 20th, 50th, and 95th percentiles in family income rose together from the 1950s to the late 1970s, then diverged as inequity widened. The gap between the upper and lower 20% of the population grew greater than in any other major industrial nation. In 1993, 66,500 federal tax returns indicated income of more than $1 million, up from 32,000 returns in 1983 (Wessel, 1998). Most of the progress toward economic equality made in the postwar boom was lost, even though by the late 1990s the unemployment rate had dropped to a level lower than it had been for 30 years.

## Public Health and Health Care

The health care sector changed notably as well. By the mid-1990s, the United States spent 14% of its GDP on medical care, compared with around 6 to 7% in Japan and less than 6% in Britain. Attempts to bring health care costs under control led to managed care through health maintenance organizations (HMOs) and other arrangements whereby costs and types of treatment were decided less by physicians and patients and more by insurance companies. By 1995, 39% percent of all physicians were salaried employees of HMOs, whereas only a decade earlier 90% had been self-employed.

The change in the health care industry was accompanied by changes in public health, many of which were confounded by broader social concerns that affected attitudes about them. Smoking was banned on airplanes, in restaurants, and in public buildings in many states. Dietary labeling on food packages spread. But the United States still suffered the world's highest murder rate; drug use expanded despite First Lady Nancy Reagan's "Just Say No" and other campaigns to educate people against the evils of substance abuse; and AIDS, unknown before the early 1980s, assumed epidemic proportions and contributed to new levels of homophobia, especially toward gay men.

Questions surrounding a woman's right to terminate an unwanted pregnancy were hotly debated. In the landmark *Roe v. Wade* decision of 1973, the U.S. Supreme Court ruled that the due process clause of the Fourteenth Amendment provides a fundamental right to privacy, which protects a woman's right to an abortion. Although the decision was highly controversial at the time and contributed to a mobilization of (predominantly Republican) anti-abortion politicians seeking to overrule it or restrict abortion rights for decades, the central tenets of *Roe* were reaffirmed in 1992's *Planned Parenthood v. Casey* and effectively remained the law of the land for nearly 50 years.

**Equal Opportunity**

During the Mass Higher Education Era, much progress had been made toward civil rights and equal opportunity for Blacks and other people of color. The Civil Rights Act of 1964 and the Voting Rights Act of 1965 were attempts to abolish discrimination against African Americans. *Brown v. Board of Education* established that "separate but equal" was inherently unequal. Gradually, beginning in the 1960s, attempts to redress the discriminatory effects of segregation evolved into policies seeking to remedy past discrimination, leading to a number of affirmative action policies in employment and college admissions. However, the air became murky as other racial or ethnic groups—including those that in the 1960 census had been listed as "other"—were added to the list of those deserving equal protection or preferential treatment.

Five distinct racial or ethnic groups were given official status by the Federal Interagency Committee on Education, which codified the groups in 1973. Along with White, Black, and American Indian, the category of Asian American was added and included those of Chinese, Indian, Filipino, Japanese, Vietnamese, Indonesian, and Hawaiian descent, as well as numerous other nationalities and population groupings reaching over nearly half the globe. The final category—ethnic Hispanic Americans—lumped together Mexicans, Cubans, people whose forebears came from Spain or Central or South America, both Black and White people who spoke Spanish, people with Spanish surnames who didn't speak Spanish, those whose families had lived in the United States for generations, and those who themselves immigrated. The arbitrariness of these racial and ethnic categories was revealed frequently, as courts, councils, and legislatures were forced to determine the group to which petitioners belonged. For example, depending on who was counting and for what purpose, Spanish-speaking Black immigrants from the Caribbean might have been labeled Hispanic or African American.

Despite the official designation of racial and ethnic groups and laws attempting to ensure equal opportunity for each, racism—both overt and covert—persisted. Laws were passed forbidding it in one context; it appeared in another. Practically every public action—tax law changes, welfare reform, the choice of school sites, student aid, the content of school textbooks, representation on governmental bodies—was viewed with an eye to which of the racial or ethnic groups appeared to gain or lose benefits. The United States, for most of its history an outpost of Europe, had escaped the worst of the religious prejudice and class warfare that wracked its parent nations for centuries. Instead, it developed its own form of tribalism, directing most of its vitriol toward those whose ancestors had been enslaved or who had journeyed to this country from the South or across the Pacific Ocean.

Nonetheless, the Consolidation Era saw an acceleration of forces striving for proportional representation and differential treatment that would remedy past discrimination and level the playing field for people of various races and ethnicities. Numerous interest groups organized to fight against discriminatory practices limiting the progress of people of color, women, people with disabilities, and other demographic groups. Affirmative action policies, in particular, were based on the idea that different groups must be treated differently to remedy past discrimination and improve outcomes for marginalized people, thus lifting outcomes for all. But while this idea was somewhat supported by the courts (see Access and Affirmative Action, under Students, later in this chapter), the concept of racial equity—controversial enough in the Contemporary Era—was not accepted widely in the Consolidation Era. More comfortable—especially for White people, who comprised nearly three-quarters of the population at the end of the era—was the idea of equality of opportunity: if all groups were provided with equal access (to college, to jobs, etc.), any failure to achieve rested not with society, but with individuals who either chose not to take advantage of certain opportunities or who did not succeed in them.

Education has long been valued for its ability to assist individuals in moving from one social class to the next; less accepted was the notion that institutions of higher education have a larger social role to improve especially the socioeconomic progress of marginalized groups. Most Americans believed that in addition to cognitive ability, luck, on-the-job competence, perseverance, motivation, personal connections, and a host of intangibles also contributed to societal and economic success. Yet fewer people acknowledged that factors related to race or ethnicity, including workplace discrimination, biases in standardized tests, parental education, access to quality schooling or enrichment opportunities—even the zip code in which one grew up—also influenced an individual's likelihood of success.

Equality has always been an elusive goal. Indeed, for most of the nation's history, Americans tended to accept inequality, even as they believed in equal opportunity and endorsed the general principle of fair competition. Thus, even as various interest groups pushed for greater racial, ethnic, and gender representation on campus, in the faculty, and in the workforce, others dismissed efforts to address the unequal outcomes of various demographic groups as unnecessary, impractical, or even antagonistic to the concept of equal opportunity. To them, individual merit should be valued above all else; anyone claiming that the system was rigged against certain groups was accused of playing the victim. For example, in the book *In Defense of Elitism*, Henry (1994) wrote that "self-proclaimed victims of society have lost sight of the proportion of their faith that reflects free will" (p. 138). Similarly, in an op-ed for the *Los Angeles Times*, Thiederman (1996) concluded that, "Equal opportunity is about individual fairness, achievement, ability and the elimination of individual victimization" (p. B9).

For many Americans in the Consolidation Era, government and institutions needed only to ensure equality of opportunity; society should bear no responsibility for equality of outcomes. And while people of color and a few scholars and legal analysts may have understood the limitations of this doctrine, a more widespread acknowledgment that equal opportunity could never be achieved without dismantling the structures and policies precluding social mobility for marginalized groups was decades away. When it entered the public consciousness late in the Contemporary Era, it would reignite many of the racial tensions and distrust of institutions evident in the 1980s and 1990s.

**Distrust in Government**

In the 1980s, the view that virtually all public sector activity was more harmful than beneficial accelerated. This antagonism toward (or at least suspicion of) government was displayed in legislation limiting terms of office, as well as by candidates for public office who promised to reduce the size of governmental programs and limit new taxes. Fewer qualified voters went to the polls: while 63% of registered voters participated in national elections in 1960, only 50% did so in 1988. Expenditures on private security, including residential and commercial guards and security systems, grew so that they were higher than allocations to the police force. By the mid-1990s, more people were employed as private security guards than as public police officers, and the state prisons under construction far outnumbered new college campuses.

Disaffection with governmental processes arises periodically; people forget that the nation's economy has always combined elements of both laissez-faire and governmental stimulation and regulation. In the nineteenth century, both federal and state governments facilitated the expansion of railroads and canals, and in the twentieth century promoted the development of radio, civil aviation, and the electronics industry. Governmental support of basic research led to enhanced processes in everything from farming, to pharmaceuticals, to the government-university-private capital nexus, to gigantic industrial corporations. Still, the United States was in one of its cyclical phases in which belief in a free-market economy, along with puritanical control of personal behavior, dominated.

Thus, the context surrounding higher education shifted during the Consolidation Era. The access that was provided to an earlier generation by the GI Bill was theoretically extended to all people, regardless of race, ethnicity, gender, disability, socioeconomic status, or prior educational preparation. College-going became ever more a necessity for entry into lucrative occupations. The rate of college-going that had leveled from 1965 to the 1980s turned up again, and by the mid-1990s reached a peak never before attained. Collective bargaining for faculty slowed and calls for professors to spend more time teaching and to pay more attention to students accelerated. Private higher education, which many had predicted would disappear, held its own as merit- and need-based governmental programs supplemented tuition payments for students from all socioeconomic groups.

## Institutions

Table 5.1 shows a statistical portrait of the conditions surrounding higher education in the Consolidation Era. The system continued expanding, although college building came almost to a halt after the frenzied pace of the 1960s, when new institutions sprang up in every state. In 1976, there were 1,898 four-year public and private nonprofit institutions; in 1993, there were 2,169. During that same interval, 50 community colleges opened, bringing the total to 1,024. The 30% enrollment growth during the era was accommodated by increased enrollments at preexisting campuses and by building 500 branch campuses. Furthermore, because 43% of students were attending part-time at the end of the era, up from 39%

Table 5.1. Statistical Portrait of the Consolidation Era, 1975–1993.

|  | 1975 | 1993 |
|---|---|---|
| U.S. population | 215,465,000 | 258,939,000 |
| Number of students | 11,185,000 | 14,305,000 |
| Number of faculty | 628,000 | 915,500 |
| Number of institutions (including branch campuses) | 3,004 | 3,638 |
| Number of degrees earned (associate, bachelor's, master's, first professional, and doctoral) | 1,665,553 | 2,167,038 |
| Current-fund revenue (in thousands of current dollars) | 39,703,166 | 170,880,503 |

Sources: NCES Digest, 2007; U.S. Bureau of the Census, 2000.

at the beginning, the institutions' capacity was not as taxed as it might have been.

**Private Institutions**

The status of the private sector is a notable characteristic of the era. In the mid-1970s, several commentators were pessimistic about the survival of private, nonprofit colleges. They looked at inflation and the financial difficulties that plagued the institutions and concluded, "By the 1990s private universities as they are now known could well have disappeared, been absorbed in state systems, or divested themselves of all but their few profitable operations . . . . Some predict Harvard will survive" (Moynihan, 1975, pp. 143, 146). Although the dire predictions did not come to pass, it is not difficult to understand why many thought this might occur. From the beginnings of colleges in America until the mid-twentieth century, the private sector had been dominant. Even after the Morrill Act and the rise of strong public universities, the private institutions' share of enrollment did not decline below half the total. But public enrollments reached parity in 1951, and by 1975 the share enrolling in private institutions declined to 26%, leading one writer to lament, "There is no end in sight" (Lyman, 1975, p. 156).

The defenders of private colleges and universities fell back continually on the argument that pluralism, a diversity of institutions, and autonomous institutions free of external control should be sustained. They deplored the term *postsecondary education*, saying that it described a place "in which proprietary schools of hairdressing or massage techniques rubbed elbows with Yale" (Lyman, 1975, p. 157). In commentary continuing well into the 1990s, private college enthusiasts criticized coordinating boards, oversight commissions, and any other forces that they believed would homogenize higher education and negatively impact private institutions.

Despite predictions of their imminent demise, privately funded colleges and universities proved resilient, cutting costs where they could and finding sufficient funds to sustain operations. The share of enrollment in private, four-year colleges held steady at not much lower than the 1975 level. Unionization of their faculty practically halted after the *National Labor Relations Board v. Yeshiva University* decision in 1980, which determined that tenure-track faculty at that institution were considered managerial and thus did not have the right to bargain collectively. Pell Grants and various student loan programs made it possible for them to continue increasing tuition, a rising stock market helped to triple their endowment income, and gifts and grants tripled as well. By 1994, private sector revenue accounted for 37% of all the funds coming into higher education.

As had been the case for a century, the private sector was dominated by research universities, nonsectarian colleges, and religiously affiliated institutions. The top five institutions in terms of current-fund revenue received from the federal government were private universities, with between one-half and two-thirds of their students enrolled at the graduate level. The sectarian colleges of the Colonial Era were elite and secularized; the remaining sectarian colleges were predominantly small and selective. The liberal arts colleges survived, although many added programs in business and the professions. Institutional diversity—prized as an ideological pillar of American higher education—was intact.

Even though nearly all private institutions expanded the types of programs they offered, thus decreasing the difference between themselves and other institutions, each had programs in which it excelled. Near the start of the era, the Carnegie Commission on Higher Education (1973a) published a classification of institutions, separating them into 18 categories from specialized schools to research universities; private institutions were represented in all of them. In the early 1980s, the National Center for Education Statistics (NCES) developed a similar classification system with 17 categories, and private institutions again appeared in all. The private institutions dominated bachelor's degrees in philosophy, religion, and theological studies and, at the graduate level, in business and psychology. They awarded bachelor's degrees to 54% of their full-timers within six years, compared to 43% of full-time students in public institutions. They enrolled 1 in 5 undergraduates but produced 1 in 3 baccalaureates. Their tuition charges doubled in the 1980s, but their students—most attending on a combination of extramurally funded loans, institutional scholarships and discounts, work-study or other self-generated income, and family support—were not driven away by the increased costs.

## Liberal Arts Colleges

The liberal arts colleges, at least those conforming to Breneman's (1994) purist definition, are one of the most distinctive components of private higher education. Whereas the private research universities look and act much like their counterparts in the public sector, the liberal arts colleges have few duplicates. Their enrollments range from a few hundred to less than 3,000; their student-faculty ratio is rarely higher than 15 to 1, hence their average class size tends to be small. They are single-purpose institutions, educating undergraduate students in the main. Their faculty reward structure centers on teaching and they exercise selective admissions and on-campus residence. They appeal to young people who seek close relationships among students and staff and those who prefer to avoid the tumult associated with large, public institutions.

Most of the liberal arts colleges were able to maintain their uniqueness. More important, from the standpoint of recruiting students, they were able to offer discounts from the posted tuition price. Each attempted to differentiate itself "from its peers by some combination of location, history, religious affiliation, single-sex or racial orientation, curricular emphasis, and perceived quality (or prestige)" (Breneman, 1994, p. 43). They competed with each other on the basis of these qualities and also on the extent to which they were able to fashion financial aid packages that brought their net cost to the student down to an acceptable level.

Even as the number of 18-year-olds in the American population declined in the 1980s, the liberal arts colleges enjoyed a substantial increase in student applications. They became more selective, admitting only 53% of their applicants in 1989, compared with 63% in 1977. After factoring in the percentage of accepted students who enrolled, their overall intake was 30 students for every 100 applicants in 1977 and 21 per 100 in 1991. Because the colleges continually strived to maintain what they considered an optimum size, student-faculty ratio, and financial balance sheet, their number of students remained stable. As an example, annual first-year enrollment at 17 women's colleges totaled 4,866 in 1977 and 4,231 in 1991—an average of 249 students per college in the latter year. First-year enrollments at Presbyterian, Methodist, and Catholic liberal arts colleges were similarly stable throughout the era, hovering at just under 300 students per year (Breneman, 1994).

The most prestigious liberal arts colleges maintained their selectivity, primarily because they were more handsomely endowed and because their allure enabled them to attract a greater number of full-pay students. At the other end of the continuum, lower-prestige institutions attracted students because they kept their tuition low and relied more heavily on extramurally funded student aid. The share of funds that the private colleges derived from all sources remained steady for 30 years prior to 1989, as the proportion gained from endowment income, gifts, and tuition declined slightly and governmental support grew. Expenditures shifted somewhat more significantly, with the percentage of funds devoted to instruction declining from 50 to 38% and that going to physical plant operation and maintenance dropping from 16 to 12%. Expenditures increased in general administration, as administrative demands grew more complex, as well as in college development, recruitment, and student services. Breneman's (1994) analysis of the liberal arts colleges concluded that they were financially sound because their key revenue sources grew more rapidly than their expenditures. In 1992, when state funding for public sector institutions was under attack, concerns about whether the community colleges and state universities would be able to offer the courses that the students wanted were prominent. Private-college recruiters were able to argue convincingly that by limiting enrollment, their institutions would be able to maintain small classes and provide the courses basic to a core curriculum.

Even so, the liberal arts colleges and other institutions in the private sector tended to have excess capacity in the mid-1990s, and calls were made to increase state grants that could be used to defray tuition. In California, for example, a $2,650 maximum grant equaled about 75% of private-college tuition in 1976, whereas by 1991—although the maximum had doubled—tuition had gone up so much that the grant would cover only about 40% of costs to students. The result was that the independent colleges, which at one time educated half of all students who received state aid, matriculated only about one-fourth of them. Private college advocates argued that increasing state funds to students in the private sector would cost the state less than if it had to expand capacity in the public institutions, but such calls largely fell on deaf ears.

The few liberal arts colleges in the public sector developed primarily in the 1960s as alternatives to larger universities. Built within existing state higher education systems, they managed to maintain their appeal much as did the private liberal arts colleges: residential settings, small classes, prescribed curricula. Some of the more successful institutions were the University of California at Santa Cruz, Evergreen State in Washington, the University of North Carolina at Asheville, and Ramapo College of New Jersey, which—along with others of the type—sustained the traditional liberal arts while adding international, multicultural, and interdisciplinary studies.

The faculty in liberal arts colleges typically spent their time differently than their colleagues at the universities. They taught for more hours and were paid less, but there was no shortage of applicants because people who had gone through those types of colleges often wanted to return to teach in them. Clark (1997) reported that faculty in the best undergraduate-centered liberal arts colleges were able to combine an interest in research with their concern for students. Astin and Chang (1995) examined a few colleges that emphasized both research and teaching and found several characteristics common among them. For one, they were all private, residential colleges spending twice as much per student on instruction and 50% more for student services than the norm. They sported frequent interactions among students and faculty; had a strong humanities orientation, including interdisciplinary, history, and foreign language courses; and emphasized student writing and student involvement in the professors' research. The faculty were both interested in students and in writing articles for publication in academic or professional journals. Their list included Bard, Bryn Mawr, Carleton, Occidental, Williams, and a half dozen others. But such institutions were rare. Most of the staff in the liberal arts colleges were strongly interested in student progress, and research was much less a consideration.

## Graduate and Professional Education

Graduate programs and the research universities in which they were housed reached a peak in influence as the Consolidation Era opened. Their academic departments had overpowered the undergraduate curriculum, helping to segment it and reducing its capacity for holistic studies. Their master's and doctoral degrees were requisite for entry to an increasing number of occupations. The institutions were involved thoroughly with service to government and the economy. Their scientific and technical roles so dominated that humanistic studies occupied an ever-smaller portion of the curriculum. Their greater size led to more administrators, and their extramural support base was cultivated continually. The university was a busy place indeed.

The numbers are instructive. By the late 1980s, doctoral-granting universities enrolled more than one-fourth of all students in the United States, and the institutions awarding the master's as their highest degree enrolled almost as many. By 1994, master's degrees were conferred in 1,347 institutions, two-thirds of them private, and doctorates in 473, half private. Concentration was such that the 70 leading institutions awarded 65% of the doctorates and 40% of master's degrees. Practitioner-oriented fields dominated: master's in business, education, health professions, and psychology were awarded in 500 or more institutions; doctorates in biological and life sciences, education, physical sciences, and psychology in at least 200. Of the 2,000 different master's degree programs, 7 in 8 were practitioner-oriented. The public institutions conferred nearly twice as many doctorates and held nearly a 3-to-2 edge in master's degree awards.

The forces affecting undergraduate education, such as expanded access and redefinition of the curriculum, had considerably less effect on graduate and professional schools. Undergraduate studies were influenced by social and political forces, both on and off campus, but fewer calls for redefining the curriculum were directed at the graduate levels. There, program content and research topics might be shaped by external constituencies, but in the main, the programs were still based on cognitive rationality and direct service to the professions. The institutional focus on research maintained its stability in the face of student protests in the 1960s and 1970s and continued despite curricular reform efforts at the bachelor's level.

Clark (1996) discussed the effect of academic growth on universities, especially the splitting and re-forming of academic disciplines. He contended that "disciplinary differentiation is many times greater than institutional differentiation" (p. 419). In other words, the disciplines operate independently from the institutions in which they are housed. When research within academe became a primary activity, faculty produced scholarly reports in increasing volume and, as the various disciplines led to specialized departments and research institutes, further expansion of scholarship within particular fields occurred. Thus, the splitting and re-forming of disciplines is a frequent occurrence, as formerly excluded fields are added and as existing fields extend their coverage. New departments are created along with new scholarly journals and new professional associations. By the 1990s, there were more than 1,000 journals in mathematics. Psychology had split into 45 major specialties; one of them—social psychology—had 17 subfields. This disciplinary fragmentation added to system complexity and led "to more esoteric academic specialties that organizationally [became] elite enclaves" (Clark, 1996, p. 424). Research universities and other institutions in the same system grew further apart as the former enhanced its research capacity and emphasized research as the primarily faculty role, while the other institutions focused primarily on teaching and access for greater numbers and different types of students.

Increases in the number of degrees awarded in professional schools and in the number of schools awarding them that had swelled in the Mass Higher Education Era continued rising through the late 1970s but then flattened out. Between 1983 and 1993 the total number of first professional degrees conferred showed little growth. Some fields actually declined—dentistry and theology most notably. Degrees in pharmacy showed the greatest increase. And nursing education continued its steady march toward requiring higher degrees for entry into practice.

The law schools moved toward an increased emphasis on clinical education, training for public policy, and a concern for relevant social activities. The number of institutions conferring the LLB or the JD increased slightly, from 166 in 1976 to 184 in 1993; degrees awarded, most in three-year programs, rose by 23%. Although the demand for legal services increased and large law firms employed greater numbers of graduates, the market for newly minted attorneys was fragmented. In some cases, the legal profession faced competition from accountants, as tax attorneys found their practice overlapped with graduates of accounting programs. Many attorneys also had to concern themselves with the laws of other nations as their practice was involved with international trade. But in general, the legal profession still was protected by state regulations regarding entry, and the various specializations accommodated each other within the schools.

The number of institutions awarding the doctor of medicine (MD) increased from 107 to 122 during the Consolidation Era, and the number of degrees awarded rose by 16%. However, this was in step with the increased population, and although some specialties seemed overpopulated, there was certainly no glut of general practitioners. Most of the private universities either received public funds or obtained grants and contracts for research, training, and patient-care activities. Some medical schools were freestanding; most were affiliated with universities, but all had some association with a teaching hospital in which they had "complete control over medical management" (Rothstein, 1992, p. 1166). Many of the basic medical science courses were taught by specialists in biological sciences, not necessarily physicians, but clinical faculty were usually members of the medical profession. Practically all the internships were taken in hospitals associated with the schools so that the faculty were involved directly. Medical research was so much a part of physician training that the joint MD–PhD was well established. One of the continuing concerns in medical education has been the relative emphasis that the programs placed on research and patient care, with a concomitant issue being specialization versus holistic studies. The growing dominance of HMOs in the delivery of medical care in the United States had yet to have a marked influence on the conduct of the medical schools.

The bachelor's of science in nursing (BSN) became the preferred degree for nurse practitioners, relegating the associate degree in nursing (ADN), conferred primarily by the community colleges, for nurses' aides and other subspecialties. Even so, the ADN was awarded to 54,000 students in 1993 and the BSN to 39,000. The master's of science degree was awarded to clinical specialists and the doctorate in nursing for those conducting research in the field. As with all professions, the conversion of degree requirements took many decades to be realized. The one certainty was that nearly all nursing education had come under the oversight of degree-granting institutions of higher education, while the clinical-practice component (but not the control) remained in the teaching hospitals.

Theological studies—the centerpiece of the Colonial Era colleges—barely held on in the universities. In no other field was the historical secularization of higher education as illustrative. Because there were no rules governing the ordination of ministers, any school could begin a program and award degrees in divinity. Therefore, most theological training took place outside the formal higher education establishment in numerous seminaries that specialized according to religious bodies and doctrinal differentiations within them. Religiously affiliated institutions constituted nearly half the private institutions of higher education in 1993—a slight increase from their proportion at the start of the era—but few specialized in training theologians.

Teacher education had moved from normal schools to four-year colleges and universities prior to the start of the Consolidation Era. Few freestanding schools of education remained. By 1993, the number of bachelor's degrees awarded in education was equaled by the number of master's degrees and doctorates in that field. Teacher education was provided in every type of college, public and private. And even though the major research universities deemphasized teacher training, most of them retained schools of education that conducted research and awarded graduate degrees. In many states, public school teachers were required to hold undergraduate majors in one of the subjects they would teach, but a fifth year of coursework or a master's degree in education was prevalent. And because practically all school systems granted salary increases to teachers who obtained higher degrees, the universities that maintained graduate programs in education continued enrolling numerous practitioners who attended part-time, even as they worked in the schools.

Accordingly, graduate and professional education remained prominent in the Consolidation Era as schools broadened their base of support and avoided most of the controversies that afflicted the undergraduate programs. The professional schools enjoyed the luxury of sustaining selective admissions policies as the number of students seeking access increased relative to the number of admits. Because graduate and professional education depended heavily on internships, apprenticeships, and clinical studies, it was more difficult to expand than was undergraduate education, much of which could be opened to greater numbers of students merely by adding chairs to a classroom. Even though some commentators continually accused graduate and professional schools of not being sensitive to the employment market, more master's and doctoral recipients were able to find employment in the fields for which they were trained than was the case for graduates at other levels.

**Community Colleges**

The community college sector reflected the consolidation that marked the beginning of the era. The number of colleges, the ratio of full- to part-time students, and the types of degrees awarded showed little change between the mid-1970s and 1993. The percentage of associate degrees conferred in occupational areas (which had reached 58% in the mid-1970s) was at just over 60% by the mid-1990s (Kisker, Cohen, and Brawer, 2023). The number of public colleges nearly tripled in the 20 years prior to 1975, going from 336 to 981, but less than 50 were added in the ensuing 20 years. The colleges accommodated the 33% increase in enrollment by adding buildings, extending instructional hours, providing classes in rented space off campus, opening branch centers, and employing additional part-time faculty. In 1976, the community colleges enrolled 34% of all students in higher education; by 1993, this had risen to 37%. The percentage of part-time students—63% in 1980—rose to 65% by 1990. At the beginning of the era, half of all community college faculty were employed part-time; by 1992, 60% were part-timers, twice the ratio employed at four-year institutions. Part-time students were taught by instructors who shared at least one of their characteristics.

Community colleges had become a permanent component of American higher education. At the end of the Consolidation Era, the colleges enrolled around 45% of all first-year students, and more than 25% of those who completed at least four courses transferred to in-state, public universities within four years of matriculation. The existence of open-access community colleges enabled the public university systems in nearly every state to maintain their selective admissions policies; without an institution available to receive nearly half those seeking higher education—80% in some states—universities would have faced immense pressure to expand their first-year classes and admit contingents of students that they considered underprepared.

Community colleges remained attractive to older students, especially those seeking to acquire skills that would enable them to enter a new career or upgrade their standing in a job they already had. In 1993, nearly 15% of community college students were age 40 or older. Tuition and fees at community colleges held steady at around 48% of the cost of attending an in-state, public, four-year institution. These lower fees meant that community college students received less financial aid. Indeed, by 1994, the colleges enrolled 48% of all undergraduates attending public institutions, but their students received only 30% of Pell Grant dollars. Nonetheless, as low-cost, well-located institutions, the colleges were in good position to accommodate a majority of the rising population of college seekers.

## The System

By the end of the Consolidation Era, the higher education system that had evolved over the centuries since the colonies were formed had reached a stage of diversity, complexity, and comprehensiveness that could never have been foreseen. It had become a set of institutions related by a medium of exchange and arranged by loosely followed principles of sequence. Each institution maintained courses, curricula, student and faculty relationships, and requirements that looked decidedly like those in other institutions.

Higher education had become, in effect, a national system that could not be described merely by examining its legal arrangements or the structure of its institutions. It was more a social system with rules of conduct, sets of shared beliefs, and expectations on the part of students, staff members, and the public.

The system's medium of exchange has been the degrees conferred and the transcripts recording student progress through the courses—the instruments by which activities in one institution are recognized as those that go on in another. If these documents are not recognized by the majority of institutions within the system, the institution that issued them is not perceived to be part of the core group. Even though most of the students in proprietary or for-profit schools can apply federal financial aid toward their tuition, the credits they earn carry no value within the graded system of higher education.

The system grows in certain standard ways. When the number of people wishing to attend increases, higher education either adds institutions or adds to the size of each unit. It often takes on functions that other social structures have carried out, as when it added occupational and professional education formerly provided through apprenticeships. In the Consolidation Era, it added the function of striving toward equity in admissions by adopting procedures designed to admit more students from historically underserved races and ethnicities. It sometimes relinquishes functions. For example, it effectually abandoned responsibility for nurturing adolescents.

Through the end of the twentieth century there was a relatively stable ratio between those who entered the system and those who exited holding certificates or degrees. In 1970, 8 million students were enrolled in higher education, and 1.27 million degrees were awarded. In 1993, 14.3 million students were enrolled, and 2.22 million degrees were awarded. The ratio was nearly the same in both years: 1 degree for every 6.5 students. This consistency was possible—despite fluctuations in the number of students entering the system—because some institutions graduated virtually everyone admitted whereas others maintained relatively high attrition rates. It came down to selectivity: in the Consolidation Era, community colleges awarded degrees to only around 10% of their students, but Princeton and Pomona graduated practically all their matriculants.

A consistent ratio also existed because standards tend to be elastic across higher education and are protected within the academic system. For example, a professor who gives a certain distribution of grades to one group of students tends to continue awarding that same distribution, even though over the years the students' performance or levels of prior preparation may have increased or decreased substantially; comparing grade distributions at colleges where there have been significant population shifts evidences this. It is a behavior peculiar to academics—an ideology that defends flexible standards. It suggests also that a dominant characteristic of professors is to sort their students—a notion that would be contested in the decades to come.

By the end of the Consolidation Era, the value higher education placed on self-preservation was clear. Its institutions, regardless of type, were exceedingly skilled at sustaining themselves; their capital campaigns, legislative lobbying, and ability to deflect criticism were well refined. Driven both by a uniquely American egalitarian impulse and a desire to maintain its most elite and selective structures and practices, the system endured. Its most stable feature was the provision of pathways that allowed students to transfer credits from college to college; its most unstable was the variability of costs among institutions.

## Students

College enrollments continued growing as more adult students, more part-time students, more female students, and more students from previously underrepresented races and ethnicities entered the system, and as students took longer to complete degree programs.

Students' proficiency at entry changed little overall. Following student demand, some fields fell out of popularity while others boomed. Costs increased, but more financial aid was available, so the net cost to students and families was more stable.

**Enrollment and Diversity**

The drive for more years of schooling is seen in data showing that between 1975 and 1993, undergraduate enrollment rose by 31% and graduate enrollment by 27%. Much of the increase was propelled by a rise in the proportion of high school graduates who enrolled in college the following fall. Although this percentage increased sharply for the first 20 years of the Mass Higher Education Era, it flattened out after 1965; for the next 18 years the rate hovered between 47 and 55%. Beginning in 1984, however, a rapid increase brought the figure to 62% by 1995.

When subdivided by race and gender, the percentage of high school graduates attending college showed some different patterns. As Figure 5.1 illustrates, female undergraduate enrollment approached parity with that of males at the start of the

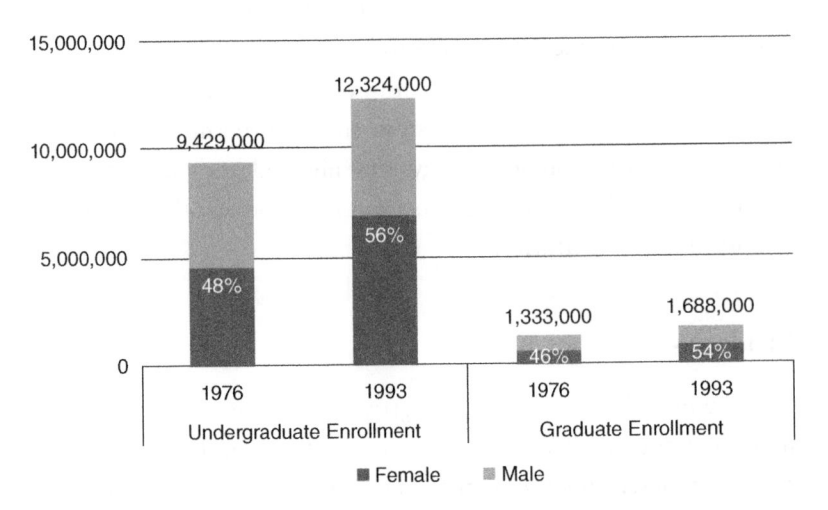

Figure 5.1. Total Enrollment and Percentage Female, 1976 and 1993.

Consolidation Era, after which enrollment of women increased by a considerably greater rate. A similar pattern was evident in graduate enrollments.

The racial and ethnic composition of college students also shifted during the Contemporary Era. In Fall 1995, just under three-quarters of all undergraduates where White, down from 83% in 1976; 11% were Black or African American (up from 9%); 8% were Hispanic or Latinx (up from 3%); and 6% were Asian or Pacific Islander, up from 2% at the start of the era. The percentage of Indigenous students remained steady at about 1% (see Figure 5.2). Although nearly all racial and ethnic groups increased their representation on college campuses, the rise in the number of Hispanic or Latinx students did not keep pace with increases in that population, and in 1993 only 22% of Hispanic 18-to-24-year-olds were enrolled in college, compared to one-quarter of African Americans and 37% of Whites. Students of color were overrepresented (in comparison to their proportion

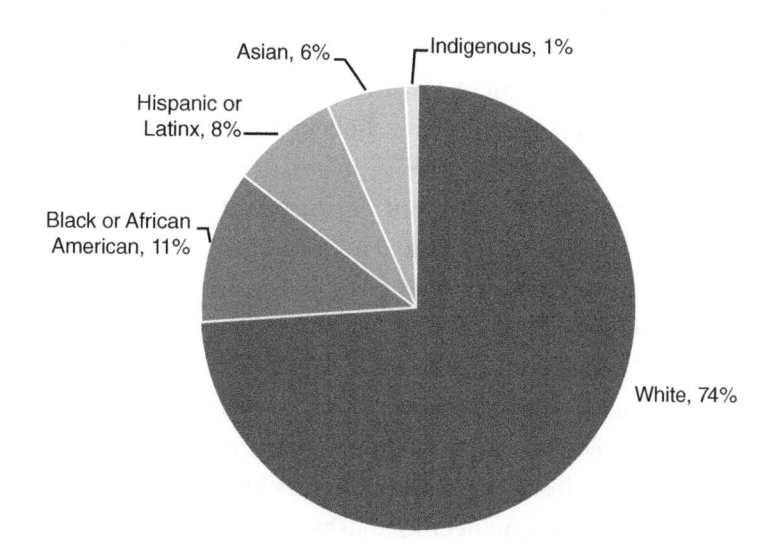

Figure 5.2. Percentage of Enrollment by Race or Ethnicity, Fall 1995.

of the 18-to-24-year-old population) in community colleges and proprietary trade schools, and underrepresented in four-year colleges and universities.

The increase in enrollments across all racial and ethnic groups surprised many analysts who had viewed the precipitous drop in the number of 18-year-olds in the population that was projected to occur between 1979 and 1992 and concluded that enrollments would drop as well. The Carnegie Council on Policy Studies in Higher Education (1980) predicted a decline of between 5 and 15% in undergraduate enrollments between the mid-1970s and the mid-1990s. Along with other analysts, they did not anticipate a higher high school graduation rate or the increased rate of college attendance by younger and older students alike. For example, the percentage of 22-to-24-year-olds enrolled in college increased from 16% in 1975 to 23% in 1995, and enrollment of 25-to-29-year-olds from 10 to 12%. During those same years, the percentage of 18-to-19-year-olds enrolled went from 47 to 59% and that of 20-to-21-year-olds from 31 to 45%. Some longitudinal data confirmed the cross-sectional numbers. Adelman (1994) analyzed the senior high school class of 1972 and found that within 15 years, 56% of the group had entered college, and roughly 2 out of 3 had attended a college, university, or proprietary school during that time. In brief, around 3 million people graduated from high school in 1972, and by 1986 over 1.8 million of them had participated in some form of postsecondary education. The enrollment picture that had looked so dismal to observers watching the decline in the number of 18-year-olds turned out to be much rosier than most had expected.

Increased enrollments led to more degrees at all levels and to a shift in the fields in which degrees were awarded (see Table 5.2). In particular, education, mathematics, foreign languages, and physical sciences lost ground, while degrees increased dramatically in the health fields, engineering, business, communications, and computer sciences. Master's degrees awarded tended to follow the patterns for bachelor's except in business, where they increased by

Table 5.2. Changes in Earned Bachelor's Degrees by Selected Field, 1975–1976 and 1994–1995.

| Field | 1975–1976 | 1994–1995 | % Change |
|---|---|---|---|
| Education | 154,437 | 105,929 | –31 |
| Mathematics | 15,984 | 13,494 | –16 |
| Modern foreign languages | 17,068 | 14,558 | –15 |
| Physical sciences | 21,458 | 19,161 | –11 |
| Architecture | 9,146 | 8,756 | –4 |
| Social sciences and history | 126,396 | 128,154 | +1 |
| Agriculture | 19,402 | 19,832 | +2 |
| Biological and life sciences | 54,085 | 55,790 | +3 |
| English | 41,452 | 51,170 | +23 |
| Health fields | 53,885 | 81,596 | +51 |
| Engineering | 38,733 | 62,331 | +61 |
| Business | 143,171 | 233,895 | +63 |
| Communications | 20,045 | 48,104 | +140 |
| Computer sciences | 5,652 | 24,737 | +338 |

Source: NCES Digest, 2007.

113% (compared to 63% among bachelor's awards), in engineering, where the 61% increase in bachelor's degrees was exceeded by a 73% rise in the number of master's degrees, and in the health professions, where the 51% increase in bachelor's degrees was accompanied by a 105% increase in master's degrees.

By 1993–1994, women earned 59% of associate degrees, 54% of all bachelor's and master's degrees, 40% of first professional awards, and 38% of doctoral degrees (see Table 5.3). Some of the more notable shifts in degrees awarded by gender were in architecture, where women's share of the degrees awarded went from 20 to 36%; in business, where master's degrees awarded to women increased

Table 5.3. Total Number of Degrees Awarded and Percentage Awarded to Women, 1976–1977 and 1993–1994.

| | 1976–1977 | | 1993–1994 | |
|---|---|---|---|---|
| Degree Type | Number Awarded | % Women | Number Awarded | % Women |
| Associate | 391,454 | 46% | 514,756 | 59% |
| Bachelor's | 925,746 | 46% | 1,165,178 | 54% |
| Master's | 311,771 | 46% | 369,585 | 54% |
| First professional | 62,649 | 16% | 75,387 | 40% |
| Doctoral | 34,064 | 23% | 42,132 | 38% |

Source: NCES Digest, 2007.

from 12 to 36% of the total; and in engineering, where master's degrees awarded to women increased from a minuscule 3.5% to 15% by the end of the era.

The diversity of students contributed to the rise of new enrollment patterns. Specifically, more students attended part-time, worked off campus, and took longer to complete their programs. Part-timers increased from 39% in 1976 to 43% in 1993. Of the students aged 16 to 24 who attended full-time, 36% worked while in college in 1973; 46% did so in 1993. The percentage of students who graduated within five years fell steadily between 1983 and 1996—from 52 to 45% at public institutions and from 60 to 57% at the privates. Dropout rates changed relatively little during this period and not at all at public institutions; the declining graduation rates were primarily a function of the longer average time-to-degree resulting from a rise in part-time attendance.

Technical training for job or skill upgrading gained in popularity. In 1995, 32% of employed workers participated in skill improvement training for their current job; nearly half the people who took job-related courses were college graduates. Many of the students just out of high school who could not find work, as well as many unemployed people who lost their jobs, matriculated at community colleges. The relationship was observed decades earlier: "Community college enrollments rise and fall remarkably in phase with the ups and downs of unemployment" (Betts and McFarland, 1969, p. 749).

**Proficiency**

The proficiency level of students entering higher education has long been a matter of concern, and ways of estimating it have taken various forms. High school grade point averages (GPAs) and patterns of courses taken provided one measure, entrance test scores another. The number of students placed in developmental education also was used as an indicator of student ability, although the criteria on which colleges made those decisions were quite varied. The pattern of courses that students took in high school evidenced efforts to enhance proficiency during the Consolidation Era. In state after state, graduation requirements were strengthened so a considerably greater percentage of high school graduates in 1994 had taken core academic subjects as compared to students graduating in earlier years; half of the 1994 graduates took at least four units in English and three each in science, social studies, and mathematics, compared with only 14% who took this array of courses in 1982. However, the percentage of first-year students enrolled in developmental classes remained steady. In 1995, as in the 1980s, around 30% of entrants took developmental classes in reading, writing, or mathematics.

If students took more units in core academic subjects in high school, why did colleges still maintain sizable developmental programs? Grade inflation was at least part of the problem. Between 1990 and 1994, the American College Testing Program collected data on around 530,000 students per year who were enrolled in more than 5,000 public schools. Using students' grades in mathematics, science, social science, and English, and comparing them with scores on all four tests of the ACT Assessment, analysts found that average test scores remained consistent across the five-year period, but the mean high school GPA increased from 2.94 to 3.04. They concluded that no significant improvement in average student achievement had occurred but that grades had improved, undoubtedly because "grading and the standards teachers use to award grades are relative" based on items other than a student's knowledge of course content, factors "such as attendance, effort, discipline, etc." (Ziomek and Svec, 1995, pp. 6–7).

Proficiency levels were also difficult to document because of the larger proportion of the population staying in school. Since the mid-1970s, the National Assessment of Educational Progress has assessed student knowledge in several subject areas. Trends for 17-year-olds showed the following: reading scores increased between 1971 and 1988 and then declined so that the 1996 scores were slightly ahead of 1971; mathematics achievement was about the same in 1996 as in 1973; science proficiency was lower in 1996 than it had been in 1969; the large gaps in achievement between White learners and students of color narrowed, especially as the proficiency exhibited by Black 17-year-olds improved relative to Whites in mathematics and science (Campbell, Voelkl, and Donahue, 1997).

The greater number of students interested in higher education led to an increase in the number participating in the advanced placement (AP) program. Between 1984 and 1995, the number of students taking AP examinations rose from 24 out of every 1,000 eleventh- and twelfth-grade students to 66 per 1,000. More academic courses taken in high school, more participation in AP programs, higher grades, stable test scores, an increased percentage of young people attending college, and greater percentages of students directed to developmental education—all these factors interacted. Some reinforced and others negated one another; a consistent pattern in student proficiency was difficult to discern.

### Access and Affirmative Action

Student access was enhanced during the Consolidation Era, not only by the increase in various forms of financial aid but also by laws and court decisions, most of which extended trends from earlier eras. Discriminatory policies reducing the likelihood that people of color, women, adult learners, and people with disabilities could attend were struck down continually. In 1982, a male applicant challenged the admissions policy of an all-female nursing school, and the Supreme Court ruled in *Mississippi University for Women v. Hogan* that public institutions could not discriminate on the basis of gender. Subsequent cases affecting private, single-sex colleges such as the Virginia Military Institute and The Citadel extended that ruling. In the 1983 case, *Bob Jones University v. United States*, the Supreme Court upheld an Internal Revenue Service decision that institutions discriminating on the basis of race would be denied tax-exempt status.

The Rehabilitation Act of 1973 and the Americans with Disabilities Act of 1990 both served to extend access to higher education for individuals with disabilities who otherwise met academic and technical standards, and these laws were upheld by the courts. In *Southeastern Community College v. Davis* (1979), the Supreme Court ruled that the college was within its rights in denying the admission of a severely deaf student to its nursing program because the student's disability would preclude her taking part in the clinical aspects of the nursing program and would create serious difficulties in practicing the profession. However, the Court noted the limitations of this case and wrote that in other circumstances institutions might be required to provide sign language interpreters for the hearing impaired. In *Doherty v. Southern College of Optometry* (1988), a federal appellate court ruled that applicants with disabilities must be admitted if they could participate in the program with the aid of reasonable accommodations. This ruling reinforced federal requirements that institutions build access ramps for students with physical disabilities and make accommodations in science laboratories so that those with visual impairments might participate.

The Age Discrimination Act of 1975 prohibited discrimination on the basis of age in any program or activity receiving federal financial assistance. In *Purdie v. University of Utah* (1978), the Utah Supreme Court ruled in favor of a 51-year-old woman who had applied to the educational psychology department and had been rejected because of her age. Earlier, a federal district court had ruled in favor of two 16-year-old plaintiffs who had sought entrance to Sonoma County Junior College in California. That court reasoned that the institution's requirement that students be 18 years old was not rational in relationship to the state's interest in educating qualified students. Other cases brought under the Age Discrimination Act similarly related age discrimination practices to issues of institutional operation and objectives. A medical school's policy of not admitting anyone over 35 years of age because of its goal of producing doctors who would have the most possible years of practice was rejected because maximizing length of practice was not part of the normal operations allowed by the Age Discrimination Act nor was it a basic objective of a medical school. However, in programs in which graduates must demonstrate a certain level of physical fitness, the courts ruled that even though a physical fitness test might have a disparate impact on older applicants, it was permissible because it had a direct and substantial relationship to the job.

The right of state universities to give preferential treatment to in-state residents was also tested by the courts. Most agreed that states have a legitimate interest in prioritizing admission of their own residents, even if this had the effect of limiting access for out-of-state students. However, challenges to a number of states' residence requirements had differing outcomes. In *Starns v. Malkerson* (1970), students at the University of Minnesota argued that a one-year residency requirement affected their fundamental right to travel interstate guaranteed under the Fourteenth Amendment, but a U.S. District court found that such a requirement did not have sufficient impact on that right to be constitutionally impermissible. However, the courts rejected other residency requirements as unconstitutional, as in *Kelm v. Carlson*

(1973), when a court of appeals invalidated a requirement that a University of Toledo law student have proof of employment in Ohio. The courts also rejected statutes mandating that students' residency at the time of application be considered their residency for their entire time as students.

Similar cases tested the rights of states to give preferential treatment to U.S. citizens or to utilize entrance examinations to track students into developmental education. The Supreme Court in 1977 ruled that New York State could not discriminate against permanent residents in granting scholarships, student loans, or other forms of financial aid without showing a compelling state interest. In this case, New York's interest in protecting its citizens or in encouraging green card holders to become citizens was not considered sufficient. Questions of the legality of entrance examinations were raised when colleges used such tests to exclude students from college-level courses and restrict them instead to developmental classes. For example, the California legislature passed a Matriculation Act in 1986 that was designed to improve entering students' reading, writing, and arithmetic through developmental education. Suit was brought against institutions that barred underprepared students from college-level courses, and as a result colleges in the state could only advise (not require) students to enroll in developmental classes if their scores fell below a specified cut-off point. This and similar rulings in other states limited but fell far short of stopping the practice of shunting a great many students—especially students of color—to developmental education.

But of all the laws and court rulings that extended access to higher education in the Consolidation Era, the most impactful by far were those related to affirmative action. As Kaplin and colleagues (2020) wrote, the federal government's initiatives regarding discrimination in the Consolidation Era "had a dual aim: to 'bar discrimination in the future' and to 'eliminate the discriminatory effects of the past'" (p. 201). In a number of cases in the 1970s, the

Supreme Court ruled that affirmative action may be appropriate to address the latter concern, even if it may adversely affect other groups, as "a sharing in the burden of past discrimination is presumptively necessary" (*Franks v. Bowman*, 1976, quoted in Kaplin et al., 2020, p. 201).

Affirmative action originally was promulgated in the mid-1960s to remedy the underrepresentation of certain groups in contracts awarded and employment within and outside of the academy. Four racial groups, along with women, were designated originally, and legislative acts and court decisions subsequently broadened the list to include people with disabilities. By the 1990s, various other subsets of the population were added as protected groups in specific applications: immigrant Portuguese in Massachusetts, Acadians in Louisiana, Hassidim in New York, gays and lesbians in a few universities. However, affirmative action was born of the civil rights struggles spearheaded by African Americans. The inclusion of women and other racial or ethnic groups both extended and diluted its original intent.

Throughout the 1960s and 1970s, affirmative action was based on the belief that talented people were excluded from admission or employment because of racial or gender prejudice. And indeed, the history of higher education gave credence to that argument; substantial race-based barriers, overt and covert alike, could be identified across the system. By the start of the Consolidation Era, most of the laws restricting access to higher education had been struck down, but discrimination persisted and the fact that not all groups participated at the same rate indicated that simply removing legal barriers to entry was not sufficient to overcome all other systemic factors that precluded or discouraged students of color from attending college.

Two major affirmative action cases reached the Supreme Court in the Consolidation Era. In the first, *DeFunis v. Odegaard* (1974), a White male was denied admission to the University of Washington's law school after which he filed suit, claiming that "less qualified minority applicants had been accepted and that, but for the affirmative action program, he would have been admitted" (Kaplin et al., 2020, p. 419). A state trial court found for DeFunis and ordered that he be enrolled. The Washington State Supreme Court later reversed the ruling, stating that the law school had an educational interest in producing a racially balanced student body, but DeFunis was permitted to remain in school during the appeal and by the time the case reached the U.S. Supreme Court, DeFunis was in his final quarter of law school and the case was dismissed as moot.

The second and more consequential case to reach the Supreme Court was *Regents of the University of California v. Bakke*. In 1978, Bakke contended that because the medical school at the University of California, Davis set aside 16 out of 100 places in each class for students of color—whose applications were considered separately—he, a White applicant, had been rejected unfairly (twice). The university justified its affirmative action program on the grounds that the state needed more doctors to work in communities of color, that there was a need to reduce the historic deficit of doctors of color, and that all learners would benefit from a diverse student body. The California Supreme Court found that while there may have been a compelling state interest for the medical school's affirmative action policy, the university had not "demonstrated that the program was the least burdensome alternative for achieving its goals" (Kaplin et al., 2020, p. 420). The California court thus ordered that Bakke be admitted and prohibited the university from giving any consideration to race in admissions.

Upon appeal, and by a 5-4 margin, the U.S. Supreme Court affirmed the first aspect of this ruling—invalidating the medical school's affirmative action program—but a different 5-4 vote reversed the second, ruling that some consideration of race was permittable in certain situations. The nine justices wrote six opinions in the *Bakke* case, none of which commanded a majority of the court. As the only justice in the majority for both votes, however, Justice Powell's opinion provided important guidance for institutions of higher education, and "most colleges and universities with affirmative action admissions plans followed the Powell guidelines" (Kaplin et al., 2020, p. 422). In particular, Justice Powell's opinion established student body diversity as a compelling state interest but discouraged the use of quotas or separate systems for reviewing applicants of color.

The Powell opinion also addressed limitations to the notion of equal opportunity, arguing that "fair appraisal of each individual's academic promise" might not be possible "in light of some bias in grading or testing procedures" (Kaplin et al., 2020, p. 422). Thus, he wrote, if race or ethnicity is only considered for the purpose of "curing established inaccuracies in predicting academic performance, it might be argued that there is no 'preference' at all" (p. 422). A reasonable extrapolation of this argument is that race-blind admissions policies might well have a disparate impact on students of color and low-income learners, who have long suffered from biases in standardized tests and whose prior academic preparation or lack of access to educational resources may have contributed to lower grades or test scores. And indeed, by the early 1990s the doctrine of disparate impact was extended to college admissions. In *United States v. Fordice* (1992), the Supreme Court ruled that Mississippi's exclusive reliance on ACT scores to restrict admission to certain of the state's public universities perpetuated racial stratification. In particular, the Court held that if the tests an applicant must take have a disparate impact on students of color (the most commonly used tests certainly did and do), and if the content of the tests was not expressly relevant to the requirements of the curriculum, their use could be restricted.

During the Consolidation Era, antidiscrimination laws and affirmative action policies led to changes in many areas of higher education. The largest gains were made by women, whose representation on the faculty grew from 23% in 1970 to 39% in 1993. African American, Indigenous, Asian, and Hispanic or Latinx faculty increased from 40,000 in 1980 to more than 65,000 at the end of the era. Increases in the percentage of people of color enrolled in college and gains in degree attainment were substantial across the board but were most pronounced among Asians. Hispanic or Latinx students, who rapidly became the most numerous officially designated ethnic group, benefited least. Yet despite uneven progress, affirmative action rulings contributed to the growing diversity of college students and would not be contested again in the courts until the mid-1990s.

**Behavior**

Throughout the Consolidation Era, the idea that students are entitled to be treated as adults and not subject to any special supervision continued. Although many parents might have preferred that the colleges exercise greater control, the concept *in loco parentis* was virtually abandoned in most of higher education. Once the Twenty-Sixth Amendment—which lowered the voting age to 18—was ratified in 1971, the concept of adulthood dropped to that age, and in most states, 18-year-olds could enter into contracts, be held liable for debts, and enjoy the other privileges of full-fledged citizenship. In the case of *Beach v. University of Utah* (1986), the court summed up the prevalent position when it said that it was unrealistic to impose on a university the role of maintaining custody over its adult students; the institution would have to babysit every student, a task beyond its resources. Furthermore, such measures were inconsistent with the relationship that institutions attempted to sustain with their students and with the objectives of a college education. Nonetheless, institutions still had to maintain a safe environment and protect students from undue risk.

The several thousand chapters of fraternities and sororities on college campuses caused special problems. A lower court decision, later reversed, held that a college was liable for damages because it failed to supervise a student who was paralyzed in an accident during a party at his fraternity house (*Whitlock v. University of Denver,*

1987). In a case brought by a student who had been injured during a fight between two fraternities at the University of Delaware, the trial court took the position that the school had a special obligation to prevent on-campus misconduct. There continued to be a strong undercurrent of opinion, especially in the lower courts, holding that institutions had some responsibility for what happened to their students, even though students were independent adults. Colleges found it more advantageous to enforce limited regulations stringently than to impose general guidelines and overambitious rules. They were supposed to educate, not police, students, but they still had to establish and enforce rules of conduct. For example, a number of states made fraternity hazing a criminal offense, but lower courts ruled that students injured during hazing activities might still name universities as defendants because the institution failed to enforce regulations preventing such activities. However, when students living off campus got in trouble with the local authorities, the institutions were successful in divorcing themselves from the cases on the grounds that it was impossible to monitor the students' behavior.

Responsibility for student employees also received some attention in the courts. In a case decided in Arizona in 1986, the court ruled that although Pima Community College was not exempt from state unemployment compensation laws, a former student who had been employed under the federal work-study program and was no longer working was not eligible for unemployment compensation because he had been a student, not an employee. In a similar case, a scholarship athlete at Indiana State University was seriously injured in football practice and lost his scholarship because he could no longer play. In 1983, the Indiana Supreme Court ruled that because there had been no attempt to enter into an employer-employee relationship in the awarding of the scholarship, the student did not meet the definition of employee and therefore could not receive workers' compensation benefits.

In comparison with the students of the 1960s, those attending in the Consolidation Era were docile in the extreme. No military draft loomed to threaten them; there was no war to protest. International tensions were markedly reduced, especially after the demise of the Soviet Union in 1991. What activism and protests there were centered for the most part on racial or ethnic groups seeking more equitable treatment in admissions and a more relevant curriculum. As the institutions yielded gradually but steadily to such demands, the reasons for campus protests withered. Hate speech and sexual harassment led to a handful of demonstrations, but as institutions enacted rules prohibiting such behavior, these issues also moved away from immediate concern. Few issues were so compelling that students across the land were ready to act in concert. Although a proposed fee increase might trigger a short-lived demonstration on one campus, it did not have the force of a Cambodian bombing or a military draft that could ignite students everywhere.

## Faculty

During the early years of the Consolidation Era, the faculty secured the gains in professionalism that they had made during the Mass Higher Education Era. In addition, faculty demographics shifted quite a bit, with marked increases in numbers of female professors and part-timers. A move toward modifying definitions of faculty productivity so that staff would spend more time teaching and less on research generated much press but was slow in modifying working conditions. Faculty salaries increased throughout the 1970s, dipped in the early 1980s, and turned up again in the 1990s, but overall they barely kept pace with the rate of inflation. Protected by a lengthy history and court decisions protecting academic freedom, institutions of higher education continued as desirable places of employment.

## Demography and Salary

The major shift in faculty demographics during the Consolidation Era was in the increased proportion of women. In the quarter-century preceding 1993, the total number of professors doubled to 915,000, with the number of men employed increasing by 62% and the number of women by 240%. By the end of the era, 39% of the professoriate was female, up from 23% circa 1970; most of that increase occurred in the early 1990s. Female professors were distributed unevenly across higher education institutions; they represented a lower-than-average percentage of the faculty at research institutions, higher than average at community colleges. However, the distribution overall was closer to parity than it had been at any time previously.

Diversification of the faculty by race or ethnicity occurred much more slowly. By 1993, a little less than 5% of full-time faculty were Black or African American (despite constituting roughly 11% of the U.S. population), 5% Asian (3% of the population), and slightly over 2% Hispanic or Latinx (9% of the population). Faculty of color were concentrated in community colleges and comprehensive public universities; representation was also above average at private doctoral-granting institutions.

The average age of the faculty remained low as early-retirement systems and a steady influx of new hires entered the professoriate. In 1992, 36% of faculty were under age 45; 37% were between 45 and 54. Part-timers were even younger—almost half were under age 45. The ratio of full-time to part-time faculty changed considerably. In 1976, roughly 70% of all professors were employed full-time; that figure dropped to below 60% by 1993. The increased hiring in the early 1990s was revealed in the length of time that full-time faculty members had been employed; in 1992 one-third were in the first seven years of their careers. Nearly 17% of new professors were faculty of color and roughly one-fourth were born outside the United States. Women were well represented among the new hires, making up almost 41% of the group.

During the Consolidation Era, faculty salaries tripled; full-timers averaged $16,831 in 1976 and $44,642 in 1993. But academic wages barely kept pace with inflation; the $16,831 in 1976 was worth $42,743 in constant 1993 dollars. In the academic year 1992–1993, faculty received an average raise of less than 4%, slightly more than the rate of inflation, which was 3%. Thus, in inflation-adjusted terms, salaries dipped in the early 1980s, rose in the latter part of that decade, and remained static through the first few years of the 1990s. The figures were affected by the increased numbers of women entering academe who were paid, on average, $10,000 less in 1993 than their male counterparts (see Table 5.4). Certainly, gender bias factored into these lower wages, but female professors also tended to be clustered in the earlier years of their careers, at lower academic ranks, and in community colleges, where salaries actually declined in inflation-adjusted dollars during the Consolidation Era. Nonetheless, in constant dollars, the average salary for female faculty was $36,711 in 1976 and $38,323 in 1993, compared to $44,681 and $48,249 for men. When examined by academic rank, average salaries for men and women showed little difference at the lower ranks, but a spread of around 13% existed at the full professor level, where men were likely to have been in their positions longer.

Table 5.4. Average Salary of Full-Time Faculty by Gender and Type of Institution, 1976 and 1993 (in Constant 1993 Dollars).

|  | 1976 | 1993 |
| --- | --- | --- |
| All faculty | $42,743 | $44,642 |
| Women | $36,711 | $38,323 |
| Men | $44,681 | $48,249 |
| Community colleges | $40,590 | $38,872 |
| Public four-year institutions | $44,646 | $46,440 |
| Private four-year institutions | $41,352 | $46,353 |

Source: NCES Digest, 2007.

Major changes were apparent in certain fields, for example in business, where average salaries for full-timers increased (in constant 1993 dollars) from $45,243 in 1988 to $49,223 in 1993. However, average salaries dropped substantially in other fields, including from $64,860 to $55,624 in health and from $42,420 to $40,972 in humanities. Salaries also differed among types of institutions. In 1993, the average salary for a full-time faculty member on a nine-month contract was $38,935 in the community colleges, $46,515 at public universities, and $46,427 in private universities.

Academic salaries may have looked high in comparison with average wages for all American workers, they but continued to lag behind those of professionals with comparable years of schooling. The AAUP estimated that professors earned 38% less than lawyers, engineers, and health care professionals, "although the gap between our earnings and our professional peer group earnings has narrowed by 16 percentage points since 1979" (Magner, 1997, p. A8). Because many professors stayed on the job longer, some institutions raised the top salary so that these faculty did not hit a salary ceiling, remaining stuck at that level of compensation until they retired. Community colleges were especially affected by sizable proportions of faculty reaching the top of the salary scale. Accordingly, several created the categories of master teacher or senior scholar so that their more productive professors could be paid more. Private universities typically had no such problem and could raise an individual professor's salary as high as the budget allowed. However, public universities often had salary scales locked in place by a systemwide or union contract and thus had to make other arrangements. Many added new steps on the salary scale. The University of California, which had phased in steps four, five, and six in the full professor ranks in the 1960s, added step seven in 1979, step eight in 1988, and step nine in 2000.

### Labor Market

Expectations for faculty preparation remained consistent: the doctoral degree was expected for those entering the faculty ranks at universities, and the master's for those joining community colleges. The number of doctorates awarded annually, which increased notably during the 1960s, topped out at 34,083 in 1975 and remained at that level through the 1980s. But it increased substantially after that, from 35,720 in 1989 to 42,132 in 1993. Master's degrees similarly increased sharply in the 1960s and early 1970s, reaching 292,450 in 1975, then flattening out. Roughly 311,000 master's degrees were awarded in 1989, but by the end of the era, almost 370,000 were conferred annually. Nearly all of these degrees were awarded in the traditional models that had been established by research universities and comprehensive institutions in earlier eras. The doctor of arts programs that began in the 1960s did not spread; few institutions were added to the two dozen or so that had begun such programs earlier. The master's of arts in teaching fared little better; traditional discipline-oriented graduate programs remained the primary preparation for college professors.

Faculty supply and demand remained in equilibrium. Various analysts predicted an oversupply of doctoral degree holders or an undersupply of qualified staff, but the labor market remained constant. Salaries did not keep pace with inflation, but the attractiveness of the academy remained high. For one thing, higher education represented a stable career in an era of instability in the broader labor market, where corporations dismissed long-term employees and cutbacks in fringe benefits became the norm. The supposed overproduction of PhDs relative to demand proved a myth, in large measure because a steadily expanding research enterprise absorbed large numbers of graduates as postdoctoral scholars and because, by 1993, 31% of the doctorates were awarded to non-U.S. citizens, up from 11% at the start of the era.

Because the institutions were concerned that senior faculty, the highest-paid members of the academy, would stay on indefinitely, around 40% of them began offering early retirement incentives by the mid-1990s. These incentive plans were adopted most often at the research universities; three-quarters of such institutions had retirement incentives in place at the end of the era. Most of the retirement systems—funded by the large number of professors entering academe, as well as institutional or state contributions—had become wealthy over the decades. But dollars alone were not sufficient to tempt sizable numbers of senior instructors who enjoyed their work, contact with students, and campus life in general. Furthermore, not every retirement led to a corresponding opening for a full-time junior faculty member. Frequently, the position was collapsed and the professor's responsibilities spread among other staff members, or a part-timer was employed to take up the retiree's responsibilities.

## Tenure, Collective Bargaining, Academic Freedom, and Due Process

The concept of tenure has been part of higher education since 1915, when the AAUP argued that academic freedom and job security were linked. In its most basic form, tenure means that after a probationary period, professors are entitled to continuous employment until they choose to leave or until the institution can show good cause for termination. The question of what constitutes good cause has been argued extensively as professors have been challenged for their views, capabilities, activities on or off campus, and even their cost. Not all institutions have tenure systems, but job rights have been protected nonetheless under prerogatives such as an individual's property interest.

Various contractual relationships define a faculty member's association with the institution. Where there are collective bargaining agreements, the contract may be no more than a form filled in by the professor in which the employee agrees to abide by the terms of the agreement negotiated between the bargaining unit and the institution. Employee handbooks and oral promises made by administrators sometimes can create contracts. AAUP guidelines have been used as evidence of binding agreements. However, in case of dispute, clear contractual language usually prevails unless there are statutes contravening the agreement. Sometimes so-called academic custom and usage is considered by a court when the statutes are not explicit about the behavior and when a contract or agreement is ambiguous.

The early years of the Consolidation Era saw an important case affecting the rights of faculty members to organize into bargaining units and have those units recognized by the governing board of their institution. In 1980, the Supreme Court ruled in *National Labor Relations Board v. Yeshiva University* that because full-time faculty at that institution had managerial responsibilities, they were not considered employees under the federal National Labor Relations Act. However, the Court said also that *Yeshiva* was a specific case; the exemption might not apply in other institutions where faculty had few if any managerial responsibilities. Subsequent rulings applied the managerial exclusion in around half the cases that were brought forward.

In 1992, around one-quarter of all faculty were represented in collective bargaining units; 96% of these were in public institutions (see Table 5.5). Thirty-one states recognized the right of faculty to bargain collectively, but of the 228,856 unionized faculty members, 65% were in California and New York. Overall, unionized faculty in 10 states accounted for 83% of the total. As Table 5.5 illustrates, 1988 represented a high-water mark for the number of institutions with collective bargaining; after that, although the number of unionized faculty grew, most of the growth was within existing units.

The concept of academic freedom was adjudicated in several cases. In *Bishop v. Aronov* (1991), a court of appeals ruled that a University of Alabama professor's First Amendment free speech and freedom of religion rights had not been violated when, in response to student complaints about his introducing religious commentaries in a physiology class, the university told him to desist. The court stated that administrators were entitled to exercise some control over style and content of speech in

Table 5.5. Faculty Unionization by Institutional Type, Selected Years 1984–1992.

| | All Institutions | | Community Colleges | | Public Four-Year Institutions | | Private Four-Year Institutions | |
|---|---|---|---|---|---|---|---|---|
| Year | Number of Institutions | Number of Faculty | Number of Institutions | Number of Faculty | Number of Institutions | Number of Faculty | Number of Institutions | Number of Faculty |
| 1984 | – | 182,964 | – | 68,996 | – | 104,367 | – | 9,087 |
| 1986 | – | 195,570 | – | 76,297 | – | 110,029 | – | 8,052 |
| 1988 | 1028 | 213,673 | 570 | 80,106 | 370 | 123,638 | 73 | 9,108 |
| 1990 | 1007 | 217,398 | 572 | 87,347 | 350 | 119,752 | 71 | 9,742 |
| 1992 | 922 | 228,856 | 565 | 100,750 | 273 | 118,624 | 71 | 8,939 |

Source: National Center for the Study of Collective Bargaining in Higher Education and the Professions, 1984, 1986, 1988, 1990, 1992.

school-sponsored activities as long as their actions were reasonably related to legitimate pedagogical concerns, such as relevance to the subject matter at hand.

In a second case regarding academic freedom (*Levin v. Harleston*, 1992), a court of appeals ruled that a philosophy professor at the City University of New York (CUNY) could not be stopped from publishing articles asserting that there were different levels of intelligence among races. Students demonstrated against what they believed was blatant racism on the part of the professor, and despite their own rules prohibiting such disruption, school officials refused to ban the demonstrations. However, the court ruled that because CUNY could not prove that the professor's controversial writings directly harmed the students, his work was to be considered free expression on issues of public concern and could not be banned.

In 1982, a court of appeals recognized a researcher's privilege to not disclose his research findings (*Dow Chemical v. Allen*). The Environmental Protection Agency had sought to use the researcher's notes and findings to decide whether several herbicides manufactured by Dow should be taken off the market. However, the court ruled that the researcher had a right to not reveal his findings because—in this case—the interests of government were not strong enough to prevail over the concept of academic freedom.

Contractual language and rules governing due process were adjudicated in the Consolidation Era also. In *Welter v. Seton Hall University* (1992), two instructors who had been terminated without the specified 12-month notice were reinstated when the New Jersey Supreme Court found that their dismissals were based on dissatisfaction with their performance. Had they committed fraud, however, or failed to disclose a second full-time job, the contract would have been voided and the professors would not have been entitled to a hearing prior to dismissal.

The diverse ways in which American colleges and universities are organized and managed lead to various interpretations of the faculty's rights to academic freedom and due process. At religiously affiliated institutions, the courts tend to shy away from questions of church governance or policy because of First Amendment protection of freedom of religion. In a celebrated case concerning an institution closely connected to the Catholic Church (*Curran v. Catholic University of America*, 1989), a court ruled that the institution was within its right to revoke a professor's ecclesiastical license, without which he could not teach Catholic theology, because he had taken several public stands against the teachings of the church. The court decided that the professor knew that ecclesiastical faculties, which are licensed by the Vatican, are different in that they have an obligation to abide by the authority of the mother church.

Federal laws prohibiting discrimination on the basis of age, gender, race or ethnicity, or disability also were tested in cases involving higher education faculty. In 1984, a court of appeals rejected a complaint brought by a faculty of nursing who said they were paid less than other professors because they were predominantly female. The court ruled that Title VII of the Equal Pay Act did not prohibit an institution from paying faculty in different disciplines on different scales; the fact that one department had a predominance of female instructors was not in itself sufficient cause to bring the claim for equal pay. However, when plaintiffs were able to provide direct or circumstantial evidence of discrimination in employment or compensation practices, they usually prevailed. For example, in 1987, a federal district court applied the Equal Pay Act to require a salary adjustment for all female faculty after the plaintiffs presented evidence that the school's president had said that male faculty should be paid more and the institution was unable to provide any legitimate reason for pay differences. Similarly, in *Clark v. Claremont University* (1992), an appellate court upheld a jury verdict concluding that racial discrimination motivated the denial of tenure to the plaintiff, who produced evidence of numerous racist remarks made by faculty involved in the tenure review process.

The Age Discrimination in Employment Act of 1967 enjoined employers from discriminating against persons 40 or more years of age, who must be employed, retained, and paid on the same basis as all other employees unless the specific nature of the work can be shown to require the use of younger people. In *Leftwich v. Harris-Stowe College*, adjudicated in 1983, the newly appointed regents of a college that had been taken over by the state college system sought to employ a new faculty. All prior instructors were invited to apply for positions at the institution, but when one professor who had scored higher on the regent's evaluation than the other two applicants was not retained, he sued, claiming discrimination on the basis of age. The facts showed that faculty who had been granted tenure before the college had been taken over by the new board were older and better paid. Thus, the court of appeals rejected the regents' claim that hiring nontenured faculty was more cost effective and promoted innovation and quality, saying that if higher salaries could be used as an argument to justify discharging older employees, the purpose of the Age Discrimination Act would be defeated. Furthermore, the court noted that assuming younger faculty would bring in new ideas—and that older professors would not—was precisely the kind of stereotypical thinking that the act was designed to eliminate.

The issue of job rights took a different turn in 1994 when the Ohio Supreme Court ruled that tenure and promotion documents at the state's public colleges should be open to inspection by all interested parties. A subsequent review of tenure decisions at Ohio State University showed that research, publications, and extramural grants still weighed most heavily in promotion decisions. "In almost every negative tenure case, inadequate research was cited as the major reason"; teaching effectiveness did not appear to enter into the decisions (Lederman and Mooney, 1995, p. 17). This finding fueled already accelerating questions about the usefulness of tenure. The idea of lifetime appointments came under further attack as laws ruling that mandatory retirement can no longer be imposed led to fears that an aging, higher-paid faculty would bankrupt institutions, and as critics argued that one of the reasons women and professors of color did not advance as rapidly as they might have was because the upper echelons of the professoriate were still occupied predominantly by White male professors who would not step aside to make room for their junior colleagues.

Because promotions at research universities were still based largely on publications and grants received, and because professors with tenure could not be removed on grounds they were superannuated, little other than persuasiveness, appeals to different standards of professionalism, and rewards for mentoring young faculty or taking on additional teaching responsibilities could be employed to change faculty behavior. Efforts to change the standards for awarding tenure or for allowing institutions to dismiss tenured professors made little headway. Grossly incompetent tenured faculty have always been subject to dismissal, but the criteria and processes for determining incompetence have rarely been spelled out to withstand challenges. In most cases the procedures have been so elaborate, the reviews so lengthy, that dismissals on the basis of incompetence are exceedingly rare.

Partly for this reason, many institutions introduced a post-tenure review to help professors maintain their currency and productivity. The post-tenure review process involves a mandatory assessment of every professor's work at periodic intervals, even after tenure is awarded. Because it is supposed to identify any impediments to improvement and to assist the professor in modifying behavior as necessary, the process theoretically aligns with the best principles of faculty evaluation—a process that has never been of much use in determining who shall be terminated but which has been useful in providing a mirror through which individuals might view and improve their own activities. Despite the addition of post-tenure reviews, however, the wave of dismissals that shook the job security of long-term employees elsewhere crashed against the walls of academe and receded with little apparent effect. And tenure remained important as the primary mechanism through which the faculty's right to academic freedom was protected.

**Productivity**

Issues of faculty productivity, never far below the surface, arose once again in the 1990s. According to the National Survey of Postsecondary Faculty (NCES, 2004), full-time instructors worked an average of 53 hours per week, with 55% of those hours devoted to teaching. The range in percentage of time dedicated to teaching went from 35% at private research universities to 69% at community colleges. Two-thirds of the professors exclusively teaching undergraduates taught between two and four classes; when faculty teaching graduate courses was factored in, the modal number was two. Multiplying the hours that faculty spent in the classroom by the number of students yielded an average of around 250 student-classroom-contact hours per week. These figures had changed little from the preceding decades, leading to the charge that professors were being paid more for the same amount of work. Put in purely economic terms, their productivity had decreased.

However, a review of the ways faculty spent their time did not answer the question of productivity. Some commentators applauded the factory model: professors were expected to be on the job for specified periods of time and to deliver certain products. Others wanted the faculty to teach more and spend less time on research. The number of students relative to the number of faculty at an institution has long been a crude but favored index of gross productivity. If the most productive faculty teach the greatest number of students, then instructors in community colleges, where the ratio of full-time equivalent (FTE) students to FTE faculty approximates 20 to 1, are the most productive. Obviously, because conducting research or guiding advanced graduate students is not part of the mission of the community college, the instructors there are expected to teach more students. But the student-faculty ratio in public four-year institutions, around 15 to 1, is higher than the 12-to-1 ratio in private institutions. Does that mean that private-college faculty are less productive? Other questions surfaced as well: Should individual faculty members be assessed on the basis of productivity, or should the measure be applied to entire departments? To what extent should productivity standards differ in research universities, liberal arts colleges, and community colleges? Would productivity be enhanced if instructors were required to stay in their offices for a specified number of hours per week? How does an hour spent speaking with a graduate student about a dissertation compare with an hour in which the instructor is lecturing, writing a grant proposal, or preparing a program to be broadcast to a wide audience?

Faculty at research universities had their own concerns with definitions of productivity. From time to time, someone would count the number of pages in published articles and suggest that the lengthier pieces indicated greater productivity. More often, the journal in which an article appeared was considered, with higher productivity suggested by articles appearing in higher-prestige publications. The dollar value of extramural grants might be noted, leading inevitably to questions of whether a dollar received for a research project was the same as a dollar solicited for student support. And in all institutions, questions of the value of institution and community service were pondered. For example, how much more productive is the chair of the committee than the committee's members? And is chairing a United Fund drive worth as much as a series of speeches to local business and professional groups?

Productivity indexes simply cannot contend with the vast array of variables related to higher education. Within the same department, some instructors work harder at classroom teaching, whereas others are highly entrepreneurial, bringing in grants for research or student support. One professor may turn out a half dozen short papers a year, whereas another might take five years to complete a book. Some spend many hours advising students, whereas others devote their time to preparing a distance education program. Add to all that the differences among academic departments in the same institution and across institutions in the same sector, and it is easy to conclude that neither the faculty as a whole nor any enlightened administrators would accept an index of productivity applied indiscriminately across the board.

Even so, the faculty were forced to justify their activities continually. One of the most persistent challenges came from legislators, state-agency officials, or members of governing boards who applied the most simplistic measures of productivity—typically the number of classes taught and the number of students in each class—to professorial salaries. In these analyses, the part-time faculty member, paid considerably less and with few responsibilities outside the classroom, appeared desirable. Salary and fringe benefits for full-time community college instructors in the mid-1990s totaled about $6,000 for each class taught, whereas a part-time lecturer with similar professional qualifications might be employed to teach a class for $2,000. In the research universities, the $15,000 or more it cost for a full-time professor to teach a class was viewed as excessive when a part-timer could be employed at less than one-third the price. The unions and academic senates fought incessantly against this line of reasoning, pointing out that a college was a community of scholars engaged in a variety of activities, not a factory employing pieceworkers. Neither they nor the budget-balancers have ever been able to convince each other of the meaning of productivity in their terms.

There are limits to viewing the workplace as a market in which people are paid on the basis of their productivity. Outside academe, piecework—paying employees by how much they turn out—has all but disappeared in industries and professions except for sales and the most routine occupations. Most employees in most occupations use sets of skills applied more generally and have knowledge and attitudes that cannot be assessed exclusively by viewing products; they are not paid according to the way they contribute at any given moment. Of all the fields, higher education depends most on a broad array of potentialities, least on a measure of products. Rewards for loyal service also enter into the equation, thus creating a bond between institution and individual. Regardless of court-protected job rights and collective bargaining agreements, norms of fairness and trust built on a lengthy tradition supersede questions of productivity.

Outside academe, the tendency in the 1990s was to reduce the number of full-timers and replace them with temporary workers. The savings were enormous, as corporations converted substantive portions of the workforce from full-time employees to part-time, fungible staffers with little loyalty to the enterprise. The ostensible reason for this shift was that corporations were pruning the dead wood; the real reason was that they could pay temporary staff considerably less for doing the same work. Universities, school systems, and civil service agencies were among the last bastions of career security and norms of professionalism. Legislators with little understanding of or sympathy for higher education as a stable institution, or an enterprise with its own peculiar standards, might have looked longingly at what was happening in corporate America as they juggled funds among competing agencies. But even when institutions were asked to provide evidence of productivity, such as graduation rates, number of classes taught per instructor, or time spent on campus, the results were invariably crude and difficult to apply with any validity to an individual faculty member. The professors' profession was too differentiated, too complex to be captured with that type of net.

### Academic Life

Just as professors in different disciplines and different types of institutions view productivity in various ways, faculty working conditions differ according to the same variables. Overall, the American academic profession is concerned primarily with teaching. Even though research has long been essential for promotion in the university sector, it takes up a relatively small amount of faculty time at institutions that do not award the doctorate. According to the 1993 NSOPF, roughly 90% of faculty listed instructional responsibilities as their major assignment (NCES, 2004). However, the ways they spent their time varied considerably by discipline, institution, and even stage of a professor's career. Professional autonomy and academic freedom were most fully realized at the research universities; high levels of personal interaction with students at the liberal arts colleges; a high degree of reclusivity and an aversion to committee work in all sectors. As a professional body, the faculty valued participation in governance; on the individual level, most preferred to have little to do with it.

During the Consolidation Era the percentage of time that faculty spent on various activities further differentiated the group. Average class size remained at 30 between 1987 and 1992, but the mean number of classroom hours taught per week increased from 9.8 to 11 as community colleges captured more of the enrollment growth. Faculty at research universities averaged 6.9 classroom hours, up from 6.5, whereas those in community colleges averaged 16.2, up from 15. Class sizes were largest at the research universities, smallest at the liberal arts colleges. The main differences among institutional types were that faculty at research universities spent 39% of their time in teaching and 32% in research, whereas those at liberal arts colleges and community colleges spent 64 and 69%, respectively, of their time teaching and 10% or less on research. Several researchers (Finkelstein, 1984, for example) examined how faculty time varied by gender, race and ethnicity, age, and institutional type, concluding that "faculty are as different from each other as they are from the population at large .... At the very least, both institutional type and prestige and academic discipline may be seen to differentiate among species of academics" (Finkelstein, 1984, p. 225).

Many studies have considered the faculty's satisfaction with their choice of career. Across all institutional types, one characteristic has been consistent: faculty derive satisfaction from the work they do and enjoy their autonomy. Their dissatisfaction relates to extrinsic demands, administrative intrusions on their workspace, and levels of compensation. In brief, the studies conducted in the Consolidation Era confirmed Herzberg's two-factor theory: personal satisfaction is related to the content of the work, whereas dissatisfaction arises from the environment surrounding the worker (Herzberg, Mausner, and Snyderman, 1959). Salary is a separate indicator of satisfaction. In 1987, 59% of full-time faculty were satisfied with their pay—this figure dropped to 55% in 1992.

Finkelstein (1984) reviewed studies examining the relationship between teaching and research and concluded that to the extent that teaching effectiveness is related to intellectual competence, it is positively associated with research productivity. In other words, involvement with research does not detract from good teaching, but conducting research is not a necessary condition for good teaching. Competent, involved professionals apparently devote much energy to every area of their work that they deem important. However, except for the faculty who willingly took on the task of working with underprepared students, most preferred to teach more engaged students. Nonetheless, nearly all instructors felt that they were good teachers and enjoyed interacting with students. They also wanted more opportunities to pursue professional development activities, including sabbatical leaves, grants for further study, and allowances for travel.

**Part-Time Faculty**

The rise of part-time faculty had an enormous impact on the trend toward professionalism. In 1995, 41% of all instructional faculty were part-timers, nearly double the percentage in 1970. Throughout higher education, the part-timers were the migrant workers of academe: students earning extra money while working toward degrees of their own, recent graduates hoping to eventually find full-time positions, people with jobs elsewhere teaching for the extra pay, retired teachers wanting to stay involved, professionals in other fields sharing their specialized knowledge. Part-time instructors helped institutions balance the budget, but at the same time they diminished faculty professionalization because they did not adhere to traditional core values beyond teaching, including research, public service, service to the institution, and commitment to a career in which they were judged by their peers. Part-time faculty were most concentrated in community colleges, where not only were they paid less, but they had less teaching experience, held lower academic credentials, had less choice in the selection of materials to be used in their courses, placed less emphasis on written assignments in determining student grades, were less likely to use instructional support services, had less out-of-class contact with students and colleagues, were less involved in departmental affairs or curriculum development, and were less likely to be members of professional associations (Kisker, Cohen, and Brawer, 2023).

The widespread use of part-timers evidenced a schism in the profession. If part-time instructors were reviewed and supervised by the career faculty, they might have been likened to paraprofessionals, aides, or support staff employed by most other professional groups. But in most cases, part-time faculty were left unsupervised to teach with the expectation that their students would enjoy the same kind of educational experience as if a full-time professor headed the class. Oversight was typically perfunctory; if they met their classes regularly and turned their grades in on time, few other demands were placed on them. The quality of learning manifested by their students was not likely to come under review. Mentoring or socializing part-time faculty to the norms and expectations of the profession was rare.

Student learning in classes taught by part-timers was rarely questioned. However, the learning attained by students in sections taught by full-time instructors was hardly a matter of review either. Faculty were evaluated (by students, peers, administrators, and the professors themselves) but student learning was not. Faculty were judged on their apparent teaching ability, their scholarship, service to the institution, and colleagueship. But all attempts to tie student learning to the ministrations of an individual instructor proved futile; the nature of institutions in which students chose their classes and instructors, and in which specific measurable objectives and pre- and posttests were rarely used, made it impossible to control enough variables to develop a valid measure of teaching effectiveness. Even so, faculty evaluation by students was commonplace. As Marchese (1997) reported, "By 1973, 29 percent of all colleges employed student evaluations; by 1983, 53 percent did; by the end of the era, the practice was all but universal." He concluded that the literature on student evaluations constituted "the largest single body of research in the world of higher-education studies" (p. 4). Nonetheless, the question of whether these evaluations related to student learning remained open.

## A Halt to Professionalization

In the Mass Higher Education Era the faculty made substantive gains in pay because of an expanding economy and a growing belief in higher education's importance to a technologically advanced economy. Also, they won the right to bargain collectively. They were insulated from many of the political and economic forces affecting colleges and universities; institutions might expand their mission, but the faculty did not have to respond to new demands. They were the arbiters of the beliefs guiding their own behavior.

As a result, however, contentions that higher education faculty had become an arrogant group resistant to change were heard often. Faculty were accused of operating in an insular environment, sustaining an elitist mentality. Scholarly recognition by one's peers was considered the highest goal, regardless of whether one's own institution or students benefited from it. The peer review process was seen more as self-protection than self-policing. Boyer (1990), for example, accused professors of devoting less time to advising students and more time to pursuing their own research interests, which were not subject to accountability by outsiders. Data showing that higher-ranked faculty spent fewer hours in the classroom were used to attack tenure, and throughout the era critics continually raised questions about the faculty's protected status. For example, if colleges were supposed to help students advance, why should the faculty use them as bases of self-protection? Why should professors enjoy autonomy and job security in an environment of corporate downsizing? What gave them the right to create their own conditions of work? All were questions that might not have been raised at a time when the faculty were so underpaid that few cared what they did. None would be resolved until the faculty themselves developed and adhered to strict codes governing their work, especially those who demanded they provide evidence of student learning.

At one time, higher education faculty were viewed as members of a guild, a profession that controlled entry to its ranks, engaged in self-governance, had informal rules about member conduct and behavior, and awarded lifetime tenure. Yet by the end of the Mass Higher Education Era and throughout the Consolidation Era, each of these characteristics was giving way: total control over entry to the profession lost some ground to affirmative action and anti-discrimination rulings; self-governance morphed into reduced participation in shared governance (with only a small minority of faculty participating in academic senate and committee activities); informal rules gave way to union contracts and institutional rules circumscribing behavior; and the greater reliance on part-time and adjunct faculty chipped away at tenure protections. By the end of the era, the trend toward professionalization essentially was reversed.

## Curriculum

Curriculum continued changing by accretion. Colleges typically added more programs and courses than they dropped. Even if one completely abandoned a set of courses, they usually remained in place at another institution. Vestiges of every prior curriculum were present somewhere in the system.

### Degrees

Shifting patterns of curriculum were reflected in the degrees awarded. By 1993, nearly 1.2 million students earned bachelor's degrees each year. The trend toward vocationalism was led by business majors, who accounted for 22% of all bachelor's awarded, up from 15% at the start of the era. When added to the degrees in education, health professions, engineering, and other occupational fields, bachelor's degrees in applied fields made up 58% of total awards, up from 54%. In addition to business, degrees in communications and protective (administration of justice) services increased notably, but those in education declined by one-third, as the master's degree became the preferred point of entry to the teaching profession. Bachelor's awarded in computer and information sciences and in law and legal studies quadrupled, and those in engineering-related technologies and parks and recreation studies doubled.

Some popular undergraduate majors carried through to the graduate level, but others served as general education programs, with graduates either leaving college with a degree suggesting preparation in the liberal arts or going on to graduate and professional schools to major in more specialized areas. Library science became almost exclusively a master's-level program, with few bachelor's or doctoral awards in that area. Bachelor's degrees in protective services totaled over 23,000, but fewer than 1,500 master's degrees were conferred in that field. Undergraduate studies in the liberal arts were dominated by majors in social sciences, history, English, communications, psychology, and the biological sciences.

The pattern of master's and doctoral degrees awarded reveals the spread of occupational studies in graduate schools. Business and education accounted for half of the 369,585 master's degrees conferred in 1993, down slightly from the percentage conferred in those fields at the start of the era. Altogether, vocationally oriented master's degrees totaled 80% of all awards, up from 76%. The increase resulted from a doubling of awards in the health professions, a 70% increase in engineering, and a 36% increase in public administration. At the doctoral level, the same fields accounted for nearly half of all degrees conferred, up from 40% awarded in those categories in 1976. However, nearly all doctoral degrees should be considered occupationally relevant, as most of the people with doctorates in the liberal arts entered teaching or governmental service, and those who gained doctorates in the sciences either stayed on as postdoctoral research scholars and instructors or took employment in research laboratories outside academe.

The sciences changed somewhat. Even though bachelor's degrees awarded in engineering rose considerably, degrees in the biological and physical sciences and mathematics declined so that, overall, the sciences dropped from 15 to 14% of all baccalaureates. The situation was reversed at the graduate level. Science degrees represented 10% of the master's degrees awarded in 1975 and 12% in 1994—an increase accounted for primarily by a doubling of engineering awards. The distribution of doctoral degrees also favored the sciences, rising from 22% of total awards in 1975 to 25% by 1995, thanks largely to the health professions. Doctorates in the biological and physical sciences increased by one-third, and those in engineering were more than double the annual number of awards at the start of the era. Doctoral study was clearly dominated by the sciences; during the Consolidation Era, the number of awards in English, foreign languages, liberal arts and humanities, and social sciences and history all declined.

Differences in course-taking patterns by men and women reflected the evolution of gender roles and opportunities. By 1993, women accounted for 59% of all associate degrees awarded, 54% of bachelor's and master's degrees, and 38% of the doctorates. Women received well over twice as many associate degrees in business and almost seven times as many in the health professions, whereas more than eight times as many associate degrees in engineering and engineering-related technologies were awarded to men. At the bachelor's level, awards in business were almost equally divided between men and women, but women continued their dominance of the health professions, receiving around five times as many bachelor's degrees in those fields. However, 86% of bachelor's degrees in engineering and engineering technology were conferred on men. In English, women received nearly twice as many bachelor's and master's degrees and roughly one-third more doctorates. Dramatic shifts in first professional degrees awarded to males and females were also apparent. Whereas in 1976 4% of degrees conferred in dentistry were awarded to women, by 1993 the number had increased to 34%. Over the same time span, medical degrees awarded to women increased from 16 to 38% of the total, and degrees in law from 19 to 43%.

Students who received bachelor's degrees took a much greater variety of courses as graduation requirements continued shifting and as more courses were accepted for degree credit. By 1984, students could receive a bachelor's degree from four out of five colleges without taking a course in a foreign language, from two of five colleges without a course in history, from half without a course in English or American literature, and from 54% without a course in mathematics (Adelman, 1994). Of the students who received bachelor's degrees in the early years of the Consolidation Era, 74% took at least one course in English composition and 70% had a course in general psychology. But no discipline other than those two was represented on the transcript of as many as half the graduates. Integrative courses in Western or world civilization were taken by fewer than 30% of all graduates and courses in philosophy by less than one-quarter. The tug of war between proponents of a free elective system and those arguing for a common core continued to be dominated by the former, while the vocationalists made steady inroads.

Concerns about the length of time students took to obtain bachelor's degrees and the quality of the learning they attained—subjects of discussion for many decades—continued. The high cost of college attendance led some observers to argue that the requirements for a bachelor's degree should be reduced to three years of full-time study. But because most students took five or more years to complete their undergraduate work, this suggestion seemed fey. Nonetheless, mandates that students graduate or lose their financial aid after completing a certain number of units gained ground, and some state systems threatened to reduce funding for courses taken by students who had completed at least 120 units and not received a bachelor's degree or, in the case of the community colleges, 60 units without obtaining an associate degree. The institutions resisted these restrictions, primarily because they provided developmental education courses for credit (but that typically did not count toward degree requirements) and because students who switched majors—and thus had to obtain more than the minimum number of credits—were penalized. The imposition of exit tests that would preclude students from obtaining bachelor's degrees unless they could demonstrate certain minimum competencies made some headway. However, the measures used to determine which students should pass from sophomore to junior year within a state system were more widespread; Florida, Georgia, and Texas were leaders in establishing such tests.

## Multiculturalism

The area of the curriculum known at the time as multiculturalism, which often included both gender and ethnic studies, became one of the most fascinating areas for review. Multiculturalism swept into the curriculum as students and some faculty argued that studying the culture of Western Europe was insufficient to understand modern America, and that the contributions, literatures, history, and art of various other races, ethnicities, religions, cultures, and people should be represented. Some of these courses had been introduced as women and students and faculty of color increased in number on college campuses, but they grew substantially during the Consolidation Era so that by the early 1990s, approximately half of all four-year colleges and universities required students to take courses that treated history, literature, or other disciplines in the humanities and social sciences from a multicultural perspective. The community colleges were less involved with race and gender studies. In 1991, 9% percent had at least one ethnic studies course in their class schedule, down from 15% in 1975; women's studies courses held steady at 3%. Social and ethnic studies combined accounted for 3% of humanities enrollments in 1977 and less than 1% in 1991. Most community colleges had co-opted multicultural studies by merging them with mainstream courses in history, literature, and interdisciplinary humanities.

Curriculum has always evolved; if it hadn't, students today would still be absorbed with the trivium, quadrivium, and Greek and Latin texts read in the original. But multiculturalism engendered controversy far out of proportion to its actual effect. To proponents, gender and racial or ethnic studies courses ensured that an ever more diverse student body saw themselves, their histories, and their cultures reflected in the curriculum, a necessary precursor to developing a sense of belonging, which is critical to learning. By including subject matter and pedagogical approaches that validated the existence and experiences of marginalized people, colleges and universities would empower women, people of color, and other oppressed populations to name problems and take action toward their liberation.

Arguments from opponents of multiculturalism ran the gamut. Some claimed it violated the tradition of cognitive rationality because gender and ethnic studies were based more on a political or social justice agenda than on reasoned research and empirical standards. To others, the multicultural movement demonstrated once again that higher education had no idea of the broad areas of knowledge its students should gain, that it was subject only to the whims of students and faculty desiring to learn and teach in their own areas of interest. Still other critics claimed that higher education was doing students a disservice by allowing them to concentrate on multicultural studies, which contributed little to their employability after graduation. (The fact that just over one-tenth of 1% of bachelor's degrees awarded in 1993 were in ethnic or cultural studies seemed not to reduce the heat in the arguments.)

Not content with examining an expansion of the curriculum as a phenomenon following in the tradition of curricular evolution, proponents and opponents alike confounded multicultural studies with representativeness, affirmative action, and competition among various ethnic groups. Accusations of debased standards, abandoned traditions, lack of academic credibility, and political agendas imposed on the past combined with critiques of the patriarchy, charges of Eurocentrism, and pleas for institutions to be more culturally responsive to keep academic writings lively. But the families sending the more than two million first-year students to college each year seemed considerably more concerned that their children gain the knowledge and skills useful to advance in society. Few followed the curricular debates, and even fewer objected when an institution required an ethnic or gender studies course or when an instructor built consideration of non-Western viewpoints into a history class. Widespread public backlash to concepts of curricular representation or structural racism would not occur for another few decades.

## Technology and Instruction

"Good morning, students, and welcome to the first class meeting of the semester. During this term we will study the concepts of, reasons for, and ways of developing . . . . Your resources include lectures, class discussions, your textbook, the library, and programs in the learning laboratory. You will write two 15-page papers and take three exams—one essay and two multiple-choice. Each paper and exam will count equally in determining your grade."

Those introductory remarks, familiar to everyone who has ever taken a college class, serve several purposes. They establish a first connection between instructor and students, one that is so important that student evaluations of instructors at the end of the course correlate significantly with impressions gained in the first couple of minutes of contact. The instructor also is creating an environment for student learning by describing the course content, instructional aids, sequence of events, and measures of attainment to be employed. Whether the introductory remarks are delivered to a class of 5 or 500, whether they are presented by a professor in person or on television, whether spoken or written, the purposes and effects are the same. The conditions of learning are described, and an implied contract is negotiated, with the instructor saying, "These are the goals of the course; these are the ways I will help you attain them; and here is how I will determine the extent to which you have succeeded." In effect, each student who remains in the class agrees to the contract by participating according to the terms outlined. Reduced to its essence, this is the teaching-learning paradigm.

The process of teaching and learning is amenable to observation, measurement, and determination of effect. Its costs can be calculated along with the time it takes to produce the desired outcome. And yet concepts of and approaches to teaching and learning have engendered endless commentary and questions of efficiency. Why should instruction cost as much as it does? Why are costs continually rising? How much are the students learning? How much of that learning is related to the cost of instruction? Are there more efficient ways of effecting learning?

The quest for efficiency in instruction has a long history. Some have proposed having faculty teach more students in larger classes; others advocated paying instructors less or utilizing greater numbers of part-time faculty. Still others have encouraged students to become more responsible for their own learning, for example through asynchronous distance learning programs. Each of these proposals has been tried many times over. Failure to find the magic bullet that yields a notable increase in efficiency is attributed variously to professors who stubbornly refuse to work longer hours, apathetic students who refuse to apply themselves to their studies, and uncaring administrators and bean-counters who look only to the bottom line of passing more students through so that tuition and state reimbursements remain high enough to balance the budget.

Many attempts to increase productivity in the Consolidation Era focused on reproducible media. Educators had long sought technology that would enrich the learning environment and reduce student dependence on a live instructor. In summing the quest, Cuban (1986) commented that the "dream has persisted from the invention of the lecture centuries ago to the early decades of this century.... In the insistent quest for increased productivity and efficiency, the lecture, film, radio, television, and microcomputer are first cousins" (p. 3). He saw an ongoing paradox of stability in change. As each new technology was introduced, the literature was filled with claims of extraordinary improvements in student learning, as well as promotional tactics devised by those who would add the innovation to the arsenal of instruction. Usually the calls for technological reform came from foundation executives, educational administrators, equipment manufacturers, and a few eager innovators from among the faculty. Academic studies followed demonstrating the effectiveness of the device. Complaints then surfaced about the logistics of use or slow adoption by instructors. Administrators accused professors of clinging to antiquated techniques; faculty charged administrators with attempting to destroy the personal relationship between teacher and student. All the while, costs of equipment soared considerably faster than its adoption. Cuban (1986) labeled this pattern "the exhilaration/scientific-credibility/disappointment/teacher-bashing cycle" (p. 5). As Oettinger (1969) concluded decades earlier, "The technology-there-is fails in the schools-as-they-are. No one can tell for sure how to marry the technology that-could-be with the schools-that-might-be" (p. 219). Eventually each innovation took its place as another aid to instruction, never to disappear, never to supplant what had gone before.

A review of a few of the technological aids introduced in the twentieth century illustrates the point. Film-oriented college courses appeared in the 1920s along with research supporting the use of film as a valuable teaching tool. In the 1930s, radio was supposed to bring the world to the classroom, to make the finest teachers available to everyone; classroom broadcasting spread rapidly once the hardware bugs were worked out and commercial or university stations provided programming. Instructional television, introduced in the 1950s, was supported initially by The Ford Foundation, then by the federal government through the National Defense Education Act. Predictably, researchers found little difference in the amount of information that students could learn from television and that was obtained in the conventional classroom. Auto-instructional programming was next, using self-paced workbooks either printed or presented through so-called teaching machines, and eventually computers entered the scene. Multimedia instruction followed, combining film, television, and audiotape with workbooks and drill.

The computer was key to the expansion of distance education, although it, too, failed to substantively change the role of faculty or substantially modify the teaching-learning paradigm. First applied to self-paced, prepackaged instructional programs, the computer then became a more flexible tool, especially as it provided access to the Internet. Whereas with radio, television, and film, programmers had to produce materials for passive listeners or viewers, the computer allowed for interaction among both groups. Like the telephone, it could be employed to bypass the authorities. Television, radio, books, and film were selective in the information they deployed but the Internet knew no such bounds. It promised ultimate freedom. Anyone could introduce materials to it; anyone could retrieve information from it. Its most sanguine advocates showed how users could re-create materials, rewrite texts, reorganize information continually. Ultimately, they believed, there would be no history, no authoritative statements, only evolving knowledge. Further, the

Internet opened a world of resources. To the extent that students knew how to judge the value of the information they derived from this infinite resource, their studies could be as broad as they wanted to make them. The resources of the campus, the faculty, libraries, and laboratories were no longer a limitation.

College faculty, as a group, were less likely to ascribe to the belief that computers and the Internet would fundamentally alter the teaching-learning paradigm. At bottom was the firmly held belief that students needed guidance. If they did not, there would be no reason for schools at any level; young people merely could seat themselves in front of computers and search the world's databases, learning anything they wanted to know. And, indeed, that was a fanciful dream long before the Internet existed. Illich (1970) felt that schools as institutions led away from the development of self-reliance and created a form of social reality divided between that which is academic and that which is not. His view of an ideal learning forum for society was to "provide all who want to learn with access to available resources at any time in their lives; empower all who want to share what they know to find those who want to learn it from them" (p. 108). This pattern of thought dates from the romantic naturalists of the eighteenth century, who contended that social institutions were corrupting, that people could learn what they needed to know without bureaucratic intervention. A counterview held that schools aided in the development of logical thought, rationality, commonly held understandings, and humanistic values; that without instruction designed according to the best principles of a democratic society, people would tend toward irrationality, tribalism, intellectual laziness, and social disintegration. The college professors of the Consolidation Era largely aligned with this view of the need for educational institutions.

However, most faculty also understood the need for technology and worked to integrate it with the instructional forms and content that they were committed to pursuing. The first application was to provide logistical support to conventional instruction. Faculty used the computer to prepare lecture notes and overhead transparencies, send email messages to colleagues and students, develop colorful classroom presentations, and otherwise replace the typewriter and blackboard. These seemed to be limited uses of the nearly $2 billion that higher education was spending annually for instructional support. But they were the most prevalent because they fit the existing college form: teachers and students interacting with one another within the confines of scheduled classes held on college campuses.

Most applications of distance learning were developed in similar fashion. An instructor presented lectures on television, used interactive video to sustain discussions with students, reacted to student work through email, and prepared and sent materials for student use. The instructor was the designer and conductor, and the students were involved to the extent that they participated on the instructor's terms. Content was predetermined, outcomes were specified, student progress was tallied, and records were maintained.

These applications of technology dominated because they kept intact the roles of professors and students. It was rather like the early automobile makers putting the engine in front because that was the position held by the horse when it pulled the carriage. The lag in full-scale application of technology to human learning was not the result of a cabal led by professors who wanted to keep their jobs, institutional managers who wanted to protect the physical plant, or funding agencies that preferred to perpetuate the familiar. It was society's way of changing incrementally, adapting the new to the former. In education, the staff and students merged all the earlier technologies into newer forms, so much so that the campuses and classrooms of the 1990s would have been familiar to the people of the 1890s.

Integrated college-wide plans for converting sizable numbers of courses into multimedia applications suitable for presentation on or off campus were not widespread in the Consolidation Era.

More often, applications of instructional technology centered on piecemeal approaches. Some colleges found funds for particular types of hardware and made them available to any who wanted to use them. Others effectively separated the applications of technology from the mainstream faculty and built technologically oriented divisions or separate entities dedicated to providing distance learning; many of these colleges without walls have a history stretching back to the time when open-circuit television was their centerpiece. But across the system, few reasoned observers believed that if only technological aids to instruction were introduced more rapidly, higher education's fiscal problems would end.

The quest for saving money through increasing productivity, with technology as the driver, merged with the desire to make people more responsible for their own education and with changes in hierarchical systems in the workplace. Industry adopted notions of team production based on organic systems operating from the bottom up. New businesses were developed by entrepreneurs working with producers, suppliers, customers, and financiers across the land. Flexibility became the rule of thumb. Educational systems, never known for their rapidity of response to societal change, were considered laggards. But technology does not operate itself; instructional programs are not self-generating. Shunting the faculty aside in favor of auto-instructional materials would not solve the problem of instructional efficiency. Learners might be free to purchase computers and search the Internet, but sequenced, designed instruction based on defined goals and content would remain important and would still need to be developed and maintained.

Thus, by no measure did information technology adopted in the Consolidation Era result in greater instructional productivity. Nonetheless, higher education was compelled to install it because it became an essential component of student literacy. Graduates entered a world where all forms of information technology were basic tools. Expenditures on technology became like expenditures on laboratory equipment. Indeed, the biological sciences could be taught in a classroom with chairs and a chalkboard, but students would not learn the way scientists function. Colleges had to install technology and their staff had to use it, even if it added to the cost of instruction.

Issues of curriculum, pedagogy, and technology all fed into a larger societal effort to bring about more learning for less money. One group tried to convince the faculty to teach larger classes or adopt aids to instruction. Another was committed to cutting costs by employing contingent instructors. A third wanted to bypass the faculty or, at best, use only the committed innovators who would work in teams along with support staff to develop instructional software, and still others would bypass the campuses entirely and rely instead on virtual universities with instructional materials derived from innumerable sources. The one opinion all of these commentators shared was that the rising number of college-age students and limited budgets at most colleges and universities would force changes as far-reaching as those seen at the start of the University Transformation Era. Their certainty that technology would lead to widespread changes in the teaching-learning paradigm, or to more cost-efficient institutions, seems quaint now, but it captured the imaginations of numerous educators and technologists of the time, as well as those who perceived an opportunity to profit from new approaches to teaching and learning.

## Governance

The steady progression toward secularization and extramural influence on higher education continued. State-level activities were particularly pronounced as calls for accountability and outcomes assessment spread from one capital to another. Accrediting bodies furthered the calls, which effectively forced the institutions to comply. Membership associations played a coordinating role, and hovering over all was the federal government, which assumed regulatory power in particular areas. As federal and state regulations multiplied, the term *compliance* entered the higher education lexicon. Institutional research and affirmative action offices expanded as more types of data and documentation were needed. The self-governing campus became a fading memory, as the big business of higher education became ever more subject to extramural management.

## Federal and State Influence

Governmental influences on higher education have always been bottom-heavy; that is, the states more than the federal government funded institutional development and provided continuing support. But the federal government has played a role, its influence shifting over the years. First, land grants stimulated new institutions; then funds for special buildings, student financial aid, and research were made available. Overall, the proportion of higher education revenue contributed by the federal government decreased from 16% in 1975 to 12% by 1993, but governmental pressure for student access continued, and a new area—institutional accountability for educational outcomes—blossomed.

The provision of (and ability to withhold) federal student aid led to governmental oversight. The U.S. Department of Justice brought suits against a number of institutions for discrimination and price fixing. The Civil Rights Act of 1991 further evidenced federal concerns about discrimination. The Student Right-to-Know and Campus Security Act, passed in 1990, required colleges to provide information about graduation rates and to submit reports on campus. The Americans with Disabilities Act of 1990 and the Rehabilitation Act Amendments of 1991 tightened requirements for educating people with disabilities. In 1994, Congress passed the Goals 2000: Educate America Act, which furthered the move toward state and local educational standards and assessments. Even so, the states carried the major responsibility for broadening access and maintaining the basic programs.

State governments have broad powers that are limited only by the federal Constitution, each state's own constitution, and powers that the federal government has preempted. The extent of state control on higher education differs from state to state, but rules cover a wide range: licensing, funding, institutional administration, labor relations, contracts, and liability. State-level boards of governors may enjoy autonomy from the state legislatures if they are noted in the state constitution, but in half the states the governing agency was created by statute and thus is more receptive to state demands (lest the statute be amended).

A few cases revealed how these differences manifested throughout the era. When the state legislature voted to close a campus of the University of South Dakota and turn it over to the state prison system, a suit challenged its power to do so (*Kanaly v. State of South Dakota*, 1985). The state supreme court ruled that although the university was statutorily created and therefore the legislature had the power to transfer its assets, the legislature also created a trust fund for the university, which had to be reimbursed for the loss of its assets. In Ohio, a court ruled in favor of laid-off employees who sought reinstatement on the grounds that they had been dismissed under misapplied rules, finding that the university was a state agency and therefore required to follow the state's administrative procedure code. However, in Michigan and California, where the universities are written into the state constitutions, courts gave them broader autonomy. For example, in 1990, the Michigan Supreme Court ruled that the legislature could attach conditions to its funding of the University of Michigan, but only to the extent that they would not interfere with the management and control of the institution because those powers were constitutionally reserved for the university. Similarly, in California, the constitutionally created university was ruled exempt from a section of the State Education Code holding that when the board of regents established salaries it must take into account the prevailing wages in different parts of the state.

State governing and coordinating boards became more influential. In Maryland, Oregon, and West Virginia, the state coordinating boards were reorganized to become part of the governors' cabinets. In several other states governors actively sought to influence the composition of the coordinating boards. As well, the governors of all 50 states adopted a series of recommendations calling on higher education to clarify the missions of various institutions, emphasize access and undergraduate education, implement assessment of student learning, and provide incentives to improve quality. In 1989, the governors came together with President George H.W. Bush to discuss these types of issues at the first national education summit.

The power of states to license private education was questioned. Traditionally, courts have ruled that state legislatures can license colleges just as they license any other business entity, provided that the qualifications of the schools in question are spelled out. In 1967, after a college challenged the state board of education's denial of a license, the New Jersey Supreme Court upheld both the board's decision and the empowering statute, concluding that the state could regulate private postsecondary institutions. And in 1982, the same court ruled that a fundamentalist Presbyterian college was not exempt from a state statute requiring degree-granting institutions to have a state-issued license. The state's interest in regulating education was deemed greater than its alleged threat to the free exercise of religion. But the states were also enjoined from regulating the activities of colleges that were chartered in other states on the grounds that only the federal government had the power to regulate interstate commerce, including interstate educational activities.

The trend toward consolidating governance of public institutions continued as Massachusetts and Maryland established statewide multi-institution boards during the 1980s. In several other states, coordinating boards were given increased authority, functioning more as governance entities. Marcus (1997) reported that 49 restructuring proposals were introduced in 29 states between

1989 and 1994. Legislatures initiated about half of them, and governors and state-level higher education authorities brought the others. The desire to reduce costs was integral to most of the proposals, but improving accountability and coordination and increasing the governor's legislative authority also ranked high. Half the states conducted studies of higher education effectiveness in the late 1980s, and 12 increased centralization. In the 1990s, Minnesota and Montana merged governance of their two- and four-year colleges. Kentucky's community colleges and technical schools were placed under a new governing board. Texas merged university systems, and New Hampshire consolidated its technical colleges. Florida's board of regents increased its control over all public higher education in the state. Other centralizing reforms took place in North Dakota, Utah, Colorado, and Tennessee.

In making these changes, legislatures wanted the state-level boards to control the institutions' ambitions and to keep their representatives from working directly with legislators to gain approval for favored activities and programs. The institutions, on the other hand, wanted the state boards to represent them to the legislature, seek increased funds, and keep the legislatures from looking too closely into institutional affairs. But the various institutions in every state's higher education system had different missions, responsibilities, and goals. Any action on the part of a state board, even an across-the-board increase in funding, gained the ire of one or another institution and invariably yielded the comment, "We deserved more than the others." Although the boards insulated the legislators to some degree, in most states the leading individual institutions had their own lobbyists, and the boards often found themselves under legislative pressure to take action favoring a single institution or institutional type.

Not all states moved in the direction of super boards, however. Connecticut authorized its institutions to submit budget requests directly to the governor and the legislature, bypassing the board of governors. Oregon permitted its colleges and universities to make purchases, enter into contracts, and manage their personnel outside the state government's central agencies. Hawaii, Virginia, and South Carolina also allowed the institutions to perform several functions that had been carried out by state bureaus. The New Jersey Board of Higher Education was replaced by a commission on higher education that had less responsibility, thus granting institutional governing boards more power, although the governor gained the ability to appoint state college trustees. Similarly, the governor of Illinois was given power to appoint board members of the University of Illinois.

The flurry of restructuring occurred because colleges and universities in all states experienced the same problems: budgets insufficient to keep up with costs, mandates to maintain open access, frequent clashes between institutional representatives and boards of trustees, and unclear or overlapping governance responsibilities. Each of the many plans was designed to help distinguish between decisions that should be made at the state or system level and those that should be made by institutions. The complex, multilevel system, composed of both centralized and decentralized elements, was under continual review, with no indication of any particular direction for all 50 states. The Education Commission of the States concluded that states should decentralize where feasible but also should redefine their central structures so that responsibilities were delineated clearly. It concluded that "higher education structures from one state should not and cannot be transferred to or imposed on another" given each state's unique history (McGuinness, 1995, p. 13).

## Associations

The numerous voluntary inter-institutional associations and consortia—some statewide, some regional, some national—exerted a form of influence. The broadest was the 80-year-old American Council on Education (ACE), with 1,600 institutional and associated members. ACE's agenda included furthering opportunities for women and people of color in higher education, developing leaders, and expanding higher education's adult- and distance-learning activities. Other associations included the Council of Independent Colleges, with a membership of 400 and a mission to advance funding for private institutions; the American Association of State Colleges and Universities (AASCU), enrolling more than 90% of the comprehensive public colleges and universities in the nation; the American Association of Colleges and Universities (AAC&U), a membership organization devoted to advancing the democratic purposes of undergraduate liberal education; the Association of Catholic Colleges and Universities; and perhaps 400 others.

Each association had an agenda representing either a consensus of what the leaders in the member institutions deemed important or what the association heads considered to be the cutting-edge issues. In the 1940s and 1950s, the American Association of Junior Colleges promoted occupational education, urging its member colleges to expand that area of the curriculum. Under different leadership in the 1960s and 1970s, the association issued numerous statements on behalf of adult education, distance learning, and programs to serve the broadest possible constituency. The group—renamed the American Association of Community Colleges (AACC)—later aligned itself with forces promoting outcomes assessment and urged its member institutions to provide information routinely on the number of people served; the number who graduate, transfer, or obtain employment; and the contribution of the college to its local economy.

In addition to its special agenda, each association tries to enhance public perception of its member institutions and influence federal legislation that benefits its colleges. The federal Lobbying Disclosure Act of 1995 (amended in 2007) precluded tax-exempt institutions and higher education associations from spending more than $40,000 per year on lobbying or from employing staff who devote 20% or more of their time to such activities unless they registered as lobby groups. Immediately, the major national associations and two-thirds of the universities with Washington offices so registered.

The associations also disseminate information on national issues affecting its member institutions, and many have staff members who speak with congressional aides and monitor the progress of pending legislation. Frequently, an association newsletter suggests that institutional leaders contact their local congressional representative and speak in favor of or in opposition to a pending bill that might affect programs or students in that sector. The groups function much as the trade and business associations, gaining funding for their efforts from institutional dues and from the sale of products and services. The extent to which they influence activities at the institutional level is unclear, but their ability to share ideas and best practices and suggest policies is certainly useful for local leaders who wish to move their institutions in particular directions.

### Accreditation

The process of accreditation evolved so that it rested on complex relationships between federal and state governments and voluntary members in each of the 6 regional accrediting associations, 8 national associations, and around 75 specialized and programmatic accreditors "recognized by the U.S. Secretary of Education as reliable authorities" (Rodenhouse, 1997, p. vi). The regional associations accredit each institution as a whole. National associations also accredit institutions but are more specialized, such as those accrediting Bible colleges or for-profit institutions. Programmatic accreditors have been established for numerous fields of study: music, engineering, nursing, law, optometry, and so on. All of these accrediting bodies are coordinated by the national Council for Higher Education Accreditation.

Just as in the Mass Higher Education Era, each accrediting agency established standards for the institutions or programs over which it had oversight. The entire process of accreditation is peculiar to the United States because there is no national ministry of education or any other official body setting standards and assessing compliance. However, although the voluntary membership associations have no legal status, their function has the effect of making them quasi-official bodies. In particular, because the federal government relies on voluntary accrediting agencies to determine which institutions are eligible to receive funding, particularly student aid, membership in voluntary associations has become voluntary in name only.

The standards set by the accreditors affected institutional conduct, and in some ways compromised institutional autonomy. Institutions that did not comply with the standards ran the risk of being denied accreditation; their students in turn risked being denied not only federal aid but also eligibility to practice their professions. Critiques of the accreditation process were common and included accusations of inconsistent expectations on the part of those doing the evaluations, inappropriate comparisons of unlike institutions, and a tendency to apply uniform criteria, which limited creativity. The standards themselves were criticized for attending more to process and input measures than to outcomes. Indeed, although the accreditation process has been effective in detecting problems such as financial trouble, inadequate facilities, or incompetent leadership, it has not been very good at determining the quality of instruction or student learning.

**Institutional Governance**

Three types of boards govern American higher education: self-perpetuating, externally appointed, and elected. The first is limited to independent institutions, and in some religiously affiliated colleges, a church body may appoint the members. These groups are comprised of individuals with commitment to the institutions rather than to an eternal constituency. Often, they have contributed funds and are expected to solicit support from other donors.

In most public colleges and university systems, state governors or legislatures (or a combination thereof) appoint governing board members. Those selected may be major contributors to political campaigns or may be selected to represent certain constituencies. Thus, they are often beholden to more than one master: the authority that appointed them, the sectors of the public that they represent, and the institutions themselves.

In many states, community colleges evolved from public schools with a tradition of locally elected school boards, and in their early history the colleges were governed by the same boards. When they separated from the lower schools, their own boards followed the pattern of being locally elected. This method of selection ensures that the board members themselves must be politicians soliciting support from various constituencies in their district. As such, they may be expected to represent the interests of their major supporters, which can lead to intense split loyalties as, for example, when a faculty union was the chief benefactor. Locally elected board members in all sectors may also use the position as a steppingstone to other political office.

A shorthand summation: in public institutions, trustees gain personal benefits from the perks and publicity that go with their positions and seek to ensure that the institution remains in good standing with the legislature. They are regulators. Trustees for private institutions work to assist the college, especially in gaining funds and courting alumni. They have considerably more influence on institutional priorities.

The roles of trustees and administrators changed little as the Consolidation Era opened. Officially, trustees were supposed to appoint, support, and evaluate the president, review the mission of the institution, approve long-term plans, oversee the educational program, ensure financial solvency, maintain the physical plant, preserve institutional autonomy, enhance the public image, serve as a court of appeal, and assess their own performance. This list of responsibilities was stated with little deviation in several books and papers dating to the 1950s. The 40,000 or so trustees serving on American college and university boards were expected to understand their responsibilities and adhere to them.

However, trustee activities have not always followed the script. Trustees have used their positions to publicize their own wishes to attain higher public office; board meetings offer a forum for them to make pronouncements on controversial topics. Trustees also have used their office to steer contracts in the direction of friends, even though such activities are considered breaches of public trust. At times, trustees let personal biases influence their work. For example, in 1997, the trustees of a California community college district argued in favor of a course teaching that the Holocaust never happened; several members of the board were affiliated with the group sponsoring the course.

Trustees may jeopardize their institutions if their actions overstep the bounds of their responsibilities. In public institutions, the state constitution or statutes describe their authority, and at private colleges and universities, the articles of incorporation and state license cover it. Liability is further bound by statutes and court decisions, as well as state corporation or trust laws. Kaplin and colleagues (2020) summarized the various types of authority, saying it may be express, implied, or apparent. Express authority is within the language of a written document. Implied authority is necessary for exercising express authority and therefore can be inferred. Apparent authority describes a situation where someone acting for the institution leads other people to believe that authority exists when in fact it does not.

As Kaplin and colleagues (2020) described, numerous cases have been brought challenging the authority of trustees. In 1977, the trustees of a private college were sued on the grounds that they had attempted to amend the bylaws of the college. A Missouri state court ruled that the board lacked the power to do so because the college's original articles of agreement dealt with the specific issue, and the trustees therefore did not have the authority to change them. In 1992, a university custodian challenged his termination on the grounds that the trustees did not have the authority to delegate hiring and firing power to the chancellor. The Louisiana Court of Appeals determined that the delegation had been proper.

The issue of institutional liability for the acts of others found its way into court frequently, and where negligence could be proven, or when risk of harm was foreseeable and unreasonable, the institutions were often found liable. For example, a student who fell on a slippery floor in a university building on her way to class sued on the grounds that the institution had a duty to exercise reasonable care to keep the premises in a safe condition. The Louisiana Court of Appeals held that the university, through the actions of its janitors who acted within the scope of their employment, breached the duty of reasonable care and was therefore liable for the student's damages. Similarly, in 1993, after a student at Gettysburg College died of heart failure during lacrosse practice, an appellate court ruled that the institution had a duty to have medical care available; the delay in securing an ambulance caused by the lack of an emergency plan made it liable for damages. But in 1980, a Florida district court found that the on-campus abduction and murder of two students was not foreseeable, hence the school had no liability. Similarly, a New York court ruled that the drowning deaths of two students during a school-sponsored canoe trip was caused by the terribly severe and unforeseen weather conditions and not by the breach of any duty of the university (Kaplin et al., 2020).

In other cases, institutions or their trustees, administrators, or faculty have been accused of defamation. In 1991, a graduate of Indiana University sued on the grounds that an apparently candid letter of reference from a professor assessing her strengths and weaknesses was defamatory. In *Olsson v. Indiana University Board of Trustees*, an Indiana Court of Appeals ruled that qualified privilege protected the professor and the institution if the communication in question was made in good faith on matters in which the letter writer had an interest or duty. Because the university was involved with teacher training, the letter was protected by qualified privilege. Similarly, a court ruled in *Shearer v. Lambert* (1976) that although a statement about an Oregon State University assistant professor by her department head was admittedly libelous, qualified privilege applied because the communication occurred in the performance of official duties. In sum, the courts established that individuals are rarely liable for acts committed as part of their official responsibilities, and institutions are rarely liable if the conditions in question are considered necessary and reasonable for the conduct of institutional affairs.

## Finance

The unprecedented increase in revenues and expenditures during the 1960s ended in the 1970s. In the decade between 1957 and 1967, expenditures rose from around $3.5 billion to $18.5 billion. The doubling of enrollments during that time did not solely account for this manifold increase. Government-sponsored research expenditures nearly tripled, and state funds coming into higher education more than quadrupled. Educators became accustomed to annual budget increases for rising salaries, funds for equipment and special projects, and capital improvement money. Those who became staff members during the surge in employment of the prior 15 years never knew privation. Those who were around for a longer time forgot how poverty-stricken they had been.

Several publications appeared in the mid-1970s cautioning that the trend was turning and that many people who were employed to build the institutions during the period of rapid growth were now out of date. The new administrators had to know how to negotiate reductions, as both public resources and the 18-year-old population steadily declined. However, the voices of a few analysts and their population projections were not sufficient to change practice. Higher education does not reinvent itself easily; its traditions run deep, and by far the greater proportion of its expenditures are as entrenched as though they were entitlements fixed by law. Nor could the institutions escape the double-digit inflation of the late 1970s that boosted the price of everything from utilities to library books. They still had to purchase technology that was essential for modernizing management systems and supplying data to state and federal agencies. They had to award raises to faculty and staff to at least partially offset the effect that inflation had on their personal budgets. And they had to hope that somehow they would muddle through, finding the funds they needed even though projections were dire.

During the Consolidation Era, shifts in funding were less dramatic when examined on a per-institution or per-student basis than they were when variations in sources of income were considered. Federal aid to students shifted away from grants in the direction of loans. State funds did not increase sufficiently to accommodate the rise in enrollments. Tuition went up rapidly so that students and their families bore an ever-increasing proportion of the total cost of instruction. Grants from philanthropic foundations moved from general awards to those given for specific purposes. Funds received from corporations were more likely to be attached to contracts for specific services. The dollars that could be used for discretionary purposes dropped. Fortunate was the institution whose leadership was able to accommodate these shifts.

**Revenue**

One note before tracing the sources of revenue: colleges are always short of money. The nature of their financial structure dictates that. Public institutions cannot run a surplus. Administrators know that failing to spend one year's appropriation may mean commensurate cuts in the next year's funding. However, if they spend all their money, their institution is at risk if its appropriation is cut. In sum, it is a no-win game; public colleges and universities can only break even or fall short. In private institutions, surplus funds can be added to the endowment only if they are so earmarked or if all campus groups are first satisfied—the latter an unlikely occurrence. If a college gains an unrestricted donation, all the staff immediately seek raises, every department suddenly needs an additional faculty member, the number of tuition discounts that the institution can give is increased, and there is always a building that needs painting. Public or private, the net effect is the same; colleges do well to break even.

A view of the revenue of institutions of higher education between 1976 and 1993 displays changes in source. As Table 5.6 illustrates, tuition was increasingly prominent as the share of revenue from governmental sources declined (federally supported student aid is included in the figures on tuition). Table 5.7 shows how sources of revenue differed between public and private institutions.

Table 5.6. Revenue of Institutions of Higher Education by Source of Funds, 1975–1976 and 1992–1993 (in Thousands of Current Dollars).

|  | 1975–1976 | | 1992–1993 | |
| --- | --- | --- | --- | --- |
| Source of Funds | Revenue | % of Total | Revenue | % of Total |
| Tuition and fees | $8,171,942 | 21% | $44,213,949 | 27% |
| Federal government | $6,447,178 | 16% | $20,489,909 | 12% |
| State governments | $12,260,885 | 31% | $40,218,148 | 24% |
| Local governments | $1,616,975 | 4% | $4,333,903 | 3% |
| Endowment income | $687,470 | 2% | $3,537,201 | 2% |
| Private gifts and grants | $1,917,036 | 5% | $9,418,804 | 6% |
| Sales and services | $7,687,382 | 19% | $38,830,491 | 23% |
| Other | $884,298 | 2% | $5,571,853 | 3% |
| Total | $39,703,166 | 100% | $166,614,258 | 100% |

*Source*: NCES Digest, 1996.

Table 5.7. Percentage of Revenue by Source, Public and Private Institutions, 1992–1993.

| Source | Public Institutions | Private Institutions |
|---|---|---|
| Tuition and fees | 18% | 41% |
| Federal government | 11% | 15% |
| State governments | 37% | 2% |
| Local governments | 4% | 1% |
| Endowment income | 1% | 5% |
| Gifts, grants, and contracts | 4% | 9% |
| Sales and services | 23% | 23% |
| Other sources | 3% | 4% |

Note: Percentages may not add up to 100 due to rounding.
Source: NCES Digest, 1996.

Because state governments were the largest single source of revenue for public institutions, the decline in the proportion of income from that source (from 31% in 1975–1976 to 24% in 1992–1993) was most hurtful. The sizable change resulted from tax-limitation initiatives, beginning with California's in 1978, and continued with increased demands for funds by other state agencies. State prisons proved a major competitor. California's "Three Strikes and You're Out" bill, passed in 1994, mandated that anyone convicted for a second felony would receive double a normal sentence; for a third felony, if the other two were for violent or serious crimes, the perpetrator would receive triple the normal sentence, with a minimum of 25 years. This added dramatically to the prison population and to mandatory state spending on corrections. The concomitant decrease in funds available for other state services forced major reductions in state funding for colleges. In the early 1980s, higher education in California received about 9% of the state's general fund, whereas just over 2% went to corrections; by 1997 the funding for prisons surpassed that going to higher education.

The situation in other states was little better. Among institutions accredited by the Southern Regional Education Board, college-going rates increased throughout the era but remained the lowest in the nation, and the share of state and local government budgets going to higher education fell. In inflation-adjusted dollars, higher education funding in the mid-1990s was equal to what it had been in 1984, yet enrollments had increased by 16%. State funding as a percentage of public institution revenue decreased by a greater percentage than the national average. And here the differences among the states were most pronounced: Georgia awarded some type of aid, including merit-based aid, to practically all of its undergraduates, but one-third of the states in the region allocated no funds to that category. Nationwide, although state spending on student aid increased through the early 1990s, by the middle of the decade that too had leveled off. Not until 1996 and 1997 would the states, aided by a strong economy, once again be able to boost institutional support by 6% each year (Nespoli and Gilroy, 1998).

**Federal Support**

Federal funds also declined as a percentage of overall income during the Consolidation Era. In 1976, federal support accounted for 16% of higher education expenditures; by 1993 it had dropped to 12%. Funds for university research increased by 41% in constant dollars, but most of that increase occurred in the 1980s; between 1990 and 1997, federal research funds increased by only 3%. Moreover, the category of "off-budget support" should be added to these figures. Almost all the funds in this category consisted of loans and work-study monies that demanded matching funds paid by participating institutions. These funds tripled between 1980 and 1997 when measured in constant dollars, an indication of the continuing shift from grants to loans. Federally subsidized or guaranteed loans were made through several programs: Federal Family

Education Loans, in which the federal government guaranteed the loans against default and subsidized them by paying interest to the lender while the borrower was in school; Federal Direct Student Loans, which accounted for one-third of the new-loan volume generated in the mid-1990s, and which made it possible for students to borrow directly from the government instead of through an intermediary bank; State Student Incentive Grants, which were matched dollar for dollar by state contributions; and Supplemental Educational Opportunity Grants, which provided funds to undergraduates who were able to demonstrate financial need (Hoffman, 1997).

Several other acts affected higher education finances either by adding funds or by increasing expenses. The Tribally Controlled Community College Assistance Act of 1978, reauthorized in 1990, provided funds for community colleges enrolling Indigenous students. In 1978, the Middle Income Student Assistance Act modified financial assistance programs to include middle-income as well as low-income students. The Challenge Grants Amendments of 1983 set up funds for which institutions might apply on a matching basis. In 1984, the Carl D. Perkins Vocational Education Act replaced the Vocational Education Act of 1963 and continued federal assistance for occupational education. In 1985, the GI Bill was renewed for veterans entering military duty after that year. A 1990 act established additional mathematics, science, and engineering scholarship programs. The Civil Rights Act of 1991 amended the Americans with Disabilities Act along with the 1964 Civil Rights Act and the 1967 Age Discrimination Act. And every few years the Higher Education Act of 1965 was revised and reauthorized in various ways. For example, in 1994, the date for penalizing colleges that had excessively high rates of student loan default was delayed for Historically Black Colleges and Universities and Tribal Colleges.

Many of the federal acts were designed to broaden access not only for students who previously had benefited from grants and loans but also for groups that might have suffered from discrimination in the past. Research in higher education continued to be subsidized on the grounds that although the Cold War had ended, the United States was in an unending economic competition with the rest of the world. On the micro-level, the federal government threatened to cut off financial aid to students in institutions that banned military recruitment on campus. Higher education and the federal government were not only indelibly wed, they continued renewing their marriage vows even as they engaged in periodic spousal disagreements. Those who opposed governmental regulation and those who opposed egalitarianism—often the same groups—were unable to overturn the sanctity of the relationship.

The federal government's funding of research increased as a percentage of institutional revenue from 8.7% in 1987 to 9.1% in 1993. The majority of this augmentation went to the public sector, even though the top five recipients were private universities: Cal Tech, Johns Hopkins, Chicago, MIT, and Stanford. Those five received more than $1 out of every $6 that the federal government contributed to higher education in the United States. By contrast, the top five public institutions—the Universities of Washington, Michigan, Wisconsin, California at San Diego, and California at Los Angeles—received about $1 in every $16. Overall, the top 25 recipients were about evenly split between public and private institutions. Federal funds, mainly for research, averaged around $340 million per institution per year in the research universities and were augmented by grants and contracts from philanthropic foundations and other donors. The funds were concentrated; 100 universities received 80% of the money. Funds for medical research and research in the biological and physical sciences dominated the awards, but research in astronomy, oceanography, and social sciences was also supported. The percentage of federal funding for research in the life sciences increased, whereas engineering's share decreased. Research in education—never a large proportion of the federal government's research effort—declined between

1980 and 1997, whereas research programs administered by the Department of Defense (DOD) increased by 19%. The most sizable percentage increase was in research funded by NASA, which tripled during those years, most of the increase coming in the 1980s. But $5 of every $8 that the federal government put into research and development was dedicated to defense, with health and space following as a distant second and third.

Programmatic emphases were the rule. The National Science Foundation funded 14 Engineering Research Centers by 1987, with the idea of cultivating interdisciplinary research in association with industry. The DOD steadily decreased its support for basic research, even as it doubled its overall funding for academic research in the five years between 1978 and 1983. Private donors similarly became more likely to award funds for specific activities. Geiger (1993) reported that "whereas in 1970 about one-third of gifts were unrestricted, less than 20 percent were in the late 1980s. For research universities the proportion was closer to 10 percent" (p. 314).

University leaders strove continually to increase their proportion of extramurally derived funds, even to the extent of developing elaborate research parks. By 1995, 25 additional research parks were formed, adding to the 10 that existed in 1975. Business incubators that assisted in the growth of new enterprises and organized research units cutting across several fields were established. The institutions developed procedures regarding the licensing of intellectual property rights, although for several years income from this source rarely exceeded the expense of administering the activity.

The spread of the funding base for research fit with the growing importance of economic development and technology transfer. The federal government could not be relied on as a source of steadily increasing funds in all areas. Annual funding for university-based research increased from $3.4 billion to $9 billion between 1975 and 1996, but this was not evenly distributed across agencies. The Departments of Housing and Urban Development, Justice, and State reduced funding over the 20-year span, and other agencies displayed peaks and valleys: Department of Education funding dropped from $160 million to $29 million in one year (1984–1985) and took eight years to recover to the higher figure; Department of Commerce funds dropped from $62 million to $36 million between 1986 and 1988, but by 1991 had regained the earlier figure; DOD outlays reached a high point in 1994 but within two years declined by 18%; Department of Transportation funding dropped by 28% between 1995 and 1996. The Department of Health and Human Services was the most consistent agency, increasing every year (from $1.3 billion in 1975 to $6.8 billion in 1996). But even within those figures, the types of research supported varied considerably, as one or another disease or social crisis captured the legislators' attention.

**Tuition**

College tuition charges came in for a considerable amount of examination, especially as they accelerated in public institutions in the 1990s. From the beginning of the Mass Higher Education Era through the 1970s, tuition increases averaged slightly more than the rate of inflation, but because family income went up as well, college remained affordable for most people. During the same period, student aid programs expanded and more low-cost community colleges opened, so both the private and public sectors attracted sizable numbers of students. By the 1980s, however, the situation changed. Tuition increased much more rapidly than either inflation or family income—about 10% per year at both private and public institutions. During that decade, the median family income increased by 50% but tuition by almost 90%. When adjusted for inflation, family income went up around 6%, and tuition by more than 30%. Even when the figures were adjusted to account for family size, disposable income, age of the head of household, or any other reasonably relevant measure, tuition costs still increased considerably more rapidly. And as tuition increased as a percentage of total revenue—reaching 45 and 69% at private four-year colleges and universities, respectively, and 22% at public institutions—the cost of higher education transferred from government to students and families.

This shift accelerated in the early 1990s. Indeed, for the three years beginning in 1991, tuition at public four-year colleges increased by 12, 10, and 8%, respectively, and at community colleges by 13, 10, and 10%. The latter figures were influenced by the tripling of fees in California—the state with by far the greatest number of community college students. Across the nation, average tuition and fees for all institutions went from $924 in 1977 to $3,517 in 1993; average costs increased at public colleges from $479 to $1,782; and at private colleges average costs went from $2,467 to $9,942. Community colleges, which long prided themselves on policies of maintaining extremely low tuition and which averaged under $500 a year as recently as 1983, passed the $1,000 mark 10 years later.

Some of the tuition rate increases at public institutions were truly phenomenal. Between 1987 and 1994, the University of California fees for in-state undergraduates went up from less than $1,500 to more than $4,000—a rate of increase nearly matched by the public universities in Michigan and Washington. Furthermore, the differential fees paid by students in graduate and professional schools increased even more markedly, as the states were reluctant to support students who were training for what were perceived to be lucrative careers. The fee override for students in law, medical, and business schools in public universities often amounted to a doubling of the regular graduate school tuition. Students who had been willing to pay more for their undergraduate education at prestigious colleges because they thought it helped their chances of gaining entrance to highly selective professional schools were paying more again after they were admitted.

The rapid rise in tuition led several institutions and states to organize prepayment plans that allowed families to pay for four years of college at the time of matriculation and thus avoid tuition increases while the student was enrolled. Another type of prepayment was introduced in 1985, when Duquesne University announced that a family could prepay tuition for a child who would attend some years later; if the child was not admissible, the payment would be refunded, but without interest. Duquesne suspended the plan less than three years later, but a number of other institutions introduced versions of it. The public sector got involved as well when, in 1986, Michigan allowed families to pay into a state-managed investment fund with the understanding that their payments would cover tuition at any public institution in the state when the child was ready to matriculate. If the student chose instead to attend a private institution or go out of state, the fund would pay the equivalent of what would be received if they had attended a public college in Michigan. Investments in the fund were deductible from state income tax, and the Internal Revenue Service ruled that income from the trust could be spread over four years and taxed at the child's rate of taxation. "By November 1988 some 27,000 families had actually signed up, investing nearly 200 million dollars" (Hauptman, 1990, p. 23).

Other states developed different types of incentives. Missouri allowed state income tax deductions for contributions to college savings accounts. Illinois sold several million dollars' worth of zero-coupon bonds; if a family held a bond for five years and used the proceeds to pay for college expenses, the state made a supplemental interest payment. By 1998, 25 states had passed legislation allowing prepaid tuition or savings plans whereby families might receive state tax deductions for contributions to college savings accounts. Federal tax deferrals were available on interest earned in the accounts. All the plans were designed to encourage families to save for their children's education. The wealthiest families—those most likely to prepay tuition—in effect bought an insurance policy covering them against tuition increases, whereas the lower-income families (who were less likely to participate) had to take their chances, hoping that higher tuition would not price their offspring out of college.

The federal government also offered various types of tax exemptions, such as allowing parents to invest up to $10,000 per year per child with the income from those funds taxed at the (presumably lower) child's rate. Other tax-based initiatives encountered difficulty because any plan connected to income tax payments invariably benefited wealthier families more. As a way around the problem, a provision in the Taxpayer Relief Act of 1997 granted tax deductions for up to $1,500 of tuition paid by lower- and middle-income families. It was designed particularly to aid students in their first two years of college.

## Student Aid

Student aid stemming from federal, state, and institutional sources continued to increase as it had since the late 1960s. Aid from all sources, less than $550 million in 1964, climbed to $10.5 billion by 1976 and to more than $26.6 billion by the end of the 1980s. When viewed in constant dollars, the aid increased more than tenfold over the 25-year span. Much of the increase was the result of student borrowing. Overall, grants accounted for 83% of all aid in the mid-1970s, but by 1990 this percentage had shrunk to 51%. Grants accounted for 80% of federal aid in 1976, a figure that dropped to 61% by 1980 and 28% by 1994 (see Figure 5.3).

Aid patterns differed according to types of students and institutions. Full-time students were more likely to receive aid than part-timers, four-year college students more than those in community colleges, graduate students more than undergraduates, students in the private sector more than those in public institutions, and students in for-profit or proprietary schools more than any others. By the end of the era, 52% of students in public institutions, 70% of those in privates, and 76% of those enrolled in proprietary schools received some form of aid. At the graduate level, 68% of all students received aid.

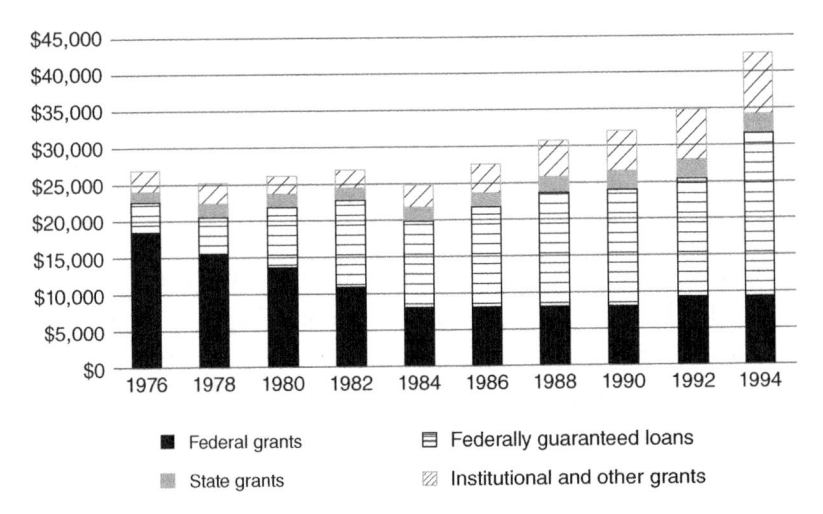

Figure 5.3. Aid Awarded to Postsecondary Students, 1976–1994 (in Millions of Constant 1994 Dollars).

Fluctuations in sources and types of aid have a long history. Guaranteed Student Loans (GSLs) began in 1965. The GSL program provided federal guarantees for loans that banks made to students, who used the funds for college expenses. The program stemmed from several premises: college is a profitable investment both for individuals and for society; would-be students typically are poor credit risks, hence they cannot readily borrow funds to finance their investment; default rates on loans to students would likely be such that banks would not make such loans except at exorbitant rates of interest to cover losses. Not least, by guaranteeing loans to students who could then give the money to any college that would accept them, the issue of aid to parochial institutions was circumvented. By the end of the 1980s, the $100 billion loaned through the GSL program was by far the largest source of aid to students.

As adult students attended in larger numbers, and as the ratio of part- to full-time students increased, the complexities of various aid programs increased as well. The Education Amendments of 1972 created the Basic Educational Opportunity Grant program (Pell Grants), retained the Educational Opportunity Grant program (adding the word "supplemental" to it), authorized State Student Incentive Grants that provided matching funds for state scholarship programs, and created the Student Loan Marketing Association—a government-sponsored corporation designed to provide funds for student loans. As needs testing was introduced, the program grew ever more complex. In the early years of Pell Grant awards, most recipients were traditional-age college students supported by their families. By 1985, the majority were older, either self-supporting or those whose families could not afford to contribute. Students attending proprietary schools benefited greatly. By 1989, students at for-profit institutions received 26% of all Pell Grants and 35% of all Stafford loans (GSLs).

Amendments to the GSL program in 1978 brought about further changes. The most significant was the removal of needs testing, thus allowing all students, regardless of income, to be eligible for Stafford loans. Because interest rates on student loans were lower than commercial rates—considerably lower in the environment of extremely high interest rates during the early 1980s—"any family with a student in college would have been irrational not to have borrowed the full amount available.... Not surprisingly, annual loan volume jumped from roughly $1.7 billion in 1977 to nearly $7.2 billion in 1981" (Breneman, 1991, p. 9). And because the GSL program was not subject to direct control through annual congressional appropriations but operated as an entitlement, the volume of such loans grew sharply as all other federal programs (such as work-study and state incentive grants) declined. The states also awarded their share of financial aid. State grant programs in 1976 totaled less than $500 million, but by 1989 exceeded $1.6 billion and in 1995 reached nearly $2.5 billion. Higher education in the United States became dependent on grants and loans made to all types of students at all levels and in all sectors.

However, a view of grants and loans awarded tells only part of the story. They must be placed in the context of tuition charges and living expenses to arrive at the net cost of college attendance. Student aid includes grants, loans, various work-study and campus-based aid, and fellowships, along with tuition discounts provided by most private sector institutions. In 1993, the average full-time undergraduate at a public four-year institution received grants totaling 30% of the average tuition and fees charged—a percentage that had been constant for the preceding decade. This figure was less than the 40% of cost that students received at the beginning of the era—a figure inflated by Vietnam War veterans attending under the GI Bill—but much more than the 10% students received from all sources prior to the opening of the Mass Higher Education Era.

During the 1980s, the proportion of student aid received in the form of loans increased. By the late 1980s, grant money fell to around 13% of the cost of attendance, whereas veterans' aid along with college work-study programs, which accounted for 20% in 1975, dropped to 2%. At the same time, loans jumped from 7% of the total cost of attendance in 1975 to more than 15% in the early 1980s and continued rising. As Table 5.8 illustrates, in 1975, the maximum Pell Grant covered 62% of the cost of a public institution and 33% at a private college or university. That share dropped to 40% and 18%, respectively, in 1987. By the latter year, maximum Stafford loans covered half the cost at public institutions and 23% at the privates. (Table 5.8 also shows the percentage of institutional costs covered by average Pell Grants and Stafford loans.)

**Expenditures and Cost Controls**

Institutional expenditures reflected the inflation of the time. Between 1976 and 1994, expenditures per student increased by 30% in constant 1994 dollars. The four-year institutions were most affected; their per-student expenditures went up by 34%, whereas those in community colleges rose by 18%. And whereas

Table 5.8. **Pell Grants and Stafford (GSL) Loans as a Proportion of College Costs, Selected Years, 1975–1987 (in Current Dollars).**

|  |  |  | Maximum Award as Percentage of Average Cost | | Average Award as Percentage of Average Cost | |
| --- | --- | --- | --- | --- | --- | --- |
| Year | Maximum Award | Average Award | Public | Private | Public | Private |
| Pell Grants | | | | | | |
| 1975 | $1,400 | $761 | 62% | 33% | 34% | 18% |
| 1980 | $1,750 | $882 | 53% | 27% | 27% | 14% |
| 1985 | $2,100 | $1,279 | 43% | 21% | 26% | 13% |
| 1987 | $2,100 | $1,350 | 40% | 18% | 26% | 12% |
| Stafford loans (GSL) | | | | | | |
| 1975 | $2,500 | $1,312 | 110% | 59% | 58% | 31% |
| 1980 | $2,500 | $2,086 | 76% | 39% | 63% | 33% |
| 1985 | $2,500 | $2,307 | 52% | 25% | 48% | 23% |
| 1987 | $2,625* | $2,466 | 50% | 23% | 47% | 21% |

*For first- and second-year students. For upperclassmen, the maximum loan was $4,000.
Source: Hauptman, 1990.

expenditures at public four-year institutions increased by 27% per student in constant dollars, in the private sector they went up by 40%. Much of the latter increase was a result of scholarships and fellowships that private institutions made available—a sum that surpassed 11% of expenditures by 1993. The Higher Education Price Index, which in 1960 was four percentage points lower than the Consumer Price Index, reached parity in 1966. At the beginning of the Consolidation Era, it was two points higher, and by the end of the era it was 17 percentage points higher. Clearly, higher education costs rose more rapidly than consumer prices in general.

As such, cost cutting became a watchword. When revenues rise, programs can be added, and even though individual unit budgets may not go up as much as the program directors desire, accommodations can be made for the most part. But when revenues increase more slowly than costs, whole programs may be put on the block. Which ones should be cut? Higher education has never been able to assess relative worth. A federal mandate for State Postsecondary Review Entities was supposed to provide guidelines for expanding or pruning programs based on criteria such as the number of graduates relative to entrants. However, the higher education community would not abide a set of federal regulations that purported to distinguish between worthy and less-worthy programs. Their complaints led to the demise of the ruling before it could be implemented.

State-level initiatives had somewhat greater success. Some states provided additional funds for programs demonstrating improved graduation or job attainment rates. Others imposed restrictions, holding forth the stick instead of the carrot (for example, by subsidizing courses that students took beyond 60 units for the associate degree and 120 units for the bachelor's at a lower level). Institutional leaders did not like that either, claiming it squelched flexibility and penalized colleges that provided sizable amounts of credit-bearing developmental instruction.

Several unique characteristics make higher education costs difficult to control. One of the intractable cost inflators is faculty salaries as related to productivity. With higher salaries paid to professional practitioners outside the academy, university salaries must increase unless higher education is to revert to a time when professors were among the lower-paid professional workers. But unless the student-faculty ratio is increased—a proposition typically resisted by both faculty and students—real teaching costs go up. Further, the fixed salary schedules whereby faculty who teach large numbers of students are paid the same as those who teach few also make it difficult to control costs.

Costs in higher education also increase because there are no universally agreed-on measures of productivity. Prestige—arguably the highest institutional value—usually increases when more resources are acquired. But adding prestigious professors and handsome buildings contributes to spiraling costs. And even research dollars that faculty attract to the institution do not help budgets; they may pay for the research, but classes must still be taught and students advised. Expansion in the number of courses an institution offers (a continuing phenomenon) represents another cost factor that is difficult to control. The more courses in the class schedule, the more specialized faculty are needed to teach them, and fewer students are available to take them. And yet which of the many courses is unworthy of being retained?

Efforts to control costs during the Consolidation Era led institutions in all sectors to take some rather obvious steps. Better building utilization was one of them, as institutions expanded summer-session course offerings and extended the hours of instruction. Offering voluntary early-retirement programs to long-term employees was another measure. Between 1990 and 1994, three such programs at the University of California led to around 2,000 faculty retirements and a savings of $200 million in salary. Even though two-thirds of the retirees were replaced, most of the new hires were at the junior level.

Other courses of action included increasing class sizes, especially in community colleges where the average size went from 27 to 31 in the decade prior to 1994. Library budgets typically took a cut, even as the cost of books and journals escalated. The proportion of funds spent on research increased because that activity was usually funded by extramurally generated dollars earmarked for the purpose. Funds for instruction decreased as a percentage of the whole, as lower-paid faculty were employed and as low-enrollment classes were cut. But higher education's ability to control costs was considerably less effective than its ability to increase its resources.

Most funding formulas fall back on the non-educationally related practice of allocating resources on the basis of program cost. By that line of reasoning, the higher the cost of offering the program, the more resources devoted to it, regardless of its social or educational merit. It is politically nearly impossible for educators to discuss in open forum the rationale for differential allocation within the system, but they can band together and argue for more resources coming in from the outside. That is also why for every hour that national associations spend giving their members specific guidelines for cutting budgets, they devote 10 more to petitioning Congress, state legislatures, and the public for increased support.

By the end of the era, higher education was still provided for in largely the same way it was when the nation was founded. Despite the higher tuition, students paid substantially less than the full cost of their education. They seemed to prefer high-spending institutions, feeling that they received more for their money, whether it came from their pockets or from a subsidy. Their cost of attending college included foregone earnings, which in all but the most expensive institutions were greater than the amount of tuition. But higher education grew so important that young people who did not attend jeopardized their earnings; they were locked out of the many professions and occupations that demanded certification. More than ever, to paraphrase a popular advertisement for the American Express card, they dared not leave home without it.

## Outcomes

Each era has been marked by modified goals, which in turn led to changed practices. And each goal revision has engendered cries of degradation, betrayal of the fundamentals, destruction of the rock on which the system was founded. Two generations after the University Transformation Era began emphasizing research, professional schools, and support for business, many academics still deplored the turn away from an emphasis on the classics, religion, and a core liberal arts curriculum. Growth in the size and number of institutions that occurred in the Mass Higher Education Era, along with rapid expansion of occupational programs, yielded commentaries that many of the new students were not qualified, that the colleges should not engage in occupational training or certification, and that the intimacy of the small campus was lost. During the Consolidation Era, system goals shifted toward more diversity in the student body, a multicultural curriculum, the inclusion of all who could benefit from higher education, and greater institutional effectiveness and efficiency.

Higher education also expanded its involvement with the broader community. The research enterprise was ever more tied to economic development and industrial ventures. Professional schools expanded their direct community service through cooperative professional ventures; hospitals opened to broader segments of the population; legal aid was provided; and attempts were made to influence governmental policy on everything from the environment to the economy. The content of collegiate studies grew to encompass a greater variety of outcomes. Few new degrees were offered, but more ways of satisfying the requirements for existing degrees developed.

## Critiques and Commentaries

Critiques of higher education flowed from within and outside the academy, just as they had for the preceding century. At the beginning of the era, several issues seemed clearly defined. Some still thought the universities should turn inward and dedicate themselves to learning and research for their own sake, benefiting society only indirectly through advances in basic knowledge and the education of able students. But this ship had sailed; higher education's purposes and outcomes were already far too intertwined with society's. On the other end of the spectrum, critics contended that higher education remained neutral, thereby endorsing or perpetuating the status quo in society, especially socioeconomic and racial stratifications. Indeed, despite large investments in financial aid, gaps in incomes grew wider. Why did higher education not devote more of its resources to leveling the playing field? Higher education was castigated also for not focusing sufficiently on moral education. Some laid at its door the breakdown in ethics as evidenced by scandals in government, drug use, sexual promiscuity, and a general lack of respect for authority. No matter how the universities attempted to ameliorate unemployment, reduce racial tensions, or enable socioeconomic mobility, it was never enough. Faculty might conduct research, consult, organize legal aid activities, provide health and dental clinics, and send students to volunteer in impoverished communities, but the problems persisted.

Ernest Boyer, president of The Carnegie Foundation for the Advancement of Teaching from 1979 to 1995, and Derek Bok, long-time president of Harvard—two of the more respected critics—contended repeatedly that higher education should increase its relationships with and efforts on behalf of the broader community. Boyer (1996) argued that higher education reached its finest moments when it served larger purposes, as when it participated in the "building of a more just society" and in making the nation "more civil and secure" (p. 13). He deplored scholars who viewed the campus "as a place where students get credentialed and faculty get tenured, while the overall work of the academy does not seem particularly relevant to the nation's most pressing civic, social, economic, and moral problems" (p. 14). Boyer also argued for a variety of different types of scholarship: conducting research that expands human knowledge, participating in integrated or interdisciplinary activities, sharing knowledge by communicating it not only to students and colleagues but also to the broader community, and applying knowledge that assists in solving social problems.

Both Boyer (1996) and Bok (1982) argued that society needed much more from higher education than it was getting. The institutions should work directly to solve basic social problems; prepare more and better teachers; act to reduce poverty, homelessness, drug abuse, and chronic unemployment; prepare students for careers in international trade; and engage more directly in moral development. And the institutions remained opportunistic: they followed the money and took on whatever projects an agency was willing to fund. At the same time, they indulged themselves in internecine warfare over student admissions, curricular emphases, and faculty promotion criteria. The idea that higher education could reform itself or even that it might maintain consistency in goals and processes was outstandingly archaic in a system as large as this one had become.

**Degrees and Wages**

Higher education's most obvious benefits begin with its enhancing of personal mobility and individual development. Between 1976 and 1993, the percentage of high school graduates who matriculated in college immediately after leaving high school increased notably, from 51 to 63%. To those numbers must be added the students who delayed entry to college but who showed up years later; two-thirds of 1980 high school sophomores enrolled by 1992 (Adelman, 1994). Higher education absorbed people from all walks of life. Enrollment rates for students from every socioeconomic quintile increased, although the most dramatic gains were made by those from the highest-income families: among this group, 83% attended college, compared with 65% two decades earlier. The percentage of males attending college immediately after high school increased from 53 to 63%, and the percentage of females matriculating directly rose from 46 to 61%. Of the 191 million people aged 18 and over at the end of the era, 38 million went to college; more than 27 million obtained a bachelor's degree, nearly 9 million held a master's degree, 2.4 million a first professional degree, and 1.7 million a doctorate.

By the end of the Consolidation Era, the notion that anyone without a college degree faced a bleak future was commonplace.

Indeed, the economic value of education had been traced for many decades, with the findings showing consistently that one's income rises with years of schooling. The penalties of not finishing high school are severe, and as people grow older, the disadvantage of not having a high school diploma compounds: at the end of the era, 86% of male high school graduates aged 25 to 34 were employed, compared with 75% of those who did not complete high school. Among females in that age group, less than half of those who did not complete high school were employed, compared to two-thirds of high school graduates. The median annual salary of 25-to-34-year-old males without a high school diploma was 80% of the salary of high school graduates; females without a diploma earned 75% of the wages paid to females who graduated from high school.

Economic rewards are also positively related to college graduation. Male and female college graduates aged 25 to 34 are more likely to be employed than their counterparts who had not been to college; 92% and 84% of male and female graduates, respectively, were employed, compared to 86% and 66% of those who did not complete college. Earnings advantages have been consistent also. The economic benefit of college-going remained steady from the early 1970s through the mid-1990s; those who completed a bachelor's degree earned more than their counterparts who had only a high school diploma. However, despite consistently earning less than males with the same level of education (see Figure 5.4), among females aged 25 to 34, the earnings premium of a bachelor's degree was greater in both 1976 and 1993 than it was for males of the same age. Furthermore, the spread between earnings of those with bachelor's degrees and those with only high school diplomas widened during the era. In 1976, a female with a bachelor's degree earned $1.36 for every dollar earned by a female with a high school diploma; by 1993 the ratio was $1.67 to $1. For males the spread widened from $1.21 per dollar to $1.61 (see Table 5.9)

Differences in median starting salaries for male and female college graduates and for those who majored in various fields

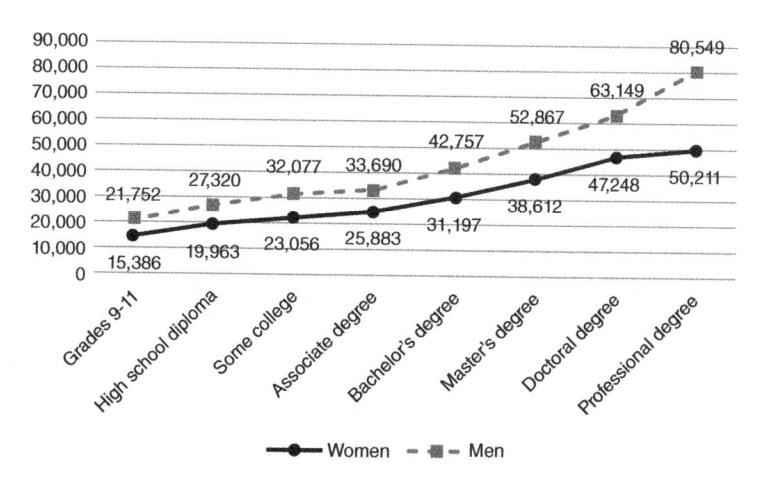

[Chart showing median annual earnings by education level for Women and Men:
- Grades 9-11: Women 15,386; Men 21,752
- High school diploma: Women 19,963; Men 27,320
- Some college: Women 23,056; Men 32,077
- Associate degree: Women 25,883; Men 33,690
- Bachelor's degree: Women 31,197; Men 42,757
- Master's degree: Women 38,612; Men 52,867
- Doctoral degree: Women 47,248; Men 63,149
- Professional degree: Women 50,211; Men 80,549]

**Figure 5.4.** Median Annual Earnings of Full-Time, Year-Round Workers 25 and Older, 1993.

showed some changes during the Consolidation Era. The median starting salary for college graduates in 1993 was $21,735. The starting salary for males was $24,058 and for females $20,252—a 19% difference for those who worked full-time. (Gender gaps in starting salaries are smaller than those in the median annual earnings of workers shown in Figure 5.4, as male salaries tended to increase faster than those for females.) Graduates in the

**Table 5.9.** Ratio of Median Annual Earnings of Full-Time, Year-Round Workers Aged 25–34, 1976 and 1993.

|  | 1976 | | 1993 | |
| --- | --- | --- | --- | --- |
| Highest Educational Level | Women | Men | Women | Men |
| Grades 9–11 | 0.78 | 0.85 | 0.75 | 0.80 |
| High school diploma | 1.00 | 1.00 | 1.00 | 1.00 |
| Some college | 1.12 | 1.09 | 1.19 | 1.16 |
| Bachelor's degree or higher | 1.36 | 1.21 | 1.67 | 1.61 |

*Source:* NCES *Digest*, 1997.

humanities, social and behavioral sciences, natural sciences, and education earned less than the median, whereas those in computer sciences and engineering, business and management, and other professional or technical areas earned more. However, the gap in earnings narrowed for most fields; for example, graduates in the humanities earned 20% less than the median in 1977 but only 11% less in 1993. Within a given field, the type of institution a graduate attended mattered little; wages were relatively consistent, regardless of whether a person began at a community college or whether it took them four, five, or six years to complete a program. The degree was the cachet.

In pure economic terms, the cost of obtaining a degree—tuition plus foregone earnings—was an investment in a person's future income. Bowen (1977) figured the value of a bachelor's degree at between 8 and 9% per year over a lifetime, and Pascarella and Terenzini (1991) calculated the rate of return at between 9 and 11%. In an extension of the belief that a scarcity of degree-holders results in a premium for those who hold degrees, the penalty for not having a degree grew as more people attained them. Green (1980) anticipated this situation, arguing that when there are only a few non-completers, schooling becomes "compulsory in ways that it was never compulsory before" (p. 101). The presence of many high school graduates put pressure on the few people without high school diplomas to obtain them; the same held true at all levels. Indeed, during the Consolidation Era, salaries for men with a college education nearly managed to keep pace with inflation; wages for those with some college but no degree experienced a decline of 27%; pay for those with a high school diploma lost 30%; and the real wages of high school dropouts declined by 34%.

Although having a bachelor's degree was the means by which people's earnings increased the most, students who earned associate degrees or occupational certificates also gained. Sanchez and Laanan (1997) reviewed studies of the earnings of community college graduates and found that from 1975 to 1994, those who entered the workforce with a bachelor's degree increased their earnings by 202%, whereas those with an associate degree or some college education showed an earnings increment of 165%. A study of the short-term effects of certification in Illinois found individuals' average earnings increased by 10% for the first six months following completion of an occupational education program; a North Carolina study found a 12% increase among certificate completers over a one-year period. Similarly, students who earned occupational certificates in California made a 47% gain in wages between their first and third year out of community college (Sanchez and Laanan, 1997).

Although institutions have been accused of ignoring the employment market when they admit students, the market is not predictable. When a sizable number of graduates are available, various businesses, industries, and agencies ramp-up the qualifications they expect in new employees, and after short periods of dislocation the surplus is absorbed. At the bachelor's level, 78% of recent graduates who were employed in 1994 had jobs related to their fields of study, and 60% reported that their jobs required a college degree. The number of new doctoral recipients increased substantially, even as the percentage who found positions in higher education fell from 68 to 52% between 1970 and 1993. Most of the graduates in physical science and engineering were employed in industry, and opportunities in public service and governmental agencies opened for those with humanities or social science degrees. But no one seemed able to refute the human capital thesis: everything else being equal, those with more education earn more and enjoy higher standards of living. The link between these variables is far from perfect, but the concept of over-education is considerably less valid.

## Research

Research remained a major function throughout the era, and the amount spent on it continued the dramatic rise that had begun in the 1950s. Between 1975 and 1994, the funds devoted to organized research increased fivefold. To these figures should be added collaborative efforts with other organizations and the funds devoted to faculty time on research, which typically were accounted for in other budget categories. Even so, research funding remained steady at 9% of current-fund expenditures.

The relationship between private industry and research in the universities shifted. The two systems interacted for many decades as industry looked to the universities to train the scientists who would staff their laboratories and to conduct the basic studies that would enhance their work. But well into the Mass Higher Education Era, industry did most of its own product development. This changed in the 1980s when industry's investment in university-based research increased notably. In previous decades, the federal government was so supportive of research that the universities did not have to expand liaisons with industrial corporations. But as federal support declined in the 1970s, industry was looked on as a patron once again. And because university research already had begun to shift from basic to applied inquiry as the government funded weapons research, the war on cancer, and social programs that ameliorated the pernicious effects of poverty, race, and environmental degradation, collaboration with industry—in genetic engineering, immunology, and electronics, for example—was a natural evolution.

One way in which industry and universities collaborated in research and development, especially in biotechnology and electronics, was in founding new corporations, with industry, venture capitalists, and universities all participating. University faculty did not have to leave their positions, funds from many sources were tapped, and all groups shared in the proceeds of whatever products might be developed. According to Geiger (1993), "Approximately 200 biotech firms were founded between 1980 and 1984," many effected by combinations of venture capitalists and university scientists (p. 303). In molecular biology departments, affiliation with a company was considered a normal state of affairs because of the long timelines and sizable funds that product development in that area demanded. The leaders of large drug companies realized that if they were to keep up, they needed to gain access to scientific developments both through the universities and through the newly founded biotech firms. In the early 1980s, contracts for research in biotechnology were negotiated routinely. "By one estimate, industry support for biotechnology in universities totaled $120 million in 1984" (Geiger, 1993, p. 304).

The relationship between industry and the universities was largely symbiotic. Cooperative ventures were seen as a way for universities to support their scientific research programs and for corporations to gain access to the latest in scientific study. The federal government assisted by amending patent law so that universities could retain title to inventions developed with federal funds. Other federal legislation supporting the collaborative efforts included tax incentives, relief from governmental regulation, and outright financial support. Many states increased the tax credits that industry could claim for investing in cooperative research projects with universities. Even small firms that derived no immediate benefit from tax breaks because they had not yet generated profits were assisted when state university researchers collaborated with them on research proposals and on joint funding. These types of arrangements also yielded support for graduate students who were then expected to remain within the state and contribute to technology transfer.

The arrangements between universities and industrial corporations were criticized by those who felt they took the universities into areas antagonistic to academic norms developed over the prior century. Some held that the universities were "too ready to allow a Trojan horse inside the walls of learning," that the "flow of research money undermines the university's independence, increases the dominant status of research relative to teaching . . . promotes some disciplines unfairly above others, and represents a state-sponsored intellectual policy the consequences of which may be as damaging to scholarship as state-sponsored industrial policies have so often been to economies" (David, 1997, p. 12).

However, two things proved certain: first, most students and faculty on campus were unaffected by the relationships with industry, as the vast majority of institutional effort went on as before. Second, industrial competitiveness was considered essential for America to hold its position at the head of world markets in biotechnology and microelectronics. Regardless of whether the majority of students or faculty approved of these collaborations, top administrators almost invariably did, and most of the leading universities organized administrative divisions precisely to solicit contracts with industry.

Increased collaboration with industry involved the universities in what Kaplin and colleagues (2020) summarized as "complex legal problems concerning contract and corporation law, patent ownership and patent licenses, antitrust laws, copyright and trademark laws . . . and conflict-of-interest regulations" (p. 895). For example, in most states, if the employment contract made no provision for the assignment of patent rights, the employee owned the patents but the employer retained royalty-free rights for business uses. In 1996, 131 universities earned $336 million from licenses and patents, an increase of 23% from the prior year. Half the total went to six institutions: California, Columbia, Stanford, Michigan State, Wisconsin, and Chicago (Blumenstyk, 1998).

The connections with industry exerted a centrifugal force on the universities. The arts and sciences, once considered the intellectual core of the institution, had shrunk anyway as the proportion of students in professional schools increased. By the 1980s, research in engineering and the sciences exacted a further toll, as organized research units were built in numerous areas that demanded collaboration across disciplinary lines. These units involved faculty from more than one department, maintained their own budgets, and had specially designated leaders; often they had their own facilities. They employed sizable numbers of graduate and postdoctoral students along with part-time faculty and full-time researchers supported by funds that the units controlled. The center directors typically had greater authority than department chairs and operated with little oversight from central university administrators. Stahler and Tash (1994) concluded that in the major research universities, these centers accounted for over one-fourth of the expenditures on research and their budgets averaged over $15 million.

University research thus moved steadily ahead. The nation's share of the world's scientific literature grew close to 40%, surpassing the combined totals for Germany, Britain, France, and Japan. Ideas and people moved from academe into business much more smoothly in the United States than elsewhere. American research universities generated economic growth by spawning patents and entrepreneurs. Graduates and faculty from the leading research universities created companies, some of which grew into sizable enterprises. David (1997) cited a study finding that "if the 4,000 or so companies founded by MIT graduates and faculty were turned into an independent nation, the income they produced would make it the 24th richest in the world. These firms account for annual revenues of some $230 billion and employ more than 1 million people" (p. 14).

## Assessment and Accountability

Pressure to justify budgets by measuring tangible contributions grew during the era. Commissions formed in every state, with each seeking ways of controlling costs and demonstrating the value of higher education. Whether or not college leaders perceived these as debasing the institutions and compromising their autonomy is irrelevant. The commissions studied, the state boards gained authority, and the institutions, often grudgingly, complied.

By 1989, two-thirds of the states had programs mandating assessment that included incentives for compliance and penalties for failing to follow the directives. The plans differed in the details of what must be tallied, but all demanded that each publicly funded institution have an assessment plan, report regularly to the state, and pay the costs of data compilation (Ewell, 1997). A review of a few of these state plans reveals their tone and consistency. The boards governing education in New York challenged the institutions to be accountable for results and to measure progress using performance indicators that, among other things, included graduation rates and employer satisfaction (The University of the State of New York, 1996). The Kentucky General Assembly mandated a higher education accountability process, including an undergraduate alumni survey, graduating student survey, indication of pass rates on licensure examinations, and persistence and graduation rates (Kentucky Council on Higher Education, 1996). The West Virginia legislature created a Higher Education Report Card revealing annual data in several categories, including student outcomes, economic and workforce development activities, campus security, and graduation rates (State College and University Systems of West Virginia, 1997). In many of the states where centralized government was less evident, the universities themselves reported data on similar goals; the University of Arizona set its own standards for student persistence, graduation rates, and time-to-bachelor's-degree, along with some institutionally specific goals such as integration of undergraduates in research and the proportion of lower-division courses taught by ranked faculty (University of Arizona, 1996).

A few scholarly groups also developed approaches to measuring outcomes. The Center for the Study of Higher Education at Pennsylvania State University prepared a listing of policy issues using the input-environment-outcomes model popularized by Alexander Astin. They defined inputs as access, affordability, financial support, and student preparation. Environmental variables spanned institutional accountability, campus climate and facilities, faculty productivity, and technology. Outcomes included lifelong learning, public service, educational effectiveness, graduate and professional education, and workforce preparation and retraining.

However, these listings of variables were advisory at best. The National Center for Education Statistics continued its widely reviewed data efforts, and the state agencies proceeded with their own outcomes-assessment indicators.

In a broad sense, the flurry of outcomes assessments was generated by higher education's success. When it enrolled but a small proportion of the population and laid claim to only a few public dollars, it did not receive much attention. But when it aided the founding of industries and kept the United States competitive in new technological areas, while at the same time enrolling a larger and ever more diverse set of students, it was viewed as a major utility. The public had high expectations; practically every state wanted to have a world-class university within its boundaries, and most young people wanted access to higher-paid and more rewarding employment. Furthermore, the timelines shortened; institutions no longer had the luxury of developing greatness over a span of centuries. Nor could they reject governmental initiatives. In the 40 years prior to the mid-1990s, federal support for research grew fiftyfold in current dollars, and institutional capacity to produce PhD's by more than ten times. The percentage of GDP that the United States spent on higher education was greater than that of any other country except Canada. Even though that percentage increased little since the start of the era, the dollar figure was large enough to capture public attention.

Much of higher education did not take kindly to attempts to convert its processes into quantifiable outcomes. Many analysts insisted that a college could not be measured in terms of outcomes, impacts, or tangible benefits because of the nature of learning and the human experience. Many of the effects of college-going on individuals are subtle, not easily quantified; causal connections of social benefits are even more difficult to assess. But those arguments convinced few people outside the academy. If faculty wanted to return to a time when they were paid as poorly as church parsons and their college matriculated only a few students housed in poorly heated buildings, they may have been able to step aside from demands for greater accountability, productivity, and results. But they had become captives of their own success. For decades they promised that if only enough funds were forthcoming, they could equalize opportunity, produce better citizens, ameliorate social problems, train workers for any emergent field, enhance the development of industry, and enrich the culture of the broader community. By the mid-1990s, it was payback time.

The Consolidation Era is notable chiefly for extending the trend toward student access (including through affirmative action rulings), for its curricular debates around multiculturalism, and because in it many of the trends that defined American higher education for the previous 350 years began to slow or show early signs of reversal. These shifts beget several questions.

- Eaton (1997) wrote that access is a "layering of multiple principles" concerned with financial status, academic preparedness, types of institutions available, and intramural assistance for women, people of color, low-income students, and those with disabilities (p. 237). By this definition, to what extent was equal access truly a reality in the Consolidation Era?

- As women, students of color, and other groups historically excluded from full participation in higher education attended college in greater numbers, and as public support for antidiscrimination policies and affirmative action gained ground, it became ever more difficult to justify practices that adversely affected these learners. Yet disparities in both access to and completion of college remained, suggesting that some discriminatory structures or attitudes persisted. In what ways did colleges and universities work to dismantle societal inequities during the Consolidation Era, and how might they have turned a blind eye or actively perpetuated them?

- Student activism was a hallmark of the collegiate experience in the Mass Higher Education Era, but campus uprisings dropped dramatically after the Vietnam War. What factors accounted for these shifts in attitudes and behaviors? Were students in the Consolidation Era disengaged in comparison to their predecessors or did their civic or community engagement take different form?

- The Consolidation Era witnessed a substantial slowing, and even reversal, of the professionalism faculty had gained in earlier eras. Given the economic and political climate of the time, was this shift inevitable? What might colleges and universities have done differently to protect or advance the professoriate as a professional class?

- The majority of curricular debates in the Consolidation Era surrounded the idea of multiculturalism, the inclusion of courses related to race, ethnicity, gender, and non-Western cultures. In what ways did these conversations mirror those occurring in the broader society? Did higher education lag behind or spur societal progress?

- Near the end of the era, many educators and technologists predicted that the adoption of new technologies would lead to widespread changes in how students accessed higher education and that technology would both improve institutional efficiency and lead to a reduction in the cost of instruction. Technology certainly made inroads in higher education, in many ways revolutionizing distance learning, but it did not substantially change the teaching-learning paradigm. Why?

- During the Consolidation Era, federal aid to students largely shifted from grants to loans, and tuition and fees as a percentage of total revenue rose from 18% at the start of the era to 41% in 1993. Did this transference of the burden of paying for college mirror broader societal or generational attitudes about individual and governmental responsibilities?

- Despite the lip service that college administrators paid to efficiency, it was considered an alien concept in higher education, while in most other endeavors it was accepted as a measure of the relationship between input, costs, and value added. To be more efficient—that is, to widen the margin between cost of production and value of the output—business enterprises sought to reduce the cost of labor and materials or build better products. But learning and instructional costs are not easily quantified, and cost-cutting is challenging in labor-intensive environments. If classes with higher student-teacher ratios or lower-paid instructors are not invariably more efficient in terms of student learning, what valid measures of institutional efficiency are available? Does our preoccupation with prestige render all attempts to assess efficiency across institutions moot?

- Even though higher education could not possibly deliver on all the pledges it made, it has never known how to back away from them. If the billions devoted to research on social issues seemed to yield no reduction in social ills, instead of reducing their claims, institutional representatives typically stated only that they needed more money. Never able to say merely, "Send your young people here and we will teach them to be good citizens and more productive workers," the higher education enterprise promised also to ameliorate social problems, cure diseases, enhance the economy, and relieve unemployment. It deflected any critiques of its ability to accomplish these goals by criticizing other institutions and ideas. Were students underprepared for collegiate studies? Blame the high schools. Were college graduation rates too low? Not enough financial aid was available to keep students enrolled. What does higher education gain by promising nothing less than social and economic progress, even if it routinely falls short in delivering it? Is there value in itself of the system's optimism and bold vision of the future? Or has higher education's willingness to move the goalposts or point fingers elsewhere made it easier to dismiss its importance?

# 6

# Equity, Accountability, Distrust, and Disinvestment in the Contemporary Era: 1994–2023

The age-old notion of the college on a hill, of an institution that both serves and exists apart from the community in which it is based, largely became an anachronism in the Contemporary Era. In the 30 years since 1994, colleges and universities have become far more vulnerable to societal forces and much institutional decision-making now occurs in the political arena and under the public eye. No longer insulated by an aura of mystique or expenditures too low to draw attention, American colleges and universities are both symbols of the nation's cultural and political conflicts and battlefields on which those skirmishes take place.

## Societal Context

A number of developments that appeared rather straightforward over the first 350 years of American higher education have reversed or shown significant course changes in the past three decades, driven or exacerbated by three major global events and several interrelated trends in American society. For example, the September 11, 2001, terror attacks led to a hugely expensive and largely open-ended War on Terror, characterized by U.S. invasions of Iraq and Afghanistan (the latter lasting 20 years), tightened immigration and deportation policies, augmented homeland security practices, and increased federal surveillance powers; the ripple effects of these changes for colleges and their students were substantial. In addition, the subprime mortgage crisis and subsequent Great Recession of 2007–2009 resulted in a financial double whammy, scoring a direct hit to college and university budgets and accelerating the longer-term trend toward disinvestment in public institutions by states and localities.

Furthermore, the COVID-19 pandemic, which resulted in over 1.1 million deaths in the United States and levels of social isolation and basic needs insecurity never before experienced by most Americans, led to numerous shifts in enrollment and institutional functioning and exacerbated and laid bare inequities among haves and have-nots. It also amplified several disturbing trends related to increased political polarization; a shrinking middle class; culture wars rooted in issues of race, religion, and identity; and greater distrust of colleges and universities. Advances in technology, including the advent of social media and mobile journalism, intensified all of these developments and contributed to an emerging *us versus them* mentality in both higher education and American society.

**Polarized Politics and a Dysfunctional Democracy**

Regardless of one's political perspective, the 30 years since the start of the Contemporary Era may have felt like a game of Chutes and Ladders, with numerous victories and significant setbacks for both progressives and conservatives. Near the end of the 1994 Congressional election campaign, Republicans issued their Contract with America—a document promising lower taxes, welfare reform, and the end of government they viewed as too big, too intrusive, and too profligate with the public's money. Upon flipping the Senate and becoming majority party in the House of Representatives for the first time in 40 years, the Republicans delivered on many of these promises, ushering in an era of fiscal conservatism and the privatization of many government services, a trend that extended to institutions of higher education.

Subsequently, the nation's economic status changed notably. Despite federal budget surpluses in the late 1990s through 2001, the annual federal budget shifted into a pronounced deficit as tax rate reductions and the Great Recession cut deeply into income; in 2009, the deficit totaled $1.42 trillion. In an attempt to stimulate the economy and both create new and recover jobs lost in the recession, President Barack Obama signed into law the American Recovery and Reinvestment Act (ARRA) of 2009. Through ARRA, the government invested roughly $830 billion in temporary relief programs, education, infrastructure, and renewable energy, and as the nation recovered, the federal deficit declined, bottoming out at $439 billion in 2015.

Social progressives gained some momentum during these years as well. In 2010, after much contentious debate, Congress passed the Affordable Care Act (better known as Obamacare). Six years later, the United States became a signatory to the Paris Climate Agreement, in the process committing billions to create green jobs at home and help developing countries mitigate climate change. LGBTQ+ rights also expanded during this period, most notably through the repeal of the military's "Don't Ask, Don't Tell" policy in 2010 and by the U.S. Supreme Court's 2015 decision in *Obergefell v. Hodges* that required all states to license marriages between same-sex couples and recognize unions that were performed out of state, effectively annulling gay marriage bans in 14 states.

In addition, between 2003 and 2020, the courts repeatedly rejected challenges to race-conscious admissions policies, establishing "student body diversity [as] a compelling state interest that can justify the use of race in university admission" (Kaplin et al., 2020, p. 426) and opening the door for a greater emphasis on diversity, equity, and inclusion at all levels of schooling. Decades of precedent were overturned in 2023, however, by the Court's ruling in the combined cases *Students for Fair Admission (SFFA) v. Harvard* and *SFFA v. University of North Carolina* that race-conscious admissions practices violated the Equal Protection Clause of the Fourteenth Amendment, a decision that effectively ended the use of affirmative action in higher education.

While progressives gained ground on social issues, a new conservative faction of the Republican Party emerged to oppose federal spending associated with ARRA, Obamacare, and other Democratic legislative victories. Members of the Tea Party primarily focused on fiscal issues and by 2016 much of their momentum either sputtered out or was harnessed by the mainstream Republican Party. However, the Tea Party tactics of disruption and obstruction normalized a new level of contentiousness in Washington, which took a decidedly nasty and personal turn as Donald Trump garnered media attention, first through his *birtherism* claims about President Obama and later in his vitriolic attacks on any and all critics, including many in the Republican Party, during the 2016 presidential campaign.

Trump's contempt for government institutions, the media, and longstanding rules of political decorum helped harness the anger and resentment of many White, predominantly rural Americans who felt abandoned by both political parties and largely left behind in the economic recovery from the Great Recession. Despite losing the popular vote to Hillary Clinton, Trump was elected president in 2016 on a wave of Make America Great Again sentiment and promptly moved to reverse a number of Obama-era achievements, including pulling out of the Paris Climate Agreement and rolling back scores of environmental regulations, imposing tough new immigration restrictions, signing into law the largest corporate tax cuts on record, and appointing ultra-conservative judges who effectively reshaped the federal judiciary. Indeed, in 2022, the Supreme Court—with the addition of three Trump-appointed conservative justices—reversed 50 years of precedent and overruled the 1973 *Roe v. Wade* decision that had established a woman's fundamental right to an abortion.

Trump's presidency had a polarizing effect on Americans across the political spectrum, dramatically accelerating a trend that had been apparent since the 1970s. Indeed, as the Pew Research Center reported, between 1971 and 2021, Congressional Democrats became "modestly more liberal on average," and Republicans showed "a much bigger increase in the conservative direction" (DeSilver, 2022). By 2016, bipartisanship was all but obsolete, and as Davenport (2017) argued, "the rapid and pervasive rise of party-line voting [had become] a cancer that is eating at the effectiveness of both the House of Representatives and the Senate." This ideological divide was exacerbated by the Supreme Court's 2010 decision in *Citizens United v. Federal Election Commission* to reverse longstanding campaign finance restrictions and enable corporations and other groups to spend unlimited amounts of money on elections, provided they do not formally coordinate with a candidate or political party. Although the *Citizens United* decision was ostensibly made in name of free speech, it "took that which had been named corrupt for over two hundred years and renamed it legitimate" (Teachout, 2014, p. 232). It also led to the establishment of shadowy Political Action Committees or Super-PACs, thereby expanding the influence of dark money from corporations, wealthy donors, and special interest groups. As Weiner (2015) wrote, *Citizens United* "reinforced the growing sense that our democracy primarily serves the interests of the wealthy few, and that democratic participation for the vast majority of citizens is of relatively little value."

Thus, by 2016, Americans were overwhelmingly frustrated with the partisan gridlock and inefficiency of Washington, and increasing numbers on both sides of the aisle expressed a belief that democracy did not work as it should. Yet the Trump administration's willingness to publicize "alternative facts," employ racial dog whistles, politicize the government's response to the COVID-19 pandemic, and make unabashedly false claims about everything from the size of inauguration crowds to the results of the 2020 presidential election, led to unprecedented levels of social fragmentation, distrust, and discord. Ultimately, Trump's lies about the 2020 election culminated in the violent storming of the Capitol on January 6, 2021, in an attempt to obstruct the counting of electoral votes that would formalize Joe Biden's victory—an event that a majority of Americans viewed as a fundamental attack on American democracy (Galston, 2023).

In many ways, Biden's presidency signified a return to normalcy in Washington and in America's relations across the globe. The COVID-19 pandemic waned and in 2023 President Biden ended the federal government's public health emergency declarations. Congress passed—with some bipartisan cooperation—major infrastructure, gun safety, election integrity, climate change, and domestic manufacturing bills. Yet distrust in democracy and in its institutions remains high and the combination of never-before seen levels of income inequality and a number of racialized events and cultural movements have ensured that Americans remain as politically divided and socially fragmented as ever. Indeed, since 2016, the United States has been considered a "flawed democracy" and was recently ranked twenty-sixth of 167 countries on the Economist Intelligence Unit's (2022) Democracy Index.

## A Changing Economy and the Shrinking Middle Class

Between 2000 and 2021, the number of working-age adults in the United States grew by 17%. At the same time, increased automation, globalization, and the greater skill required for jobs that could not be performed by machines or shipped overseas led to declining numbers of occupations that both paid a living wage and did not require education beyond high school. According to Georgetown's Center on Education and the Workforce, by 2018, two out of every three jobs required some postsecondary education or training, and the best-paid and most desirable required at least a bachelor's degree (Carnevale et al., 2018). Enrollments—especially in community colleges and broadly accessible institutions—boomed during the Great Recession as large numbers of displaced workers sought to upskill or reskill. Jobs requiring some postsecondary education or training less than a bachelor's degree topped the lists of fastest-growing occupations, and in the second decade of the twenty-first century, community colleges and some comprehensive universities built certificate and degree programs to train ever greater numbers of nurses, solar panel installers, wind turbine technicians, and skilled workers in advanced manufacturing and health care fields. The rise of the Skilled Technical Workforce indicates that the bachelor's degree is no longer the only viable portal to the middle class, and a greater number of students—especially adult learners—are eschewing the traditional, linear path to a college degree in favor of shorter-term credentials, including industry-relevant and stackable certificates. Yet these new ways of "doing college" (Gaston and Van Noy, 2022, p. 28) contributed to the dearth of opportunity for those with only a high school education; in 2023, the greatest disparities (in attitudes, incomes, and career opportunities) existed not between workers holding sub-baccalaureate credentials and those with advanced degrees, but among people who had at least some postsecondary experience and those who did not.

As changes to the composition of the workforce generally proceeded in one direction, other indicators of America's economic health throughout the Contemporary Era were more variable, showing a steady rise during the first few years of the twenty-first century, a substantial dip during between 2007 and 2009, followed by a long period of pronounced improvement until the COVID-19 pandemic upended everything in 2020, at least for a short while. Unemployment, for example, rose substantially during the Great Recession, then dropped consistently from late 2009 until job losses due to the pandemic caused it to skyrocket in Spring 2020. In April of that year, the unemployment rate peaked at nearly 15%, before dropping to 6.7% by the end of 2020 and to roughly 3.5% by

Spring 2022, where it remained consistent for some time (Bureau of Labor Statistics, 2023).

Similarly, between 2007 and 2009, $8 trillion was wiped out of the stock market, and Americans lost $9.8 trillion in wealth "as home values plummeted and their retirement accounts vaporized" (Merle, 2018). Yet soon afterward, the United States entered the longest bull market in history, which lasted almost exactly 11 years until the COVID-19 pandemic brought it to a close. During that time, interest rates dropped steadily, real wages increased, and people—especially those with money in the market—generally felt rich. Consumer spending, which had slowed during the recession years, once again shot up, accounting for more than two-thirds of gross domestic product in 2022 (CEIC, 2023).

Yet while much wealth was created in the second decade of the twenty-first century, it was far from evenly distributed. The federal minimum wage has remained at $7.25 per hour since 2009, and while it is now substantially higher in several states (exceeding $15 in California, Massachusetts, and Washington), 15 states remain pegged to the federal minimum. Furthermore, as analysts from the Pew Research Center (Kochhar and Sechopoulos, 2022) showed, the percentage of American adults that make up the middle class has steadily shrunk from 61% in 1971 to 50% in 2021. More Americans have joined the upper income tier (21%, compared to 14% in 1971), but the lower income tier has also expanded, now comprising 29% of American adults. And although household incomes have risen considerably, those for lower-income households were slower to grow than those for middle-income households (45%, compared to 50% growth over the half century), and both rates were dwarfed by the 69% growth experienced by upper-income households. Black adults saw some of the biggest gains in income during this period but continued to be overrepresented in the lower income tier.

The result of these shifts is a historic level of income inequality. In 2020, just over one-fifth of American adults earned half of all income in that year; the 50% of Americans in the middle class accounted for 42% of aggregate income, and the 29% of adults in the lowest income tier accounted for only 8% of aggregate annual income (Kochhar and Sechopoulos, 2022). Once accumulated wealth is considered, inequality in America is even more stark. Even before the pandemic exacerbated financial inequities, roughly one-fifth of Americans had "zero or negative net worth," and the three richest Americans—Bill Gates, Warren Buffet, and Jeff Bezos—together held more wealth than 50% of the American population (Collins and Hoxie, 2017, p. 2).

This wealth gap—along with massive government bailouts of the banking industry in 2008—contributed to the public's growing distrust of government and financial institutions. And over time, the notion that both Washington and Wall Street are fundamentally unfair morphed into more generalized suspicions about the fairness of all institutions, including those in the media and in higher education. The postsecondary sector's centrality in the culture wars of the twenty-first century, in which race, religion, and other aspects of identity are front and center, also contributed to changing perceptions of the nation's colleges and universities.

## Race, Identity, and the Twenty-First Century Culture Wars

As progressives gained ground on social issues in the Contemporary Era, it became easy for many—especially those living in blue states and major metropolitan areas—to believe that the arc of Martin Luther King Jr.'s moral universe was indeed bending toward justice. Until 2023, affirmative action had been upheld in the courts. Gay marriage was legal. Health care was established as a basic human right. Eleven states and numerous metropolitan areas identified themselves as sanctuary cities, discouraging local law enforcement from reporting the immigration status of individuals unless it involved investigation of a serious crime. More than 150 confederate monuments were removed from public spaces in the South, and the United States invested heavily in alternative energy sources, electric vehicles, and common-sense climate reforms.

Yet racial, class, and identity-based tensions simmered just under the surface, and during Trump's presidency two diametrically opposed cultural movements came to a head. The first was fueled, as Lawrence Glickman (2020) wrote in *The Atlantic*, by "a psychology of white resentment." Given voice and legitimacy by a president who refused to condemn their actions and far-right commentators and media outlets that espoused their views, White supremacist and White nationalist groups emerged from the shadows in which they had long operated, promoting their views on social media and organizing public events, including the 2017 Unite the Right rally in which a White nationalist murdered one person and injured 35 counterprotesters in Charlottesville, Virginia.

At the same time, the Black Lives Matter movement, which began in 2014 following highly publicized killings of Michael Brown, Trayvon Martin, Eric Garner, and several other African Americans, was supercharged in Spring 2020 following the police murders of Breonna Taylor and George Floyd, who died after a White police officer knelt on his neck for over nine minutes while Floyd lay handcuffed on a Minneapolis street. Floyd's murder—the video of which was watched over 1.4 billion times in the first 12 days after his death—galvanized a nation that was largely working or studying from home in the early months of the COVID-19 pandemic; the *New York Times* estimated that between 15 and 26 million Americans took to the streets in 2020 to protest racialized violence and call for criminal justice reform. Perhaps for the first time in history, outrage over the murder of a Black man resulted in a nationwide reckoning about race and racism in America's workplaces, classrooms, and legislatures.

But just as the Civil Rights Movement of the 1960s prompted a backlash in which "White people with relative societal power perceived themselves as victimized by what they described as overly aggressive African Americans demanding equal rights," the social justice movements of the twenty-first century shifted the focus "from those denied equality under the law and demanding justice to those who imagined threat or inconvenience in the possibility of social change" (Glickman, 2020). The years since 2020 have seen angry conservative backlashes against everything from COVID mask mandates to education about structural racism, sexual orientation, and gender identity. Since 2021, at least 44 states have taken steps to restrict the teaching of critical race theory or limit how teachers can discuss racism and sexism (Schwartz, 2023). In 2022, Florida Governor Ron DeSantis signed a bill forbidding classroom instruction on sexual orientation or gender identity in kindergarten through the third grade, and in 2023, a state board approved an extension of this "Don't Say Gay" bill to include all grades. In several states, Republicans have passed laws restricting access to gender-affirming health care for teens and preventing teachers from addressing students with pronouns other than those corresponding to their sex at birth.

In addition, bans on books featuring LGBTQ+ themes or characters, characters of color, or content related to race or racism became widespread in Republican-controlled states (PEN America recorded 1,477 book bans in the first half of the 2022–2023 school year alone). In a further act of censorship, the Republican-controlled state house in Missouri passed a budget in 2023 that would completely defund all libraries in the state. While much of the conservative backlash focused on K–12 education, colleges and universities increasingly were dragged into the fray as lawmakers in Texas, Florida, and other states advanced legislation that would end or limit tenure for professors in public colleges and universities and ban diversity, equity, and inclusion offices or activities on campus. These laws represent a fundamental attack on academic freedom, and if passed and upheld in the courts, would imperil higher education's ability to promote free inquiry and critical thought, not to mention provide equitable supports for students. This should be a chilling prospect for anyone who has benefited from or aspires to attend an institution of higher education, yet in the current era of political polarization, it is unclear if Americans can set aside their differences to preserve the institutions that have, for nearly 400 years, enabled the nation's scientific, technological, social, cultural, and economic progress.

**Divergent Views of American Higher Education**

The culture wars of the twenty-first century, in which issues of race and identity were superimposed onto longstanding political and economic differences, contributed to deeply divergent views about and a general distrust of American higher education. In 2019, the Pew Research Center summarized several of its own surveys, finding "an undercurrent of dissatisfaction—even suspicion—among the public about the role colleges play in society, the way admissions decisions are made and the extent to which free speech is constrained on college campuses" (para. 2). And, the report showed, "these views are increasingly linked to partisanship" (para. 2).

One study, for example, found that 61% of Americans (including 52% of Democrats and 73% of Republicans) believe that the higher education system is going in the wrong direction. Both Democrats and Republicans cited rising tuition and other costs as a primary source of their discontent, but nearly 8 in 10 Republicans identified "professors bringing their political and social views into the classroom" as a major reason for their dissatisfaction. Similarly, a recent poll conducted by Inside Higher Ed showed that 83% of Republicans agreed with the statement that "most college professors teach liberal propaganda," a sentiment shared by only 17% of Democrats. Furthermore, while 71% of Democrats agreed that "higher education is the best way to get ahead in the U.S.," only 37% of Republicans concurred (Jaschik, 2022).

According to James Davidson Hunter, author of the 1991 book *Culture Wars*, Republican distrust of institutions of higher education is rooted in nothing less than a "fear of extinction." As he explained, colleges and universities remain the primary route to the middle and upper classes. Yet because most faculty and staff in these institutions hold progressive political views, conservatives view them and the institutions they represent as "an *existential threat* to their way of life, to the things that they hold sacred" (quoted in Stanton, 2021, italics in the original).

These feelings are exacerbated by media stories that reinforce polarizing views of higher education. In 2022, the Lumina Foundation sponsored an analysis of the primary narratives related to higher education appearing in over 40,000 news, magazine, and blog sources spanning conservative, liberal, and mainstream outlets at national, regional, and local levels. Finding that narratives related to "woke-ism," the fairness of affirmative action or student debt cancellation policies, and the notion that "college is no longer relevant" accounted for roughly one-third of total media impact, the Lumina Foundation's Debra Humphreys (2023) argued that ideas damaging to the future of higher education had "firmly rooted themselves in the [media] landscape" (p. 9). Furthermore, she illustrated how the "woke-ism" narrative had spilled over from conservative to mainstream media outlets, allowing such attitudes to gain a larger foothold in the national conversation.

However, not all media narratives related to higher education were negative. Indeed, 68% of total coverage was supportive of colleges and universities. In particular, the narrative around higher education's ability to level the playing field, which accounted for 22% of total impact, suggested that "the public's appetite for discussing race, equity, and opportunity is quite high" (Humphreys, 2023, p. 9). This narrative, along with those related to saving the American Dream and community colleges being "higher ed's best kept secret," do much to counter negative views of higher education. Yet because traditional news media are no longer beholden to the doctrine of fair and balanced news coverage, and because social media algorithms perpetuate feedback loops and create echo chambers in which content consumers are continually fed news and information aligned with their views and interests, the extent to which Americans already suspicious of colleges and universities are exposed to narratives that might enhance support for higher education is unclear.

In the third decade of the twenty-first century, colleges and universities have once again become settings for conflict over changing American values. But this time, they are also targets in the nation's broader culture wars over race, identity, social justice, free speech, and individual rights. Debates over whether the U.S. postsecondary system has done more to increase opportunity or perpetuate privilege that were once the domain of scholars are now commonplace on social media, and politicians and commentators alike view attacks on the colleges as effective mechanisms for motivating voters or increasing ratings. It is in this context that faculty must teach, students must learn, and administrators and trustees must guide their institutions toward a just and financially sustainable future.

## Institutions

Higher education expanded throughout much of the Contemporary Era, reaching a high-water mark in 2018 before declining numbers of high school graduates, institutional consolidation in some states, and the COVID-19 pandemic combined to reverse the trend. Table 6.1 offers an overview of the Contemporary Era. Notable is the 38% increase in enrollment between 1994 and 2018, as well as the subsequent 5% drop between 2018 and 2021 (which was larger in community colleges and other broadly accessible institutions). In the latter year, 3,931 accredited nonprofit colleges and universities awarded associate or bachelor's degrees. In addition, more than 2,000 proprietary or for-profit institutions provided everything from short-term occupational certificates to graduate degrees. Despite recent enrollment losses, the number of credentials awarded by the traditional sector expanded so that nearly 750,000 certificates, over 1 million associate degrees, more than 2 million bachelor's degrees,

Table 6.1. Statistical Portrait of the Contemporary Era, 1994–2021.

| | 1994 | 2005 | 2015 | 2021 |
|---|---|---|---|---|
| U.S. population | 263,435,673 | 295,895,287 | 321,418,821 | 329,725,481 |
| Number of students | 14,278,790 | 17,487,475 | 19,988,204 | 18,659,851 |
| Number of faculty | 924,000 | 1,290,426 | 1,552,256 | 1,489,415 |
| Number of institutions (including branch campuses) | 3,688 | 4,276 | 4,583 | 3,931 |
| Number of degrees earned (associate, bachelor's, master's, first professional, and doctoral) | 2,217,700 | 2,936,337 | 3,892,869 | 4,090,291 |
| Current-fund revenue (in thousands of current dollars) | 189,120,570 | 385,971,374 | 573,080,211 | 665,434,991 |

*Sources:* NCES *Digest*, 2023; U.S. Bureau of the Census, 2023.

nearly 850,000 master's and first professional degrees, and 190,000 doctorates were conferred each year. Tuition, room, and board for undergraduate residential students at four-year institutions averaged nearly $26,000 per year overall, with the private sector more than twice as high as the public. Seventy-two percent of students received some type of financial aid. Of the 242 million adults in the United States, 40% participated in some form of adult education annually. Over 18 million students were enrolled in institutions of higher education, at a cost of $665 billion.

**Research Universities**

Commonality among institutions is greatest among the most prominent. While different sectors of the U.S. system vary widely in finances, curricular emphases, accessibility, degrees awarded, ties to corporations, sports, physical campuses, student services, and so forth, doctoral-granting universities—both public and private—tend to closely resemble one another. Although some private research universities enroll only a few thousand students and some of the largest flagship public universities over 100,000, variation among these institutions occurs primarily in the number of Nobel Laureates on the faculty, the number of courses or programs taught online, the amount of federal research dollars awarded, or whether a particular university has an associated medical or engineering school. Doctoral-granting universities in the United States also have larger endowments than other institutions; endowments among the 20 institutions with the largest range from just under $6 billion at Cornell to over $55 billion at Harvard. These and similar universities bring in millions (if not billions) of federal and private research dollars, maintain sprawling campuses, reward faculty primarily for research activity, engage in selective admissions practices, and offer students a broad array of specialized courses and amenities.

Doctoral-granting universities are the most exclusive institutions of higher education, but because of their size, the 131 classified as having very high levels of research activity enroll more than one-fifth of all students. This combination of prestige and market share means that, for better or worse, the policies and practices at research universities are mimicked by other types of institutions seeking to improve their reputations. Perhaps the best example of higher education's isomorphic tendencies during the Contemporary Era is in the practice of student recruitment. In tacit acknowledgement that the academic quality of an incoming first-year class is the most influential predictor of high graduation rates and other positive institutional outcomes, between 1994 and 2023, research universities engaged in fierce competition for the best and brightest students. To admit top students and maintain high yields, they solicited ever greater numbers of applications, instituted early-decision or early-action admissions programs, poured money into residence halls and research and athletic facilities, and marketed honors programs that would provide students with special privileges and benefits such as smaller classes and research opportunities. Although only 1% of four-year institutions admit less than 10% of applicants and an additional 5% admit between 10 and 30% (DeSilver, 2019), these practices were imitated by many other colleges and universities, which contributed in part to substantially higher tuition and fees at all types of four-year institutions.

Between 1995–1996 and 2007–2008, universities—especially private universities—increased merit-based financial aid at double the rate of need-based aid in order to discount their sticker price and lure top-performing students away from less expensive institutions. Even Ivy League universities found it necessary to compete for top high school graduates; in 2001, Princeton announced it would cover all incoming students' financial aid needs with grants instead of loans, a move that brought competition for students to a new level. However, the trend toward merit-based aid stalled in 2008 following several reports showing that the increase overwhelmingly benefited students from families in the highest income quartile. Since then, several institutions and states shifted more resources to need-based aid to provide equitable opportunities for students who might not otherwise be able to afford college. Indeed, in 2022, Princeton enhanced its grant-based financial aid policy by pledging that students from families earning less than $100,000 will pay nothing for tuition, room, and board.

Most research universities have long participated in competitive sports. Harvard and Yale were national football powers in the first half of the twentieth century, and in 1935, a player from the University of Chicago was the first winner of the Heisman Trophy. In the late twentieth century, however, athletics programs at flagship public universities grew to record proportions. College football, in particular, reached a new level when the Bowl Championship Series was instituted in 1998 and generated even more money when the College Football Championship (CFP) replaced it in 2014. (In 2016–2017 the Big Ten conference brought in over $132 million for its teams' participation in the CFP.) In 2019, the last year before the COVID-19 pandemic skewed the numbers, Division I athletics generated $15.8 billion in revenue. In 2021, the Supreme Court ruled that these profits must be shared with the athletes themselves, and shortly afterward the NCAA voted to allow student athletes to receive an expanded array of education-related benefits in exchange for the use of their name, image, and likeness.

Despite the huge amount of revenue generated annually by athletics, only a few universities earned enough money from media rights, bowl revenues, ticket sales, royalties and licensing, donor contributions, and other sources to support their athletic departments; the vast majority of intercollegiate sports programs required significant subsidy from their parent institution. In 2019, only 25 of the 130 schools in the Football Bowl Subdivision reported positive net revenues; the median program ran an operating deficit of $18.8 million (PBS, 2023). Universities were willing to continue their investment in football and other athletic teams, however, as sports continued to be an integral part of the extra-curriculum for students and a way of entertaining (and potentially gaining financial support from) alumni and local communities.

Despite serving as a loss leader for most institutions, participation in big-time athletics is emblematic of another trend among research universities in the Contemporary Era: an increased orientation toward the market and greater commercialization of education and scientific research. As former Harvard president Derek Bok wrote in 2003, "universities have become much more active in selling what they know and do to individuals and corporations" (p. vii), and this trend has since accelerated. Whether increased entrepreneurship is due to a greater number of business executives on university governing boards and in collegiate C-suites or has resulted from decades of reductions in governmental support for institutions of higher education (or some combination of the two), the modern research university has become a global enterprise. Even the most elite institutions engage in revenue-generating behavior ranging from patent licensing, to building research centers or institutes to attract federal and philanthropic research dollars, to purchasing formerly for-profit universities to expand their global reach and profit from enrollment in courses and programs that fall outside their core offerings. Although all types of colleges and universities now engage in some level of educational entrepreneurship, such behavior is concentrated among institutions where scientific research is a mission priority.

**Comprehensive and Land Grant Universities**

In the Contemporary Era, comprehensive and land grant universities both took steps to look and act like the more prestigious research universities and grew into a class of their own, one focused less on exclusivity and more on providing high-quality education and support to students, especially those from minoritized or low-income communities. In some cases, actions that mimicked those in the research universities—enhanced student recruitment, a greater focus on alternative revenue generation, the provision of doctoral degrees—were defended as necessary to extend educational opportunity to historically underserved groups. For example, coordinating commissions and long-range plans such as California's 1960 Master Plan for Higher Education had long delineated which degrees state universities could and could not award. Yet in the Contemporary Era, many such institutions actively worked to expand their curriculum upward, arguing, for example, that the ability to confer doctoral degrees in education, engineering, health services, and other areas was necessary to provide equitable pathways to advanced degrees and to meet labor market demands. By 2023, the California State University system, once limited by the Master Plan to awarding nothing higher than a master's degree, offered 23 PhD programs in various disciplines, 30 EdD programs, as well as 17 Doctor of Nursing Practice, Doctor of Audiology, or Doctor of Physical Therapy programs across its 23 campuses.

As new degree programs and institutional emphases were added, others evolved or gravitated toward available funding. Following passage of the 2008 farm bill, which established the Agriculture and Food Research Initiative (AFRI), the federal government appropriated millions of dollars in competitive research grants: $445 million in 2022 alone. While AFRI grants are not limited to land-grant institutions, they are some of the primary beneficiaries due to their longstanding commitment to agricultural teaching, research, and extension. To enhance their research capacity, some leading agricultural universities such as Texas A&M and Colorado State University eliminated or combined traditional departments such as animal science, horticulture, agronomy, entomology, and rural sociology, and increased their liaisons with corporate farming. Others created new interdisciplinary programs focusing on resource and land management, land use and disaster planning, and climate change mitigation strategies. Despite these broader trends, niche efforts tied to regional economies, such as a brewing program or a research center devoted to a local ecological problem, were still common in land-grant institutions, and both they and other comprehensive universities maintained baccalaureate, master's, and first professional programs in the humanities, liberal arts, sciences, education, and business.

Although some comprehensive and land-grant universities have somewhat selective admissions requirements, most accept the vast majority of applicants and thus fall into Crisp, McClure, and Orphan's (2022) definition of broadly accessible four-year institutions, a category that also includes some private colleges, Minority-Serving Institutions, and baccalaureate-granting community colleges. Collectively, these institutions extend baccalaureate and graduate education to historically marginalized communities and, like community colleges, strive to implement equitable policies and practices to support students. As Gonzales and Robinson (2023) wrote, although broadly accessible institutions "hold teaching as a central priority, many nurture research activities and agendas that center community and place, and thus facilitate possibilities for epistemic justice" (p. 467).

However, another contemporary trend threatens comprehensive and land-grant institutions' ability to serve historically marginalized groups: the removal or restriction of developmental education programs for academically underprepared students. In 1999, in response to a scathing critique of the City University of New York's (CUNY) academic standards and student outcomes, CUNY's Board of Trustees approved a plan that eliminated all developmental education at its senior colleges, making it the sole purview of CUNY's community colleges. Comprehensive universities across the country soon did likewise, drawing support from legislators concerned about the rising costs of developmental education and attainment-focused organizations such as Complete College America, which in 2012 referred to developmental education as higher education's "Bridge to Nowhere."

Between 1994 and 2018, the percentage of universities offering developmental courses dropped from 85 to 74% in the public four-year sector, and from 69 to 58% in private four-year institutions. Since 2000, numerous states have written or tightened existing policies to restrict the types of institutions that can offer developmental education, make it optional for students, or limit the time learners may spend in developmental programs (Doran, 2022). For example, a 2012 Connecticut bill limited underprepared students to one semester of developmental coursework, excluding developmental classes attached to credit-bearing courses. While such legislation may promote the implementation of best practices in developmental education—including corequisite, accelerated, and contextualized models—Doran (2022) cautioned that it also may serve to restrict university access for historically marginalized students.

**Community Colleges**

As open-access institutions with a mission to serve their communities and provide developmental, liberal arts, integrative, and occupational education and training, community colleges have been essential in expanding the higher education enterprise to all learners, especially those from historically marginalized or minoritized communities. In 2020, community colleges enrolled 4.7 million students, down from 5.4 million pre-pandemic. Yet the high-water mark for community college enrollments came in 2010, when 7.2 million recent high school graduates and adults alike entered the institutions to upskill or further their education during the Great Recession. The enrollment decline between 2010 and 2019 can be attributed to several factors, notably the number of students re-entering the job market, substantial efforts by state universities to recruit a larger percentage of high school graduates, and a reclassification of institutions in which community colleges that offered one or more baccalaureate degrees were removed from the category (Kisker, Cohen, and Brawer, 2023). Nonetheless, in 2020 one-third of all students beginning postsecondary education enrolled first in a community college, and of those who delayed entry until they were 30 or older, nearly two-thirds began in such institutions. Of the 14.8 million people who earned a bachelor's degree between 2008 and 2017, 52% had attended a community college (Foley, Milan, and Hamrick, 2021).

The extent of community college enrollment varies widely among states: in Iowa, Mississippi, Wyoming, California, and New Mexico, community colleges enrolled over 40% of all undergraduates, while community colleges in several other states enrolled less than 15%. (In some cases, however, this small market share was due to the fact that most or all of the state's community colleges were authorized to award the baccalaureate and thus were counted as four-year institutions.) Disaggregating enrollment figures by race and ethnicity further reveals the community colleges' contributions to access, as proportions of Hispanic or Latinx and African American students enrolled in community colleges exceed their shares of the national population; this holds true for most states as well (Kisker, Cohen, and Brawer, 2023).

The community college's impressive market share can be attributed to two factors: location (over 90% of Americans live within 25 miles of a community college, and close to 50% of community college students live within 10 miles of the college they attend), and the cost of attendance. In the first decade of the twenty-first century, when public and private four-year universities raised tuition and fees by as much as 9% a year, community colleges kept their prices low. Furthermore, enhancements to the Pell Grant program and the emergence of College Promise and other state-sponsored tuition- or debt-free college plans ensured that community colleges remain the most affordable options for postsecondary study. In 2020, community college tuition and fees averaged $3,501 per year, although this ranged from $1,270 in California to over $7,000 in New Hampshire.

As in years past, community colleges provided the essential lower-division coursework necessary for transfer to a four-year university, as well as occupational certification and degree programs preparing learners for professions in which some college, but not necessarily a bachelor's degree, is required for entry. In the Contemporary Era, however, much effort was made to integrate liberal arts and occupational programs and ensure that both areas provided pathways to further education as well as the workforce. Community colleges also participated extensively in developmental education; a 2016 report suggested that community college students and their families spent $920 million annually on pre-college courses (Jimenez et al., 2016), although that figure may have decreased as the colleges emphasized corequisite, accelerated, and contextualized models over stand-alone and prerequisite developmental courses. Community colleges are also essential in connecting the K–12 and postsecondary sectors. Each year several hundred thousand high school students participate in dual enrollment programs, and some colleges have worked to integrate grades 11–14 via early college high school and P-TECH programs in which learners earn their high school diploma as well as an associate degree in two or three years instead of the traditional four.

Despite their contributions to access (indeed, because of it), community colleges contribute to a hierarchical structure of postsecondary education, and in turn influence university reputations. Showing that 12 of the 17 state universities ranked in the top 100 institutions in the world were in states where community college enrollments exceeded the national median, Goldin and Katz (2008) suggested that the presence of the low-cost, open-access institutions enabled the universities to engage in highly selective admissions practices and allocate more funds to research and graduate programs without denying access to higher education for the rest of the states' youth. However, in recent years community colleges have focused on developing occupational certificate and applied baccalaureate programs so that their students—many of whom are low-income or from historically marginalized races and ethnicities—can access credentials and well-paying jobs without having to transfer to a four-year university. In addition to preparing the vast majority of workers entering the skilled technical workforce, by 2021 at least 139 community colleges in 24 states were approved to offer the baccalaureate in applied areas such as business, education, nursing, health professions, and technology (this number has since increased substantially). Florida and Washington have the greatest number of community colleges conferring bachelor's degrees; by 2021, every single one of Florida's 28 colleges operated baccalaureate programs, and 29 of Washington's 34 colleges did the same (Love, Bragg, and Harmon, 2021).

In recent decades, as states and localities systematically disinvested in public higher education in general and in community colleges in particular, the institutions have engaged in numerous public–private partnerships, corporate training arrangements, and other entrepreneurial approaches to serving students and communities. Throughout the Contemporary Era practically all community colleges collaborated with one or more companies to provide employees with job-specific technological, management, or workplace literacy skills, and a few generated millions of dollars annually from such arrangements. Although critics of contract training and other entrepreneurial activities argue that they have compromised academic values and shifted the community college's focus away from liberal arts programs, transfer curricula, and citizenship development, others acknowledge the potential of entrepreneurship to diversify and stabilize community college revenues. Many community college leaders concurred with Kisker (2021), who reasoned that "community college entrepreneurship—in and of itself—is neither good nor bad. What matters is that entrepreneurial opportunities are pursued in a way that prioritizes the needs of college stakeholders . . . and that they are evaluated by their ability to further the college's mission" (p. 33).

Community colleges often have been derided for persistence and completion rates that are lower than those in other sectors, but accurately measuring such rates has always been problematic for community colleges, whose students enter with a diverse range of goals and expectations; often stop and start their education multiple times, sometimes "swirling" between institutions (de los Santos and Wright, 1990); and because two-thirds of students (and 78% of adults) attend part time, which necessarily extends time-to-degree or transfer. Transfer rates similarly differ depending on which factors are included in the calculation (the number of years measured, intentions of incoming students, whether transfers to out-of-state or private institutions are counted). In the 1980s and 1990s, the percentage of students who transferred consistently held around 20 to 25%, but in recent years roughly one-third of first-time community college students transferred to a senior institution. Perhaps more importantly given the varied missions of the institution and intentions of its students, 65% of full-time and 52% of part-time learners earned a degree or certificate, transferred, or were still enrolled after six years (National Student Clearinghouse, 2022b). Given their lower cost and responsiveness to business and community needs, community colleges have garnered much attention from legislators, industry groups, and philanthropic organizations and have become lynchpins in regional economic development and workforce training efforts.

**Minority-Serving Institutions**

A substantial number of community colleges and broadly accessible comprehensive or land-grant universities are designated as Minority-Serving Institutions (MSIs), in recognition of their role in educating various marginalized or minoritized populations and to enable special assistance grants to improve the retention and support of targeted populations. The diverse sector of MSIs includes Historically Black Colleges and Universities (HBCUs) and Predominately Black Institutions (PBIs); Tribal Colleges and Native American Serving Non-Tribal Institutions (NASNTIs); Hispanic-Serving Institutions (HSIs); as well as Asian American and Native American Pacific Islander Serving Institutions (AANAPISIs) and Alaska Native and

Native Hawaiian Serving Institutions (ANNHs). Some institutions, specifically HBCUs and some Tribal Colleges, are classified as MSIs due to their historical origin or mission focus, while most other MSIs are so categorized because they meet federally defined enrollment thresholds of students from the specified race or ethnicity and with demonstrated financial need. MSIs collectively enroll roughly 20% of undergraduates and 40% of all undergraduate students of color. Given projections showing that the United States will become majority-minority by 2044, as well as the deficit framing inherent in the term "minority-serving," Blake (2017) and others have advocated that these institutions instead be called "equity-oriented institutions," but this is not likely to occur absent changes in federal legislation that directs funding to MSIs.

Although the MSI designation was not formalized until the Higher Education Act of 1965, some private HBCUs date to the mid-nineteenth century; most public HBCUs were created following the second Morrill Act, which stipulated in 1890 that states must either demonstrate that admission to land-grant institutions was not restricted by race or establish new institutions for Black students. In 2021, the nation's 99 remaining HBCUs—predominately four-year institutions, evenly split between public and private—enrolled roughly 287,000 students. Although approximately 75% of HBCU students are African American, less than 10% of Black students attend one of these institutions. However, another 9% attend one of 67 PBIs, defined as two- or four-year colleges whose undergraduate student body is at least 40% Black and at least 50% low-income or first-generation. Despite their origins as separate and decidedly unequal institutions—and centuries of being underfunded and undervalued (Harris, 2021)—HBCUs contributed mightily to the educational and social progress, not only of African Americans, but of the nation in general. Their substantial influence on the American Civil Rights Movement; the legal profession and the NAACP; medical and health programs; religious education; music, art, and culture; and collegiate and professional sports are painstakingly detailed in Lovett's (2015) *America's Historically Black Colleges and Universities: A Narrative History*.

Like that for African Americans, the history of higher education for Indigenous peoples is steeped in racism and shameful treatment of America's original inhabitants. Tribal Colleges have their roots in boarding schools developed for the purpose of assimilating Indigenous children into mainstream society (Thelin, 2019). Yet following the 1965 Higher Education Act, Native American and Alaska Native tribes established their own institutions to serve Indigenous students and protect tribal cultures, values, and traditions. The first—Diné College in Arizona—was established by the Navajo Nation in 1968; the American Indian College Fund now recognizes 33 Tribal Colleges and Universities in 14 states, some with numerous satellite campuses. Most are small, serving only a few hundred students, but some—such as Diné and Navajo Technical University (New Mexico)—serve well over 1,000 learners. Along with ANNHs and NASNTIs—non-tribal institutions where Indigenous students make up at least 10% of the student body—Tribal Colleges and Universities have been essential in extending access to Indigenous students.

HSIs emerged as a designated category in 1992, following years of advocacy and exponential growth in the Latinx population. HSIs are defined as two- or four-year colleges where Hispanic or Latinx students comprise at least 25% of the undergraduate full-time-equivalent (FTE) student body and at least half of all Hispanic students are low-income. As Brown (2022) noted, soon after receiving HSI designation, many institutions amended their mission statements, recruitment practices, and curriculum and pedagogical approaches to acknowledge their new identity. In 2020–2021, two-thirds of all Hispanic or Latinx undergraduates were enrolled in one of 559 HSIs. This percentage is likely to increase, as in 2023 there were 393 emerging HSIs with FTE enrollments between 15% and 24.9% Hispanic (Hispanic Association of Colleges and Universities, 2023).

Designated in the 2007 College Cost Reduction and Access Act, AANAPISIs represent the newest category of MSIs and serve one of the most ethnically diverse and least understood groups. Located throughout the United States and Pacific Islands, AANAPISIs are defined as colleges or universities with undergraduate enrollments that are at least 10% Asian American and Pacific Islander (AAPI) and where at least 50% of degree-seeking students are considered low-income. AANAPISIs comprise only 4.4% of all American colleges and universities, yet together they enroll nearly 40% of all AAPI students (Nguyen, Hoang, and Ching, 2022).

**Private Colleges and Universities**

Most private, four-year colleges continued to thrive during the Contemporary Era, due in part to their ability to confer degrees upon a greater percentage of their students. Indeed, 57% of first-time, full-time students at private, nonprofit institutions earned a bachelor's degree within four years (and 68% completed within six), compared to 42% and 63%, respectively, of public college or university students. What accounts for this difference? One answer may lie in the private college's ability to restrict student entry. Yet while this explains why prestigious private institutions such as Stanford, Yale, Northwestern, and Duke boast bachelor's degree completion rates approaching 95%, it does not fully account for the private-public graduation gap, since more than half of all private four-year colleges offer admission to 80% or more of their applicants (Crisp, McClure, and Orphan, 2022). Furthermore, the private college advantage in graduation rates holds even among open-access and broadly accessible institutions.

An explanation for the graduation gap thus points to higher per capita expenditures (nearly 30% higher in 2019–2020) and to many of the institutional factors that have characterized private higher education since the Colonial Era: small classes, high levels of student-faculty interaction, tightly knit residential campus communities, and large percentages of full-time students. Rudolph's

(1962) notion of the "collegiate way"—the idea that a college community should function much like a family in which everyone lives together, learns together, and exerts positive influences on one another's social, academic, and personal development—is clearly just as important to the success of contemporary private colleges as it was to those founded in the eighteenth and early nineteenth centuries.

However, not all private colleges thrived in the Contemporary Era; some small four-years and numerous private two-year colleges did not. These institutions—many of which are church-affiliated—comprised a majority of the junior college sector between 1915 and 1949, but since then have declined in number, merging with other institutions or closing their doors. By 2019, after decades of dwindling enrollments and increased operational costs, 56% of private two-year colleges operating at the start of the Contemporary Era ceased to exist. Only 85 such institutions remained in 2019–2020, and several (as well as a handful of small, private four-year colleges) have since closed.

Nonetheless, private colleges collectively generated huge sums of money during the Contemporary Era as national policies that reduced taxes on the wealthiest Americans enabled those individuals to pay higher tuitions for their sons and daughters, as well as donate substantial sums to their alma maters. Development officers at private colleges expanded their efforts, and many donors heeded the call: gifts and grants to private institutions tripled during the era to more than $31 billion in 2019–2020. Due to higher tuition (and thus greater amounts of financial aid), as well as growth in the number of federal research grants and contracts, private universities received increasing payouts from Washington during the Contemporary Era. Indeed, the top six institutions receiving the most money from the federal government in 2018 were all private; the $11.4 billion these universities collectively received accounted for 14% of all federal revenue to higher education in that year.

Despite increased federal support for private higher education during the Contemporary Era, or perhaps because of it, many legislators, parents, and students deplored the rising tuition and fees. Many of these critiques were leveled at private colleges, even though the 59% increase in tuition, fees, room, and board at these institutions between 1994 and 2020 paled in comparison to the 83% increase at public four-year colleges, which of course started from a much lower base. In 2022–2023, tuition, room, and board at private four-year institutions cost an average of $53,430. The average price of a private education was higher in New England, where a greater number of colleges draw students from across the country, than it was in areas of the country where private colleges serve a more regional population, and higher among doctoral-granting institutions than colleges awarding the bachelor's as their highest degree (College Board, 2022).

Although some students undoubtedly were priced out of the private higher education market during the Contemporary Era (or at a minimum were scared away by high sticker prices), higher tuitions meant bigger pots of money from which institutions could award need-based scholarships, and huge investments in institutional aid reduced the net cost of attending private institutions to a price comparable to that of a public university for many middle- and low-income families. The fact that 92% of private college students received some sort of financial aid did not quell the critics, however, and in 2008, Congress passed legislation aimed at stemming the rising cost of college. The Higher Education Opportunity Act requires the U.S. Department of Education to post each college's net tuition online and spotlight the 5% of institutions with the largest percentage increases over the last three years in a bid to shame colleges into limiting future tuition hikes. However, although annual tuition increases slowed to little more than the rate of inflation in the second decade of the twenty-first century, inflation was so pronounced in the years following the COVID-19 pandemic (16% between 2020 and 2023 alone) that private colleges ultimately were forced to raise tuition again just to keep up with labor and operating costs.

**Liberal Arts Colleges**

Despite national attention to the price of college and decades of predictions that the demise of liberal arts colleges was imminent, these institutions maintained a significant place in the American higher education system due in large measure to aggressive financial aid policies, small class sizes and close student-professor relationships, campus amenities, and residential environments. But the liberal arts colleges are still threatened by the popularity of career-oriented (i.e., non-liberal arts) majors and by competition for top students. In 2023, the 89 liberal arts colleges (classified by the Carnegie Foundation as baccalaureate colleges with an arts and sciences focus) enrolled less than 1% of all undergraduates. Ostensibly, these students—like their predecessors in years past—chose to attend such institutions for the advantages mentioned above, for the prestige of attending a small or elite college, or for undergraduate research opportunities that would otherwise be reserved for graduate students.

There is some evidence, however, that these are not the only reasons twenty-first century students make enrollment decisions. According to a 2019 UCLA survey of first-year students, although 83% reported that they chose to go to college "to learn more about things that interest me," and 75% chose "to gain a general education and appreciation of ideas," 84% selected "to be able to get a better job," 79% stated "to get training for a specific career," and 73% indicated "to be able to make more money" (Stolzenberg et al., 2020, p. 49). Statistics such as these—along with evidence that "disappointingly few" students, faculty, administrators, or trustees "seem to understand the term [liberal arts] in any kind of depth"—have led some to argue that "higher education has lost its way and stands in considerable peril" (Fischman and Gardner, 2022, pp. 63, xi).

Yet there seems to be little consensus on what liberal arts institutions should do to protect their place in the postsecondary landscape. Some, such as Fischman and Gardner (2022), argue that these and other colleges should focus on their core educational mission, which is to help students "analyze, reflect, connect, and communicate on issues of importance and interest" (p. 80). Others believe the only way to save liberal arts colleges—and the liberal arts in general—is to create niche programs, connect the liberal arts to a career, and participate in consortia that enable the sharing of courses and professors as well as back-office functions (Gose, 2021). Most liberal arts institutions have embraced both paths in recent years, doubling down on their liberal mission while adding classes and majors, such as business management, where utility to the job market is more obvious to students. Many also have promoted research showing that after 40 years, the return on investment (ROI) in a liberal arts college is 25% higher than the median ROI for all institutions and lags only behind doctoral universities with the two highest levels of research activity (Carnevale, Cheah, and Van Der Werf, 2020). Thus, fears that all liberal arts colleges will see substantial drops in enrollment seem unjustified; just as they have for nearly 400 years, these institutions will surely adapt to new market pressures, but the number that will be able to do so while maintaining their characteristic liberal focus remains in question.

**Graduate and Professional Education**

Graduate and professional education grew in importance during the Contemporary Era, evidenced by a 49% increase in the number of Americans 25 and older holding a master's, first professional, or doctoral degree between 2000 and 2021 (U.S. Bureau of the Census, 2023). Today, nearly 40% of bachelor's degree recipients enroll in a graduate program within four years of completing college (Baum and Steele, 2017). The system accommodated rising graduate enrollments both by expanding existing programs and by adding new ones at universities in states where restrictions on the types of advanced degrees certain institutions may offer had been loosened. By 2019, master's degrees were conferred in 1,852 institutions, and doctorates in 1,039. Public universities awarded slightly more than half of all master's and doctoral degrees, although privates awarded more first professional degrees in law, the medical professions, and theology. As in the Consolidation Era, graduate study was concentrated at larger research institutions; in 2019–2020, 56% of all master's and 54% of doctoral degrees were awarded by universities enrolling more than 15,000 students.

The number of doctoral degrees awarded in academic (i.e., nonprofessional) disciplines increased by 24% during the Contemporary Era. More than one-third of those awarded in 2019–2020 went to non-U.S. citizens. Following changes in the workforce, nearly two-thirds of all doctorates awarded in 2019–2020 were in STEM disciplines and computer science; doctoral degrees in the humanities and social sciences comprised one-quarter of all awards and 10% were in education. Upon graduation, 29% of doctoral recipients entered the faculty ranks, 47% joined corporate or government research labs or university-based centers, and an additional 24% went into administration or professional services.

First professional degrees were similarly tied to market cues. For several years, pharmacists featured prominently on the Bureau of Labor Statistics' lists of the fastest growing occupations; between 1995–1996 and 2019–2020, pharmacy degrees increased by 468%. Doctor of osteopathic medicine degrees increased 266% during that time, and those in dentistry showed a 77% increase. Veterinary, medical, and optometry degrees also increased substantially during the Contemporary Era while others, such as law and theology, declined. Overall, the 96,014 first professional degrees awarded in 2019–2020 represented a 25% increase over 25 years.

The number of master's degrees awarded annually more than doubled during the Contemporary Era, from 403,609 in 1994–1995 to 866,894 in 2020–2021. Seven fields (business, education, engineering, computer and information sciences, health professions, psychology, and public administration and social services) accounted for nearly 80% of awards in the latter year; master's degrees in education and business alone accounted for 41% of the total. Fields with the greatest percentage increase of master's degrees closely paralleled the fastest growing professions or those that promised lucrative starting salaries; throughout the Contemporary Era, master's degrees in computer and information sciences increased by 412%, those in the health professions by 320%, mathematics and statistics by 245%, the biological and biomedical sciences by 195%, and engineering technologies by 210%. As the nation invested heavily in the War on Terror following September 11, 2001, master's degrees in homeland security, law enforcement, and firefighting increased by 525% and degrees in military technology and applied sciences by 604%. Similarly, America's interest in fitness and nutrition led to a 487% increase in master's degrees in those areas. Gender preferences were still apparent although not as pronounced as in earlier years, with women dominating education and the health professions (earning 78 and 82%, respectively, of master's degrees in those fields), and men earning most degrees in computer and information sciences (67%). However, master's degrees in business, which had once been awarded overwhelmingly to men, were roughly evenly distributed between the genders in 2019–2020.

The rise in master's degrees in business, especially in business administration (the MBA), warrants particular attention. The first business schools were formed in the late nineteenth and early twentieth centuries as larger, more complex corporations replaced family-run businesses and required professional managers who possessed the measurement and management skills to fill increasing numbers of bureaucratic positions. As institutions designed to serve industry, business schools are perhaps the most obvious examples of market forces at work in higher education. The traditional curriculum is tied to skills needed in the marketplace (economics, management, and accounting), and many schools also offer programs related to fast-growing industries. For example, in 2023, the Tepper School of Business at Carnegie Mellon University offered five different tracks of its full-time MBA program, including entrepreneurship, business analytics, and energy and sustainability. It also offered four separate joint MBA and master's degree programs and a joint MBA/JD program with the University of Pittsburgh.

Programs and courses in entrepreneurship are particularly attractive to students, and some business schools offer grants or incubation services to help students start small businesses. Although a passion for accounting or marketing may have driven some students to enroll in MBA and other business programs, most did so believing that receipt of the degree would lead to a bigger paycheck; indeed according to *Fortune* magazine (Driscoll, 2021), MBA recipients can expect to earn 75% more than people with only a bachelor's degree in business. Full-time MBA and other business programs attracted students who believed that the resulting career and pay boosts would exceed the costs of tuition and two years of foregone salary, but in the Contemporary Era business schools increasingly accommodated students who could not afford to leave their jobs by adding part-time and online MBA programs (the Tepper School at Carnegie Mellon offers both, as well as an accelerated track). These evening and weekend programs became especially popular after the 1997 Tax Relief Act enabled working students to deduct tuition payments on their federal tax returns.

**Proprietary Institutions**

The higher education system is usually considered to include the 3,931 public or nonprofit degree-granting community colleges, four-year colleges, and universities. However, a parallel system of postsecondary for-profit or proprietary schools has grown, fueled especially by the availability of federal financial aid for its students. Unlike public and nonprofit institutions, which must invest any profits back into the institution and adhere to certain governance structures and strict accreditation requirements in exchange for tax exemptions, the roughly 2,100 proprietary schools enrolling over 1.2 million students are operated as businesses, and profits accrue to owners or shareholders. This dissimilarity in economic models, as Whitman (2022) stated, is not simply a difference in tax status; it goes to the heart of institutional motivations, how the two sectors view and treat students, and how success is defined and measured.

Proprietary colleges frequently have highly focused missions limited to specific industries or fields of study and primarily provide career programs with "measurable skill outcomes that are more likely to pass in cost-benefit analyses for students" (Iloh, 2016, p. 432). The sector encompasses both degree-granting two- and four-year schools and nondegree-granting institutions, which primarily award workforce certificates. Although nondegree-granting institutions make up 73% of all for-profits, the vast majority of enrollment (67%) is in degree-granting four-year institutions, most of which also award associate degrees and certificates; many also offer graduate degrees. Roughly half of for-profit institutions enroll fewer than 500 students per campus and focus on a small set of programs preparing students for careers in, for example, cosmetology, technology, business, or health care. However, the majority of students attend larger online institutions, including the super-systems that have numerous campuses across multiple states and offer a wide range of degrees and certificates.

Faculty in for-profit colleges, nearly all working part-time, are hired and fired by the schools' owners and administrators; tenure and academic governance are nearly nonexistent. Whereas the staff in a public institution must seek approval from numerous sources before developing a new curriculum, a process often taking 18 months, for-profit institutions can have those same programs up and running within weeks. Tuition at for-profit institutions is typically pegged to the maximum amount reimbursable by federal financial aid, and as a result these schools are financed almost exclusively by governmental grants and federally subsidized loans taken out by students.

The proprietary sector has a long history. Several proprietary business schools began in the nineteenth century and others opened subsequently. By World War I, they enrolled a quarter of a million students. An Association of Independent Colleges and Schools, representing primarily business schools, was founded in 1912; the National Accrediting Commission of Cosmetology Arts and Sciences began in 1924; and the National Association of Trade and Technical Schools was founded in 1965. The sector grew notably, however, after the Servicemen's Readjustment Act of 1944 enabled their students to receive financial aid. Following World War II, roughly three million returning servicemembers used their GI Bill benefits to attend for-profit technical or trade institutions or to take correspondence courses. Indeed, as Whitman (2022) reported, "the total number of for-profit or proprietary schools in the U.S. tripled in the five years that followed FDR's signing of the GI Bill, from 1,878 to 5,635" (p. 12). However, due to "wildly misleading claims about quality training and well-paid jobs that awaited them upon their graduation" (p. 12), tens of thousands of veterans were prepared for careers for which they could not obtain a job and Congress soon amended the GI Bill to curb abuses by for-profit institutions.

Nonetheless, more federal aid to proprietary school students became available in 1965 with the passage of the National Vocational Student Loan Insurance Act, and in 1972 the Higher Education Act amendments made proprietary institutions full partners in the receipt of federal student aid. In the 40 years that followed, proprietary institutions grew at a phenomenal rate, increasing by 1,000% between 1976–1977 and 1996–1997. The unprecedented growth continued into the 2000s; enrollments tripled in the first decade of the twenty-first century, helped by a relatively lax regulatory environment, the expansion of financial aid to online institutions, a growing demand for postsecondary credentials, increased emphasis on job training and workforce development, and, especially, a great many private investors seeking new ways to profit from the intersection of these various conditions (Kisker, Cohen, and Brawer, 2023). By 2010, the 2.4 million students taking courses at for-profit colleges comprised 11% of all postsecondary enrollments, and these institutions raked in over $4 billion in Pell Grants—quadruple the amount they received 10 years earlier. The University of Phoenix alone brought in over $1 billion in Pell Grant funding in 2009–2010 (Education Trust, 2010).

However, since 2011, the for-profit sector has contracted substantially, due to increased regulation, widespread student debt defaults, and media attention to the abuses and fraudulent recruiting practices of many of the largest proprietary schools. The Obama administration rescinded federal recognition of the Accrediting Council for Independent Colleges and Schools (ACICS), arguing that it had failed by allowing a number of high-profile colleges to engage in misleading marketing tactics. And in 2014, the U.S. Department of Education enacted a set of regulations mandating public disclosure of key performance data and a cutoff of federal financial aid to institutions where more than a certain percentage of graduates had debt-to-income ratios higher than a specified limit. Although the gainful employment rule also applied to certificate programs at public and nonprofit colleges, because the proprietary sector accounted for half of all student loan defaults, the impact on it was substantial and led to the near-immediate implosion of the behemoths Corinthian Colleges and ITT Technical Institute. Several years later, following accusations that they had defrauded students, the Education Corporation of America and the Education Management Corporation also closed. The University of Phoenix survived, but in 2019 paid $191 million to the Federal Trade Commission to settle claims of fraud and deceptive marketing. These and other proprietary school shutdowns left tens of thousands of students struggling to pay off debt incurred in the programs, although in 2021, President Biden's administration canceled $1 billion in student loans for over 72,000 defrauded borrowers (Sheffey, 2021).

The proprietary sector had a short-lived renaissance when President Trump named Betsy DeVos, a longtime investor in for-profit schools, as secretary of education. DeVos rolled back the gainful employment rule and restored federal recognition of the disgraced ACICS, but the resurgence was short-lived. In 2022, President Biden's education department once again removed ACICS from the list of federally recognized accreditors and proposed new gainful employment regulations in 2023. To get around these rules, a number of formerly for-profit institutions converted to nonprofit status, and several more sold their operations to public or nonprofit universities (including the University of Phoenix, which in 2023 announced an impending sale to a nonprofit entity created by the University of Idaho). By 2023, most new postsecondary businesses sought to collaborate rather than compete with traditional higher education (Kisker, Cohen, and Brawer, 2023).

Nonetheless, although the for-profit sector is not as prominent as it was circa 2010, it maintains a significant presence in the postsecondary landscape, enrolling disproportionate numbers of adults, low-income learners, and students of color, especially African Americans. Indeed, while only 1 out of every 20 students in higher education is enrolled at a degree-granting, for-profit institution, 1 in 8 Black students, 1 in 7 Pacific Islanders, 1 in 14 Indigenous students, and 1 out of every 14 first-generation students attends a for-profit school (Cottom, 2017). And these numbers do not even consider the students enrolled at nondegree-granting institutions.

Furthermore, the proprietary institutions are key contributors to national and statewide educational attainment initiatives. In 2020–2021, they awarded 27% of all certificates below the associate degree, 6% of associate degrees, 7% of bachelor's, and

6% of master's degrees. For-profit participation in first professional and doctoral education remains marginal. As Kisker, Cohen, and Brawer (2023) wrote, "Given their tendency to serve adults, students of color, low-income learners, veterans, women, and various other minoritized groups, if for-profit institutions were regulated properly, they could be a great force for bringing marginalized people into the workforce. But that is a big 'if'" (p. 534). Indeed, misleading recruitment practices aimed especially at African American and low-income populations remain commonplace (Cottom, 2017), and loan defaults by students from that sector remain high: 12 years after enrolling at a proprietary institution, 53% percent of students—and 75% percent of Black students—defaulted on their federal student loans (Whitman, 2022). Until or unless such abuses are corrected, for-profit colleges will continue to be viewed with skepticism and derision by much of the higher education community, even as community colleges and other broadly accessible institutions seek to adopt many of the proprietary sector's client-centered approaches to student retention and support.

**The System**

American higher education as a system functioned during the Contemporary Era much as it did in the previous century, with a diverse set of institutions absorbing changes in enrollment, responding to market pressures for new or career-oriented curricula, churning out more and more degrees and certificates, and seeking extramural funding to replace that which had been provided in earlier eras by federal and state governments. Within the system, different institutions had different priorities: the research institutions lived up to their title; the liberal arts colleges and many private universities preserved residential patterns of the past; comprehensive universities, community colleges, and proprietary institutions ensured the broad-based access upon which the whole system depends; and MSIs spanning all categories sought to improve the retention and support of students from historically marginalized races or ethnicities.

As a way of reducing costs and enhancing system cohesion, many researchers, policymakers, and foundation executives championed organizational and funding changes that would create what they hoped would be a seamless pathway from kindergarten through the baccalaureate, with community colleges facilitating these connections. Throughout the Contemporary Era, public institutions collaborated to improve student transfer and the articulation of credits to majors and upper-division requirements at universities, and the community colleges, in particular, strengthened dual enrollment, early college high schools, and other programs aimed at giving historically underserved students a head start in college. The states have generally supported these initiatives through policy changes, but to date most have kept governance and funding for the different sectors separate.

Indeed, the system largely continues to function as a set of nested boxes or concentric circles, with the liberal arts colleges and research universities at the core. Further out are the comprehensive institutions, then community colleges, and at the exterior, the proprietary schools. Each sector is perceived by its staff, alumni, supporters, funding agents—the public at large—as having a certain worth. The core institutions are most selective in admissions, they employ faculty with the highest credentials, and they offer the greatest amenities. Their per capita costs and the support they receive through public funding, tuition, and donations are considerably greater. Their endowments are larger; they dominate the list of institutions ranked by wealth. Other institutions play different, no less valuable roles, but their position in the system is marked by several distinct characteristics. They accept a greater percentage of applicants. Their faculty may concentrate more on teaching than research and fewer hold doctoral degrees. Their revenues and costs are lower and their curricula are more likely to be directed toward preparing people for employment in fields requiring fewer years of study.

These differences are more marked the further the institution is from the core of the system. Students and faculty find difficulty moving from the exterior toward the center. Hardly any community college instructors subsequently join the faculty at research universities. Practically no credits earned at proprietary schools can be applied to degrees at liberal arts colleges, whereas credits from the core institutions are accepted at almost all the others. (In fact, few proprietary credits are accepted even by community colleges, although increasing numbers of community college students transfer to for-profit four-year schools.)

The diversity within the system is at once a strength and a weakness. It is a strength because it enables some types of institutions to respond quickly to various opportunities, from research collaborations to preparing people for jobs in newly emergent fields. It is a weakness because it condones program duplication, constrains efforts at cost reduction, and perpetuates socioeconomic divisions. As a whole, the system has become more vulnerable to outside influence, and although public research universities and prestigious private institutions are the most frequent targets of political ire and public dissatisfaction, negative media narratives and polarized perceptions of the sector threaten support for and enrollment in all institutions. (Interestingly, although community colleges have been championed by legislators and the media alike for their affordable price and centrality to regional economic and workforce development efforts, they, too, have suffered from reduced state and local allocations.)

In recent years, a number of commentators have questioned the ongoing viability of the system, pointing to ever-escalating costs, post-pandemic enrollment losses, and increasing percentages of Americans who consider college to be a questionable investment (despite overwhelming evidence to the contrary). Yet despite these very real challenges, American higher education remains a point of reference for the rest of the world. As this book illustrates, European influence on American higher education came in two stages. First was the college form, especially the curriculum and the residential pattern, imported from England. Subsequently, the German model of research, academic freedom, and public service was appended. But all that happened well over 100 years ago. Now, 19 American universities anchor the Times Higher Education's 2023 list of the top 30 universities in the world and comprise 9 of the 10 wealthiest. More importantly, the Europeans and much of the rest of the world admire the American system's ability to ensure access to all who desire higher learning and its success in combining research and service, academic and occupational curricula, and graduate and undergraduate studies, all within the same set of institutions. They appreciate the diversity of forms and respect how transfer pathways, while imperfect, enable social mobility for individuals and groups. Thus, despite the (many) challenges of the Contemporary Era, colleges and universities remain central to American society and to its status in the world.

## Students

College and university enrollments rose throughout the Contemporary Era, and the student bodies on campuses across the country came closer to representing the gender, racial, and ethnic makeup of the broader society. Following two major affirmative action cases in the 1990s and early 2000s, most institutions enhanced efforts to improve access and enhance equity and inclusion on campus. Civic engagement and campus activism increased, and administrators sought to balance efforts to create safe and inclusive environments with their legal duty to protect free speech. Students' mental health struggles and already high incidence of basic needs insecurities were exacerbated by the COVID-19 pandemic and its aftermath, and violence on campus continued to rise. Major technological advances forever changed the ways students communicate, learn, and spend their time, leading to new ways of engaging students in class, both on- and offline. These shifts affected students' experiences and ability to succeed in college, and although graduation rates continued to rise, racial and socioeconomic equity gaps persisted.

**Enrollment and Diversity**

Undergraduate enrollments increased by nearly 30% during the Contemporary Era, fueled by rising numbers of high school graduates, increased participation among students of color and, for a time, greater percentages of high schoolers going directly to college. Between 1994 and 2009, the percentage of high school graduates enrolling in college the following fall increased from 62% to 70%, after which it declined slowly until 2019 and then dramatically during the COVID-19 pandemic, once again resting at 62% in 2021. Graduate enrollments, on the other hand, increased steadily between 1994 and 2021. Female students, who reached parity with their male counterparts early in the Consolidation Era, now comprised 58 and 61%, respectively, of total undergraduate and graduate enrollment, up from 56 and 53% in 1994 (see Figure 6.1). Although the spectacular enrollment gains made by women in a mere half century lie in stark contrast to the previous

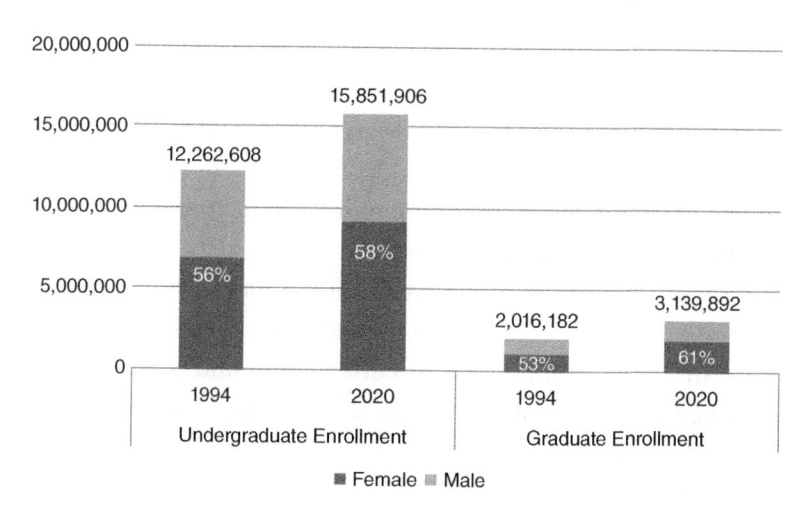

Figure 6.1. Total Enrollment and Percentage Female, 1994 and 2020.

350 years of male-dominated academia, these numbers—as well as those showing that on average men earn lower grades and are less likely to achieve bachelor's degrees—led many institutions to consider how they can improve efforts to recruit, retain, and support male students, especially men of color.

The racial and ethnic composition of college student bodies shifted dramatically during the Contemporary Era. In Fall 2020, just over half of all undergraduates were White, down from 60% in 1994; 13% were Black or African American (up from 12%); and 21% were Hispanic or Latinx (up from 10% at the start of the era). The percentage of Asians, Pacific Islanders, Indigenous, and non-resident students all held steady or increased slightly, and in 2020, 4% of students represented two or more races (see Table. 6.2). Although even the most exclusive institutions enhanced efforts to recruit diverse student bodies, certain racial or ethnic groups remained over- or underrepresented in some types of institutions. For example, Hispanic or Latinx students enrolled disproportionately in public community and four-year colleges, while Black or African American students were more likely to attend for-profit institutions. Although White students remained the single largest racial group across all of higher education, only in private, nonprofit colleges did they comprise a majority of students. These changing demographics prompted greater attention to the ways in which institutions of higher education both extend and constrain opportunity for various groups and led to numerous programs and policies intended to support and retain students from historically marginalized races and ethnicities.

Most institutions also implemented programs to support the substantial numbers of LGBTQ+ students enrolled on their campuses; in 2021, 18% percent of college men and 31% percent of college women identified as gay, lesbian, bisexual, pansexual, queer, or questioning (Paresky and Abrams, 2021). In addition, 1 in 20 Americans under age 30 identified as a gender other than that which was assigned at birth (2% identified as transsexual and

Table 6.2. Percent of Undergraduate Enrollment by Type of Institution and Race/Ethnicity, Fall 2020.

| Race/Ethnicity | % of Total | % of Community Colleges | % of Public Four-Year Institutions | % of Private Nonprofit Institutions | % of Private For-Profit Institutions |
|---|---|---|---|---|---|
| White | 51% | 47% | 50% | 58% | 41% |
| Black or African American | 13% | 13% | 12% | 12% | 28% |
| Hispanic or Latinx | 21% | 27% | 23% | 13% | 19% |
| Asian | 7% | 6% | 7% | 6% | 4% |
| Pacific Islander | 0.3% | 0.3% | 0.2% | 0.3% | 1% |
| Indigenous | 1% | 1% | 1% | 0.5% | 1% |
| Two or more races | 4% | 4% | 4% | 4% | 4% |
| Nonresident | 3% | 1% | 3% | 5% | 1% |

Source: NCES Digest, 2023.

3% as nonbinary). However, "the vast majority of U.S. colleges and universities are poorly positioned to understand and address LGBTQ+ student equity . . . because they do not collect systematic data on student sexual identities and trans or nonbinary gender identities" (Beattie, 2023). Unlike information on students' race, ethnicity, gender, and age, which institutions must report annually to the U.S. Department of Education, information on sexual orientation or gender identity is not required, and—citing concerns related to policy, government reporting, and privacy or safety, as well as student information system issues—many colleges do not collect it (Doan, 2021). Given data showing that LGBTQ+ students frequently experience hostile campus environments, that 1 in 10 are sexually harassed during their college years, and that they are far more likely to report mental health struggles while in college than their heterosexual and cisgender peers (Conron et al., 2022, p. 5), it is clear that institutions must do more to both understand the LGBTQ+ students on their campuses and to affirm and support their social, emotional, and academic well-being.

As student bodies became ever more diverse, some enrollment trends evident in previous eras endured while others reversed. The percentage of students who work while in college continued to rise dramatically, reaching 43% of full-time and 78% of part-time undergraduates in 2015, before dropping to 40% and 74% in 2020 (the drop may be due, in part, to job and enrollment losses during the COVID-19 pandemic). In 2020, roughly 10% of full-time and 40% of part-time students worked 35 or more hours per week, leading researchers to distinguish between *students who work* and *employees who study* (Baum, 2010). Despite ample evidence that on-campus work is more likely to facilitate students' academic and social integration, only about 10% of working students held jobs on campus, and many of those who did also worked off campus (American Council on Education, 2006).

Although the percentage of students attending colleges and universities part time rose from 39 to 43% during the previous era, by 2021, part-timers dropped back to 39% of all enrollments. And while growth in the share of students over age 25 continued, reaching 39% after the Great Recession, it subsequently declined to roughly one-third of all enrollments in 2019. The reduced percentages of part-time and older students in the Contemporary Era were due primarily to greater numbers of high school graduates, as undergraduate classes filled with younger, full-time students. However, this pattern may soon begin to change, as the number of high school graduates is projected to peak in 2024 and then slowly decline (some states have already hit this enrollment cliff). As it does, competition for recent high school completers (and their attendant tuition dollars) will intensify among all institutions of higher education.

Competition among institutions likely will exacerbate already high levels of competition among applicants and their families for admission to exclusive research universities and liberal arts colleges. Indeed, increasing levels of stress and anxiety about the admissions process was a hallmark of the Contemporary Era, even as more institutions adopted the common application, reduced their reliance on standardized test scores and letters of recommendation, and shed other criteria that disadvantaged lower- and middle-income students and those from historically underserved races and ethnicities. Indeed, some of these adjustments actually contributed to lower acceptance rates at some universities, as the size of most first-year classes remained static while greater numbers of students submitted applications to more schools. This perceived scarcity in admission to elite institutions led some wealthy parents to attempt to game the system. In 2019, the FBI filed charges against 57 people as part of the so-called varsity blues scandal; most pleaded or were found guilty in court of (collectively) funneling millions of dollars through a private admissions counselor and falsifying their children's athletic or extracurricular achievements to gain admission at the University of Southern California, Stanford, Yale, Georgetown, and similar institutions.

Despite greater competition in admission to some institutions, the most impactful enrollment trends during the Contemporary Era were toward a greater diversity of students and increased access for first-time and returning students alike. The 18-to-22-year-old White male attending full time would never again be the typical college student.

**Access, Equity, and Inclusion**

The issue of access to higher education, ever present throughout the previous half century, took on added urgency in the Contemporary Era as studies repeatedly showed diminished economic prospects for workers without a college degree or certificate. Acknowledging that most of the students exiting the K–16 educational pipeline before its end did so between the tenth and the thirteenth grades, educators and policymakers focused much of their attention on connecting the secondary and postsecondary systems. Beginning in 2010, 46 states adopted the Common Core State Standards, meant to improve high school graduates' readiness for college and careers. Yet after several studies found only minimal (and sometimes negative) changes in literacy rates and college preparedness, 24 states repealed or substantially revised their core standards. However, another approach to connecting high school and college expanded rapidly; by 2022, 48 states had dual enrollment policies allowing students to earn college credit while still in high school, and at least 30 created K–16 commissions, although the power of these commissions to coordinate secondary and postsecondary funding and operation varied widely. Reform efforts aimed at the high school–to-college transition have shown mixed results; the most successful are those that involve collaboration among high school and college staff.

Heightened immigration, especially from Mexico and other Latin American countries, led to debates about college access for a new group of students: undocumented immigrants. Although the Supreme Court ruled in 1982 that children brought illegally into the United States may not be denied a free public education, this right was never explicitly extended to postsecondary institutions, and the 1996 Illegal Immigration Reform and Immigrant Responsibility Act made undocumented students ineligible for tuition, scholarship, and financial aid benefits unless a state passed specific legislation providing for such eligibility. In 2001, Congress first proposed the federal DREAM (Development, Relief, and Education for Alien Minors) Act, which would have granted legal status to certain undocumented immigrants who were brought to the United States as children and went to school here.

However, while the DREAM Act has been reintroduced in Congress at least 11 times, it has never been ever enacted. In its place, 19 states have passed laws allowing undocumented students who meet certain requirements (such as attending high school in the state for a specified number of years and graduating or receiving a GED) to pay in-state tuition at public colleges and universities. Seven of these (California, Colorado, Minnesota, New Mexico, New York, Texas, and Washington) allow undocumented students to receive state financial aid; an additional six states allow undocumented students to pay in-state tuition at specific institutions or college systems; and Massachusetts and Virginia allow in-state tuition for Deferred Action for Childhood Arrivals (DACA) students. (In 2012, the Obama administration created the DACA program to provide work authorization and protection from deportation for undocumented youth who have lived in the United States for many years.) These recent legislative changes have enabled far more undocumented students to enroll in higher education; the Center for American Progress (Peréz, 2014) estimated that nearly half of all undocumented immigrants aged 18–24 who had graduated from high school were enrolled in postsecondary education, mostly community colleges. Unfortunately, only about 60% of undocumented students earn a high school diploma. College access for undocumented students will improve exponentially if the federal DREAM Act is ever enacted.

The terror attacks of September 11, 2001 also affected access to American colleges and universities, as questions regarding the admission of foreign students were continually confounded with issues of national security. As part of the 2001 Patriot Act, Congress implemented a series of measures designed to regulate the flow of international students and scholars into the United States. Some measures placed additional visa restrictions on foreign students, and others were designed to track and monitor the more than 600,000 nonresidents attending American colleges and universities. Despite reports of cumbersome visa restrictions and delays, access for international students was restricted only temporarily, and by 2008 the effects of the Patriot Act on international student enrollment had all but evaporated. Similarly, international student enrollment dropped slightly as travel was curtailed during the COVID-19 pandemic, but increased opportunities to learn online meant that most students could continue their studies from locations outside the United States.

Recent legislation has expanded access for veterans and military servicemembers. The 2008 Veterans Education Assistance Act ensured benefits comparable to those enjoyed by servicemembers after World War II, covering 100% of in-state tuition for four years at a public university (or an equivalent amount at a private institution) for any member of the military who served on active duty for three or more years. It also provided monthly stipends for housing and $1,000 per year for books and supplies, increased the amount of time veterans may use their educational benefits, and allowed them to transfer unused educational benefits to family members. The 2017 Veterans Education Assistance Act—better known as the Forever GI Bill—further expanded these benefits by, for example, eliminating time limits for some servicemembers and their dependents, offering additional benefits for veterans pursuing STEM-related careers, increasing benefits for servicemembers who served fewer than 18 months, and expanding benefits for reservists, National Guardsmen, and military dependents.

Affirmative action was hotly debated in the Contemporary Era. Although the 1978 Supreme Court case *Regents of the University of California v. Bakke* established that a diverse student body was a compelling state interest, several subsequent court cases and state laws challenged or clarified the legality of race-conscious admissions policies. In the 1996 *Texas v. Hopwood* case, the Fifth Circuit Court of Appeals ruled that the University of Texas's law school violated the Fourteenth Amendment by using a separate admissions review process for applicants of color. Following *Hopwood* and the passage of several state laws prohibiting discrimination or preferential treatment on the basis of race (such as California's Proposition 209, passed in 1996), some institutions sought alternative measures of ensuring diverse student bodies. Universities in Texas, California, and Florida adopted percentage plans to increase the number of students of color without giving certain groups preferential treatment. Texas's percentage plan, for example, guaranteed admission to all state colleges or universities for any high school student whose grade point average was in the top 10% of their high school class. California increased funding for outreach programs designed to recruit students of color, and many universities instituted comprehensive, individual reviews of applicants' files to evaluate "individual achievements, including those that had a racial dimension" (Newfield, 2008, p. 107).

In 2003, two affirmative action cases, both arising from admissions practices at the University of Michigan, reached the Supreme Court. *Grutter v. Bollinger* and *Gratz v. Bollinger*, heard and decided as companion cases, garnered national attention and spurred numerous amicus briefs from supporters and opponents of affirmative action alike. In *Grutter*, rejected White applicants challenged the University of Michigan Law School's admissions policy that aimed to achieve a diverse student body but did not define diversity solely in terms of race or ethnicity. In *Gratz*, rejected White applicants challenged an affirmative action plan used by the university's College of Literature, Science, and Arts. Unlike the law school's policy, the undergraduate admissions plan relied on a point system: all applicants were awarded a certain number of points for their high school GPA, SAT score, personal achievements, and so forth, but Black, Hispanic, and Native American applicants were awarded an additional 20 points for being a member of an underrepresented group. In addition, the college had a separate review process for students of color or low-income applicants whose scores may not have otherwise qualified them for admission.

The Supreme Court upheld the law school's affirmative action plan in a 5–4 decision, but invalidated the college's admissions policy 6–3, ruling that it violated the Equal Protection Clause of the Fourteenth Amendment because the point system failed to provide individualized consideration of each applicant. In short, the Court's decisions in *Grutter* and *Gratz* reaffirmed that student body diversity was indeed a compelling state interest that could justify the use of race in university admissions but stated that affirmative action plans must be narrowly tailored and flexible enough to ensure individualized consideration of all the ways an applicant might contribute to a diverse educational environment. The extent to which courts should apply strict scrutiny to the notion of diversity as a compelling state interest and to the narrow tailoring of admissions processes was tested several times between 2003 and 2020, most notably in the two *Fisher v. University of Texas at Austin* cases (known as Fisher I and Fisher II), although in both the university's race-conscious holistic review process was left intact.

Following decisions upholding the legality of using narrowly tailored affirmative action policies, advocates for historically underserved students extended the concept of diversity from campus admissions offices to curricula, student support, faculty development and recruitment, campus climate, and other arenas of college life. Rationales for such diversity, equity, and inclusion (DEI) initiatives included the need for college professors to more closely resemble their students in race and ethnicity, the need to make the curriculum more relevant to students of color, and the need to make campus environments more inclusive and supportive of historically marginalized or minoritized scholars. By 2023, DEI offices were commonplace, some attention was paid to the ways in which institutional policies and practices contributed to racial and social stratifications, and numerous programs were implemented to improve support for historically underrepresented groups.

However, these actions led to a considerable backlash from conservatives who decried any attempt to improve equity for marginalized groups as unfair, preferential treatment, and to additional cases targeting the legality of affirmative action. In 2023, the Florida legislature passed Senate Bill 266, which banned DEI personnel and practices, and months later Texas followed suit by passing Senate Bill 17, which banned DEI offices in public colleges and universities across the state. By July 2023, anti-DEI legislation was introduced in 22 states, becoming law or receiving final legislative approval in 7 (Chronicle of Higher Education, 2023).

And in 2023, a Supreme Court dominated by Republican-appointed justices sided with the anti–affirmative action group Students for Fair Admission (SFFA) in two linked cases against Harvard College and the University of North Carolina, effectively ending affirmative action nationwide. SFFA, run by conservative activist Edward Blum, alleged that admission of Asian Americans was suppressed by affirmative action policies at the two institutions and thus violated the Equal Protection Clause of the Fourteenth Amendment. Writing for the 6–3 majority, Chief Justice John Roberts concurred, finding that "Because Harvard's and UNC's admissions programs lack sufficiently focused and measurable objectives warranting the use of race, unavoidably employ race in a negative manner, involve racial stereotyping, and lack meaningful end points, those admissions programs cannot be reconciled with the guarantees of the Equal Protection Clause" (*SFFA, Inc. v. President and Fellows of Harvard College*, 2023, p. 8). "Eliminating racial discrimination" Roberts argued, "means eliminating all of it"

(p. 4). However, he affirmed that "nothing prohibits universities from considering an applicant's discussion of how race affected the applicant's life," thus leaving the door open for holistic reviews of essays in which applicants discuss their race or ethnicity (or any other aspect of their identity) "so long as that discussion is concretely tied to a quality of character or unique ability that the particular applicant can contribute to the university" (p. 8).

In a visceral dissent to Roberts's opinion, Justice Sonia Sotomayor wrote, "Today, this Court overrules decades of precedent and imposes a superficial rule of race blindness on the Nation. The devastating impact of this decision cannot be overstated. The majority's vision of race neutrality will entrench racial segregation in higher education because racial inequality will persist so long as it is ignored" (*SFFA v. Harvard*, 2023, pp. 68–69). Americans are divided as sharply as the justices in their views of the *SFFA* decisions and in their opinions about the use of race in college admissions. Thus, even after five decades, affirmative action continues to generate conflict, both within higher education and between institutions and some of their constituents. But it also has served the system well by forcing it to become more cognizant of social injustice—something not prominent throughout most of the sector's history.

This increased awareness led faculty and administrators to apply an equity-minded approach to many aspects of higher education functioning, and most have considered how other marginalized groups, including gay, lesbian, transgender, and nonbinary individuals, experience and can be supported through college. Colleges and universities were among the first organizations to normalize the use of pronouns other than those corresponding to one's sex at birth. And in 2021, the U.S. Department of Education's Office for Civil Rights issued a Notice of Interpretation that extended Title IX of the 1972 Education Amendments—which prohibited discrimination on the basis of sex in any educational program or activity offered by an institution receiving federal financial assistance—to include discrimination based on sexual orientation or gender identity. As with affirmative action policies, Americans are sharply divided on this issue, and many question the fairness of allowing transgender females to compete in women's athletics. In an attempt to balance the rights of both transgender and biological women, in Spring 2023, the Department of Education proposed a new rule that would prohibit schools and colleges from issuing blanket bans on transgender athletes, instead allowing them to reject such athletes only when questions of physicality and fairness arise. Yet despite its broad implications, this draft policy gave institutions much latitude in developing their own policies and thus, as the *New York Times*' Remy Tumin (2023) wrote, is likely "far from the last word on the matter."

**Preparation and Proficiency**

Examination of several indicators of students' preparation for and proficiency after college paints a mixed picture. Many more students completed high school during the Contemporary Era, and upon adopting Common Core standards in the years after 2010, most states stepped up efforts to encourage all students to take a college-prep curriculum, including four years of English and three each of math, science, and social studies. Each year, several hundred thousand high school students participated in dual enrollment, and in 2021 nearly 1.2 million students (35% of U.S. public high school graduates) took at least one Advanced Placement exam, a 39% increase from 2001 (College Board, 2023a).

However, average scores on SAT and ACT exams taken by college-bound seniors paint a slightly different picture. Although math SAT scores improved from 506 in 1995 to 520 in 2005, they subsequently declined sharply (bottoming out at 508 in 2016) until the test was redesigned in 2017. The critical reading portion of the SAT showed a similar pattern (rising from 504 to 508 between 1995 and 2005 before dropping to 494 in 2016), as did the short-lived writing section, which was implemented in 2006 and declined steadily until the 2017 redesign (College Board, 2020). Average ACT scores remained relatively static for another decade after SAT scores began to decline but similarly showed across-the-board drops between 2015 and 2020. In addition, only 59% of ACT-tested high school graduates in 2019 met the ACT college readiness benchmark in English. Forty-five percent met the benchmark for reading—a decline from the peak of 55% reached in 1999—39% for math, and 36% for science. Just over 1 in 4 (26%) met the college readiness benchmarks in all four subjects. Even more discouraging: only one-third of students who took the entire core curriculum met the ACT College Readiness Benchmarks in all four subjects (ACT, 2019).

Furthermore, scores on the National Assessment of Educational Progress (NAEP) given annually to twelfth graders showed a decline in 17-year-olds' reading ability between 1994 and 2019, although scores on the math and science portions remained static. Equity gaps between White test-takers and their Hispanic and African American peers were substantial and persistent in the NAEP and other standardized tests. Socioeconomic status also affected the results: parental education correlated positively with reading scores, while the percentage of students qualifying for free or reduced-price lunch at the test-taker's school showed a straight-line, negative correlation. Since low-income students were more likely to enroll in community colleges and other broadly accessible institutions, these figures do much to explain those institutions' heavy involvement with developmental education. According to Barnett, Fay, and Pheatt (2016), 40% of all college students, and 68% of those in community colleges, arrive on campus underprepared for college-level work.

Discrepancies in student achievement at the high school level thus led to further status differentiation among sectors of higher education. Prestigious public and private universities engaged in fierce competition for top high school students, while community colleges and broadly accessible universities accepted most or all comers, regardless of their level of preparation. Despite increased representation of low-income and racially minoritized students at exclusive institutions, it has become increasingly difficult to rebut arguments that American schools and colleges operate much like caste systems, with the bulk of opportunities and rewards going to students born into economic, social, and educational privilege.

The extent to which colleges adequately prepare students for advanced degrees or for the workforce also has been questioned in recent years. The percentage of bachelor's degree recipients who took the Graduate Record Exam (GRE) held steady at around 34% through 2008, increased to 41% of all baccalaureate recipients in 2011, then dropped to 26% in 2019 and 23% in 2020 (the drop in 2020 was likely pandemic-related). As they had throughout the Consolidation Era, verbal scores on the GRE slid from 479 in 1994 to 456 in 2009 before the test was redesigned and rescaled in 2011. Since then, verbal scores have remained consistent. Quantitative scores on the GRE showed the opposite pattern, rising from 553 in 1994 to 590 in 2009 and then—on the redesigned GRE—increasing from 151 in 2011 to 154 in 2020. In 2003, the former section on analytical reasoning was replaced with a section on analytical writing; scores on this section have declined from 4.2 in its first year to 3.6 in 2020.

Whether GRE scores accurately reflect the preparation or proficiency of all college graduates is debatable. Yet several other indicators point to the fact that many students graduate college without the capabilities necessary to succeed in their careers. Among the top skills employers identified as being very important to graduates' ability to succeed in the workforce (work effectively in teams, think critically, analyze and interpret data, and apply knowledge and skills in real-world settings), preparation gaps—the difference between the percent of employers who deem a skill to be very important and the share reporting that recent graduates were very well prepared in that area—ranged from 14 to 21%. Indeed, among the 15 skills employers viewed as important, only

2 (digital literacy and civic engagement) showed preparation gaps less than 10% (Finley, 2020). These data may contribute to rising public perceptions, especially among Republicans, that colleges and universities are no longer "the best way to get ahead in the U.S." (Jaschik, 2022). However, they also have led to numerous program revisions aimed at helping all students—especially those enrolled in more applied degree and certificate programs—gain the soft skills that employers demand and that historically have been emphasized only in liberal arts disciplines.

**Student Engagement**

Since the 1970s, researchers have shown repeatedly that the more students engage with faculty and peers and become involved in curricular and extracurricular activities, the greater their likelihood of persisting and succeeding in college. Unsurprisingly, students who reside on campus and attend full time are more likely than their part-time and commuter peers to discuss coursework with other students, consult with faculty outside of class, and spend time in the library or in student clubs. But most twenty-first century college students reside and work off-campus, and various attempts have been made to assess the magnitude and effects of their engagement as well. Pace (1979), Astin (1977, 1993), and Tinto (1975) developed measures of student involvement and integration during earlier eras, and Kuh and McClenny extended their work more recently, one with the National Survey of Student Engagement (NSSE), the other with the Community College Survey of Student Engagement (CCSSE). Both assess the way that involvement is affected by college practices and expectations and publicize the programs and institutions where course requirements, support services, financial aid, and a host of other areas of assistance are designed to maximize student engagement.

NSSE and CCSSE survey large samples of students across numerous institutions, asking questions about students' time management; self-perceived gains; interactions with peers, faculty, and staff; types of activities they are encouraged to undertake; and the degree of support they feel they receive from the college. They ask if coursework challenges students to analyze and synthesize concepts, the extent to which students prepare for class or write multiple drafts of papers, and whether services such as tutors are available and how frequently they use them. CCSSE focuses especially on student involvement in the classroom, including how often students work on projects with other learners, the time they spend preparing class assignments, and their interactions with instructors. Findings from both surveys consistently show that students who attend full time, work fewer hours per week off-campus, and have been involved in learning communities, First-Year Experience programs, or similarly designed orientation and student-success activities are more likely to persist in college, earn higher GPAs, graduate, and value their college experiences—findings that transcend their abilities when they entered college. Although this type of research seemingly demonstrates the obvious, it encourages faculty and staff to consider how they can redesign curricula, pedagogical approaches, and support structures to better and more equitably support student learning and development.

## Civic Engagement, Campus Activism, and Free Speech

One way in which college students have long engaged on campus is via civic and democratic engagement, a broad category encompassing academic behaviors like taking a course with a civic or service-learning designation; participating in extracurricular activities such as student clubs, candidate or election-issue forums, or deliberative dialogues; and engaging in activities more closely associated with political or democratic processes, including registering to vote, voting, or campaigning for a candidate or issue (Kisker, 2016). Facilitating students' civic learning and democratic engagement has long been a priority for both community colleges and four-year institutions as it falls squarely into higher education's core value of preparing engaged citizens.

Since 2012, the Institute for Democracy and Higher Education (formerly housed at Tufts University and now located within the Association of American Colleges & Universities) has collected data on registration and voting behavior at nearly 1,200 colleges and universities across the United States. Since the project's inception, students' political participation has steadily increased, but such involvement rose dramatically between the 2016 and 2020 presidential elections, following "student outrage over the horrifying death of George Floyd and others targeted because of their skin color; divisive, discriminatory rhetoric and actions of the [Trump] administration; and apathetic political leaders brushing aside issues students care about such as global climate change and systemic inequality" (Thomas et al., 2021, p. 3). In 2020, 66% of students at surveyed institutions voted, compared to 52% four years prior. Furthermore, 80% of students who registered to vote in that year actually did vote, signaling that "they are vested in their own futures and the health of democracy" (p. 4). Students under age 30 voted in higher numbers than their older peers; females were more likely than males to vote (although both showed double-digit increases from 2016); and White, Black, and multiracial students voted at higher rates than their Asian and Hispanic or Latinx counterparts, although the increase since 2016 was greatest among Asian Americans (Thomas et al., 2021).

In addition, students have long engaged in peaceful (and, at times, not-so-peaceful) protest and other forms of campus activism. Students' right to demonstrate has been affirmed repeatedly by the courts, and although activism was muted for decades after the campus unrest of the 1960s and 1970s, it picked up in 2003 when many students protested the U.S. invasion of Iraq. Most of the antiwar demonstrations were a far cry from the protests and sit-ins of previous generations, however, almost certainly because there was no military draft. Greater proportions of part-time and commuter students also may have had a dampening effect. However, beginning in the second decade of the twenty-first century, student activism increased substantially, with many of the protests mirroring larger social movements. For example, in association with the Occupy Wall Street movement of 2011, students at colleges across the country staged sit-ins and rallies to protest economic inequality. The most prominent of these, at the University of California at Davis, ended violently when police used pepper spray to disburse students occupying the campus quad. The incident was captured on mobile phones and the images went viral, sparking similar protests at other institutions. In 2013, the university was forced to pay $30,000 in damages to each pepper-sprayed student.

Similarly, a campus protest in 2014 helped call national attention to the Black Lives Matter (BLM) movement. That year, students at St. Louis University stood in solidarity with the family of Michael Brown, an 18-year-old Black man who had been fatally shot by a White police officer in nearby Ferguson, Missouri. Over the next several years, college students across the country organized their own chapters and participated in numerous BLM rallies to protest racial injustice. College campuses once again provided the settings for some BLM rallies in Fall 2020, but the bulk of BLM demonstrations that year occurred between George Floyd's murder in late May and the end of June, a time when most college campuses were closed due to the COVID-19 pandemic.

In addition to the Occupy and BLM movements, several other national and global issues led to heightened levels of student activism during the 2010s and early 2020s. The sharp increase in hate speech, White nationalism, and racist incidents in the years after Donald Trump was elected president—the Anti-Defamation League (2018) recorded 147 instances of racist fliers, banners, or stickers on college campuses in Fall 2017, more than triple the number of cases reported in Fall 2016—prompted numerous campus rallies. Conservative and progressive students alike held demonstrations related to the removal or relocation of Confederate monuments, and many students organized protests against sexual assault, to decry global inaction on climate change, or to advocate for gay marriage and greater protections for transgender people. In 2022, after the Supreme Court overturned *Roe v. Wade* and gave the states latitude to restrict a woman's right to an abortion for the first time in 49 years, students at Dartmouth College and many other institutions staged rallies protesting the decision and in support of reproductive freedom.

Campus activism increased once again as the Israel–Hamas war erupted in Fall 2023. Several universities responded in ways that promoted dialogue and free expression while holding space for students' (and other college stakeholders') deeply felt emotions and beliefs. However, these educative acts were largely overshadowed by some constituents' fury about overly cautious or equivocated responses by several college leaders to the Hamas attacks, a perceived failure to denounce anti-Semitic actions at some institutions, and a wave of demonstrations on campuses across the country that resulted in "an extraordinary surge of harassment, threats and bigotry," both anti-Semitic and anti-Arab (Lerer and O'Brien, 2023). These protests differed from others in the Contemporary Era—and even those that occurred in the 1960s and 1970s—not because they thrust college and universities onto the front lines of the nation's culture wars, nor because many politicians and some in the media proclaimed they were proof of a liberal conspiracy or "woke agenda" within higher education. None of this was new. What set these demonstrations apart from those that came before was the unprecedented divisiveness they engendered within campus communities, along with very real concerns about students' safety, leading to "painful and public rifts among donors, alumni, students, administrators and faculty members" (Lerer and O'Brien, 2023).

Furthermore, as internet studies scholar Safiya Noble shared, online and social media coverage of the Israel–Hamas war and associated campus unrest "brought what were formerly political and ideological debates on campuses to the world, reshaping the nature and context of conversations grounded in learning."

The lack of nuance in these communications, as well as their tendency to be magnified within ideological echo chambers, contributed greatly to the ensuing divisiveness, because "click-baity memes, videos, and posts are less about creating shared understanding and more about the profits that can be generated from inflammatory arguments for social media companies" (S. Noble, personal communication).

Despite the media attention paid to campus activism in Fall 2023, student activism during the Contemporary Era was not solely confined to national or international issues. As in earlier eras, many demonstrations were organized to protest various policies, actions, or inactions of the colleges or universities themselves. Students rallied for greater racial sensitivity, more inclusive and culturally relevant coursework, and greater diversity among faculty and staff. Students were especially vocal in their demands for social justice and institutional commitments to antiracism, and protests at Claremont McKenna College and the University of Missouri resulted in the resignations of high-profile deans or presidents and, in the case of the University of Missouri, the hiring of the university's first chief diversity officer. Protests against university responses to accusations of rape or sexual assault were also common and some—including the so-called mattress protest at Columbia University—garnered national media attention. In 2013, Emma Sulkowicz claimed she had been raped by a fellow university student. After a campus adjudication process did not find the man to be at fault, Sulkowicz carried a 50-pound dormitory-style mattress everywhere she went to represent the weight she carried because of the assault and the fact that her rapist walked free on campus. Her actions were covered widely in the press and sparked similar demonstrations at other institutions.

Despite the range of issues protested on college campuses, activism during the Contemporary Era may be less remembered for the topics of students' demonstrations than it will be for the tactics they used, at times, to protest speech they found offensive or dehumanizing. Although college students have long boycotted various speakers or staged counterprotests, students of the Contemporary Era frequently chose instead to disrupt or prevent the speech altogether. Social conservatives, as well as those who had made provocative statements about various marginalized groups, were most often the targets of these "invasive disruptions" (Davis, Morgan, and Cho, 2023, p. 221).

For example, in 2017, Middlebury college students associated with the American Enterprise Institute, a conservative think tank, invited Charles Murray to speak on campus. Murray is best known for his 1994 book *The Bell Curve*, which argued that socioeconomic differences between Blacks and Whites might be attributable to racial differences in intelligence. Students were infuriated that the college would cosponsor a speech by someone with White supremacist views, and roughly 200 people massed to protest his talk. Shouting slogans like "Black Lives Matter" and "Your message isf hatred, we will not tolerate it," students effectively prevented Murray from speaking until Middlebury officials moved him to a private room to live-stream his speech (Gee, 2017). Similarly, in 2023, students at the State University of New York at Albany shouted, sang, chanted, and danced the conga to disrupt a speech by Ian Haworth, a conservative who previously had made discriminatory comments about transgender people. University officials were forced to move Haworth's speech to a much smaller room on campus and restrict entry once it reached capacity. As reported in Inside Higher Ed (Alonso, 2023), campus protesters interrupt speeches to the point they cannot go on roughly 10 times each year.

As with the Middlebury example, students often are incensed that their institution would allow what they view as hateful and harmful speech on campus and frequently have viewed university protections of such speech as tacit support for it. For their part, college and university administrators typically respond that they have a duty to protect academic freedom, free speech, and the unfettered exchange of ideas, but they are also highly constrained by the law. Indeed, university attempts to adopt speech codes or prohibit or punish particular types of messages, including hate speech, have been struck down repeatedly in the courts on First Amendment grounds. Since the 1970s, colleges and universities have been forced to weigh the legal and political ramifications of barring offensive speech against its potential to diminish equal educational opportunity for targeted individuals or groups. Efforts to achieve a balance have proven tricky. As Thomas (2018) summarized, colleges and universities may not prohibit or censor speech unless it explicitly endorses violence or dangerous actions, raises imminent safety concerns, disrupts in-class education, or involves repeated harassment of individuals (not groups) due to their social identity.

Furthermore, when students shout down speakers or otherwise preclude their presentations, college faculty and administrators are frequently forced into the uncomfortable position of having to protect the speaker or silence or remove the protesters, even if staff also find the speech to be offensive. As Kaplin and colleagues (2020) wrote, several court decisions have emphasized that "freedom to protest does not constitute freedom to disrupt" (p. 659), and that "the First Amendment knows no heckler's veto" (p. 666). Thus, colleges and universities are often caught between their legal duty to protect (even offensive) speech and their educational responsibility to provide safe, inclusive, and equitable campus environments.

In recent years, a number of university leaders have spoken in defense of free speech and civil discourse, while at the same time pleading for respectful conversations across difference. Cornell President Martha Pollack, for example, spoke to students at the university's Fall 2022 convocation, arguing that "free speech, as difficult and as challenging as it is, is not only the bedrock of higher education. It's also the bedrock of democracy and a free society. Chipping away at that bedrock—even for what we think are good reasons, like protecting others—diminishes our capacity as a learning community to do our work, and it puts our democracy at risk" (Jesse, 2023). Other campus leaders have made similar points, although it is unclear whether these statements will result in students being more likely to tolerate or engage with ideas they view as offensive or whether the speeches will be enough to assuage media commentators and policymakers advocating for legislative restrictions on academic freedom.

**Attitudes and Behavior**

Various metaphors have been applied to young people in the past century. Each generation has been tagged with descriptors such as Lost, Greatest, Silent, Beat, Baby Boom, X, and so forth by commentators wishing to applaud or deplore its behavior. Most first-time students in the Contemporary Era fall into one of two generational categories: Millennials or Gen Z. Millennials—those born between 1980 and 1995—frequently have been described as lazy, entitled, narcissistic, and unreliable, often for their tendency to challenge the hierarchical status quo and a perceived unwillingness to put in the time previous generations did to earn a good grades, gain more responsibility, and advance in the workplace. However, as Williams (2015) pointed out, Millennials "were raised during the boom times and relative peace of the 1990s, only to see their sunny world dashed by the Sept. 11 attacks and two economic crashes, in 2000 and 2008. Theirs is a story of innocence lost" (para. 10). Perhaps for this reason, Millennials have been far more engaged than many previous generations in political, service learning, and charitable activities.

Like the Millennials, many in Gen Z—individuals born after 1995—embrace diversity and equity and value finding their own and honoring others' unique identities. In this way, Gen Z is "Millennials on steroids" (Williams, 2015, para. 8). Stanford researcher Roberta Katz described Gen Z as "a highly collaborative cohort that cares deeply about others and [has] a pragmatic attitude about how to address a set of inherited issues like climate change" (cited in De Witte, 2022, para. 1). Gen Z is highly self-reliant and, as the first generation to be raised on smartphones, technologically savvy. They are often described as being more mature and in control than their Millennial counterparts, perhaps because, as Williams (2015) wrote, they carry "the weight of saving the world and fixing our past mistakes on their small shoulders" (para. 8).

As in previous years, many students viewed their time on campus as prolonged adolescence, which meant that some—especially full-time students attending residential institutions—spent a significant amount of time partying. Alcohol consumption remained widespread: according to the most recent National Survey on Drug Use and Health (SAMHSA, 2021), 49% of full-time college students aged 18 to 22 drank alcohol in the past month and of those, 27% engaged in binge drinking, defined as consuming five or more drinks on a single occasion. However, there is some evidence that Gen Z does not consume alcohol to the same extent as previous generations; just 10 years earlier, nearly two-thirds of full-time college students had reported drinking and the rate of binge drinking hovered around 44% for most of the 2000s. However, marijuana use among college students increased sharply in the second decade of the twenty-first century, reaching the highest level in 35 years (likely helped by the legalization of that drug in 22 states and the District of Columbia between 2012 and 2023). In 2020, 12% of college students reported using marijuana in the past 30 days (up from 5% in 2017) and 44% reported using it in the past year, compared to 38% in 2015. In addition, 19% reported vaping tobacco in the past month and 9% reported using hallucinogens in the previous year. Monthly cigarette use, however, declined to 4% of all college students (National Institutes of Health, 2021).

Interestingly, several studies have documented a decline in the sexual activity of young people (both those in college and those who are not). Per Twenge, Sherman, and Wells (2017), 15% of 20-to-24-year-olds in Gen Z reported having had no sexual partners;

the corresponding figure among Millennials had been 6%. A few studies have sought to understand the factors leading to lower levels of sexual activity, finding that, for young women, a decline in alcohol consumption contributed to a lack of interest in casual sex, and for young men, an increased interest in online and computer gaming was the main reason. The larger number of college students and other young adults who live with their parents may also contribute to lower levels of sexual activity (South and Lei, 2021).

**Mental Health and Basic Needs Insecurities**

Of all the attitudes and behaviors that characterize college students in the Contemporary Era, the most distinguishing—and most disturbing—may be the high levels of stress, anxiety, depression, and other emotional disorders they reported experiencing. In 2019, the American College Health Association reported that 87% of college students felt overwhelmed, 85% felt emotionally exhausted, two-thirds reported overwhelming anxiety, and 45% felt so depressed it was difficult to function. More than half felt things were hopeless, and 13% had seriously considered suicide in the previous year. Figures such as these help to explain why, since 2010, suicide has been among the leading causes of death for college students (Centers for Disease Control and Prevention, 2020).

Sadly, students' mental health challenges were exacerbated by the COVID-19 pandemic, as the combination of increased isolation, greater health and economic stressors, and academic demands led to far more students reporting they were in crisis or experiencing symptoms of depression or anxiety. In the 2020–2021 school year, more than 60% of college students met the criteria for one or more mental health problems, a nearly 50% increase from 2013. Rates of mental health challenges varied by race and ethnicity and other aspects of identity, with Indigenous, Pacific Islander, transgender, nonbinary, gay, lesbian, and bisexual students showing the largest increases in depression, anxiety, and suicidal ideation (Lipson et al., 2022; Donadel, 2023). While most colleges and universities have implemented or enhanced emotional support and wellness resources, the rates at which students utilize mental health services are low in general and tend to be far lower for students of color (Francis and Horn, 2016). Given these statistics, it should be no surprise that mental health tops the list of college students' biggest concerns (Donadel, 2023).

In addition, recent research has pointed to frighteningly high percentages of students with basic needs insecurities—a major problem even before it was exacerbated by the COVID-19 pandemic. According to the Hope Center for College, Community, and Justice, in 2021, 34% of college students had experienced food insecurity in the last 30 days, 48% had unstable or transitory housing, and 14% were homeless. Fifty-eight percent of all college students experienced one or more of these basic needs insecurities; percentages were higher among students attending community colleges. In addition, many students lacked access to reliable Internet service or consistent transportation. As Goldrick-Rab and Cochrane (2019) pointed out, African Americans, those identifying as LGBTQ+, and students considered independent for financial aid purposes are at particular risk of basic needs insecurity, as are those who have served in the military, lived in foster care, or experienced incarceration.

**Violence on Campus**

Following passage of the 1990 Student-Right-to-Know and Campus Security Act (CSA), Congress required U.S. colleges and universities to report to the Department of Education annually on campus crime statistics and security policies. Amendments to the CSA expanded the mandate to include data on sexual assault and hate crimes. Yet while the CSA certainly improved transparency, it did little to prevent violent episodes on campus. Between 2000 and 2010, there were more than a dozen campus shootings, most notably the Virginia Tech massacre where, on April 16, 2007, a student with a history of severe depression shot and killed 5 faculty members and 27 students in two separate shooting sprees before killing himself. The Virginia Tech massacre was the deadliest mass shooting on campus in U.S. history and served to refocus attention on college safety and security. In the months and years that followed, many colleges installed electronic locks in dormitories and classroom buildings, instituted emergency notification systems to quickly alert students of danger on campus, and employed technology to monitor students' social media to identify potential threats to campus communities.

As a result of these improvements, campus crime dropped by 20% overall in the second decade of the twenty-first century. However, only burglary, arson, and motor vehicle thefts dropped; sex offenses, murder, and negligent homicides increased. Excluding the Virginia Tech massacre, which skewed the numbers, an average of 17 murders occurred on college campuses every year between 2001 and 2019, and the number of (reported) forcible sex offenses increased 435% during that time, reaching 11,767 separate instances in 2019. Gun violence was a recurring theme, resulting in 172 injuries and 73 fatalities at colleges or universities between 2013 and 2022. Of the 12 mass shootings that have occurred on college campuses since 1966, 9 transpired in the Contemporary Era, killing at least 70 people and injuring more than 75 others. In all but three of these instances, the shooter was a current or former student. While most college students will never experience a violent attack on campus, the threat of it looms large, and campus safety remains a top concern for both students and staff.

**Completion**

Increased enrollments and more jobs requiring advanced training led to a greater number of credentials at all levels during the Contemporary Era. Certificates below the associate degree increased by 66% between 1994 and 2010 then declined slightly as many large for-profit institutions imploded (ending up 60% higher than at the start of the era). During that time, associate degrees

Table 6.3. Total Number of Degrees Awarded and Percentage Awarded to Women, 1994–1995 and 2020–2021.

| Degree Type | 1994–1995 | | 2020–2021 | |
| --- | --- | --- | --- | --- |
| | Number Awarded | % Women | Number Awarded | % Women |
| Certificate | 620,669 | 60% | 991,381 | 57% |
| Associate | 539,691 | 60% | 1,036,431 | 61% |
| Bachelor's | 1,160,134 | 55% | 2,066,455 | 58% |
| Master's | 403,609 | 55% | 866,894 | 61% |
| Doctoral | 114,266 | 41% | 194,059 | 55% |

Source: NCES Digest, 2023.

nearly doubled, bachelor's awards rose by 78%, master's by 115%, and doctoral degrees by 70% (see Table 6.3). The percentage of doctoral degrees awarded to women increased dramatically during the era, and by 2020, women earned the majority of credentials at all levels. Nonetheless, some fields, such as engineering and computer science, continued to be dominated by males.

The fields in which bachelor's degrees were awarded shifted, although not as dramatically as those for master's and doctoral degrees. As Table 6.4 illustrates, disciplines related to immediate employment possibilities such as computer and information sciences, the health professions, and the biological and biomedical sciences, showed some of the biggest percentage gains. As with graduate degrees, bachelor's awards in fitness and kinesiology grew commensurately with the nation's growing interest in physical fitness and the number of degrees in homeland security, law enforcement, and firefighting rose substantially after 9/11 and the War on Terror. As these fields grew, other longstanding disciplines lost ground. The number of bachelor's degrees in English and education both decreased during the Contemporary Era, and although awards in foreign languages, the social sciences, and the liberal arts

Table 6.4. Changes in Earned Bachelor's Degrees by Selected Field, 1995–1996 and 2020–2021.

| Field | 1995–1996 | 2020–2021 | % Change |
|---|---|---|---|
| English | 49,928 | 35,762 | −28 |
| Education | 105,384 | 89,398 | −15 |
| Foreign languages, literatures, and linguistics | 14,832 | 15,518 | +5 |
| Liberal arts and sciences, general studies, humanities | 33,997 | 41,909 | +23 |
| Social sciences and history | 126,479 | 160,827 | +27 |
| Physical sciences and technologies | 19,716 | 29,238 | +48 |
| Business | 226,623 | 391,375 | +73 |
| Psychology | 73,416 | 126,944 | +73 |
| Visual and performing arts | 49,296 | 90,022 | +83 |
| Engineering and engineering technologies | 77,997 | 145,041 | +86 |
| Communications and related programs | 48,173 | 95,332 | +98 |
| Multi/interdisciplinary studies | 26,885 | 54,584 | +103 |
| Mathematics and statistics | 12,713 | 27,092 | +113 |
| Biological and biomedical sciences | 61,014 | 131,499 | +116 |
| Homeland security, law enforcement, firefighting | 24,810 | 58,009 | +134 |
| Health professions | 85,755 | 268,018 | +213 |
| Parks, recreation, leisure, fitness, kinesiology | 12,974 | 54,294 | +318 |
| Computer and information sciences | 24,506 | 104,874 | +328 |

*Source:* NCES *Digest,* 2023.

all increased, their rate of growth was far below the average (78%) across all disciplines.

Time-to-degree continued to rise. Given the preponderance of part-timers attending community colleges, the average time-to-associate degree was 5.6 calendar years, the same or longer than the average time-to-bachelor's degree among students at four-year public (5.6 years) or four-year private institutions (5.4 years). Bachelor's degree earners from for-profit institutions required an average of 8.8 years to complete their program (National Student Clearinghouse, 2016). Given these numbers, six-year graduation rates became the preferred statistic; in 2020, 65% of four-year public and 76% of four-year private college students earned a bachelor's degree within this amount of time. Roughly one-third of students beginning at a community college completed a degree within six years of enrollment. However, given the diversity of education and training goals among community college students, most institutions now utilize a broader metric for student success. Indeed, the national Student Achievement Measure counts transferring to another two- or four-year college, earning a degree or certificate, and continued enrollment as successful outcomes; nationally, 56% of all community college students (65% of full-timers and 52% of part-timers) achieved one of these successful outcomes after six years (National Student Clearinghouse, 2022a, 2022b).

As in previous eras, socioeconomic and racial inequities in bachelor's degree completion were prevalent. In 2019, 8 out of every 10 dependent students from the highest income quartile attained the baccalaureate by age 24, compared to 7 in 10 from the second-highest quartile, 35% from the third, and 28% from the lowest income quartile (The Pell Institute for the Study of Opportunity in Higher Education, 2019). The facts that wealthier students were much more likely to attend institutions with large endowments and competitive admissions processes, attend full-time, and live on campus do much to explain the socioeconomic equity gap in bachelor's attainment rates. Equity gaps are also apparent when examining bachelor's completion rates by race and ethnicity.

After six years, 67% of White students who began at a four-year college or university earned a bachelor's degree, compared to 45% of Blacks or African Americans, 59% of Hispanic or Latinx students, 77% of Asians, 52% of Pacific Islanders, 42% of Indigenous learners, and 60% of those from two or more races. When transfers to another institution and continued enrollment are considered, overall success rates ranged from 62% for Indigenous students to 87% among Asian Americans (see Figure 6.2). Equity gaps in associate degree completion rates are similar.

One oft-cited explanation for racial equity gaps in college completion is that they are largely due to socioeconomic disparities. And indeed, as Stanford's Center for Education Policy Analysis (CEPA, 2023) showed, equity gaps are strongly correlated with racial gaps in income, poverty, unemployment, and educational attainment. Yet, CEPA argued, because racial equity gaps are still present in states where racial socioeconomic disparities are "near zero" (typically states with small Black or Hispanic populations), socioeconomic disparities are not the sole cause of racial equity gaps.

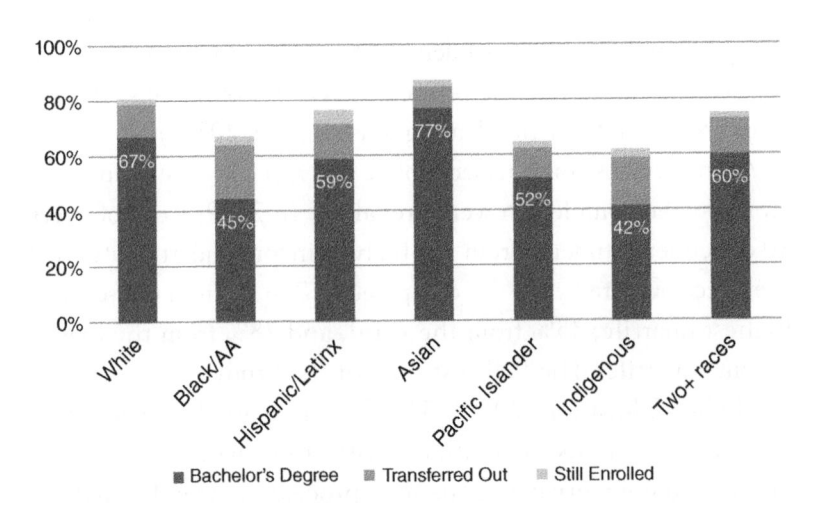

**Figure 6.2.** Outcomes Six Years After Starting a Four-Year College or University by Race and Ethnicity, 2014 Cohort.

Structural factors, including "the availability and quality of early childhood education, the quality of public schools, patterns of residential and school segregation, and state educational and social policies" also contribute to variations in educational attainment by race or ethnicity. Furthermore, the fact that Black and Hispanic students are more likely to attend for-profit institutions—as well as community colleges and broadly accessible universities that have less money to spend on student support services and where greater percentages of students attend part-time—also helps explain equity gaps in college completion. Nonetheless, if institutions of higher education are to dismantle the structural barriers that inhibit college success for low-income and racially marginalized students, they must double-down on strategies to implement equitable support services, culturally relevant pedagogies, and other approaches to ensuring that college campuses are safe and inclusive environments for all students.

## Faculty

Faculty trends that began in the Consolidation Era, including higher proportions of part-time and nontenure-eligible instructors, continued in the more recent era accompanied by other, more welcome changes in the professoriate, including greater racial, ethnic, and gender diversity. As the labor market shifted and expectations for research, teaching, and service increased, faculty lost much of their professional independence. This—along with the fact that professors have been blamed repeatedly for many of higher education's woes, including higher costs, a greater focus on externally funded research, and the academy's alleged liberal bias—led to high levels of dissatisfaction and burnout. Although faculty still enjoy substantial academic freedom in the classroom and in their scholarship, recent legislative efforts to restrict tenure and free expression on campus threaten what little remains of the vaunted life of a college or university professor.

## Tenure

Over the past 50 years, the total number of faculty increased along with enrollment, but part-time and nontenure-eligible positions grew disproportionately. Indeed, of the nearly 1.5 million faculty in 2020, 44% were part-timers. This figure is lower than in 2011, when the professoriate was evenly split between full- and part-timers, but is higher than the 41% of part-timers at the beginning of the era and double the percentage of faculty who were employed part-time in 1970 (22%). The percentage of full-time faculty working on contingent appointments (i.e., who were not eligible for tenure) also increased, and not just because nearly all part-timers are contingent. According to the American Association of University Professors (AAUP, 2022a), across all institutional types (excluding for-profits), 35% of full-time faculty were not eligible for tenure, including 31% of full-timers at doctoral universities and nearly half of full-time professors at community colleges.

In nearly all applications, contingent faculty have few job protections and may be dismissed readily without cause. However, even among full-time tenured and tenure-track faculty, job security and tenure protections eroded during the Contemporary Era. According to the AAUP (2022b), between 2017 and 2022, 18% of all four-year institutions (including one-quarter of publics, one-quarter of doctoral universities, and 39% of large institutions) tightened tenure standards. In addition, 54% replaced retiring tenured professors with contingent appointments; this occurred most often at medium or large public institutions, especially those granting the master's as the highest degree. The percentage of institutions that replaced tenured with fixed-term positions increased threefold between 2004 and 2022. Finally, 58% of institutions responding to the AAUP survey indicated that they had a post-tenure review process, up from 46% in 2000. Post-tenure review was more likely to exist in public institutions (68%) than in private universities (51%), likely due to legislative requirements "or a perceived need by public institutions to conduct such a review in the face of legislative hostility toward tenure" (p. 8). Although periodic reviews of tenured professors (which are separate and distinct from annual performance reviews) do not necessarily threaten their job security, the AAUP (2022b) "considers policies that place the burden of proof on faculty members to demonstrate that they should be retained as inimical to academic freedom and tenure" (p. 7).

However, in recent years lawmakers in Georgia, Florida, Missouri, Iowa, Texas, and Wisconsin have moved even further to restrict or abolish tenure at public institutions. As Irene Mulvey, president of AAUP, argued, the threat these bills pose extend far beyond state borders and affect even tenured and tenure-track faculty in blue states. "Tenure is not for the individual," she stated, "tenure exists to protect academic freedom, which is essential to democracy" (as quoted in Cineas, 2023, para. 19). As the number of tenured and tenure-track faculty diminish, there are fewer people who can stand up for the rights of their colleagues to research, teach, and write without interference from policymakers, board members, governors, or state legislators. "It's up to all of us in the profession to protect our colleagues who do not have the protections of academic freedom," she wrote (para. 19). "If you don't have academic freedom, you end up in an authoritarian state where the government gets to tell you what is true and what you can and can't learn" (para. 16). Thus, anti-tenure legislation in a handful of states brings serious repercussions for academic freedom across the nation. As Mulvey put it, "The damage to higher education is essentially a domino and democracy itself is at the end of [the] line" (para. 30).

### Demography

As the professoriate trended toward a part-time, contingent workforce, it continued to diversify, with women and faculty of color gaining ground throughout the era. In Fall 2020, women comprised 51% of all faculty, and 48% of full-timers, affirming the steady (but not yet complete) progress that women have made in faculty ranks. Women also comprised 53% of assistant professors, which suggests a continual increase in new hires, although the fact that one-quarter of assistant professors work on contingent appointments may mean that many of these new female faculty are not eligible for tenure. Indeed, according to the AAUP (2020), more than half of female, full-time faculty hold non-tenure-track positions.

A gradual increase in the number of faculty of color, especially among Asian and Hispanic or Latinx professors, is also apparent, although the demographic makeup of the professoriate still does not mirror the U.S. population. At the turn of the twenty-first century, 6% of full-time faculty were African American or Black, 3% were Hispanic or Latinx, 9% were Asian or Pacific Islander, 1% were Indigenous, and the remaining 80% were White. By 2020, the percentage of White, full-time faculty dropped to 67%, although the percentage of Black or African Americans remained the same (6%) and the share of Indigenous faculty dropped to less than 1%. Hispanic/Latinx and Asian/Pacific Islander faculty both gained ground (to 5 and 11%, respectively, of all full-time faculty), but most of the change came in the larger share of the professoriate who were two or more races (1% in 2020), nonresidents (6%), or who declined to state their race or ethnicity (3%).

**Salary**

In constant dollar terms, average faculty salaries increased by only 10% during the Contemporary Era, but fringe benefits gained so that they amounted to 20 to 30% of salaries. By 2020–2021, average full-time salaries across all sectors reached $91,908, with assistant professors earning an average of $77,903 and full professors $127,767. Although the average faculty member could earn a similar amount at four-year public and private institutions in the mid-1990s, by 2020–2021, average salaries had increased by 17% at private institutions but only 6% at public colleges and universities, resulting in an average nine-month salary that was roughly

$8,000 lower at publicly funded institutions. Average salaries for full-time community college faculty remained essentially static during the Contemporary Era, after accounting for inflation. The gender pay gap shrank slightly between 1995 and 2021, with average salaries for women increasing by 15% while those for men increased by 11%. However, because women had started at a much lower base, and because they remained overrepresented in community colleges, among assistant professors, and in English and the humanities, at the end of the era they earned 83% as much as their male counterparts (up from 81% in 1995; see Table 6.5).

One of the more notable characteristics in full-time faculty salaries was the persistent differentiation in pay between professors by discipline. Simply stated, the closer a discipline is to the corporate world, the higher the pay for its professors. Average salaries for full professors of law or business were more than 150% of the average pay for a full professor of English, and those for economics and computer and information sciences faculty were not far behind. As well, most college presidents earned three to five times the salary paid to their senior faculty members, and head football coaches in Football Bowl Subdivision institutions garnered roughly 17 times

Table 6.5. Average Salary of Full-Time Faculty by Gender and Type of Institution, 1995 and 2021 (in Constant 2021 Dollars).

|  | 1995 | 2021 |
|---|---|---|
| All faculty | $83,650 | $91,908 |
| Women | $72,379 | $83,198 |
| Men | $89,628 | $99,754 |
| Community colleges | $73,659 | $73,187 |
| Public four-year institutions | $87,020 | $92,497 |
| Private four-year institutions | $86,392 | $100,660 |

Source: NCES Digest, 2023.

as much, an average of $2.7 million per year. (At the onset of the Great Depression, when a reporter commented to baseball legend Babe Ruth that his salary was higher than President Hoover's, he allegedly responded, "I had a better year.") These salary differences usually are rationalized by attributing them to so-called market forces, the same rationalizations used to justify low pay for part-time faculty.

Across all sectors of higher education, the pay differential between full-time, tenured professors and contingent faculty is enormous. At universities awarding the master's as the highest degree, nine part-time faculty, each teaching three courses per year, might be employed at the same cost as one full-time assistant professor (AAUP, 2022a). In California community colleges in 2020, the hourly pay for part-time instructors was $69.11, or just over $3,500 per course, while full-timers earned between $77,500 and $116,250 for teaching at most 10 courses per year. In other words, even first-year faculty teaching full-time earned double the average for part-timers; those at the high end of the salary spectrum took home more than three times as much. Other states showed similar patterns. In 2020, the average nine-month salary for full-time community college faculty in Illinois was $80,469 plus retirement compensation and other benefits, approximately $9,500 per course, while part-timers earned $807 per credit hour: roughly $2,400 per course (Kisker, Cohen, and Brawer, 2023). Relying on part-time faculty allows administrators to respond to market demands while saving money, but as Clark (1988) pointed out, "Nothing deprofessionalizes an occupation faster and more thoroughly than the transformation of full-time posts into part-time labor" (p. 9).

Do the majority of part-time faculty work at multiple institutions to cobble together an academic career, or do they work full-time in careers outside of academe and take part-time teaching positions for various personal or professional reasons? The answer is: it depends on the teaching field. According to Levin, Kater, and Wagoner (2006), in the community colleges, most part-timers in fields that are closely tied to the private sector do not desire full-time academic positions, but rather teach in addition to their full-time careers outside academe. Part-timers in disciplines further from the market, however, are more likely to desire full-time faculty appointments. If a full-time position is unavailable, these professors tend to hold multiple part-time teaching positions at different institutions.

**Labor Market and Collective Bargaining**

As the demographic and salary data presented previously illustrate, the faculty labor market is undergoing a profound change evidenced by the decreasing availability of full-time, tenure-track positions in all sectors and the corresponding increase of other academic appointments. A greater reliance on nontenure-track appointments has given rise to a bifurcated labor market consisting of full-time tenure track, full-time nontenure track, and part-time faculty, as well as graduate teaching assistants. Except for teaching assistants, who are available only in universities offering graduate programs, each of these groups exists in every sector of higher education. Research universities have the highest percentage of full-time and tenure-eligible faculty who hold the most lucrative positions. However, they rely extensively on graduate student instructors to teach lower-level undergraduate courses to free up faculty to focus on their research. According to the Bureau of Labor Statistics (2022), there were 135,000 postsecondary teaching assistants in Spring 2022, earning an average annual salary of $41,900.

Contingent faculty not only teach for less money, they also give administrators more control over academic programs. Unionization has been largely unsuccessful in protecting the number of full-time or tenure-track positions or in providing part-timers with the same benefits as their full-time colleagues. Just over 25% of all higher education faculty were represented by collective bargaining agents in 2019. Community colleges have the highest percentage of unionized faculty, followed by four-year public institutions. Only a small percentage of faculty are unionized at private colleges or universities, although this sector saw the most growth in unionization over the past decade due to "a more friendly legal environment toward labor rights at the [National Labor Relations Board] during the Obama Administration and a less adversarial response to faculty unionization by some higher education institutions" (National Center for the Study of Collective Bargaining in Higher Education and the Professions [NCSCBHEP], 2020, p. 15).

Union membership as a percentage of total faculty has remained relatively static over the last few decades, primarily because the number of states recognizing the right of faculty to bargain collectively has not changed. However, the number of unionized faculty increased through the expansion of existing units and the formation of new units in states where collective bargaining is already authorized. In 2012, California and New York accounted for nearly half of all organized faculty, and between 2013 and 2019 union growth was concentrated in those states, followed by Florida and Massachusetts (NCSCBHEP, 2020). Many of the recent additions to faculty unions have been part-time instructors, graduate research and teaching assistants, and postdoctoral scholars. The United Auto Workers is the dominant national union representing postdoctoral scholars and academic researchers, and they also represent the vast majority of newly organized graduate and undergraduate student employees.

Increased unionization among contingent and low-paid instructors, combined with a litany of complaints and frustrations stemming largely from working conditions during the COVID-19 pandemic, led to a surge of labor unrest, what NCSCBHEP's executive director called a "post-pandemic strike wave" (as cited in Iafolla, 2023). Although labor strife on campus rose throughout the 2010s, union work stoppages hit a 17-year high in 2022. That year, faculty, graduate teaching and research assistants, and other academic workers went on strike 15 times. The largest, at the University of California's 10 campuses, involved roughly 48,000 graduate student workers and lasted for nearly six weeks. Showing support for the strikers, more than 300 professors refused to cross the picket lines, effectively cancelling classes and postponing the submission of student grades until the strike ended.

Despite this and similar examples of faculty standing up for the rights of their graduate student workers, in collective bargaining negotiations the interests of full-time and tenure-track faculty are typically paramount. Even in bargaining units where tenure-track and contingent faculty are both represented, agreements on issues such as salary adjustments serve to benefit tenure-track faculty disproportionately. Furthermore, contingent faculty often are excluded from areas of general negotiations that relate to working conditions. As a result, they may seek separate union representation, which pits their interests against those of their colleagues on the tenure track, whether they are organized or not. Therefore, faculty unionization embodies a paradox: while it can improve faculty work conditions, pay, and benefits, the priorities and interests of full-time and tenure-track faculty are often at odds with those of part-time or nontenure-track instructors, a situation that continues to favor those with more stable and desirable appointments.

Whether the trend toward a part-time, contingent professoriate intensifies in the coming years will depend on the relative strength of faculty organizations that contend teaching positions should be filled by full-timers, and of the opposition—that is, managers who prefer employing lower-cost part-timers. Where an institution's leaders see the necessity for rapid response to new demands and where they have problems balancing the budget, they will extol the virtue of a fungible faculty, claiming that it is easier to deploy specially trained instructors to teach new types of courses than to retrain permanent staff. Where faculty groups are able to counter those moves, administrators may build new types of units modeled on contemporary extension divisions and employ the needed faculty off-book. As the rise in employment of part-time and nontenure-track instructors has revealed, there is no need for managers (or policymakers) to make a frontal assault on tenure. They can merely stop replacing the professors who leave.

**Productivity and Expectations**

Despite larger numbers of part-time and contingent instructors, faculty productivity and expectations for promotion, contract renewal, and tenure have remained relatively stable. Classroom hours or student contact hours are the most widely used measures of faculty productivity across the sectors, with scholarly publication and research grants added as metrics at most master's and doctoral institutions. The time that faculty spend on their professional activities reflects these emphases. According to the last National Study of Postsecondary Faculty (NSOPF), published in 2004, 62% of faculty time was devoted to teaching, 18% to research, and 20% to administrative and other work, with distinct differences apparent between sectors and academic disciplines, a finding replicated by the Delaware Cost Study (Hemelt et al., 2018). Full-time faculty reported an average of 11.1 classroom hours and 308 student contact hours per week. Those at private doctoral institutions had the lowest number of hours in both categories, while those at public community colleges were the highest. Nearly all part-time faculty reported teaching as their principal activity, and there was little deviation in those numbers between sectors and among academic disciplines (NCES, 2004).

Among full-time faculty, however, classroom and contact hours varied substantially by discipline. Engineering faculty in four-year institutions spent the fewest hours in the classroom and had the fewest weekly student contact hours, while fine arts faculty reported the most hours in the classroom and health sciences faculty who supervised clinical practice generated the highest number of student contact hours. It is difficult to maintain uniform teacher-student ratios across all academic departments, especially between the sciences and the humanities. Science faculty generate considerably greater extramural support for teaching assistants and postdoctoral scholars. (However, the faculty in areas that gain few grants and contracts still have benefited from the reduced teaching loads inaugurated by the scientists.) Irreconcilable differences appear also between occupational programs where accreditation standards may mandate a maximum number of laboratory stations that one professor may supervise, and courses taught in classrooms where the only limit to the number of students enrolled is the number of available chairs.

Thirteen years after the 2004 NSOPF report, the University of Maryland (2017) conducted a time diary study of faculty at 17 institutions (including 1 community and 2 baccalaureate colleges; all others were master's or doctoral universities), finding that full-time faculty spent 53% of their time teaching and 6% on advising or mentoring students, 14% on research, 13% on campus service, and an additional 14% on "other work-related activities." Although this study did not differentiate between institutional types, it did shed some light on differences by gender, race or ethnicity, and faculty rank. Female faculty spent less time each day on research than their male colleagues (1:06, compared to 1:32). Faculty of color spent *more* time on research than their White colleagues (1:43, compared to 1:13) but less on campus service (0:55 per day, compared to 1:26). Contrary to accusations that faculty become lazy after receiving tenure, the study's authors found that tenured full professors worked more hours per day (11:04) than tenure-track associate professors (10:23), who in turn worked more than assistant professors (9:59) and those not eligible for tenure (10:05).

According to a national survey of 145,000 faculty (Blankstein, 2022), more than two-thirds believe that expectations for achieving tenure, promotion, or contract review at their institution are clear and fair. These typically include an assessment of teaching, academic research, and other professional responsibilities, including (at doctoral and master's universities) the amount of extramural funding generated. However, as expectations for fundraising and grant writing have increased, more faculty—especially those in fields where this expectation is highest, such as the sciences and medicine—indicated that there is too much emphasis on revenue generation in their tenure and promotion processes.

However, most faculty believed that their institution's expectations for academic research and publication were "about right"; of those who disagreed, similar percentages felt that research was given too little or too much consideration. Publication in refereed journals remained the most highly valued research activity in promotion, contract renewal, and tenure processes, and in 2021, roughly 90% of faculty across all disciplines indicated that they shared their scholarly research in peer-reviewed journals. About 65% shared their findings through conference presentations, and just under 60% often or occasionally published their research in scholarly monographs or edited volumes. Professors in the sciences and medical fields relied more heavily on peer-reviewed journals and conference presentations, while those in the humanities and social sciences published more often in edited books and monographs (Blankstein, 2022).

In recent years, more than 90% of all faculty spent some time engaged in work related to diversity, equity, and inclusion (DEI) and most believed that work to be important. However, the bulk of this "invisible labor" was performed by faculty of color, usually women of color, who were disproportionately called upon to mentor historically underserved students and lead departmental equity and inclusion efforts (Flaherty, 2019). Yet because only 22% of institutions include DEI criteria in tenure standards (AAUP, 2022b), faculty who do the heavy lifting may not be rewarded—and indeed may be punished—for the time and effort they spend on DEI work. To rectify this workload imbalance, which contributes to lower levels of satisfaction and engagement and an increased likelihood of burnout, O'Meara and colleagues (2022) argued that colleges and universities must take collective responsibility for DEI and social justice efforts, revise annual and merit review criteria so that faculty who engage in diversity-related teaching and service are better rewarded for those efforts, and implement multiple pathways to promotion and tenure.

## (Dis)Satisfaction with Academic Life

Although faculty spend most of their time teaching, their abilities in this regard are little taken into account in hiring processes. Selection committees typically give most credence to candidates' academic credentials, letters of recommendation, prior experience, and publications. Some go a step further and invite the finalists to make a presentation to a class or meet with a few students for an hour or so. But evidence of teaching ability as related to student learning is not in the equation; the time involved and the logistics of arranging an evidential teaching-learning situation are too daunting. The decision to employ is made in the fey hope that the probationary period will reveal teaching prowess.

Yet whether or not faculty are effective teachers from the start (most aren't initially; teaching is both an art and a skill that needs to be honed), most find that teaching, mentoring, and advising students are the most satisfactory aspects of their work, even in online environments (Blundell, Castañeda, and Lee, 2020; Latif and Grillo, 2001). Indeed, likely because faculty spend so much time with students, numerous surveys have shown that they are generally satisfied with their work life, even as they have expressed dissatisfaction with their working conditions. Indeed, the list of conditions leading to faculty frustration, fatigue, and burnout are long and have existed for some time. These include threats to tenure, academic freedom, and job security; pressure from administrators and others to act in ways that would improve student and institutional accountability; persistent experiences of overt or covert racism, sexual harassment, or gender bias; and unrelenting pressure (especially at research institutions) to publish and generate external funding.

By 2020, the added stress of teaching during a pandemic led to a resurgence of faculty dissatisfaction; articles with titles such as

"On the Verge of Burnout" and "The Season of Our Professorial Discontent" appeared frequently, describing the professoriate's increasing mental exhaustion, which was heightened among women, caregivers, faculty of color, and those in the LGBTQ+ community (Chronicle of Higher Education, 2020). Furthermore, in the years that followed, many professors—both full- and part-time—found themselves unprepared to handle the sharp increase in students with basic needs insecurities or mental health challenges, as well as the emotional labor required to support them. High levels of stress and dissatisfaction have stoked fears that, as in the K–12 system, there will be a Great Resignation of college and university professors in the coming years. And indeed, a 2021 survey from the *Chronicle of Higher Education* found that over half of college and university professors have considered retiring early or changing careers (Musgrave, 2022). Whether this occurs will depend largely on the extent to which colleges and universities can acknowledge faculty stress, address unsustainable and inequitable workloads, and provide resources for faculty well-being, but it also may depend on their collective ability to reverse trends that have largely turned the professoriate into a part-time, fungible workforce. Absent such a move, the faculty of the future are not likely to enjoy the same insular, protected life as their predecessors.

### Due Process and Academic Freedom

The faculty's right to due process in employment—the idea that by following various guidelines they may enjoy a reasonable expectation of continuing contracts or the awarding of tenure—was firmly established by several court cases in the 1970s. However, application of this right changed along with the nature of the professoriate, with faculty rights diminishing and those of institutions dominating. Specifically, because part-time and nontenure-track faculty cannot claim the same expectation of continued employment as their tenured colleagues, they frequently do not have the same claim to due process that a permanent faculty enjoys. Most contingent faculty serve at the pleasure of the institution and can be dismissed without cause, which severely limits any due process claim they might make.

However, the faculty's right to academic freedom established in the University Transformation Era—the freedom to study and teach what they wish and to comment on the affairs of government, business, and other trends and events without institutional or extramural repercussion—generally has been upheld, and in 2006 the AAUP explicitly extended these rights to part-time and contingent faculty. However, since the 1970s several court cases pitted a professor's right to academic freedom against an institution's right to make autonomous decisions related to university functioning. Some of these decisions narrowed the parameters of faculty academic freedom rights. For example, in the 1994 case of *Waters v. Churchill*, the Supreme Court stated that an institution's claim to academic freedom could take precedence over that of an individual faculty member if the institution could prove that the faculty member's speech was disruptive to university operations. Fifteen years later, in *Buchanan v. Alexander*, a federal appellate court similarly sided with an institution after it dismissed a tenured professor, finding that she violated the university's sexual harassment policies by discussing her sex life and that of her students in class. The court concluded that because the professor's sexually explicit statements did not address a matter of public concern, they were not protected under the First Amendment.

However, in several other cases, the faculty's right to academic freedom prevailed over institutional autonomy. In the 1996 case *Cohen v. San Bernardino Valley College*, an English professor was accused of creating a hostile learning environment for some of his students due to his "frequent use of profanity and vulgarities, his sexual comments, and his use of topics of a sexual nature for class writing assignments" (Kaplin et al., 2020, p. 334). Although a district court initially found in favor of the college, an appellate court overturned the decision, ruling that the college's policy was "unconstitutionally vague" (p. 336). The cases of *Silva v. University of New Hampshire* (1994) and *Hardy v. Jefferson Community College* (2001) were similarly decided in favor of faculty speech rights. In *Silva*, a professor was reprimanded and suspended without pay for repeatedly using sexual allusions in class. However, the court ruled that the professor's statements "advanced his valid educational objective of conveying certain principles related to the subject matter of his course" (p. 337). In *Hardy*, a professor gave a lecture on how language is used to marginalize various groups of people and conducted an exercise in which he asked students to suggest words that "served the interests of the dominant culture" (p. 338). When students responded by naming several terms used to denigrate gay people, African Americans, and females, an offended student took actions that eventually led to the college's decision not to employ Hardy the following semester. Hardy filed suit and prevailed, with the court ruling that his speech was "germane to the subject matter of his lecture on the power and effect of language" (p. 338) and that it had not "undermined his working relationship within his department, interfered with his duties, or impaired discipline" (p. 339).

The boundaries of faculty academic freedom when it conflicts with institutional autonomy were further drawn by the 2006 *Garcetti v. Ceballos* decision in which the Supreme Court determined that if a public employee (i.e., a faculty member) speaks as a private citizen on a matter of public concern, that speech is protected. However, if the faculty member's speech is "made pursuant to carrying out official duties," it does not qualify for First Amendment protection and thus does not insulate the employee from institutional discipline (Kaplin et al., 2020, p. 308). However, the majority opinion in *Garcetti* explicitly stated that the ruling did not apply to cases "involving speech related to scholarship and teaching" (p. 308) and numerous court cases since "appear to be sensitive to and supportive of a scholarship and teaching exemption to *Garcetti*" (p. 356).

In the twenty-first century, however, academic freedom rights have been more often challenged by external constituents than by institutions themselves and—reflecting larger political or ideological conflicts—frequently have involved allegations of political, racial, or religious bias in the academy. In these cases, the courts have consistently upheld the academic freedom rights of faculty and institutions. For example, in 2001, a student at Indiana University–Purdue University at Fort Wayne planned to present a play that his departmental faculty had approved for his senior thesis. A group of taxpayers and state legislators tried to prevent the performance on grounds that the play's content was offensive to many Christians, but federal courts denied the plaintiff's motion for an injunction. Three years later, at the University of North Carolina at Chapel Hill, taxpayers and students challenged an orientation program in which students were directed to read a book on the Islamic faith, arguing that the book was merely an exercise in political correctness. The federal district court "rejected the plaintiff's claims on the merits" (Kaplin et al., 2020, p. 311).

Over the past two decades there have been several additional challenges to professors' or institutions' academic freedom in designing courses or course materials, leading classroom discussions, or assigning grades. As Kaplin and colleagues (2020) wrote, "the challengers typically cite particular decisions that they claim foster indoctrination or otherwise reflect a political (usually liberal) bias. [They] often claim that such decisions violate student academic freedom, thus adding an additional dimension of conflict to the situation" (pp. 311–312). Given established precedent, as well as a district court's ruling in *Cohen v. San Bernardino Valley College* that the college "must avoid restricting creative and engaging teaching, even if some over-sensitive students object to it" (p. 335), few of these cases have prevailed. Nonetheless, those who challenge academic freedom may not need to win in court to achieve their goals. As illustration: in 2021, trustees of the University of North Carolina at Chapel Hill initially declined to offer tenure to Pulitzer

Prize-winning journalist Nikole Hannah-Jones, reportedly due to conservative objections to her role as creator of the *1619 Project*, which reframed the country's history by centering the consequences of slavery and the contributions of Black Americans. Although the trustees eventually reversed course, Hannah-Jones instead elected to join the faculty at Howard University. Given the political polarization of the Contemporary Era, the deep distrust of colleges and universities felt by many conservatives, and legislative efforts to restrict or roll back tenure in several states, the Hannah-Jones example may well serve as a political playbook for those intent on eroding academic freedom in the academy.

## Curriculum

The curriculum continued to evolve: colleges and universities developed new approaches to supporting underprepared students; faculty sought to augment and reframe general education to better achieve its civic and educative purposes; occupational specialization persisted and institutions developed new pathways to degrees, certificates, and industry relevant credentials. As well, advances in technology and artificial intelligence led to transformations in everything from library holdings; to the ways students communicate, learn, and access information; to strategies for teaching and learning in both online and in-person classrooms. A global pandemic rapidly accelerated engagement in online learning. And faculty incorporated critical and culturally responsive pedagogies, which—like the multiculturalism of the Consolidation Era—drew the ire of those who did not subscribe to an academic ethos grounded in critical inquiry, self-reflection, and the incorporation of diverse perspectives.

### Developmental Education

Developmental education, defined as courses or supplementary programs in reading, writing, or mathematics for college students whose high schools did not adequately prepare them for college-level work (or for whom time away from academe meant these skills needed to be refreshed), was provided in two-thirds of all institutions that enroll first-year students. This was true in 99% of public community colleges, 75% of public four-year colleges, 61% of four-year proprietary schools, and 58% of four-year private institutions. Most colleges did not award degree credit for developmental courses but counted them toward institutional credit so that students could receive financial aid.

Despite their prevalence, the effectiveness of developmental programs has been in dispute since they began. Numerous studies have shown that students referred to developmental education are less likely to reach various credit milestones and eventually earn a degree or certificate than those who began in college-level classes; these effects are magnified among those requiring three or more developmental courses. One problem has been that colleges and universities have relied on assessment and placement tests that failed to distinguish between students who would benefit from developmental education and those who could succeed in college-level courses with additional support. Too many students—especially those from minoritized backgrounds—were directed toward developmental studies based on tests of limited validity; a 2012 study found that 3 out of every 10 students were misassigned to developmental English; error rates for math placement were lower, but not trivial (Belfield and Crosta, 2012). To remedy this, many institutions began considering students' high school GPAs or other measures in combination with placement tests to refer students more accurately to developmental or college-level classes.

In addition to implementing multiple measures of assessment and placement, many colleges and universities have moved away from stand-alone developmental programs, choosing instead to limit the amount of time students may spend in developmental education or change the way in which developmental support is offered. Some of the most impactful developmental reforms include short-term skills refresher courses; corequisite models in which students who are assessed as needing developmental instruction are placed in first college-level courses but provided with additional learning support, such as tutoring or a paired extra-help course in the same subject; and contextualized, major- or career-specific developmental courses, especially in math. Popular contextualized math pathways include those focused on quantitative literacy for students pursuing humanities majors, statistics courses for health and social science majors, and algebra courses for those pursuing a STEM-related career (Rutschow et al., 2019). Chapter 8 in Kisker, Cohen, and Brawer's 2023 book on community colleges discusses developmental education, its effects, and recent reforms at length.

**The Core Curriculum**

Twenty years ago, after examining the transcripts of students entering college from the high school classes of 1972, 1982, and 1992, Adelman (2004) labeled the set of courses most often completed by bachelor's degree recipients as the *empirical core curriculum*. This set of 30 courses represented roughly one-third of all credits earned and had been reasonably consistent over time, including approximately equal numbers of classes in humanities and languages, science and mathematics, social sciences, and business, along with a few other fields such as music performance and physical education. The top individual courses were English composition, general psychology, calculus, general chemistry, and Spanish.

Not surprisingly, there was great overlap between the empirical core curriculum and courses that would satisfy students' general education (GE) requirements, which, since the University Transformation Era, typically have been distributed across various disciplines to ensure that students gained a broad knowledge base in addition to more specialized study in their major. At nearly every degree-granting college and university, students have long been asked to complete one or more courses in the humanities and arts, social and behavioral sciences, natural sciences and technology, mathematics or quantitative reasoning, and composition or writing; in recent decades, many also have required a course focused on gender or cultural studies. The idea, of course, was that by taking a sampling of courses from across the curriculum, all college graduates would have a common core of knowledge which would enable them to think critically, communicate effectively, and work well with others. A general education would also, proponents hoped, help students become "ethical human beings and effective citizens," developing qualities including respect for others and "a willingness to assume civic, political, and social responsibilities" (Accrediting Commission for Community and Junior Colleges, 2001, p. 5).

However, in 2011, Arum and Roska published *Academically Adrift*, an extensive analysis of the extent and quality of college-level learning, finding that many students showed no meaningful gains on key measures of learning, including critical thinking, during their college years. Although more recent reports challenged some of these findings—especially those related to critical thinking—a number of scholars argued that GE distribution requirements have contributed to a lack of demonstrated learning in college, as they "have become a box-checking exercise that can be met through an extensive list of options," one dictated by "a series of rather unsavory political compromises, designed to placate various interests and prop up enrollment in departments lacking substantial student demand" (Mintz, 2023). Students take the GE courses, but as a recent survey attested, less than one-third seem to understand their purpose or how the knowledge gained may be "foundational to success in work, citizenship and life" (Hart, 2022). To counter this, faculty at numerous colleges and universities—supported by organizations such as the American Association of State Colleges and Universities (AASCU) and the Association of American Colleges and Universities (AAC&U)—have attempted to reframe the core curriculum so that it better achieves its civic and educative purposes. Within community colleges, Kisker, Cohen, and Brawer (2023) advocated for an integrative approach to GE that builds on the colleges' existing work related to critical thinking; equity, inclusion, and belonging; service learning and civic engagement; and environmental sustainability and climate change.

Similarly, Mintz (2023) suggested that faculty can create more meaningful GE experiences by building interconnected lower-division courses that deal with existential issues such as ethics, evil, identity, love, or tragedy as viewed through multiple literary or philosophical traditions; by integrating international and cross-cultural perspectives into humanities courses; and by examining "urgent issues of our time—climate change, equity, immigration—from multidisciplinary perspectives" (para. 31). Although examples of all these approaches can be found on campuses across America, few institutions have embraced them as the centerpieces of their core curriculum; according to the AAC&U (2016), 79% of institutions still utilize a distribution model for general education, although most also offer some integrative features. Nonetheless, a slow-moving reformation in general education has begun, centering less on the formal integration of academic disciplines—that ship sailed roughly 150 years ago—than on ideals of relevance and civic and community engagement.

**Occupational Specialization**

Despite the longstanding importance of a core curriculum to educators, few students have ever enrolled merely to learn; nearly all have expected to gain skills, knowledge, and connections useful in bettering their income or lifestyle. In a broad sense, all curriculum is occupationally relevant, but over time, most colleges have directed more of their instructional efforts toward specific jobs and professions. The earliest job training programs prepared people for law, medicine, and the ministry. As the universities developed, they added journalism, business, architecture, education, social work, dentistry, public administration, and engineering. And when community colleges were formed, they picked up automotive repair, nursing, and technologies supportive of the health and engineering professions, eventually adding programs leading to skilled technical occupations such as aircraft mechanics and solar panel and wind turbine technicians.

By 2020, 55% of associate degrees, 64% of bachelor's, 83% of master's, and 82% percent of doctoral degrees were awarded to students majoring in professional or applied fields. (Actually, since nearly all PhD recipients gained employment in research labs, government service, or in schools or colleges, those degrees should be considered occupationally relevant regardless of academic specialty.) In addition, except for some community college certificates that indicated a student had completed a transferrable core curriculum, nearly every postsecondary nondegree credential (NDC) was occupational in nature.

While the trend toward occupational specialization continued from earlier eras, the Contemporary Era is unique in that what had been considered a one-way street from community college through graduate school gave way to a more diverse set of educational and training pathways through which students could move laterally and vertically and at their own pace over the course of their careers. Traditional transfer pathways continued—for example, from community college to university, or from bachelor's to master's degree—but were joined by transfer pathways and degrees in applied areas, including the community college baccalaureate. Community colleges and other broadly accessible institutions expanded the use of competency-based courses and programs and the awarding of credit for prior learning. As well, colleges and universities at all levels began awarding NDCs and stackable credentials to help learners upskill or change careers. While stackable credentials are most often designed to lead from short-term, employment-oriented programs to more advanced degrees, students don't always follow the prescribed sequences and some, as

DesRochers explained, do college "backwards" (as cited in Gaston and Van Noy, 2022, p. 28).

Indeed, by 2023, it was common to find a student with a master's in computer science hoping to further specialize by enrolling in a community college cybersecurity or artificial intelligence certificate program. Disaffected lawyers went back to school to become firefighters or teachers, and associate, bachelor's and graduate students alike picked up industry-relevant credentials and digital badges to bolster their employment prospects. Indeed, in 2022, Gaston and Van Noy argued that we might think about occupational credentials as less of a stack, and more of a LEGO construction, where "pieces are made to fit together in a variety of directions for a variety of purposes" (p. 29). Such a model envisions that most if not all workers will experience a continually evolving educational and career journey, with pieces (i.e., degrees, certificates, and other credentials) fitting together in ways that are simultaneously unique to the learner yet easily articulated among institutions of higher education. In an age where societal and technological advancements are constantly changing the knowledge and skills required for various occupations, a postsecondary system that provides multiple entry and exit points, enabling students of all ages to continue learning, seems ideal.

**Libraries and Learning Resources**

Traditional examinations of libraries have focused on collections, circulation data, and operating expenditures. NCES tallied data from 3,654 postsecondary libraries in 2019–2020, reporting over 2.7 billion books, media, and databases; more than 1 billion circulation transactions; and $8.3 billion in operating expenditures (half on salaries). Harvard and Yale headed the list of academic institutions with the largest collections, just as they had nearly two centuries earlier, although the flagship research universities in Illinois, California, and Michigan were close behind. Although 3 out of every 4 for-profit institutions had some sort of library, the entire sector together offered only about 228,000 books, media, or other resources.

But collection size becomes increasingly less relevant as libraries move toward virtual collections and as their services focus more on instructional support than research productivity. Most have reduced costly subscriptions to physical journals in favor of electronic journal subscriptions that faculty and students can access via the Internet at a cost for licensing that is related to institutional size. Physical books now make up only 37% of all books held by academic libraries, and physical media (including audiovisual materials) make up only 20%; most media holdings are now digital. In addition, librarians often point students and faculty toward the vast trove of free materials available online—for example: government publications, pre-prints of journal articles, podcasts, online tutorials—as well as numerous Open Educational Resources (OER), including reading materials, lesson plans, course activities or labs, simulations, illustrations, and so forth. Although only 15% of faculty (and 25% of those teaching introductory courses) reported using OER as required material in their courses in 2019–2020, these percentages represented a threefold increase from 2015–2016. Adoption of OER was highest among faculty teaching in MSIs (Seaman and Seaman, 2021).

**Technology Use and Online Learning**

Just as technology has transformed academic libraries, technological advances have fundamentally reshaped campus operations, student behaviors, and teaching and learning processes. In the twenty-first century, technology is infused into nearly all aspects of campus functioning. For example, colleges and universities have embraced learning management and student information systems; created online portals to help students create their own degree plans and maps; utilized technology-based early alert systems to facilitate timely responses to student problems as soon as they become evident; and built or licensed cloud-based data warehouses and dashboards to manage enrollments and enable faculty and staff to explore visual representations of equity gaps and student progress and outcomes data. Furthermore, most institutions have enabled remote access to various student services; even before the COVID-19 pandemic forced colleges to move services online, most campuses offered registration, financial aid, transcription, tutoring, and other resources online or via smartphone apps.

Technology similarly changed how students interact with their institutions. At the start of the Contemporary Era, most learners attended lectures, laboratories, and faculty office hours in person; turned in paper copies of homework assignments; and wrote letters home to family and friends. By the turn of the century, many students had their own computers and nearly all were able to access those in libraries or campus computing centers to write essays or complete assignments. Email and instant messaging became ubiquitous, and a few early adopters had mobile phones.

Since then, advances in computing and cellular technology, as well as the Internet and its attendant uses, have fundamentally altered the ways students communicate, learn, and access information. Many students today have both a smartphone and a laptop or other personal computer. They are more likely to communicate through social media, smartphone app, or text message than via email; one study found that 72% of students treat emails from student groups like spam; more than half admit to not always reading emails from their institution or academic department; and nearly 40% percent do not always read emails from their advisers (Joa, Gabay, and Ha, 2016). And with the assistance of institutional subscriptions to online journals and OER, learners can access research and class materials without ever setting foot in a library.

As technology advanced, more students took advantage of opportunities to engage in hybrid or online courses and programs. Even before the COVID-19 pandemic, more than one-third of college students took at least one virtual course, and 18% exclusively attended online (up from 16% and 5%, respectively, in 2003). In Fall 2020, when most campuses reopened for in-person learning, nearly three-quarters of all students continued to take one or more virtual courses and 46% were learning entirely at a distance. Three years post-pandemic, most college students preferred in-person learning, but roughly one-third still favored a hybrid learning model or expressed an interest in learning online. Online and hybrid learning had been normalized, even at the most selective residential institutions.

However, higher education's technological response to the COVID-19 pandemic laid bare what many had known for years, which is that "institutions are not providing equitable student support services to online students, with the most significant gaps identified in student advising and counseling services" (Bouchey, Gratz, and Kurland, 2021, p. 30). Thus, for the first time, traditional colleges and universities were forced to think deeply how they can provide high-quality, equitable instruction and student support, both through new structures created specifically for online learners and by tailoring existing strategies to students learning at a distance. In the years since 2020, colleges and universities developed a number of virtual support services, including online orientations that introduce students who may never set foot on a campus to the resources and services available to them and online apps or landing pages where students can access everything they need, including real-time responses from faculty and advisers and just-in-time resources such as tutoring and tech support. Similarly, in the post-pandemic era, online counseling, advising, and financial aid assistance have taken on added importance, as students—both online and in person—face numerous stressors related to their mental, social, and financial well-being. When done well, support for online learners serves to enhance campus-based services, in effect improving support for all students (Bouchey, Gratz, and Kurland, 2021).

However, there is considerable evidence that at least some students do not fare as well in online courses as they would in a face-to-face environment. A working paper published by the National Bureau of Economic Research (Altindag, Filiz, and Tekin, 2023) found that even before the COVID-19 pandemic, students in online courses were more likely to withdraw from classes and less likely to receive passing grades than peers learning in person. The Community College Research Center (2013) found that students in developmental courses fared especially badly in online courses and that equity gaps between White and Black students were larger in virtual environments. Finding that students of color, those living in rural areas, and those from low-income and basic-needs-insecure backgrounds "struggle mightily in online courses," Sublett (2022) concluded that "available evidence suggests fully online learning . . . impedes student success and equity" (pp. 27, 30). Thus, in the post-pandemic era, colleges and universities are thinking much more strategically about when and to whom they offer online and hybrid courses, as well as how they can effectively support all learners, regardless of modality.

Institutions also have been forced to consider the costs of teaching and providing support to students learning online. Despite eager pronouncements to the contrary in the late 1990s and early 2000s, online learning has not cut costs or increased productivity. A well-designed online course integrating content, assessment, and student support is expensive to produce and maintain. Furthermore, many institutions have imposed enrollment restrictions on online courses to ensure quality, and because per-student labor costs are not much changed, there is "a negligible association between online credits and instructional costs" (Hemelt and Stange, 2020). The late George Keller (2008), a long-time analyst of instructional design, once summed the situation bluntly, saying "Perhaps the most fatuous and delusional expectation of information technology enthusiasts is that substituting IT for traditional teaching arrangements will enable colleges and universities to reduce their costs appreciably. Precisely the opposite has occurred" (p. 76). Indeed, the costs of instructional technology doubled as a percentage of institutional budgets between 1990 and 2015. They skyrocketed during the COVID-19 pandemic, but since then nearly 3 in 4 colleges and universities have reported reductions in their information technology budgets, even as the costs of maintaining virtual learning options and online support services remain high.

Technology costs will almost certainly continue to climb as faculty and administrators identify new ways of communicating with and engaging students, both online and in person. Indeed, over the past three decades, professors have adopted a number of technology tools to build community in the classroom, enable on- and offline group work, monitor student progress and success, and engage learners in classroom exercises and assessments. Learning management systems (LMS), which were employed in 15% of college courses in 2000, are now used by nearly all colleges and universities; the most comprehensive provide students with access to academic calendars, course assignments, a dashboard to chart their progress, tools to communicate with classmates and faculty, shortcuts to tutoring, technical support, and wellness services, and a digital home for essays, assignments, resources, and assessments. By the end of the Contemporary Era, technology became thoroughly infused into collegiate teaching and learning, in the process fostering more accessible, collaborative, and personalized learning environments.

However, recent advances in technology and a reliance on digital sources of information have raised a number of concerns related to digital equity, student wellness, and academic integrity. For example, more than 1 in 8 undergraduate students who live off-campus lack consistent access to broadband Internet and must rely on cellular data to access online resources or engage in virtual or hybrid courses. Indigenous students, as well as low-income learners and those living in rural areas, are least likely to have stable broadband access (Skinner, Burtch, and Levy, 2022). Noble (2018) has written extensively about how social media platforms and search engine algorithms magnify and propagate racist, classist, sexist, homophobic, and anti-Semitic views. And Lynch

(2018) and others have shown that an overreliance on technology can exacerbate students' already high levels of social disconnection, depression, and anxiety.

Most recently, the development of large language models such as ChatGPT that can "generate text that can be indistinguishable from text written by humans" has resulted in "much hype and doomsday predictions when it comes to student assessment in higher education" (Rudolph, Tan, and Tan, 2023, p. 1). Given ChatGPT's ability to summarize material and write in a given style or genre (e.g., essay, research paper, haiku, song lyrics), some faculty and staff are understandably concerned that it could lead to widespread cheating or honor code abuses. Others are worried it will rob students of their creativity, motivation, or ability to think critically. Still others raise reliability concerns—up to half of the time ChatGPT produces erroneous outputs, what computer scientists call "hallucinations"—as well as privacy and equity concerns: What happens to all the data generated by students' queries? Following ChatGPT's release in November 2022, colleges and universities scrambled to update their academic integrity and honor codes, provide faculty, staff, and students with information about allowed and improper uses of ChatGPT and similar technologies, and promote software such as GPTZero that (also imperfectly) detects whether a given piece of text was written by AI.

But although the emergence of ChatGPT led to an "initial panic" among educators, with some institutions banning its use altogether, many faculty now believe that if used properly, generative AI may be beneficial for teaching and learning, as it has the capacity to make lessons more interactive and individualized, save teachers time on administrative tasks, encourage students to validate information and challenge assumptions, and augment collaborative educational practices such as the "think-pair-share" exercise (Heaven, 2023). Ultimately, because of the ease with which ChatGPT and similar AI technologies can be used to cheat on summative assessments, they may force a sector-wide reckoning about the desired learning outcomes of various assignments, including whether a final product should be valued over the processes and learning required to create it and whether an assessment has shallow or deeper instrumental value (e.g., whether it simply results in a passing grade or leads to a transferable skill).

As the ChatGPT example illustrates, the rapid pace of technological change means that colleges and universities will be continually challenged to stay abreast of recent developments, update technology use policies and practices, and identify ways in which virtual reality, machine learning, AI, and other technologies can be used to enhance learning, critical thinking, and intellectual judgment instead of detract from them. This is no small task. Luckily, ChatGPT offered some advice, in the form of a sonnet:

> In halls of learning, where wisdom takes flight,
> A faculty seeks ways to teach with might,
> Large language models hold promise untold,
> Yet challenges rise, as tales must be told.
> To gain the benefits, faculty wise,
> Embrace the tools, but with discerning eyes.
> Augment your teaching, let models assist,
> Not replace you, but as guides they persist.
> Structured interactions, critical minds fed,
> Encourage students to go forth and tread,
> Beyond model's answers, seek truth's embrace,
> And nurture skills, independent space.
> So, faculty, blend models with your art,
> For in this dance, true learning shall impart.[1]

---

[1] ChatGPT output in response to May 19, 2023, prompt: "In the form of a sonnet, how might college faculty utilize large language models to attain its benefits and minimize negative implications for teaching and learning?" Interestingly, when the output was cut and pasted into GPTZero, the AI detection software responded by saying, "Your text is likely to be written entirely by a human." Sigh.

### Critical and Culturally Responsive Pedagogies

The multicultural movement of the Consolidation Era succeeded in expanding the canon to include more diverse voices and opened the door for examinations of race, gender, and class in both new and traditional disciplines. In the Contemporary Era, educators moved beyond multiculturalism to interrogate the ways in which educational structures and systems have perpetuated racism, classism, and other intra-group inequities. The application of critical race theory (which emerged in 1970s legal scholarship) to education spurred a widespread examination of how postsecondary programs and practices serve to elevate or depress the educational and economic prospects of marginalized or minoritized groups and led to pedagogical approaches designed center their experiences.

Chief among these new pedagogical approaches is culturally responsive teaching. Defined as "a pedagogy that recognizes the importance of including student's cultural identities in all aspects of learning," culturally responsive teaching "empowers students socially, intellectually, politically, and emotionally" (Pappamihiel and Moreno, 2011, p. 333). It necessitates faculty interrogation of their own identities and validation of their students' cultural heritages to boost educational attainment, especially for students from races or ethnicities that have been historically marginalized in higher education. Following the teachings of Paulo Freire (1970), culturally responsive teaching emphasizes the use of real-world social issues that can equip learners "with the tools to name problems and take positive action for social change" (Garrett, Miller, and Gilbert, 2021, p. 110).

Although culturally responsive teaching and similar liberation pedagogies have become more common in higher education classrooms, Garrett, Miller, and Gilbert (2021) found that they are not always embraced in colleges with lower proportions of students of color or in many rural institutions, where White faculty often maintain curricular structures and pedagogical practices that fail to recognize the cultural identities and resources of students of color in the name of "fairness" or "treating everyone equally" (p. 107). Furthermore, in recent years, such pedagogies have drawn the ire of conservative commentators and lawmakers who claim that any practices that highlight the racialized history of America or the experiences of marginalized people are simply attempts to indoctrinate students into a progressive political ideology. While classroom topics and pedagogical approaches have long been defended by the courts on academic freedom and free speech grounds, such protections may be tested in the coming years as Republican lawmakers in Florida, Texas, and elsewhere pass bills prohibiting spending on collegiate diversity, equity, and inclusion efforts and banning the teaching of "theories that systemic racism, sexism, oppression, and privilege are inherent in the institutions of the United States and were created to maintain social, political, and economic inequities" (Florida Senate Bill 266, 2023, p. 5). Whether or not these laws hold up in court, they will almost certainly achieve their desired effect in the near term, which is to stall or reverse the progress institutions of higher education have made to provide welcoming, inclusive, and equitable environments for all students, especially those from historically marginalized races and ethnicities.

### Academic Ethos

As colleges and universities experience substantial changes in curricular emphases, pedagogical approaches, and uses of technology, one might wonder, "What is the essence of academe?" Although the evolution of academic disciplines mandates that they continually revise methodology and topics of study, throughout history many of these changes have been denounced as betraying higher education's heritage. In the past 75 years alone, scholars have bemoaned the acceptance of alternative viewpoints, especially those holding that there is no hierarchy of knowledge, that no method of inquiry, pattern of discourse, or area of study is inherently valid (e.g., Nisbet, 1971). Others admonished social scientists for their relative indifference to social problems or for imitating the methodologies utilized by natural scientists (e.g., Mills, 1959; Soros, 2008). Accusations in the 1980s and 1990s that multiculturalism and other efforts to expand the canon beyond patriarchal, Western European perspectives would inevitably lead to lower standards and a loss of academic credibility presaged the current conservative backlash to critical race theory and DEI efforts on campus. And each technological revolution elicited strong emotions about the future of teaching and learning, "ranging from doomsday predictions to unbridled euphoria" (Rudolph, Tan, and Tan, 2023, p. 1).

Yet despite the hysteria, curricular evolution continued as it always had. The social sciences turned toward attempts to solve social concerns, spurred in part by students' demands for a more relevant curriculum and the public's desire to find solutions to community problems. The sciences, which had long been viewed empirically pure, logical, and positive, centered on objective experiments and rational statements, were criticized for ignoring the unexamined biases of researchers and for effecting environmentally harmful industrial processes and fearsome weaponry. The study of literature and history embraced a broader array of perspectives, and the canon was gradually expanded rather than eliminated.

For nearly 400 years, the disciplines have risen, fallen, and been reconstituted continually as the curriculum and the society in which it is situated evolved. At a system level, however, curriculum reform occurred at a glacial speed, and the enterprise was large enough to contain traditions long past their prime. The classics, Greek, and Latin still represented a significant proportion of the curriculum for generations after the mainstream of American thought moved away from the trivium and the quadrivium. Yet by the Contemporary Era the disciplines began to serve multiple masters: the professions, the university, and the community at large. The latter has become the most demanding master of all, and shifting political and social forces now pull colleges and universities in varying directions.

Reason, culture, and excellence have long been the leading concepts undergirding higher education. Reason (truth, rationality) is the organizing principle for the academic disciplines. Culture is the unifier, the sum of a society's values and knowledge. Excellence (quality) has no content; what is studied matters less than that it is researched and taught well. The history of higher education is reflected in the light of these concepts. As codified in the eighteenth and early nineteenth centuries, the premier disciplines (law, medicine, and theology) sought to reconcile established tradition with rational inquiry. The late-twentieth-century disputes over which perspectives should be reflected in the curriculum revealed the importance of culture, of naming the traditions and experiences that define us, differentiate us, and bind us together in a common humanity.

These ideals are again being challenged, this time by those outside academe who are concerned less with the integrity of the disciplines or the continuity of a liberal arts tradition than by a fear that when presented with opportunities to think critically, to consider wicked problems from multiple perspectives, and to interact with different kinds of people, students may come to hold views or develop values that differ from those of their parents. Ultimately, they fear the academic ethos, the "Hippocratic oath for the academic profession" (Shils, 1978, p. 165): education not for indoctrination but for liberation. Pedagogy that leads not to any particular perspective but to the examination of one's own values and beliefs. Considered in this way, the evolution of the disciplines—and of their associated pedagogies and technologies—is nothing less than higher education's imperfect progress in the pursuit of reason, culture, and excellence.

## Governance

Higher education administration has long exhibited a duality: a bureaucratic hierarchy organized under the office of a president or chancellor (who in turns answers to a board of trustees) and a collegial structure through which faculty make decisions regarding curriculum and the employment of their colleagues. In recent years, however, boards of trustees have taken a more active role in managing campus affairs; an increased orientation to the market introduced new governance actors, each demanding evidence of accountability and return on investment; and shared governance was further threatened by increased administrative control over enterprise operations and by the continued trend toward a part-time, contingent academic workforce. Accreditation agencies were challenged to keep up with ever greater numbers of online courses and programs and to crack down on the abuses of the for-profit sector. Higher education governance, which had become increasingly complex over the previous 150 years, was now big business and received near-constant scrutiny from those within and outside academe.

### Accountability and an Orientation to the Market

The Contemporary Era saw colleges and universities making a distinct turn toward the market, with leaders acting to shelter existing resources and to generate new ones. Presidents and their staff spent increasing amounts of time fundraising and assisting in the acquisition of large federal research grants. Those at public institutions also spent considerable time lobbying state legislators and philanthropic grant makers for greater support. Public and government relations offices grew considerably, and even broadly accessible institutions and community colleges vastly increased marketing efforts and expenditures. Much time and energy were spent considering how colleges and universities might expand their influence and enrollments through the construction of research parks, entrepreneurial partnerships, enhanced campus amenities, noncredit offerings, and other activities related to the higher education enterprise.

An obvious manifestation of higher education's orientation to the market was the increased use of accountability measures or performance indicators, which linked academic metrics to budgetary concerns and, in the extreme, to objectives that were not necessarily related to teaching and learning. (An example of the latter is when an institution's expenditures are divided by the number of degrees awarded to derive an index of productivity; reduced to the absurd, online diploma mills are the most productive of all institutions!) Although public institutions have theoretically always been accountable to the states and communities from which they draw taxpayer support, in the Contemporary Era states, accrediting bodies, grant makers, and the federal government demanded that the institutions demonstrate their responsiveness to community needs and provide reports of their stewardship of public funds (i.e., document the institutions' return on the public's investment).

Nearly all states now have some form of mandated accountability in place, specifying a few to several dozen goals. Thirty-three states allocate funding to two- or four-year public institutions (or both) through an outcomes-based funding policy, thus linking institutional support to institutional performance. However, these policies have proven cumbersome to manage and have not always resulted in the desired outcomes, especially those related to equity. According to the Education Trust (Elliott, Haynes, and Jones, 2021), of the 33 outcomes-based funding policies currently in place, most "have done little to improve resource equity or boost student success overall" (para. 4).

Nonetheless, the collection and publication of data related to institutional effectiveness, as well as student progress and success, required colleges and universities to make substantial investments in data infrastructure and to hire staffers to produce the hundreds of reports required by various agencies. Demands for accountability increased as more and more students engaged in higher learning, as tuition levels comprised ever greater percentages of average household incomes, and as states and the federal government increased their contributions. Counterintuitively, demands for accountability also increased when states and localities pulled back on the amount of support they provided and legislators questioned the efficiency or effectiveness of institutional budgeting processes. (As the section on Finance details, in labor-intensive organizations such as colleges and universities, there is little fat to trim from institutional budgets, despite many lawmakers' exhortations to the contrary.)

Demands for accountability grew further as colleges and universities engaged in philanthropic and entrepreneurial revenue generation; more funding sources begot more governance actors, and each of these required their own reporting on the efficiency or effectiveness of resources expended. The public, too, required more data: the Student-Right-to-Know and Campus Security Act of 1990 obliged institutions to provide information on graduation rates, security policies, campus crime statistics, institutional procedures for allocating financial aid, and detailed figures on the cost of attendance, including tuition and fees, books and supplies, room and board, and local cost of living. The 2008 Higher Education Opportunity Act required institutions to set annual cost reduction benchmarks, report reasons for tuition increases, and provide information enabling the public to estimate the net cost of attendance (after applicable grants and discounts). The 2014 gainful employment regulations enacted by Obama's Department of Education mandated public disclosure of key performance data and a cutoff of federal financial aid to institutions where more than a certain percentage of graduates had debt-to-income ratios higher than a specified limit. Although the rules were suspended by the Trump administration, Biden's Department of Education proposed even more stringent gainful employment regulations in May 2023 that would, among other things, create a "watch list of programs that . . . provide a low financial value to students" and a new website that will track a range of data on college programs (Knott, 2023).

The availability of all this information invited policymakers, commentators, and the general public to come to their own conclusions—educated or not—about the effectiveness of higher education and whether attending college is worth the cost. Some seized on bits of information—the number of DEI officers employed at a given university, for example, or graduation rates among African Americans, or pseudo-scientific rankings of various collegiate majors based on their graduates' average salaries—and weaponized them, betting that their attacks on the institutions would bolster ratings or political support among constituents. Ideologically based critiques of America's colleges and universities are nothing new; what changed in the Contemporary Era was the vast amount of data that could be cherry-picked to support the assertions.

**Presidents**

The larger the institutions became, the more they began to look like corporations, with complex organization charts illustrating the myriad roles of senior and mid-level administrators as well as the staffers working in their offices. The presidency evolved in the direction of the market as well. Historically, college and university presidents came up through the faculty ranks before taking on administrative responsibilities and ultimately ascending to the C-suite. And while more than half of all presidents in four-year colleges and universities still took this route (especially in doctoral institutions, where two-thirds had previous faculty experience), many more—especially those in community colleges—rose solely through the administrative ranks and nearly 10% came from outside academe (American Council on Education, 2023; this percentage was down substantially from 2016, when 15% of presidents were recruited from business or industry).

Regardless of their paths to the presidency, the primary roles of presidents shifted ever more toward fundraising, government and public relations, and budgetary matters. Formerly more prominent in private institutions, these functions spread across the system, from public research universities to community colleges. According to the Deloitte Center for Higher Education Excellence (2017), the essential skills required for the presidency were "administrative and financial acumen, fundraising ability, and political deftness" (p. 2). As college presidents spent most of their time interacting with external stakeholders, provosts took on the role of the top academic leader, responsible for academic affairs and for resolving internal disputes. Despite this role evolution, presidents were far more likely to be removed by votes of no-confidence from their faculty than for failing to meet fundraising targets or other financial metrics.

According to the American Council on Education (2023), the mean tenure for current presidents in 2022 was 5.9 years, down from 8.5 years in 2006. Yet despite some diversification of the presidential ranks, most are still older White men. The percentage of female presidents increased from less than one-quarter to just over one-third between 2006 and 2022, and in the latter year 73% were White; only 17% of college and university presidents were Black or African American, 6% Hispanic or Latinx, 3% Asian, and 2% multiracial. Less than 1% of college or university presidents were Middle Eastern or Arab American, Indigenous, or from another racial/ethnic group. The average age of the college president remained steady at 60 years of age (American Council on Education, 2023).

As presidents took on ever more corporate responsibilities, their salaries increased commensurately, far outpacing increases in faculty wages. In 2021, the average presidential salary ranged from $225,000 at community colleges to $250,000 and $387,000, respectively, at public and private baccalaureate institutions, and $495,000 and $824,000, respectively, at public and private doctoral universities (Chronicle of Higher Education, 2021). Yet much variation was masked within these means, and CEOs at the most elite public and private universities garnered $1 million or more, as well as allowances for housing, autos, and other benefits. The University of Pennsylvania's president earned $3.9 million in 2016, 20 times the median salary of professors at Penn that year (Bryant, 2022). Yet in negotiations over salaries and prerequisites, presidential pay is not compared with that of professors, but with the CEOs of comparable colleges and universities, as well as with those in the corporate world.

## Administrative Bloat or the Costs of Compliance and Equitable Support?

Presidential salary increases were one frequently mentioned reason for rising costs during the Contemporary Era. Administrative bloat—described as the "ballooning growth of administrative functions and personnel in U.S. higher education" (Williamson, Hughes, and Head, 2018, p. 15)—was also cited as a prime contributor. In truth, administrative costs *have* increased substantially since the start of the Contemporary Era, especially at community colleges. In constant 2021 dollars, expenditures on administrative functions (institutional support, as well as academic support and student services) per full-time-equivalent (FTE) student increased 35% between 1999 and 2020 at private, four-year institutions, while expenditures on instruction, research, and public service increased by only 20%. At four-year public institutions, per-FTE administrative costs increased by 13% between 2009 and 2020, while faculty costs remained steady. And at community colleges, per-FTE administrative costs increased by 46%, while instructional costs grew by half that amount (23%).

Where was all this money going? Certainly, some can be attributed to higher levels of competition among institutions for the most well-prepared students. In addition to offering top-notch campus amenities, many colleges and universities also boasted of low student-to-support-staff ratios as a way of illustrating the myriad resources available to learners. The growing reliance on information and educational technology—as well as institutions' efforts to provide instruction and support at a distance—also contributed mightily to administrative costs. As Williamson, Hughes, and Head (2018) illustrated, however, much of the growth in administrative expenditures also can be traced to state efforts during the Consolidation Era to streamline operations at public universities and community colleges through the creation of statewide governing and coordinating boards and other structures that serve as intermediaries between institutions and legislatures. In doing so, the researchers argued, states were successful in reducing faculty power and influence in shared governance, but as a result "may have actually created an environment that has contributed to increasing administrative bloat" (p. 17).

Another major contributor to rising administrative costs was the amount of human and other resources necessary to comply with ever greater governmental regulations and demands for accountability. A 2014 examination of the costs of regulatory compliance at 13 colleges and universities found that such efforts comprised between 3 and 11% of total, non-hospital operating expenditures (an average of 6.4%) and took up between 4 and 15% of faculty and staff time (Vanderbilt University, 2015). Expenditures related to the administration of grants and contracts accounted for nearly one-quarter of compliance costs at research institutions, but across the board, accreditation was a primary driver. Accreditation, Morris (2010) pointed out, is a burdensome yet "extremely important, high-stakes activity since colleges and universities must be accredited in order to participate in a myriad of federal programs" (p. 295). Coordinating accreditation self-studies and visits and gathering supporting documentation requires a substantial amount of administrative time and effort. As an example, the University of Georgia at Athens' accreditation process required 15,000 pages of supporting documentation to address 800 pages of core requirements from the Southern Association of Colleges and Schools (Morris, 2010).

A final reason for rising administrative costs relates to the fact that students attending U.S. colleges and universities are both far more numerous and far more diverse—racially, ethnically, socioeconomically, and otherwise—than they were 30 years ago. A diverse student body requires a greater variety of resources and support services to ensure that the institution is in compliance with federal equal opportunity regulations and to build equitable and inclusive learning environments. In previous eras, faculty were far more involved in academic and student support functions, but as these services gained in complexity (and as full-timers made up diminishing percentages of the faculty), much of the work to provide career guidance, health and mental health services, advisement, tutoring and mentoring, veterans' or DEI support services, and so on was taken over by administrative experts.

But these rationales for growth in noninstructional expenditures frequently fall on deaf ears, as administrative bloat provides a convenient foil for faculty groups who are (understandably) more concerned about the rise of a part-time, fungible instructional workforce than the amount of money spent on compliance, IT, and student support, as well as lawmakers and commentators who claim to be irate about rising tuition and fees even as they advocate for lower levels of governmental support for colleges and universities. Indeed, some accusations of administrative bloat are overtly misleading: Zywicki and Koopman's (2017) claim that "even as more and more resources have poured into universities from tuition dollars and public and private support, an increasing amount of these dollars have been gobbled up by administrators and other university bureaucrats instead of supporting academic programs" (p. 3) promotes the false notion that money spent on anything outside the classroom has nothing to do with supporting students' ability to learn or persist in higher education. Zywicki and Koopman's reasoning relies heavily on arguments promoted by the right-wing Goldwater Institute (Greene, Kisida, and Mills, 2010), and in many ways their (and similar) accusations of administrative bloat resemble fiscally conservative arguments for starving the beast (i.e., reducing governmental spending on social programs). Actually, Zywicki and Koopman (2017) were honest about their intentions in this regard, stating that "[t]he explanation that we provide is that the role of the administration in the modern, nonprofit university can be best understood as analogous to the nature of a bureaucracy in another famously nonprofit industry, the government" (p. 3).

**Shared Governance and Leadership**

As American higher education evolved from a set of small residential colleges into a system of complex enterprises with myriad core and ancillary purposes, and as managerial power increased within the organizations, internal governance processes also shifted. Long before the Contemporary Era, the concept of collegial governance—faculty and administrators working together to collectively make institutional decisions—disappeared from all but a few tiny private campuses. It was replaced by the concept of shared governance in which faculty and administrators had "distinct areas of delegated authority and decision making" (Kezar and Holcombe, 2017, p. v). Indeed, the AAUP's 1966 "Statement on Government of College and Universities," issued and endorsed by the major institutional and governance associations, delineated specific areas of influence, stating that "the faculty has primary responsibility for such fundamental areas as curriculum, subject matter and methods of instruction, research, faculty status, and those aspects of student life which relate to the educational process." The governing board and the president would review faculty decisions in those matters but take a counter position "only in exceptional circumstances" (p. 139).

As a practice, shared governance varied widely among institutions. Those without faculty unions, with more collaborative cultures, and with procedures for socializing new faculty to governance roles enacted structures and processes to maintain shared responsibility for student development and achievement. At others, a zero-sum mentality or lack of trust between administrators and faculty—or their bargaining units—precluded any meaningful collaboration in institutional decision-making (Kisker, Cohen, and Brawer, 2023). It didn't help that participation in shared governance was primarily only an option for full-time or tenure-track faculty, which marginalized the part-time, contingent workforce and resulted in unsustainable amounts of committee work for the full-timers (Kater and Kisker, 2018).

Thus, by the 1990s, charges that shared governance was a "myth," that the days of faculty sovereignty were over, and that greater administrative control led to "academia [beginning] its slow yet unequivocal decline toward mediocrity and potential irrelevance" (for example, Hughley, 2023) were balanced only by laments from administrators, funders, and others who believed that the primary outcome of shared governance was gridlock, delayed decision-making, and an inability to respond quickly to community and economic needs. As Rosenberg (2014) wrote, many faculty saw administrators chiefly as managers who were more concerned with the bottom line than with educational quality, while administrators viewed many faculty members as "utterly indifferent to something as important as 'the bottom line'" (para. 11). Furthermore, the "exceptional circumstances" noted in the AAUP's statement occurred more frequently, as various other constituent groups exerted pressure on the board and administrators. Astute practitioners learned to maneuver within the thicket—bypassing, persuading, using loopholes, and otherwise finding ways of getting their work done. The processes described in organization charts and procedures manuals by no means told the true story of academic management and decision-making.

As a result, a number of scholars and educators have proposed new approaches to higher education governance. Kisker and Kater (2021) argued that faculty and staff must stop mythologizing the 1960s mental model of shared governance in which power is apportioned among opposing groups and instead engage in governance processes where the unique strengths and qualifications of stakeholders—faculty, staff, administrators, and students—are relevant across a spectrum of institutional decision-making. Kezar and Holcombe's (2017) conception of shared leadership similarly capitalizes on the importance of leaders throughout the organization, not just those in traditional positions of authority, and highlights the value of institutional structures and processes that can promote and sustain shared decision-making. In both models, participatory governance sheds the traditional demarcations between instructional and administrative territories and becomes "the process of coming to a decision, not the decision itself; its heart and soul are the conversations that occur every day, in every corner of the college, about how to enhance teaching and learning, better serve the community, or strengthen the organization" (Kisker and Kater, 2021, p. 5). So envisioned, shared leadership has the potential to capitalize on stakeholders' broad knowledge of and expertise within organizations, enable the networked leadership necessary to address increasingly complex budgetary challenges, and create broad ownership of strategies to deal with rapid social, political, economic, and technological changes (Kezar and Holcombe, 2017).

**Accreditation**

American higher education has a history of institutional autonomy, diversification, and self-regulation through accreditation. In general, accreditation serves the public by monitoring quality in higher education and easing the transfer of credit, functions that gained in both importance and complexity during the Contemporary Era. Accrediting agencies also insulate colleges and universities, to some extent, from government oversight, instead ensuring accountability "through the current decentralized structure of higher education in which institutions, programs, and accrediting organizations sustain full responsibility for academic quality rather than cede this important responsibility to the federal government" (Eaton, 2003, p. 2). Because only students in accredited institutions are allowed access to the billions of dollars in grants and loans that states and the federal government make available each year, the accreditation agencies have become a powerful shadow government.

In the early years of accreditation, the agencies assessed institutional quality primarily by documenting institutions' laboratory space, library holdings, faculty qualifications, financial stability, and so on. To gain accreditation today, colleges and universities must document planning and evaluation processes that cover all aspects of their operations: fiscal accountability, curriculum development, student performance, facilities maintenance. In addition, as demands for accountability increased in the Contemporary Era, accrediting agencies sought to assess the magnitude of state returns on investment, typically the preparation of a skilled workforce and the number and quality of graduates to fill jobs, as well as data related to student progress and outcomes, such as time-to-degree, pass rates on licensure exams, persistence and retention, milestone achievement, and transfer rates. The accrediting agencies also have been concerned with direct evidence of student learning and the supports in place to improve student persistence and attainment. And in recent years, they have implemented standards associated with diversity and equity. Industry-based skills standards have grown as well, thereby effecting a form of accreditation manifest by business and industry. These standards were not uniform across regional or programmatic associations, and not all have been enforced strictly, but enough of them have been set in place that they suggest a trend in intent, if not in substance.

In recent years, much of the controversy surrounding accreditation has been in relation to its ability to enforce student protections and ensure the quality of for-profit institutions. Although a handful of regional accreditors accept proprietary colleges into their ranks, most are accredited by one of several national organizations, including the Accrediting Commission of Career Schools and Colleges, in operation since 1965, and others that focus on a specific type of school, such as business, technology, art, or online learning. As Kisker, Cohen, and Brawer (2023) reported, oversight of for-profit accreditation has tightened considerably in recent years:

> In 2012, a U.S. Senate report argued that national accreditors did not have the capacity to adequately evaluate the

largest for-profit institutions, because "the self-reporting and peer-review nature of the accreditation process exposes it to manipulation by companies that are more concerned with their bottom line than with academic quality and improvement" [For-Profit Higher Education: The Failure to Safeguard the Federal Investment and Ensure Student Success, p. 8]. Soon after, the national accreditor ACICS lost federal recognition (twice) for failing to act in its watchdog capacity, forcing the schools it oversaw to seek accreditation elsewhere. As more and more attention is paid to the fraudulent business practices perpetrated by some proprietary institutions, the enormous amount of student loan debt held by graduates of these schools, and the relevancy (or lack thereof) of graduates' credentials to the marketplace, the accreditation of for-profit institutions is likely to come under even more scrutiny, with the intent of gaining greater transparency about college functioning and student outcomes. (p. 525)

Accreditation of distance or online programs has been a thorny issue also. Historically, distance learning guidelines and standards have varied considerably, not least because traditional standards of faculty contact, library access, and campus facilities did not apply. However, in recent years, accreditation of online programs has come to resemble regular accreditation processes more closely, with measurement of student outcomes, institutional planning, and implementation of evidence-based instructional strategies at the heart of the assessments. In particular, the disparate outcomes experienced by many students enrolled in online courses and programs—especially students of color and those from low-income backgrounds—have prompted accreditors to focus more on how colleges provide remote students with access to college resources, including academic advising and career or emotional counseling.

As Kisker, Cohen, and Brawer (2023) detailed, critiques of the accreditation process take many forms. One concern is that the regional accrediting associations vary in their standards and treatment of colleges with different emphases, although the Council for Higher Education Accreditation works to ensure minimum standards. Another criticism has to do with the amount of time required to receive approval for new programs, especially those leading to short-term credentials. A more recent concern has emerged following the U.S. Department of Education's decision in 2019 to repeal regional monopoly rules, which allowed formerly regional accrediting associations to cross into each other's territory and compete for clients. As Reed (2020) described, this move made it easier for colleges to "accreditor shop"—perhaps allowing them to work with the accreditor that is best suited to their programmatic emphases—but it also opened the door for accreditors to relax standards and requirements to keep existing or entice new business. Although Reed and others feared that accreditation standards will revert to the least common denominator now that they can reach beyond their traditional borders, others argued that this change will enable innovation—both at the colleges and within the accreditors themselves—and that the competition will lead to stronger standards, especially in measures associated with equity and diversity (Busta, 2020). The major effects are still unknown, but the issue has been further complicated by legislation such as Florida Senate Bill 7044 (2022), which requires the state's universities to seek new accreditors every five years and prohibits them from maintaining the same accreditor two cycles in a row in a blatant attempt to weaken the authority of regional accreditors and consolidate power over higher education within the state government.

## Finance

In 1980, Bowen summed up higher education finance by stating that universities will raise all the money they can and spend all the money they raise. That has not changed in good times or bad.

All of higher education is in a continual search for funds. Its buildings are aging, its staff needs raises, its technologies need upgrading. Yet the system always seems to acquire enough to continue functioning; as state allocations diminished as a percentage of overall revenues, public institutions increasingly turned to private sources. Indeed, privatization and the public's belief that higher education is predominantly a private good have proceeded in tandem. And colleges, universities, and postsecondary associations have abetted the trend by repeating the mantra, "Go to college and make more money." A long-term shift away from public funding and toward private sources of revenue (including students) occurred as states reduced allocations, tuitions increased, and as federal and state aid to students shifted from need- to merit-based grants, and from grants and scholarships to loans. Educational entrepreneurship and the privatization of academic research increased, as did fundraising and philanthropy. Budgeting and cost containment in colleges and universities became an exercise in determining relative value and balancing conflicting demands.

## State Disinvestment and Targeted Federal Support

Higher education's finances during and after the Great Recession of 2007–2009 were illustrative of general trends in revenue and, specifically, the diminished share coming to public institutions from states and localities. Early in 2008, state support showed the highest annual increase in more than 20 years, with 15 states reporting double-digit gains. Appropriations rose faster than inflation in most states as record numbers of high school graduates entered both two- and four-year colleges and as workers displaced in the economic downturn returned to higher education, community colleges in particular, to upskill or reskill. But those gains were ephemeral; by the end of the year most states faced declines in revenue, with $85 billion in deficits predicted for fiscal year 2010. In short, rapidly increasing enrollments ran headlong into reduced state incomes, as the housing and stock market slumps of 2008 led to drastically reduced sales- and income-tax receipts, capital gains taxes, and real estate transfer taxes. Between 2007–2008 and 2010–2011, the inflation-adjusted total amount of state allocations to public colleges and universities dropped by 12%; per-FTE funding dropped 22%. As the nation recovered, state allocations began to tick up again, but by 2019–2020 were only 93% of what they were in 2007–2008 (per-FTE allocations were only 86% of what they had been).

As Palmer and Romano (2018; Romano and Palmer, 2016) showed, this pattern was far from unique and indeed repeated many times over, with the end result being a decades-long trend toward public disinvestment in higher education, despite shorter-term ups and downs from one year to the next. Indeed, the share of public higher education revenue provided by the states—which was 61% in 1976—dropped to 46% in 1981 and to 36% by the start of the Contemporary Era. Since then, the percentage coming from the states halved again, hitting 18% in 2021 (see Table 6.6). Although these percentages are affected by other trends as well—in particular, an increase in federal funding, especially following the Great Recession and during the COVID-19 pandemic, as well as higher levels of investment and endowment income—the trend toward state disinvestment is clear.

At 34%, state funding continues to be the largest source of revenue for community colleges, but this share is a far cry from the 60% that came from the states in 1980 (Kisker, Cohen, and Brawer, 2023). Among flagship state universities, the percentage of revenue from state allocations varied from 3% at the University of Virginia and 4% at the University of Michigan to more than one-third of total funding at the Universities of Massachusetts at Amherst, Idaho, Alaska-Fairbanks, Connecticut, and Buffalo (Reger, 2023). In general, the more research grants and contracts a public university has, the lower the percentage of funding from the state. Indeed, many public sector institutions once viewed as state-supported are now more accurately described as state-located.

Table 6.6. Revenue of Public Institutions of Higher Education by Source of Funds, 1994–1995 and 2020–2021 (in Thousands of Current Dollars).

| | 1994–1995 | | 2020–2021 | |
| --- | --- | --- | --- | --- |
| Source | Revenue | % of Total | Revenue | % of Total |
| Tuition and fees | $21,908,104 | 18% | $81,877,170 | 16% |
| Federal government | $13,191,843 | 11% | $75,240,084 | 15% |
| State governments | $42,854,681 | 36% | $92,484,134 | 18% |
| Local governments | $4,756,884 | 4% | $15,790,403 | 3% |
| Endowment income | $693,313 | 1% | $60,390,483 | 12% |
| Gifts, grants, and contracts | $4,737,529 | 4% | $29,253,566 | 6% |
| Sales and services, auxiliary enterprises | $14,989,680 | 13% | $60,608,327 | 12% |
| Hospitals | $12,527,982 | 11% | $66,728,115 | 13% |
| Other | $3,652,477 | 3% | $20,639,718 | 4% |
| Total | $119,312,493 | 100% | $503,011,998 | 100% |

*Sources:* NCES *Digest*, 1997, 2023.

In addition to allocations from states and (for community colleges) localities, higher education revenue sources included tuition and fees; sales, services, and auxiliary enterprises; gifts, grants, and contracts; and federal contributions. Funding for public institutions was dominated by tuition and fees (16%) and support from federal, state, and local sources (together constituting 36% of revenue). Private sources of revenue (including tuition and fees, endowment earnings, and private gifts and grants) made up nearly three-quarters of all funds to private colleges and universities, and federal grants and contracts added another 8% (see Table 6.7).

Table 6.7. **Percentage of Revenue by Source, Public and Private Institutions, 2020–2021.**

| Source | Public Institutions | Private Institutions |
| --- | --- | --- |
| Tuition and fees | 16% | 19% |
| Federal government | 15% | 8% |
| State governments | 18% | 1% |
| Local governments | 3% | 0% |
| Endowment income | 12% | 46% |
| Gifts, grants, and contracts | 6% | 8% |
| Sales and services, auxiliary enterprises | 12% | 5% |
| Hospitals | 13% | 9% |
| Other | 4% | 4% |

Source: NCES *Digest*, 2023.

Except for certain types of institutions (MSIs, Gallaudet University for the deaf and hard of hearing, military service academies), federal support has never taken the form of general operating funds awarded to institutions. Instead, it has been allocated to certain programs (medical, advanced manufacturing), particular purposes (libraries, residence halls), and research in specified fields. However, federal outlays to higher education have increased substantially in recent years. Between 2010 and 2018, the Federal Trade Adjustment Assistance for Community College and Career Training (TAACCCT) grant program sent an unprecedented $2 billion to community colleges in the form of economic stimulus and workforce development grants. But this amount was dwarfed by the $76 billion in American Rescue Plan and Higher Education Emergency Relief Funding (HEERF) from the federal government to institutions of higher education to "prevent, prepare for, and respond to the coronavirus pandemic" (U.S. Department of Education, 2023, p. 2). As a result of this increase in federal support, student financial assistance, which had once accounted for nearly 40% of federal funds to colleges and universities, amounted to only 18% of all federal outlays in 2021.

As federal contributions and earmarks increased, the professional associations expanded efforts to influence legislation. Until the Contemporary Era, most of them lobbied only when their own constituents' interests were affected. But after the 1994 congressional elections brought a Republican majority threatening to cut student aid, limit affirmative action, and reduce funding for the Department of Education, they accelerated lobbying efforts. Proprietary institutions worked especially hard to consolidate power through intense lobbying and campaign donations to PACs benefiting members of the House and Senate education committees, but they were not alone in doing so. In 2010, public and nonprofit higher education collectively spent $96.4 million to hire Washington lobbyists. But this amount declined after Congress banned earmarks in 2011; the sector spent only $74.5 million to lobby Congress in 2019, with many universities choosing instead to hire firms to help them land major grants from the National Science Foundation, the National Institutes of Health, the National Endowment for the Humanities, and other federal agencies (Murakami, 2020).

In 2010, colleges and universities had to fight for every penny received from states or the federal government. Since then, competition for state dollars has become arguably more intense, but the feds have shown a willingness to invest heavily in higher education, at least in response to national or global emergencies or in ways that the government believes will lead to improved economic or workforce outcomes. What this means for higher education is unclear; if current patterns continue, the percentage of institutional operating funds from public sources will decline and a greater share of government support will be tied to specific programs or areas of interest. Revenues of public universities will look even more like those of their private counterparts than they do today, with the majority of unrestricted operating funds coming from private sources, including tuition. This will undoubtedly lead to increased costs for students and families unless colleges and universities are far more successful than they have been in shifting some portion of entrepreneurial or philanthropic revenue from specific line items to the general fund.

**Tuition and Student Aid**

Reflecting the trend toward private sources of funding for institutions of higher education, tuition in American colleges and universities increased throughout the Contemporary Era. Most of this rise occurred between 1994–1995 and 2010–2011, when tuition and required fees increased by 90% (in inflation-adjusted dollars) at public, four-year institutions, 47% at community colleges, and 36% at private, four-year institutions. Between 2011–2012 and 2021–2022, however, tuition simply kept pace with inflation at public, four-year institutions and rose less than 1% per year at community colleges and private institutions. In 2021–2022, tuition and required fees averaged $3,564 at community colleges, $9,596 at four-year public institutions, and $37,222 at private four-year institutions (up from an inflation-adjusted $2,236, $5,027, and $25,208, respectively, at the start of the era).

On average, tuition for out-of-state students at public, four-year institutions was nearly three times higher than for in-state residents. In what Klein (2022) called "The Great Student Swap," between 2002 and 2018, nearly every state flagship university expanded its proportion of out-of-state or international students to benefit from the considerably higher tuition payments; the total share of out-of-state students attending flagship universities increased by an average of 55% over that time, leading to an average 15% decline in in-state enrollments. According to the Urban Institute (Roy and Su, 2022), while in-state residents comprised 75% of first-year students at public flagship universities in 2000, in 2018 less than two-thirds (63%) were in-state residents.

Higher tuitions were accompanied by increases in student aid from the federal government, states, and institutions, although the average amount of aid awarded did not keep pace with tuition increases. Nonetheless, the average amount of grant and scholarship aid increased substantially during the Contemporary Era; maximum Pell Grants rose from $2,300 in 1994–1995 to $7,395 in 2023–2024 and a number of laws expanded eligibility for the Pell grant program to more students, including part-timers and those attending year-round. Although helpful to students and their families, Pell Grants, as well as state and institutional grants and scholarships, rarely covered the full cost of a college education, including room, board, transportation, and living expenses, let alone foregone earnings. In 2021–2022, 81% of full-time community college students received some sort of financial aid, as did 85 and 91%, respectively, of students at public and private four-year institutions. In addition to grants and scholarships, a great many learners also took out federal government-backed loans to finance their college education. In 2021–2022, 2.2 million students took out more than $84 billion in direct loans plus tens of billions more in private loans. By 2023, the average bachelor's degree recipient had borrowed more than $30,000 to finance their education.

Federal direct aid to students since the 1960s was designed to assist those who could not otherwise afford to attend college. But gradually, financial aid became at least as beneficial in relieving costs for those who would most likely attend anyway. Between 2009–2010 and 2020–2021, grant and scholarship aid to students from the lowest and second-lowest income quintiles attending public, four-year institutions rose by 12 and 17%, respectively, but these increases were dwarfed by the 58 and 84% increases in grants and scholarships to students from the highest and next-highest quintiles. Increases in grant and scholarship aid to students at private institutions were similarly correlated with income levels. In addition, the National Association of State Student Grant and Aid Programs (2022) showed that need-based grants constituted about 62% of state-funded student financial aid in 2020–2021, whereas it had comprised 84% of the total in the mid-1990s. The shift from need- to merit-based grants during the Contemporary Era, combined with lower ratios of grants to loans in student aid packages, has largely benefited students from middle- and upper-income families, despite the fact that financial aid may not be the determining factor in whether or not they attend college, whereas "federal grants targeted to students from lower-income families do influence college enrollment in this group." Thus, McPherson and Shapiro (2002) concluded, "the recent redistribution of federal dollars appears to be going in the wrong direction" (p. 81).

Promise Programs, too, have aided students from middle- and upper-income tiers as much or more than those from lower-income backgrounds. These programs, which now exist in 32 states, provide free tuition for the first two years of college with some income, merit, geographic, or programmatic limitations (Campaign for Free College Tuition, 2023). In addition to state-level Promise Programs, local Promise Programs now exist in every state but Alaska, Idaho, and Mississippi (College Promise, 2021). Nearly all provide last-dollar support—in other words, they cover the difference between tuition and fees and any need-based financial aid awarded to students—for high school graduates who enroll full time in a public college or university and make satisfactory progress toward a degree. As a result, higher-income students receive larger grants than their lower-income peers, whose tuition and fees are primarily covered by federal and state aid. While Promise Programs undoubtedly make the first two years of college more affordable for many students, first-dollar programs—such as that passed in New Mexico in 2022—may be more beneficial for those from low-income backgrounds, as they enable students to apply Pell and other grants toward the additional costs associated with college, such as textbooks, transportation, housing, and childcare. In addition, Palmer and Romano (2018) noted the inefficiency of last-dollar programs, arguing that a far more efficient use of resources would be to increase financial support for those who need it most and simplify and provide guidance for filling out the Free Application for Federal Student Aid (FAFSA), thereby making it much easier for low-income families to qualify for and receive support.

Unlike federal and state aid, which is intended to produce a more highly educated populace, institutional aid is largely an enrollment management tool. Offsetting tuition with institutional aid enables continual increases in published price, effectively utilizing the tuition dollars of full-pay students to subsidize those for lower-income classmates (much as undergraduate tuitions subsidize the education of those enrolled in graduate programs). Although higher sticker prices may affect enrollment at less-exclusive institutions, at the most selective colleges they don't seem to scare away qualified students from wealthier families; Pisacreta and colleagues (2021) found that more than half of students at selective public and private institutions came from families in the top income quintile, while fewer than 15% came from families with incomes in the bottom 40%.

What is the ideal ratio of tuition and fees to total educational cost? Beginning in the 1970s, economists repeatedly argued that students should pay one-third of direct costs, and government and philanthropy should be responsible for two-thirds, challenging the pattern of low tuition then prevalent in some states. (It took 30 years for that recommendation to be realized.) Low tuition is attractive to middle- and low-income students who might be discouraged by high sticker prices, but it is sustainable only when participation rates or expenditures are also low. As enrollments and costs rise, the high-tuition, high student-aid model advocated by many economists becomes logical. However, its main drawback is that in practice, aid is never provided in measures equivalent to tuition increases. Furthermore, because some demographic groups are less comfortable than others with the idea of financing their children's education, a high-tuition, high-aid model ensures that access to selective colleges and universities is less than equitable.

From the public's perspective, colleges—acting like business corporations—increase tuition frequently because of "increased costs or increased profit taking of some sort" (Whitney, 2006, p. 34). They don't realize that except for the proprietary sector, higher education has always depended on donations and public subsidies to balance its budgets, and tuition increases in public institutions are now usually associated with constant-dollar reductions in public support. As state allocations continue to decrease as a proportion of revenues to public institutions, colleges and universities will be forced to make up the difference by shifting costs to private sources (including students) and through more entrepreneurial approaches to revenue generation.

## Privatization and Entrepreneurship

Until the housing and financial sector bubbles bust in 2008, the United States evidenced its faith in the private sector by standing aside as unregulated markets rose to unsustainable levels; the education sector was not excluded from this trend. Privatization of higher education refers to the growing role of market ideology in academic life. In essence, public colleges and universities are encouraged to focus more on efficiency and outcomes, and less on process, ideas, and community value. As such, many institutions of higher learning began to function as economic contributors, with students as consumers, and academic research as a product. This trend was not limited to U.S. institutions—indeed, a 1994 World Bank report encouraged universities across the globe to shift from state funding to student fees, consultancies, and donations—but it led to profound changes in the way American colleges and universities are funded and operated.

The privatization of U.S. higher education is a product of late-twentieth century market enthusiasm, an unwavering faith in a free market economy with little or no governmental oversight or regulation of capital, industrial, and knowledge markets. Over the past 30 years, the belief that private institutions can perform better and more efficiently than public ones was pervasive among legislators and taxpayers, and led to regressive distributions of tax cuts, deregulation of the energy and financial markets, and proposals to privatize traditional governmental entitlements such as Social Security. This encouraged legislators to reduce appropriations for higher education even while calling for greater access and accountability.

To survive with reduced appropriations and higher expectations, public colleges and universities sought increasing amounts of funding from private sources. Much of this capital outsourcing occurred gradually, but the Contemporary Era witnessed several more dramatic moves toward the market, particularly in response to fiscal crises and natural disasters. For example, after Hurricane Katrina devastated New Orleans in 2005, Tulane University eliminated 14 doctoral programs and combined others, allowing "those that remain—mostly in the sciences, where outside research funds are more plentiful—to thrive" (Selingo, 2006). Similarly, the precipitous drop in per-student allocations following the Great Recession spurred greater entrepreneurial and revenue-generating behavior across all types of institutions, including community colleges, which responded by expanding public-private workforce training partnerships, building corporate colleges, creating online programs with multiple start dates throughout the year, privatizing auxiliary services, and so forth (Kisker, 2021). Institutional responses to events such as these reinforce Naomi Klein's (2007) notion of disaster capitalism, the idea that economic crises and other disasters provide opportunities to change the relative roles of government and private enterprise in funding public institutions.

Whether gradual or dramatic, downturns in state appropriations led to sharp tuition hikes and intensified fundraising across all sectors of higher education. Colleges and universities publicized their emphasis on market-relevant curricula, such as business and computer science, that could attract corporate donations and career-focused students. Many institutions also began adapting business practices to reduce costs, including cash-flow evaluation of academic units and outsourcing auxiliary activities such as student dining. Some universities encouraged corporations to endow faculty chairs, and many others invited corporate sponsorships and financing of sports arenas and other campus facilities. Although most college leaders saw such entrepreneurial actions as increasingly necessary in the face of state disinvestment, many legislators took them as further proof that the institutions had all the resources they needed; as Breneman (2005) wrote, "The older argument for subsidies—namely the public or social benefits of an educated populace—commands less attention in a world driven by market values" (p. 4).

Reduced state appropriations also led to several experiments in higher education funding, although not all have worked as planned. Some, like Virginia's charter universities, accepted lower levels of state support in exchange for increased autonomy from state regulations, including the ability to set their own tuition, fees, and accounting mechanisms. However, only 6 of Virginia's 16 universities were allowed to assume full responsibility for managing their financial operations, and two different governors quashed institutional attempts to set their own prices, either by requesting that tuition remain flat or by holding money back in retaliation for tuition increases (DeFusco, 2022). In perhaps the most striking move toward a free market system, in 2005, Colorado dramatically revamped its higher education funding policy, instituting per-credit-hour stipends that follow students to the colleges in which they enroll, replacing Colorado's former system of allocating money directly to institutions based on FTE enrollments. Students can use their stipend at any public college or university in the state, and if they also qualify for Pell Grants, can use up to 50% of the total per-credit amount at in-state private colleges. The intent of this policy was to pressure colleges and universities to pay more attention to consumer preferences in price and course offerings. In return, Colorado granted public institutions enterprise status, giving them greater flexibility to set their own tuitions and requiring them to engage in performance-based, fee-for-service contracts to pay for mission-related functions that are not covered by stipend funding.

**Privatizing Research**

The effects of privatization are perhaps most dramatic at elite universities, where research is often funded by industry, and where complex patenting and licensing operations are in place to market faculty members' inventions (extracting royalties for the university, of course). Although research universities have long cooperated with industry to bring breakthroughs in science and technology to the market, many scholars worry that corporations now have a stranglehold on university research, especially in medicine, pharmacology, and biotechnology. As Washburn (2005) wrote, "The problem is not university-industry relationships per se; it is the elimination of any clear boundary lines separating academe from commerce" (p. x).

The roots of what Slaughter and Leslie (1997) termed *academic capitalism* reach back to the mid-1970s, when President Nixon called on the National Science Foundation (NSF) to stimulate nonfederal investment in university research and development, and to improve the application of results. Shortly afterward, the NSF required investigators to obtain joint university-industry funding so that more research would be industry-relevant. Corporate involvement in academic inquiry was further aided by the 1980 Business Patent Procedures (aka Bayh-Dole) Act, which permitted universities to patent and license federally sponsored research. As a result of the Bayh-Dole Act and the 1986 Federal Technology Transfer Act, which encouraged government labs to forge cooperative agreements with industry, universities instituted policies that emphasized the value of higher education to national economic activity (Slaughter, 1998). However, Bayh-Dole only accelerated what had been a force for more than a century since the Morrill Act fostered land-grant colleges with a mission of research benefiting agriculture. The idea that higher education should assist in economic development was ingrained in its culture.

The commercialization of inventions and patents yielded sizeable sums to the universities that spent the most on research and whose research labs contributed marketable products. As Nag, Gupta, and Turo (2020) reported, between 2005 and 2020, the United States spent more than $1 trillion on federally sponsored university research. In 2018, the government invested $71 billion in university research. That same year, universities developed 828 new products, 1,080 new start-ups, 26,217 new inventions, and 17,087 new patent applications. They also generated roughly $2.94 billion in academic technology transfer (licensing revenue generated by taking academic inventions to market), which corresponded to roughly $147 billion in sales of products derived from academic technology. As Nag, Gupta, and Turo (2020) wrote, "not bad in terms of ROI from $71 billion"!

However, because nearly all licensing revenues are generated by a small subset of licenses, most university technology transfer offices do not generate enough income to cover their operating expenses (Valdivia, 2013). Except for the exceedingly rare cases in which research yields a profitable product, the universities lose money on the research grants they receive. The costs of laboratory and office space, contract management, and patent-related legal expenses usually sum to more than what a grant or contract will cover for indirect costs (for example, the feds do not allow research dollars to be spent on filing patents to protect inventions). Furthermore, congressional appropriations for the National Foundation on the Arts and Humanities are minuscule in comparison with those for the National Science Foundation and the National Institutes of Health. Research in the social sciences and humanities receives little federal funding, and any new theatres or art galleries on college campuses are almost certainly funded at least in part by private donors or philanthropic foundations.

Over the past three decades, drug and medical device makers surpassed the federal government as the primary source of research funding. And private agents, including foundations, business corporations, and venture capitalists, contribute more. Greater corporate sponsorship of and involvement in academic research has had notable effects. It is increasingly common for universities and some of their faculty to own equity in a company sponsoring a drug trial, which means that both have a direct financial interest in the outcome. At a minimum, these conflicts of interest preclude any claims of disinterested inquiry, and some scholars have raised questions about the ethical implications of engaging in research where one outcome may bring millions of dollars to the faculty member and university, while another might result in the corporate sponsor essentially picking up his ball (i.e., funding) and going home. This conflict of interest is exacerbated by the fact that hundreds of universities—and even some community colleges, such as GateWay in Arizona—opened business incubators or venture capital funds to promote and profit from commercially promising academic research. The privatization of academic inquiry also results in less free-flowing information among scholars and the public; the question of who owns academic research has grown increasingly contentious as many scientists sign contracts requiring them to keep their research methods and results secret for a period of time (presumably until the industry sponsor approves the outcomes), and as others file restrictive patents or engage in exclusive licensing of their discoveries.

Not surprisingly, commentators have been vocal in their support and criticism of government- and industry-supported research. Proponents argue that without corporate involvement, faculty would have a much harder time bringing their inventions to commercial use, and point to significant advances in information technology, artificial intelligence, machine learning, biotechnology, and other fields that resulted from cooperation with industry. Furthermore, they cite the billions of dollars spent on academic research each year, as well as the millions that universities collect annually in licensing and royalties, and ask if universities would be able to continue supporting leading-edge research without help from industry or the government.

Critics respond by arguing that exclusive licensing of federally funded academic research stifles competition and facilitates monopolistic pricing, essentially forcing taxpayers to pay twice—once through tax dollars supporting the research, and again through higher prices once the invention reaches the market (Washburn, 2005). Furthermore, few institutions codify or sustain consistent research themes, choosing instead to appoint staff to monitor the funding agencies and cast their proposals according to funds available. Greenberg (2007) considered this a variant on Parkinson's Law: "Research expands to absorb the money available for its conduct" (p. 29).

The debate about corporate involvement in academic research mirrors a larger dispute concerning the overall effects of privatization and increased entrepreneurship on college and university campuses. An extreme view is that privatization tempts colleges and universities to serve corporations and donors ahead of the public, restricts access for low-income students and families who are turned off by higher tuition prices, forces colleges to scale back course offerings in non-market-affiliated fields, and encourages public institutions to abandon their core public purposes, thereby contributing to legislators' and the public's belief that higher education is primarily a private good, with most of its benefits accruing to individuals. For many, this is a scary proposition; the 2001 Enron scandal, 2008 crash of Wall Street financial institutions, and more recent bank bailouts provided ample evidence that unfettered markets may not work.

One thing is clear: whether one applauds the market-driven reforms and opportunities resulting from diminished state funding or decries the ways that market ideology has limited the discovery and sharing of knowledge and ideas, the trend toward privatization and entrepreneurship shows no signs of reversing. This is no doubt a relief to college administrators seeking to balance budgets in the face of limited general fund allocations, as well as an ominous sign for faculty and others who decry heightened levels of academic capitalism. Yet as Kisker (2021) wrote, educational "entrepreneurship—in and of itself—is neither good nor bad. What matters is that entrepreneurial opportunities are pursued in a way that prioritizes the needs of college stakeholders . . . and that they are evaluated by their ability to further the college's mission" (p. 33).

**Fundraising and Philanthropy**

Fundraising increased in tandem with the privatization of academic research and heightened entrepreneurial behavior among all institutional types. Although philanthropic donations would never generate sufficient revenue to replace diminishing state funds, college leaders had no choice but to continue seeking more from that source. At the start of the Contemporary Era, private gifts, grants, and contracts accounted for 4% of all revenue in public institutions and 9% in private colleges and universities. By 2020–2021, 6% of revenues to public institutions and 8% of those to private institutions came from these sources (see Table 6.7). The vast majority of philanthropic funds were restricted to certain uses, typically applied research, scholarships, or buildings. Schools of business and engineering were especially successful in attracting support because they tended to have alumni and friends in the corporate sector. Museums, endowed chairs, and galleries also received funds from private donors. These types of facilities by no means enhanced institutional productivity, but they added prestige to the campuses fortunate enough to receive them, along with an endowment sufficient to pay for their continuing maintenance. An overall breakout showed that in 2017–2018, the last year for which data are available, private support was received in the following proportions: 26% from alumni, 18% from other individuals, 14% from corporations, 30% from foundations, and 11% from other sources. The total amounted to $47 billion, more than double the amount received in 1994–1995, after adjusting for inflation.

The increased emphasis that public universities gave to private fundraising put them in direct competition with their counterparts in the private sector. In 2020–2021, the public institutions collected $29 billion in private gifts and grants, while the private institutions received $34 billion. The largest gifts went to private institutions and public doctoral universities: in 2022, Stanford University received $1.1 billion to establish the Doerr School of Sustainability, the University of Oregon landed $425 million to create the Ballmer Institute for Children's Behavioral Health, Harvard University received $350 million in continued support for the Wyss Institute for Biologically Inspired Engineering, the University of Pennsylvania brought in $125 million to recruit and educate nurse practitioners to work in underserved communities, and Loyola University in Chicago received $100 million to kickstart an initiative to support students from historically underserved races and ethnicities (Philanthropy News Digest, 2023).

In public and private institutions alike, the drive to increase funding from the private sector led to sizable investments in staff. It was not unusual for a major university to have 300 people working in the development office. The institution's president had to be involved, along with numerous people skilled in fundraising. The development officers proceeded with deliberate plans, targeting wealthy donors and establishing personal relationships with them where possible; they emphasized the prestige of their institution, the scope of its programs, and the way it served the public. They were careful to tailor their requests to purposes favored by particular donors. Fundraising in both the public and private sector became so important that the issue dominated presidential selection; presidents who could relate well to private donors and corporate or foundation officials or who had a demonstrated track record of raising philanthropic funds were highly sought-after.

Increased fundraising and philanthropic activity helped bolster college endowments, which reached record levels during the Contemporary Era. By the end of the 2020 fiscal year, college and university endowments held more than $691 billion in assets; the 120 institutions with the largest—headlined by Harvard ($41.9 billion), Yale ($31.2), the University of Texas System ($29.8), Stanford ($27.7), Princeton ($25.6), and the Massachusetts Institute of Technology ($17.4)—accounted for 75% of the total. Among liberal arts colleges, Williams topped the list, with $2.7 billion, followed by Amherst ($2.6), Wellesley ($2.3), and Pomona ($2.3). Even community colleges have built endowments by soliciting funds from alumni, local employers, and other donors. At $486 million, Miami Dade College's endowment is the largest by far; the next five range from $51.9 million at Northampton Community College (Pennsylvania) to $74.3 million at Valencia College (Florida). According to figures compiled by the Center for Community College Advancement (Finkel, 2019), community college endowments grew an average of 76% (after adjusting for inflation) between 1998 and 2018, with average holdings growing from $5.3 million to more than $14.3 million. Across all institutional types, endowment spending averaged 4.2% in 2022, down from 4.8% the year prior.

## Determining Relative Value and Balancing Conflicting Demands

Much of the recent writing about higher education has been concerned with problems of declining resources. And most of the responses recommend various forms of redesign or restructuring so that the institutions will function more efficiently. Yet a basic problem remains, which is that higher education has had no way of determining relative value. The premises that all knowledge is of equal worth, and that only professionals in specialized areas can determine the value of their work, have led to the conclusion that all comparisons among institutional missions or academic departments are spurious. Accordingly, programs may be duplicative, outmoded, or excessively expensive, but costs vary dramatically across academic disciplines and between course levels, and there are no easy ways to reallocate funds within institutions or to shift resources from one institution to another.

Formula budgeting, with specific percentages allocated for building operations, faculty workloads, administrative support, and student aid—a long-time favorite of institutional managers—typically is based on revenue expectations, which in turn are often based on FTE students. But when the number of students rises or falls rapidly, and institutional support changes along with them, managers must make decisions about where to spend the increases or make the cuts. Institutional missions—such as research, service, and instruction—are interdependent and difficult to disaggregate, and the formulas often neglect differences in efficiency and quality. Lingenfelter (2007) summed up the problem: "The more formulas attempt to account for complex goals and conditions, the more they become unwieldy, incomprehensible, and mistrusted" (p. 660).

As such, some institutions have implemented responsibility-centered management, giving a lump sum plus authority for budget allocation to individual units. This acknowledges that no central authority can compare relative worth, that each individual department can adjudicate allocations more efficiently. And institutions have reduced expenses by implementing voluntary early retirement programs in which staff members determine whether and when to leave based on their own personal considerations. Yet while institutions may tinker at the margins, because central administrators have no way of knowing who the best and worst staff members are—and if it had such information, no way of mandating that the worst leave—it is helpless in guiding the process.

Other institutions have implemented practices that seek to decouple enrollment considerations (and the attendant per-FTE funding) from internal budgeting processes to improve strategic decision-making. For example, Valencia College (Florida) utilizes what it calls purpose-based budgeting, which bases internal allocations on accurate projections of future costs rather than former budgets, enabling the college to direct supplemental funding toward strategic priorities (Kisker, 2021). Similarly, Romano and Palmer (2016) advocated for greater use of activity-based costing, arguing that this method of pricing out "the functions or activities that are part of a college's mission" can help managers "identify cost drivers and non-value adding activities, which in turn assists in the reallocation of resources to activities that provide the greatest value" (p. 148). Because activity-based costing considers the price of various institutional functions, which may cut across academic programs or units, it can help colleges separate enrollment considerations from strategic decision-making (Kisker, 2021). Yet because it requires a wholesale revision of longstanding budgeting practices, as well as extreme transparency and high levels of communication across campus, activity-based costing is not easy to implement, and may be especially high stakes in states where funding is attached to institutional performance or achievement of specified outcomes.

A second problem is that efficiency is not rewarded in the academic marketplace; the public values least the most efficient institutions. Proprietary schools that have no campuses, libraries, or full-time faculty are quite efficient at awarding college credits and degrees at a cost so low that they return profits to their corporate owners. (Their effects on students' employment prospects and debt burdens cannot be so envied.) The colleges and universities with beautiful grounds and other amenities, full-time faculty teaching small classes, and sophisticated libraries and laboratories are least efficient in terms of cost-per-degree. Yet they top all the lists of "The Best Colleges in America," and students clamor to enroll. Despite calls for and claims of increased productivity, so long as students seek colleges with numerous campus amenities and that offer close interaction with professors and other students, institutions will be somewhat limited in their efforts to increase efficiency.

Extrinsic demands create other complications. Funding comes from many sources, and some funding agencies specify how their monies shall be allocated. Accrediting agencies influence expenditures on laboratories, libraries, and educational technology. State legislatures impose programs in fields that can help fulfill workforce demands. The federal government supports some activities and withdraws from them when new priorities emerge. Indeed, the feds have never had a comprehensive or consistent policy toward higher education. Rather, beginning with the Northwest Ordinance of 1787 that provided each new state with two townships of land to be used for support of a college, its actions have been piecemeal: operational support for service academies, Gallaudet, and MSIs; the Morrill Act in the nineteenth century; the GI Bill in the twentieth; and COVID-19 relief and support for community college workforce programs in the twenty-first.

Because comparative value is impossible to assess, and efficiency rewarded only in theory, when budget reductions become necessary, institutions most often implement across-the-board cuts, sharing the pain uniformly by taking equivalent funds proportionately from each unit. Smaller cuts in a broad range of operations are considerably more feasible than larger, narrowly tailored reductions, and it is politically far safer to replace a couple of high-cost faculty with several part-timers than it is to collapse an entire department. When that proves insufficient, an institution may close or combine schools or departments that have the least political force, that are too weak to protest effectively, that have the least amount of support within or outside the institution.

In many ways, higher education in the twenty-first century is immersed in the same waters that engulfed health care in the last decades of the twentieth. In the 1970s, more expensive tests, hospitals, and physicians led to an alarming percentage of the gross domestic product going to medicine. In the 1980s, managed care grew rapidly, and costs were contained; for most patients, hospital stays and visits with physicians became shorter. Attempts to slow the increased costs of college and to accommodate all who seek higher learning may similarly lead to most students having less time with professors, more involvement with technology, and more opportunities for asynchronous learning. In the meantime, all institutions, for-profit and nonprofit alike, will continue searching for ways to cut costs, maximize revenues, and demonstrate market relevance; in the process, the lines demarcating the sectors will become even more hazy than they are now.

Still open are questions of value to the broader community. How many professional practitioners does society need in each area? What is the worth of an archive of the culture, a housing for classicists? No funding formula can even begin to address these issues, yet they are fundamental to the conduct of higher education. The recurrent budget crises have forced a flurry of activity, but major changes in the direction of more purposeful or efficient functioning have yet to appear (online education, certainly, has not resulted in the cost savings many of its early proponents predicted). By its nature higher education is inefficient if measurements focus on inputs and outputs. Its various units stagger along, as messy as democracy, and perhaps as valuable.

## Outcomes

The types of outcomes noted in the Consolidation Era—greater access to the postsecondary system, more degrees, enhanced research capabilities, and personal and societal benefits—continued as prominent measures, although metrics related to equity, as well as receipt of short-term certificates and other nondegree credentials, took on added importance. Research in the sciences grew ever stronger as the drive for prestige and institutional support remained paramount and as relationships between corporations and university-based researchers became increasingly intertwined. Although external critiques had never been particularly influential in guiding institutional behavior, they took on added importance in the Contemporary Era as colleges and universities were attacked for their perceived role in the nation's cultural and political conflicts and as policymakers in some states chipped away at long-standing areas of institutional autonomy, including tenure, academic freedom, and programs and practices related to diversity, equity, and inclusion.

**Tracking Outcomes**

In the Contemporary Era, most states maintained databases containing information on students enrolled in public colleges and universities, and some also included data from in-state private institutions, enabling longitudinal tracking of students within states, even as students transferred from one school to another. Data on gender, race or ethnicity, enrollment, major field of study, and degrees attained were compiled and used to complete the mandatory federal Integrated Postsecondary Education System (IPEDS) reports. Most institutions also linked student progress with state employment records to calculate wages earned or field of employment and some, on occasion, matched student records with other databases such as public assistance and incarceration to gain a sense of higher education's contributions to the public good.

However, because institutions of higher education are only asked to report the number of students who are enrolled for credit to IPEDS, we do not yet have an accurate national picture of noncredit student demographics, multiterm enrollment patterns, or outcomes, despite the fact that nearly 40% of community college enrollments are in noncredit courses. In recent years IPEDS held two Technical Review Panels to discuss how its surveys might be improved to better capture noncredit enrollment and activity but to date opted not to gather such data, focusing instead on improving data quality and reducing the reporting burden for institutions. Nonetheless, a group of scholars working with the National Center for Science and Education Statistics (D'Amico et al., 2022) continues to push the issue; they and others have illustrated the consequences of failing to collect noncredit data, including the artificial inflation of per-student expenditures, especially in community colleges (e.g., Romano and D'Amico, 2021).

Nonetheless, the longitudinal tracking of students enrolled for credit, and the ability to measure outcomes across state lines, has grown dramatically with the establishment of the National Student Clearinghouse (NSC), which provides a "near-census" method of tracking student enrollment and transcript data (the database includes over 97% of all students in U.S. public and private colleges and universities). While the NSC has been used by individual institutions and employers to verify degrees or analyze students' transfer destinations for some time, in 2010 it established a research center, which has since published numerous reports on student mobility, transfer, and completion, as well as how the COVID-19 pandemic affected postsecondary enrollment and persistence. The NSC's ability to follow students across state lines and through public, private, and for-profit institutions has enabled a much more robust way to determine transfer and completion rates, and data can be disaggregated by race or ethnicity, gender, and other demographic categories. Not surprisingly, these rates are considerably higher than those captured by the U.S. Department of Education, and thus the NSC has been instrumental to institutions' ability to respond to accountability mandates with data that tell a more complete story of student success and mobility.

**The Drive for Degrees**

Although research showing that, on average, people with more years of schooling earned more money continued enjoying wide circulation, the causal connections between income and diplomas remained obscure. People with degrees have gained cognitive skills and behavioral patterns that make them more productive. But they also have access to higher-paying jobs that are closed to nondegree holders. Thus, credentials may be confounded with competence.

Put another way, in workforce development, the credential's main use is in getting a job where competence is heightened through socialization and experience. This effect is most prominent in service occupations such as teaching.

Goldin and Katz (2008) contended that supply and demand explain the long-run evolution of the premium paid to college graduates. When the relative demand for graduates is greater than the supply, as it was early in the twentieth century, the wage difference is high. From 1915 to 1940, as the rate of college going increased threefold, the premium paid to college graduates narrowed. Subsequently, as the growth of service (teaching, health professions) and technology-based industries accelerated from the 1980s onward, the difference in wages paid to bachelor's degree holders over those with high school diplomas increased; in 2021, it was 78% for men and 70% for women (up from 54% for men and 57% for women in 1994). As the United States reaches an enrollment cliff—the number of high school graduates is expected to peak in 2024 and then begin to decline—and as automation and artificial intelligence take over jobs that require little critical thinking or analysis, this premium may continue to climb.

The drive for degrees will continue, as accountability requirements and public sentiment demand ever higher completion rates and the elimination of equity gaps. Colleges and universities, too, will continue to push for more degree recipients, both to demonstrate their contributions to society and to ensure enrollments in various courses and programs. The doctoral degree provides a case in point. Questions of whether the doctorate is important for teaching undergraduates have been raised periodically and never answered definitively. But several characteristics of the system ensure that the number of degrees awarded rises steadily. First, faculty positions in research universities and in broadly accessible institutions aspiring to higher status are reserved for doctoral degree holders. Second, attaining the doctorate moves the recipient higher on the salary schedule in community colleges, thus bringing an immediate reward. And third, hardly any graduate school faculty consider the market for their alumni when they decide on the number of students to admit. Their concern is to maintain their own enrollments, lest their departmental budget be cut or, in times of fiscal exigency, their entire division eliminated.

However, the traditional, linear path to a college degree may be challenged as the skilled technical workforce grows, and as pathways to the middle class expand to include short-term, industry-relevant credentials and stackable certificates. The bachelor's degree will remain important for its prestige factor and because it provides a ticket to the next level of education for those seeking advanced degrees, but more and more students—especially adult learners—will attend colleges in fits and starts, fitting certificates, degrees, and other credentials together in unique ways and expecting their credits to articulate automatically among institutions of higher education. Colleges and universities will be challenged, not only to respond to students' changing needs, but to anticipate them and design support structures that recognize the diversity of student goals and address the experiences of returning learners, as well as those with prior experience in the military or the workforce. IPEDS and other large-scale data collection efforts will also need to evolve to better account for nondegree credentials as well as new understandings of what it means to attend and succeed in college.

**Assessing Learning**

For decades, higher education researchers have attempted to document the learning manifest by students in particular programs or institutions. An industry producing standardized assessment tools grew to accommodate these efforts, with the Educational Testing Service and the American College Testing Program the most prominent publishers. A listing of the tests and surveys available to measure student progress would fill several pages. The Academic Profile Test, Collegiate Assessment of Academic Proficiency, and

Collegiate Learning Assessment all have been used as measures of general education or critical thinking, although only the last (rebranded CLA+) continues to be used widely. Most rely on scores made by samples of first-year students and upperclassmen or graduating seniors to estimate learning gains. All have limitations, whether in the content of the instrument (Can any two- or three-hour exam measure all that might be learned in college?) or in the pattern of administration: whether cross-sectional or longitudinal, how does one account for the students who dropped out before taking the post-test? Or those who attended other institutions for significant portions of their undergraduate years? As well, can one really judge the "value add" of a college education through a test in which students have no stake in the outcome? (Such questions have been raised repeatedly, especially since the publication of *Academically Adrift* in 2011.)

These problems in assessing student learning are magnified when researchers attempt to control for students' entering abilities, gender, race or ethnicity, and so on, and when scholars try to attribute the observed differences to particular experiences such as cocurricular activities or the number of hours the students spend with professors or tutors. Never mind the biggest caveat of all, the fact that within-institution gains in student learning have been shown to be consistently greater than average between-institution gains. For these reasons, evidence of student learning is rarely requested by accreditors and state agencies, who find it far easier to ask for outcomes such as degrees awarded, job attainment rates, graduate school entry, licensure exam pass rates, and similar measures of student progress and success.

Nonetheless, arguing that focusing solely on input and output measures obscures the primary purpose of the enterprise—student learning and the development of skills and competencies necessarily to thrive in life and in the workplace—several organizations have developed tools to more broadly recognize what one should gain in college. For example, the Lumina Foundation's Degree

Qualifications Profile initiative established learning outcomes and competencies along five dimensions: intellectual skills, broad knowledge, specialized knowledge, applied learning, and civic learning, specifying levels of performance on each dimension for associate, bachelor's, and master's degrees. And the Education Design lab has launched nine employer-validated 21st Century Skills Micro-credentials and digital badges, which institutions may award to students upon demonstration of proficiency in self-directed learning, empathy, oral communication, critical thinking, resilience, intercultural fluency, collaboration, initiative, and creative problem-solving. Assessment of student learning has long been losing ground as accreditors, state agencies, and others push for data on completion, but in an ironic twist, it may be bolstered by employer demands for a workforce trained in the integrative skills—critical thinking, intercultural competency, collaboration, connecting disparate concepts and experiences—that colleges have promoted for nearly 400 years.

**Personal Benefits**

The benefits that individuals derive from going to college have been traced for many decades, with psychological and cognitive development studies being the most prominent areas of inquiry. Feldman and Newcomb (1969) summarized many of the studies conducted during the Mass Higher Education Era, and in 1977 Bowen attempted to put a dollar value on the changes experienced by individuals in the college years (many others have since followed suit; articles comparing the ROI of various collegiate majors can be found widely on the Internet). In 1991 and again in 2005 Pascarella and Terenzini summarized 2,500 studies conducted since Feldman and Newcomb's work; the third edition of *How College Affects Students* (Mayhew et al., 2016) updated that literature. Astin (1993) studied various types of college effects, concentrating especially on full-time students just out of high school. Pace (1979) reviewed comprehensive achievement tests administered to broad samples of undergraduates over a 50-year span. Accordingly, a rich literature is available that traces the effects of all types of colleges. In summarizing findings from thousands of studies conducted over several decades, the analysts found certain consistencies:

Learning and cognitive changes:

- College has a substantial cognitive impact, with students gaining most in verbal ability.

- Students gain substantive knowledge in specific academic areas; the more they study a subject, the more they know about it.

- Smaller gains are shown in the areas of rationality and critical thinking, although they are enhanced after even one year of college.

- Substantial increases in intellectual tolerance are made, as are modest increases in intellectual integrity, creativity, wisdom, aesthetic sensibility, and understanding of truth.

Psychosocial changes:

- Religious orientation decreases (except for students in religious institutions), but less than among young people not enrolled in college.

- Psychological well-being shows moderate increases in the long term, especially in the areas of confidence and self-sufficiency, but in the short term, college attendance may contribute to higher levels of stress, anxiety, and depression. These effects may be heightened among women, students from historically underserved races and ethnicities, and LGBTQ+ learners.

- College-educated parents devote more time to their children and enhance tendencies toward further education among them, thus effecting an intergenerational outcome. They are also considerably more likely to provide their teenage children with information about community, national, and international events and to attend concerts, plays, and religious services with them.

- College-educated adults are healthier and take greater advantage of health services.

- College graduates are more confident, independent, self-directed, and likely to believe they can control what happens to them.

Changes in attitudes and values:

- College-educated people are more likely to vote and engage in other forms of civic or political participation.

- College-going contributes to increased social activism and greater endorsement of civil liberties such as a woman's right to an abortion, legalized marijuana, and women's liberation, but is negatively associated with a belief that the government should have more oversight of social problems.

- Those who have attended college—and especially those who experienced cross-racial interactions, engaged in racial or cultural workshops, or enrolled in an ethnic studies course—exhibit more compassion toward people of other cultures and viewpoints and are more likely to recognize and act on injustice.

- College-educated people show greater acceptance of diverse sexualities and gender identities and are less homophobic than those who do not attend college.
- Attitudes and values formed in college are likely to persist for many years into adulthood, and intellectual growth continues far beyond college graduation.

Economic and career changes:

- College graduates are less likely to be unemployed and more likely to work longer hours but are not necessarily more satisfied with their jobs.
- College helps individuals move between social classes. Education or the level of schooling attained is a major determinant of a person's socioeconomic status.
- College graduates earn more, on average, than those with lower levels of educational attainment (see Table 6.8 and Figure 6.3).

Table 6.8. Ratio of Median Annual Earnings of Full-Time, Year-Round Workers 25 and Older, 2021.

| Highest Educational Level | Women | Men |
|---|---|---|
| Grades 9–11 | 0.83 | 0.83 |
| High school diploma | 1.00 | 1.00 |
| Some college | 1.14 | 1.15 |
| Associate degree | 1.26 | 1.30 |
| Bachelor's degree | 1.70 | 1.78 |
| Master's degree | 2.10 | 2.19 |
| Doctoral degree | 2.77 | 3.07 |
| Professional degree | 2.82 | 3.15 |

*Source:* NCES *Digest*, 2023.

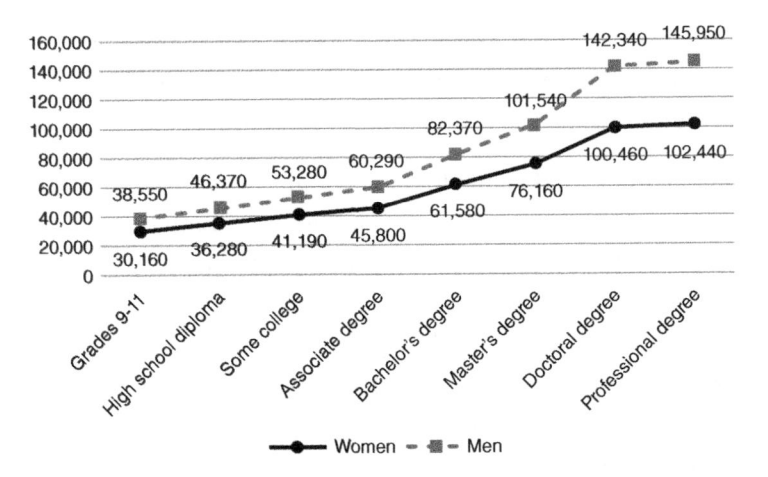

**Figure 6.3. Median Annual Earnings of Full-Time, Year-Round Workers 25 and Older, 2021.**

As Table 6.8 shows, the earnings premiums associated with subsequent levels of education are substantial. Compared with the average earnings of a high school graduate, those who did not complete secondary school earned, on average, 83% as much per year. Attending at least some college ensured an earnings premium of 14 to 15%; associate degree recipients earned 26 to 30% more. On average, bachelor's degree recipients earned 70 to 78% more than high school graduates, master's degree holders earned more than double, and those with doctorates or professional degrees earned nearly three times as much (for women) or more than three times as much (for men). Despite women earning the majority of degrees at all levels, the higher education earnings premium is substantially larger for males than for females; in other words, receipt of a bachelor's or advanced degree has a greater effect on men's earning potential. As such, at all levels of educational attainment, women continue to earn between 70 and 82% of what their male counterparts do (see Figure 6.3). Similarly, the earnings premium of a bachelor's (or higher) degree is stronger for Whites and Asians and for students with a college-educated parent than they are for Black, Hispanic or Latinx, and first-generation students. Factors contributing to these labor market inequities include racial or gender differences in employment possibilities tied to students' majors, the selectivity of institutions attended (graduates of the most selective colleges and universities tend to earn more), and racial or gender discrimination in the labor market (Fry, 2021; Nichols and Anthony, 2020).

The consistent findings noted in the preceding pages point to socially desirable yet personal outcomes of college attendance. They vary by age, gender, race or ethnicity, pattern of college attendance, and numerous other characteristics and situations, but when all are aggregated, evidence for the value of college is quite clear. The most powerful cognitive effects are in oral and written communication, abstract reasoning, critical thinking, and the ability to deal with conceptual complexity. Attitudinally, students tend to move away from authoritarian, dogmatic thinking, embrace civil liberties and individual autonomy, and demonstrate greater cultural awareness and openness to others, including those from races or ethnicities different than their own and those in the LGBTQ+ community. Yet contrary to conservative assertions that college-going produces progressive ideologies, Mayhew and colleagues' (2016) meta-analysis of how college affects students found that for most learners, "liberal views were already well established in the first year of college" (p. 253).

Furthermore, as Mayhew and colleagues (2016) explained, the magnitude of between-college effects is typically much smaller than whether someone attended college at all (net effects) or what students did while in school (within-college effects), despite substantial differences in entering characteristics of students at different types of colleges and universities. In other words, the effects of institutional type have proven to be quite modest and may only occur because certain types of colleges promote certain experiences and environments, which *do* affect student outcomes. Astin (1993) attributed the most significant between-college effects to student involvement in college life, especially residing on campus, a contention substantiated repeatedly by various ongoing studies of student engagement.

In addition, Mayhew and colleagues (2016) found that four-year schools promote higher bachelor's degree completion than community colleges (among students who desire that degree); that community college graduates are more likely than those of four-year institutions to work in a job related to their field of study; that religious schools bolster civic and religious or spiritual outcomes more than nonreligious institutions; that attending a MSI or women's college "leads to various outcomes that are at least as favorable as attending other schools" (p. 542); and that "total expenditures and state allocations, as well as specific expenses that directly support student learning and student success" promote higher graduation rates (p. 543). Tuition levels, and the existence of performance funding or articulation agreements, Mayhew and colleagues (2016) found, did not have a direct effect on graduation rates.

**Societal Benefits**

The concept of *public good* has been defined variously, but in higher education generally refers to the idea that an educated populace benefits society at large, and that college graduates bolster the economy and strengthen our democracy. However, as the preceding section made clear, higher education is also a private good—it benefits individual students—and economists and others have found it notoriously difficult to separate individual gain from societal benefits. For example, college graduates who qualify as professionals earn higher salaries (private good) even while they provide essential services and tax revenue to the community (public good). Adam Smith's eighteenth-century definition, "self-interest, in the aggregate, could most efficiently provide the common good," while imperfect, seems most generally accepted (Pusser, 2006, p. 26). However, that definition does not cover the social benefits generated, for example, by university-based research that yields cures for diseases, slows climate change, or results in more efficient ways of producing food for greater numbers of people, nor does it take into account taxpayer savings stemming from reduced criminal justice costs and lower levels of public assistance.

Support for education has long been justified on the grounds that it is in the compelling interest of the state or the nation. During the Cold War, arguments for federal funding turned on that rationale, and similar justifications led to the awarding of $76 billion in HEERF funding during the COVID-19 pandemic. Throughout the decades, scholars have found that higher education assists in the maintenance of civic order; reduces crime, incarceration rates, and criminal justice costs; increases community, physical, and mental health; and enhances the human capital needed for a growing economy and changing workforce. Researchers have sought ways of measuring these broad social effects, including tracking welfare recipiency. Not surprisingly, years of schooling are inversely related to receiving public assistance. In 2021, 27% of adults 25 and older without a high school diploma—and 14% of adults with only a high school diploma—received SNAP benefits (formerly known as food stamps), a figure that dropped to 3% among those with a bachelor's degree (College Board, 2023b).

Moreover, college graduates tend to be healthier, exercise more, and are more engaged in their communities; a Pew Research study found that while 70% of college graduates were involved in one or more community groups, less than half of those with only a high school diploma were similarly engaged (Sandstrom and Alper, 2019). As well, adults with some postsecondary education are at least twice as likely to volunteer their time and make charitable contributions. They are 24% more likely to be employed and 2.2 times less likely to be unemployed. They are 4.9 times less likely to be incarcerated (Trostel, 2015). They are also more likely to vote: in the 2020 presidential election, 77% of 25-to-44-year-old citizens with at least a bachelor's degree voted, compared to 46% of high school graduates (College Board, 2023b). Indeed, college attendance has a lasting effect on civic engagement and volunteerism that extends even to off-year elections (Perrin and Gillis, 2019).

Furthermore, through their work as doctors, teachers, scholars, engineers, entrepreneurs, social workers, civic leaders, and other professions, college graduates directly improve the social conditions of their communities and society writ large. The values associated with academe—social responsibility, concern for the environment, intellectual curiosity, and knowledge creation—are spillover effects that, while difficult to calculate, nonetheless contribute to the public good and taxpayers' return on investment.

Other measures of higher education's contributions to the public good are more straightforward. In particular, numerous studies have shown that higher education:

- Generates better products and intellectual capital through research.

- Contributes to economic development through the preparation of a trained workforce and the multiplier effect of businesses and entire industries started by graduates or university staff in collaboration with entrepreneurs.

- Develops literacy. The community colleges and broadly accessible institutions especially have been engaged in direct language training for immigrants and in enhancing the basic skills of students whose high schools provided insufficient preparation.

- Contributes to the socioeconomic mobility of students, and in the process widens economic and social divisions between those with some postsecondary education or training and those without.

- Is an economic engine, employing over 3.8 million people and spending $655 billion per year.

Analysts have long tried to place a dollar value on each of these outcomes but have been frustrated by all the contaminating variables. Nonetheless, higher education's requests for continued funding rest on a combination of premises: direct contributions to the economy, enhanced productivity yielded by trained workers, and progress toward a more just and equitable society. Many scholars have contended that higher education is more than an engine of economic activity, that it is the home of ideas, "a site of history, culture, and symbolic importance in the broader political economy" (Pusser, 2006, p. 19). These contentions still have at least some resonance; as Baumol, Blackman, and Wolff (1989) pointed out, "If future income and job-benefit returns to the student were all that education had to offer, there would be little reason for governments to subsidize it as they do" (p. 199). Yet from an economic perspective, the weakest arguments for supporting higher education are that it has intrinsic educational value. Institutions and programs showing measurable economic and social benefits are much easier to defend than those claiming to have value in and of themselves.

Do the public benefits that higher education yields justify the public resources devoted to it? Where do private gain and public good overlap and diverge? How much is the university itself worth? These perennial questions have never been adequately answered. That colleges are cultural archives, that they arouse intellectual curiosity, and that they enhance social justice are compelling reasons to support academe, but to policymakers the notion that higher education is a public good has been largely overshadowed by the dominant view that its primary function is to act as the gateway to employment and higher earnings.

## Critiques and Commentary

The contemporary structure of higher education is little changed from the pattern put in place in the middle years of the University Transformation Era when the American university separated into undergraduate and graduate colleges. The academic departments became dominant along with professorial tenure and a pyramidal management structure. Intercollegiate sports and vast alumni networks were developed. State support of public higher education expanded and was seen as an entitlement for decades, until a continuous cycle of recessions and per-FTE cuts in allocations resulted in a long-term trend toward disinvestment. Institutional goals were preparation for work, general education (which in most cases was nothing more than a smorgasbord of specialized courses organized according to political accommodations between departments), and new knowledge generation. The four-year baccalaureate, with 120 credits required for graduation, academic majors, and semesters or quarters with summers off became the pattern for most students. For faculty, the norms stabilized around teaching and advising students, engaging in committee and community service, and preparing scholarly publications. Separate professional schools, each a fiefdom, dominated the universities, and graduate degrees were conferred with scarcely a nod to the number of professionals required in each field or, in the case of academic doctorates, preparing their recipients for teaching.

Calls for institutional reform came from many sources. Legislators continually insisted on institutional accountability and reduced expenditures. Students and groups aligned with social justice movements demanded more equitable representation of students and faculty from historically underserved races and ethnicities, as well as the provision of equitable supports and structural changes that would enable marginalized or minoritized students to persist and complete at the same rates as their White, Asian, and wealthier peers. Students, faculty, and others rebelled against a curriculum they said was too parochial, archaic, and Eurocentric, and pressed for literature, pedagogies, and perspectives that better reflected the voices and experiences of marginalized Americans and other cultures around the world. Employer groups wanted people prepared for work in specialized occupations, but who also had the integrative or soft skills necessary to succeed and advance in their careers. Most recently, some conservative policymakers and commentators have accused the institutions of promoting a "woke" agenda by examining the ways in which colleges and universities—and indeed the United States itself—have reinforced racial and socioeconomic stratifications and by fostering ideas of equity, inclusion, and diversity that (the commentators believed) were dangerous and anti-American (or at least anti-White). All contended that higher education was unable or unwilling to do more than rearrange a few deck chairs on the *Titanic*, even as journalists repeatedly shouted that higher education was "in crisis," had experienced a "tumble from grace," or—most generously stated—was having a "low moment" (Thelin, 2019, p. 400).

Pressure for change stemmed from reactions to phenomena that were unknown or barely on the horizon 150 years ago: mass enrollments and greater racial and socioeconomic diversity among learners; students of all ages; online learning and advanced educational technology; an explosion of short-term, industry-relevant certificates and other nondegree credentials; multibillion-dollar budgets; complex management systems; campuses with buildings designed exclusively for research or for providing amenities to students; and licensing agreements with private corporations (among research universities) and entrepreneurial and public-private partnerships (across all institutional types). And, not least, per capita student costs that at times escalated, at least at four-year institutions, far faster than the rate of inflation.

The calls for reform were not new, nor were disagreements about where blame was to be lain. Commentators from within the academy pointed to diminishing state allocations, as well as the high costs associated with providing equitable support to students, especially those whose prior education or years in the workforce left them underprepared for college-level work. Those outside the system blamed the massive expenditures and continually rising costs on administrative bloat or institutional greed and, ironically, both progressive and conservative commentators accused higher education of not focusing enough on the needs of marginalized or minoritized populations or, conversely, focusing *solely* on their needs. The only point of agreement to be found was that higher education needed to transcend, as Kisker (2021) wrote, its history of incremental change and engage in more substantive modification.

Yet transformative changes that kept intact higher education's access, quality, and service missions were few and far between. Research universities and community colleges demanded faculty members with different expertise, but graduate preparation in the disciplines varied little. In a world in which rapid advancements in technology require a nimble and responsive approach to education and training, most colleges and universities were stymied by lengthy curriculum development and shared governance processes. The academic departments still control what is taught and by whom—prioritizing discipline-based approaches to seeking and transmitting knowledge—which may be satisfactory for research universities where new knowledge is continually created, but which ill serves the other 90% of higher education. And yet, institutional and state articulation agreements ensured that the disciplinary pathways and requirements of the university were replicated by any institution preparing students for transfer. Furthermore, the public and private four-year institutions frequently failed to accommodate adults who cared little for campus amenities, and who—because of their attendance patterns and education or training objectives—typically were served well only by community colleges, extension divisions, and the for-profit sector.

Thus, much of the criticism about higher education's intractable nature is legitimate, if only because a system with open-ended goals can always be reproved for not doing better. Higher education's emphasis on economic development has succeeded in gaining support, but linking degrees with personal earnings and employment further fuels the public's expectation that a degree or certificate alone guarantees these results. A Public Agenda report (Schleifer, Friedman, and McNally, 2022) indicated that 86% of Americans believed that a college education can help working adults advance in their career and 64% agreed that most people with a high school diploma would make a better living if they got a college education. In the competition for public support, the colleges have no choice; they must continually strive to convince taxpayers and legislators that they are receiving a good return on their investment. Yet Chambers (2005) cautioned about listing personal and social benefits of higher education: "The more social outcomes are attributed solely to higher education, the more the public expects higher education, alone, to deliver on those outcomes" (p. 11). Keller (2008) noted this presumption more colorfully: "In a crazy compliment to the field of education, many people seem to believe that, if only we had better teaching, and improved curriculum, and greater accountability, schools and colleges could transform the country's health, manners, economy, and behavior. The faith is touching but bizarre" (p. xi). The flip side to this, of course, is that "in the absence (or failure) of public policies to provide equitable pathways out of poverty and to rewarding and economically sustaining careers, the job falls to the institutions that have the most contact and influence with learners seeking to improve their educational and economic prospects" (Kisker, Cohen, and Brawer, 2023, p. 479). America's colleges and universities alone may not be able to solve all of society's ills, but expectations that they do more than they currently are will not soon diminish.

Numerous surveys of college and university presidents revealed a nuanced understanding of (and concern for) many of the critiques and calls for reform (e.g., Immerwahr, Johnson, and Gasbarra, 2008; Inside Higher Ed, 2023). Presidents consistently agreed that access, equity, quality, cost, and the value of degrees are their top concerns, but noted that these are intrinsically linked and interdependent. Change in one affects the others. Improving the quality of higher education and providing equitable support for students requires either putting more money in the system or making colleges and universities less accessible. Cutting costs must eventually lead to cuts in either quality or access and thus call into question the value of degrees. These linkages are logical yet not always obvious to the public. More than half of people surveyed by Immerwahr, Johnson, and Gasbarra (2008) said that the colleges could spend a lot less and still maintain quality, while 58% also said that colleges could take more students without affecting the quality or increasing prices. Over half regarded colleges primarily as businesses, and 40% believed that waste and mismanagement contributed to driving up the costs of college.

Public-opinion surveys are usually regarded as unreliable by researchers in higher education, but institutional supporters and managers often refer to them as harbingers of forthcoming problems and opportunities. And because of the reciprocal relationship between public opinion and legislative action, the public's lack of understanding and increasing distrust of higher education may, in the long run, influence what happens to the system more than all its lobbyists put together. As such, the polls described in the Societal Context section of this chapter—especially those showing that large percentages of Republicans believe that "most college professors teach liberal propaganda," and that majorities of both parties "believe higher education is going in the wrong direction" (e.g., Jaschik, 2022)—validate faculty and administrative fears that their longstanding traditions of institutional autonomy, tenure, and academic freedom, as well as their efforts to provide safe, inclusive, and equitable environments for all students, will continue to come under attack (and not just because of the financial resources dedicated to them). While to date some legislative attempts to restrict tenure or ban it outright have failed or were rolled back (as in Texas and Iowa), others have been passed (in Georgia, for example).

Furthermore, several bills signed into law by Florida governor Ron DeSantis amount to, as the AAUP (2023) proclaimed, a "politically and ideologically driven assault unparalleled in US history. If sustained, this onslaught threatens the very survival of meaningful higher education in the state, with dire implications for the entire country" (p. 1). In particular, Florida Senate Bill 266 limited what colleges can offer as programs, majors, or minors; instituted post-tenure reviews; took responsibility for hiring, firing, and promoting their peers away from the faculty, giving it to presidents (and expressly stating that presidents should not be bound by the opinions or recommendations of faculty in making these decisions); prohibited the teaching or discussion of structural racism in general education classes; required annual economic security reports linking every degree with earnings; and banned any programs or campus activities that "advocate for diversity, equity, and inclusion, or promote or engage in political or social activism" (Florida Senate, 2023, p. 11). Texas Senate Bill 17, signed into law in June 2023, similarly banned DEI offices and initiatives in public institutions, and anti-DEI legislation has been passed or received final legislative approval in five additional states (Chronicle of Higher Education, 2023). Whether these and similar bills were inspired by public opinions about higher education or simply utilized the polls as justification for undermining institutions that counter authoritarian tendencies and White nationalist beliefs is beside the point. As the legislation in Florida and Texas illustrates, those intent on ensuring that America's system of higher education maintains a racialized caste system—or at least that it does nothing to dismantle it—will continue to shape the public's negative perceptions of colleges and universities and then use those same beliefs to rationalize further incursions into institutional autonomy.

## Summary and Trends

This book has recounted the major trends in higher education since the Colonial Era, several of which slowed or showed distinct signs of reversal in the most recent eras. Institutions grew larger and more varied. Students gained access as institutional types emerged or evolved to serve all comers. However, although colleges and universities instituted a number of equity-driven policies and practices, especially in the Contemporary Era, substantial equity gaps between White, Asian, and wealthier students and their Black, Hispanic or Latinx, Indigenous, and lower-income peers persisted. Faculty professionalization progressed steadily, reaching a peak in the Mass Higher Education Era, before losing ground to part-time, fungible labor. The curriculum expanded, especially toward occupational studies.

Institutional governance moved toward secularization and comprehensive, state-level units before decentralizing and taking on a more corporate approach to management. Public funding for higher education increased throughout its first 350 years, then waned in the late twentieth and early twenty-first centuries, forcing institutions to act entrepreneurially and/or turn to private sources of support. As a result of these shifts in governance and funding, an ever expanding number of governance actors demanded more accountability for student and institutional outcomes, in the process arming both legislators and the general public with a plethora of data points from which to support increasingly divergent and partisan views of the system. Although higher education's outcomes—individual mobility, societal and economic development, evolution of the professions, and advancement of knowledge—have remained steady since the University Transformation Era, students, parents, employers, policymakers, and even many faculty and administrators tended to emphasize and prioritize the individual and economic benefits of college over those associated with the public good.

Which of the trends might have been predicted when the nation was formed? Large multipurpose institutions? No. The plethora of professions that would demand years of schooling prior to practice, and an economy that would allow young people to delay entry into the workforce until they were well into their twenties, were not on the horizon. Student access? Perhaps, because it embodies the egalitarian, democratic ideal on which the nation was founded. Attention to student equity? Definitely not, as women and students of color were initially shunted to decidedly separate and unequal institutions and financial aid was not widely available until the mid-twentieth century. Faculty professionalization (and then deprofessionalization)? No. The first had to await the nineteenth-century German concept *Lehrfreiheit* and the professionalizing of several other occupational groups, and the second followed a global restructuring of work that required a more efficient and nimbler (and thus less secure) workforce.

A curriculum more directly related to occupations? Perhaps. The trend was on the horizon in the last few years of the Colonial Era, as the newer colleges attempted to provide a curriculum beneficial to a variety of commercial interests. Diversified financing? Yes, because from the start, the colleges relied on combinations of public funds, tuition, and donations, although the eventual magnitude and then reduction of state contributions was not foreseeable. Secular governance? Yes, because governance was interdenominational in several institutions, and attempts were made early on to involve civic leaders. But state-level governance and multi-institutional systems would have been hard to visualize because the early colleges functioned independently in scattered locations. Expectations that higher education would ameliorate social problems and enhance the economy? No. The early colleges were influential in developing men of public affairs, but the economy did not depend on college-spawned inventions or a workforce trained in postsecondary institutions.

Which trends will remain intact in the decades to come? The growth of new institutions has slowed considerably and hardly any new nonprofit campuses will be built. State, federal, and private or philanthropic funds will be available to expand campus facilities but it will not be enough to establish entire institutions. It may not even be enough to sustain many small private institutions, as the combination of higher tuitions, low enrollments, and fewer opportunities for entrepreneurial revenue-generating partnerships have already taken a toll, forcing many to close their doors or merge with nearby institutions.

The concept of open access, well grounded in the Mass Higher Education Era, will survive but with limitations; smaller percentages of students will attend full-time or primarily in-person, and even fewer will have the residential campus experience. Diversity will remain a core value as it has since the Mass Higher Education Era, although institutions will have to implement creative recruitment practices and holistic reviews of applications to ensure that race neutrality in admissions does not, as Justice Sotomayor feared, "entrench racial segregation" (as cited in Kaplin et al., 2020, pp. 68–69). Similarly, while attention to equity in the student experience and in various outcome metrics is likely to continue, recent efforts in Florida, Texas, and elsewhere to restrict diversity, equity, and inclusion practices may require faculty and administrators in those states to be creative about how they provide and describe these services for some time. Nonetheless, educators will find it hard to ignore the clear evidence that welcoming, inclusive, and supportive environments—both on campus and online—are foundational to student learning, persistence, and attainment. Equity has become one of higher education's guiding principles and so long as institutions retain some level of autonomy from the state, social justice efforts will eventually prevail.

Faculty professionalization, on the other hand, has already made a U-turn, stymied by the massive influx of part-timers and both full- and part-time instructors on contingent appointments. The curriculum will continue broadening, as academic inquiry sustains its pattern of generating new subspecialties and as additional occupational groups seek higher education's cachet. New credentials, including industry-relevant and stackable certificates, will gain prominence as recent high school graduates and adult students alike progress along various educational pathways in ways that suit their lives and evolving career goals. All the external pressures on curriculum favor vocationalism, and most institutional types will have to take on more sub-baccalaureate training and/or admit greater numbers of returning students to offset declining numbers of high school graduates. (The only real question is whether universities will do this primarily through extension divisions or partnerships with formerly for-profit entities or whether they will integrate new programs and credentials into traditional departments and disciplines.)

Secular governance has become dominant. State-level control has already lost ground to decentralization, and some institutions have gone further, seeking charter or enterprise status, effectively trading governmental restrictions for increased accountability requirements. Privatization has changed the conditions of institutional finance, as public colleges and universities at all levels have been forced to seek alternative funding streams to mitigate the effects of state disinvestment and to accommodate rising costs and enrollments. Furthermore, what some commentators identified as higher education's *edifice complex*—continuous capital investment in plants, research buildings, and athletic facilities—is likely to continue. Beautifying student facilities (dorms, gyms, student centers) has become an integral part of institutional marketing. Rising tuition and market competition have turned higher education into a product to be sold, and students and parents increasingly want to know what options or amenities come with their bill. Dorms are passé—housing is in. Dining halls are now food courts, with an array of cuisines from different parts of the globe.

Students' approaching colleges and universities as consumers is not new; what is changing is higher education's eagerness to treat them as such. Thus, the tendency to view higher education less as a set of social institutions than as a business enterprise will continue. As a result, colleges and universities will increasingly find themselves judged according to the same standards that are applied to any business: "To what extent does this entity add value? . . . And can comparable value be added more efficiently by other means?" (Schuster and Finkelstein, 2006, p. 10). But higher education's spirit is too mercurial to be captured in the crude measures available. It serves many functions, provides something for anyone seeking it, and is a national asset of incomparable value.

We can predict only the most powerful trends in higher education because unforeseeable events convert specific projections into little more than informed guesses. For decades colleges and universities had experimented with distance education and online learning, but few could have predicted how the COVID-19 pandemic would dramatically accelerate this trend across all institutional types. Even the technophiles of the early twenty-first century might have a hard time believing that, three years post-pandemic, roughly one-third of all college students would still favor online or hybrid learning models (or that the costs of online instruction would, in most cases, exceed those of traditional classrooms). Similarly, while one might have assumed that student activism would rise as the nation once again reckoned with issues of race and identity, would anyone have predicted that mainstream Republicans—let alone elected officials—would so vehemently protest the concept of structural racism or engage in dehumanizing attacks on the LGBTQ+ community before Trump's presidency fanned the flames of an *us versus them* mentality, a belief that justice for minoritized populations is necessarily an existential threat to White conservatives' way of life?

Thus, while only the crudest outlines of higher education's future are yet visible, the study of America's colleges and universities remains fascinating, with many questions open in each topic:

- Throughout the Contemporary Era, comprehensive universities expanded to offer doctoral degrees, community colleges conferred applied baccalaureates, and nearly every institutional type evolved in ways that would strengthen or expand its market share, including the provision of industry-relevant and other nondegree credentials. What might this continued evolution look like in the coming years, especially as institutions can no longer count on increasing numbers of high school graduates? Will it lead to heightened competition or collaboration across sectors? What positive or negative effects might result?

- As concepts of equity and inclusion ascended toward the same level of importance as student access, colleges and universities modified many practices to better admit and support learners from marginalized or minoritized backgrounds. Yet America's system of higher education has, over the years, perpetuated privilege at least as much as it has enhanced opportunity, and the 2023 Supreme Court decision banning affirmative action, as well as legislative restrictions on DEI initiatives in some states, will likely have dampening effects on efforts to alter structures and policies that have long precluded social and economic mobility for some groups. What tactics might faculty and administrators take to ensure equitable and inclusive learning environments for all students without risking further incursions into institutional autonomy or threats of reduced funding?

- Since at least the 1960s, college students have been characterized by their progressive views and activist behaviors, and courts have long sided with students' right to free speech and peaceful protest. Yet in the Contemporary Era students showed an increased willingness to shout down speakers whose views they found offensive, which sometimes pit them against college and university leaders who might otherwise have been sympathetic to the students' views. And in response to the Israel–Hamas war, some students turned their vitriol on one another, prompting real concerns about the safety of Jewish students and those with pro-Palestinian viewpoints alike. How might institutions of higher education support and enable student activism and democratic engagement and still protect free speech and an unfettered exchange of ideas? Can college campuses be the battlefields on which the nation's cultural and political conflicts take place without also making themselves targets or prompting harmful internal divisions?

- Faculty professionalization was on the wane long before the Contemporary Era, but both frontal attacks on tenure and the long-term trend toward a part-time, fungible academic workforce in the name of fiscal sustainability accelerated in this most recent period. The president of AAUP argued that the erosion of tenure and academic freedom protections threaten nothing less than democracy itself. What, if anything, can be done to slow or reverse this tide? Might there be a tipping point beyond which efforts to preserve academic freedom and prevent authoritarianism are too little, too late?

- The curriculum shifted in the Contemporary Era much as it had in previous decades, trending ever more toward programs and disciplines more closely aligned with careers and the fastest-growing occupations. At the same time, employers aware of the rapid pace of technological and industrial change pleaded with colleges and universities to focus more on the twenty-first century skills necessary for success in life and in a changing workforce. Might this renewed focus on integrative competencies such as critical thinking, communication, collaboration, and intercultural fluency portend a renaissance for traditional higher education learning outcomes once associated primarily with the liberal arts? How might the incorporation of AI-based teaching and learning strategies as well as critical and culturally relevant pedagogies play into this dynamic?

- As state funding for public institutions declined as a percentage of the total (and in real per-FTE terms), and as all institutions increased revenues from private sources, the number of governance actors expanded, and accountability mandates increased tenfold. Higher costs of compliance—as well as the resources required to provide a larger and increasingly diverse student body with equitable support—contributed to substantial growth in noninstructional expenditures. This led to numerous charges of administrative bloat, which some policymakers then used to justify further reductions in governmental support. How might colleges and universities better make the case for expenditures outside the classroom but in areas critical to supporting student persistence and success? At what point will institutions have to reconcile these increased expenditures with reduced spending on salaries for full-time, tenure-eligible faculty?

- As nonfinancial aid funding to colleges and universities from states and the federal government declines or is increasingly tied to specific initiatives or programmatic emphases, a greater percentage of operating revenues will come from grants, donations, and other private sources. What might this mean for the public mission of America's colleges and universities, or for how institutions make decisions about curricular priorities?

> Will it pressure college leaders to continue raising tuition and fees? What other effects might it have on student access, curricular quality, or institutional efficiency?

- In a society characterized by polarized politics and a dysfunctional democracy, historic levels of income inequality, a populace divided over issues of race and identity, deeply divergent views about and distrust of institutions of higher education, and ideologically driven attempts to erode institutional autonomy, how might America's colleges and universities refocus attention on their worth to society? Will Americans ever be able to come together to defend the institutions that have acted, for nearly 400 years, as the archives of our culture, the defenders of our democracy, and the gateways to social and economic opportunity? What would be the consequences of failing to preserve the system?

Although it is tempting for supporters and scholars of American higher education to view the contemporary context in which colleges and universities operate in a dystopian light, it is important also to recall the strengths of a system that has served, for more than 150 years, as an architype of excellence and egalitarianism both in the United States and across the globe. And while colleges and universities must continually parry threats from outside academe—including attacks on tenure, academic freedom, and DEI initiatives, state disinvestment, and students' rising mental health and basic needs insecurities—the status of American higher education, both at home and abroad, is bolstered by its economic and symbolic value. Perhaps most important now is its ability to adapt to changing conditions and to do so in a transparent manner, showing how institutional decisions align with the academy's longstanding values and mores, including institutional autonomy, academic freedom and free expression, equal access and equitable support, and a commitment to acting for the public good. No one knows exactly how colleges and universities—or the society in which they are embedded—will change in coming years. The only certainty is that the diverse system will continue experimenting with forms and content, learning and adapting as it goes, while retaining meaningful traditions developed over the past 390 or so years. The American people deserve no less from institutions that—in their pursuit of reason, culture, and excellence—are manifestations of the nation's self.

# References

Accrediting Commission for Community and Junior Colleges. (2001). Primary purposes of ACCJC.

ACT. (2019). College readiness benchmark attainment.

Adams, J.T. (1931). *The Epic of America*. New York: Blue Ribbon Books.

Adelman, C. (1994). *Lessons of a Generation: Education and Work in the Lives of the High School Class of 1972*. San Francisco: Jossey-Bass.

Adelman, C. (2004). *The Empirical Curriculum: Changes in Postsecondary Course-Taking: 1972–1999*. Washington, D.C.: U.S. Department of Education.

Alonso, J. (2023). Shouting down speakers who offend. *Inside Higher Ed* (13 April). https://www.insidehighered.com/news/students/free-speech/2023/04/13/shouting-down-speakers-who-offend (accessed 1 November 2023).

Altindag, D.T., Filiz, E.S., and Tekin, E. (2023). Is online education working? National Bureau of Economic Research working paper 29113.

Ambrose, S.E. (1996). *Undaunted Courage: Meriwether Lewis, Thomas Jefferson, and the Opening of the American West*. New York: Simon & Schuster.

American Association of Colleges and Universities. (2016). Recent trends in general education design, learning outcomes, and teaching approaches. https://files.eric.ed.gov/fulltext/ED582012.pdf (accessed 15 May 2023).

American Association of University Professors (AAUP). (1940). 1940 statement of principles on academic freedom and tenure.

American Association of University Professors (AAUP). (1966). Statement on government of colleges and universities.

American Association of University Professors (AAUP). (2020). Data snapshot: IPEDS data on full-time women faculty and faculty of color.

American Association of University Professors (AAUP). (2022a). The annual report on the economic status of the profession, 2021–22.

American Association of University Professors (AAUP). (2022b). The 2022 AAUP survey of tenure practices.

American Association of University Professors (AAUP). (2023). Preliminary report of the special committee on academic freedom and Florida.

American College Health Association. (2019, Spring). National college health assessment.

American Council on Education. (1937). The student personnel point of view: A report of a conference on the philosophy and development of student personnel work in the college and university. *American Council on Education Studies, Series I* 1 (3).

American Council on Education. (2006). Working their way through college.

American Council on Education. (2023). The American college president, 2023 edition.

Anti-Defamation League. (2018). White supremacist propaganda surges on campus.

Arum, R. and Roska, J. (2011). *Academically Adrift: Limited Learning on College Campuses*. Chicago: University of Chicago Press.

Astin, A.W. (1977). *Four Critical Years: Effects of College on Beliefs, Attitudes, and Knowledge*. San Francisco: Jossey-Bass.

Astin, A.W. (1993). *What Matters in College? Four Critical Years Revisited*. San Francisco: Jossey-Bass.

Astin, A.W. and Chang, M.J. (1995). Colleges that emphasize research and teaching: Can you have your cake and eat it too? *Change* 27 (5): 44–49.

Barnett, E.A., Fay, M.P., and Pheatt, L. (2016). Implementation of high school-to-college transition courses in four states. Columbia University, Teacher's College, Community College Research Center.

Bate, W.J. (1975). *Samuel Johnson*. Orlando: Harcourt Brace.

Baum, S. (2010). Student work and the financial aid system. In: *Understanding the Working College Student: New Research and Its Implications for Policy and Practice* (ed. L. Perna), 3–22. Sterling, VA: Stylus.

Baum, S. and Steele, P. (2017). Who goes to graduate school and who succeeds? Urban Institute.

Baumol, W.J., Blackman, S.A.B., and Wolff, E.N. (1989). *Productivity and American Leadership*. Cambridge, MA: MIT Press.

Beattie, I.R. (2023). Don't ask, can't tell: LGBTQ+ student data promote equity. *Footnotes*, 50(2). https://www.asanet.org/footnotes-article/dont-ask-cant-tell-lgbtq-student-data-promote-equity/ (accessed 8 May 2023).

Belfield, C. and Crosta, P.M. (2012). Predicting success in college: the importance of placement tests and high school transcripts. Columbia University, Teacher's College, Community College Research Center working paper no. 42.

Betts, J.R. and McFarland, L.L. (1969). Safe port in the storm: Impact of labor market conditions on community college enrollments. *Journal of Human Resources* 30 (4): 741–765.

Birnbaum, R. and Eckel, P.D. (2005). The dilemma of presidential leadership. In: *American Higher Education in the Twenty-First Century*, 2e (eds. P.G. Altbach, R.O. Berdahl, and P.J. Gumport). Baltimore, MD: Johns Hopkins University Press.

Blake, D. (2017). The case for rebranding minority-serving institutions. *Diverse Issues in Higher Education* (17 January). https://www.diverseeducation.com/students/article/15099800/the-case-for-rebranding-minority-serving-institutions (accessed 26 April 2023).

Blankstein, M. (2022). Ithaka S+R US faculty survey 2021. Ithaka S+R. https://sr.ithaka.org/wp-content/uploads/2022/07/SR-Report-US-Faculty-Survey-2021-07142022.pdf (accessed 11 May 2023).

Bledstein, B.J. (1976). *The Culture of Professionalism: The Middle Class and the Development of Higher Education in America*. New York: Norton.

Bloom, A. (1974). The failure of the university. *Daedalus* 103 (4): 58–66.

Blumenstyk, K.G. (1998). Royalties on inventions bring $336-million to top U.S. research universities. *Chronicle of Higher Education* 44(25): A44.

Blundell, G.E., Castañeda, D.A., and Lee, J. (2020). A multi-institutional study of factors influencing faculty satisfaction with online teaching and learning. *Online Learning* 24 (4): 229–253.

Bok, D. (1982). *Beyond the Ivory Tower: Social Responsibilities of the Modern University*. Cambridge, MA: Harvard University Press.

Bok, D. (2003). *Universities in the Marketplace: The Commercialization of Higher Education*. Princeton, NJ: Princeton University Press.

Boorstin, D.J. (1991). *The Americans: The Colonial Experience*. London: Sphere Books.

Bouchey, B., Gratz, E., and Kurland, S. (2021). Remote student support during COVID-19: perspectives of chief online officers in higher education. *Online Learning* 25 (1): 28–40.

Bowen, H. (1977). *Investment in Learning*. San Francisco: Jossey-Bass.

Bowen, H. (1980). *The Costs of Higher Education*. San Francisco: Jossey-Bass.

Bowen, H. and Schuster, J. (1986). *American Professors: A National Resource Imperiled*. New York: Oxford University Press.

Boyer, E.L. (1990). *Scholarship Reconsidered: Priorities of the Professoriate*. Princeton, NJ: Carnegie Foundation for the Advancement of Teaching.

Boyer, E.L. (1996). The scholarship of engagement. *Journal of Public Service and Outreach* 1 (1): 11–20.

Breneman, D.W. (1991). *GSLs: Great Success or Dismal Failure?* Fishers, IN: United Student Aid Funds.

Breneman, D.W. (1994). *Liberal Arts Colleges: Thriving, Surviving, or Endangered?* Washington, D.C.: Brookings Institute.

Breneman, D.W. (2005). Entrepreneurship in higher education. In: *Arenas of Entrepreneurship: Where Nonprofit and For-Profit Institutions Compete*. New Directions for Higher Education, no. 129 (ed. B. Pusser), 3–9. San Francisco: Jossey-Bass.

Broome, E.C. (1903). *A Historical and Critical Discussion of College Admission Requirements*. New York: Columbia University Press.

Brown, T.T. (2022). The evolving missions and functions of accessible colleges and universities. In: *Unlocking Opportunity Through Broadly Accessible Institutions* (ed. G. Crisp, K.R. McClure, and C.M. Orphan), 65–81. New York: Routledge.

Bryant, J. (2022). Who are the highest-paid university presidents? *Best Colleges* (26 August). https://www.bestcolleges.com/news/analysis/2021/05/08/highest-paid-university-presidents/ (accessed 23 May 2023).

Bureau of Labor Statistics. (2022). Occupational employment and wages, May 2022: 25-9044 teaching assistants, postsecondary. https://www.bls.gov/oes/current/oes259044.htm (accessed 8 May 2023).

Bureau of Labor Statistics. (2023). Civilian Unemployment Rate. https://www.bls.gov/charts/employment-situation/civilian-unemployment-rate.htm (accessed 12 April 2023).

Burke, C.B. (1982). *American Collegiate Populations: A Test of the Traditional View*. New York: University Press.

Busta, H. (2020). CHEA president: As accreditation rules change, colleges can benefit from choices. *Higher Ed Dive* (26 September). https://www.highereddive.com/news/chea-president-as-accreditation-rules-change-colleges-can-benefit-from-ch/585940/ (accessed 29 September 2022).

Butts, R.F. (1939). *The College Charts Its Course*. New York: McGraw-Hill.

Campaign for Free College Tuition. (2023). Our momentum: How soon will your state's colleges be tuition free? https://www.freecollegenow.org/#momentum (accessed 25 January 2023).

Campbell, J.R., Voelkl, K., and Donahue, P.L. (1997). Report in brief: NAEP 1996 trends in academic progress. National Center for Education Statistics.

Carnegie Commission on Higher Education. (1973a). A classification of institutions of higher education.

Carnegie Commission on Higher Education. (1973b). The purposes and performance of higher education in the United States: Approaching the year 2000. A report and recommendations. Columbus, OH: McGraw-Hill.

Carnegie Council on Policy Studies in Higher Education. (1980). *A Summary of Reports and Recommendations.* San Francisco: Jossey-Bass.

Carnegie Foundation for the Advancement of Teaching. (1977). *Missions of the College Curriculum: A Contemporary Review with Suggestions: A Commentary.* San Francisco: Jossey-Bass.

Carnegie Foundation for the Advancement of Teaching. (1982). *The Control of the Campus: A Report on the Governance of Higher Education.* Princeton, N.J.: Princeton University Press.

Carnegie Foundation for the Advancement of Teaching. (1994). A classification of institutions of higher education.

Carnevale, A.P., Cheah, B. and Van Der Werf, M. (2020). ROI of liberal arts colleges: Value adds up over time. Georgetown Center on Education and the Workforce.

Carnevale, A.P., Strohl, J., Ridley, N., and Gulish, A. (2018). Three educational pathways to good jobs: High school, middle skills, and bachelor's degree. Georgetown Center on Education and the Workforce.

Census and Economic Information Center (CEIC). (2023). United States private consumption: % of GDP. https://www.ceicdata.com/en/indicator/united-states/private-consumption--of-nominal-gdp (accessed 11 April 2023).

Center or Education Policy Analysis (CEPA). (2023). The educational opportunity monitoring project: Racial and ethnic achievement gaps. Stanford University. https://cepa.stanford.edu/educational-opportunity-monitoring-project/achievement-gaps/race/ (accessed 6 May 2023).

Centers for Disease Control and Prevention. (2020). Web-based injury statistics query and reporting system (WISQARS): Fatal injury data, leading causes of death reports, 1981–2020.

Chambers, T.C. (2005). The special role of higher education in society. In: *Higher education for the public good: emerging voices from a national movement* (eds. A.J. Kezar, T.C. Chambers, J.C. Burkhardt, and associates), 3–22. San Francisco: Jossey-Bass.

Chronicle of Higher Education. (2020). "On the verge of burnout": Covid-19's impact on faculty well-being and career plans. https://connect.chronicle.com/rs/931-EKA-218/images/Covid%26FacultyCareerPaths_Fidelity_ResearchBrief_v3%20%281%29.pdf (accessed 12 May 2023).

Chronicle of Higher Education. (2021). Median salaries of college presidents, 2020–21. https://www.chronicle.com/article/median-salaries-of-college-presidents-2020-21 (accessed 23 May 2023).

Chronicle of Higher Education. (2023). DEI legislation tracker. https://www.chronicle.com/article/here-are-the-states-where-lawmakers-are-seeking-to-ban-colleges-dei-efforts?cid=gen_sign_in (accessed 10 July 2023).

Cineas, F. (2023). The "anti-intellectual attack" on higher ed will take years to undo. *Vox* (17 June). https://www.vox.com/policy/23762357/republican-attack-higher-education (accessed 18 June 2023).

Clark, B.R. (1988). The absorbing errand. Remarks presented at the national conference of the American Association of Higher Education (March 1988).

Clark, B.R. (1995). *Places of Inquiry: Research and Advanced Education in Modern Universities*. Berkeley, CA: University of California Press.

Clark, B.R. (1996). Substantive growth and innovative organization: New categories for higher education research. *Higher Education* 32: 417–430.

Clark, B.R. (1997). The modern integration of research activities with teaching and learning. *Journal of Higher Education* 68 (3): 241–255.

College Board. (2020). 2020 SAT suite of assessments annual report.

College Board. (2022). Trends in college pricing and student aid 2022.

College Board. (2023a). AP program results: Class of 2021.

College Board (2023b). Education pays 2023: The benefits of higher education for individuals and society.

College Promise. (2021). College Promise catalog of local and state programs (Fall). https://assets.website-files.com/61ba001bb59d0528645a4bf9/627bca118d528a61414d78da_guide-programs-2021-fall.pdf (accessed 25 January 2023).

Collins, C. and Hoxie, J. (2017). Billionaire bonanza: The Forbes 400 and the rest of us. Institute for Policy Studies.

Committee on the Objectives of a General Education in a Free Society. (1945). *General Education in a Free Society: A Report of the Harvard Committee*. Cambridge, MA: Harvard University Press.

Committee on Veterans Affairs. (1973). Final report on educational assistance to veterans: A comparative study of three G.I. bills. Senate Committee Print No. 18. U.S. Government Printing Office.

Community College Research Center. (2013). What we know about online course outcomes.

Complete College America. (2012). Remediation: Higher education's bridge to nowhere. https://completecollege.org/wp-content/uploads/2017/11/CCA-Remediation-final.pdf (accessed 25 April 2023).

Conron, K.J., O'Neill, K., Marzullo, M.R., et al. (2022). Los Angeles, community college and the experiences of LGBTQ people: Findings from a national probability survey. The Williams Institute, UCLA School of Law.

Cottom, T.M. (2017). *Lower Ed: The Troubling Rise of For-Profit Colleges in the New Economy*. New York: The New Press.

Crisp, G., McClure, K.R., and Orphan, C.M. (eds.). (2022). *Unlocking Opportunity Through Broadly Accessible Institutions*. New York: Routledge.

Cuban, L. (1986). *Teachers and Machines: The Classroom Use of Technology Since 1920*. New York: Teachers College, Columbia University.

D'Amico, M.M., Basis, V., Nissen, P., and Van Noy, M. (2022). Iowa noncredit data snapshot. Rutgers School of Management and Labor Relations. https://smlr.rutgers.edu/sites/default/files/Documents/Centers/EERC/Iowa%20State%20Report_Final%208.17.22tc_0.pdf (accessed 10 July 2023).

Davenport, D. (2017). A growing cancer on Congress: The curse of party-line voting. *Forbes* (13 December). https://www.forbes.com/sites/daviddavenport/2017/12/13/a-growing-cancer-on-congress-the-curse-of-party-line-voting/?sh=11c35ee46139 (accessed 11 April 2023).

David, P. (1997). The Knowledge Factory. *Economist* 345 (8037): 1–22.

Davis, C.H.F. III, Morgan, D., and Cho, K.S. (2023). Activism and student movements in college: Actors, contexts, tactics, and strategies of postsecondary political engagement. In: *American Higher Education in the 21st Century: Social, Political, and Economic Challenges*, 5e (ed. M.N. Bastedo, P.G. Altbach, and P.J. Gumport), 207–234. Baltimore, MD: John Hopkins University Press.

de los Santos, A. and Wright, I. (1990). Maricopa's swirling students: Earning one-third of Arizona State University's bachelor's degrees. *Community, Junior, and Technical College Journal* 6 (60): 32–34.

De Witte, M. (2022). Gen Z are not "coddled." They are highly collaborative, self-reliant and pragmatic, according to new Stanford-affiliated research. *Stanford News* (3 January). https://news.stanford.edu/2022/01/03/know-gen-z/ (accessed 4 May 2023).

DeFusco, J. (2022). Youngkin's push to keep tuition flat paying off as another university approves a one-time credit. ABC 8 News Capitol Connection (16 September). https://www.wric.com/news/politics/capitol-connection/youngkins-push-to-keep-tuition-flat-paying-off-as-another-university-approves-one-time-credit/ (accessed 24 January 2023).

Deloitte Center for Higher Education Excellence. (2017). Pathways to the university presidency: The future of higher education leadership. https://www2.deloitte.com/content/dam/insights/us/articles/3861_Pathways-to-the-university-presidency/DUP_Pathways-to-the-university-presidency.pdf (accessed 23 May 2023).

DeSilver, D. (2019). A majority of U.S. colleges admit most who apply. Pew Research Center (9 April). https://www.pewresearch.org/short-reads/2019/04/09/a-majority-of-u-s-colleges-admit-most-students-who-apply/ (accessed 21 April 2023).

DeSilver, D. (2022). The polarization in today's Congress has roots that go back decades. Pew Research Center (10 March). https://www.pewresearch.org/fact-tank/2022/03/10/the-polarization-in-todays-congress-has-roots-that-go-back-decades/ (accessed 11 Apri, 2023).

Dexter, F.B. (1896). *Biographical Sketches of the Graduates of Yale College with Annals of the College History. Vol. 2: 1745–1763*. New York: Henry Holt.

Doan, K.B. (2021). Community college practices regarding the collection of LGBTQ+ student data. New Directions for Institutional Research. *Special Issue: The Evolution of Diversity, Equity, & Inclusion, Institutional Research, & Data* 2021 (189–192): 29–42.

Donadel, A. (2023). Mental health remains the top concern for students. *University Business* (12 January). https://universitybusiness.com/mental-health-remains-the-top-concern-for-students/ (accessed 4 May 2023).

Doran, E. (2022). Current trends in developmental education policy and their implications for broad access institutions. In: *Unlocking Opportunity Through Broadly Accessible Institutions* (ed. G. Crisp, K.R. McClure, and C.M. Orphan), 137–151. New York: Routledge.

Driscoll, K. (2021). Will your online MBA result in a higher salary? *Fortune* (24 April). https://fortune.com/education/articles/will-your-online-mba-result-in-a-higher-salary/ (accessed 27 April 2023).

Eaton, J.S. (1997). The evolution of access policy: 1965–1990. In: *ASHE Reader on Public Policy and Higher Education* (ed. L.F. Goodchild, C.D. Lovell, E.R. Hines, and J.I. Gill), 237–245. Amarillo, TX: Ginn Publishing.

Eaton, J.S. (2003). *Almanac of External Quality Review 2003*. Council for Higher Education Accreditation.

Economist Intelligence Unit (2022). Democracy Index 2022. The Economist Group. https://www.eiu.com/n/campaigns/democracy-index-2022/ (accessed 12 April 2023).

Education Trust. (2010). Subprime opportunity: the unfulfilled promise of for-profit colleges and universities.

Elliott, K.C., Haynes, L., and Jones, T. (2021). Re-imagining outcomes-based funding. The Education Trust (1 April). https://edtrust.org/resource/re-imagining-outcomes-based-funding/ (accessed 1 June 2023).

Emerson, R.W. (1838). An oration delivered before the Phi Beta Kappa society at Cambridge, August 31, 1837, 2e. Boston: Munroe.

Ewell, P.T. (1997). The role of states and accreditors in shaping assessment practice. In: *ASHE Reader on Public Policy and Higher Education* (ed. L.F. Goodchild, C.D. Lovell, E.R. Hines, and J.I. Gill), 305–314. Amarillo, TX: Ginn Publishing.

Feldman, K.A. and Newcomb, T.M. (1969). *The Impact of College on Students*. San Francisco: Jossey-Bass.

Finkel, E. (2019). Endowments: They're not just for elite universities anymore. *Community College Daily* (11 November). https://www.ccdaily.com/2019/11/endowments-theyre-not-just-for-elite-universities-anymore/ (accessed 31 May 2023).

Finkelstein, M. (1983). From tutor to academic scholar: Academic professionalization in eighteenth and nineteenth century America. *History of Higher Education Annual* 3: 99–121.

Finkelstein, M. (1984). *The American Academic Profession: A Synthesis of Scientific Inquiry Since World War II*. Columbus, OH: Ohio State University Press.

Finley, A. (2020). How college contributes to workforce success. Employer views on what matters most. American Association of Colleges and Universities.

Fischer, D.H. (1989). *Albion's Seed: Four British Folkways in America*. New York: Oxford University Press.

Fischman, W. and Gardner, H. (2022). *The Real World of College: What Higher Education Is and What It Can Be*. Cambridge, MA: MIT Press.

Flaherty, C. (2019). Undue burden. *Inside Higher Ed* (3 June). https://www.insidehighered.com/news/2019/06/04/whos-doing-heavy-lifting-terms-diversity-and-inclusion-work (accessed 11 May 2023).

Flexner, A. (1908). *The American College: A Criticism*. New York: Century.

Flexner, A. (1910). *Medical Education in the United States and Canada: A Report to The Carnegie Foundation for the Advancement of Teaching*. New York: The Carnegie Foundation for the Advancement of Teaching.

Flexner, A. (1930). *Universities: American, English, German*. New York: Oxford University Press.

Florida Senate, SB 7044 (2022). https://www.flsenate.gov/Session/Bill/2022/7044/BillText/er/HTML (accessed 26 May 2023).

Florida Senate, SB 266 (2023). https://www.flsenate.gov/Session/Bill/2023/266/BillText/er/HTML (accessed 19 May 2023).

Foley, D., Milan, L., and Hamrick, K. (2021). The increasing role of community colleges among bachelor's degree recipients: Findings from the 2019 National Survey of College Graduates. National Science Foundation.

Francis, P.C. and Horn, A.S. (2016). Counseling services and student success. Research brief. Midwestern Higher Education Compact.

Franklin, B. (1931). *Benjamin Franklin's Proposals for the Education of Youth in Pennsylvania*. Philadelphia: University of Pennsylvania Press. (Originally published in 1749 as *Proposals Relating to the Education of Youth in Pensilvania*.)

Freire, P. (1970). *Pedagogy of the Oppressed*. New York: Continuum.

Fry, R. (2021). First-generation college graduates lag behind their peers on key economic outcomes. Pew Research Center.

Galston, W.A. (2023). Polls show Americans are divided on the significance of January 6. Brookings Institute (6 January). https://www.brookings.edu/blog/fixgov/2023/01/06/polls-show-americans-are-divided-on-the-significance-of-january-6/ (accessed 11 April, 2023).

Garbarino, J.W. (1977). State experience in collective bargaining. In: *Faculty Bargaining in Public Higher Education: A Report and Two Essays*. San Francisco: Jossey-Bass.

Garbarino, J.W. with Aussieker, B. (1975). *Faculty Bargaining: Change and Conflict*. Report prepared for the Carnegie Commission on Higher Education and the Ford Foundation. New York: McGraw-Hill.

Garrett, S.D., Miller, V., and Gilbert, C. (2021). The challenge of culturally responsive teaching in rural community colleges. In: *Teaching and Learning in the 21st Century Community College*. New Directions for Community Colleges, no. 195 (ed. M. T. Hora), 107–118. San Francisco: Jossey-Bass.

Gaston, P.L. and Van Noy, M. (2022). *Credentials: Understand the Problems. Identify the Opportunities. Create the Solutions*. Sterling, VA: Stylus.

Gee, T. (2017). How the Middlebury riot really went down. *Politico Magazine* (28 May). https://www.politico.com/magazine/story/2017/05/28/how-donald-trump-caused-the-middlebury-melee-215195/ (accessed 3 May 2023).

Geiger, R.L. (1986). *To Advance Knowledge: The Growth of American Research Universities, 1900–1940*. New York: Oxford University Press.

Geiger, R.L. (1993). *Research and Relevant Knowledge: American Research Universities Since World War II*. New York: Oxford University Press.

Geiger, R.L. and Sorber, N.M. (eds.). (2013). *The Land-Grant Colleges and the Reshaping of American Higher Education*. New York: Routledge.

Giele, J.Z. (1995). Two paths to women's equality. In: *Temperance, Suffrage, and the Origins of Modern Feminism*. New York: Twayne.

Gladieux, L.E. and Hauptman, A.M. (1995). The college aid quandary: Access, quality, and the federal role. Brookings Institution and College Board.

Glickman, L. (2020). How White Backlash Controls American Progress. *The Atlantic* (22 May). https://www.theatlantic.com/ideas/archive/2020/05/white-backlash-nothing-new/611914/ (accessed 23 April 2023).

Goldin, C. and Katz, L.F. (2008). *The Race Between Education and Technology.* Cambridge, MA: Harvard University Press.

Goldrick-Rab, S. (2016). *Paying the Price: College Costs, Financial Aid, and the Betrayal of the American Dream.* Chicago: University of Chicago Press.

Goldrick-Rab, S. and Cochrane, D. (2019). Addressing the basic needs of California community college students. Temple University, Hope Center for College, Community, and Justice.

Gonzales, L.D. and Robinson, T.N. (2023). Broad-access institutions: Sites of possibility and opportunity. In: *American Higher Education in the 21st Century: Social, Political, and Economic Challenges*, 5e (ed. M.N. Bastedo, P.G. Altbach, and P.J. Gumport), 449–476. Baltimore, MD: John Hopkins University Press.

Goodchild, L.F. and Wechsler, H.S. (eds.). (1997). *ASHE Reader on the History of Higher Education*, 2e. Needham Heights, MA: Simon & Schuster Custom Publishing.

Gose, B. (2021). The road ahead for liberal-arts colleges. *Chronicle of Higher Education Trends Snaphot.* https://connect.chronicle.com/rs/931-EKA-218/images/RoadAheadLiberalArts_AWS_TrendsSnapshot_v4.pdf (accessed 27 April 2023).

Grant, G. and Riesman, D. (1978). *The Perpetual Dream: Reform and Experiment in the American College.* Chicago: University of Chicago Press.

Green, T. (1980). *Predicting the Behavior of the Educational System.* Syracuse, NY: Syracuse University.

Greenberg, D.S. (2007). *Science for Sale: The Perils, Rewards, and Delusions of Campus Capitalism.* Chicago: University of Chicago Press.

Greene, J.P., Kisida, B., and Mills, J. (2010). Administrative bloat at American universities: The real reason for high costs in higher education: Goldwater Institute.

Hamlin, A.T. (1981). *The University Library in the United States.* Philadelphia: University of Pennsylvania Press.

Handlin, O. and Handlin, M.F. (1971). *Facing Life: Youth and the Family in American History*. Boston: Little, Brown.

Hannah-Jones, N. (2021). Origins. In: *The 1619 Project: A New Origin Story* (ed. N. Hannah-Jones and The New York Times Magazine), xvii–xxxiii. New York: One World Publishing.

Hansen, W.L. and Weisbrod, B.A. (1969). The distribution of costs and direct benefits of public higher education: The case of California. *Journal of Human Resources* 4 (2): 176–191.

Harris, A. (2021). *The State Must Provide: Why America's Colleges Have Always Been Unequal—And How to Set Them Right*. New York: Ecco.

Harris, S. (1972). *A Statistical Portrait of Higher Education*. Report prepared for the Carnegie Commission on Higher Education. New York: McGraw-Hill.

Hart, J. (2022). Are we taking Gen Ed for granted? *Inside Higher Ed* (25 May). https://www.insidehighered.com/views/2022/05/26/addressing-disconnects-gen-ed-opinion (accessed 15 May 2023).

Harwarth, I., Maline, M., and DeBra, E. (1997). Women's colleges in the United States: History, issues, and challenges. U.S. Department of Education.

Hauptman, A.M. (1990). The tuition dilemma. Brookings Institution.

Heaven, W.D. (2023). Fear about ChatGPT among educators giving way to optimism. *Government Technology* (6 April). https://www.govtech.com/education/higher-ed/fear-about-chatgpt-among-educators-giving-way-to-optimism (accessed 19 May 2023).

Hemelt, S.W. and Stange, K.M. (2020). Why the move to online instruction won't reduce college costs. Brookings Institution.

Hemelt, S.W., Stange, K.M., Furquim, F., et al. (2018). Why is math cheaper than English? Understanding cost differences in higher education. NBER working paper 25314. National Bureau of Economic Research.

Henry, W.A., III. (1994). *In Defense of Elitism*. New York: Doubleday.

Herbst, J. (1980). The institutional diversification of higher education in the new nation: 1780–1820. *Review of Higher Education* 3 (3): 15–18.

Herbst, J. (1981). Church, state and higher education: College government in the American colonies and states before 1820. *History of Higher Education Annual* 1: 42–54.

Herbst, J. (1982). *From Crisis to Crisis: American College Government 1636–1819*. Cambridge, MA: Harvard University Press.

Herzberg, F., Mausner, B., and Snyderman, B.D. (1959). *The Motivation to Work*. New York: Wiley.

Hesburgh, T.M. (1984). The "events": A retrospective view. *Daedalus* 103 (4): 67–71.

Hispanic Association of Colleges and Universities. (2023). About Hispanic-serving institutions (HSIs). https://www.hacu.net/hacu/About_HSIs.asp (accessed 26 April 2023).

Hoffman, C.M. (1997). Federal support for education: Fiscal years 1980 to 1997. National Center for Education Statistics.

Hofstadter, R. (1952). *The Development and Scope of Higher Education in the United States*. New York: Columbia University Press for the Commission on Financing Higher Education.

Hofstadter, R. and Smith, W. (eds.). (1961). *American Higher Education: A Documentary History*, 2 vols. Chicago: University of Chicago Press.

Hughley, A.W. (2023). Submitted: The myth of shared governance in higher education. *College Heights Herald* (1 January). https://wkuherald.com/70262/opinion/submitted-the-myth-of-shared-governance-in-higher-education/ (accessed 25 May 2023).

Humphreys, D. (2023). Advancing civic learning in a fraught political environment. Paper presented at the Civic Learning and Democracy Engagement Leadership Forum, Baltimore, MD (15 March 2023).

Hunter, J.D. (1991). *Culture Wars: The Struggle to Control the Family, Art, Education, Law, and Politics in America.* New York: Basic Books.

Hurd, J. (1966). Did Webster really say it? *Dartmouth Alumni Magazine* (January): 22-23.

Hope Center for College, Community, and Justice. (2021). #RealCollege2021: Basic needs insecurity during the ongoing pandemic. Temple University.

Hutchins, R.M. (1936). *The Higher Learning in America.* New Haven, CT: Yale University Press.

Iafolla, R. (2023). College, university strike wave continues its swell into 2023. Bloomberg Law (24 January). https://news.bloomberglaw.com/daily-labor-report/college-university-strike-wave-continues-its-swell-into-2023 (accessed 9 May 2023).

Illich, I. (1970). *Deschooling Society.* New York: HarperCollins.

Iloh, C. (2016). Exploring the for-profit experience: An ethnography of a for-profit college. *American Educational Research Journal* 53 (3): 427–455.

Immerwahr, J., Johnson, J., and Gasbarra, P.V. (2008). The iron triangle: College presidents talk about costs, access, and quality. Report No. 08–2. National Center for Public Policy and Higher Education.

Inside Higher Ed. (2023). College presidents increasingly worried about perceived value of degrees. https://www.insidehighered.com/news/survey/college-presidents-increasingly-worried-about-perceived-value-degrees (accessed 8 June 2023).

Jaschik, S. (2022). Democrats, Republicans and higher education. *Inside Higher Ed* (25 October). https://www.insidehighered.com/quicktakes/2022/10/26/democrats-republicans-and-higher-education (accessed 21 April 2023).

Jencks, C. and Riesman, D. (1968). *The Academic Revolution.* New York: Doubleday.

Jesse, D. (2023). Presidents are changing their tune on free speech. *Chronicle of Higher Education* (3 May).

Jimenez, L., Sargrad, S., Morales, J., and Thompson, M. (2016). Remedial education: The cost of catching up. Center for American Progress.

Joa, C.Y., Gabay, I., and Ha, L. (2016). Does U.S. college students' social media use affect school e-mail avoidance and campus involvement? Paper presented at the 14th annual conference on Telecommunications and Information Technology in Louisville, KY (6–10 April 2016).

Jordan, D.S. (1903). *The Call of the Twentieth Century: An Address to Young Men*. Boston: American Unitarian Association.

Jordan, W.D. and Litwack, L.F. (1994). *The United States*. 7e. Upper Saddle River, NJ: Prentice Hall.

Kaplin, W.A., Lee, B.A., Hutchens, N.H., and Rooksby, J.H. (2020). *The Law of Higher Education*, 6e (student version). San Francisco: Jossey-Bass.

Karabel, J. (2005). *The Chosen: The Hidden History of Admission and Exclusion at Harvard, Yale, and Princeton*. Boston: Houghton Mifflin.

Kater, S.T. and Kisker, C.B. (2018). Redefining shared responsibility: Governance in the 21st century community college. In: *Understanding Community Colleges*, 2e (ed. J.S. Levin and S.T. Kater), 227–246. New York: Routledge.

Keller, G. (2008). *Higher Education and the New Society*. Baltimore, MD: Johns Hopkins University Press.

Kentucky Council on Higher Education. (1996). Annual accountability report series for Kentucky higher education.

Kerr, C. (1963). *The Uses of the University*. The Godkin Lectures at Harvard University. Cambridge, MA: Harvard University Press.

Kett, J.F. (1977). *Rites of Passage: Adolescence in America, 1790 to the Present*. New York: Basic Books.

Kezar, A.J. and Holcombe, E.M. (2017). Shared leadership in higher education: Important lessons from research and practice. American Council on Education.

Kisker, C.B. (2016). An inventory of civic programs and practices. In: *Civic Learning and Democratic Engagement*. New Directions for Community Colleges, no. 173 (ed. B. Ronan and C.B. Kisker), 13–22. San Francisco: Jossey-Bass.

Kisker, C.B. (2021). *Creating Entrepreneurial Community Colleges: A Design Thinking Approach*. Cambridge, MA: Harvard Education Press.

Kisker, C.B. and Kater, S.T. (2021). Contemporary challenges and opportunities in US community college governance. In: *Encyclopedia of Educational Innovation* (ed. M.A. Peters and R. Heraud). Singapore: Springer.

Kisker, C.B., Cohen, A.M., and Brawer, F.B. (2023). *The American Community College*, 7e. San Francisco: Jossey-Bass.

Klein, A. (2022). The great student swap. Brookings Institution.

Klein, N. (2007). *Shock Doctrine: The Rise of Disaster Capitalism*. New York: Metropolitan Books.

Knott, K. (2023). New, stronger gainful employment regs released. *Inside Higher Ed* (18 May). https://www.insidehighered.com/news/government/student-aid-policy/2023/05/18/new-stronger-gainful-employment-regs-released (accessed 22 May 2023).

Kochhar, R. and Sechopoulos, S. (2022.) How the American middle class has changed in the past five decades. Pew Research Center (20 April). https://www.pewresearch.org/short-reads/2022/04/20/how-the-american-middle-class-has-changed-in-the-past-five-decades/ (accessed 21 April 2023).

Kreger, J.L. (1998). An industrial designer in academe: Albert Kahn and the design of Angell Hall. *LSAmagazine* 21 (2): 4–12.

Kuttner, R. (1997). *Everything for Sale*. New York: Knopf.

Ladd, E.C. and Lipset, S.M. (1975). *The divided academy: Professor and Politics*. New York: McGraw-Hill.

Latif, D.A. and Grillo, J.A. (2001). Satisfaction of junior faculty with academic role functions. *American Journal of Pharmacy Education* 65: 137-143.

Lederman, D. and Mooney, C.J. (1995). Lifting the cloak of secrecy from tenure. *Chronicle of Higher Education* 41(31): 17–18.

Lemann, N. (1995). The great sorting. *Atlantic Monthly* 276: 84–100.

Lerer, L. and O'Brien, R.D. (2023). Pointing to anti-Israel protests, Republicans see "Woke Agenda" at colleges. *New York Times* (1 November). https://www.nytimes.com/2023/11/01/us/politics/republicans-israel-war-protests-college-campuses.html (accessed 1 November 2023).

Levin, J.S., Kater, S., and Wagoner, R.L. (2006). *Community College Faculty: At Work in the New Economy*. New York: Palgrave Macmillan.

Levine, A. and Dean, D.R. (2012). *Generation on a Tightrope: A Portrait of Today's College Student*. San Francisco: Jossey-Bass.

Lingenfelter, P.E. (2007). The financing of public colleges and universities in the United States. In: *Handbook of Research in Education Finance and Policy* (ed. H.F. Ladd and E.B. Fiske), pp. 651–670. New York: Routledge.

Lipson, S.K., Zhou, S., Abelson, S., et al. (2022). Trends in college student mental health and help-seeking by race/ethnicity: Findings from the national healthy minds study, 2013–2021. *Journal of Affective Disorders* 306 (1): 138–147.

Lombardi, J.V., Capaldi, E.D., Reeves, K.R., et al. (2003). The sports imperative in America's research universities. The Center for Measuring University Performance.

Love, I., Bragg, D., and Harmon, T. (2021). Mapping the community college baccalaureate: An inventory of institutions and programs comprising the current landscape. New America Foundation.

Lovett, B.L. (2015). *America's Historically Black Colleges and Universities: A Narrative History, 1937–2009*. Macon, GA: Mercer University Press.

Lovett, C.M. (1993). American professors & their society. *Change* 25 (4): 26–37.

Lucas, C.J. (2006). *American Higher Education: A History*, 2e. New York: Palgrave Macmillan.

Lyman, R.W. (1975). In defense of the private sector. *Daedalus* 104 (1): 156–159.

Lynch, M. (2018). Consequences of the new digital childhood. *The Tech Advocate* (6 July). https://www.thetechedvocate.org/consequences-of-the-new-digital-childhood/ (accessed 18 May 2023).

MacDonald, G.B. (ed.). (1973). *Five Experimental Colleges*. New York: HarperCollins.

Magner, D.K. (1997). Increases in faculty salaries fail to keep pace with inflation. *Chronicle of Higher Education* 43 (43): A8–A9.

"Making America Rich." (1998). *Wall Street Journal* (26 March), p. A22.

Marchese, T. (1997). Student evaluations of teaching. *Change* 29 (5): 4.

Marcus, L.R. (1997). Restructuring state higher education governance patterns. *Review of Higher Education* 20 (4): 399–418.

Mayhew, M.J., Rockenbach, A.N., Bowman, N.A., et al. (2016). *How College Affects Students: 21st Century Evidence That Higher Education Works*, 3e. San Francisco: Jossey-Bass.

McGuinness, A.C., Jr. (1995). Restructuring state roles in higher education: A case study of the 1994 New Jersey Higher Education Restructuring Act. Education Commission of the States.

McKeachie, W.J. (1963). Research on teaching at the college and university level. In: *Handbook on Teaching* (ed. N.L. Gage). Skokie, IL: Rand McNally.

McLachlan, J. (1974). The choice of Hercules: American student societies in the early 19th century. In: *The University in Society*, Vol. 2 (ed. L. Stone). Princeton, NJ: Princeton University Press.

McMaster, J.B. (1909). *A Brief History of the United States*. Sacramento: California State Series.

McPherson, M.S. and Shapiro, M.O. (1991). Keeping college affordable: Government and educational opportunities. Brookings Institution.

McPherson, M.S. and Shapiro, M.O. (2002). Changing patterns of institutional aid: Impact on access and education policy. In: *Condition of Access: Higher Education for Lower Income Students* (ed. D.E. Heller, pp. 73–96. Westport, CT: American Council on Education/Praeger.

Meriwether, C. (1907). *Our Colonial Curriculum, 1607–1776*. Washington, D.C.: Capital.

Merle, R. (2018). A guide to the financial crisis—10 years later. *Washington Post* (10 September). https://www.washingtonpost.com/business/economy/a-guide-to-the-financial-crisis--10-years-later/2018/09/10/114b76ba-af10-11e8-a20b-5f4f84429666_story.html (accessed 16 April 2023).

Mills, C.W. (1959). *The Sociological Imagination*. New York: Oxford University Press.

Mintz, S. (2023). Gen Ed: Its past, present and possible future. *Inside Higher Ed* (2 April). https://www.insidehighered.com/blogs/higher-ed-gamma/gen-ed-its-past-present-and-possible-future (accessed 15 May 2023).

Morris, L.V. (2010). The problem of defining and communicating quality in the 21st century. *Innovative Higher Education* 35 (5): 295–296.

Moynihan, D.P. (1975). The politics of higher education. *Daedalus* 104 (1): 128–147.

Murakami, K. (2020). College lobbying declined after earmarks. *Inside Higher Ed* (12 February). https://www.insidehighered.com/news/2020/02/13/higher-education-lobbying-has-declined-will-change (accessed 30 May 2023).

Musgrave, P. (2022). The season of our professorial discontent: The pandemic irrevocably changed the student-teacher relationship—and not for the better. *Chronicle of Higher Education* (9 June). https://www.chronicle.com/article/the-season-of-our-professorial-discontent (accessed 12 May 2023).

Nag, D., Gupta, A., and Turo, A. (2020). The evolution of university technology transfer: By the numbers. *IPS Watchdog* (7 April). https://ipwatchdog.com/2020/04/07/evolution-university-technology-transfer/id=120451/ (accessed 31 May 2023).

Nash, G.B., Crabtree, C., and Dunn, R.E. (1997). *History on Trial: Culture Wars and the Teaching of the Past*. New York: Knopf.

National Association of State Student Grant and Aid Programs. (2022). 52nd annual survey report on state-sponsored student financial aid. 2020–2021 academic year.

National Center for Education Statistics (NCES). (1970–2023). Digest of education statistics. U.S. Department of Education.

National Center for Education Statistics (NCES). (2004). National study of postsecondary faculty, 2003–2004. U.S. Department of Education.

National Center for the Study of Collective Bargaining in Higher Education and the Professions (NCCBHEP). (1984–1994). *Directory of Faculty Contracts and Bargaining Agents in Institutions of Higher Education* (vols. 1–21).

National Center for the Study of Collective Bargaining in Higher Education and the Professions (NCCBHEP). (2020). 2020 supplementary directory of new bargaining agents and contracts in institutions of higher education, 2013–2019.

National Institutes of Health. (2021). Marijuana use at historic high among college-aged adults in 2020.

National Student Clearinghouse. (2016). Time to degree – 2016.

National Student Clearinghouse. (2022a). Completing college: National and state reports.

National Student Clearinghouse. (2022b). Yearly success and progress rates: Fall 2015 beginning postsecondary student cohort.

Nespoli, L.A. and Gilroy, H.A. (1998). Lobbying for funds. *Community College Journal* 68 (4): 10–14.

Nevins, A. (1962). *The Origins of the Land-Grant Colleges and State Universities*. Washington, D.C.: Civil War Centennial Commission.

Newfield, C. (2008). *Unmaking the Public University: The Forty-Year Assault on the Middle Class*. Cambridge, MA: Harvard University Press.

Nichols, A.H. and Anthony, M., Jr. (2020). Graduation rates don't tell the full story: Racial gaps in college success are larger than we think. Education Trust.

Nisbet, R.A. (1971). *The Degradation of the Academic Dogma: The University in America, 1945–1970*. New York: Basic Books.

Nguyen. M.H., Hoang, S.B., and Ching, C.D. (2022). Supporting students of color at broad access colleges and universities: The potential of federal policy. In: *Unlocking Opportunity Through Broadly Accessible Institutions* (ed. G. Crisp, K.R. McClure, and C.M. Orphan), pp. 119–136. New York: Routledge.

Noble, S.U. (2018). *Algorithms of Oppression: How Search Engines Reinforce Racism*. New York: New York University Press.

O'Meara, K., Culpepper, D., Misra, J., and Jaeger, A. (2022). Equity-minded faculty workloads: What we can and should do now. American Council on Education.

Oettinger, A.G. (1969). *Run, Computer, Run: The Mythology of Educational Innovation*. Cambridge, MA: Harvard University Press.

Orlans, H. (1962). The effects of federal programs on higher education: A study of 36 universities and colleges. Brookings Institution.

Pace, C.R. (1979). *Measuring Outcomes of College: Fifty Years of Findings and Recommendations for the Future*. San Francisco: Jossey-Bass.

Palmer, J.C. and Romano, R.M. (2018). State fiscal support for community colleges. In: *Understanding Community Colleges*, 2e (ed. J.S. Levin and S.T. Kater), pp. 247–264. New York: Routledge.

Pappamihiel, N.E. and Moreno, M. (2011). Retaining Latino students: Culturally responsive instruction in colleges and universities. *Journal of Hispanic Higher Education* 10 (4): 331–344.

Paresky, P.B. and Abrams, S.J. (2021). Sex and politics on campus. *Psychology Today* (19 November). https://www.psychologytoday.com/us/blog/happiness-and-the-pursuit-leadership/202111/sex-and-politics-campus (accessed 8 May 2023).

Park, R. (1978). Some considerations on higher education of women. In: *The Higher Education of Women: Essays in Honor of Rosemary Park* (ed. H. Astin and W.Z. Hirsch). New York: Praeger.

Pascarella, E.T. and Terenzini, P.T. (1991/2005). *How College Affects Students: Findings and Insights from Twenty Years of Research*. San Francisco: Jossey-Bass.

Pell Institute for the Study of Opportunity in Higher Education. (2019). Indicators of higher education equity in the United States: 2019 historical trend report. Council for Opportunity in Education.

Peréz, Z.J. (2014). Removing barriers to higher education for undocumented students. Center for American Progress.

Perrin, A.J. and Gillis, A. (2019). How college makes citizens: Higher education experiences and political engagement. *Socius: Sociological Research for a Dynamic World* 5: 1–16.

Peters, W.E. (1910). *Legal History of the Ohio University, Athens, Ohio: Compiled from Legislative Enactments, Judicial Decisions, Trustee's Proceedings, etc.* Cincinnati, OH: Press of the Western Methodist Book Concern.

Pew Research Center (2019). The growing partisan divide in views of higher education. https://www.pewresearch.org/social-trends/2019/08/19/the-growing-partisan-divide-in-views-of-higher-education-2/ (accessed 21 April 2023).

Philanthropy News Digest. (2023). Large gifts to universities totaled nearly $4 billion in 2022 (6 January). https://philanthropynewsdigest.org/news/large-gifts-to-universities-totaled-nearly-4-billion-in-2022 (accessed 31 May 2023).

Pisacreta, E.D., Schwartz, E., Bond Hill, C., and Kurzweil, M. (2021). Federal policies for increasing socioeconomic diversity at selective colleges and universities. Ithaka S+R.

Public Broadcasting System (PBS). (2023, Mar. 18). Analysis: Who is Winning in the High-Revenue World of College Sports? (18 March). https://www.pbs.org/newshour/economy/analysis-who-is-winning-in-the-high-revenue-world-of-college-sports (accessed 24 April 2023).

Pusser, B. (2006). Higher education, markets, and the preservation of the public good. In: *Earnings from Learning* (ed. D.W. Breneman, B. Pusser, and S.E. Turner). Albany, NY: State University of New York Press.

Rashdall, H. (1936). *The Universities of Europe in the Middle Ages*. Oxford: Clarendon Press.

Reed, M. (2020). No more regional accreditors: A small change that portends much larger changes. *Inside Higher Ed* (16 September). https://www.insidehighered.com/blogs/confessions-community-college-dean/no-more-regional-accreditors (accessed 29 September 2022).

Reger, A. (2023). Budgets and endowments of flagship state universities. Connecticut General Assembly, Office of Legislative Research.

Rodenhouse, M.P. (ed.). (1997). *1997 Higher Education Directory*. Falls Church, VA: Higher Education Publications.

Rogers, C. (1969). *Freedom to Learn*. Columbus, OH: Merrill.

Romano, R.M. and D'Amico, M.M. (2021). How noncredit enrollments distort community college IPEDS data: An eight-state study. *The AIR Professional File* Fall: 15–31.

Romano, R.M. and Palmer, J.C. (2016), *Financing Community Colleges: Where We Are, Where We're Going*. Lanham, MD: Rowman and Littlefield.

Rosenberg, B. (2014). Shared or divided governance? *Inside Higher Ed* (28 July). https://www.insidehighered.com/views/2014/07/29/essay-new-approach-shared-governance-higher-education (accessed 25 May 2023).

Rothstein, W.G. (1992). Medical education. In: *The Encyclopedia of Higher Education* (ed. B.R. Clark and G. Neave). New York: Pergamon Press.

Roy, J. and Su, J. (2022). Trends in enrollment growth at public flagship universities. Urban Institute.

Rudolph, F. (1962). *The American College and University: A History*. New York: Knopf.

Rudolph, F. (1977). *Curriculum: A History of the American Undergraduate Course of Study Since 1636*. San Francisco: Jossey-Bass.

Rudolph, F. (1991). *The American College and University: A History*, 2e. Athens, GA: University of Georgia Press.

Rudolph, J., Tan, S., and Tan, S. (2023). ChatGPT: Bullshit spewer or the end of traditional assessments in higher education? *Journal of Applied Learning and Teaching* 6(1), 342–362.

Rutschow, E.Z., Cormier, M.S., Dukes, D., and Cruz Zamora, D.E. (2019). The changing landscape of developmental education practices: Findings from a national survey and interviews with postsecondary institutions. Columbia University, Teacher's College, Center for the Analysis of Postsecondary Readiness.

Sanchez, J.R. and Laanan, F.S. (1997). Economic returns to community college education. *Community College Review* 25 (3): 73–87.

Sandstrom, A. and Alper, B.A. (2019). Americans with higher education and income are more likely to be involved in community groups. Pew Research Center.

Schleifer, D., Friedman, W., and McNally, E. (2022). America's hidden common ground on public higher education: What's wrong and how to fix it. Public Agenda.

Schneider, H. and Schneider, C. (eds.). (1929). *Samuel Johnson: His Career and Writings*. New York: Columbia University Press.

Schuster, J.H. and Finkelstein, M.J. (2006). *The American Faculty: The Restructuring of Academic Work and Careers*. Baltimore, MD: Johns Hopkins University Press.

Schwartz, S. (2023). Map: Where Critical Race Theory Is Under Attack. *Education Week* (23 March). https://www.edweek.org/policy-politics/map-where-critical-race-theory-is-under-attack/2021/06 (accessed 23 April 2023).

Seaman, J.E. and Seaman, J. (2021). Digital texts in the time of COVID: Educational resources in U.S. higher education, 2020. Bay View Analytics.

Selingo, J. (2006). Tulane U. sets the pace for recovery. *Chronicle of Higher Education* (26 May). https://www.chronicle.com/article/tulane-u-sets-the-pace-for-recovery/ (accessed 31 May 2023).

Sheffey, A. (2021). 5 of the biggest for-profit colleges that were accused of defrauding their students. *Business Insider* (23 March). https://www.businessinsider.com/for-profit-colleges-alleged-fraud-student-loans-debt-cancelation-education-2021-3 (accessed 9 February 2023).

Shepherd, L.L. (2023). *Resistance from the Right: Conservatives and the Campus Wars in Modern America*. Chapel Hill, NC: University of North Carolina Press.

Shils, E. (1978). The academic ethos. *The American Scholar* 47(2), 165–190.

Shores, L. (1966). *Origins of the American College Library, 1638–1800*. Nashville, TN: George Peabody College.

Sinclair, U. (1923). *The Goose-Step: A Study of American Education*, 2e. Pasadena, CA.: Upton Sinclair.

Skinner, B.T., Burtch, T., and Levy, H. (2022). Variation in broadband access among undergraduate populations across the United States (EdWorkingPaper: 22-667). Brown University, Annenberg Institute for School Reform.

Slaughter, S. (1998). National higher education policies in a global economy. In: *Universities and Globalization: Critical Perspectives* (ed. J. Currie and J. Newson), pp. 45–70. Thousand Oaks, CA: Sage.

Slaughter, S. and Leslie, L.L. (1997). *Academic Capitalism: Politics, Policies, and the Entrepreneurial University*. Baltimore, MD: Johns Hopkins University Press.

Sloan, D. (1971). Harmony, chaos, and consensus: The American college curriculum. *Teachers College Record* 73 (2): 221–251.

Snow, L.F. (1907). *The College Curriculum in the U.S.* New York: Teachers College.

Snyder, T.D. (ed.). (1993). *120 years of American education: A statistical portrait*. National Center for Education Statistics.

Soros, G. (2008). *The new paradigm for financial markets: The credit crisis of 2008 and what it means*. Public Affairs.

South, S.J. and Lei, L. (2021). Why are fewer young adults having casual sex? *Socius* 7.

Stahler, G.J. and Tash, W.R. (1994). Centers and institutes in the research university: Issues, problems and prospects. *Journal of Higher Education* 65 (4): 540–555.

Stanton, Z. (2021). How the "Culture war" could break democracy. *Politico* (20 May). https://www.politico.com/news/magazine/2021/05/20/culture-war-politics-2021-democracy-analysis-489900 (accessed 12 April 2023).

State College and University Systems of West Virginia. (1997). *West Virginia higher education report card*.

Stolzenberg, E.B., Aragon, M.C., Romo, E., et al. (2020). *The American freshman: National norms fall 2019*. University of California, Los Angeles, Higher Education Research Institute.

*Students for Fair Admission, Inc. v. President and Fellows of Harvard College*, 600 U.S. (2023). https://www.supremecourt.gov/opinions/22pdf/20-1199_hgdj.pdf (accessed 10 July 2023).

Sublett, C. (2022). The access-equity dualism of online learning in community colleges. In: *Expanding Community College Opportunities: Access, Transfer, and Completion*. New Directions for Community Colleges, no. 198 (ed. C.C. White and A.B. Clayton), pp. 25–36. San Francisco: Jossey-Bass.

Substance Abuse and Mental Health Services Administration (SAMHSA). (2021). *Key substance use and mental health indicators in the United States: Results from the 2021 national survey on drug use and health*.

Teachout, Z. (2014). *Corruption in America: From Benjamin Franklin's Snuff Box to Citizens United*. Cambridge, MA: Harvard University Press.

Ten Brook, A. (1875). *American State Universities, Their Origin and Progress; A History of Congressional University Land-Grants*. Cincinnati, OH: Robert Clarke.

Texas Senate SB 17 (2023). https://capitol.texas.gov/tlodocs/88R/billtext/pdf/SB00017I.pdf (accessed 16 June 2023).

Thelin, J.R. (2019). *A History of American Higher Education*, 2e. Baltimore, MD: Johns Hopkins University Press.

Thelin, J.R. (2021). *Essential Documents in the History of Higher Education*, 2e. Baltimore, MD: Johns Hopkins University Press.

Thiederman, S. (1996). Creating victims to compensate victims. *Los Angeles Times* (27 November), p. B9.

Thomas, N. (2018). Educating for democracy in undemocratic contexts: Avoiding the zero-sum game of campus free speech versus inclusion. *eJournal of Public Affairs* 7 (1).

Thomas, N., Gismondi, A., Gautam, P., and Brinker, D. (2021). Democracy counts 2020: Record-breaking turnout and student resiliency. Tufts University, Jonathan M. Tisch College of Civic Life, Institute for Democracy and Higher Education.

Thwing, C.F. (1910). *A History of Education in the United States Since the Civil War*. Boston: Houghton Mifflin.

Tinto, V. (1975). Dropout from higher education: A theoretical synthesis of recent research. *Review of Educational Research* 45 (1): 89–125.

Tollett, K. (1975). Community and higher education. *Daedalus* 104 (1): 278–297.

Trostel, P. (2015). It's not just the money: The benefits of college education to individuals and to society. Lumina Foundation.

Trow, M.A. (1989). American higher education: Past, present, future. *Studies in Higher Education* 14 (1): 5–22.

Tumin, R. (2023). Title IX and the new rule on transgender athletes explained. *New York Times* (7 April). https://www.nytimes.com/article/title-ix-transgender-athletes-school-sports.html (accessed 1 November 2023).

Twenge, J.M., Sherman, R.A., and Wells, B.E. (2017). Sexual inactivity during young adulthood is more common among U.S. millennials and iGen: Age, period, and cohort effects on having no sexual partners after age 18. *Archives of Sexual Behavior* 46: 433-440.

U.S. Bureau of the Census. (1791). Return of the whole number of persons within the several districts of the United States, according to "An act providing for the enumeration of the inhabitants of the United States."

U.S. Bureau of the Census. (1864). Population of the United States in 1860; Compiled from the original returns of the eighth census, under the direction of the Secretary of the Interior.

U.S. Bureau of the Census. (2000). U.S. Census 2000.

U.S. Bureau of the Census. (2023). American community survey. https://data.census.gov/all (accessed 1 November 2023).

U.S. Department of Education. (2023). Higher education emergency relief funding: 2021 annual performance report.

U.S. Senate. (2012). For profit higher education: the failure to safeguard the federal investment and ensure student success.

University of Arizona. (1996). Measurable goals for undergraduate education.

University of Maryland, Advance Program for Inclusive Excellence and the Time Use Laboratory. (2017). Faculty time use study: An opportunity for institutions to better understand faculty work. https://www.uww.edu/documents/ir/University-Wide%20Surveys/Faculty%20Time%20Use/FINAL%20Summary%20Report-%20Faculty%20Time%20Study%202017%20Implementation.pdf (accessed 11 May 2023).

The University of the State of New York. (1996). Leadership and learning.

Valdivia, W.D. (2013). University start-ups: Critical for improving technology transfer. Brookings Institution, Center for Technology Innovation.

Vanderbilt University. (2015). The cost of federal regulatory compliance in higher education: A multi-institutional study. https://news.vanderbilt.edu/files/Regulatory-Compliance-Report-Final.pdf (accessed 15 May 2023).

Veblen, T. (1957). *The Higher Learning in America: A Memorandum on the Conduct of Universities by Businessmen*. New York: Sagamore Press. (Originally published 1918.)

Veysey, L.R. (1965). *The Emergence of the American University*. Chicago: University of Chicago Press.

Vine, P. (1997). The social function of 18th century higher education. *History of Education Quarterly* 16: 409–424.

Ward, I. (2023). Modern conservatism was born on college campuses. So why does the GOP hate them? *Politico Magazine* (4 September). https://www.politico.com/news/magazine/2023/09/04/conservatives-obsessed-with-college-campuses-00113755 (accessed 20 September 2023).

Washburn, J. (2005). *University, Inc. The Corporate Corruption of American Higher Education*. New York: Basic Books.

Wayland, F. (1850). Report to the Corporation of Brown University on changes in the system of collegiate education. Brown University.

Wechsler, H.S. (1997). An academic Gresham's Law: Group repulsion as a theme in American higher education. In: *ASHE Reader on the History of Higher Education*, 2e (ed. L.F. Goodchild and H.S. Wechsler), pp. 416–431. Needham Heights, MA: Simon and Schuster Custom Publishing.

Wechsler, H.S., Goodchild, L.F., and Eisenmann, L. (eds.). (2008). *ASHE Reader on the History of Higher Education*, 3e. Boston: Person Learning Solutions.

Weiner, D.I. (2015). Citizens United five years later. Brennan Center for Justice. https://www.brennancenter.org/our-work/research-reports/citizens-united-five-years-later (accessed 11 April 2023).

Wessel, D. (1998). The wealth factor. *Wall Street Journal* (2 April), p. A1.

Whitman, D. (2022). For-profit colleges and the myth of institutional equity. New American Foundation. https://www.newamerica.org/education-policy/reports/for-profit-colleges-and-the-myth-of-institutional-equity/ (accessed 9 February 2023).

Whitney, K.M. (2006). Lost in transition: Governing in a time of privatization. In: *Governance and the Public Good* (ed. W.G. Tierney). pp. 29–50. Albany, NY: State University of New York Press.

Williams, A. (2015). Move over Millennials, here comes Generation Z. *New York Times* (18 September). https://www.nytimes.com/2015/09/20/fashion/move-over-millennials-here-comes-generation-z.html.

Williamson, T.W., Hughes, E.S., and Head, P.L. (2018). An exploration of administrative bloat in American higher education. *Planning for Higher Education* 46 (2): 15–22.

Wolfle, D. (1954). *America's Resources of Specialized Talent. Report of the Commission on Human Resources and Advanced Training*. New York: HarperCollins.

Wolfle, D. (1972). *The Home of Science: The Role of the University*. New York: McGraw-Hill.

Ziomek, R.L. and Svec, J.C. (1995). High school grades and achievement: Evidence of grade inflation. ACT Research Report Series, 95–3. American College Testing Program.

Zywicki, T. and Koopman, C. (2017). The changing of the guard: The political economy of administrative bloat in American higher education. George Mason University, Antonin Scalia School of Law.

# Name Index

**A**

Abelson, S., 624
Abrams, S.J., 470, 628
Accrediting Commission for Community and Junior Colleges, 521, 605
ACT, 482, 605
Adams, J.T., 106, 108, 605
Adelman, C., 330, 366, 409, 520, 605
Alonso, J., 490, 605
Alper, B.A., 585, 631
Altindag, D.T., 528, 605
Ambrose, S.E., 27, 605
American Association of Colleges and Universities, 522, 605
American Association of University Professors, 139, 232, 502, 503, 504, 506, 512, 593, 605, 606
American College Health Association, 494, 606
American Council on Education, 472, 539, 540, 606
American Council on Education 1937, 166, 606
Anthony, Jr., M., 583, 628
Anti-Defamation League, 487, 606
Aragon, M.C., 633
Arum, R., 521, 606
Astin, A.W., 12, 319, 478, 484, 583, 606
Astin, A.W. 1977, 12, 292, 484, 606
Aussieker, B. 1975, 617

**B**

Barnett, E.A., 482, 607
Basis, V., 612
Bate, W.J., 18, 607
Baumol, W.J., 587, 607
Baum, S., 457, 472, 607
Beattie, I.R., 472, 607
Belfield, C., 519, 607
Betts, J.R., 333, 607
Birnbaum, R., 260, 607
Blackman, S.A.B., 587, 607

Blake, D., 451, 607
Blankstein, M., 511, 512, 607
Bledstein, B., 11, 124, 179, 185, 608
Bloom, A., 299, 608
Blumenstyk, K.G., 416, 608
Blundell, G.E., 513, 608
Bok, D., 408, 443, 608
Bond Hill, C., 629
Boorstin, D.J., 21, 608
Bouchey, B., 527, 608
Bowen, H., 12, 224, 233, 268, 269, 270, 284, 285, 291, 293, 294, 412, 608
Bowman, N.A., 12, 625
Boyer, E.L., 362, 408, 608
Bragg, D., 449, 624
Brawer, F.B., 12, 121, 240, 324, 361, 446, 447, 463, 464, 465, 506, 520, 522, 544, 547, 548, 551, 591, 623
Breneman, D.W., 204, 316, 317, 401, 561, 608, 609
Brinker, D., 634
Broome, E.C., 28, 29, 73, 126, 609
Brown, T.T., 452, 609
Bryant, J., 540, 609
Bureau of Labor Statistics, 432, 507, 609
Burke, C.B., 65, 609
Burtch, T., 529, 632
Busta, H., 549, 609
Butts, R.F., 35, 609

**C**

Campaign for Free College Tuition, 557, 609
Campbell, J.R., 334, 610
Capaldi, E.D., 624
Carnegie Commission on Higher Education, 204, 289, 291, 315, 610
Carnegie Council on Policy Studies in Higher Education, 300, 330, 610
Carnegie Foundation for the Advancement of Teaching, 204, 232, 239, 242, 610

## Name Index

Carnevale, A.P., 430, 457, 610
Castañeda, D.A., 513, 608
Census and Economic Information
    Center, 432, 610
Center of Education Policy
    Analysis, 500, 610
Centers for Disease Control and
    Prevention, 494, 611
Chambers, T.C., 591, 611
Chang, M.J., 319, 606
Cheah, B., 457, 610
Ching, C.D., 453, 628
Cho, K.S., 490, 613
Chronicle of Higher Education, 479, 514,
    540, 593, 611
Cineas, F., 503, 611
Clark, B.R., 118, 238, 239, 318, 320, 321,
    506, 611
Cochrane, D., 495, 618
Cohen, A.M., 12, 121, 240, 324, 361, 446,
    447, 463, 464, 465, 506, 520, 522,
    544, 547, 548, 551, 591, 623
College Board, 455, 481, 482,
    585, 611, 612
College Promise, 557, 612
Collins, C., 433, 612
Committee on the Objectives of a General
    Education in a Free Society, 242
Committee on Veterans Affairs, 194, 612
Community College Research
    Center, 528, 612
Complete College America, 445, 612
Conron, K.J., 472, 612
Cormier, M.S., 631
Cottom, T.M., 464, 465, 612
Crabtree, C., 9, 627
Crisp, G., 445, 453, 612
Crosta, P.M., 519, 607
Cruz Zamora, D.E., 631
Cuban, L., 371, 612
Culpepper, D., 628

### D

D'Amico, M.M., 573, 574, 613,
    630
Davenport, D., 429, 613
David, P., 416, 417, 613
Davis III, C.H.F., 490, 613
Dean, D.R., 12, 624
DeBra, E., 11, 619
DeFusco, J., 561, 613

Deloitte Center for Higher Education
    Excellance, 539, 613
de los Santos, A., 450, 613
DeSilver, D., 429, 441, 614
De Witte, M., 493, 613
Dexter, F.B., 28, 614
Doan, K.B., 472, 614
Donadel, A., 494, 495, 614
Donahue, P.L., 334, 610
Doran, E., 446, 614
Driscoll, K., 460, 614
Dukes, D., 631
Dunn, R.E., 9, 627

### E

Eaton, J.S., 420, 546, 614
Eckel, P.D., 260, 607
Economist Intelligence Unit, 430, 614
Education Trust, 463, 615
Eisenmann, L., 83, 636
Elliott, K.C., 537, 615
Emerson, R.W., 79, 615
Ewell, P.T., 418, 615

### F

Fay, M.P., 482, 607
Feldman, K.A., 12, 289, 578, 615
Filiz, E.S., 528, 605
Finkel, E., 568, 615
Finkelstein, M., 31, 80, 359, 360, 615
Finkelstein, M.J., 598, 631
Finley, A., 484, 615
Fischer, D.H., 14, 615
Fischman, W., 456, 457, 615
Flaherty, C., 512, 616
Flexner, A., 149, 172, 184, 616
Florida Senate SB 266, 533, 593, 616
Florida Senate SB 7044, 549, 616
Foley, D., 447, 616
Francis, P.C., 495, 616
Franklin, B., 25, 47, 616
Freire, P., 249, 532, 616
Friedman, W., 591, 631
Fry, R., 583, 616
Furquim, F., 619

### G

Gabay, I., 526, 622
Galston, W.A., 430, 616
Garbarino, J.W., 230, 231, 233, 234, 617
Gardner, H., 456, 457, 615

Garrett, S.D., 532, 617
Gasbarra, P.V., 591, 592, 621
Gaston, P.L., 2, 431, 524, 617
Gautam, P., 634
Gee, T., 490, 617
Geiger, R.L., 11, 12, 41, 114, 119, 128, 138, 173, 174, 175, 219, 275, 276, 288, 297, 395, 414, 415, 617
Giele, J.Z., 102, 617
Gilbert, C., 532, 617
Gillis, A., 586, 629
Gilroy, H.A., 392, 627
Gismondi, A., 634
Gledieux, L.E., 210, 617
Glickman, L., 434, 435, 617
Goldin, C., 448, 575, 618
Goldrick-Rab, S., 12, 495, 618
Gonzales, L.D., 120, 445, 618
Goodchild, L.F., 618
Goodchild, L.F., 83, 636
Gose, B., 457, 618
Grant, G., 244, 618
Gratz, E., 527, 608
Greenberg, D.S., 565, 618
Greene, J.P., 543, 618
Green, T., 412, 618
Grillo, J.A., 513, 623
Gulish, A., 610
Gupta, A., 563, 626

# H

Ha, L., 526, 622
Hamlin, A.T., 98, 99, 618
Hamrick, K., 447, 616
Handlin, M.F., 17, 619
Handlin, O., 17, 619
Hannah-Jones, N., 61, 518, 619
Hansen, W.L., 293, 619
Harmon, T., 449, 624
Harris, A., 11, 451, 619
Harris, S., 209, 212, 213, 619
Hart, J., 521, 619
Harwarth, I., 11, 619
Hauptman, A.M., 210, 398, 403, 617, 619
Haynes, L., 537, 615
Head, P.L., 541, 637
Heaven, W.D., 530, 619
Hemelt, S.W., 510, 528, 619
Henry III, W.A., 311, 619
Herbst, J., 19, 49, 63, 92, 96, 620
Herzberg, F., 360, 620
Hesburgh, T.M., 299, 620

Hispanic Association of Colleges and Universities, 452, 620
Hoang, S.B., 453, 628
Hoffman, C.M., 393, 620
Hofstadter, R., 49, 69, 113, 132, 136, 138, 620
Holcombe, E.M., 544, 545, 546, 622
Hope Center for College, Community, and Justice, 495, 621
Horn, A.S., 495, 616
Hoxie, J., 433, 612
Hughes, E.S., 541, 637
Hughley, A.W., 545, 620
Humphreys, D., 437, 620
Hunter, J.D., 436, 621
Hurd, J., 67, 621
Hutchens, N.H., 622
Hutchins, R.M., 183, 621

# I

Iafolla, R., 508, 621
Illich, I., 373, 621
Iloh, C., 461, 621
Immerwahr, J., 591, 592, 621
Inside Higher Ed, 436, 591, 621

# J

Jaeger, A., 628
Jaschik, S., 436, 484, 592, 621
Jencks, C., 64, 621
Jesse, D., 492, 621
Jimenez, L., 448, 622
Joa, C.Y., 526, 622
Johnson, J., 591, 592, 621
Jones, T., 537, 615
Jordan, D.S., 113, 622
Jordan, W.D., 9, 307, 622

# K

Kaplin, W.A., 12, 228, 230, 337, 338, 339, 340, 386, 387, 416, 491, 515, 516, 517, 596, 622
Karabel, J., 127, 622
Kater, S.T., 506, 545, 622, 623, 624
Katz, L.F., 448, 575, 618
Keller, G., 528, 591, 622
Kentucky Council on Higher Education, 418, 622
Kerr, C., 118, 165, 622
Kett, J.F., 133, 622
Kezar, A.J., 544, 545, 546, 622

Kisida, B., 543, 618
Kisker, C.B., 11, 121, 240, 324, 361, 446, 447, 449, 463, 464, 465, 485, 506, 520, 522, 544, 545, 547, 548, 551, 560, 566, 570, 590, 591, 622, 623
Klein, A., 555, 623
Klein, N., 560, 623
Knott, K., 538, 623
Kochhar, R., 432, 433, 623
Koopman, C., 543, 637
Kreger, J.L., 137, 623
Kurland, S., 527, 608
Kurzweil, M., 629
Kuttner, R., 191, 623

## L

Laanan, F.S., 412, 413, 631
Ladd, E.D., 221, 233, 623
Latif, D.A., 513, 623
Lederman, D., 353, 624
Lee, B.A., 622
Lee, J., 513, 608
Lei, L., 494, 633
Lemann, N., 213, 295, 624
Lerer, L., 488, 624
Leslie, L.L., 562, 632
Levine, A., 12, 624
Levin, J.S., 506, 624
Levy, H., 529, 632
Lingenfelter, P.E., 569, 624
Lipset, S.M., 221, 233, 623
Lipson, S.K., 494, 624
Litwack, L.F., 9, 307, 622
Lombardi, J.V., 116, 624
Love, I., 449, 624
Lovett, B.L., 11, 120, 157, 452, 624
Lovett, C.M., 78, 80, 624
Lucas, C.J., 19, 35, 624
Lyman, R.W., 314, 625
Lynch, M., 529, 625

## M

MacDonald, G.B., 244, 625
Magner, D.K., 346, 625
"Making America Rich", 306, 625
Maline, M., 11, 619
Marchese, T., 362, 625
Marcus, L.R., 380, 625
Marzullo, M.R., 612
Mausner, B., 360, 620
Mayhew, M.J., 12, 578, 583, 584, 625

McClure, K.R., 445, 453, 612
McFarland, L.L., 333, 607
McGuinness, Jr., A.C., 381, 625
McKeachie, W.J., 248, 625
McLachlan, J., 88, 625
McMaster, J.B., 9, 625
McNally, E., 591, 631
McPherson, M.S., 266, 557, 625, 626
Meriwether, C., 34, 36, 37, 41, 626
Merle, R., 432, 626
Milan, L., 447, 616
Miller, V., 532, 617
Mills, C.W., 534, 626
Mills, J., 543, 618
Mintz, S., 521, 522, 626
Misra, J., 628
Mooney, C.J., 353, 624
Morales, J., 622
Moreno, M., 532, 628
Morgan, D., 490, 613
Morris, L.V., 542, 626
Moynihan, D.P., 278, 314, 626
Mulvey, 503
Murakami, K., 554, 626
Musgrave, P., 514, 626

## N

Nag, D., 563, 626
Nash, G.B., 9, 627
National Association of State Student Grant and Aid Programs, 557, 627
National Center for Education Statistics, 627
National Center for Education Statistics, 355, 359, 510, 627
National Center for the Study of Collective Bargaining in Higher Education and the Professions, 627
National Center for the Study of Collective Bargaining in Higher Education and the Professions, 350, 508, 627
National Institutes of Health, 493, 627
National Student Clearinghouse, 450, 499, 627
National Study of Postsecondary Faculty, 510, 511
NCES *Digest*, 199, 278, 282, 313, 331, 332, 345, 390, 391, 411, 439, 471, 497, 498, 505, 552, 553, 581
Nespoli, L.A., 392, 627

Nevins, A., 115, 627
Newcomb, T.M., 12, 289, 578, 615
Newfield, C., 477, 627
Nguyen, M.H., 453, 628
Nichols, A.H., 583, 628
Nisbet, R.A., 533, 628
Nissen, P., 612
Noble, S.U., 489, 529, 628

## O

O'Brien, R.D., 488, 624
Oettinger, A.G., 371, 628
O'Meara, K., 512, 628
O'Neill, K., 612
Orlans, H., 276, 277, 628
Orphan, C.M., 445, 453, 612

## P

Pace, C.R., 290, 484, 628
Palmer, J.C., 551, 558, 570, 628, 630
Pappamihiel, N.E., 532, 628
Paresky, P.B., 470, 628
Park, R., 77, 629
Pascarella, E.T. /, 12, 288, 289, 412, 578, 629
Pell Institute for the Study of Opportunity in Higher Education, The, 499, 629
Peréz, Z.J., 475, 629
Perrin, A.J., 586, 629
Peters, W.E., 69, 629
Pew Research Center, 436, 629
Pheatt, L., 482, 607
Philanthropy News Digest, 567, 629
Pisacreta, E.D., 558, 629
Public Broadcasting System, 442, 629
Pusser, B., 584, 587, 630

## R

Rashdall, H., 19, 35, 630
Reed, M., 549, 630
Reeves, K.R., 624
Reger, A., 551, 630
Ridley, N., 610
Riesman, D., 64, 244, 618, 621
Robinson, T.N., 120, 445, 618
Rockenbach, A.N., 12, 625
Rodenhouse, M.P., 383, 630
Rogers, C., 249, 630
Romano, R.M., 551, 558, 570, 574, 628, 630

Romo, E., 633
Rooksby, J.H., 622
Rosenberg, B., 545, 630
Roska, J., 521, 606
Rothstein, W.G., 322, 630
Roy, J., 555, 630
Rudolph, F., 11, 23, 26, 29, 30, 32, 34, 35, 37, 50, 85, 96, 148, 158, 453, 630, 631
Rudolph, J., 530, 534, 631
Rutschow, E.Z., 520, 631

## S

Sanchez, J.R., 412, 413, 631
Sandstrom, A., 585, 631
Sargrad, S., 622
Schleifer, D., 591, 631
Schneider, C., 52, 631
Schneider, H., 52, 631
Schuster, J., 224, 233, 608
Schuster, J.H., 598, 631
Schwartz, E., 629
Schwartz, S., 435, 631
Seaman, J., 525, 631
Seaman, J.E., 525, 631
Sechopoulos, S., 432, 433, 623
Selingo, J., 560, 632
Shapiro, M.O., 266, 557, 625, 626
Sheffey, A., 464, 632
Shepherd, L.L., 216, 632
Sherman, R.A., 493, 635
Shils, E., 535, 632
Shores, L., 41, 632
Sinclair, U., 182, 632
Skinner, B.T., 529, 632
Slaughter, S., 562, 563, 632
Sloan, D., 89, 632
Smith, W., 49, 136, 138, 620
Snow, L.F., 38, 84, 86, 87, 632
Snyderman, B.D., 360, 620
Snyder, T.D., 19, 63, 110, 199, 267, 632
Sorber, N.M., 12, 617
Soros, G., 534, 633
South, S.J., 494, 633
Stahler, G.J., 417, 633
Stange, K.M., 619
Stange, K.M., 528, 619
Stanton, Z., 437, 633
State College and University Systems of West Virginia, 418, 633
Steele, P., 457, 607

Stolzenberg, E.B., 456, 633
Strohl, J., 610
*Students for Fair Admission, Inc. v. President and Fellows of Harvard College,* 427, 633
Sublett, C., 528, 633
Substance Abuse and Mental Health Services Administration, 493, 633
Su, J., 555, 630
Svec, J.C., 334, 637

**T**

Tan, S., 530, 534, 631
Tash, W.R., 417, 633
Teachout, Z., 429, 633
Tekin, E., 528, 605
Ten Brook, A., 22, 77, 633
Terenzini, P.T., 12, 288, 289, 412, 578, 629
Texas Senate SB 17, 593, 634
Thelin, J.R., 11, 589, 634
Thiederman, S., 311, 634
Thomas, N., 486, 491, 634
Thompson, M., 622
Thwing, C.F., 118, 634
Tinto, V., 484, 634
Tollett, K., 302, 634
Trostel, P., 585, 634
Trow, M.A., 24, 68, 93, 634
Tumin, R., 481, 634
Turo, A., 563, 626
Twenge, J.M., 493, 635

**U**

University of Arizona, 418, 635
University of Maryland, 511, 635
University of the State of New York, The, 418, 635
U.S. Bureau fo the Census, 19, 63, 313, 635

U.S. Bureau of the Census, 63, 439, 457, 635
U.S. Department of Education, 554, 635
U.S. Senate, 547, 635

**V**

Valdivia, W.D., 563, 635
Vanderbilt University, 542, 636
Van Der Werf, M., 457, 610
Van Noy, M., 2, 431, 524, 612, 617
Veblen, T., 182, 636
Veysey, L.R., 11, 636
Vine, P., 54, 636
Voelkl, K., 334, 610

**W**

Wagoner, R.L., 506, 624
Ward, I., 216, 636
Washburn, J., 562, 565, 636
Wayland, F., 90, 636
Wechsler, H.S., 83, 128, 618, 636
Weiner, D.I., 429, 636
Weisbrod, B.A., 293, 619
Wells, B.E., 493, 635
Wessel, D., 307, 636
Whitman, D., 461, 462, 465, 637
Whitney, K.M., 559, 637
Williams, A., 492, 493, 637
Williamson, T.W., 541, 637
Wolff, E.N., 587, 607
Wolfle, D., 103, 213, 276, 637
Wright, I., 450, 613

**Z**

Zhou, S., 624
Ziomek, R.L., 334, 637
Zywicki, T., 543, 637

# Subject Index

18-year-olds, number (decline), 317
1202 commissions, impact, 254–256

## A

Academe, essence (question), 533–534
Academic affairs, 259
*Academically Adrift* (Arum/Roska), 521, 577
Academic capabilities, criteria (usage), 128
Academic capitalism, 562–563
Academic career
  conceptualization, 31
  entry, 288
  initiation, 80
  part-time faculty assembly, 506–507
Academic department, rise, 138–139
Academic ethos, 533–535
Academic freedom
  concept, 225–228
  rights, challenges, 517
Academic Profile Test, 576
Academic research
  institution expectations, 512
  Pentagon support, decline, 219
Academic salaries, level (perception), 346
Academic studies, 371
Academic workforce, trend, 536
Accounting systems, uniformity, 160–161
Accreditation, 261–264
  function, 546–549
  process
    criticism, 548–549
    evolution, 383–384
  standards, setting, 384
  types, 168
Accrediting Commission of Career Schools and Colleges, 547
Accrediting Council for Independent Colleges and Schools (ACICS)
  failure, 463–464
  federal recognition, loss, 548

Activism, 214–219. *See also* Student activism
  appearance, 215
  campus activism, 468, 485–492
  community shortcomings, viewpoints, 244
  conservative political activism, 216
  decline, 303
  direction, 243
  focus, 343
  impact, 299
  political activism, promotion/engagement, 593
  protests, 217–218
  social activism, 3
  social justice activism, 299
Addams, Jane, 102
Administrative bureaucracies, rise, 165–167
Administrative costs, increase, 283, 542
Administrators, roles, 385–386
Adult Education Act, 253
Adult education, expansion, 207
Adulthood, entry (delay), 103
Affirmative action, 310, 334–341
  basis, 338
  cases, 477–478
  impact, 222
  limitation, 554
  plan, 478
Affirmative Action Executive Order, 285
African Americans, opportunities (constraints), 108
Age Discrimination Act (1967), 393
Age Discrimination Act (1975), 335–336
Age Discrimination in Employment Act (1967), 353
Agriculture and Food Research Initiative (AFRI), establishment, 444
Agriculture, research (development), 178

646  Subject Index

Alaska Native and Native Hawaiian Serving Institutions (ANNHs), 450–452
Alcohol consumption, presence, 493
Alien and Sedition Acts, 192
Alternative facts, publicizing, 429–430
American Association of Community Colleges (AACC), 382
American Association of Junior Colleges, occupational education (promotion), 382
American Association of State Colleges and Universities (AASCU), 521–522
  enrollments, 382
  formation, 203–204
American Chemical Society, organization, 140
American college president, authority, 48
American College Testing (ACT) College Readiness Benchmarks, 482
American College Testing (ACT) Program, 481–482, 576
  founding, 214
  student data, 333–334
*American Community College, The* (Kisker/Cohen/Brawer), 12
American Council on Education (ACE), 381–382
  college expectations, 161
American Economic Association, formation, 140
American Education Society, founding, 96
American Federation of State, County, and Municipal Employees, membership gains, 191
American Federation of Teachers, membership, 191, 233–234
American higher education
  history, supplementary reading, 11–12
  system, function, 465–466
  trends/events, 6e
  viewpoints, divergence, 436–438
American Historical Association, formation, 140
American Philological Association, founding, 140
American Psychological Association, 140
American Recovery and Reinvestment Act (ARRA), 427–428

American Rescue Plan and Higher Education Emergency Relief Funding (HEERF), 535–554, 585
American Revolution, birth, 18
Americans with Disabilities Act of 1990, 335, 377, 393
*America's Historically Black Colleges and Universities* (Lovett), 11, 452
Amherst College, department of education formation/suggestion, 86–87
Angell, James, 164
Antiwar demonstrations, 486–487
Applied sciences, teaching, 71–72
Armaments race, 188–189
Artistic/literary standards, impact, 180–181
Asian American and Native American Pacific Islander Serving Institutions (AANAPISIs), 450, 453
Asian American and Pacific Islander (AAPI) undergraduate enrollments, 453
Associates degrees, percentage, 324
Association of American Universities (AAU)
  formation, 114, 139
  library/laboratory requirements, 161
  Statement of Principle, publication, 139
Athletics, loss leader, 443
Atomic Energy Commission (AEC), formation, 274
Attitudes (changes), education (impact), 580–581
Automated instruction, 247

**B**

Baby Boomers, 492
  college attendances, 214
Bachelor's degrees
  attainment, 289
  completion rates, 453
  earnings, 582–583
    changes, 331t, 498t
  programs, admission requirements, 126t
Bachelor's of arts programs, admission, 124–125
Bank of the United States, founding, 59
Bargaining units, 544–545
Barnard, Frederick, 164

Basic Education Opportunity Grants (Pell Grants), authorization/creation, 212, 279–280, 401–402
*Beach v. University of Utah*, 341
Beat Generation, 492
*Bell Curve, The* (Murray), 490
Between-college effects, magnitude (reduction), 583–584
Biden, Joe (presidency victor), 430
*Bishop v. Aronov*, 349
Black Lives Matter (BLM) movement, initiation, 434, 487, 490
Black students, enrollment (encouragement), 211
Blum, Edward, 479
*Board of Regents v. Roth*, 228
*Bob Jones University v. United States*, 335
Bok, Derek, 408
Boosterism, importance, 92
Boyer, Ernest, 408
Brainpower, loss, 212–213
Brain Trust (Roosevelt), 142
Broadly accessible institutions
  agenda, 445
  competency-based courses/programs usage, expansion, 523
  comprehensive institutions, relationship, 202
  direct language training, 586
  enrollment, increase, 430–431, 438
  faculty
    positions, higher status (aspirations), 575–576
    teaching hours, changes, 137
  graduation rates, 453
  low-income student enrollment, 482
  marketing efforts/expenditures, increase, 536
  Minority-Serving Institution designation, 450
  state colleges, relationship, 121
  student
    acceptance, 482–483
    attendance, 501
    retention/support, client-centered approach, 465
Brown, Michael (killing), 434, 487
*Brown v. Board of Education*, 195, 308
Buchanan, James (Dickinson College student), 74

*Buchanan v. Alexander*, 515
Budget crises, 572
Bush, George H.W. (domestic spending reduction), 306
Business affairs, 259
Business Patent Procedures Act (Bayh-Dole Act), 562–563
Butler, Nicholas Murray, 164

## C

California State College and University System, 203
Campus
  activism, 468, 485–492
    increase, 488
    media attention, 489
  political polarization, 216
  violence, 495–496
Canal constructions, 59
Career
  changes, education (impact), 581
  preparation, 52
  security, 358
Career-ladder pattern, emergence, 80–81
Carl D. Perkins Vocational Education Act, 303
Carnegie Commission on Higher Education recommendations/publications, 250–252, 279, 300–301
Carnegie Corporation, 160
Carnegie Foundation for the Advancement of Teaching, 160–161, 456
  funding, 172
Catt, Carrie Chapman, 102
Center for Educational Policy Analysis (CEPA) analysis, 500–501
Center for the Study of Higher Education (Pennsylvania State University), policy issues, 418–419
Centrifugal curriculum, 152–154
Challenge Grants Amendments, 393
ChatGPT, usage, 530–531
Chronicle of Higher Education, position listings, 223
Church
  European institution, development, 20
  membership, growth, 60
*Citizens United v. Federal Election Commission*, 429

648  Subject Index

City College of New York, impact, 65
City University of New York (CUNY), academic standards/student outcomes (criticism), 445
Civic engagement, 468–469, 485–492
Civil corporation (college pattern), 91–92
Civil Rights Act of 1964, 196, 308, 393
 Title VII, 198, 284–285
Civil Rights Act of 1991, 377
Civil Rights Movement, 434–435
 college involvement, 214
Civil War, 9, 61, 68, 105–107, 147
 costs, 109
 excesses/profiteering, 107
Claremont McKenna College protests, 489
*Clark v. Claremont University*, 352
Classical curriculum, survival, 89
Classics
 abandonment, 245
 teaching, 34, 43
Class ranks, computation, 160
Clean Air Act, impact, 192
Clergyman, number (decline), 163–164
Coffman, Lotus, 164
Cognitive changes, education (impact), 579
Cognitive rationality, 320
*Cohen v. San Bernardino Valley College*, 515, 517
Cold War, impact, 187–189, 226, 274–275, 305, 394
Collaborative learning, 243
Collective bargaining (faculty), 230–235, 348–355, 507–510
College-affiliated learned societies, student engagement, 102
College Cost Reduction and Access Act, 453
College Education Examination Board, examinations development, 129–130
College Entrance Examination Board, promise, 150
College Football Championship (CFP), money (generation), 442
College Level Examination Program, College Board establishment, 246–247
College of New Jersey
 financial support, absence, 50–51

formation, 22
organization, 46–47
College of Philadelphia
 formation/founding, 23, 51, 95
 Scottish influence, 40
College of Rhode Island, formation, 22
College of the Western Reserve, 84
College of William and Mary
 chartering, 50
 organization, 45
 professorship, establishment, 38
 student, preparation/characteristics, 28
College of William and Mary,
 Christianization mission, 22
Colleges. *See* Colonial colleges
 access, 292
 debates, 474–475
 September 11 terror attack, impact, 476
 admissions requirements, broadening, 124–125
 attendance
  mobility, enhancement, 54
  personal/social benefits, 289–292
 attitudes/values, changes, 580–581
 autonomy, preservation, 250–251
 budgets/physical plants, weakness, 97, 99
 church auspices, impact, 100–101
 completion, racial equity gaps, 500–501
 confidence, loss, 300
 costs, Pell grants/Stafford (GSL) loans (proportion), 403t
 degrees
  linear path, 576
  prestige, 241
 development studies, 240–241
 discipline, 74
 discriminatory admissions criteria, 134
 economic/career changes, 581
 economic generator, 181
 entrance, pressure (increase), 126–127
 establishment, reasons, 24
 formation
  ease, 65–66
  increase, 62–63
 founding, 148
 four-year college/university, outcomes, 500f
 functioning, transparency, 548
 governance (emergent nation), 91–95

Subject Index    649

graduates, premium payment, 575
interdenominational freedom,
    emphasis, 48–49
learning/cognitive changes, 579
mission, 570
parental expectations, 28
patterns, 91–92
personal benefits, 578–584
population, expansion, 122
private donor dependence, 95
protests, 218
psychosocial changes, 579–580
royal charters, 48
savings accounts, contributions
    (state income tax deduction
    allowance), 398–399
small colleges
    diffusion, 57
    societal context, 57–62
students. *See* Underserved students.
    attraction, 69–70
    racial/ethnic composition, 470
teaching (profession), idea
    (development), 31
tuition, increases, 559
value, demonstration, 55
women, entry, 76–77
College-wide plans, integration, 374–375
Collegiate Assessment of Academic
    Proficiency, 576
Collegiate form, establishment, 13
Collegiate Learning Assessment
    (CLA+), 577
Collegiate life, codification, 132–133
Collegiate way, 454
Colonial colleges, 23t
    financing, 49–51
    outcomes, 51–56
    questions, 55–56
Colonial Era, 7
    colleges
        attendance, 26
        financing, 49–51
        outcomes, 51–55
    collegiate form, establishment, 13
    curriculum, 32–43
        requirements, 33–34
        viewpoint, 39
    faculty, presence, 30–32
    governance features, 44

institutions
    governance, 43–49
    growth/organization, 19–26
    integrated studies, commonness, 81
    population, increase, 14–15
    religious orientation, decline, 25
    slavery, 14–15
    societal context, 13–18
    statistical portrait, 19t
    students
        attendance, 26–30
        numbers, problems, 77–78
Colonial institutions, governing
    principles, 44–45
Colonies, social/cultural context, 15
Columbia, applicant requirements, 128
Columbia Bureau of Applied
    Social Research, study
    methodologies, 297
Commission on Financing Higher
    Education, 250
Commissions, coordination, 255
Committee of Ten, formation, 148–149
Common Core State Standards,
    adoption, 474
Communism, impact/opposition, 187–189
Community
    effort, impact, 92
    pride, 177
    service, 302
Community colleges. *See* Junior colleges
    consolidation/attraction, 324–325
    diversity, 206
    enrollment, variation, 446–450
    evolution, 385
    lower-division coursework, 447–448
    market share, factors, 447
    persistence/completion rates,
        derision, 449–450
    revenues, diversification/
        stabilization, 449
    transfer rates, 450
Community College Survey of Student
    Engagement (CCSSE), 484–485
Compliance, term (usage), 377
Comprehensive Health Manpower
    Training Act, 253
Comprehensive institutions,
    growth, 202–204
Comprehensive-school designation, 203

Comprehensive state universities,
    expansion, 208
Comprehensive universities
    characteristics, 443–446
    evolution, 202–203
Congressional appropriations, 563–564
Consolidation Era, 7, 305
    accreditation process,
        evolution, 383–384
    affirmative action, 334–341
    antidiscrimination laws,
        impact, 340–341
    Bachelor's degrees, earning
        (changes), 331t
    college costs, Pell grants/Stafford (GSL)
        loans (proportion), 403t
    community colleges,
        consolidation, 324–325
    compliance/penalties,
        assessment, 417–418
    costs, control, 405
    criticism, 407–409
    curriculum, 363–376
    degrees, awarding, 364–367, 409–413
    economic rewards, 410
    economic status, change, 427
    enrollments, increase, 330–331
    faculty, 343–363
        academic freedom/due
            process, 348–355
        academic life, 358–360
        demographics, shift, 344
        full-time faculty, average salary, 345t
        labor market, 346–348
        productivity, 355–360
        professionalization,
            cessation, 362–363
        tenure/collective bargaining, 348–355
        trends, 501
        unionization, 350t
    federal support, decline, 392–396
    finance, 388–406
    full-time students, aid (receiving), 399
    full-time workers, median annual
        earnings, 411f
        ratio, 411t
    funding, shifts, 389
    governance, 376–388
        institutional governance, 384–388
    government, distrust, 311–313
    graduate education, peak, 319–324
    health care sector, change, 307–308
    higher education
        assessment/accountability, 417–420
        associations, impact, 381–383
        criticism, 407–409
        federal/state influence, 377–381
        institutions, revenue, 390t
        system, changes, 325–327
    income inequality, changes, 306–307
    industry
        collaboration/connections, 416–417
        universities, symbiotic
            relationship, 415
    institutions, 313–327
        expenditures/cost controls, 402–406
        revenue, 390t
    labor force, changes, 306–307
    liberal arts colleges, uniqueness
        (maintenance), 316–319
    multiculturalism, impact, 367–369
    multicultural movement, 532
    opportunity, equality, 308–311
    outcomes, 406–420
    part-time faculty, impact, 360–362
    political polarization, increase, 426
    postsecondary students, aid
        (award), 400f
    private institutions, status, 314–316
    productivity, increase (attempts), 371
    professional education, degrees
        (increase), 319–324
    proficiency, enhancement, 333
    public health, change, 307–308
    public/private institutions, revenue
        percentage, 391t
    research
        federal government funding,
            increase, 394–395
        importance, continuation, 413–417
    revenue, sources, 389–392
    salaries, pace, 412
    social benefits, causal
        connections, 419–420
    societal context, 305–313
    statistical portrait, 313t
    students, 327–343
        access, 334–341, 420
        aid, 399–402
        behavior, changes/problems, 341–343

Subject Index 651

enrollment/diversity, 328–333
enrollment, race/ethnicity
  percentage, 329f
females, presence (percentage), 328f
proficiency, concern, 333–334
total enrollment, 328f
women, degrees (total), 332t
system goals, shift, 407
technology, instruction
  (relationship), 369–376
trustees/administrators, roles, 385–386
tuition, examination, 396–399
wages, 409–413
Consumer spending, changes, 432
Contemporary Era, 425
academic ethos, 533–535
academic life, faculty
  (dis)satisfaction, 513–514
accountability, 425
accreditation, function, 546–549
administrative bloat, 541–544
American higher education, viewpoints
  (divergence), 436–438
Bachelor's degrees, changes, 498t
campus
  activism, 485–492
  violence, 495–496
change, pressure, 589
civic engagement, 485–492
college/university
  accountability, 536–539
community colleges, enrollment
  (variation), 446–450
compliance, cost, 541–544
comprehensive universities,
  characteristics, 443–446
core curriculum, 520–522
critical/culturally responsive
  pedagogies, 532–533
criticism, 587–593
culture wars, 433–436
curriculum, 518–535
democracy, dysfunction, 426–430
developmental education, 518–520
disinvestment, 425
dissatisfaction, undercurrent, 436
distrust, 425
economy, changes, 430–433
enrollment, increase, 438, 440, 469
entrepreneurship, impact, 559–562

equity, 425
faculty, 501–518
  academic freedom, 514–518
  collective bargaining, 507–510
  demography, changes, 503–504
  due process, 514–518
  labor market, impact, 507–510
  productivity/expectations, 510–513
  salary, increase, 504–507
  tenure, 502–503
federal support, 550–555
finance, 549–572
four-year college/university,
  outcomes, 500f
free speech, issue, 485–492
fringe benefits, 504–505
full-time faculty, average salary, 505t
fundraising, increase, 566–568
governance, 535–549
  leadership, sharing, 544–546
graduate/professional education,
  growth, 457–460
higher education
  degrees, obtaining/drive, 574
  isomorphic tendencies, 441
  personal benefits, 578–584
  relative value,
    determination, 568–572
  societal benefits, 584–587
  system, function, 465–468
identity, changes, 433–436
institutions, 438–468
  presidents, roles, 539–541
land grant universities,
  characteristics, 443–446
learning
  assessment, 576–578
  resources, usage, 524–525
liberal arts colleges, significance
  (continuation), 456–457
liberal arts, occupational programs
  (integration), 448
libraries, relevance (change),
  524–525
market orientation, 536–539
middle class, reduction, 430–433
Minority-Serving Institutions (MSIs),
  diversity, 450–453
occupational specialization, 522–524
online learning, increase, 525–531

Contemporary Era (*continued*)
  outcomes, 572–593
    tracking, 573–574
  philanthropy, increase, 566–568
  politics, polarization, 426–430
  private colleges/universities, success, 453–456
  privatization, impact, 559–562
  proprietary institutions, parallel system, 460–465
  public institutions, revenue, 552t
  public/private institutions, revenue (percentage), 553t
  questions, 598–602
  race, impact, 433–436
  research
    funding, 564
    privatization, 562–566
  research universities, prominence/competition, 440–443
  societal context, 425–438
  state disinvestment, 550–555
  statistical portrait, 439t
  students, 468–501
    access/equity/inclusion, issues, 474–481
    activism, 489
    aid, 555–559
    attitudes/behavior, 492–494
    basic needs insecurities, 494–495
    course completion, 496–501
    degrees, total, 497t
    engagement, 484–492
    enrollment/diversity, 469–474
    females, percentage, 469f
    mental health, 494–495
    preparation/proficiency, 481–484
    total enrollment, 469f
    women, degrees (number), 497t
  technology, usage, 525–531
  threat, 2–3
  transformative changes, 590
  trends, 593–603
  tuition, increase, 555–559
  undergraduate enrollment, percent, 471t
Contingent faculty, salary (decrease), 507–508
Contract training, criticism, 449
Core curriculum, 520–522
Corequisite models, 520
Corinthian Colleges, implosion, 463

Cornell
  faculty members, voting trustee appointment, 234–235
  founding, 112
Cornell, Ezra, 115, 171
Corporate giving, search, 280
Correspondence courses, opening, 158
Cost-per-degree, 570
*Costs of Higher Education, The* (Bowen), 12
Council for Higher Education Accreditation
  accrediting bodies coordination, 383
  function, 549
Council of Guidance and Personnel Associations, appearance, 165
Council of Independent Colleges, membership, 382
Course-taking patterns, differences, 365–366
COVID-19 pandemic
  HEERF funding, 585
  impact, 468–469, 472, 487, 494–495, 508, 526–527, 551, 574
Credit-bearing developmental instruction, 404
Cultural heritage, preservation, 291
*Culture of Professionalism, The* (Bledstein), 11
Culture wars, 433–436
*Culture Wars* (Hunter), 436
*Curran v. Catholic University of America*, 352
Curriculum
  atomistic approach, 248–249
  barriers, 36–37
  broadening, 133–134
  centrifugal curriculum, 152–154
  changes, 88
    accretion, impact, 363–364
  classical curriculum, survival, 89
  classical texts/Christian doctrine, usage, 20
  colonies, 32–43
  core curriculum, 520–522
  course
    disparateness, 153
    division, 235–236
    derivation, 35
    development, 547
    evolution, 38–39, 368, 534

Subject Index   653

expansion, 83, 369
experimental colleges, impact, 244
fractures, reaction, 154
human capital formation,
    relationship, 236
issues, 376
origin, 36
parallel curriculum, impact, 87
precollege work, 241–242
prescribing, 153–154
redefinition, 320
stability, drawback, 33
transformation, 145
    faculty, impact, 145–146
uniformity, 86
variety, principles, 81–82
*Curriculum* (Rudolph), 32

**D**

Dartmouth College
    case, 4, 9, 66–67
    impact, 9, 67
Declaration of Independence, equality
    (qualification), 18
Defamation, accusation, 387–388
Deferred Action for Childhood Arrivals
    (DACA) students, in-state
    tuition, 475
*DeFunis v. Odegaard*, 338–339
Degree Qualifications Profile initiative
    (Lumina Foundation), 577–578
Delaware Cost Study, 510
Democracy, dysfunction, 426–430
Democracy Index (Economist Intelligence
    Unit), 430
Denominational college, 84
DeSantis, Ron
    classroom instruction law, 435
    laws, enactment, 592–593
de Tocqueville, Alexis, 16
Developmental programs,
    effectiveness, 519
Development, Relief, and Education for
    Alien Minors (DREAM) Act,
    475
DeVos, Betsy (employment rule
    rollback), 464
Digital badges, usage, 578
Disaster capitalism, 560
Disciplinary differentiation, 320–321

Discipline-based approaches,
    prioritization, 590
Discrimination
    claims, 222
    remedy, 310
Discriminatory policies, impact, 335
Disparate treatment/impact, 222
Distance education (expansion), computer
    (impact), 372–373
Distance learning, applications
    (development), 374
Distance programs, accreditation, 548
Diversity, equity, and inclusion (DEI),
    533, 539, 543
    criteria, 512
    initiatives, 478–479
    offices, ban, 593
Doctoral degrees, 575–576
    award pattern, 364–365
    number, award (increase), 458
    production, increase, 287–288
Doctoral-granting universities,
    exclusivity, 440–441
*Doherty v. Southern College of
    Optometry*, 335
Donations, size (increase), 171
"Don't Ask, Don't Tell" policy, repeal,
    427
"Don't Say Gay" bill, state board
    approval, 435
*Dow Chemical v. Allen*, 351
Due process clause, 228–230, 308
Duquesne University, tuition
    prepayment, 398

**E**

Earmarks, Congressional ban, 554
Economic changes, education
    (impact), 581
Economy, changes, 430–433
Education
    adult education, expansion, 207
    developmental education, 518–520
    ideals, challenge, 535
    modelling, 86–87
    state coordination, 254–258
    trends, evolution, 7
    value, 310–311
Educational entrepreneurship, 566
Educational institutions, need, 373

Educational Resources Information Center
    (ERIC), 276
Educational Testing Service
    (ETS), 214, 576
Education Amendments of 1972, Title IX,
    197–198, 211, 285, 401, 480
Education Amendments of 1974, 253
Education Commission of the States,
    decentralization conclusions, 381
Education Corporation of America,
    closure, 463
Education Management Corporation,
    closure, 463
Education Professions
    Development Act, 253
Educators, annual budget increases, 388
Electives, addition, 85
Eliot, Charles, 112, 147–148, 165
    inaugural address, 138
    tenure, 117–118
Emancipation Proclamation, 61
*Emergence of the American University, the*
    (Veysey), 11
Emergent Nation Era, 7
    colleges
        financing, 95–100
        governance, 91–95
    curriculum, 81–91
        old forms, collectivity, 89–90
    faculty, professionalization, 78–81
    higher education outcomes, 100–104
    institutions, 62–72
    questions, 103–104
    small colleges, diffusion, 57
    societal context, 57–62
    statistical portrait, 63t
    students
        characteristics, 72–78
        growth, 72–73
Emmanuel College, graduates, 21
Empirical core curriculum, 520
Employer-employee relationship, 342
Employment Retirement Income Security
    Act of 1974 (ERISA), 285
Endowments
    increase, 173–177
    receipts, proportion, 175
Energy Policy Conservation Act,
    impact, 192
Enlightenment dream, 139–140

Enrollments
    decoupling, 569–570
    doubling, 388
Enslaved people
    forced labor, 58
    freedom/emancipation, 61,
        106, 108, 196
Entrance exams, development, 143
Entrepreneurship
    allowance, 168–169
    impact, 559–562
    increase, 565
Equal Employment Opportunity Act, 285
Equality, goal (elusiveness), 311
Equal opportunity, 308–311
    application, 127
    cases, shift, 198
    civil rights, relationship, 194–198
    concept, antagonism, 311
    expansion, efforts, 196
    federalll regulations,
        compliance, 542–543
    limitations, 340
    progress, 196
Equal Pay Act, Title VII (court ruling), 352
Equal Protection Clause,
    violations, 428, 479
Equity, 474–481. *See also* Diversity, equity,
    and inclusion
    approach, 326
    commitment, 7–8
    Contemporary Era, 425
    digital equity, 529
    embracing, 492
    gaps, 482, 499–501, 526, 528
    gender equity, appearance, 211, 287
    idea, distance, 299
    LGBTQ+ student equity, 472
    Mass Higher Education Era, 263
    public discussion, 437–438
    questioning, 269
    racial equity, 298, 310
    racial/socioeconomic equity gaps, 469
    resource equity, improvement, 537
    student equity, attention, 5
Equity-oriented institutions, 451
*Essential Documents in the History of Higher
    Education* (Thelin), 11
Ethnicities. *See* Underserved races/
    ethnicities

Subject Index 655

Executive Order 11375 (Johnson), 197
Exit tests, imposition, 367
Extramural influence, progression, 376–377
Extrinsic demands, impact, 571

**F**

Facilities maintenance, 547
Faculty
 academic freedom, 348–355, 514–518
 academic life, 358–360
 academic life, (dis)satisfaction, 513–514
 activities, justification, 357
 affirmative action, impact, 222
 arrogance, 362–363
 autonomy, 135, 359–360
 average age, 344
 bureaucratization, resistance, 166
 collective bargaining, 230–235, 348–355, 507–510
 compensation, 272
 continuing contracts, right, 229–230
 demographics, shift, 344
 demography, changes, 220, 503–504
 disciplinary commitment, problem, 79–80
 diversification, 344
 due process, 228–230, 348–355, 514–518
 expectations, 510–513
 exploitation, rationalization, 99
 fringe benefits, 504–505
 full-time faculty, average salary, 345t
 groups, moves (countering), 509–510
 guild perspective, 363
 incentive plans, 347–348
 labor market, 346–348
 militancy, 232–233
 part-time faculty, impact, 360–362, 506–507
 pay (erosion), inflation (impact), 271–272
 preparation, expectations, 346–347
 presence (colonies), 30–32
 productivity, 355–358, 510–513
 definitions, modification, 343
 professionalism, trend, 360–361
 professionalization, 78–81, 140
  advancement, 224
  approach, 5, 234–235
  cessation, 362–363
 contribution, 78–79
 increase, 141–142
 ranking, practice, 141
 research interest, 297–298
 sabbatical leaves, 137
 salary, 220–225, 504–507
  increase, 345
  inflation-adjusted dollar decline, 345
  inflation rate, contrast, 282–283
  sources, 221–222
 sovereignty, 545
 student evaluation, 362
 supply and demand, equilibrium, 347
 tenure, 228–230, 348–355, 502–503
 unionization, 230–231, 350t
 work engagement, 512–513
Faculty of color, number (increase), 504
Family income, attendance patterns (correlation), 210
Federal Direct Students Loans, 393
Federal Family Education Loans, 392–393
Federal government, power (growth), 59
Federal Interagency Committee on Education, racial/ethnic group status, 309
Federal Reserve, establishment, 107
Federal/state employees, organizing right, 230–231
Federal student aid, provision, 377
Federal tax deferrals, availability, 398–399
Federal Trade Adjustment Assistance for Community College and Career Training (TAACCCT) grant program, 553–554
Federal Trade Commission, establishment, 107
Fee-for-service contracts, 562
Financial sector bubble, 559
Financing
 colonial colleges, 49–51
 emergent nation colleges, 95–100
 patterns, 265
First-year students, institutional expenditures/median parental income, 294t
Fiscal accountability, 547
*Fisher v. University of Texas at Austin* (Fisher I) (Fisher II), 478
*Five Experimental Colleges* (MacDonald), 244

*Florida ex rel. Hawkins v. Board of Control*, 195
Floyd, George (killing), 434, 486, 487
Forever GI Bill, 476
Formula budgeting, 569
For-profit colleges, faculty (hiring/firing), 461–462
For-profit institutions
  evaluation, problems, 547–548
  regulation, 465
Foundations
  funds, attraction, 173
  prominence, increase, 170–171
Four-year college/university, outcomes, 500f
Four-year program, abandonment, 90
Four-year residential college experience, value, 131–132
Frankling, Benjamin (College of Philadelphia organization), 47
*Franks v. Bowman*, 338
Fraternities, formation, 76
Free elective system, 366
Free market, federal government enhancement, 66
Free speech, issue, 485–492
Free Speech Movement, 215
Full-time community college instructors, salary/fringe benefits, 357
Full-time equivalent (FTE) enrollments, 561–562
Full-time equivalent (FTE) students, basis, 569
Full-time equivalent (FTE) students to FTE faculty, ratio, 355–356
Full-time faculty
  average salary, 345t, 505t
  salaries, increase, 223–224
Full-time instructors, work (time allotment), 355
Full-time students
  aid, receiving, 399
  undergraduate FTE study body, 452
Full-time tenured faculty, 502
Full-time, tenure-track positions, availability (decrease), 507
Full-time workers, median annual earnings, 411f, 582f
  ratio, 411t, 581t
Fundraising
  campaigns, 95–96
  increase, 566–568
  systematic fundraising efforts, 171–172

**G**

*Garcetti v. Ceballos*, 516
Garner, Eric (killing), 434
GateWay, 564
General education (GE)
  applications, 155
  integrative approach, 522
  problems, 154
  requirements, 520–521
  term, usage, 242
General Education Board
  endowment stimulation, 173
  generosity, 172
*Generation on a Tightrope* (Levine/Dean), 12
Generation Z, characteristic, 492–494
Georgia Female College, 77
Germany, American college graduates travel, 79
GI Bill. *See* Servicemen's Readjustment Act
Gilman, Daniel, 112, 164
Goals 2000: Educate America Act, 377
Governance
  Colonial Era, features, 44
  Consolidation Era, 376–388
  Contemporary Era, 535–549
  forms, 94–95
  leadership, sharing, 544–546
  pattern, 92–93
  University Transformation Era influences, relationship, 167–169
Governing boards
  composition/oversight, 162–163
  decisions, 166–167
  rhetoric/reality, 256–257
Government, distrust, 311–313
Grade point averages (GPAs), computation, 160
Graduate education
  growth, 457–460
Graduate education, status, 319–324
Graduate Record Examination (GRE)
  installation, 129–130
  recipients, 483
  scores, 483–484

Graduates, public influence, 53
Graduate study/research, adoption, 118
Grammar, memorization/analogical reasoning, 40
*Gratz v. Bollinger*, 477
Gray, Asa, 103
Great Books (St. John's College), 122–123
Great Depression, 133, 200
  higher education financing, suffering, 175–176
Greatest Generation, 492
Great Recession, 2, 426, 431, 446, 473, 550–551
  economic recovery, 428
  unemployment, increase, 431–432
Great Resignation, 514
Greek, instruction/study, 17, 28, 34, 37, 47, 73, 83
Greely, horace, 58
*Grutter v. Bollinger*, 477
Guaranteed Student Loans, availability/history, 207, 400
Gun violence, theme (recurrence), 496

# H

Hall, G. Stanley, 112
Hamas attacks, college leader responses, 488
Harding, Warren G., 193
*Hardy v. Jefferson Community College*, 516
Harper, William Rainey, 135–136, 164
Harvard University
  disputes, usage, 42
  elective system, universality, 115–116
  establishment, 21–22
  gifts, 567
  money, receiving, 50
  state investment, 96
  student, preparation/characteristics, 28
Hatch Act, passage, 178
Hate speech, increase, 487–488
Health care
  establishment, 433–434
  sector, change, 307–308
Health Professions Educational Assistance Act, 253
Hebrew, instruction, 17
Henry, Henry, 102
Hierarchical management systems, development, 163

Higher education. *See* American higher education
  assessment/accountability, 417–420
  associations, impact, 381–383
  benefits, 409
  "Bridge to Nowhere," 445–446
  change, research emphasis (impact), 296
  charitable foundation support, 280–281
  conception, disaffection, 109–110
  conflicting demands, balance, 568–572
  constraint, Civil War (impact), 9
  context, shift, 312–313
  contributions, 586
  costs
    increase, 405
    reduction, desire, 380
  enrollments, expansion, 208
  expenditures, 285–286
  federal expenditures, increase, 267
  federal/state influence, 377–381
  federal support, 273–280
    decline, 392–396
  finances, increase, 264
  funds, search, 550
  governance, 161–169
    approaches, 545–546
  history, study (framework), 1, 3
  institutions
    expenditures, 278t
    Republican distrust, 436–437
    revenue, 390t
    voluntary support, 282t
  insulation, decision, 3
  isomorphic tendencies, 441
  labor market, difference, 271
  mass higher education, 187
    statistical portrait, 199t
  media narratives, relationship, 437–438
  National Center for Education Statistics qualification, 10
  national foundation, debate, 277–278
  occupational groups, association, 113
  outcomes (emergent nation), 95–100
  pay differential, 506
  personal benefits, 578–584
  privatization, 559–560
  professional preparation, relationship, 100
  property, value (increase), 264–265
  public good contribution, 586–587

658   Subject Index

Higher education (*continued*)
  public institutions, revenue, 552t
  purposes, objectives (sets), 289–290
  relative value, determination, 568–572
  resources, coordination
    (improvement), 255
  secular governance, increase, 161–162
  shifts, increase, 110
  social role, 310–311
  societal benefits, 584–587
  societal outcome, 291–292
  state disinvestment, 550–555
  student interest, 334
  support, sources, 264–267
  system
    changes, 325–327
    cohesion/diversity, 466–467
    function, 465–468
    growth, 169
    medium of exchange, 326
  total expenditures, increase, 283–284
  White students, majority, 470
  worth, 293
Higher Education Act (1965), 207, 254, 393, 451–452
Higher Education Act amendments (1972), 462–463
Higher Education Facilities Act, 253
Higher Education Opportunity Act, 538
  net tuition online posting, 455–456
Higher Education Price Index, Consumer Price Index (relationship), 403
Higher Education Report Card, creation, 418
High schools
  curriculum (dictation), colleges (impact), 149
  enrollments, growth, 150
  student achievement, discrepancies, 482–483
Hispanic/Latinx students, enrollment (encouragement), 211
Hispanic-Serving Institutions (HSIs), 450
Historically Black Colleges and Universities (HBCUs), 4, 8, 119, 450–451
  basic skills, programs (development), 157
  comprehensive-school designation, impact, 203
  development/evolution, 120

penalization, delay, 393
student
  enrollment, 120
  involvement, 214
Historically underserved races/ethnicities.
  *See* Underserved races/ethnicities
Holistic education, 242
Holistic evaluation, notion, 129
Holistic studies, capacity (reduction), 319
Homestead Act (1862), 59, 106
Honors programs, introduction, 158
House Un-American Activities Committee, hearings, 193
Housing bubble, 559
*How College Affects Students* (Mayhew), 578–579
Human development, college change, 103
Hurricane Katrina, impact, 560
Hutchins, Robert, 164, 183, 226

I

Identity, changes, 433–436
Immigration laws, impact, 189
Income
  inequality, changes, 306–307, 432–433
  spreading, Internal Revenue Service ruling, 398
*In Defense of Elitism* (Henry), 311
Indigenous population, civilizing (idea), 25
Indigenous students, enrollment (encouragement), 211
Individual mobility, emphasis, 101–102
Industrial competitiveness, importance, 416
Industrialists, excesses, 107–108
Industrialization, triumph, 106
Industrial production, shift, 190
Inflation rate, faculty salaries (contrast), 282–283
Information technology, results, 375–376
Institute for Democracy and Higher Education, registration/voting behavior data, 486
Institutional accountability, 588–589
Institutional administration, rise, 138–139
Institutional aid, impact, 558
Institutional autonomy, 10
  academic freedom, contrast, 515–516
  American higher education history, 546
  boundaries, 139

compromise, 384
erosion, 602
federal interferences, questions, 176
government, impact, 286
incursions, 593, 599
preservation, 385–386
traditions, 592
Institutional conduct, influence, 167–168
Institutional expenditures, inflation (relationship), 402–403
Institutional functioning, raising, 172
Institutional functions, percentage allocations (differences), 269
Institutional governance, student participation scope (expansion), 261
Institutional liability, issue, 387
Institutions
  administrative structure division, 259
  admission, competition, 474
  autonomy, maintenance, 93
  building, growth, 64
  commonality, 440
  competition, 116, 473
  comprehensive institutions, growth, 202–204
  conduct, public (influence), 257
  curriculum, transformation, 145
  differences, 227
  efficiency (index), 267–271
  emergent nation, 62–72
  enrollments, growth, 143
  entrepreneurship, allowance, 168–169
  establishment
    religious groups, impact, 65
    states, impact, 68
  expansion, 201–202
  expenditures/cost controls, 402–406
  faculty members, association, 348–349
  for-profit institutions, evaluation (problems), 547–548
  governance, 43–49
    faculty, role, 139
  growth/organization (colonies), 19–26
  growth/spread, 70, 119
  higher education institutions, revenue, 390t
  institutional governance, 384–388
  post-tenure review, 354–355
  public institutions, revenue, 552t
  public/private institutions, revenue percentage, 391t
  reclassification, 446–447
  research institutions, growth, 114
  revenue sources, 265, 267
  self-reliance, development, 373
  undergraduate/graduate courses, 239t
  voluntary support, 282t
Instruction
  conditions, 248
  evolution, 90–91
  forms, impact, 247–248
Instructional efficiency, problem, 375
Instructional forms, variations (spread), 159
Instructional reformation, atomistic approach, 248–249
Instructors, student evaluations, 370
Integrated Postsecondary Education System (IPEDS) reports, 573, 576
Intercollegiate athletics, emergence, 132
Intercollegiate sports, 4
Interdenominational freedom, emphasis, 48–49
Interdisciplinary courses, 154–155
Interstate Commerce Act, 107
Inventions/patents, commercialization, 563
IQ tests, usage, 213
Isolated community, virtue (belief), 30
ITT Technical Institute, implosion, 463

## J

Jet Propulsion Laboratory (California Institute of Technology), 297
Jim Crow laws, 120
Job/skill upgrading, technical training (popularity), 332–333
John C. Green School of Science (Princeton), 125
Johns Hopkins
  research, commitment, 144–145
  School of Political Science, establishment, 142
Johnson, Lyndon B., 196–197
Johnson, Samuel, 18
Joliet Junior College, emergence, 121
Jordan, David Starr, 164
Junior colleges
  emergence, 121
  problems, 206

## Subject Index

### J

Junior-level faculty appointments, 221–222
Just-in-time resources, usage, 527

### K

*Kanaly v. State of South Dakota*, 378
Keller Plan, 247
*Kelm v. Carlson*, 336–337
Kent State University, Ohio National Guard shooting, 216–217
Kentucky General Assembly, higher education accountability process mandate, 418
Kerr, Clark, 244, 252, 300
*Keyishian v. Board of Regents*, 228
King, Jr., Martin Luther (moral universe), 433–434
King's College
  formation, 22
  royal charter, receiving, 47
  student, preparation/characteristics, 28
Knowledge
  generation, 588
  university product, 236
Korean War, 192, 213
Ku Klux Klan, racism/violence, 192–193

### L

Labor force
  changes, 189–191, 306–307
  competition, shift, 190
Labor market
  bifurcation, 507
  difference, 271
  impact, 507–510
  inequities, 583
Labor unions, power/backlash, 191
Lafayette School of Mines, 71
Land, geographic openness, 17
*Land-Grant Colleges and the Reshaping of American Higher Education, The* (Geiger/Sorber), 12
Land grant universities, characteristics, 443–446
Latin, instruction/study, 28, 34, 41, 47, 73, 83
Latinx/Hispanic students. *See* Hispanic/Latinx students
*Law of Higher Education, The* (Kaplin), 12
Lawrence Livermore Laboratory (University of California), 297
Lawrence Scientific School, admission requirements, 125
Leadership, governance (sharing), 544–546
Learning
  assessment, 576–578
  changes, education (impact), 579
  freedom, concept, 152–153
  process, 370
Learning management systems (LMS), usage, 529
Learning resources, usage, 524–525
*Leftwich v. Harris-Stowe College*, 353
*Levin v. Harleston*, 351
LGBTQ+ student
  community, 514, 583
  equity, 472
  identification, 495
Liberal arts colleges
  Carnegie Commission definition, 204
  direction, change, 204–206
  excess capacity, 318
  faculty, time allotment (difference), 318–319
  number, decrease, 204–205
  return on investment, 457
  selectivity, 317–318
  significance, continuation, 456–457
  uniqueness, maintenance, 316–319
Liberal arts emphasis, continuation, 180–181
Liberal conspiracy, proof, 488
Liberal propaganda, teaching (Republican belief), 592
Libraries
  archive function, 55
  budgets, reduction, 405
  relevance, change, 524–525
Lincoln, Abraham, 61
Literacy rates, changes, 474
Lobbying Disclosure Act (1995), 382–383
Lobbying efforts, acceleration, 554
Lost Generation, 492
Louisiana Purchase, 57–59
Lowell, A. Lawrence, 164, 165
Loyalty, concepts, 156
Lumina Foundation, Degree Qualifications Profile initiative, 577–578

### M

Manifest Destiny, idea, 61
Marginalized populations, 450, 590
Marginalized students, 588
Marshall Plan, The, 188
Martin, Trayvon (killing), 434
Massachusetts Institute of Technology (MIT)

Subject Index        661

military connections, 297
organization, 113–114
Mass Higher Education Era, 7, 187
  academic freedom, concept, 225–228
  benefits, inequality, 293
  campus
    changes, 214
    political polarization, 216
  Carnegie Commission on
      Higher Education
      recommendations, 250–252
  civil rights, importance, 194–198
  Cold War, impact, 187–189
  college access, 292
  colleges
    attendance, personal/social
      benefits, 289–292
    effects, differences, 292–295
  communism, impact, 187–189
  community colleges, diversity, 206
  comprehensive institutions,
      growth, 202–204
  criticism, 298–303
  curriculum, 235–249
    forces, 239–246
  degrees, award, 321
  degrees, number (changes), 286–289
  economic prosperity, 189–191
  education, state coordination, 254–258
  employer expectations, 241
  enrollment, increase, 286–287
  environmental concerns, 191–194
  equal opportunity cases, 198
  equal opportunity, changes, 194–198
  expenditures, rise, 282–283
  faculty, 219–235
    collective bargaining, 230–235
    demography/salary, 220–225
    tenure/due process, 228–230
  finance, 264–286
  higher education
    federal support, 273–280
    institutions, expenditures, 278t
    institutions, voluntary support, 282t
    support, sources, 264–267
  inauguration, 105
  income, schooling
      (relationship), 288–289
  innovations, 246
  institutions
    accreditation, 261–264
    changes, 198–208
  efficiency (index), 267–271
  expenditures, 294t
  founding, 202
  governance, 249–264
  management, 258–261
  periphery, 207–208
  shifts, 207–208
  undergraduate/graduate courses, 239t
  instruction innovations, 246
  instruction, innovations, 246–249
  junior colleges, problems, 206
  labor force, changes, 189–191
  liberal arts colleges, direction
      (change), 204–206
  outcomes, 286–303
  philanthropy, increase, 280–282
  private junior colleges, problems, 206
  private/public universities, current-fund
      revenue (percentage), 266t
  product development, 414
  productivity, technological adoptions
      (impact), 268
  research, importance
      (contention), 295–298
  research universities, increase, 200–201
  science/humanism, political dimensions
      (reversal), 237
  social concerns, 191–194
  societal context, 187–198
  staff salaries, 271–274
  statistical portrait, 199t
  student access/activism, 208–209
  students
    access, increase, 208–214
    activism, increase, 208, 214–219
    first-year students, institutional
      expenditures/median parental
      income, 294t
  trends, 187–188
  tuition, increase, 396
Master Plan for Higher Education
    (California), 252, 444
Master's degrees, award
  increase, 458–459
  pattern, 364–365
Master's degrees in business,
    increase, 459–460
Matriculation Act (1986), 337
McCarran Internal Security Act, 193
McCarran-Walter Immigration Act,
    193
McCarthyism, spread, 225–226

McCarthy, Joseph (anti-communist campaign), 193–194
*McLaurin v. Oklahoma State Regents for Higher Education*, 195
*McLendon v. Morton*, 229
"Mechanical" philosophy, 47
Median starting salaries, differences, 410–412
Medical Library Assistance Act, 253
Medical schools, freestanding status, 322
Mental/moral discipline, importance, 180–181
Merit-based grants, 550
Miami Dade College, endowment, 568
Michigan Institute for Social Research, study methodologies, 297
Michigan State Agricultural College, 71
Middle class, reduction, 430–433
Middle Income Student Assistance Act, 393
Millennials, characteristic, 492–494
Milwaukee Technical Institute, faculty unionization, 231
Minoritized populations, 450, 590, 598
Minoritized students, 483, 588
Minority-Serving Institutions (MSIs), 465–466, 553, 584
  diversity, 445, 450–453
*Mississippi University for Women v. Hogan*, 335
Modern Language Association, formation, 140
Morrill Land Grant Act (Morrill Act), 4, 8–9, 110, 115, 120, 176, 314, 571
Motor Vehicle Safety Act, impact, 191–192
Multi-campus system, evolution, 256
Multiculturalism, impact, 367–369, 518
Multiversity, 244–245
Municipal colleges, formation/financial support, 65
Murray, Charles, 490

## N

National Accrediting Commission of Cosmetology Arts and Science, initiation, 462
National Aeronautics and Space Administration (NASA), authorization, 274
National Assessment of Educational Progress (NAEP)
  scores, 482
  student knowledge assessment, 334
National Association for the Advancement of Colored People (NAACP), 451
  progress/success, 195, 197
National Association of Financial Aid Officers, founding, 258
National Association of Trade and Technical Schools, founding, 462
National Center for Education Statistics
  classification system, 315–316
  data efforts, review, 419
  establishment, 253
National College Women's Equal Suffrage League, formation, 133
National Council of Teachers of English, formation, 140
National Defense Education Act, 236, 276, 279, 288, 295, 372
National Education Association
  bargaining recognition, 233–234
  Committee of Ten, formation, 148–149
  Educational Policies Commission, 250
National Institute of Mental Health, 274–276
National Institutes of Health (NIH) budget, 275–276
National Labor Relations Act, 230
*National Labor Relations Board v. Yeshiva University*, 315, 349
National Merit Scholarship Program, impact, 213
National Opinion Research Center (University of Chicago), 297
National Organization for Women, founding, 197–198
National professional associations, connections, 179
National Science Foundation (NSF)
  engineering funding, 395
  formation, 273–274
  impact, 562–563
National Student Clearinghouse (NSC), near-census enrollment tracking method, 574
National Survey of Student Engagement (NSSE), 484–485
National university, establishment (attempt), 66–67
National Vocational Student Loan Insurance Act, 253, 462

Subject Index 663

Native American Serving Non-Tribal Institutions (NASNTIs), 450, 452
Natural sciences, research (growth), 177–178
Need-based aid, 442
Need-based grants, 550, 557
New England Puritans, mission, 15–16
New Jersey Board of Higher Education, replacement, 381
New World, expansion, 58
Noble, Safiya, 488–489
Non-market-affiliated fields, course offerings (reduction), 565
Northampton Community College, endowment, 568
North Central Association, standards (adoption), 167
Northeast Association of Colleges and Secondary Schools, formation, 167
North/South conflict, 61
Northwest Territories, ceding, 57
Nott, Eliphalet, 85–86, 96
Nurse Training Act, 253

### O

*Obergefell v. Hodges*, 427
Oberlin College, women (enrollment), 76–77
Occupational Safety and Health Act, 285
Occupational Safety Health Administration, formation, 191
Occupational specialization, 522–524
Off-budget support category, addition, 392–393
Office of Civil Rights, affirmative action requirements, 222–223
Office of Educational Research and Improvement, 277
Office of Naval Research, formation, 274
Ohio State University, tenure decisions (review), 353–354
*Olsson v. Indiana University Board of Trustees*, 387–388
Online learning, increase, 525–531
Online programs, accreditation, 548
Open-access institutions, mission, 446
Open Educational Resources (OER), 525
Open market, federal government enhancement, 66
Organized labor, setbacks, 306

Other work-related activities, 511
Out-of-state students, tuition, 555–556

### P

Paris Climate Agreement, 428
Part-time faculty
  impact, 360–362
  ratio, 223
  usage, profession schism, 361
Part-time instructors, percentage (growth), 219–220
Part-time students, attendance, 472–473
Patriot Act (2001), 476
*Paying the Price* (Goldrick-Rab), 12
Pedagogy, reliance, 42
Peer-group relationships, importance, 76
Pell Grants, 212, 279–280, 401–402, 463
  funding, 463
People's Republic of China (PRC), UN admission delay, 188
Performance-based fee-for-service contracts, 562
Permanent residents, discrimination (absence), 337
*Perpetual Dream, The* (Grant/Riesman), 244
*Perry v. Sindermann*, 229
Personal connections, benefits, 54
Per-student allocations, decrease, 560
Per-student labor costs, stasis, 528–529
Philanthropic foundations
  grants, 389
  research generosity, 281
Philanthropic funds, restriction, 566–567
Philanthropy
  funds source, 176–177
  growth, 170–173, 280–282, 566–568
*Pickering v. Board of Education*, 228
*Planned Parenthood v. Casey*, 308
Political Action Committees (SuperPACs), establishment, 429
Political activism, promotion/engagement, 593
Political economy, 587
Politics, polarization, 426–430
Pollack, Martha, 491–492
Port Huron Statement, 215
Post-pandemic enrollment losses, 467–468
Postsecondary education, 314
  requirement, 430–431

## Subject Index

Postsecondary for-profit/proprietary schools, parallel system, 460–461
Postsecondary landscape, protection, 457
Postsecondary students, aid (award), 400f
Practicality, claims, 238
Predominantly Black Institutions (PBIs), 450
Presidents (colleges/universities)
  administrative/financial acumen, 540
  managerial power, 93
  role, 539–541
    change, 260
  salary, increases, 541
  surveys, 591–592
President's Commission on Higher Education report/recommendation, 8, 249–250
Primary narratives (Lumina Foundation), 437
Princeton, qualifications priority, 129
Private colleges
  founding, 92
  monetary support, difficulty, 68
  sums, generation, 454
Private colleges/universities, success, 453–456
Private donations, revenue source, 170
Private education (licensing), states power (impact), 379
Private higher education, characterization, 453–454
Private institutions
  Bachelor's degree completion rates, 453
  endowments, building, 174–175
  status, 314–316
Private junior colleges
  disappearance, 208
  problems, 206
Private-public graduation gap, 453
Private/public institutions, revenue percentage, 391t, 553t
Private/public universities, current-fund revenue (percentage), 266t
Private universities
  disappearance, possibility, 314
  merit-based financial aid, increase, 441–442
Privatization
  impact, 559–562
  research privatization, 562–566

Productivity
  enhancement, 587
  increase, 371, 375
  indexes, usage, 356–357
Professional degrees, award (dramatic shifts), 366
Professional education
  degrees, increase, 319–324
  growth, 457–460
Professionalism
  culture, 179
  defining, efforts, 135
Professional programs, accreditation, 262–263
Professional schools, costs (increase), 172
Professors
  hiring, 30–31
  pay differential, 506
  teaching hours, reduction, 137
  underpayment, 99–100
Program coordination, funds (increase), 270
Promise Programs, 557–558
*Proposals Relating to the Education of Youth in Pensilvania* (Franklin), 25
Proprietary colleges, missions (focus), 461
Proprietary institutions, parallel system, 460–465
Proprietary sector, history, 462
Psychosocial changes, education (impact), 579–580
P-TECH programs, 448
Public Agenda report, 591
Public colleges
  increase, 324
  monetary support, difficulty, 68
Public good
  concept, 584
  higher education, contributions, 586
Public health, changes, 307–308
Public institutions
  characteristics, 94
  domination, 174
  funding, 552
  governance, consolidation, 379–380
  revenue, 552
  size, increase, 199–200
  sums, receiving, 97
  surplus, absence, 389–390
Public-opinion surveys, unreliability, 592

Public/private sector, fundraising, 567–568
Public schools, paucity, 27
Public secondary schools, development, 73
Public universities
 development, 173–174
 emphasis, increase, 567
Public Works Administration,
 assistance, 176
*Purdie v. University of Utah,* 336
Pure Food Act, 107, 192
Purpose-based budgeting, 570

## Q
Queen's College
 financial support, 50–51
 formation, 22
Quincy, Josiah, 87

## R
Race. *See* Underserved races/ethnicities
 impact, 433–436
Race-blind admissions policies, 340
Racial equity gaps, 500–501
Racial/ethnic groups
 designation, 309–310
 enrollments, increase, 330
Racist incidents, increase, 487–488
Radical egalitarianism, 299
Railway lines, building, 59
Rationality, impact, 113–114
Reagan, Nancy ("Just Say No"
 campaign), 308
Reagan, Ronald (domestic spending
 reduction), 305–306
Reconstruction Era, Abolitionists (moral
 outrage), 108
*Regents of the University of California v.
 Bakke,* 339, 477
Rehabilitation Act Amendments
 of 1991, 377
Rehabilitation Act of 1973, 211–212, 335
Religious multiplicity, commonness, 60
Religious orientation, decline, 25
Religious revivalism, reappearance, 101
Religious sects, formation, 24
Rensselaer Polytechnic Institute, 83
*Research and Relevant Knowledge*
 (Geiger), 11
Research, federal funding
 (effects), 276–277
Research findings, nondisclosure, 351
Research institutions, growth, 114
Research presence, growth, 102–103
Research, privatization, 562–566
Research universities
 class sizes, 359
 increase, 200–202
 industries, symbiotic
  relationship, 296–297
 prominence/competition, 440–443
 promotions, basis, 354
Reserve Officers' Training Corps
 (ROTC), 117, 279
*Resistance from the Right* (Shepherd),
 216
Restructuring, impact, 306–307
Revenue
 private donations, revenue source, 170
 sources, 389–392
Rhode Island College, governing board
 authority, 46
Right-to-work laws, Taft-Hartley Act
 (impact), 191
Roberts, John, 479–480
Rockefeller Foundation, 160
Rockefeller, John D., 135–136
*Roe v. Wade,* 308, 428
 overturning, 488
Roosevelt, Franklin D. (Brain Trust), 142
Royal charters, usage, 47–49
Rush, Benjamin, 66

## S
Sabbatical leaves, 137
Scholars, support (absence), 82–83
Scholastic Aptitude Test (SAT),
 240, 481–482
 development, 129
 usage, 213
Scholasticism, 41
Schooling, drive, 328
Science degrees, percentage, 365
Scientific inquiry, principles (impact), 34
Scientific methods, application, 82
Scottish universities, reformation, 39–40
Secondary schools
 attendance, growth, 151
 colleges, relationship, 150–151
Section 504 (Rehabilitation Act of
 1973), 211–212

Secularization, 302
  progression, 376–377
Selection committees, impact, 513
Selective admissions, criteria, 129
Self-educators, rise, 101–102
Self-governance, measure, 49
Self-interests, pursuit, 93
Servicemen's Readjustment Act (GI Bill), 4, 8, 105, 194, 200, 207, 252, 462
  financial aid, 209, 571
  renewal, 393
  specifications, 261–262
  Vietnam War veteran usage, 402
Service-to-the-community role, 111
SFFA v. Harvard, 480
SFFA v. President and Fellows of Harvard College, 479
SFFA v. University of North Carolina, 427–428
Shared governance, mental model, 545–546
Shared leadership, 546
Shearer v. Lambert, 388
Shelton v. Tucker, 228
Sherman Anti-Trust Act, 107
Silent Generation, 214, 492
Silva v. University of New Hampshire, 516
Single-parent households, number (rise), 240
Skilled Technical Workforce, rise, 431
Skills Micro-credentials, usage, 578
Skills, teaching, 156–157
Slavery, 14–15
Small colleges
  diffusion, 57
  societal context, 57–62
Smith, Adam, 584–585
Smith-Lever Act of 1914, 176, 178
Smith, William, 25
SNAP benefits, 585
Social activism, 3
  increase, 580
Social class, escape, 5
Social justice activism, 299
Social progressives, momentum, 427
Social reform movements, growth, 61
Social sciences, fractionation, 146–147
Social Security Act, 284–285
Societal benefits, rationalization, 263
Society of Friends, The (Indian interaction), 14

Southeastern Community College v. Davis, 335
Southern Association of Colleges and Schools, core requirements, 542
Southern Regional Education Board, institutional accreditation, 392
Southern segregationists, resistance, 196
Soviet Union, demise, 343
Stafford loans, 401–402
Staff salaries, examination, 271–273
Stanford
  gifts, receipt, 567
  industry connections, 296–297
  opening, 147
  research funding, increase, 201
Stanton, Elizabeth Cady, 102
Starns v. Malkerson, 336
State appropriations, decrease, 560–562
State colleges
  distinction, 203–204
  growth, 121–122
  land, government awards, 69
State disinvestment, 550–555
State governing/coordinating boards, influence, 379
State-level governance, 257–258
State-level initiatives, 404
"Statement on Government of College and Universities" (AAUP), 544
State Must Provide, The (Harris), 11
State Postsecondary Review Entities, mandate, 404
State Student Incentive Grants, authorization, 401
State universities, distinction, 203–204
Statewide boards, effect, 257
Stevens Institute of Technology, 71
St. John's College, 122–123, 155–156
Stone, Lucy, 102
Structural factors, impact, 501
Student activism, 2, 243–245, 258
  display, 208–209
  enabling, 600
  faculty complicity, 220, 223–224
  focus, 303
  goals, 261
  hallmark, 421
  increase, 208–209, 214–219, 487
    assumption, 598
  influence, 299
  shock, 300

Subject Index    667

Student Loan Marketing Association,
    creation, 401
*Student Personnel Point of View, The*
    (publication), 166
Student Right-to-Know and Campus
    Security Act (CSA), 377,
    495–496, 538
Students
  acculturation, 32–33
  achievement, discrepancies, 482–483
  affairs, 259
  aid, 555–559
  assistance, purpose, 180
  attendance (colonies), 26–30
  basic need insecurities, 494–495
  campus activism, 485–492
  characteristics (emergent nation), 72–78
  civic engagement, 485–492
  college
    attraction, continuation, 210
    impact, 289–290
  custody, maintenance (role), 341
  degrees, total, 497t
  discipline resistance, 75
  diversity, 328–333, 469–474
  employees, responsibility, 342
  engagement, 484–492
  enrollment, 328–333, 469–474
    growth, 158
    near-census tracking method, 574
    race/ethnicity percentage, 329f
  entry requirements, changes
    (examination), 127–128
  equity, 474–481
  federal direct aid, 556–557
  females, presence (percentage),
    328f, 469f
  first-year students
    institutional expenditures/median
      parental income, 294t
    UCLA survey, 456
  government, change, 260–261
  graduation, 292–293
  inclusion, 474–481
  income per student, variation, 174
  interests, engagement, 88–89
  learning
    assessment, 577
    depth, grades indication, 159–160
    part-timers, impact, 361–362
    quality, 366–367
  life, patterns (origin), 29
  mental health challenges, 494–495
  number, increase, 144
  outcomes, 548
  part-term student attendance, 472–473
  performance, 547
  postsecondary students, aid
    (award), 400f
  preparedness, 239–240
  proficiency, stasis, 328
  protests, 218–219
  racial/ethnic composition, 329–330
  representation, 299–300
  revenue, increase, 268
  scholarship needs, 172
  total enrollment, 328f, 469f
  uprisings, 226–227
  versatility, 54
  women, degrees (total), 332t, 497t
Students' Army Training Corps (SATC),
    formation, 117
Students for Fair Admission (SFFA), anti-
    affirmative action group, 479
*Students for Fair Admission (SFFA)
    v. Harvard*, 427
Student-to-support-staff ratios, 541–542
Study
  areas, transformation, 146
  freedom, concepts, 152–153
Sub-specializations, formation, 146
Sulkowicz, Emma (rape claim), 489
Super boards, approach, 380–381
Supplemental Educational Opportunity
    Grants, 393
Supplemental Instruction (SI), 247
*Sweatt v. Painter*, 195
*Sweezy v. New Hampshire*, 227–228
System-wide regulations,
    compliance, 259–260

T

Taft-Hartley Act, impact, 191
Tappan, Henry, 94, 112, 164
Targeted federal support, impact,
    550–555
Task Force for Reform in Higher
    Education, 250
Tax receipts, reduction, 551
Tax Relief Act (1997), 460
Taylor, Breonna (killing), 434
Teacher education, changes, 323

Teaching
  costs, considerations, 528–529
  effectiveness, intellectual competence (relationship), 360
  process, 370
  profession, communist exclusion, 226
  stress, 513–514
Technical colleges, formation, 83
Technical Review Panels, 573–574
Technological aids, review, 372
Technology
  applications, 374
  costs, 529
  instruction, relationship, 369–376
  usage, 525–531
Tenure
  bargaining units, 509
  decisions, review (Ohio State University), 353–354
  faculty, 228–230, 348–355, 502–503
  post-tenure review, 354–355
  restriction/abolishment, 503
  system, usage, 219–220
Tenure-track faculty, 502
Tepper School of Business (Carnegie Mellon University), MBA programs, 460
*Texas v. Hopwood*, 477
Theological studies, 323
"Three Strikes and You're Out" bill (California), 391–392
TIAA-CREFF pension fund, formation, 172
Ticknor, George, 112
Time-to-degree, increase, 499
Title IX (Education Amendments of 1972), 197–198, 211, 285, 480
Title VII (Civil Rights Act), 198, 284–285
  discrimination claims, 222
Title VII (Equal Pay Act), court ruling, 352
*To Advance Knowledge* (Geiger), 11
Treaty of Paris (1783), 57
Tribal Colleges, 451
  penalization, delay, 393
Tribally Controlled Community College Assistance Act, 393
Truman, Harry S., 188, 193, 195
Trump, Donald
  birtherism claims, 428
  cultural movements, tensions, 434
  discriminatory rhetoric/actions, 486
  election lies, 430
  presidency, polarization, 429
Trustees
  authority, challenges, 386–387
  roles, 385–386
Tuition
  examination, 396–399
  fees, ratio, 558–559
  increase, 555–559
  student aid, increase (combination), 556
Tulane University, doctoral programs (elimination), 560
Tutors, hiring, 30–31
Two-factor theory, 360

## U

UCLA programs, developmental emphasis, 152
Undergraduate curriculum, chaos, 152
Undergraduate enrollment, percent, 471t
Undergraduate/graduate courses, 239t
Underserved communities, work (impact), 567
Underserved groups, educational opportunity (extension), 444
Underserved races/ethnicities
  criteria, changes, 473
  psychological well-being, 579
  representation, equitability, 588
  students
    admissions, increase, 326
    support, 567
Underserved racial/ethnic groups, assistance, 211
Underserved students
  advantages, giving, 466
  diversity concept, extension, 478–479
  mentoring, 512
Undocumented immigrants, college access, 474–475
Union College, presidency (strength), 85
Unionization, 230–233
  membership, 508
  weakening, 306–307
United States Merchant Marine Academy, collective bargaining, 231
*United States v. Fordice*, 340
Universities
  academic growth, effect, 320–321

Subject Index 669

access, September 11 terror attack (impact), 476
boards of trustees, composition, 182–183
confidence, loss, 300
developmental courses, dropping, 446
differences, 136
emergence, 111
establishment/formation, 71, 112–113
extramurally derived funds, increase (leader attempt), 395
founding, 148
four-year college/university, outcomes, 500f
mission, 117
pressure, 111–118
research, advancement, 417
transformation, 105
  era, statistical portrait, 110t
uniqueness, 116–117
University-based researchers/corporations, relationships, 572–573
University of California
  board of directors, alumni seat designation, 162
  Board of Regents, impact, 150
  entrance exams, development, 143
  faculty expenses, budget provision, 137–138
  founding, 115
  professor ranks, 346
University of Chicago, 156
  divisions, separation, 159
  founding, 165
University of Illinois, founding, 115
University of Michigan, 94
  opening, 73
University of Minnesota, 154–155
  General College, opening, 122–123
University of Missouri protests, 489
University of North Carolina School of Applied Science, 71
University of Oregon, gifts, 567
University of Paris, education model, 20
University of Pennsylvania, state investment, 96
University of Phoenix, Pell Grant funding, 463
University of State of New York, formation, 70

University of Virginia Department of Applied Chemistry, 71
University of Virginia, Jefferson plan, 84–85
University of Washington, female students (attendance), 131
University of Wisconsin, Experimental College (focus), 122
University Transformation Era, 7, 105
  academic capabilities, criteria (usage), 128
  administrative bureaucracies, increase, 165–167
  appropriations, impact, 173–177
  Bachelor's degree programs, admission requirements, 126t
  colleges
    admissions, 124–130
    attendance, growth, 130–133
    experience, 156–157
  curriculum
    breadth, 144–147
    broadening, 133–134
    centrifugal curriculum, 152–154
    changes, 143–161
    human capital formation, relationship, 236
  endowments, increase, 173–177
  enrollment, growth, 123–124
  faculty
    appointment, 141
    evolution, 134–143
  general education, changes, 154–156
  governance, influences (relationship), 167–169
  higher education
    criticism, 181–184
    governance, 161–169
    secular governance, increase, 161–162
    shifts, increase, 110
  industrialization, triumph, 106
  institutions
    changes, 109–123
    financing, 170–177
    presidential power, exercise (variation), 163–165
    vertical moves, 118–123
  instructional forms, broadening, 157–161

Subject Index

University Transformation Era (*continued*)
　intercollegiate athletics, emergence, 132
　junior colleges, functioning, 121
　middle years, 587–588
　outcomes, 177–184
　philanthropy, growth, 170–173
　preparatory programs, growth, 147–152
　research, emphasis, 406–407
　social mobility, expectations, 133–134
　societal context, 105–109
　students
　　admissions, 124–130
　　enrollment, 123–134
　　study quality, changes, 125–126
U.S. Bureau of Education, accredited institution list, 168
U.S. Constitution, 105
　Article VI, 60
　Thirteenth Amendment, 61
U.S. Department of Education, Notice of Interpretation, 480–481
U.S. Freedmen's Bureau, collaboration, 120
U.S. Military Academy, 83
U.S. presidents, college training, 53
U.S. Supreme Court rulings, impact, 194–195, 228–230, 308, 335–342, 349, 427–429, 442, 474, 477–480, 515–517

## V

Valencia College
　endowment, 568
　purpose-based budgeting, 570
Values (change), 2
　education, impact, 580–581
Varsity blues scandal, 473
Veterans Education Assistance Act, 476
Veterans Readjustment Act, 262
Vietnam War, 215–217, 402
Virginia Tech massacre, 495–496
Vocational Education Act, 253, 393
Vocationalism
　impact, 145
　trend, 364
Voting Rights Act (1965), 197

## W

Wagner Labor Relations Act, 284–285
Wald, Lillian, 102
Wall Street crash, 565–566
War on Terror, 425–426, 459, 497
*Waters v. Churchill*, 515
Wayland, Francise, 112, 170
Wayne State University, 154–155
Wealth gap, 433
Webster, Daniel, 67
*Welter v. Seton Hall University*, 351
Wheeler, Benjamin, 164
White, Andrew, 112
White nationalism, increase, 487–488
*Whitlock v. University of Denver*, 341
Winthrop, John ("city on a hill"), 16
Woke agenda, 488
Woke-ism, 437
*Women's Colleges in the United States* (Harwarth/Maline/DeBra), 11–12
Women's colleges, rise, 4
Woolsey, Theodore, 112
Work, changes, 189–190
Workforce
　change, 585
　composition, changes, 431–432
　configuration, change, 307
Working conditions, shift, 224–225
Workplace, market viewpoint, 357–358
World War II, United States (emergence), 187
World War I, United States (emergence), 108–109

## X

Xenophobia, 192–193

## Y

Yale, Elihu, 50
Yale Report, 83–84, 155–156, 242–243
Yale University
　curriculum, modeling, 37–38
　formation, 46
　Latin requirements, sustaining, 148
　Society of Alumni organization, 96
Young Americans for Freedom, 216

Printed and bound by CPI Group (UK) Ltd, Croydon, CR0 4YY
14/03/2024
14470869-0003